Handbook of Research on Promoting Sustainable Public Transportation Strategies in Urban Environments

Zafer Yilmaz
TED University, Turkey

Silvia Golem
University of Split, Croatia

Dorinela Costescu
Polytechnic University of Bucharest, Romania

A volume in the Practice, Progress, and Proficiency in Sustainability (PPPS) Book Series

Published in the United States of America by
    IGI Global
    Engineering Science Reference (an imprint of IGI Global)
    701 E. Chocolate Avenue
    Hershey PA, USA 17033
    Tel: 717-533-8845
    Fax: 717-533-8661
    E-mail: cust@igi-global.com
    Web site: http://www.igi-global.com

Copyright © 2023 by IGI Global. All rights reserved. No part of this publication may be reproduced, stored or distributed in any form or by any means, electronic or mechanical, including photocopying, without written permission from the publisher.
Product or company names used in this set are for identification purposes only. Inclusion of the names of the products or companies does not indicate a claim of ownership by IGI Global of the trademark or registered trademark.
Library of Congress Cataloging-in-Publication Data

Names: Yilmaz, Zafer, 1974- editor. | Golem, Silvia, 1980- editor. |
    Costescu, Dorinela, 1969- editor.
Title: Handbook of research on promoting sustainable public transportation
    strategies in urban environments / Zafer Yilmaz, Silvia Golem, and
    Dorinela Costescu, editor.
Description: Hershey, PA : Engineering Science Reference, [2023] | Includes
    bibliographical references and index. | Summary: "Urban transportation
    is a multidisciplinary subject that consists of many topics, i.e.,
    designing the unimodal or intermodal public transportation system in the
    cities, energy usage in these systems, transportation information
    systems to gather information related to possible passengers, the
    economics of public transportation, etc. The traditional urban
    transportation systems around the globe are now being transferred into
    green public transportation systems in an effort to mitigate CO2
    emissions and provide nature-friendly transportation systems in cities
    and, ultimately, to increase citizens' wellbeing. Green public
    transportation is a common goal for all countries, and this will be the
    most interesting technological area not only for developed cities but
    also developing cities. Nowadays, cities are expected to transform their
    traditional transportation systems to cutting-edge high technology green
    transportation systems in the near future due to regulations applied by
    the related authorities such as the EU, UN, etc. At the same time,
    cities are undergoing a transformation from traditional to smart cities,
    which is an inevitable process due to speedy developments in
    technologies and smart systems. This is why green public transportation
    systems must be developed and adjusted so as to be applicable in future
    smart cities"-- Provided by publisher.
Identifiers: LCCN 2022039906 (print) | LCCN 2022039907 (ebook) | ISBN
    9781668459966 (hardcover) | ISBN 9781668459980 (ebook)
Subjects: LCSH: Urban transportation--Environmental aspects. |
    Transportation--Technological innovations. | Sustainable urban
    development.
Classification: LCC HE305 .P75 2023 (print) | LCC HE305 (ebook) | DDC
    388.4--dc23/eng/20221020
LC record available at https://lccn.loc.gov/2022039906
LC ebook record available at https://lccn.loc.gov/2022039907

This book is published in the IGI Global book series Practice, Progress, and Proficiency in Sustainability (PPPS) (ISSN: 2330-3271; eISSN: 2330-328X)

British Cataloguing in Publication Data
A Cataloguing in Publication record for this book is available from the British Library.

All work contributed to this book is new, previously-unpublished material. The views expressed in this book are those of the authors, but not necessarily of the publisher.

For electronic access to this publication, please contact: eresources@igi-global.com.

Practice, Progress, and Proficiency in Sustainability (PPPS) Book Series

Ayman Batisha
International Sustainability Institute, Egypt

ISSN:2330-3271
EISSN:2330-328X

Mission

In a world where traditional business practices are reconsidered and economic activity is performed in a global context, new areas of economic developments are recognized as the key enablers of wealth and income production. This knowledge of information technologies provides infrastructures, systems, and services towards sustainable development.

The **Practices, Progress, and Proficiency in Sustainability (PPPS) Book Series** focuses on the local and global challenges, business opportunities, and societal needs surrounding international collaboration and sustainable development of technology. This series brings together academics, researchers, entrepreneurs, policy makers and government officers aiming to contribute to the progress and proficiency in sustainability.

Coverage

- Eco-Innovation
- Knowledge clusters
- Sustainable Development
- Green Technology
- Socio-Economic
- Technological learning
- Environmental informatics
- Innovation Networks
- Strategic Management of IT
- Global Content and Knowledge Repositories

IGI Global is currently accepting manuscripts for publication within this series. To submit a proposal for a volume in this series, please contact our Acquisition Editors at Acquisitions@igi-global.com or visit: http://www.igi-global.com/publish/.

The Practice, Progress, and Proficiency in Sustainability (PPPS) Book Series (ISSN 2330-3271) is published by IGI Global, 701 E. Chocolate Avenue, Hershey, PA 17033-1240, USA, www.igi-global.com. This series is composed of titles available for purchase individually; each title is edited to be contextually exclusive from any other title within the series. For pricing and ordering information please visit http://www.igi-global.com/book-series/practice-progress-proficiency-sustainability/73810. Postmaster: Send all address changes to above address. Copyright © 2023 IGI Global. All rights, including translation in other languages reserved by the publisher. No part of this series may be reproduced or used in any form or by any means – graphics, electronic, or mechanical, including photocopying, recording, taping, or information and retrieval systems – without written permission from the publisher, except for non commercial, educational use, including classroom teaching purposes. The views expressed in this series are those of the authors, but not necessarily of IGI Global.

Titles in this Series

For a list of additional titles in this series, please visit: www.igi-global.com/book-series

Implications of Industry 5.0 on Environmental Sustainability
Muhammad Jawad Sajid (Xuzhou University of Technology, China) Syed Abdul Rehman Khan (Xuzhou University of Technology, China) and Zhang Yu (ILMA University, Pakstan)
Business Science Reference • © 2023 • 328pp • H/C (ISBN: 9781668461136) • US $250.00

Climatic and Environmental Significance of Wetlands Case Studies from Eurasia and North Africa
Abdelkrim Ben Salem (Faculty of Sciences, Mohammed V University, Rabat, Morocco) Laila Rhazi (Faculty of Sciences, Mohammed V University, Rabat, Morocco) and Ahmed Karmaoui (Moulay Ismail University, Meknès, Morocco & Moroccan Center for Culture and Science, Moocco)
Engineering Science Reference • © 2023 • 208pp • H/C (ISBN: 9781799892892) • US $195.00

Climate Change, World Consequences, and the Sustainable Development Goals for 2030
Ana Pego (Nova University of Lisbon, Portugal)
Engineering Science Reference • © 2023 • 306pp • H/C (ISBN: 9781668448298) • US $250.00

Positive and Constructive Contributions for Sustainable Development Goals
Cristina Raluca Gh. Popescu (University of Bucharest, Romania & The Bucharest University of Economic Studies, Romania)
Engineering Science Reference • © 2023 • 281pp • H/C (ISBN: 9781668474990) • US $245.00

Leadership Approaches to the Science of Water and Sustainability
Kristin Joyce Tardif (University of Arkansas, Fort Smith, USA)
Engineering Science Reference • © 2022 • 219pp • H/C (ISBN: 9781799896913) • US $215.00

Eco-Friendly and Agile Energy Strategies and Policy Development
Mir Sayed Shah Danish (University of the Ryukyus, Japan) and Tomonobu Senjyu (University of the Ryukyus, Japan)
Engineering Science Reference • © 2022 • 272pp • H/C (ISBN: 9781799895022) • US $240.00

Handbook of Research on Global Institutional Roles for Inclusive Development
Neeta Baporikar (Namibia University of Science and Technology, Namibia & University of Pune, India)
Information Science Reference • © 2022 • 398pp • H/C (ISBN: 9781668424483) • US $270.00

Analyzing Sustainability in Peripheral, Ultra-Peripheral, and Low-Density Regions
Rui Alexandre Castanho (WSB University, Poland)
Engineering Science Reference • © 2022 • 334pp • H/C (ISBN: 9781668445488) • US $240.00

701 East Chocolate Avenue, Hershey, PA 17033, USA
Tel: 717-533-8845 x100 • Fax: 717-533-8661
E-Mail: cust@igi-global.com • www.igi-global.com

List of Contributors

Budak, Aysenur / *Gebze Technical University, Turkey* 293
Çelik, Gizem / *TED University, Turkey* 203
Costescu, Dorinela / *Polytechnic University of Bucharest, Romania* 25, 98
Ćukušić, Maja / *Faculty of Economics, Business, and Tourism, University of Split, Croatia* 68
Durmaz, Nida / *Gebze Technical University, Turkey* 293
Erjavec, Jure / *School of Economics and Business, University of Ljubljana, Slovenia* 120
Etamé, Jacques / *University Institute of Technology, University of Douala, Cameroon* 250
Etémé Bessala, Séverin Bertand / *University Institute of Technology, University of Douala, Cameroon* 250
Golem, Silvia / *Faculty of Economics, Business, and Tourism, University of Split, Croatia* 68, 333
Groznik, Aleš / *School of Economics and Business, University of Ljubljana, Slovenia* 44
Heyes, Adam / *Faculty of Economics, University of West Bohemia, Czech Republic* 223
Irgin, Pelin / *Independent Researcher, Canada* 164
Jašić, Tea / *Faculty of Economics, Business, and Tourism, University of Split, Croatia* 68
Kresa, Zdenek / *Faculty of Economics, University of West Bohemia, Czech Republic* 223
Krizmanič, Bor / *School of Economics and Business, University of Ljubljana, Slovenia* 44
Manfreda, Anton / *School of Economics and Business, University of Ljubljana, Slovenia* 1, 120
Moskolai Ngossaha, Justin / *Faculty of Science, University of Douala, Cameroon* 250
Nagode, Kristina / *School of Economics and Business, University of Ljubljana, Slovenia* 1
Nincevic Pasalic, Ivana / *Faculty of Economics, Business, and Tourism, University of Split, Croatia* 182
Ninčević Pašalić, Ivana / *Faculty of Economics, Business, and Tourism, University of Split, Croatia* 68
Popa, Mihaela / *Polytechnic University of Bucharest, Romania* 25
Raicu, Serban / *Polytechnic University of Bucharest, Romania* 25
Roman, Eugenia Alina / *Polytechnic University of Bucharest, Romania* 98
Singh, Aditya / *Lovely Professional University, India* 267
Tamba, Jean Gaston / *University Institute of Technology, University of Douala, Cameroon* 250
Tluchor, Jan / *Faculty of Economics, University of West Bohemia, Czech Republic* 223
Tomat, Luka / *School of Economics and Business, University of Ljubljana, Slovenia* 1
Yılmaz, Zafer / *TED University, Turkey* 203
Yücel, Öykü / *Faculty of Economics and Administrative Sciences, TED University, Turkey* 141
Yücel, Seda Damla / *TED University, Turkey* 313

Table of Contents

Preface xv

Section 1
Concepts and Theoretical Framework

Chapter 1
The Smart Society Concepts and Elements for Assuring a Green Future 1
Kristina Nagode, School of Economics and Business, University of Ljubljana, Slovenia
Luka Tomat, School of Economics and Business, University of Ljubljana, Slovenia
Anton Manfreda, School of Economics and Business, University of Ljubljana, Slovenia

Chapter 2
Performance of Urban Public Transportation Networks 25
Serban Raicu, Polytechnic University of Bucharest, Romania
Dorinela Costescu, Polytechnic University of Bucharest, Romania
Mihaela Popa, Polytechnic University of Bucharest, Romania

Chapter 3
The Role of Electromobility in the Energy-Related Smart Grids 44
Bor Krizmanič, School of Economics and Business, University of Ljubljana, Slovenia
Aleš Groznik, School of Economics and Business, University of Ljubljana, Slovenia

Chapter 4
Information Systems and Technologies for Green Public Transportation 68
Ivana Ninčević Pašalić, Faculty of Economics, Business, and Tourism, University of Split, Croatia
Maja Ćukušić, Faculty of Economics, Business, and Tourism, University of Split, Croatia
Silvia Golem, Faculty of Economics, Business, and Tourism, University of Split, Croatia
Tea Jašić, Faculty of Economics, Business, and Tourism, University of Split, Croatia

Chapter 5
Challenges in the Development of Urban Intermodal Mobility Systems 98
Dorinela Costescu, Polytechnic University of Bucharest, Romania
Eugenia Alina Roman, Polytechnic University of Bucharest, Romania

Chapter 6

Nudging Towards Sustainable Public Transportation.. 120
Anton Manfreda, School of Economics and Business, University of Ljubljana, Slovenia
Jure Erjavec, School of Economics and Business, University of Ljubljana, Slovenia

Chapter 7

Use of Green Bonds to Promote Green Projects... 141
Öykü Yücel, Faculty of Economics and Administrative Sciences, TED University, Turkey

Chapter 8

An Overview of Sustainable Public Transportation in Higher Education.. 164
Pelin Irgin, Independent Researcher, Canada

Section 2
Case Studies and Empirical Research Findings

Chapter 9

The Use of Information and Communication Technologies and Renewable Energy in Europe:
Implications for Public Transportation 182
Ivana Nincevic Pasalic, Faculty of Economics, Business, and Tourism, University of Split, Croatia

Chapter 10

Comparison of Traditional and Green Public Transportation Vehicles in Terms of CO2
Emissions 203
Gizem Çelik, TED University, Turkey
Zafer Yılmaz, TED University, Turkey

Chapter 11

Attractiveness of Urban Public Transport From the Point of View of Young Passengers:
Experience From the Czech Republic.. 223
Zdenek Kresa, Faculty of Economics, University of West Bohemia, Czech Republic
Jan Tluchor, Faculty of Economics, University of West Bohemia, Czech Republic
Adam Heyes, Faculty of Economics, University of West Bohemia, Czech Republic

Chapter 12

Social Big Data for Improving Urban Mobility Services: The Case of Douala, Cameroon.............. 250
Séverin Bertand Etémé Bessala, University Institute of Technology, University of Douala,
Cameroon
Justin Moskolai Ngossaha, Faculty of Science, University of Douala, Cameroon
Jean Gaston Tamba, University Institute of Technology, University of Douala, Cameroon
Jacques Etamé, University Institute of Technology, University of Douala, Cameroon

Chapter 13

The Development and Significance of Bengaluru Suburban Rail Project... 267
Aditya Singh, Lovely Professional University, India

Chapter 14
Evaluation of the Barriers to the Use of Sustainable Transportation Systems in City Logistics
With an Integrated Grey DEMATEL-ANP Approach 293
Nida Durmaz, Gebze Technical University, Turkey
Aysenur Budak, Gebze Technical University, Turkey

Chapter 15
Relationship Between Intellectual Property Rights and Entrepreneurial Ecosystems 313
Seda Damla Yücel, TED University, Turkey

Chapter 16
A Walking-Friendly Environment? How to Measure It 333
Silvia Golem, Faculty of Economics, Business, and Tourism, University of Split, Croatia

Compilation of References 347

About the Contributors 392

Index 398

Detailed Table of Contents

Preface... xv

Section 1
Concepts and Theoretical Framework

Chapter 1
The Smart Society Concepts and Elements for Assuring a Green Future 1
    Kristina Nagode, School of Economics and Business, University of Ljubljana, Slovenia
    Luka Tomat, School of Economics and Business, University of Ljubljana, Slovenia
    Anton Manfreda, School of Economics and Business, University of Ljubljana, Slovenia

The cities and society are bound to change, and the residents want them to be pleasant places to live. Modern digital technology can provide different solutions that can solve several problems that cities are facing and can be applied to existing infrastructure as well. However, merely implementing the technology is not enough, and cities need to exploit the potential of digital resources, accept and utilize digital resources to support their strategies, and leverage each technology. Since digitalization has a broad impact on both organizations and society, this chapter will review the concept of digitalization as an enabler and facilitator of smart cities together with presenting the concept of a smart society and its impact on the green future. Several research areas are outlined in the chapter with important elements of a smart city and society that assure a green and sustainable future.

Chapter 2
Performance of Urban Public Transportation Networks.. 25
    Serban Raicu, Polytechnic University of Bucharest, Romania
    Dorinela Costescu, Polytechnic University of Bucharest, Romania
    Mihaela Popa, Polytechnic University of Bucharest, Romania

Despite the objectives of sustainable development, which aim to reduce pollution and energy consumption, many cities face issues caused by traffic congestion and inadequate public transportation. In this framework, the chapter emphasizes the challenges of public transportation services and analyses a comprehensive set of criteria for evaluating public transportation performances. The functions of public transportation and their linked criteria for performance evaluations are discussed. Then, the particularities of effectiveness and efficiency in public transportation networks are explained. Effectiveness is defined as the level of achievement of preset tasks of public transportation. Efficiency is related to the ratio between the outputs and the used resources. Additionally, different indicators must be defined for production and commercial efficiency. The presented analysis supports developing an effective and efficient urban transportation system in a dynamic social environment, with rapid changes in user requirements.

Chapter 3
The Role of Electromobility in the Energy-Related Smart Grids 44
Bor Krizmanič, School of Economics and Business, University of Ljubljana, Slovenia
Aleš Groznik, School of Economics and Business, University of Ljubljana, Slovenia

The chapter describes the major components of the power grid. It then describes and explains the trends in the consumption and generation of electricity, with a particular focus on increasing the share of renewable energy sources. The concept of the smart grid is then described, including a discussion of the smart meter and the prosumer concept. The second part of the chapter is dedicated to electromobility. This section describes the main characteristics of electric vehicles and the trend of their diffusion, battery technologies, charging stations, smart charging, and the vehicle-to-grid concept.

Chapter 4
Information Systems and Technologies for Green Public Transportation 68
Ivana Ninčević Pašalić, Faculty of Economics, Business, and Tourism, University of Split, Croatia
Maja Ćukušić, Faculty of Economics, Business, and Tourism, University of Split, Croatia
Silvia Golem, Faculty of Economics, Business, and Tourism, University of Split, Croatia
Tea Jašić, Faculty of Economics, Business, and Tourism, University of Split, Croatia

Overloaded infrastructure is one of the main challenges cities are facing nowadays. Cities attempt to overcome these challenges by applying different innovative concepts and technologies, some of which are smart city initiatives. One of the elementary features of smart cities is the modernization of public transport and a well-designed transportation infrastructure. Modern information systems are used in public transportation in many ways, with the main purpose of facilitating and improving public transport for citizens. This chapter overviews the implementation of some standard information systems in public transportation and explains their purposes, way of functioning, and advantages for both users and providers. The aim of this chapter is to demonstrate relevant information systems used in public transport in several European cities - Rome, Paris, London, and Split. It is clearly shown that each city has its own version of a particular information system that achieves the goals of smart mobility.

Chapter 5
Challenges in the Development of Urban Intermodal Mobility Systems 98
Dorinela Costescu, Polytechnic University of Bucharest, Romania
Eugenia Alina Roman, Polytechnic University of Bucharest, Romania

Technological progress and the economic and social environment dynamics lead to changing mobility needs. Modifying travel practices, increasing the pressures for fast and predictable services, and expanding the demands of users for individualized offers determine requirements for diversifying the mobility supply in an integrated framework that must meet sustainable development objectives. In this framework, intermodal public transport plays a significant role. The chapter introduces the definitions of multimodality and intermodality in urban mobility systems. Intermodal transportation accounts for the different capabilities of diverse modes, including their availability, speed, density, costs, limitations, and, therefore, their most appropriate operating. The functions of intermodal public transportation are discussed. It is emphasized that solutions for sustainable mobility can be developed through a better understanding of the opportunities and challenges of the new mobility services.

Chapter 6
Nudging Towards Sustainable Public Transportation 120
Anton Manfreda, School of Economics and Business, University of Ljubljana, Slovenia
Jure Erjavec, School of Economics and Business, University of Ljubljana, Slovenia

The chapter presents the importance of public transportation in coping with contemporary environmental issues. However, the aim is not to present public transportation as the only method of transportation leading towards a green future. New services and solutions should be carefully developed in cooperation with residents considering their needs, culture, habits, and existing procedures. Transforming the mindset of residents should be considered as well. Therefore, the authors present the readers with different theories, models, tools, and frameworks, illustrated with existing cases for promoting behavioral change amongst individuals, focusing specifically on nudging mechanisms. While the focus of the chapter is mainly on nudging towards sustainable public transportation, the authors illustrate nudging with examples from other areas as well and argue how such uses can also be applied to promote sustainable public transportation. This chapter is therefore aimed at policymakers and other stakeholders involved in promoting sustainable public transportation modes.

Chapter 7
Use of Green Bonds to Promote Green Projects 141
Öykü Yücel, Faculty of Economics and Administrative Sciences, TED University, Turkey

With increasing concern in environment and sustainability and rising costs, the need for alternative financing mechanisms has arisen. Especially in developing countries, where financial resources are scarce, it is necessary to come up with new ways of financing options to cover for the upfront investment needs of green projects. Recently green bonds are commonly used to finance green projects. Like conventional bonds, green bonds are fixed income securities, however proceeds of green bonds can only be used in financing or re-financing new or existing green projects that have environmental benefits. In this chapter the author details the concept and types of green bonds, figures on how developed and integrated green bond market is, green bond principles and measurement of objectives, regulatory bodies, investment advantages and risks, investment alternatives, real-life examples as well as suggested greenium (green premium) and concept for investors.

Chapter 8
An Overview of Sustainable Public Transportation in Higher Education 164
Pelin Irgin, Independent Researcher, Canada

Very few engineering and business/management education programs emphasize the importance of sustainable public transportation in urban environments, even though agencies and practitioners recognize it. Many undergraduate and graduate students have little training on how a sustainable public transport system is planned, designed, and operationalized, which is critical for a better understanding of sustainability and equity in public transportation. Content and instructional materials in sustainable public transportation education are still not readily available for practitioners. Therefore, this chapter aims to examine the public content and instructional materials on the websites of various universities in North America and Europe and to understand their commitment to education in sustainable public transportation, specifically to "sustainable public transportation" courses offered in the programs. It addresses how sustainability and equity in public transportation are integrated with textual and visual materials used in engineering and business/management education programs.

Section 2
Case Studies and Empirical Research Findings

Chapter 9
The Use of Information and Communication Technologies and Renewable Energy in Europe:
Implications for Public Transportation 182
    Ivana Nincevic Pasalic, Faculty of Economics, Business, and Tourism, University of Split, Croatia

Information and communication technologies (ICTs) can help in cutting up to 20% of global carbon emissions by assisting consumers, different industries, and the public sector in energy savings and energy efficiency improvement. This chapter explores the relationship between ICTs and the development of renewable energy in European countries. In the first part of the research, the author conducted a cluster analysis to measure the differences in the use of ICTs in Europe through information society indicators. The results of the clustering (hierarchical and K-means) showed the existence of four clusters, and the increased differences between clusters from 2015 to 2020. The second part of the research confirms the existence of differences between clusters in the share of energy consumption from renewable sources, and the differences proved to be statistically significant. The results are discussed in terms of implications for public transportation, concluding that local governments must start and/or keep using ICTs for urban solutions for the future to be greener and sustainable.

Chapter 10
Comparison of Traditional and Green Public Transportation Vehicles in Terms of CO2
Emissions 203
    Gizem Çelik, TED University, Turkey
    Zafer Yılmaz, TED University, Turkey

There is a high demand in energy consumption of cities due to growth in population, and more pollution due to high CO2 emissions. Effective methods for increasing energy efficiency include the adoption of green vehicles to the transportation systems. The chapter aims to evaluate traditional public transportation technologies, introduce alternative future green transportation technologies in smart and sustainable cities, and make comparison between traditional and green public transportation systems. Istanbul is chosen to apply a case study to explain the importance of using green transportation ways in terms of CO2 emissions. The results of different transportation modes in different routes are compared. The results found for different scenarios on the routes in this case study ensure that the most eco-friendly options would be the walking, cycling, and public transportation ways for the passengers, although they may not provide the optimal solutions in terms of total duration and distance traveled.

Chapter 11
Attractiveness of Urban Public Transport From the Point of View of Young Passengers:
Experience From the Czech Republic 223
    Zdenek Kresa, Faculty of Economics, University of West Bohemia, Czech Republic
    Jan Tluchor, Faculty of Economics, University of West Bohemia, Czech Republic
    Adam Heyes, Faculty of Economics, University of West Bohemia, Czech Republic

This chapter uses the customer-oriented approach to help enhance understanding of the use of sustainable public transportation (PT) systems in urban areas to support climate change actions. It studies the views and experiences of young passengers (Generation Z) in a heavily used Central European PT system. Three surveys were conducted to study the effect of the coronavirus epidemic on the behavior of passengers. Additionally, automated passenger counting data were utilized. The surveys identified that despite the epidemic, the most important factors of customer experience were those that related to the total travel time. Findings further included the fact that the PT is starting to be used more frequently in 2022 after decline in 2020 and 2021. The decline was not caused by a massive outflow of regular passengers, but in general by passengers having fewer reasons to travel. Discussions are underway as to how to increase the attractiveness of PT systems.

Chapter 12
Social Big Data for Improving Urban Mobility Services: The Case of Douala, Cameroon............... 250
    Sévérin Bertand Etémé Bessala, University Institute of Technology, University of Douala, Cameroon
    Justin Moskolai Ngossaha, Faculty of Science, University of Douala, Cameroon
    Jean Gaston Tamba, University Institute of Technology, University of Douala, Cameroon
    Jacques Etamé, University Institute of Technology, University of Douala, Cameroon

In the context of developing countries such as Cameroon, which is the case study, urban mobility is still mainly based on the traditional model, and the major tools of urban mobility governance are practically not in place. Only the main cities have an urban development plan. These cities are marked by poor knowledge of urban mobility issues due to lack of data and studies on the continuous monitoring of the performance of urban mobility. In this context, how can innovative solutions based on big data technologies and sophisticated approaches be integrated to address the challenges of sustainable urban mobility? In this study, a methodological framework based on a system engineering approach has been proposed to guide mobility decision makers and users in the implementation and use of urban mobility services. The result of this study helps to extract knowledge and massive data for a better decision making in the context of developing countries and proposes a model of urban mobility system to be deployed as a recommendation to decision makers.

Chapter 13
The Development and Significance of Bengaluru Suburban Rail Project 267
    Aditya Singh, Lovely Professional University, India

The suburban rail project in Bengaluru city in the Karnataka state of India will address the local mass travel needs from Bengaluru city to nearby towns or satellite cities. The chapter discusses the development stages of the Bengaluru Suburban Rail Project. The necessity, essential features, and significant advantages of the suburban rail project are presented. The project is expected to reduce traffic congestion problems in Bengaluru city and its nearby towns. Supplementary benefits related to time savings and increased passenger comfort are also estimated. Further, the challenges and risks faced by the project are discussed. Some future potential extensions of the project are considered.

Chapter 14
Evaluation of the Barriers to the Use of Sustainable Transportation Systems in City Logistics
With an Integrated Grey DEMATEL-ANP Approach.. 293
    Nida Durmaz, Gebze Technical University, Turkey
    Aysenur Budak, Gebze Technical University, Turkey

The rapid increase in journeys, freight transport, and the use of private vehicles in cities causes environmental problems such as the decrease in urban environmental quality as well as economic and social problems in transportation. In this context, the concept of the city logistics shows up to improve and maintain logistics activities in settlements. It is necessary to define the barriers to the use of sustainable transportation systems in city logistics and to plan strategic steps by prioritizing these barriers according to their importance. In this study, an integrated approach of Grey DEMATEL-ANP is proposed to model these barriers in the city logistics for Istanbul. The proposed method determines the cause-effect relationships and relative weights of the key barriers. The results of this study may help decision makers and practitioners to address the key barriers highlighted and provide the theoretical guideline to use the sustainable transport systems across city logistics successfully.

Chapter 15
Relationship Between Intellectual Property Rights and Entrepreneurial Ecosystems........................ 313
 Seda Damla Yücel, TED University, Turkey

Intellectual property rights (IPR) are critical for developing new inventions and creations, transforming them into social and economic value, and increasing inventors' and creators' competitiveness. The main functions of IPR are preventing competitors from owning, using, selling, and monetizing related inventions and creations, access to markets and networks, and obtaining venture capital. Entrepreneurship contributes significantly to economic growth and is crucial to creating opportunities and improving the performance of new businesses. Its impact varies from economy to economy based on its outputs, a nation's industrial and technological prowess, and its legislative framework for developing entrepreneurs. Technological development is inevitable considering the increasing population, existing infrastructure, services offered to society, limited resources, the expected quality of life, and the city's ecological imprint. Therefore, creative and technological solutions will be essential, especially in building dynamic approaches while creating smart cities for the future.

Chapter 16
A Walking-Friendly Environment? How to Measure It.. 333
 Silvia Golem, Faculty of Economics, Business, and Tourism, University of Split, Croatia

One of the main aims of the smart city paradigm is to reduce the environmental footprint of urban growth by managing the urban mobility in a citizen-friendly way. Facilitating and encouraging citizens to walk is a way to make the modern form of urban mobility greener and safer. Evidence of the benefits of walking and walkable urban forms has appeared in different strands of literature, suggesting the multidisciplinary nature of it. The main aim of this chapter is to document and review the existing measures of urban walkability, along with the relevant cases where the attempts to measure walkability were made, thereby contributing a wider literature which aims to identify and understand factors that are most relevant for urban walkers.

Compilation of References 347

About the Contributors 392

Index 398

Preface

The title of this book is *Handbook of Research on Promoting Sustainable Public Transportation Strategies in Urban Environments*. Therefore, as expected, the emphasis is on sustainable public transportation strategies, but with an added focus on the multidisciplinary aspects of correlations between urban environment and mobility.

Public transportation in urban environments is a multidisciplinary subject that consists of many topics, i.e., designing the unimodal or intermodal public transportation system in the cities, energy usage in these systems, transportation information systems to gather information related to possible passengers, the economics of public transportation, etc. The traditional urban transportation systems around the globe are now being transferred into green public transportation systems in an effort to mitigate CO_2 emissions and provide nature-friendly transportation systems in cities and, ultimately, to increase citizens' well-being. Green public transportation is a common goal for all countries, and this will be the most interesting technological area not only for developed cities but also for developing cities. Nowadays, cities are expected to transform their traditional transportation systems to cutting-edge high technology green transportation systems in the near future due to regulations applied by related authorities such as the EU, UN, etc. At the same time, cities are undergoing a transformation from traditional to smart cities which is an inevitable process due to very fast developments in technologies and smart systems. Therefore, new public transportation strategies must be developed and adjusted so as to be applicable in future smart cities.

This book provides relevant theoretical frameworks, the latest empirical research findings, and an overview of the latest technological developments on the subject. It is prepared for all professionals (managers, finance directors, entrepreneurs, academicians, etc.) who want to improve their understanding of public transportation strategies in an urban environment with additional motivation for future smart cities. This volume will help the students to improve their knowledge about the upcoming transportation systems since they will be the end-users of those systems in the very near future. Hence, this makes the book potentially a required or recommended book for transportation and smart cities-related courses. This book also provides a multi-disciplinary perspective on current and cutting-edge research exploring and extending our understanding of the use of public transportation systems in smart cities (i.e., network design, supply chain of green transportation, operations, finance, and information management systems, etc.) to support climate change actions. It includes issues that are theoretical, technical, cognitive, organizational, and managerial that focus on the design, development, implementation, use, and evaluation of public transportation systems in urban environments to support the mitigation of CO_2 emissions. These were revealed through quantitative, qualitative, or case-based methods in the book.

The chapters to follow present a wide variety of domains and perspectives from promoting sustainable public transportation strategies in urban environments. And it is an international perspective, both in terms of the varied geographical points of origin for the research and for the authors' locations. This work reaches into four different continents namely Asia, Africa, Europe, and North America including the countries such as Cameroon, Canada, Czech Republic, China, Croatia, India, Romania, Slovenia, as well as Turkey. And this is probably not an exhaustive list. This range of countries validates both the interest in and importance of sustainable public transportation.

Although this book is a completed volume, and the research and thinking presented in these chapters provide some determination to their specific topics, each chapter also raises many additional questions that deserve further inquiry and investigation. In other words, while each chapter answers one or more questions, each chapter also raises additional inquiries that deserve attention and exploration. There is much still to learn about the strategies of public transportation in urban environments to ensure sustainable ways of public transportation in very near smart cities.

ORGANIZATION OF CHAPTERS

The chapters of this book present a variety of topics. The book is divided into two sections: "Concepts and Theoretical Framework" and "Case Studies and Empirical Research Findings."

Section 1. Concepts and Theoretical Framework

The chapters in this section focus on the concepts and theoretical framework of sustainable public transportation strategies in urban environments.

In Chapter 1, Kristina Nagode, Luka Tomat, and Anton Manfreda explore the smart society concepts and elements for assuring a green future. The cities and society are bound to change, and the residents want them to be pleasant places to live in. Modern digital technology can provide different solutions that can solve several problems that cities are facing and can be applied to existing infrastructure as well. However, merely implementing the technology is not enough and cities need to exploit the potential of digital resources, accept and utilize digital resources to support their strategies and leverage each technology. Since digitalization has a broad impact on both organizations and society, this chapter will review the concept of digitalization as an enabler and facilitator of smart cities together with presenting the concept of a smart society and its impact on the green future. Several research areas are outlined in the chapter together with important elements of a smart city and society that are assuring a green and sustainable future.

In Chapter 2, the authors Serban Raicu, Dorinela Costescu, and Mihaela Popa focus on the performance of urban public transportation networks. Despite the objectives of sustainable development, which aim to reduce pollution and energy consumption, many cities face issues caused by traffic congestion and inadequate public transportation. In this framework, the chapter emphasizes the challenges of public transportation services and analyses a comprehensive set of criteria for evaluating public transportation performances. The functions of public transportation and their linked criteria for performance evaluations are discussed. Then, the particularities of effectiveness and efficiency in public transportation networks are explained. Effectiveness is defined as the level of achievement of preset tasks of public transportation. Efficiency is related to the ratio between the outputs and the used resources. Additionally, different

xvi

Preface

indicators must be defined for production and commercial efficiency. The presented analysis supports developing an effective and efficient urban transportation system in a dynamic social environment, with rapid changes in user requirements.

In Chapter 3, Bor Krizmanič and Aleš Groznik explain the role of electromobility in energy-related smart grids. The chapter describes the major components of the power grid. It then describes and explains the trends in the consumption and generation of electricity, with a particular focus on increasing the share of renewable energy sources. The concept of the smart grid is then described, including a discussion of the smart meter and the prosumer concept. The second part of the chapter is dedicated to electro-mobility. This section describes the main characteristics of electric vehicles and the trend of their diffusion, battery technologies, charging stations, smart charging, and the vehicle-to-grid concept.

In Chapter 4, Ivana Ninčević Pašalić, Maja Ćukušić, Silvia Golem, and Tea Jašić explain information systems and technologies for green public transportation. Overloaded infrastructure is one of the main challenges cities are facing nowadays. Cities attempt to overcome these challenges by applying different innovative concepts and technologies, one of which is smart city initiatives. One of the elementary features of smart cities is the modernization of public transport and well-designed transportation infrastructure. Modern information systems are used in public transportation in many ways, with the main purpose of facilitating and improving public transport for citizens. This chapter overviews the implementation of some standard information systems in public transportation and explains their purposes, way of functioning, and advantages for both users and providers. The aim of this chapter is to demonstrate relevant information systems used in public transport in several European cities - Rome, Paris, London, and Split. It is clearly shown that each city has its own version of a particular information system that achieves the goals of smart mobility.

In Chapter 5, the authors Dorinela Costescu and Eugenia Alina Roman deal with challenges in the development of urban intermodal mobility systems. Technological progress and the economic and social environment dynamics lead to changing mobility needs. Modifying travel practices, increasing the pressures for fast and predictable services, and expanding the demands of users for individualized offers determine requirements for diversifying the mobility supply in an integrated framework that must meet sustainable development objectives. In this framework, intermodal public transport plays a significant role. The chapter introduces the definitions of multimodality and intermodality in urban mobility systems. Intermodal transportation accounts for the different capabilities of diverse modes, including their availability, speed, density, costs, limitations, and, therefore, their most appropriate operating. The functions of intermodal public transportation are discussed. It is emphasized that solutions for sustainable mobility can be developed through a better understanding of the opportunities and challenges of the new mobility services.

In Chapter 6, the authors Anton Manfreda and Jure Erjavec focus on nudging toward sustainable public transportation. The chapter presents the importance of public transportation in coping with contemporary environmental issues. However, the aim is not to present public transportation as the only method of transportation leading toward a green future. New services and solutions should be carefully developed in cooperation with residents considering their needs, culture, habits, and existing procedures. Transforming the mindset of residents should be considered as well. Therefore, the authors present the readers with different theories, models, tools, and frameworks, illustrated with existing cases for promoting behavioral change amongst individuals, focusing specifically on nudging mechanisms. While the focus of the chapter is mainly on nudging towards sustainable public transportation, they illustrate nudging with examples from other areas as well and argue how such uses can also be applied to promote

xvii

Preface

sustainable public transportation. This chapter is therefore aimed at policymakers and other stakeholders involved in promoting sustainable public transportation modes.

In Chapter 7, the author Oyku Yucel deliberates on the use of green bonds to promote green projects. The need for alternative financing mechanisms has arisen with increasing concerns about the environment and sustainability and rising costs. Especially, in developing countries where financial resources are scarce, it is necessary to come up with new ways of financing options to cover the upfront investment needs of green projects. Recently, green bonds are commonly used to finance green projects. Like conventional bonds green bonds are fixed-income securities, however, proceeds of green bonds can only be used in financing or re-financing new or existing green projects that have environmental benefits. In this chapter, concept, and types of green bonds, figures on how developed and the integrated green bond market are, green bond principles and measurement of objectives, regulatory bodies, investment advantages and risks, investment alternatives, real-life examples as well as suggested greenium (green premium) concept for investors will be discussed.

In Chapter 8, the author Pelin Irgin focuses on an overview of sustainable public transportation in higher education. Very few engineering and business/management education programs emphasize the importance of sustainable public transportation in urban environments even though agencies and practitioners recognize it. Many undergraduate and graduate students have little training on how a sustainable public transport system is planned, designed, and operationalized, which is critical for a better understanding of sustainability and equity in public transportation. Content and instructional materials in sustainable public transportation education are still not readily available for practitioners. Therefore, this chapter aims to examine the public content and instructional materials on the websites of various universities in North America and Europe and to understand their commitment to education in sustainable public transportation, specifically to "sustainable public transportation" courses offered in the programs. It addresses how sustainability and equity in public transportation are integrated with textual and visual materials used in engineering and business/management education programs.

Section 2. Case Studies and Empirical Research Findings

The chapters in this section focus on case studies and empirical research findings related to sustainable public transportation strategies in urban environments.

In Chapter 9, the author Ivana Nincevic Pasalic explores the use of information and communication technologies and renewable energy in Europe. Information and Communication Technologies (ICTs) can help in cutting up to 20% of global carbon emissions by assisting consumers, different industries, and the public sector in energy savings and energy efficiency improvement. This chapter explores the relationship between ICTs and the development of renewable energy in European countries. In the first part of the research, the author conducted a cluster analysis to measure the differences in the use of ICTs in Europe through information society indicators. The results of the clustering (hierarchical and K-means) showed the existence of four clusters and the increased differences between clusters from 2015 to 2020. The second part of the research confirms the existence of differences between clusters in the share of energy consumption from renewable sources, and the differences proved to be statistically significant. The results are discussed in terms of implications for public transportation concluding that local governments must start and/or keep using ICTs for urban solutions, for the future to be greener and sustainable.

In Chapter 10, the authors Gizem Çelik and Zafer Yilmaz apply a comparison of traditional and green public transportation vehicles in terms of CO_2 emissions. The chapter aims to evaluate traditional public

xviii

Preface

transportation technologies, introduce alternative future green transportation technologies in smart and sustainable cities and make a comparison between traditional and green public transportation systems. Istanbul is chosen to apply a case study to explain the importance of using green transportation ways in terms of CO_2 emissions. The results of different transportation modes in different routes are compared. The results found for different scenarios on the routes in our case study ensure that the most eco-friendly options would be the walking, cycling, and public transportation ways for the passengers although they may not provide the optimal solutions in terms of total duration and distance traveled.

In Chapter 11, the authors Zdenek Kresa, Jan Tluchor, and Adam Heyes explain the attractiveness of urban public transport from the point of view of young passengers. Experience from the Czech Republic. This chapter uses the customer-oriented approach to help enhance understanding of the use of sustainable public transportation (PT) systems in urban areas to support climate change actions. It studies the views and experiences of young passengers (Generation Z) in a heavily used Central European PT system. Three surveys are conducted to study the effect of the coronavirus epidemic on the behavior of passengers. Additionally, automated passenger counting data are utilized. The surveys identify that despite the epidemic, the most important factors of customer experience are those related to the total travel time. Findings further include the fact that the PT is starting to be used more frequently in 2022 after a decline in 2020 and 2021. The decline is not caused by a massive outflow of regular passengers, but in general by passengers having fewer reasons to travel. Discussions are underway as to how to increase the attractiveness of PT systems.

In Chapter 12, the authors Séverin Bertand Etémé Bessala, Justin Moskolai Ngossaha, Jean Gaston Tamba, and Jacques Etamé analyze social big data for improving urban mobility services. In the context of developing countries such as Cameroon, which is the case study, urban mobility is still mainly based on the traditional model and the major tools of urban mobility governance are practically not in place. Only the main cities have an Urban Development Plan. These cities are marked by poor knowledge of urban mobility issues due to a lack of data and studies on the continuous monitoring of the performance of urban mobility. In this context, how can innovative solutions based on Big Data technologies and sophisticated approaches be integrated to address the challenges of sustainable urban mobility? In this study, a methodological framework based on a system engineering approach has been proposed to guide mobility decision-makers and users in the implementation and use of urban mobility services. The result of this study helps to extract knowledge and massive data for better decision-making in the context of developing countries and proposes a model of urban mobility system be deployed as a recommendation to decision-makers.

In Chapter 13, the author Aditya Singh explains the development and significance of Bengaluru suburban rail project. The suburban rail project in Bengaluru City in the Karnataka state of India will address the local mass travel needs from Bengaluru City to nearby towns or satellite cities. The chapter discusses the development stages of the Bengaluru Suburban Rail Project. The necessity, essential features, and significant advantages of the suburban rail project are presented. The project is expected to reduce traffic congestion problems in Bengaluru City and its nearby towns. Supplementary benefits related to time savings and increased passenger comfort are also estimated. Further, the challenges and risks faced by the project are discussed. Some future potential extensions of the project are considered.

In Chapter 14, the authors Nida Durmaz and Aysenur Budak focus on the evaluation of the barriers to the use of sustainable transportation systems in city logistics with an integrated grey DEMATEL-ANP approach. The rapid increase in journeys, freight transport, and the use of private vehicles in cities causes environmental problems such as the decrease in urban environmental quality as well as economic and social problems in transportation. In this context, the concept of city logistics shows up to improve and maintain logistics activities in settlements. It is necessary to define the barriers to the use of sustainable transportation systems in city logistics and to plan strategic steps by prioritizing these barriers according to their importance. In this study, an integrated approach of Grey DEMATEL-ANP is proposed to model these barriers in the city logistics for Istanbul. The proposed method determines the cause-effect relationships and relative weights of the key barriers. The results of this study may help decision-makers and practitioners address the key barriers highlighted, and provide the theoretical guideline to use sustainable transport systems across city logistics successfully.

In Chapter 15, the author Seda Damla Yücel explains intellectual property rights and entrepreneurship in smart cities. intellectual property rights (IPR) are critical for developing new inventions and creations, transforming them into social and economic value, and increasing inventors' and creators' competitiveness. The chapter focuses on the main functions of IPR are preventing competitors from owning, using, using, selling, and monetizing related inventions and creations, access to markets and networks, and obtaining venture capital. The chapter also explains how entrepreneurship contributes significantly to economic growth and is crucial to creating opportunities and improving the performance of new businesses. Its impact varies from economy to economy based on its outputs, a nation's industrial and technological prowess, and its legislative framework for developing entrepreneurs. Technological development is inevitable considering the increasing population, existing infrastructure, services offered to society, limited resources, the expected quality of life, and the city's ecological imprint. Therefore, creative and technological solutions will be essential, especially in building dynamic approaches while creating smart cities for the future.

In Chapter 16, the author Silvia Golem talks about a walking-friendly environment. One of the main aims of the smart city paradigm is to reduce the environmental footprint of urban growth by managing urban mobility in a citizen-friendly way. Facilitating and encouraging citizens to walk is a way to make the modern form of urban mobility greener and safer. Evidence of the benefits of walking and walkable urban forms has appeared in different strands of literature, suggesting the multidisciplinary nature of it. The main aim of this paper is to document and review the existing measures of urban walkability, along with the relevant cases where the attempts to measure walkability were made, thereby contributing a wider literature that aims to identify and understand factors that are most relevant for urban walkers.

Zafer Yilmaz
TED University, Turkey

Silvia Golem
University of Split, Croatia

Dorinela Costescu
Polytechnic University of Bucharest, Romania

Section 1
Concepts and Theoretical Framework

Chapter 1
The Smart Society Concepts and Elements for Assuring a Green Future

Kristina Nagode
https://orcid.org/0000-0002-1440-4589
School of Economics and Business, University of Ljubljana, Slovenia

Luka Tomat
School of Economics and Business, University of Ljubljana, Slovenia

Anton Manfreda
https://orcid.org/0000-0003-0469-5201
School of Economics and Business, University of Ljubljana, Slovenia

ABSTRACT

The cities and society are bound to change, and the residents want them to be pleasant places to live. Modern digital technology can provide different solutions that can solve several problems that cities are facing and can be applied to existing infrastructure as well. However, merely implementing the technology is not enough, and cities need to exploit the potential of digital resources, accept and utilize digital resources to support their strategies, and leverage each technology. Since digitalization has a broad impact on both organizations and society, this chapter will review the concept of digitalization as an enabler and facilitator of smart cities together with presenting the concept of a smart society and its impact on the green future. Several research areas are outlined in the chapter with important elements of a smart city and society that assure a green and sustainable future.

DOI: 10.4018/978-1-6684-5996-6.ch001

Copyright © 2023, IGI Global. Copying or distributing in print or electronic forms without written permission of IGI Global is prohibited.

INTRODUCTION

Digitalization has far-reaching effects on both companies and society. Digital transformation, which is receiving a great deal of attention in academia and business, is changing companies' key business operations, management concepts, products, processes and organizational structures. Numerous definitions can be found in the literature, but practitioners also perceive the phenomenon from different angles. Managing digitalization is becoming increasingly difficult due to the constantly evolving innovations and the difficulty of managing the associated technologies. Moreover, these technologies have the potential to affect the quality of life of every individual as well. Finally, these issues are challenging not only for organizations and individuals, but also for cities and society. This transformation is affecting a wide range of areas, including mobility, the environment, public governance and, most importantly, the lives of current and future citizens.

Throughout human history, an important need has been to live together, to create a safer environment for populations, and to achieve a better quality of life through easier management of people and resources. Aware of this, people invented places where they could more easily provide these services and learn to live together. However, many cities today face challenges resulting from rapid urbanization and the inability of infrastructure to cope. By the end of 2050, the urban population is expected to account for about 70% of the total population (United Nations, 2018). As a result, several smart city initiatives are emerging as smart cities address key issues of modern life.

In rapidly growing cities around the world, mobility and transportation cause a variety of problems that need to be solved. Smart cities can provide solutions by using digital technologies that enable sensing, data processing and communication between objects connected to the Internet. Overall, smart city initiatives, along with smart mobility initiatives, should aim to improve the quality of life and ensure a green future for residents by taking their needs into account and avoiding the unnecessary construction of unwanted or useless infrastructure that would overwhelm and annoy citizens. To support the development of such a smart city, several aspects need to be considered. Among them, digital transformation, sustainability, and smart society are the concepts that are referred to as the most important.

With this in mind, this chapter first presents established definitions and research areas related to the concept of digital transformation as key to the emergence of smart cities, as well as research areas related to the concept of smart cities and society. Finally, the problems and challenges presented are not only relevant to cities, but the transformation relates to society as a whole. Next, the concept of sustainability and green future is presented, which is one of the most important pillars for ensuring smart mobility and transportation in smart cities, in contrast to the current and future challenges such as climate change, population growth, and rapid urbanization. Sustainability is an important concept that aims to prevent overuse of limited resources and protect the environment. This is followed by the presentation of the concept of smart society, which is an important aspect that needs to be taken into account to enable better economic prosperity, social well-being and sustainable and efficient governance. Finally, we present smart mobility and transportation as one of the most influential aspects of smart development.

The focus is on the main components and elements of a smart society with special attention to smart mobility as the most user-centric element of any smart city. The aim of the chapter is therefore to carefully present the main ideas and link the concepts of digital transformation, sustainability, and a smart society with smart mobility and transportation leading to a green future.

DIGITAL TRANSFORMATION AND ITS IMPACT ON ORGANIZATIONS AND SOCIETY

The Concept of Digital Transformation

The term "digital transformation" (DT) was introduced by Bharadwaj (2000), who examined the relationship between IT and business performance, focusing on the importance of using digital technologies to support business processes that enable gaining competitive advantage to meet the challenges of the emerging digital economy. Next, the concept DT was further developed by Bauer, who looked at DT in various sectors such as dentistry, e-commerce (Bauer & Brown, 2001), and healthcare services (Bauer, 2002). Subsequently, numerous articles have been published on DT looking at the concept from different aspects. The distribution of publications over the last few years is shown in Figure 1.

Figure 1. Number of DT publications through time from 2012-2021
Source: (Clarivate Analytics, 2022); own analysis

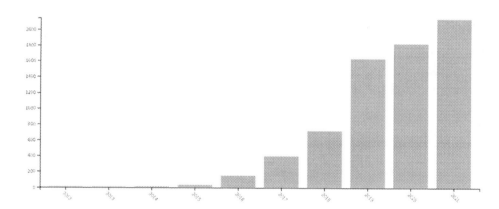

Nevertheless, a more holistic approach to DT is needed, so Matt, Hess, and Benlian (2015) proposed a conceptual DT framework that emphasizes four key dimensions: Technology use reflects a company's approach and ability to explore and leverage new digital technologies; Value creation changes reflect the impact of digital transformation on a company's value creation; Structural changes refer to the changes in organizational structures, processes, and capabilities needed to deal with and leverage new technologies; and the Financial dimension refers to both a company's need to act in response to a struggling core business and its ability to finance a digital transformation. The literature shows that DT can be viewed from both a social and an economic perspective, with different objectives, as can be seen in Table 1.

Anyhow, at its core, DT refers to the application of technology to build new business models, processes, software and systems enabling profitable revenue, greater competitive advantage, and higher efficiency of the business processes and their performance. Businesses thus transform processes and business models, empowering workforce efficiency and innovation, and personalizing customers or in the case of smart city citizen experiences (Schwertner, 2017). It was shown that DT is not all about technology. While digital technology provides opportunities to boost efficiency in processes' performance on one

Table 1. DT objectives from an economic and social perspective

Economic perspective	Social perspective
• Implement new and innovative business models. • Increase income generation, productivity and value addition in the economy. • Improve the regulatory framework and technical standards.	• Foster the development of a more innovative and collaborative culture in industry and society. • Change the education system to provide new skills and future orientation to persons so that they can achieve excellence in digital work and society. • Create and maintain digital communication infrastructures and ensure their governance, accessibility, quality of service and affordability. • Strengthen digital data protection, transparency, autonomy and trust • Improve the accessibility and quality of digital services offered to the population

Source: (Ebert & Duarte, 2018)

hand and increase customer experience and satisfaction on the other, it is of utter importance for the organizations that its people have the right mindsets to change current organizational practices. Thus, organizations need to consider the following key elements (Tabrizi et al., 2019):

- Setting their business strategy before investing in anything related to DT.
- Customer experience needs to be designed from the outside in.
- DT should rely on inside personnel who have intimate knowledge about what works and what doesn't in their daily operations.
- Employees, especially their fear of being replaced, need to be recognized, handled and managed,
- Key personnel mindsets need to be willing to accept agile decision making, rapid prototyping and flat structures.

Organizations need to carefully consider how to transform their business to obtain benefits and avoid risks from DT. They must strategically approach DT concentrating on the common organization's nexus and with sufficient technical skills and business knowledge enabling them to build and maintain the enthusiasm of the management and employees to embrace the needed changes and attain competitive advantages (Tomat & Trkman, 2019).

DIGITAL TRANSFORMATION RESEARCH REVIEW

Since DT has become an important area of research in contemporary business studies, many literature reviews have been proposed to show the current state of the field. However, since most of them are qualitative reviews, they lack objectivity to comprehensively reflect current developments. Therefore, this section presents a bibliographic review of the literature from DT. Such an approach can be used to identify the current state of knowledge and explore the state of the art, as well as to create science maps to understand specific scientific fields and examine current trends. Using science mapping, it is possible to extract the relevant parameters from the specific scientific literature and classify them into clusters to achieve objectivity of information about a specific field (Tranfield et al., 2003). In order to represent the current state of knowledge in the field DT, the co-occurrence analysis was performed to identify the clusters of the most important terms that co-occur in the studied papers and to create a graphical representation of the links between the recognized terms.

The Smart Society Concepts and Elements for Assuring a Green Future

The Web of Science was selected to conduct a co-occurrence analysis because it allows for the identification of relevant publications in the studied area, as it is the main online academic service that provides online publication databases of the leading scientific journals in the fields of interest (Boyack et al., 2005). To identify the relevant publications, the following search string was used: TS = ("Digital transformation"). In this way, publications were identified that contained the term *digital transformation* in any of the searchable fields in the Web of Science. In addition, publications were narrowed down to articles in the following Web of Science categories: Business, Management and Information Science, Library Science. The time window for articles was set from 1.1.2016 to 31.7.2022, as the number of publications on DT increased rapidly from 2016 (see Figure 1). Based on these parameters, 1250 publications were identified and further analyzed using the bibliographic method of coincidence.

Different software tools and applications exist for performing bibliometric analysis, such as VOSViewer, BibExcel, Sitkis, and SciMat. As VOSViewer is one of the most popular and free to use, it has been selected for this study. Additionally, it allows for the construction of the co-occurred terms network as well as it allows for visualization of identified clusters.

To perform co-occurrence analysis, full records and cited references (author, title, source, abstract, keywords…) of identified publications have been exported from the Web of Science and imported into VOSviewer. The co-occurrence unit of analysis was set to author keywords only. The minimum number of occurrences of a term was set to 8 resulting in the 78 term phrases being included in the analysis. Furthermore, identified terms have been manually monitored and those that were not relevant have been excluded from further analysis. The identified terms have been divided into 3 clusters that are shown in Figure 2.

Figure 2. Co-occurrence network of DT publication phrases within scientific articles
Source: own analysis

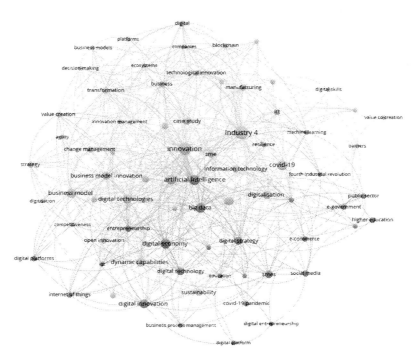

As seen in Figure 2 three clusters have been identified. The biggest two are coloured in red and green and consists of 27 terms. The third, smallest cluster (coloured in blue) consists of 21 items. The first most significant cluster (coloured in red) is conquered by the terms *digital innovation, big data, artificial intelligence, IoT, digital strategy and digital economy* suggesting that the majority of the research in this cluster tackles the emergence of new modern digital technologies being used in the organizations. These papers are more practically oriented researching the implementation and adoption of these technologies in the real sector.

The second most significant cluster (coloured in green) is conquered by the terms *Industry 4., Innovation", Business model, Technologies, Technological innovation and Dynamic capabilities* suggesting that the majority of the research in this cluster tackles capability of organizations to purposefully adapt an organization's resource base by performing innovative upscales of their performances to address challenges of ever-changing dynamic business environments they are currently operating in. Papers in this cluster research business model innovation, which can arise from a successful DT implementation process.

The third cluster (coloured in blue) is conquered by the terms *Covid-19, Digitalization, Digitalisation, Industry 4.0, Information technology, Change management, Leadership, Supply management and Innovation management* suggesting that the papers in this cluster approach the DT from more managerial perspective seeing DT as a driver to improve decision making in the organizations to increase their performance.

Several specific terms can be observed in all three clusters forming strong correlations amongst them. For example, *digital technologies* from the green cluster strongly relate to *artificial intelligence* and *big data* in the red cluster and *industry 4.0, covid-19* and *resilience* in the blue cluster. Or, *digital economy* from the red cluster strongly relates to *digitization, industry 4.0, knowledge management* and *competitiveness* in the blue cluster and *innovation, business model innovation, business model* and *dynamic capabilities* in the green cluster. Nevertheless, the recent Covid-19 pandemic also boosts the research in the DT field. Hence, *covid-19* from the blue cluster is strongly correlated to *technology, digital technologies and value creation* in the green cluster and *big data, digital innovation* and *digital strategy* in the red cluster.

To complement the network map analysis, density map visualization can be considered. The colour intensity of each term in a density map reflects the density of items in a network. As can be seen from Figure 3 similar clusters and findings from the network map can arise from the density visualization.

IMPACT OF DIGITAL TRANSFORMATION ON ORGANIZATIONS AND SOCIETY

Nowadays, organizations are facing various challenges arising from new digital technologies and dynamic environments forcing them to constantly innovate and change their processes and business models to adapt to the "new age" customer needs. As digital technologies are developing, the traditional concept of doing business has been majorly disrupted and organizations need to change and implement new and innovative business models. To build new business models, processes, and systems that provide profitable revenue, greater competitive advantage, and higher efficiency, organizations need to digitally transform (Schwertner, 2021). Thus, DT impacts organizations in many ways enabling them to benefit in various areas and from different technological and business-related perspectives. The major benefits of DT for organizations are presented below (Virtru, 2018):

Figure 3. Co-occurrence density map of DT publication phrases within scientific articles
Source: own analysis

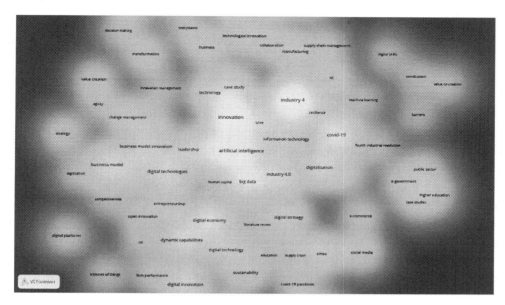

- Enhanced data collection: DT enables translation of the raw data into valuable insights across various touchpoints producing single views of different aspects of the organization (e.g. production, finance or business opportunities).
- Stronger resource management: DT is a system for gathering the right data and incorporating it fully for business intelligence at a higher level.
- Data-driven customer insights: DT encompasses every area of a business and can lead to process innovation and efficiency across units.
- A better customer experience: DT enables creating a customer-centric business strategy.
- Encourages digital culture: DT provides customers with control of how their data is collected and used and empowers them with the autonomy to make decisions around their data.
- Increased profits: DT improves efficiency and profitability.
- Increased agility: DT increases the business' agility to improve speed-to-market by allowing for faster innovation and adaptation while providing a pathway to improvement.
- Improved productivity: DT enables automatization of many manual tasks and integrates data throughout the organization empowering team members to work more efficiently.

On the other hand, DT also brings risks to the organization. The major risks of DT for organizations are presented below (Căpușneanu, 2021):

- Cyber-security risk: Digital environment can be mitigated by unauthorized access organizations lacking to assure the confidentiality and integrity of technology systems (e.g., platform strengthening, network architecture, security application, vulnerability management and security monitoring).

- Operations risk: Lack of internal or external event prevention procedures that may adversely affect the ability to meet business objectives through its defined operations (e.g., inadequate controls in operating procedures).
- Technology risk: Technological failures or obsolete technologies, which have a major impact on systems, people and processes (examples of risk areas:
- scalability, file compatibility and accuracy, and the functionality of implemented technology).
- Data Leakage risk: Failing to implement data protection procedures across the digital ecosystem at different stages of the data lifecycle.

While DT has tremendous impact on individuals, businesses, and organizations, it also has significant impact on society (Gimpel & Röglinger, 2015). For example, constantly evolving and digitally supported business cycles based on current technological paradigms are modernizing the way society as a whole operates, including its economic, social, cultural, and political organization (Freeman et al., 2001).

From a historical perspective, we have seen significant advances in many areas such as medicine, military technology, cultural development, and communication technologies.

Usually, the emergence of a new technological revolution is seen as both an opportunity and a threat to the common behavioral practices of organizations and society in general. Thus, competitive structures that seek profit and want to survive in market competition force changes in business and economy, while society is held back by a strong inertia due to routine, ideology, and vested interests, leading to a gap between the techno-economic and socio-institutional spheres (Papenhausen, 2009). However, the increasing use of digital technologies in recent years, as well as the growth of information and communication, has triggered an "information overload" among people, pushing their mental capacities to their limits as they try to adapt to the new digital economy (Hilbert, López, & Vásquez, 2010). For example, the rise of artificial intelligence (AI) is outperforming humans in numerous intellectual tasks and becoming one of the key elements of current societal development as people rely on AI to make many of their important decisions using various technologies (e.g., self-driving cars, cancer diagnosis, electricity distribution, stock markets, etc.). In addition, AI has also significantly influenced people's cultural, economic, social, and political views (Pariser, 2011).

Overall, the new digital technologies DT lead to an inseparable and organically intertwined sociotechnological system that brings advantages and disadvantages to society. The main disadvantages include loss of privacy, political polarization, psychological manipulation, addictive behaviors, social anxiety and distraction, misinformation, and mass narcissism (Hilbert, 2022). On the other hand, digital technologies are driving human social development by influencing organizational processes and introducing new business models that create a whole new variety of products and services that influence human behavior (Morze & Strutynska, 2021).DT is posing challenges both to economies and society focusing on different areas, such as the labour market, education, health and wellbeing, etc., hence significant mindset changes will need to be made to adapt people and accelerate their inclusion into the processes of digital transformation of the society, which could be done through the creation of the modern digital environments, digitalization of different aspects of human processes, development of digital skills, etc. Hence, Morze & Strutynska (2021) proposed a general model of DT, which is presented in Figure 4 and is consisting of five main components:

- The reasons that lead to the need for the digital transformation of the area/industry

- The use of digital technologies to change business processes in the industry to increase its efficiency.
- Preparation of workers, employers, and the population as a whole for life in new socio-economic conditions.
- Effective use of existing data, including the use of modern tools for their analysis.
- Inclusion of new products, services, policies, markets, environment and development of the digital society as a whole

Figure 4. General DT model
Source: (Morze & Strutynska, 2021)

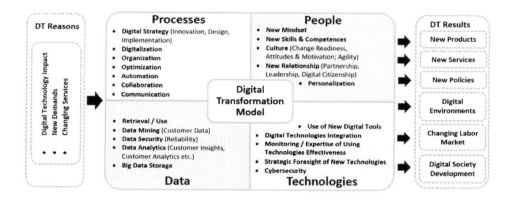

DT is an important and "not so easy to succeed" process that needs to be continuously evolved in the organization. Yet, DT is not affecting only organizations and their business, but society as a whole. As DT is not only technological, it is changing the way people work, entertain their selves and spend their free time impacting almost every piece of modern society (such as politics, health, work, etc.). The technological advancements and innovations will change the way people interrelate with the environment, marking a certain step forward in the digital era in which all segments of society are being digitalized, strongly impacting the social dimensions striving towards the security of workers, social inclusion, social status and, finally, the social peace (Komarčević, Dimić, & Čelik, 2017).

SUSTAINABILITY AND GREEN FUTURE CONCEPT

The Concept of Sustainability and a Green Future

Sustainability has become a huge part of the academic debate across various fields, such as environmental sciences, engineering, business and economics, energy fuels and others. Furthermore, it formed its field of sustainability research, with 59.292 articles published in environmental sciences and ecology research areas in the past years. The popularity of the concept is noted from the rapid growth of the use of the term since the 1990s in academic publications (see figure 5), resulting in 225.293 publications on the topic in the July of 2022 (of that 173.774 articles) (Clarivate Analytics, 2022; own analysis).

Figure 5. The number of academic publications on the sustainability topic from 1998 to 2021
Source: (Clarivate Analytics, 2022); own analysis

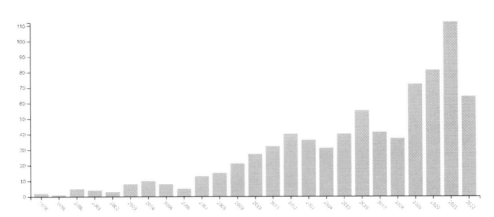

The importance of sustainability is also evident in the corporate environment, with the sustainability sector generating around 1 billion US dollars in annual revenues globally. While this is not much when considering the entire market, market research forecasts from UN sustainable development goals forecast indicate that future markets for their products and services could account for 12 trillion US dollars a year by 2030 (Elkington, 2018).

The concept of sustainability has become increasingly popular after the 1980s and has since then been defined many times from various perspectives. The understanding of the issue has been evolving from a more environmental focus, to an economic and social one. In the 1980s and 1990s, the pressure for change in corporations became evident, and the sustainable development concept emerged (Elkington, 2018). In the academic literature, there have been more than 100 definitions of the concept since then, but the most used one remains the one proposed by the Word commission on environment and development in its report "Our common future" in 1987, claiming that sustainable development is "the development that meets the needs of current generations without compromising the ability of future generations to meet their needs and aspirations" (Brundtland, 1987). As noted, sustainability is a very broad concept and serves as the ultimate goal. It can be applied to different systems in society, such as governments, organizations, and individuals. On the organizational level, concepts like sustainable development (Beck & Cowan, 1996), corporate citizenship (Collins & Porras, 1994), sustainable entrepreneurship, triple bottom line (Elkington, 1997), and business ethics (Commission of the European Communities, 2001) and corporate social responsibility (Commission of the European Communities, 2002) emerged.

Perhaps the most used of these has been the triple bottom line, which suggests three pillars of sustainability: economic, environmental and social, also known as profit, planet and people (3 P's). Economic sustainability refers to the profit that organizations achieve, while environmental and social sustainability refers to the conservation of resources (Elkington, 2018). Together, they are the basis of corporate social responsibility (CSR) that leads to corporate sustainability. However, this scheme needs to be carefully evaluated as well, since CS and CSR used to be historically completely separate from each other but have now become very much intertwined (van Marrewijk, 2003). The triple bottom line (TBL) approach, which considers people and the planet also being in the companies focus besides the profit, has also been criticized after its initial wave of popularity, even by the author himself. In 2018,

The Smart Society Concepts and Elements for Assuring a Green Future

Elkington re-estimated the TBL for Harvard Business Press, suggesting some changes. He implied that in the past two decades, the TBL was not used correctly and claimed that there has been too big of an importance put on the financial aspect of economic sustainability and, in some cases, environmental, whereas the social and other economic sustainability aspects have been put aside. Moreover, he says inter-generational equity is supposed to be the core of the concept (Elkington, 2018).

In the 1990's the sustainable development concept evolved from its focus on corporations to the consumer level, with the introduction of the green consumer concept (Elkington et al., 1990). During that time, there have also been many public demonstrations aspiring to provoke policy changes to help decrease the negative effects of corporations on the environment. Non-governmental organizations played a big role in this movement as well, making the 'green' movement global (Elkington, 2018).

In 2015, the United Nations developed sustainable development goals (SDGs) in the Agenda 2030 (United Nations, 2015), which has been signed by 40 nations until 2021 and offered 920,7 million US dollars only in 2020 for its implementation. The signed nations have pledged to commit to fulfilling the SDGs by the year 2030.

Nevertheless, a system change is still needed. Governments are falling behind with the development of sustainability policies and SDGs are often unsuccessfully implemented. Reevaluation of the concept and its measurement has been done before by many researchers, resulting in a big variety of similar concepts and measurement tools, namely: *concepts* like social responsibility, ethics, corporate governance, social accountability or sustainability; *measurement tools of sustainable development:* corporate sustainability reporting, world sustainability society, the environmental sustainability index, environmental performance index etc. (Elkington, 2018).

SUSTAINABILITY RESEARCH REVIEW

A bibliometric study was conducted on the sustainability topic based on the Web of Science (WoS) online publications database in august 2022. The search was done based on the topic *sustainability* to identify all of the publications that contain the term in title, abstract, or author keywords. The resulting database was further refined by the following filters: research areas were set to *information science library science*, the document type was set to *articles*, and the WoS index was set to *social sciences citation index – SSCI and science citation index expanded – SCI-EXPANDED*. The result was a database of 773 articles, that were used for the co-occurrence bibliometric analysis.

The co-occurrence analysis was performed with the VOSviewer software tool as one of the most popular ones. The identified publications were first exported from the WoS in a text file format with their full records and cited references and imported into the VOSviewer. The co-occurrence unit of analysis was set to author keywords, excluding the *sustainability* keyword, as it is present in all of the units of analysis by default.

The results showed the keywords with the highest number of occurrences, as well as clusters of correlated keywords on the topic.

The identified author keywords were divided into 6 clusters (see figure 6):

- Cluster 1 (red): collaboration, environment, ICT, India, information management, innovation knowledge management, open access, smart city, transparency, websites.

- Cluster 2 (green): academic libraries, digital divide, digital libraries, higher education, information literacy, internet, libraries, public libraries, strategy, sustainable development, telecommunications
- Cluster 3 (dark blue): bibliometrics, big data, big data analytics, circular economy, corporate social responsibility, covid-19, performance, social media, social sustainability
- Cluster 4 (yellow): case study, environmental performance, environmental sustainability, green is, green it, institutional theory, knowledge sharing, literature review
- Cluster 5 (purple): blockchain, developing countries, e-government, education, ict4d, information systems, supply chain
- Cluster 6 (light blue): artificial intelligence, climate change, competitive advantage, firm performance, information technology

The biggest clusters are the green one and the red one, both with 10 words, followed by the dark blue one with 9 words, the yellow one with 8 words, the purple one with 7 words, the light blue one with 5 words, and the light blue one with 5 words as well. The red cluster is conquered by the terms *knowledge management, innovation, collaboration,* and *India*. The green cluster is conquered by the terms *sustainable development* and *academic libraries*. The dark blue cluster is conquered by the terms *social media, big data*, and *circular economy*. The yellow cluster is conquered by the terms *environmental sustainability* and *green is*. The purple cluster is conquered by the terms *developing countries* and *information systems*. The light blue cluster is conquered by the terms *information technology* and *competitive advantage*. The information science and library science research on the topic of sustainability puts the greatest emphasis on the managerial and librarian perspective, specifically on the interconnectivity, innovativeness, and use of data and technology. The yellow cluster of research is the only one that focuses more specifically on sustainability.

Figure 6. Co-occurrence network of sustainability publication phrases within scientific articles

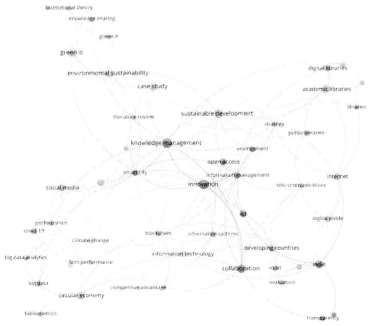

The Smart Society Concepts and Elements for Assuring a Green Future

From identified clusters and most frequently used keywords it is evident that sustainability research in information science and library science mainly focuses on the implementation of new technologies, the data and information analytics and management in organizations and governments, and their environmental sustainability performance. There is a lack of research on the social sustainability aspects of information systems and libraries, as one of the mentioned three pillars of sustainable development.

SMART SOCIETY IN THE GREEN FUTURE ERA

The Elements of a Smart Society

Digitalization has led to constant and rapid changes in today's society - be it cities, states, or countries - that require interaction and collaboration among citizens, organizations, and government to successfully achieve their goals. Government should help communities prepare for the changes ahead, support them in the adaptation process, and ensure that the changes benefit them and do not leave them feeling disconnected. In doing so, they must consider their particular strengths and challenges. A society that improves the well-being of its citizens, the strength of its economy, and the efficiency of its institutions using digital technologies deployed by governments is considered smart. The ultimate goal of smart societies, therefore, is neither smartness nor technology, but to enable a good life for people. The question that arises is how can new technologies deliver societal benefits? At the state level, countries should first assess their current societal state and then compare it to a benchmark country or other social system. The benchmark includes three categories: the people, the institutions, and the economy. Benchmarks for people and their well-being include inclusiveness, environment and quality of life, state of talent and human condition, and talent development. Institutional effectiveness is measured by freedoms (online and offline), trust, security, and public services. Economic resilience indicators include global connectivity, economic robustness, entrepreneurship, and innovation capacity. The indicators for the measures are shown in Figure 7 below. Based on the results, the country can identify its gaps and develop an appropriate strategy to address them, possibly using digital technologies (Chakravorti et al., 2017).

In Society 5.0, cybernetic space and physical space are very closely interconnected (UNESCO, 2015) with the aim to improve quality of life, social responsibility and sustainability (Carayanis et al., 2022). The value in it is created from the knowledge that is formed based on the gathered data and information (Society 5.0 A People-centric Super-smart Society, 2018). It is a very trendy concept, first developed in Japan, one of the most technologically developed countries. Society 5.0 and smart society are going in the same direction with SDGs from the Agenda 2030 by addressing sustainable, inclusive, human-centred societies (UNESCO, 2015). The shift to the human-centric approach has happened also in the case of industry 4.0, which further evolved to industry 5.0, that aims to have a positive impact on society, environment, and economy, following sustainable development goals (Breque et al., 2021). Both, society 5.0 and industry 5.0 are therefore relying on the same core elements: human-centricity, sustainability, and resilience. They aim to tackle challenges associated with interactions between people and machines (Breque et al., 2021), based on knowledge to improve competitiveness, productivity, and social well-being.

Figure 7. People, economy and institutions of smart society
Source: (Chakravorti et al., 2017)

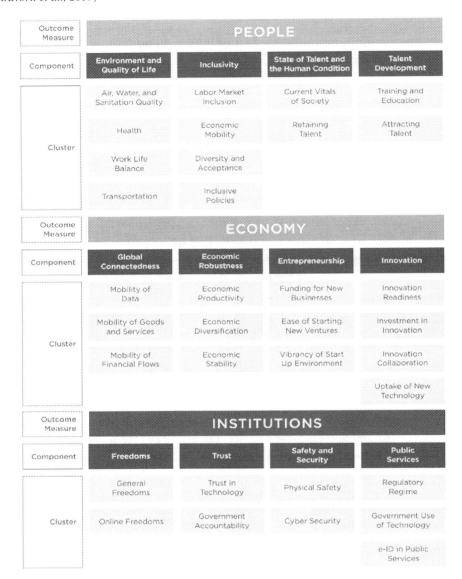

A smart city is another closely related concept to the smart society and society 5.0. It has been presented many years ago, but the idea flourished after 2011. It presents a response to rapid urbanization, which has been causing various challenges in urban environments. It is defined as a city, that puts people at the heart of development, incorporates information and communication technologies into urban governance and uses these elements as tools to promote effective government formation that includes participatory planning and citizen participation. By promoting integrated and sustainable development, smart cities are becoming more innovative, competitive, attractive and resilient, thus improving lives (Bouskela, 2016). Just as smart societies go hand in hand with sustainable development, also smart cities have emphasized sustainability in recent years.

The Smart Society Concepts and Elements for Assuring a Green Future

Smart society elements include people, institutions, and the economy (Chakravorti et al., 2017). Some of their sub-elements that are closely related to sustainable development include air, water and sanitation quality, work-life balance, training and education, economic productivity etc. Smart city elements on the other hand include elements such as smart government, manufacturing, citizens, mobility, transportation, security, grids/energy, health, buildings, farming/agriculture, open data and home (Longzhi et al., 2018). In terms of their sustainability, perhaps the most important elements are smart transportation and agriculture as they are one of the biggest polluters of the environment (European commission, 2021).

SMART SOCIETY RESEARCH REVIEW

A bibliometric study was conducted on the smart society topic based on the Web of Science (WoS) online publications database in august 2022. The search was done based on the topic *smart society* to identify all of the publications that contain the term in title, abstract, or author keywords. The resulting database was further refined by the following filters: the document type was set to *articles*, and the WoS index was set to *social sciences citation index – SSCI* and *science citation index expanded – SCI-EXPANDED*. The result was a database of 55 articles, that were used for the co-occurrence bibliometric analysis. By conducting a descriptive analysis on WoS we found out that approximately half of the articles are from the engineering research area, and only 3.6% are from the information science and library science area. There are no articles on the topic before the year 2011, therefore only articles past that year have been included in the analysis. Nevertheless, the number of articles is rising exponentially (see figure 8).

The co-occurrence analysis was performed with the VOSviewer software tool as one of the most popular ones. The identified publications were first exported from the WoS in a text file format with their full records and cited references and imported into the VOSviewer. The co-occurrence unit of analysis was set to author keywords, excluding the *smart society* keyword, as it is present in all of the units of analysis by default. The minimal threshold was set to 2, resulting in 20 keywords used in the map. The number of clusters was set to three.

Figure 8. The number of academic publications on the smart society topic from 2011 to 2022
Source: (Clarivate Analytics, 2022); own analysis

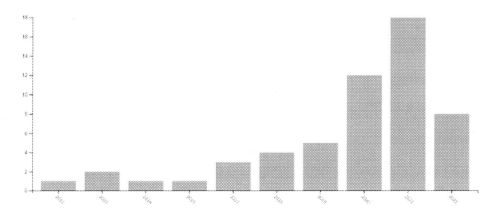

15

The results showed the keywords with the highest number of occurrences, as well as clusters of correlated keywords on the topic.

The identified author keywords were divided into 3 clusters (see figure 9). The biggest cluster is the red one with 7 words, followed by the green one with 6 words, and the blue one with 3 words. The red cluster is conquered by the terms *internet of things* (IoT) and *security* and presents the most significant cluster. The blue cluster follows it and is conquered by the term *artificial intelligence*, while the green one is conquered by the terms *society 5* (also called society 5.0) and *smart city*. From that, we can conclude that the majority of research is focusing more on the adoption of the internet of things in practice (red cluster) and on the development of new forms of societies, while the rest is focused on the development of required technologies for ensuring smart societies, such as AI and machine learning.

From identified clusters and most frequently used keywords it is evident that smart society research mainly focuses on the implementation of new technologies in smart cities and societies, such as the internet of things, artificial intelligence, machine learning, blockchain and others. One of the important research topics is also security of new technology use.

Figure 9. Co-occurrence network of smart society phrases within scientific articles
Source: own analysis

SMART MOBILITY AND TRANSPORTATION

As presented in the previous chapter, concepts of digital transformation, sustainability and smart society are of crucial importance to assure smart mobility and transportation of the cities of the future through digital technologies and innovative approaches. Among all the important elements of the smart city concept, we highlight smart mobility and transport, as this element is the most user-centric or generally the most visible to the end user. Mobility and transportation are one of the most important drivers of economic and social development as they connect people to educational institutions, jobs, health services, recreation centers, etc., but they also have negative impacts on the environment, such as resource depletion, pollution, and congestion (Rassafi & Vaziri, 2005).

Transport systems are accountable for up to 25% of world energy consumption and GHG emissions, moreover, the emissions are increasing rapidly (UN IPCC in Bamwesigye & Hlavackova, 2019). Some of the negative social influences of transportation include incidents, vulnerability to fuel price increases, loss of time and physical inactivity while commuting and so on (Woodrow & Grant, 2016).

Sustainable transportation ensures safe and consistent access to basic individual and societal needs, preserves social and environmental resources for future generations, is efficient and affordable, provides a variety of transport modes to choose from, and is environmentally friendly with low emission levels (Litman & Burwell, 2006).

The Smart Society Concepts and Elements for Assuring a Green Future

In smart cities, smart mobility initiatives aim to solve some of these problems through the use of digital technologies. In developing smart cities, it is also important to work toward sustainability in integrating smart mobility and other smart initiatives. Both sustainable transportation, as well as smart mobility should aim to improve the quality of life in communities and are closely linked (Bamwesigye & Hlavackova, 2019).

We further examined the relation towards mobility in a study conducted on the topic of smart cities in 2020 and 2021 on 3,078 respondents. Respondents were asked to state their level of agreement with the possible barriers of the mobility shift and their use of a car on a scale from 1 (strongly disagree) to 5 (strongly agree).

The results of the question regarding the barriers to the mobility shift (see figure 10) show that the strongest barriers are the lack of public infrastructure, the undefined strategy of the country and the lack of knowledge and awareness. Respondents also agree that little or no smart mobility promotion, conservative policies of local decision-makers, and a high cost for the end user are stopping the mobility shift, but to a lesser extent. Furthermore, they do not perceive the unattractiveness of the market for foreign investors, and the poor availability of technology as strong barriers to the mobility shift.

Figure 10. Barriers to the mobility shift
Source: own analysis

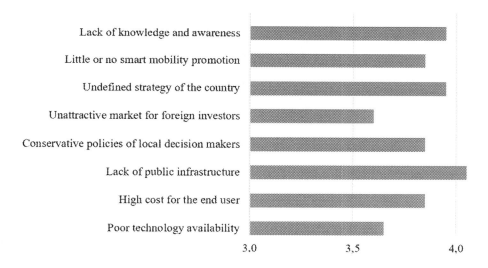

The results of the question regarding the use of a car (see figure 11) show that respondents only agree slightly that a lack of well-secured parking spaces in the city is hindering them from owning a car (answer 5) and in contradiction, that despite all the other transportation options and costs, owning a car still means too much to them to give it up at any time. We can propose that the existing car owners are not likely to give up car use yet, because the convenience of it is greater than the challenges that come with it. While the respondents without a car are not likely to decide to get one while living in the city. They disagree the most about them shifting from owning a car to using public transportation, even if it would be organized well or replacing it with car-sharing options completely. Furthermore, respondents disagree slightly that a variety of alternative modes of transport would be able to completely replace their need of owning a car, and that car ownership is purely an economic decision of comparing the cost of it compared to the cost of alternative transportation. We can propose that a variety of alternatives is needed for citizens to even think about giving up their car ownership and that the current public transportation system is not giving them all the benefits that they get from owning a car.

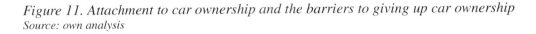

Figure 11. Attachment to car ownership and the barriers to giving up car ownership
Source: own analysis

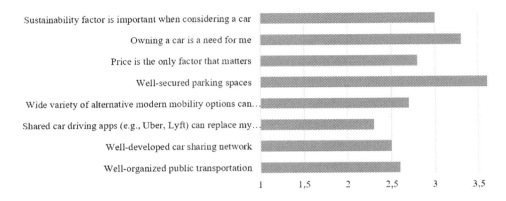

To conclude, the biggest barriers to moving to alternative modes of transportation are the lack of public infrastructure, the undefined strategy of the country and the lack of knowledge and awareness. People are very reluctant to shift from owning a car to using public transportation or replacing it with car-sharing options completely, even if it is well-organized. They are also reluctant to shift to alternative modes of transport, even if there is a variety of options. The existing car owners are not likely to give up car use yet, because the convenience of it is greater than the challenges that come with it. Although, the respondents without a car are not likely to decide to get one while living in the city, because of the parking and other issues that come with it. Regarding the sustainability aspects of owning a car, they are neutral about it.

Both figures show that the transition is not and will not be an easy process, calling for the cooperation of several relevant stakeholders. However, as smart cities and societies grow, also the transport demand grows as well. Smart cities need to incorporate Mobility as a Service (MaaS) as a smart mobility plan to better manage the use of transport and the flow of demands and availability. The basic concept behind it is to integrate all modes of transport into a single-entry point from the user standpoint and be always available for access. MaaS aims to avoid the time spent in traffic and congestion all the while providing a better and healthy lifestyle to the citizens. It also has other impacts especially in reducing pollution by minimizing the emission of toxic gasses.

The EU capital cities have long suffered from hours wasted in traffic congestion and rush hours. It minimizes productivity by causing delays in the morning commute to work as well as causing stress levels to rise due to road rage and lack of patience, sometimes it could escalate to accidents with serious injuries or more.

The Smart Society Concepts and Elements for Assuring a Green Future

The value of MaaS is to give its users a simplistic way to navigate the city, by switching from private to collective ownership that is more cheap, easy to use and sustainable. This idea allows city councils and policymakers to rethink the way transportation works and focus more on mobility rather than the means.

To achieve these goals, there is a need for collective work and collaboration between governmental agencies, private firms, and individuals. Service providers shall integrate all their services in a single platform where all the information on modes of transport is kept up to date in a real-time fashion, payments and ticket purchasing are very safe and the user interface is intuitive and easy to use.

Integration is a keyword when it comes to MaaS. There are five levels of integration identified (Sochor et al, 2018):

Level 0 No integration: in this level, each service provider is responsible for their trips, collecting data and providing clients with their transportation services.

Level 1 Integration of Information: In this level transportation companies work closely with open platforms to provide them with open and standardized data about the timeline of their transportation. These open platforms, such as Google and Moovit, have users rather than customers. The purpose is to provide users with information to assist them in their travel decisions and earn a small commission by forwarding them to the provider's platform or generating Ads on their pages.

Level 2 Integration of payment: This level focuses on providing single tickets for trips. It has to use the integration of information to provide the user with options to choose from. Users of this level are registered users for carsharing, profile needed services or ad hoc users for a single trip ticket. The value for its customers is the easy access, and for suppliers is the exposure to customers from this platform.

Level 3 Integration of the service offer: In this level trips and modes of transport are bundled in packages and presented as package payments or subscription-based. The operators aim to identify the best suppliers per transportation type and generate legal contracts with the local transportation agencies. Also, they could provide a roaming service where customers can use their native service while visiting other cities/countries.

Level 4 Integration of societal goals: This level reaches more towards sustainability goals. It can be implemented in any of the previous levels depending on the city's goals and politics. The two major actors in this level are transportation service providers and cities. These two can influence users' behaviour towards a societal or environmental goal. So, it is mandatory to cooperate between the two actors as well as the operators who run the transportation platform to fulfil both the citizen's and the city's needs. This cooperation could manifest in data exchange on transportation timelines and non-sensitive user data to manage traffic and congestion problems.

More and more cities are embracing different modes of micro-mobility to reduce congestion and provide cleaner mobility to address extensive air pollution and fight with the several presented challenges. While driverless vehicles and consumer-owned electric vehicles are not expected to hit the mass market anytime soon, micro-mobility is being embraced as a means to reduce congestion, traffic and chronic air pollution. Micro-mobility goes hand in hand with sustainable transport with its lightweight vehicles such as bicycles, e-scooters and others. People are willing to use micro-mobility even more, and the covid-19 pandemic even increases this willingness. Due to higher awareness about personal hygiene and physical distancing people were encouraged to use micro-mobility rather than public transportation. Other types of transport such as car sharing, electric scooters and electric bicycles will also significantly shape the future mobility transportation systems.

After all, smart cities are built on technology that improves the lives of citizens and provides support for future services, including future autonomous mobility. The impacts of autonomous vehicles will extend across society and the shift in transportation and mobility will require new policies, different infrastructure and the cooperation of various stakeholders to properly support the transformation into intelligent transport (Manfreda et al., 2021).

Some of the benefits that smart mobility offers to the city are providing innovative traffic and transportation infrastructure, saving resources, improving efficiency, providing accessibility to urban services, improving the quality of life for residents, reducing costs, and more efficient energy usage. Public transportation is one of the key elements in smart and sustainable cities affecting all spheres of a modern city. Having important social, economic and environmental impact, it is of utter importance that should be properly managed.

CONCLUSION

Throughout human history, an important need has been to live together, to create a safer environment for the population, and to achieve a better quality of life through easier management of people and resources. With this in mind, people have invented places where they could more easily provide these services and learn to live together. However, many cities today face challenges arising from rapid urbanization and the inability of infrastructure to cope with it, and by the end of 2050, the urban population is expected to account for about 70% of the total population (United Nations, 2018), leading to various threats, risks, and challenges to society, such as. such as profound social instability, high population density, risks to critical infrastructure, potential water crises, lack of affordable housing, traffic congestion, the potential for devastating spread of disease, inadequate electricity supply and distribution, poverty, or inefficient transportation systems. In addition, future urban populations will be exposed to the impacts of climate change. Modern organizations, and consequently individuals, cities, and society as a whole, face several challenges arising from the dynamic environments in which they operate. To address these challenges, several smart city initiatives are emerging to address the key issues of modern life.

The main challenges addressed in this chapter relate to digital transformation, sustainability, smart society in the age of the green future, and smart mobility and transportation. These concepts are and will therefore be crucial to achieving the green future that society is striving for. Thus, digital transformation is an essential part of the comprehensive development of society, economy, and business and affects the daily life of the entire society and is perceived as one of the most important global trends of this era. Thus, almost all areas of society (e.g., politics, governance, education, science, lifestyles, collective intelligence networks, the construction of open systems, and health) are being transformed by technological progress (Verina & Titko, 2019). Consequently, it will play a critical role in ensuring a resource-efficient and socially inclusive economy that encourages society to adopt greener lifestyles and make ecologically responsible choices to protect the environment and conserve natural resources for current and future generations.

In light of the above, it is important to ensure conceptual sustainability in future societal development by meeting the needs of current humanity without compromising the ability of future generations to thrive in a green environment. However, as explained in the subsection Sustainability and Green Future Concept, sustainability is a very broad concept and should be tackled as the ultimate goal for future development applied to various systems in society, such as governments, organizations, and individuals.

Therefore, the SDGs should be carefully followed and implemented, paying particular attention to social responsibility, ethics, corporate governance, social accountability, and sustainability (Elkington, 2018).

Digital transformation and sustainability are leading to constant and rapid changes in today's society, which tends to become "smart." Therefore, relevant authorities need to provide an environment that supports the upcoming changes that will benefit the whole society; in particular, the well-being of citizens, the strength of the economy, and the effectiveness of institutions using digital technologies deployed by governments are considered smart. On a conceptual level, the future smart societies aim to provide a better life for people on the wave of emerging digital technologies.

However, in the future smart society, the focus should be on smart mobility and transportation. The concept of smart mobility is based on the introduction of smart technologies used in transportation systems and mobility networks that connect different technology-based parts of mobility, changing the way transportation infrastructure is used by users. Thus, the integration of smart mobility devices into smart cities and their transport networks could lead to significant improvements in various transport-related areas such as road safety, healthcare, accidents, pollution, etc. On the other hand, there are also some potential threats to society that could result from smart mobility, such as resource depletion or traffic congestion (Rassafi & Vaziri, 2005).

Despite the advantages and the undoubted benefits that the introduction of smart technologies will bring to our cities, we must realize that we will face many challenges. The efficiency of such communities comes at a price. It requires a high financial investment, and even more important is the regulation and legal protection. Smart cities will collect, store, and analyse data about residents at every opportunity. This can pose a security risk, as it is very difficult to limit potential invasions of privacy or even the potential risk of hacker attacks. Yet, all of this should not be seen as an impeding element, but as a challenge that can be tackled with a clear vision and good knowledge of the goal, we want to achieve.

REFERENCES

Bamwesigye, D., & Hlavackova, P. (2019). Analysis of Sustainable Transport for Smart Cities. *Sustainability*, *11*(7), 2140. doi:10.3390u11072140

Bauer, J. (2002). Rural America and the Digital Transformation of Health Care: New Perspectives on the Future. *Journal of Legal Medicine*, *23*(1), 73–83. doi:10.1080/0194764023172766678 PMID:11957332

Bauer, J., & Brown, W. (2001). The digital transformation of oral health care: Teledentistry and electronic commerce. *The Journal of the American Dental Association*, *132*(2), 204–209. doi:10.14219/jada.archive.2001.0156 PMID:11217594

Beck, D. E., & Cowan, C. C. (1996). *Spiral dynamics: mastering values, leadership and change*. Blackwell Publishing.

Bharadwaj, A. (2000). A resource-based perspective on information technology capability and firm performance: An empirical investigation. *Management Information Systems Quarterly*, *24*(1), 169–196. doi:10.2307/3250983

Bouskela, M. (2016). *The Road toward Smart Cities: Migrating from Traditional City Management to the Smart City*. Inter-American Development Bank. doi:10.18235/0000377

Boyack, K. W., Klavans, R., & Börner, K. (2005). Mapping the backbone of science. *Scientometrics*, *64*(3), 351–374. doi:10.100711192-005-0255-6

Breque, M., De Nul, L., & Petridis, A. (2021). *Industry 5.0, towards a sustainable, human-centric and resilient European industry.* European Commission, Directorate-General for Research and Innovation. https://op.europa.eu/en/publication-detail/-/publication/468a892a-5097-11eb-b59f-01aa75ed71a1/

Brundtland, G. H. (1987). *Our Common Future: From One Earth to One World.* UN. http://www.un-documents.net/ocf-ov.htm

Căpuşneanu, S., Mateş, D., Tűrkeş, M. C., Barbu, C. M., Staraş, A. I., Topor, D. I., Stoenica, L., & Fűlöp, M. T. (2021). The impact of force factors on the benefits of digital transformation in Romania. *Applied Sciences (Basel, Switzerland), 11*(5), 2365. doi:10.3390/app11052365

Carayanis, E. G., & Morawska-Jancelewicz, J. (2022). The futures of Europe: Society 5.0 and Industry 5.0 as driving forces of future universities. *Journal of the Knowledge Economy, 13*(4), 3445–3471. doi:10.100713132-021-00854-2

Chakravorti, B., Chaturvedi, R. S., & Troein, C. (2017). *Building smart societies – A blueprint for action.* Tufts: The Fletcher School. https://sites.tufts.edu/digitalplanet/files/2020/06/Building-Smart-Societies.pdf

Collins, J., & Porras, J. I. (1994). *Built to Last: Successful Habits of Visionary Companies.* HarperCollins Publishers.

Commission of the European Communities. (2001). *Green Paper: Promoting a European framework for Corporate Social Responsibility.* Europa. https://ec.europa.eu/commission/presscorner/detail/en/DOC_01_9

Commission of the European Communities. (2002). *Corporate Social Responsibility: A business contribution to Sustainable Development.* Eurofound. https://www.eurofound.europa.eu/observatories/emcc/articles/business/corporate-social-responsibility-a-business-contribution-to-sustainable-development

Ebert, C., & Duarte, C. H. C. (2018). Digital transformation. *IEEE Software, 35*(4), 16–21. doi:10.1109/MS.2018.2801537

Elkington, J. Hailes, Julia., & Makower, J. (1990). The green consumer. Penguin Books.

Elkington, J. (1997). *Cannibals with forks: The Triple Bottom Line of 21st Century Business.* Capstone Publishing Limited.

Elkington, J. (2018). *25 Years Ago I Coined the Phrase "Triple Bottom Line." Here's Why It's Time to Rethink It.* Harvard Business Review. https://hbr.org/2018/06/25-years-ago-i-coined-the-phrase-triple-bottom-line-heres-why-im-giving-up-on-it

European Commission. (2021). *Transportation and the green deal.* Europa. https://ec.europa.eu/info/strategy/priorities-2019-2024/european-green-deal/transport-and-green-deal_en

Freeman, C., & Louçâ, F. (2001). *As time goes by: from the industrial revolutions to the information revolution.* Oxford University Press.

Freeman, C., & Louçã, F. (2001). As Time Goes By: From the Industrial Revolutions to the Information Revolution. Oxford University Press pp. viii, 40.

Gimpel, H., & Röglinger, M. (2015). *Digital transformation: changes and chances–insights based on an empirical study.* University Bayreuth. https://eref.uni-bayreuth.de/29908/

Hilbert, M. (2022). Digital technology and social change: The digital transformation of society from a historical perspective. *Dialogues in Clinical Neuroscience, 22*(2), 189–194.

Hilbert, M., López, P., & Vásquez, C. (2010). Information societies or "ICT equipment societies?" Measuring the digital information-processing capacity of a society in bits and bytes. *The Information Society, 26*(3), 157–178.

Hitachi-UTokyo Laboratory. (2018). *Society 5.0: A People-centric Super-smart Society.* Springer. https://doi.org/10.1007/978-981-15-2989-4

Komarčević, M., Dimić, M., & Čelik, P. (2017). Challenges and impacts of the digital transformation of society in the social sphere. *SEER: Journal for Labour and Social Affairs in Eastern Europe, 20*(1), 31–48.

Litman, T., & Burwell, D. (2006). Issues in sustainable transportation. *International Journal of Global Environmental Issues, 6*(4), 331–347.

Longzhi, Y., Noe, E., & Neil, E. (2018). *Outlier discrimination and correction in intelligent transportation systems: Privacy and security aspects of e-government in smart cities.* Elsevier.

Manfreda, A., Ljubi, K., & Groznik, A. (2021). Autonomous vehicles in the smart city era: An empirical study of adoption factors important for millennials. *International Journal of Information Management, 58*, 102050.

Matt, C., Hess, T., & Benlian, A. (2015). Digital transformation strategies. *Business & Information Systems Engineering, 57*(5), 339–343.

Morze, N. V., & Strutynska, O. V. (2021). Digital transformation in society: Key aspects for model development. *Journal of Physics: Conference Series, 1946*(1), 012021.

Papenhausen, C. (2009). A cyclical model of institutional change. *Foresight, 11*(3), 4–13.

Pariser, E. (2011). *The filter bubble: What the Internet is hiding from you.* Penguin Group.

Rassafi, A. A., & Vaziri, M. (2005). Sustainable transport indicators: Definition and integration. *International Journal of Environmental Science and Technology, 2*(1), 83–96.

Schwertner, K. (2017). Digital transformation of business. *Trakia Journal of Sciences, 15*(1), 388–393.

Schwertner, K. (2021). The Impact of Digital Transformation on Business: A Detailed Review. In J. Metselaar (Ed.), *Strategic Management in the Age of Digital Transformation* (pp. 1–29). Proud Pen.

Sochor, J., Arby, H., Karlsson, I. M., & Sarasini, S. (2018). A topological approach to Mobility as a Service: A proposed tool for understanding requirements and effects, and for aiding the integration of societal goals. In *1st international conference on mobility as a service (ICoMaaS) Proceedings (vol. 27, pp. 3-14).* Chalmers university of technology.

Tabrizi, B., Lam, E., Girard, K., & Irvin, V. (2019). Digital transformation is not about technology. *Harvard business review*. https://hbr.org/2019/03/digital-transformation-is-not-about-technology

Tomat, L., & Trkman, P. (2019). Digital transformation–the hype and conceptual changes. *Economic and Business Review*, *21*(3), 2.

Tranfield, D., Denyer, D., & Smart, P. (2003). Towards a methodology for developing evidence-informed management knowledge by means of systematic review. *British Journal of Management*, *14*(3), 207–222.

UNESCO. (2015). *UNESCO science report: towards 2030*. UNESCO. https://unesdoc.unesco.org/ark:/48223/pf0000235406

United Nations. (2015). *Transforming our world: the 2030 Agenda for Sustainable Development (A/RES/70/1)*. UN. https://sdgs.un.org/2030agenda

United Nations. (2018). *World urbanization prospects: The 2018 revision*. UN. https://www.un.org/development/desa/pd/content/world-urbanization-prospects-2018-revision

van Marrewijk, M. (2003). Concepts and Definitions of CSR and Corporate Sustainability: Between Agency and Communion. *Journal of Business Ethics*, *44*(2), 95–105.

Verina, N., & Titko, J. (2019). Digital transformation: conceptual framework. In *Proc. of the Int. Scientific Conference "Contemporary Issues in Business, Management and Economics Engineering'2019"*, (pp. 9-10). Vilnius, Lithuania.

Virtru. (2018). What are the Benefits of Digital Transformation? *Virtu*. https://www.virtru.com/blog/8-benefits-digital-transformation

Woodrow, C. I., & Grant, C. (2016). *Smart green cities: toward a carbon neutral world*. Routledge: Taylor and Francis.

KEY TERMS AND DEFINITIONS

Bibliometric Analysis: A statistical method to analyze the relationships and impacts of publications within a given area of research.

Digital Transformation: The concept of using and applying digital technologies to create new or modify existing business models, processes, and customer experience enabling profitable revenue and greater competitive advantage.

Smart City: The concept that includes the combination of urbanism and information and communication technologies with some aspects of creativity in society. It incorporates information and communication technologies into urban governance to promote effective government formation that includes participatory planning and citizen participation.

Smart Mobility: Smart mobility is one of the core elements of a smart city. It refers to the application of modern digital technologies in transportation systems including new management strategies, business models and processes in order to emphasize sustainability.

Sustainability: The concept that aims to prevent the overuse of limited resources and protect the environment.

Chapter 2
Performance of Urban Public Transportation Networks

Serban Raicu
Polytechnic University of Bucharest, Romania

Dorinela Costescu
https://orcid.org/0000-0002-1562-5834
Polytechnic University of Bucharest, Romania

Mihaela Popa
https://orcid.org/0000-0002-9071-508X
Polytechnic University of Bucharest, Romania

ABSTRACT

Despite the objectives of sustainable development, which aim to reduce pollution and energy consumption, many cities face issues caused by traffic congestion and inadequate public transportation. In this framework, the chapter emphasizes the challenges of public transportation services and analyses a comprehensive set of criteria for evaluating public transportation performances. The functions of public transportation and their linked criteria for performance evaluations are discussed. Then, the particularities of effectiveness and efficiency in public transportation networks are explained. Effectiveness is defined as the level of achievement of preset tasks of public transportation. Efficiency is related to the ratio between the outputs and the used resources. Additionally, different indicators must be defined for production and commercial efficiency. The presented analysis supports developing an effective and efficient urban transportation system in a dynamic social environment, with rapid changes in user requirements.

DOI: 10.4018/978-1-6684-5996-6.ch002

Copyright © 2023, IGI Global. Copying or distributing in print or electronic forms without written permission of IGI Global is prohibited.

INTRODUCTION

Urban structures and everyday life modifications have influenced mobility practices in the last decade, mainly characterized by broadening travel needs (Van Audenhove et al., 2014). Public transportation (PT) and non-motorized travel are increasingly considered mandatory components of the sustainable development of cities (COM, 2020; Veryard & Perkins, 2018). Moreover, the pandemic of Covid-19 has hugely impacted learning and working conditions, with significant consequences on the daily mobility pattern and concerns about safety travelling (Das et al., 2021; Vickerman, 2021). Therefore, the PT system must be constantly adapted to new requirements to ensure the social, environmental, and urban planning objectives.

Especially in the last period, statistics show low PT performances in European cities (Eurostat, 2021). In addition to the competition with private car usage, PT is a community service that must be supplied quasi-permanently, not only in peak periods. Despite the increased operating deficit, the socio-economic relevance of PT in time and space is unquestionable. It is essential to provide methods for adequate sizing of the PT supply, e.g., the social role of public transportation is recognized, but from an environmental point of view, is it justified to operate a bus on a line for an average of 5 passengers/hour? The answers to this category of questions need correct definitions of PT tasks. Additionally, appropriate methods for assessing the relationships between the effectiveness of public policies and PT efficiency must be available to decision-makers.

Although the term performance is frequently applied in the transport sector, it is utilized for different meanings. The concept most often refers to the quality/price ratio, which integrates the sense of efficiency rather than effectiveness (from a socio-economic point of view). Generally, public policies consider a set of performance measures based on specific objectives at the administrative level. Three main categories of indicators are notable (D'Arcier, 2012):

- **Indicators for Socio-Economic Effectiveness** measure the benefits of public policies for citizens; they reflect citizens' viewpoints (e.g., reducing congestion, reducing pollution, enhancing the urban environment, etc.).
- **Indicators for Service Quality** assess the improvement of PT attributes perceived by users (the viewpoint of users).
- **Indicators for Efficiency** aim at the optimum of the consumed resources function of the supplied offering (the viewpoints of operators and funding authorities).

The assessment of public transport performances, depending on the implemented operating technologies, is essential for increasing its attractiveness to users. Additionally, public transport operators must identify solutions for improving the effectiveness and efficiency of the service. The service functions and public transport performance indicators result from the correlated examinations of the public transport system (infrastructures, vehicles, implemented technologies, offered services), mobility system (the assembly of mobility demands and offerings in an area) and specific urban structure and shape. The factors that determine the performance of an urban public transport network are synthesized based on the links between commercial efficiency and the main goals of the public transport system – social, environmental, and urban planning.

Performance of Urban Public Transportation Networks

This chapter discusses the particularities of PT effectiveness and efficiency. To properly understand the necessary actions for sustainable mobility, the PT functions and their linked criteria for performance evaluations are explained. Mainly, it is emphasized that the correlation between effectiveness and efficiency must be clarified to avoid the simplicity and inaccuracy of assessing the component lines of a PT network. The presented criteria and indicators constitute a basis for guiding the management actions of a PT system.

DIFFICULTIES IN THE EVALUATION OF PUBLIC TRANSPORTATION PERFORMANCE

Collective Urban Public Transportation vs Individual Car Usage

Developing zones where people live and work mainly determines the origins and destinations of urban travel, the intensities and lengths of travel, and energy consumption. Daily urban mobility, expressed in person-km/time unit (year, day, hour, depending on the level of analysis) or person-trips/inhabitant/year, has increased in recent decades. The mobility increase, caused by the growth of the urban population, the intensification of socio-economic activities and the decentralization of cities, has been characterized by the rise in the share of the use of cars in daily trips.

After the Industrial Revolution, European cities had to provide residences for the population attracted by the various new jobs of the expanding industry within their historical limits. As a result, the cities expanded and generated massive daily commuting flows between residence zones and activity locations, mainly ensured by collective PT (also a consequence of the technical progress of the 19th century). The invention of the internal combustion engine, followed by the mass production of cars with more efficient propulsion-braking, support guidance, comfort systems and driving control, gradually shaped the urbanization process. Thus, in the 1920-1965 period, PT and telephony favoured a process of suburbanization characterized by a separation of housing from industry and an intense commute from the vicinity of the cities to their centre on PT networks - the hygienist city conception of Corbusier (Le Corbusier, 1971). Then, after 1965, the car determined the suburbanization of workplaces and commercial spaces, a dispersion of them compared to the previous phase in which the cluster towards the city centre revealed the role of PT lines. Car usage, complemented by the development of motorway networks with interchanges and ring roads, determined the diffusion of urbanization in rural areas.

Mobility solutions were designed for cars, allowing an increase in distances and the number of trips. Since the 1970s, running and parked cars have been invading the streets of historical cities that are incapable of adapting despite the authorities' efforts. Residents see their living environment affected.

Two conclusions can be drawn from a brief examination of the travel demand evolution and the choices for fulfilling them. The first refers to the sensitive and not adequately defined relationships between urban planning – transportation – traffic – living style. The second, linked with the first, illustrates the inability of the decision-makers to foresee the consequences of taking over some possible successful practices without carefully analyzing them. E.g., after the Second World War, when the automotive industry and car trade registered increasingly accelerated growth, the slogan "car for all" was adopted without considering the noticeable differences between the road traffic infrastructures in regions, especially those between the new cities and the historical ones. A quasi-general enthusiasm for the possession of this means of travel was generated in European cities. Due to the congruence between the provided mobility characteristics and the dominant ideology, the car as a means of individual travel was seen as the liberator from the fixed line route, traffic schedules and the shared vehicles typical of public transport. The car implied a private personal realm, individual management of time and space, a vector of autonomy and freedom, and an available means for daily trips. Obtaining a driver's license has become routine, symbolic access to release and mobility. Moreover, the car is also seen as a lifestyle in that the brand, version, colour, accessories and possible customizations are expressions of a different attitude (Hickman et al., 2019).

But, beyond the positive social representations of the car, as a symbol of individual freedom, numerous polemics reveal the gap between its unacceptable social and environmental consequences and the collective values (Pharoah, 1992). The deficiencies of car travel attachment contrast with the PT positive valences and non-motorized travel. The rapid extent of the consequences of car usage in urban mobility with all the incorporated technological innovations has adverse effects (Anciaes et al., 2022; Banister & Hickman, 2013; Newman & Kenworthy, 2015):

- **Accessibility Decreases** due to time spent in traffic congestion and searching available parking lots, especially in central areas.
- **Degradation of the Street as a Public Space** for informal communication (mainly caused by land use for road infrastructures for moving, parked and stationary cars).
- **Noise and Atmospheric Pollution** more intensively felt by the poor population due to the spatial segregation of housing.
- **Increased Crashes** with more considerable exposure for pedestrians, children and the elderly and higher risks for motorcyclists and cyclists than car users.
- **Worsening Daily Mobility Conditions** for those who do not use cars (pedestrians and cyclists, as well as PT users) due to the urban area's fragmentation by major traffic arteries, the

Table 1. Urban travel modal share in twelve European Member States covering diverse areas

Travel distance per person per day by main travel mode for urban mobility on all days (%)	Romania	Greece	Poland	Netherlands	Austria	Denmark	Latvia	Portugal	Germany	Croatia	Italy	Slovenia
By car as drivers	30.4	44.6	48.2	49.6	50.6	53.8	54.8	57.3	58.0	59.6	63.7	65.2
By car as passengers	26.4	15.4	10.6	12.6	13.5	11.3	13.0	12.9	11.8	13.3	10.6	15.4
By taxi (as passengers)	2.5	1.3	0.0	0.0	1.1	0.3	0.5	0.4	0.2	0.4	0.2	0.2
By motorcycle and moped	0.1	7.0	0.6	2.0	1.0	0.9	0.3	1.3	0.6	0.1	2.8	0.2
By bus and coach	27.6	11.5	25.9	3.7	4.0	4.1	13.1	10.8	2.3	9.9	7.2	6.8
Urban rail	1.9	12.8	2.9	0.0	13.0	4.4	4.9	4.0	5.4	5.0	2.5	0.0
By train (regular and high speed)	3.9	0.1	2.9	7.5	9.0	5.5	5.2	5.1	8.6	2.8	3.8	1.3
Cycling	0.3	0.5	4.7	16.0	3.4	7.5	2.2	0.5	5.5	2.1	1.9	3.3
Walking	6.9	5.8	1.8	5.1	3.9	4.1	6.1	5.8	4.0	4.5	6.8	6.5
Others	0.0	1.0	2.4	3.5	0.6	8.1	0.1	1.7	3.6	2.5	0.6	1.1

Source: (Eurostat, 2021)

All these consequences generate indirect external costs supported by the entire community. Urban public authorities seek to limit them through multiple efforts: substituting the need to travel (by online services, remote work), promoting clean mobility, congestion charging (especially in central urban areas), improving PT offers and urban planning (through actions at the tactical, respectively strategic level) (Cairns et al., 2002; De Borger et al., 2005; Gössling & Cohen, 2014; Hickman et al., 2019; Pharoah, 1992). Nevertheless, the car is the dominant mode of travel in European cities (Table 1), with less than two persons on average per car (Eurostat, 2021).

However, there are examples of transportation systems developed in correlation with urban planning, with positive consequences in increasing the PT share (Figure 1). The solutions for improving the attractiveness of PT can be identified according to the interactions between particularities of the mobility demand and characteristics of the urban zones.

Figure 1. Weights of PT in commuting to work in European capitals
Source: own processing based on EC 2016 data

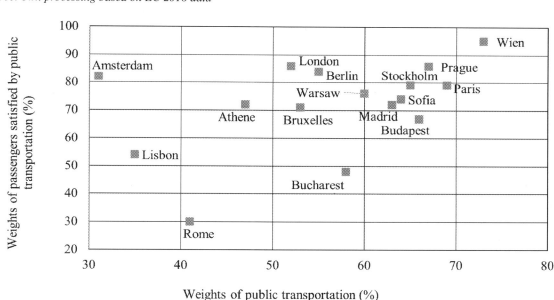

Goals of Public Transportation

There are two options for the motorized movement of the population: one that brings money to the State - car usage, and another that consumes the State's budget - PT. Confronted with the negative consequences of the quality of urban life produced by the excessive increase in car traffic, the authorities have to get involved. But just as tobacco and alcohol yield returns but should not be encouraged, car usage (through the inability to solve the travel fluency at peak hours and the implied high social costs - noise, air pollution, crashes, etc.) must be fenced off. Consequently, the State is committed to financially supporting the investment and operation of urban PT to increase its attractiveness. That means that urban collective PT has become public goods with well-defined missions (D'Arcier, 2012; Litman, 2016; Raicu & Costescu, 2020; Van Egmond et al., 2003):

1. **Social Goal**: ensure access to work and other activities for the captive or low-income residents. It involves providing service in peripherical areas (in districts with low-income people) and supplementary to the usual schedule (e.g., for maintenance staff, during the night, or in the early morning). The objectives of this task and the diversity of mobility behaviour tend to favour measures for expanding PT networks, ensuring the broadest possible spatial coverage to increase the opportunities for PT use, even in the case of low-intensity passenger flows. In these cases, social functions are fulfilled even if PT is supplied at a minimum level due to financial constraints.
2. **Protecting the Environment**: offering an alternative to private car usage; the attractiveness of the urban PT must determine the private car users to change their modal options, especially for daily trips with destinations in congested zones. Parking restrictions, speed limits, toll taxes, and rising fuel prices are measures that can lead to an increase in the share of PT in urban mobility and reduce congestion. However, PT must improve its performance. Express lines, dedicated lanes, speed and frequency, reasonable regularity, and comfortable connections enhance the attractiveness of PT. The effectiveness depends on the capability of PT to take over long trips (e.g., between the centre and peripheries) and the ones inside the outskirts where the trips by car have increased. Even if the low densities in the peripheral spaces discourage the modal redistribution, action must be taken to promote transport intermodality to reduce the length of car trips.
3. **Contribution to Urban Planning**: generally, it refers to investments for network development, especially those for high transit capacity. Research for better integration of mobility – urban planning for the development of new areas or the restructuring of old districts has highlighted the substantial role of high-capacity public transport infrastructures (metro, light rail, tram) and transit-oriented development (TOD) (Deboosere et al., 2018; Staricco & Brovarone, 2018).

Focusing on these goals (Figure 2), some compromises are required in the PT network configuration (e.g., maximizing the service coverage and ensuring the efficiency of the PT network).

Figure 2. Primary goals of urban PT
Source: after D'Arcier, 2010

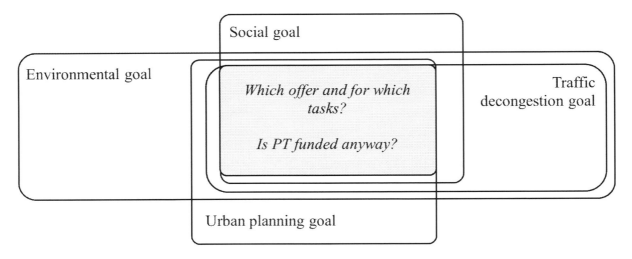

Therefore, regardless of the competencies of those who decide on a particular configuration and operating solutions, it is challenging to design the urban collective PT network in extended urban spaces. Adapting the network to potential demand under financial, political and social constraints remains challenging.

Functions of Public Transportation

PT performance analysis differs from other public services in at least two aspects (Raicu et al., 2022; R. Raicu & S. Raicu, 2005). On the one hand, PT performance depends not only on the quality provided during the journey but also on the accessibility to the different points of interest (work, study, health services, shopping, entertainment, etc.) (Curtis & Scheurer, 2017). On the other hand, PT is not the only option to satisfy mobility demands (D'Arcier, 2012). Consequently, PT must be integrated into a mobility system, including infrastructures, travel technologies (walking, cycling, private car, scooters) and related services (including parking supply and supplementary add-value services) (Raicu & Costescu, 2021; Raicu & Costescu, 2020; Raicu et al., 2009). Thus, the PT performance must consider three domains (Figure 3): the PT system (infrastructures, vehicles, technologies, services), the mobility system (overall travel demand and available travel options/offers), and the urban system (characterized by shape, size and morphology which determine the particularities in transportation operating) (D'Arcier, 2012; Van Egmond et al., 2003).

Figure 3. Domains in the evaluation of the performance of PT

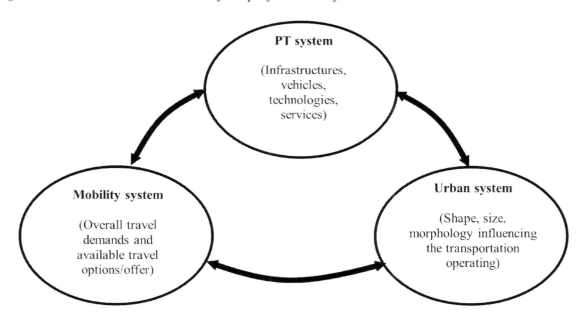

Starting from the PT tasks, a set of functions can be highlighted (Table 2). The service performance evaluation criteria can be formulated for each item (D'Arcier, 2012; Litman, 2016; Negre et al., 2008; Raicu & Costescu, 2020).

Table 2. Functions of PT and criteria for performance assessment

Functions of PT	Criteria for evaluation of PT performance
I. Spatial accessibility of the inhabitants for work, commerce, health care, study, leisure, etc. (through an adapted service offer)	• Spatial coverage by public transport lines• Temporal access (frequency adapted to demand, minimal frequency of regular services, adapted frequency in periods with temporal peaks of demand)• Intermodal integration (ensuring continuity and stability of trips)
II. Accessible transport to all inhabitants	• Ensuring access for people with reduced mobility • Supporting the access of people with low income
III. Reducing individual motorized travel by increasing the attractiveness of the public transport	• Adequate comfort in vehicles and access points (stations, stops, transfer facilities)• Appropriate passenger information system on operating hours, conformity with schedules • Guaranteeing the functional reliability of the network • Ensuring the trustworthiness of service operating (no frequent incidents, strikes, etc.)
IV. Ensuring communication relations with passengers and the urban community	• Recording and considering suggestions and complaints• Transparent administration adapted to mobility requirements
V. Improving the quality of the environment by limiting negative externalities	• Dynamics of local and global levels of environmental impact
VI. Ensuring an economical operation acceptable for passengers and the community	• Ensuring the permanence of the inheritance of the public transport system • Guaranteeing the financial support of the service (distribution of sources of income and expenses for the preservation of the operation)• Ensuring a good quality/social cost ratio

Source: after D'Arcier, 2012

Such a criteria system helps orientate actions for managing a PT system. But it is barely valuable to explain the obtained results and indicate the network's sources of efficiency or inefficiency. In other words, it is suitable for organizational needs and too synthetic for explaining performance. Therefore, the analysis must be supplemented with analyzes of production efficiency and commercial efficiency.

SYNTHETIC MEASURES OF PUBLIC TRANSPORTATION PERFORMANCE

Effectiveness

Effectiveness numerically characterizes the capability of a system for fulfilling its tasks assigned in the urban mobility system. Criteria and indicators of effectiveness must reflect PT tasks. The choice of effectiveness criteria is equivalent to the correct formulation of the objectives and the scope of possible solutions.

Establishing the criterion of effectiveness for PT systems is a complicated issue. Generally, random exogenous and endogenous factors change the PT performance over time. Therefore, average values should be used in defining the effectiveness criterion. At the same time, the incidence of contradictory factors corresponding to the disjoint interests of the involved stakeholders (infrastructure administrators, PT operators, users, community) enforce the use effectiveness criteria accompanied by specifying some limiting requirements. E.g., the "number of passengers" on a line in a particular origin-destination relationship (or in all relationships and on all lines of the PT network) could constitute an effectiveness criterion only accompanied by specifications regarding the comfort and (or) trip time, fare, etc. Also, "travel time" in a particular origin-destination relationship does not constitute a well-chosen effectiveness criterion because it does not contain the elements related to the access times to the initial station,

Performance of Urban Public Transportation Networks

waiting times at the station, and walking from the end station to the destination. Of course, the "total trip time" from the residence to the point of interest is a more appropriate criterion. It includes both the insertion of the public transport line in the urban area, respectively the accessibility for the user, as well as the average speed on the trip distance.

The criteria regarding road safety, implicitly included in the PT tasks, are also applied. Frequently, the "number of crashes" in a particular area and period is used. Nevertheless, it is considered unsatisfying, even if separations into "minor" and "severe" crashes or specifications regarding "injuries" and "deaths" are made. The "cost of accidents" (more difficult to evaluate) can constitute a more appropriate indicator of effectiveness, including the effectiveness of active and passive safety measures in urban mobility systems.

The mentioned argue some requirements for choosing the effectiveness criterion. They must be as complete as possible, easy to calculate, have a physical meaning, and refer to an ideal operating characteristic (so that the recorded values can be set on the 0-1 scale).

Efficiency

Efficiency, like engine efficiency defined in physics, quantifies the ratio between effect (output) and effort (input) (Raicu, 2007). Efficiency differs from effectiveness, defined as the achievement degree of preset objectives. In PT systems, efficiency requires specific examinations because the purposes of mobility and transport policies are complex and differently reflected in the serving system (Baumstark et al., 2005).

Therefore, different forms of efficiency consistent with the targeted results are necessary. Most frequently, production efficiency and commercial efficiency are used. The first, production efficiency, corresponds to some standard performance indicators in the industry. The second corresponds to specific service problems regarding the appropriateness of the offer to the size and spatial-temporal attributes of the demand.

- **Production Efficiency** is a classic issue of transportation economics. Since the 1970s, when car competition affected the profitability of PTs, it has become a permanent concern for performance improvement. Since then, the mechanisms of public subsidies have been implemented and contributed to the decrease in the commercial efficiency of the PT network (Bly, 1987; Kerin, 1987; De Borger et al., 2002).

  The production efficiency analysis aims to identify the factors that intervene in the operating costs of a network. Besides the usual parameters related to capital, workforce and energy, many other variables must be underlined to understand the differences between networks. They can refer to speed (technical and operating) and attributes of the network shape and configuration (connectedness, connectivity, isotropy, accessibility, slope and length of the lines, population, etc.) (De Borger et al., 2002; Kerstens 1999).

  Baumstark et al. (2005) emphasize the nature of contractual relationships in explaining the efficiency differences between networks. Without contesting the wide variety of conditions related to the local context, the attitude of the public managing authorities is considered particularly important for defining the public transport offer and operating conditions. The managing authorities are the ones that establish the key components for the network performance, such as fare schemes and the nature of the offer (investments in infrastructure and vehicles, type of vehicles, operating conditions, level of service). Different levels of the PT network performance can be differentiated in relation to the involved stakeholders (managing authorities, transport operators), recording terms (short/medium/long), and the level of global performance required by the objectives of the mobility policies.

- **Commercial Efficiency** is not a direct derivative of production efficiency (although production efficiency has a fundamental role in minimizing operating costs). The overall design of the network is undoubtedly an essential factor for PT attractiveness. Additionally, it is influenced by the population (in particular, by the population density in the coverage area) and also by the modal share (in competition with car usage). The path of the lines, the proposed level of service (LOS) and the investments assumed for operation must be considered in evaluating commercial efficiency.

  It is interesting to analyze the relative values rather than the absolute values of the commercial efficiency indicators. Relative values allow for identifying lines or components of the network with poor performance (to investigate the causes) and highlighting actions to improve performance. The causes can be structural (e.g., the inadequacy of the type of service at the level of demand) or the gap between the offered service and the expectations of the targeted users (e.g., too low frequency, travel time too long compared to competing modes). In such cases, a more insightful analysis of the demands of the increasingly diversified users is required.

The differences between production and commercial efficiency are noticeable (Figure 4). Production efficiency is a structural objective for the transport operator because the activity output depends on it. But concomitantly, the public managing authority is interested in results like any customer buying a service. The standards imposed by the managing authority directly affect the magnitude of the transportation operator's resources (financial, material, energy and workforce). Several constraints specific to service do not allow optimizing the transport operating process as in other industrial domains: intermediate stocks cannot be accumulated (transportation is instantaneous and localized), operating levels can be modified over time (daily, weekly, yearly) only with significant socio-economic impact, a smooth variation of traffic conditions (speed, regularity, etc.) is not possible. Certain conditions imposed as offer standards (e.g., operating time, frequency, comfort, etc.) mean an oversizing of the engaged resources with direct effects on costs. In conclusion, optimization under constraints is complex and often requires marginal adaptations of the contractual specifications.

But the examination of commercial efficiency reveals different problems in terms of public policies. Referring to the performance of the network and its usage (number of passengers relative to operated vehicles-km), adapting the offer to the demand inevitably becomes necessary. The most straightforward solutions suppose removing services with a low degree of use (during periods with low demand) or limiting services in less dense areas (suburbs, in particular). But any of these actions contradict the objectives of sustainable mobility (because this approach would not reduce the share of cars in the urban mobility system).

The characteristics of operating and commercial efficiency suggest that incentive clauses must be provided in the contractual relationship between the public managing authority and the public transport operators. An adapted contractual relationship must be ensured through the "lump sum contribution" (employed net costs), which establishes a distribution of the operational and commercial risks. Therefore, contractual mechanisms favouring network optimization must be analyzed (especially in a difficult financial context for communities).

Performance of Urban Public Transportation Networks

Figure 4. The relationship between operating and commercial efficiency
Source: after Baumstark et al., 2005

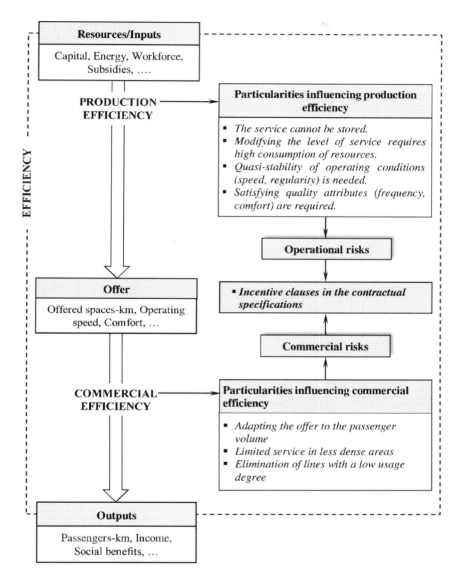

Correlations Between Effectiveness and Efficiency

Assessing the performance of a PT network is particularly complex when several viewpoints are considered. First, the correlation between effectiveness and efficiency must be clarified in order to avoid the simplicity of the financial allocation for the component lines of the network. Figure 5 summarizes the numerous interactions that influence the network's performance and highlights the need for public financing for the gap between operating expenditures and revenues. The upper part of Figure 5 reveals that the PT network covers an area characterized by an ensemble of locations (residences, work/study, retail, services, recreation) and alternative, competitive or complementary travelling/transport offers.

Performance of Urban Public Transportation Networks

The objectives of public policy reflected in the Sustainable Urban Mobility Plan (SUMP) are found in the operational plan at the level of the PT offer: the technical hierarchies of the supply appropriate to the estimated passenger flows and the established levels of service (frequency, operating time, speed, regularity, etc.).

Production efficiency fundamentally depends on the design of the network but also the priorities given to PT lines and the incentive procedures defined in the contracts with the transport operators.

Commercial efficiency equally depends on how the lines that form the network were designed in relation to the covered land, the attractiveness of the offered levels of service, and on the applied charging and fare schemes.

Effectiveness considers the characteristic of the accomplished mobility needs of PT users in relation to the completed trips (reason, distance, hourly/daily periodicity).

Figure 5. Factors influencing the performance of an urban public transport network
Source: after D'Arcier, 2012

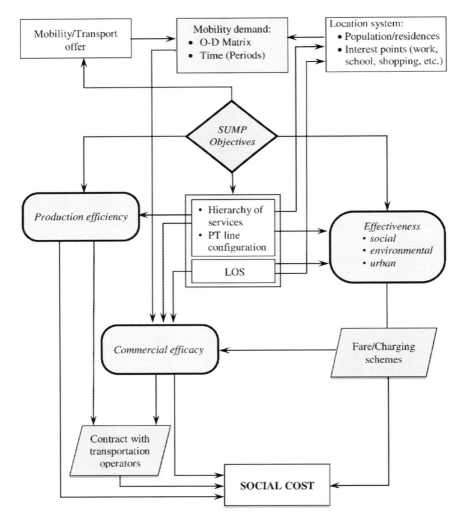

Performance of Urban Public Transportation Networks

To explain the overall level of network performance, an analysis at the PT line level is also necessary. The PT line must be examined in terms of network access points. This analysis highlights the role of correlations in organizing the network, i.e., how the overall logic of the network corresponds to the needs of mobility in the area, multiplying the travel relations. In other words, this relationship analysis evaluates the network effect generated by the topological structuring of the public transport lines (Costescu et al., 2021).

The study of the network effect inevitably leads to the need to define a hierarchy of the network lines. It is necessary to reveal how a relatively reduced number of high-capacity lines are fed by a substantial number of lines with lower production and commercial efficiency but which significant service coverage in the ensemble (Massot & Orfeuil, 2005).

In a separate examination, the lines of the PT network have very varied performances (depending on the served area and the offered LOS). But at the aggregate level, they all contribute to the network's overall performance.

PERFORMANCE AT THE PUBLIC TRANSPORTATION LINE LEVEL

Statistical analysis of the commercial efficiency of different lines of a PT network shows significant dispersions (Carvalho et al., 2015; D'Arcier, 2012; Fitzová et al., 2018; Özgün et al., 2021; Van Egmond, 2003). Significant differences in terms of the commercial efficiency of the lines within the same networks are caused by the PT technology (metro, tram, bus), covered land (center, periphery, primary nodes), the itineraries, connections provided within the network and LOS. For most networks, significant differences are determined by the covered land (urban, suburban, peripheral), the distance to the city center, the population density and the socio-economic activity density. Differences are also attributed to the shape of the PT line (radial, diametral, tangential) and the provided function (access to the center or to a secondary pole, a high-capacity corridor that ensures local, regional or interregional connections).

However, it should be noted that the multiplication of criteria for differentiating PT lines can lead to an excessive number of categories that can include an insufficient number of PT lines (or even only one). Therefore, the analysis of the commercial efficiency of the PT lines should be limited (at least initially) to a reduced number of typologies (primary connections, major diffusions, secondary diffusions). The explanatory variables of the commercial efficiency variations within each typology can be attributed either to LOS and the position of each line in the network or to land insertion (in terms of covered population and travel motivations). Two categories of explanatory variables can be considered:

- **Variables Describing the Significant Differentiations Related to the Line Typology:**
  - Line length: longer lines cover larger areas and have more potential for capturing residents' interest.
  - Operating speed: journey time remains a decisive factor in PT attractiveness compared to other modes of travel (especially private cars).
  - Operating time: besides commuting to work, usually during peak hours, the start and end operating times for a PT line influence the perception regarding the offer quality.
  - Sinuosity index: the aim to cover the entire urban area often leads to complex itineraries that extend the travel time over an acceptable limit in certain relationships.

- Frequency: the waiting time represents one of the main PT disadvantages. Relative to the estimated passenger flows, the frequency varies during the operating time; in some periods, it can be considered improper by potential users.
- Service schedule: different frequencies in peak and off-peak periods characterize the service; a high deviation of frequencies creates a perception of appropriate operating only in peak hours and overall reduced attractiveness.
- The number of stops or the distance between stops: it is considered that an acceptable covered area corresponds to a 300 m walking distance around a bus stop. Therefore, dense stops penalize the travel time due to frequent vehicle stops.

- **Variables Describing the Line Insertion:**
  - Population density in the coverage area of the line stops.
  - Employee density: commuting to work represents a substantial component of urban mobility demand impacting PT network design.
  - Location of educational institutions (schools, colleges, universities): commuting for the study represents a significant component of urban mobility demand impacting PT services.
  - Location of commercial facilities.
  - Location of intermodal terminals: connections with other local, regional, and interregional transport networks influence the PT services.

Table 3. Indicators specific to PT lines

Class	Indicators
C1. Performance of the offer	- Type of the PT line (connection, dispersion, etc.)- Line length- Sinuosity index- Frequency- Operating speed- Vehicles-km/day- Population in the coverage area- Percentage of stations accessible within 30 minutes
C2. Utilization (commercial efficiency)	- Type of the PT line- Passengers/day- Passenger-km/day- Passenger/vehicle-km- Average trip length
C3. Social performance	- Type of the PT line- Trips by PT/inhabitant/years separated per social group (actively employed population, unemployed, students, seniors, other categories of inactive population)- Total trips, with the percentage of trips of non-residents
C4. Performance on traffic decongestion	- Cars-km for individual trips longer than 3.5 km reduced by transferred to PT system- Trips by PT to work (vehicles-km)- Trips by PT for other reasons (vehicles-km)- Total production (passengers-km)
C5. Performance in reduction of CO_2 emissions	- Daily CO_2 emissions of PT- Daily CO_2 emissions of cars- PT emissions/car emissions- Passengers-km transferred to PT- Reduction of CO2 emissions due to increase of PT attractiveness (CO_2 emissions of cars/passengers-km)

Source: based on D'Arcier, 2012

The synthetical analysis tool (dashboard) must include data synthesis groups and indicators specific to PT lines. Five classes of criteria (C1 – C5) are relevant for performing the analysis (Table 3). The PT indicators, grouped into the five classes, can be categorized for lines of the same type or on each PT technology of the network (bus, trolleybus, tram, metro, urban/suburban railway, etc.).

Correlations between the commercial efficiency of a public transport line and explanatory variables involve laborious statistical calculations, which often are difficult due to the unavailability of data re-

Performance of Urban Public Transportation Networks

garding some factors (Fitzová et al., 2018). Moreover, even when correlations have been highlighted, they can lead to contradictory conclusions (D'Arcier, 2012).

An analysis tool is necessary to compare the production and commercial efficiency indicators of different lines (and with average values for lines in the same category). Limiting the number of indicators (selected by supply, mobility needs and public policy objectives) is recommended to identify the most significant performance discrepancies among different lines.

CONCLUSION

In a congested urban environment, with diverse modal options of travel (among which car usage has a significant weight), PT offerings must be designed and sized in such a way as to ensure the judicious use of urban space and high performance of the operating of the transportation system. In this regard, it is essential to understand the role of PT in the urban system as a whole and to reveal the principles that must be applied in the development and operation of urban public transport systems in order to satisfy mobility needs. The assessment of PT performance adapted to implemented operating technologies is necessary for increasing PT attractiveness for different categories of users.

The analysis of PT performances differs from other public services. PT performance depends not only on the quality provided during the journey but also on the accessibility to the different locations (work, study, health and social services, etc.). In addition, PT is not the only option to satisfy mobility needs. Therefore, PT must be integrated into a mobility system, including infrastructures, travel technologies (walking, cycling, private car, scooters) and related services (including parking supply).

In order to analyze the evolution of PT performance and to establish a basis for identifying measures to improve it, the role of the PT system must be described. This clarification is also essential because the planned PT supply and its financing methods are established according to the goals assigned to the PT system.

Several levels of the performance evaluation must be defined regarding involved decision-makers, phases for registering changes (short, medium, or long term), and objectives of urban mobility policies.

Considering the complexity of urban mobility policies, distinct approaches to effectiveness and efficiency are essential in PT systems. Effectiveness defines the level of achievement of the predetermined tasks. Efficiency refers to the ratios between outputs and consumed resources. In addition, separate assessments are required for production efficiency (which identifies the factors influencing operating costs) and commercial efficiency (specific to service issues, reflecting the adaptation of the offer to the size and attributes of the travel demand).

Generally, the effectiveness and efficiency of PT systems are challenging to assess because measurable objectives are rarely defined. The lack of clear objectives regarding the targeted tasks and functions over specific time horizons impedes the effectiveness assessment. Often, it seems easier to evaluate efficiency based on outputs and ex-post-recorded data. Generally, the focus is on production efficiency, which must be a permanent objective to improve performance according to the operating costs on the network. In many situations in which authorities subsidize PT operators, a decrease in production efficiency is noticed.

Contractual relationships between public managing authorities and operators strongly influence the effectiveness and efficiency of PT systems and explain the differences between various urban transportation systems. Besides the influence of local particularities, it has been demonstrated that authorities can influence the key elements of the overall PT performance through investments distributed across different modes of transport in infrastructure and vehicles, appropriate fare and charging schemes, and the established LOS.

In order to understand the differences between the networks and the criteria for their structuring and line design, in addition to the usual variables (financial, material, human, energy resources), other variables specific to the technical characteristics of the transport modes must be taken into account, e.g., network structure and shape (connectedness, connectivity, accessibility), population density and urban spread, length and slope of the PT lines, enforced traffic restrictions, etc.

The performance indicators of a PT network reveal the complexity of relationships between production and financial efficiencies and the effectiveness in satisfying the potential urban mobility needs. They indicate the factors explaining the disparities of PT lines in terms of commercial efficiency. Finally, they underlay the development of a synthetic tool for the comparative analysis of the performances of different classes of PT lines that structure a PT network.

REFERENCES

Anciaes, P., Jones, P., Mindell, J. S., & Scholes, S. (2022). The cost of the wider impacts of road traffic on local communities: 1.6% of Great Britain's GDP. *Transportation Research Part A, Policy and Practice, 163*, 266–287. doi:10.1016/j.tra.2022.05.016

Banister, D., & Hickman, R. (2013). Transport futures: Thinking the unthinkable. *Transport Policy, 29*, 283–293. doi:10.1016/j.tranpol.2012.07.005

Baumstark, L., Ménard, C., Roy, W., & Yvrande-Billon, A. (2005). *Modes de gestion et efficience des opérateurs dans le secteur des transports urbains de personnes [Management methods and efficiency of operators in the urban passenger transport sector].* Mobilité, territoires et développement durable [Mobility, territories and sustainable development].

Bly, P. H. (1987). Managing public transport: Commercial profitability and social service. *Transportation Research Part A, General, 21*(2), 109–125. doi:10.1016/0191-2607(87)90004-5

Cairns, S., Atkins, S., & Goodwin, P. (2002). Disappearing traffic: The story so far. *Municipal Engineer, 15*(1), 13–22. doi:10.1680/muen.2002.151.1.13

Carvalho, M., Syguiy, T., & Nithack e Silva, D. (2015). Efficiency and Effectiveness Analysis of Public Transport of Brazilian Cities. *Journal of Transport Literature, 9*(3), 40–44. doi:10.1590/2238-1031.jtl.v9n3a8

COM. (2020). Sustainable and Smart Mobility Strategy – putting European transport on track for the future. Communication from the Commission to the European Parliament, the Council, the European Economic and Social Committee and The Committee of the Regions. European Commission.

Costescu, D., Stere, A. S., & Serban, A. M. (2021). Network of Dedicated Bus Lanes: A Solution to Increase the Accessibility of the Urban Intermodal Transport. *Romanian Journal of Transport Infrastructure, 10*(2), 1–15. doi:10.2478/rjti-2021-0008

Performance of Urban Public Transportation Networks

Curtis, C., & Scheurer, J. (2017). Performance measures for public transport accessibility: Learning from international practice. *Journal of Transport and Land Use, 10*(1), 93–118.

D'Arcier, B.F. (2010). La situation financière des transports publics urbains est-elle "durable "? [The financial situation of public city transportation- is it durable?] *Les Cahiers scientifiques du transport [Journal of Scientific Transportation], 58,* 3-28.

D'Arcier, B.F. (Coord.) (2012). *Measure de la performance des lignes de transport public urbain [Measure of the performance of city public transport lines].* APEROL: Amélioration de la Performance Economique des Réseaux par l'Optimisation des Lignes [Improving the Economic Performance of Networks by Line Optimization].

Das, S., Boruah, A., Banerjee, A., Raoniar, R., Nama, S., & Maurya, A. K. (2021). Impact of COVID-19: A radical modal shift from public to private transport mode. *Transport Policy, 109,* 1–11. doi:10.1016/j. tranpol.2021.05.005 PMID:36570699

De Borger, B., Kerstens, K., & Costa, Á. (2002). Public transit performance: What does one learn from frontier studies? *Transport Reviews, 22*(1), 1–38. doi:10.1080/01441640010020313

De Borger, B., Proost, S., & Van Dender, K. (2005). Congestion and tax competition in a parallel network. *European Economic Review, 49*(8), 2013–2040. doi:10.1016/j.euroecorev.2004.06.005

Deboosere, R., El-Geneidy, A. M., & Levinson, D. (2018). Accessibility-oriented development. *Journal of Transport Geography, 70,* 11–20. doi:10.1016/j.jtrangeo.2018.05.015

EC. (2016). Quality of Life in European Cities. 2015. Flash Eurobarometer 419, Directorate-General for Regional and Urban Policy, European Commission, Publications Office of the European Union.

Eurostat (2021). *Passenger mobility statistics.* Eurostat. https://ec.europa.eu/eurostat/statistics-explained/index.php?title=Passenger_mobility_statistics

Fitzová, H., Matulová, M., & Tomeš, Z. (2018). Determinants of urban public transport efficiency: Case study of the Czech Republic. *European Transport Research Review, 10*(2), 42. doi:10.118612544-018-0311-y

Gössling, S., & Cohen, S. (2014). Why sustainable transport policies will fail: EU climate policy in the light of transport taboos. *Journal of Transport Geography, 39,* 197–207. doi:10.1016/j.jtrangeo.2014.07.010

Hickman, R., Mella Lira, B., Givoni, M., & Geurs, K. (Eds.). (2019). *A Companion to Transport, Space and Equity.* Edward Elgar. doi:10.4337/9781788119825

Kerin, P. D. (1987). Why Subsidize State Transport Authorities? *The Australian Quarterly, 59*(1), 60–72. doi:10.2307/20635413

Kerstens, K. (1999). Decomposing Technical Efficiency and Effectiveness of French Urban Transport. *Annales d'Economie et de Statistique, 54*(54), 129–155. doi:10.2307/20076181

Le Corbusier. (1971). La Charte d'Athènes. [The Athens Charter]. Points.

Litman, T. (2016). *When are bus lanes warranted? Considering economic efficiency, social equity, and strategic planning goals.* Victoria Transport Policy Institute. https://www.vtpi.org/blw.pdf

Massot, M. H., & Orfeuil, J. P. (2005). La mobilite au quotidien, entre choix individuel et production sociale. *Cahiers Internationaux de Sociologie, 1*(118), 81–100. doi:10.3917/cis.118.0081

Negre, L. (Coord.) (2008). *Charte des services publics locaux. Indicateurs de performance des réseaux de transport public [Charter of local public services, Performance indicators of public transport networks]*. Institut de la Gestion Déléguée, Association des Maires de France.

Newman, P., & Kenworthy, J. (2015). *The End of Automobile Dependence. How Cities are Moving Beyond Car-Based Planning*. Island Press. doi:10.5822/978-1-61091-613-4

Özgün, K., Günay, M., Doruk, B., Bulut, B., Yürüten, E., Baysan, F., & Kalemsiz, M. (2021). Analysis of PT for Efficiency. In: Hemanth, J., Yigit, T., Patrut, B. & Angelopoulou, A. (Eds) Trends in Data Engineering Methods for Intelligent Systems. ICAIAME 2020. Lecture Notes on Data Engineering and Communications Technologies, (vol 76). Springer Cham.

Pharoah, T. (1992). *Less Traffic, Better Towns*. Friends of the Earth.

Raicu, R., & Raicu, S. (2005). Complex aspects of transport quality. In C. A. Brebbia & L. Wadhwa (Eds.), *Urban Transport XI. WIT Transactions on The Built Environment* (Vol. 77, pp. 281–290). WIT Press.

Raicu, S. (2007). *Transportation Systems*. AGIR Press. (*In Romanian*)

Raicu, S., & Costescu, D. (2020). *Mobility. Traffic Infrastructures*. AGIR Press. (*In Romanian*)

Raicu, S., & Costescu, D. (2021). Mobility - polysemy with interdisciplinary valences. *Journal of Engineering Sciences and Innovation, 6*(4), 459–472.

Raicu, S., Dragu, V., Popa, M., & Burciu, S. (2009). About the high capacity public transport networks territory functions. In C. A. Brebia (Ed.), *Urban Transport XV. WIT Transactions on The Built Environment* (pp. 41–50). WIT Press. doi:10.2495/UT090051

Raicu, S., Popa, M., & Costescu, D. (2022). Uncertainties Influencing Transportation System Performances. *Sustainability, 14*(13), 7660. doi:10.3390u14137660

Staricco, L., & Brovarone, E. V. (2018). Promoting TOD through regional planning. A comparative analysis of two European approaches. *Journal of Transport Geography, 66*, 45–52. doi:10.1016/j.jtrangeo.2017.11.011

Van Audenhove, F. J., Korniichuk, O., Dauby, L., & Pourbaix, J. (2014). *The Future of Urban Mobility 2.0. Imperatives to shape extended mobility ecosystems of tomorrow*. Arthur D. Little & The International Association of Public Transport (UITP). http://www.adlittle.com/downloads/tx_adlreports/2014_ADL_UITP_Future_of_Urban_Mobility_2_0_Full_study.pdf

Van Egmond, P., Nijkamp, P., & Vindigni, G. (2003). A comparative analysis of the performance of urban public transport systems in Europe. *International Social Science Journal, 55*(176), 235–247. doi:10.1111/1468-2451.5502005

Veryard, D., & Perkins, S. (Coord.) (2018) *Integrating Urban Public Transport Systems and Cycling. Summary and Conclusions. ITF Round Table 166*. International Transport Forum.

Vickerman, R. (2021). Will Covid-19 put the public back in public transport? A UK perspective. *Transport Policy*, *103*, 95–102. doi:10.1016/j.tranpol.2021.01.005 PMID:33558796

KEY TERMS AND DEFINITIONS

Accessibility: Capability of reaching destinations. It can be assessed at different levels of transport network or system based on various metrics (distances, time, money, other quality factors).

Clean mobility: Solutions provided by integrated infrastructures, vehicles, and technologies that satisfy the needs of people travel and goods movement, ensuring the reduction of negative effects compared to previous periods and contributing to the achievement of pollution targets defined at city or region levels.

Commercial Efficiency of Public Transportation: Capability of judicious use of the supplied public transportation. It reflects the viewpoints of public transportation operators and funding authorities, assessed on operation output (passenger-km) and consumed resources (financial, energy, human and material resources).

Production Efficiency of Public Transportation: Capability of fulfilling public transportation tasks assigned in the urban mobility system. It can be assessed based on technical indicators (attributes of the network, technical and operating speeds, transportation output in vehicles-km or spaces-km) and consumed resources (financial, energy, human and material resources).

Public Transportation Performance: The ability of the public transportation system to fulfil the social, economic and environmental goals set by public policies. It can be assessed based on a broad set of indicators reflecting socio-economic effectiveness, production and commercial efficiency.

Socio-Economic Effectiveness: Evaluations of the benefits of public policies for citizens; its indicators reflect the viewpoints of the citizens (e.g., reducing congestion, reducing pollution, enhancing the overall urban environment).

Urban Mobility System: Set of traffic and transport infrastructures, technologies for all modes of travel (walking, cycling, private car and scooter usage, public transportation offerings) and related services (including parking supply) satisfying the mobility demand at the urban level.

Chapter 3
The Role of Electromobility in the Energy–Related Smart Grids

Bor Krizmanič

https://orcid.org/0000-0001-8272-6902

School of Economics and Business, University of Ljubljana, Slovenia

Aleš Groznik

School of Economics and Business, University of Ljubljana, Slovenia

ABSTRACT

The chapter describes the major components of the power grid. It then describes and explains the trends in the consumption and generation of electricity, with a particular focus on increasing the share of renewable energy sources. The concept of the smart grid is then described, including a discussion of the smart meter and the prosumer concept. The second part of the chapter is dedicated to electromobility. This section describes the main characteristics of electric vehicles and the trend of their diffusion, battery technologies, charging stations, smart charging, and the vehicle-to-grid concept.

INTRODUCTION

Since the great inventions of the light bulb and the electric motor in the 19th century, the importance of electricity in our lives has increased enormously. Today we cannot imagine life without electricity, but we often forget the system that allows us to use it. Electricity is provided by the power grid, which is the critical infrastructure of any country.

We are experiencing major changes in the generation, supply, and consumption of electricity. In the face of all these changes, the stability of the grid cannot be taken for granted. For example, research has shown that uncoordinated charging of electric vehicles, where vehicles start charging as soon as they are plugged in, may well cause grid problems at the local level (Clement-Nyns et al., 2010). However, new technologies can ensure that the current grid transforms, empowers many smaller players, and becomes more resilient. Changes in the energy sector are also reflected in long-term growth in capital spending. An International Energy Agency (IEA) analysis found that global energy investment will increase by

DOI: 10.4018/978-1-6684-5996-6.ch003

The Role of Electromobility in the Energy-Related Smart Grids

more than 8% to reach \$2.4 trillion by 2022. The level of investment is expected to exceed pre-COVID levels. It is also important to highlight that in recent years, the majority of energy investments have been in renewable energy and grid investments in the energy sector and are also driven by increased spending on end-use efficiency (International Energy Agency, 2022b).

The purpose of this chapter is to introduce the reader to the traditional power grid and highlight the key current and future trends affecting it, with a focus on the electrification of mobility. Therefore, this chapter first explains the main components of the power grid and then introduces three major trends that are currently impacting the power grid: general electricity consumption, renewable energy sources, and advanced consumption modes. The chapter then looks to the future and introduces the concept of a smart power grid, a power grid of mobility. The last part of the chapter is dedicated to electromobility and its importance for the power grid.

POWER GRID

The power grid, also known as the electrical grid, is a network of components that delivers electricity to consumers. First, it is important to understand a conventional power grid's basic elements and concepts. The main components of the power grid are:

- **Generating Plants**, also known as power plants or stations, produce electricity using either combustible fuels such as coal, natural gas, and biomass or noncombustible energy sources such as wind, solar energy, and nuclear fuels. Today, they are usually located near energy sources and far from densely populated areas. The other parts of the power grid are therefore critical to delivering electricity from the generation source to the consumer.
- **Electrical Substations** to adjust the voltage to the required level. Electric power normally flows through several substations with different voltage levels between the generating plants and the final consumer. Components called transformers are used to transfer electrical energy from one circuit to another (with different voltage levels).
- **Electric Power Transmission Network** is used to transmit electricity over long distances. The higher the voltage of a transmission line, the more power it can carry. Transmission networks are used to transmit electricity from large production plants to areas of concentrated consumption, where they are connected to distribution networks at substations or even directly to the largest industrial consumers (e.g. ironworks). The transmission network also serves as a link between the national power grids of different countries. The transmission network consists of overhead lines, and less frequently, cable lines and distribution or substations. Since transmission networks transmit large amounts of power, they are high- and medium-voltage networks. There are no clear and universally accepted boundaries, however, transmission networks in principle operate above 30 kV, typically even higher (e.g. 110 kV, 220 kV, and 400 kV) (International Electrotechnical Commission, 2022).
- **Electric Power Distribution Network** is used to deliver electricity to individual customers. The step-down transformer is used to reduce the voltage so that the electricity can reach the end customers through the distribution lines. Therefore, it consists of substations and transmission lines of various lower voltage classes (normally below 30 kV) to distribute electricity to end users (Kaplan, 2009 & International Electrotechnical Commission, 2022).

45

Different parts of the grid may be owned and organized differently in different countries. Countries also differ in the organization of transmission and distribution system operators, of which there may be several or only one.

Power grids vary in size and may cover entire countries or continents. The grid is usually synchronous, meaning that all distribution areas operate at synchronized three-phase alternating current (AC) frequency. This allows the transmission of AC electricity throughout the region and connects a large number of power generators and consumers. In Continental Europe, for example, power grids are interconnected in the largest synchronous power grid in the world, the Continental Synchronous Area or synchronous grid of Continental Europe. It connects the grids of 24 countries, including most of the countries in the European Union. In North America, including the United States and Canada, there are two major interconnected grids (Western and Eastern Interconnection) and three smaller interconnected grids (Texas, Alaska, and Quebec Interconnection).

While supply and demand is a fundamental concept in virtually every other industry, the current power grid has great difficulty with it because, as mentioned earlier, electricity must be consumed at the moment it is generated. Without the ability to accurately and precisely determine demand at any given moment, keeping the "right" supply on hand for all contingencies is problematic at best. This is especially true at times of peak demand, i.e., at times when electricity demand is highest in a given period. As presented below, problems in balancing supply and consumption can also be caused by the unstable production of electricity.

CURRENT TRENDS IN THE POWER GRID

The electrification of mobility will have a strong impact on the operation of the power system in the future, but it is also affected by some already existing trends. Below are described the three most important paradigms that we must take into account when considering the inclusion of electric vehicles in the power grid.

Electricity Consumption

In recent years, it has become clear that electricity will play a key role in the energy transition to a clean energy future. Electricity is a so-called secondary energy source. Primary energy sources include oil, natural gas, coal, nuclear, solar, and wind (Energy Information Administration, 2022). In a power grid, power plants use different primary energy sources to generate electricity. In this way, we can reduce and adjust what the electricity is generated from. Today, of course, the trend is toward renewable energy sources (RES) and away from fossil fuels. But not everything is that simple, because different energy sources have different characteristics.

The basic and objective trend is that electricity consumption is increasing worldwide. Figure 1 shows a graph of electricity consumption for the entire world between 1990 and 2019, due in part to population growth and industrialization at the global level (International Energy Agency, 2022a). Electricity consumption is also increasing due to factors other than electromobility. For example, electricity is increasingly used to heat and cool buildings. For example, the high concentration of air conditioners in warmer climates has been a problem for power grid operations for years (Smith, Meng, Dong & Simpson, 2013). Heat pumps are also increasingly replacing other fossil fuel heating systems (e.g., natural

The Role of Electromobility in the Energy-Related Smart Grids

gas and oil). Integrating heat pumps on a larger scale is also challenging in terms of balancing electricity peaks. On the other hand, heat pumps could also be used as energy storage in the power grid in the future (Pedersen, Andersen, Nielsen, Stærmose, & Pedersen, 2011).

We have to keep in mind that electricity is not a solution for all energy-related issues. As mentioned before, electricity is a secondary source of energy, that is, we need other sources of energy to produce it. To achieve the environmental goals that humanity has recently set for itself, it makes sense to generate electricity from renewable sources whenever and wherever possible. Therefore, the share of renewable energy sources is increasing.

Figure 1. Electricity consumption, World 1990-2019 Electricity (source: International Energy Agency, 2022a)

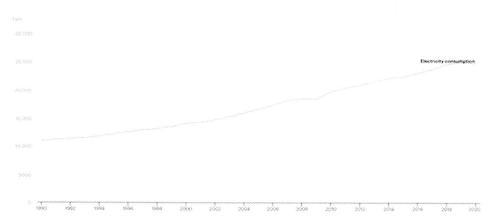

Increasing Share of Renewable Energy Sources

Climate change will require technological and social change in all aspects of our lives in the future (Allen et al., 2018), including the transition from fossil fuels to renewable energy sources (Stikvoort, Bartusch, and Juslin, 2020). Renewable energy is defined by Lund as "an energy that is produced by natural resources-such as sunlight, wind, rain, waves, tides, and geothermal heat-that are naturally replenished within a time span of a few years" (Lund, 2009).

In general, renewable energy sources and their form of use are: Hydropower (electricity generation), solar energy (solar home system, solar dryer, solar stove), direct solar energy (photovoltaic, thermal electricity generation, water heater), geothermal energy (urban heating, electricity generation, hydrothermal, hot dry rock), Wind (power generation, wind generators, windmills, water pumps), wave energy (numerous designs), tidal energy (dam, tidal stream), and modern biomass (heat and power generation, pyrolysis, gasification, fermentation) (Demirbaş, 2016).

Figure 2 shows global electricity generation by energy source. We can see that coal and gas are the largest energy sources for electricity generation.

Figure 2. Global electricity production by source, World (source: Ritchie & Roser, 2022)

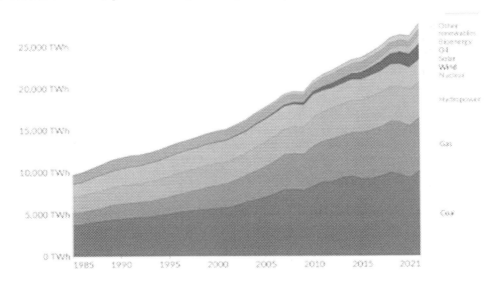

There are large differences between countries and different parts of the world in the use of RES for electricity generation. Figure 3 shows the share of electricity generation from renewable sources (all RES together) by country in 2021. We can see that there are indeed big differences between regions and curtsies. For example, the central part of Africa around the Equator gets almost all its electricity from RES. Similarly, South America reaches high proportions from RES. Within Europe, there is a heterogeneous distribution of shares from RES, while Scandinavian countries generate almost all their electricity from RES, Eastern European countries are far behind (Ritchie & Roser, 2022).

Figure 3. Share of electricity production from renewables by countries, 2021 (source: Ritchie & Roser, 2022)

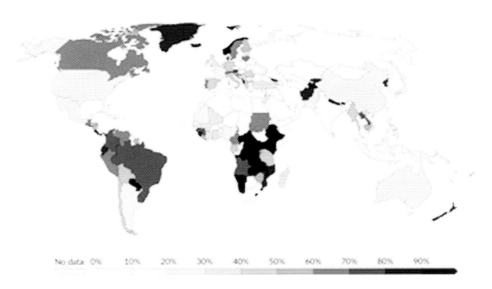

The Role of Electromobility in the Energy-Related Smart Grids

Figure 4 combines maps showing the share of electricity generation from hydropower, solar power, and wind power in 2021. A more detailed view with a separate display for the share of electricity generated from hydropower, solar power, and wind power shows that in Central Africa most electricity is generated from hydropower plants. The same is true for Scandinavian and some southern European countries, as well as countries in the southern part of South America. The picture is reversed to a greater extent for electricity generation from solar energy. Here, the largest shares are achieved by the more developed countries. All of Europe achieves relatively high shares, and the same is true of the United States, China, India, Australia, and several other large countries. And in general, the share of electricity generation from solar power is much lower than that from hydropower. Parallels can be seen in the shares of electricity production from wind power with the distribution of production from solar power. (Ritchie & Roser, 2022).

The use of fossil fuels is bad for the environment and does not meet greenhouse gas (GHG) emission reduction goals and guidelines. On the other hand, fossil fuels have very good properties for power generation because they are very good for long-term storage for energy. Their storage is relatively inexpensive or even does not cause any costs (e.g. coal mine near the power plant). In addition, they can be used at any time when needed. This is very suitable for the operation of the electric system since its task is to ensure a sufficient amount of electricity for a given consumption.

On the other hand, the use of renewable energy sources, although less harmful to the environment, is not without negative effects on it. For example, the construction of hydroelectric power plants or large solar power plants causes great interference with the natural environment. However, they do not cause greenhouse gas emissions and are renewable, which is currently the focus worldwide.

The power grid will need to integrate a larger share of renewable energy sources that have volatile generation patterns. This poses a major challenge for grid operators (Carrasco et al., 2006). For example, the generation of electricity from sunlight is inherently uneven. Generation depends on numerous geographic factors. On a daily basis, electricity generation from PV naturally varies widely because electricity can only be generated during daylight hours. In principle, PV light production peaks around midday, but pore water drops to zero at night. In addition to the alternation of day and night, production is also affected by the weather. The latter is problematic due to its unpredictability (van den Akker et al., 2012). In addition to the diurnal variations in electricity production, there are also variations on an annual basis. In principle, more power can be generated in the summer than in the winter. How much variation there is between seasons depends on the latitude of the plant's location. The closer the site is to the equator (lower latitude), the more consistent the power generation (Øgaard, Riise, Haug, Sartori, & Selj, 2020).

Furthermore, the problem is not only the dips in PV power production but also the simultaneous production that can lead to problems at the local level, in the distribution grid. Large surpluses of electricity fed into the grid by local solar power plants can exceed the capacity of cables and substations. For example, if all the houses on a particular street had rooftop PV systems, they would produce a lot of electricity in the summer. At the same time, however, household consumption would be low because many people would be on vacation. This would result in a large surplus of electricity that would exceed the capacity of the substations in the street and cause a power outage in the entire street.

Figure 4. Maps displaying the share of electricity produced from hydro, solar, and wind (from top to bottom) in 2021 (source: Ritchie & Roser, 2022)

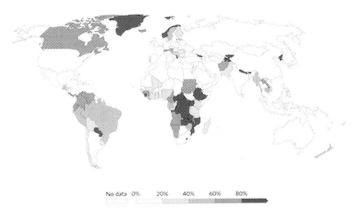

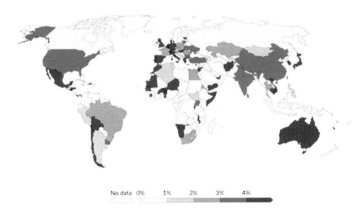

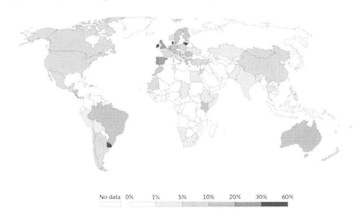

Active Consumers and Prosumer

With the development of new technologies, consumers can become more active and involved in the process of energy production, delivery, and consumption. In order to successfully integrate more small renewable energy sources and improve the efficiency of the power grid, energy consumers must become more active. Being an active electricity consumer means that, unlike previous passive consumers who did not adjust their consumption and simply paid the electricity bill at the end of the month, they adjust their electricity consumption and may even produce and store it themselves. In recent years, several active electricity consumer concepts have gained traction. Prosumer is one of the most commonly used concepts. There are several definitions and, accordingly, different scopes for this term. Prosumer is a combination of the two words "producer" and "consumer". According to Eureletric's definition, a prosumer is "a customer who produces electricity primarily for their own use but may also sell the excess electricity" (Eureletric, 2015).

The concept of prosumers allows for the development of two approaches that can be used for a more sustainable approach to the energy system. The first represents a large number of self-sufficient consumers that would produce and fully consume the energy themselves. This pathway is unlikely, and this approach will focus on a smaller number of consumers who need or are able to supply themselves with sufficient energy due to geographic constraints. The second approach is prosumers connected to the grid. They would not only be passive customers but would also provide certain energy services to the grid. Prosumers will complement the existing energy system and even compete with other traditional players in the system (Parag & Sovacool, 2016).

Solar photovoltaic (PV) systems on rooftops are by far the most common method for energy consumers to become prosumers. Most PV installations, especially in the EU, have been built under a government subsidy program. The most common support scheme is the feed-in tariff (FIT), which offers a price above the market price to producers of renewable energy sources with long-term contracts. The use of the FIT scheme, particularly in Europe, is slowly declining. In Germany, for example, the feed-in tariff scheme has been replaced by a simpler self-consumption scheme (Botelho, et al., 2021). Until recently, prosumers were not under much pressure to become more active, but this is slowly changing. As government incentives for prosumers and others' use of renewable energy sources slowly decline, prosumers will need to monetize their investments, which will drive new business models (Murdock, et al., 2018). One of the global trends currently is self-consumption and regulations that address collective self-consumption, e.g., EU Directive 2018/2001. These trends are influencing the development of new business models.

SMART GIRD

Many changes are forcing the traditional power grid to change. The power grid must accommodate both increasing power consumption and increasing renewable energy sources. Managing a large share of such sources in the system requires large investments in new information and communication technology devices and a more flexible power distribution mechanism (Botelho, et al., 2021). Coping with these challenging trends requires an increasingly complex electric power system. In recent years, the new concept of so-called "smart grids" has emerged. One of many definitions of the term "smart grid" defines it as "an electricity network that enables devices to communicate between utilities and consumers to manage demand, protect the distribution network, conserve energy, and reduce costs" (Kylili &

Fokaides, 2015). This concept describes the integration of hardware, software, computer monitoring and control technologies, and advanced communication networks into a power grid. A smart grid will allow consumers to better manage their consumption based on various information, which could include the price of energy at a given time (Shabanzadeh & Moghaddam, 2013).

The driving factors for the emergence of a smart grid range from environmental reasons (renewable energy adoption, energy conservation, and demand reduction) to more operational reasons such as operational efficiency, customer satisfaction, and utility economics. An important feature of the smart grid is that it allows the exchange of information in both directions between the different parts of the power grid. In the traditional power grid, power flows from the generation side of the grid to the consumer, and the flow of information (about consumption) flows in the opposite direction. In the smart grid, the communications infrastructure, in combination with the power infrastructure and more active consumers, enables power and information to flow in both directions in a smart grid environment. (Figure 5). The boundaries between consumers and generators will disappear as consumers become more active and adjust their behaviour based on information from the grid. Adjusting electricity consumption to the state of the grid is called demand response. For example, if the electric utility grid has a low percentage of electricity from renewable energy sources, depending on consumption, the price of electricity may be higher and consumers will be encouraged to consume less, and vice versa (Moshari, Yousefi, Ebrahimi & Haghbin, 2010).

Figure 5. Two-way power and information flows in the smart grid environment (Source: Fazeli, Zangeneh & Kalantar, 2014)

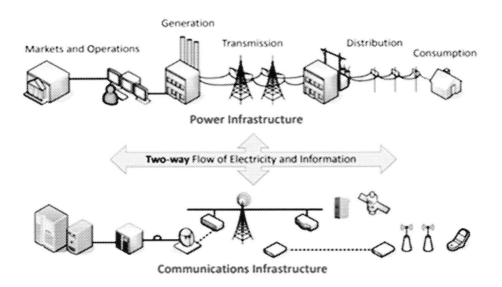

In practice, there are many ways to make the network smarter. One example is the establishment of a so-called virtual power plant (VPP) in Vermont. The electric utility company Green Mountain Power (GMP) has set up a network of residential battery systems to save on electricity prices. GMP has installed

The Role of Electromobility in the Energy-Related Smart Grids

4000 Tesla Powerwalls home battery packs at its customers' homes. The concept is quite simple and is known as energy arbitrage. When there is a surplus of electricity in the network, and conditions are favorable for electricity generation from RES, electricity prices are low. At that time, the batteries are charged and during the period when there is relatively little electricity and the price is higher, they are discharged. GMP also uses Tesla's Autobidder software for its real-time trading and control platform to better utilize energy storage capacity. According to GMP in 2020 and 2021, when the number of batteries in the system was still smaller, batteries saved over $3 million annually. During a heat wave in the summer of 2022, the batteries saved nearly $1.5 million in just one week. In the future, GMP expects even greater savings from the battery system and is already planning the installation of additional batteries (Lambert, 2022 & Pickerel 2021).

Although the smart grid represents a great perspective for the further development of the power system, it is not without problems and challenges. First of all, upgrading the current system with new technology will require substantial investments in infrastructure. However, given all the external factors (described trends), it will not be possible to avoid all investments in the grid. Among the other challenges related to smart grids, communication problems are often mentioned. In the smart grid, current grid communication solutions will struggle to keep up with the increase in data exchange from various sensors (e.g., smart meters) and devices (e.g., home batteries). In the current grid, a lot of the communication is done through Power Line Communication (PLC), which is based on the transmission of modulated carrier signals over the existing low-voltage lines. PLC encounters many problems such as interference and noise issues, channel congestion and channel instability, etc. Also, other forms of communication such as wireless and cellular communication such as unreliability, interference, compatibility of different protocols, etc. In addition to communication problems, there are also system security and privacy issues. With the increasing number of different smart devices in the network, increasing communication and remote management of the system, it is increasingly difficult to ensure system security. Denial of service (DoS) attacks and other forms of attacks on the power infrastructure have already occurred in the past. A smart power grid with many electronic devices provides many targets for attackers (hackers). By monitoring electricity consumption more closely using smart meters and collecting data about devices in households (e.g., registers about installed solar panels, heat pumps, home charging stations for electric vehicles, etc.), grid operators will have a very good insight into people's lives. This means that it will be necessary to pay close attention to protecting consumer privacy and anonymizing data (Colak et al., 2016).

Smart Meter

As already mentioned, traditional electricity grids are designed to deliver electricity to consumers and bill them monthly. There is little or no direct exchange of information between the subject, who is at the beginning of the electricity supply chain, and the consumer. As we will see later in the course, smart grids attempt to solve this problem. A critical part of the modern smart grid is the so-called advanced metering infrastructure (AMI), which is "an integrated system of smart meters, data management systems, and communication networks that enable two-way communication between utilities and customers" (Aggarwal & Kumar, 2021). Smart meters are a critical technology to enable an active consumer and a key component of the future power grid. A smart meter is an electronic device that primarily records the consumption of electrical energy (e.g., electricity usage). It can also collect data on amperage, voltage level, and power factor. The information from smart meters can help consumers get a better view of electricity consumption and regulate it according to various factors (price, aggregate consumption, etc.). The data will also be sent to electricity suppliers for system monitoring and customer billing. The installation of smart meters in homes enables a bidirectional flow of information between homes and the grid, which also enables dynamic pricing (Molina-Markham, et al., 2010).

Smart meters enable the deployment of smart metering systems that bring the financial benefits mentioned above. Smart meters can reduce business losses and control energy consumption in real-time or near real-time. They can also detect energy theft, improve grid reliability, and lead to better revenue and rate management. The latter is particularly important for bringing smaller (i.e., residential) generators into the grid, as innovative rate structures can be introduced and more accurate bills can be generated based on meter data. It will encourage consumers to change their behaviour and optimize energy consumption, even generating electricity on their own property and feeding it back into the grid. Therefore, smart metering architecture is critical to achieving the goal of a smart grid (Kaur, 2021).

Inclusion of Active Energy Consumers

Most of the energy produced by prosumers comes from renewable energy sources, which are volatile and fluctuate in their production. A modern energy consumer in smart grids will not only be able to produce and sell electricity, but will also be able to regulate energy consumption based on the energy surplus or deficit in the grid, store energy, and trade with other consumers. A general term for such consumer is active energy consumer. Due to the development of information and communications technology (ICT), more accessible and affordable renewable energy technologies (e.g., photovoltaic), and the development of a smart grid, the concept of the consumer or active customer has become more important in the field of energy systems (Botelho, et al., 2021).

Compared to a traditional power grid, a grid with integrated prosumers has some advantages and opportunities that can improve system efficiency in several ways. One of the most important ways to improve efficiency is to introduce smart control and communication technology. So-called smart appliances include major household energy consumers such as heating systems, air conditioners, refrigerators, and other electrical appliances. These smart appliances will be able to receive real-time energy price data and automatically adjust their performance (Parag & Sovacool, 2016). In addition, prosumers can also have some energy storage capacities. This way, consumers can also manage their energy more efficiently. Energy storage can also be provided by batteries in electric vehicles, which makes it more affordable and possible. To use electric vehicles and enable the exchange of electric energy, they must be equipped with electronic equipment such as an interface for grid connection, a meter, and a bidirectional communication interface (Lopes, Soares & Almeida, 2010).

We now present a practical example of incorporating active power consumers into the grid with the aim of improving its performance. For example, in 2020, the Slovenian company Gen-I d.o.o. created a system for response load management with centralized management of heat pumps of household consumers in the area of the substation, which often exceeded their rated voltage due to overloads. The solution was implemented for the distribution system operator (DSO) Elektro Ljubljana d.d. Gen-I has reached an agreement with 17 households from the area of the substation, which use heat pumps for heating, to integrate them into the system. The total power of the heat pumps is a maximum of 30 kW, but the power is reduced from a maximum of 20 kW. The reason for this is that the heat pumps have different time intervals of normal duty cycles and full power is not always available. Based on the real-time observed loads in the network, DSO Elektro Ljubljana initiates a Gen-I call to reduce consumption.

Then, using ICT through the central utilization system, Gen-I tries to ensure lower consumption by delaying the switch-on by switching off the heat pumps. Gen-I has 15 minutes to reduce consumption after receiving the DSO call. Overall, the projects are delivering very good results. Such solutions can increase the capacity of the grid without much additional investment, or at least delay investment in the grid. The capacity of the flexibility system can be increased by including households in the flexibility system. In the future, the next step would be to incorporate predictive analytics into the system to predict higher loads in the future. This would allow heat pumps to be turned on in advance, even before peak loads occur, making it even easier to turn them off during times of increased demand (Hozjan, 2022).

ELECTROMOBILITY

Technological advances and environmental commitments increasingly link mobility and energy. Sustainable transportation, including electric vehicles, is an environmentally friendly form of transportation that reduces emissions of greenhouse gases and other pollutants during transportation. In recent years, it has become clear that electricity will play a key role in the transition to a clean energy future. Of course, electromobility is not just about electric vehicles; the transformation of mobility needs to be considered more broadly. In addition to the vehicles, stakeholders must also provide the charging infrastructure and appropriate systems to facilitate the integration of electric vehicles into the power grid.

Electric Vehicles

Electric vehicles (EVs), also known as plug-in electric vehicles (PEVs), do not pollute local air and are therefore CO_2 neutral. For this reason, countries and industries have developed very ambitious plans to introduce electric vehicles (Santos, 2017). ENTSO-E defines electric vehicles as "road vehicles with an electric engine and battery which need to charge electricity from a power grid". These vehicles can be pure electric vehicles (BEVs) or plug-in hybrid electric vehicles (PHEVs) (ENTSO-E, 2021). Unlike Internal Combustion Engine Vehicles (ICVs), electric vehicles do not use an internal combustion engine for their propulsion. A BEV is defined by Balthasar, Tait, Riera-Palou, and Harrison (2012) as "a vehicle that draws all of its power from the electric grid, using only batteries for onboard energy storage". According to the same author's definition, a PHEV is also "a vehicle that draws part of its power from the electric grid via batteries, meeting the rest of its propulsion needs with an alternative energy source onboard (e.g., gasoline)". Hybrid electric vehicles (HEVs) also use an internal combustion engine and an electric powertrain, but unlike PHEVs, they do not draw power from the grid. Therefore, HEVs have no impact on the electric grid.

The number of electric vehicles is expected to increase rapidly and significantly in the coming years. In their study, Rietmann, Huegler, and Lieven (2020) forecast that 30% of passenger cars worldwide will be electric vehicles by 2032. A recent comprehensive survey on electric vehicles in the EU found that 51% of Europeans are considering buying a car. Electric Vehicles at the time of the survey (EasyPark Group, 2021). Due to Directive 2014/94/EU, all EU member states are required to present a national policy framework for alternative fuels infrastructure in the transport sector, and the number of electric vehicles is expected to grow rapidly and significantly in the coming years. In their study, Rietmann, Huegler, and Lieven (2020) forecast that 30% of passenger cars worldwide will be electric vehicles by 2032. A recent comprehensive survey on electric vehicles in the EU found that 51% of Europeans are

The Role of Electromobility in the Energy-Related Smart Grids

considering buying a car. Electric Vehicles at the time of the survey (EasyPark Group, 2021). Based on Directive 2014/94/EU, all EU member states are required to submit national policy frameworks for alternative fuels infrastructure in the transport sector.

It should also be noted that many countries will no longer allow the purchase and registration of new passenger cars with internal combustion engines in the foreseeable future. For example, as part of the green transition, the EU is adopting the Fit for 55 legislative package, which mandates a 100 percent reduction in CO2 emissions for new cars and vans by 2035. This means that after 2035, no new vehicles can be registered that do not run exclusively on carbon-neutral fuels (Shop, 2022).

The number of electric vehicles is expected to increase rapidly and sharply in the coming years. In their study, Rietmann, Huegler, and Lieven (2020) predict that by 2032, 30% of passenger cars worldwide will be electric vehicles. According to the European Automobile Manufacturers Association (ACEA), 9.1% of new cars in the EU were battery electric and 19.6% hybrids in 2021. Figure 6 shows the comparison of the shares of newly registered cars in the EU by fuel type from 2018 to 2021. We see that in 2018 the combined share of new petrol and diesel cars was 92.3% and in 2021 it was already only 59.6% (European Automobile Manufacturers' Association, 2022a).

Figure 6. Share of newly registered cars in the EU by fuel type (source: summarized by European Automobile Manufacturers' Association, 2022a)

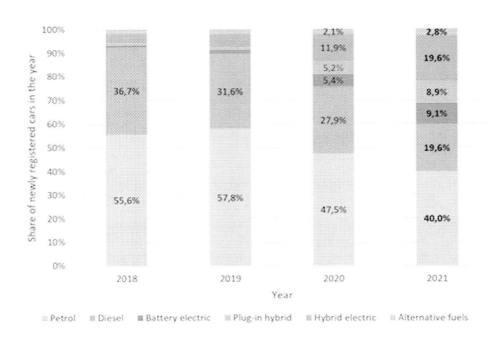

The Role of Electromobility in the Energy-Related Smart Grids

Battery Technologies

There are different types of batteries, such as lithium-ion batteries, lead-acid batteries, and molten salt batteries. The different types differ in their characteristics, e.g., duration of energy storage, energy density, battery aging, and cost. Various battery technologies are also used in electric vehicles, but usually lithium-ion batteries.

One of the most important characteristics is energy density efficiency because it determines how much energy the battery can store relative to its volume and weight. Overall, batteries have a relatively low energy density, so batteries in electric cars require larger and heavier energy storage systems than cars with an internal combustion engine. Better energy density efficiency of energy storage systems results in a lighter vehicle, which leads to better driving dynamics and of course improves efficiency (Huber, Schaule, Jung & Weinhardt, 2019).

Battery aging is also very important, as the reduction of capacity with time and use is one of the main problems with their use. Batteries degrade during use and also during storage due to a variety of chemical mechanisms (Ritchie et al., 2001). Degradation of performance with the number of charge cycles is particularly important for electric cars. Battery temperature has a strong influence on its performance and also on the degree of aging or degradation. The range of an electric car in cold temperatures decreases sharply due to poor battery performance. For this reason, special heat pump systems are installed in some vehicles to better control the temperature of the battery. There are also different opinions about the environmental impact of electric cars on the life cycle compared to internal combustion engine vehicles. Many critics point out that an electric vehicle is more environmentally friendly than an internal combustion engine vehicle throughout its life cycle. The life cycle assessment strongly depends on the expected lifetime of the electric vehicle (Huber, Schaule, Jung & Weinhardt, 2019).

Charging Stations

Charging of electric vehicles is a really important aspect of electromobility. There are different technologies for charging electric vehicles. They are divided into conductor-based and inductive-based charging. There are also charging attempts with battery swapping. By far the most common method is conductor-based charging, which is divided into direct current (DC) and alternating current (AC) technologies. For example, slow charging at private household charging stations is done with DC voltage, while fast charging is done with AC voltage and reaches a very high power, possibly up to 350 kW, which would put a heavy load on the grid (ENTSO-E, 2021). Fast charging stations that require very high power may exceed the capacity of the distribution grid and require special connections to the transmission grid. In addition to public charging stations, there are, of course, private charging stations. There will likely be the largest number of such charging stations, but compared to public charging stations, they will be slower and thus place less strain on the power grid.

There is an indirect network effect of the deployment of charging stations on the diffusion of electric vehicles. The benefits of electric vehicle are higher the greater the number of charging stations (Li, Tong, Xing & Zhou, 2017). In practice, this means that a network of charging stations must be established and a certain density of these stations must be achieved for an electric vehicle to be usable. With the rapid growth of public charging stations, some European countries are already approaching a fairly large network of charging stations that can meet the needs of the current number of users. (European Federation for Transport and Environment AISBL, 2020). Table 1 shows the number of charging points per

EU country and their percentage of the EU total in 2021, keeping in mind that a charging station can include one or more charging points. In absolute terms, most electric vehicle charging points in the EU are located in the Netherlands. Although this country is not one of the largest in the Union, its 90,284 charging points represent 29.4% of all charging points in the EU. It is followed by Germany and France with 59,410 and 37,128 charging points, respectively. In 2021, a total of 306,864 charging points were installed in the EU (European Automobile Manufacturers' Association, 2022b).

Table 1. Charging points per EU country and percentage of EU total in the year 2021 (source: summarized by European Automobile Manufacturers' Association, 2022b)

EU country	No. of charging points	Share in EU
Austria	13,110	4.3%
Belgium	13,695	4.5%
Bulgaria	531	0.2%
Croatia	1,730	0.6%
Cyprus	57	0.0%
Czech Republic	2,189	0.7%
Denmark	5,752	1.9%
Estonia	385	0.1%
Finland	5,497	1.8%
France	37,128	12.1%
Germany	59,410	19.4%
Greece	514	0.2%
Hungary	2,541	0.8%
Ireland	1,542	0.5%
Italy	23,543	7.7%
Latvia	420	0.1%
Lithuania	207	0.1%
Luxembourg	1,782	0.6%
Malta	98	0.0%
Netherlands	90,284	29.4%
Poland	2,811	0.9%
Portugal	4,124	1.3%
Romania	1,161	0.4%
Slovakia	1,367	0.4%
Slovenia	1,309	0.4%
Spain	10,480	3.4%
Sweden	25,197	8.2%
EU total	**306,864**	

The Role of Electromobility in the Energy-Related Smart Grids

Due to the relatively high maximum charging power of electric vehicles and to facilitate the development and diffusion of the technology, regulators and industry have developed standards for electric vehicle charging. In particular, efforts are being made to standardise plug types and communication protocols. Connectors are defined in the international standard IEC 62196. Currently, type 2 (defined in IEC 62196) is the most commonly used plug type in the EU, also due to EU regulatory requirements (ENTSO-E, 2021).

Smart Charging

The traditional utility value chain includes power generation, trading, transportation, distribution, retail, and (Richter, 2013). Electrification of road transport affects all parts of the network. Considering that one of the main reasons for switching to electric vehicles is to switch to clean energy, it makes sense that the electricity consumed by these vehicles should come from renewable sources. However, it is difficult to integrate renewables into the grid because their production patterns are inherently volatile.

The grid has to simultaneously cope with increasing electricity consumption and a higher share of renewables. In addition, BEVs have higher peak demand compared to other residential electricity users. Since many electric vehicle owners charge their vehicles at night, this can lead to a high degree of simultaneity in charging demand. Even with low market penetration, these peak demands can pose a challenge to the grid (Clement-Nyns, Haesen, and Driesen, 2009). This indicates that to ensure a stable and uninterrupted power supply to the electric grid, some control and management of electric vehicle charging is required. Electric vehicle charging is at the interface between the energy and transportation sectors and is a key factor for the successful development of both sectors (ENTSO-E, 2021). Electric vehicle charging needs to be flexible to match power demand to available energy. This must be done in an intelligent way, as electric vehicles must meet the mobility needs of users regardless of their load flexibility. Therefore, the concept of smart charging has evolved. Smart charging (SC), also known as directed charging or coordinated charging, has several definitions (Delmonte, Kinnear, Jenkins, and Skippon, 2020). One of the many definitions defines a smart charging system as "an information system that optimizes the charging process to achieve one or more goals while reaching a desired state of charge (SoC) within a specified time frame" (Huber, Schaule, Jung, & Winhart, 2019). In addition to the required SoC, the technical, financial, and socio-environmental goals are other fundamental objectives (Sovacool, Axsen, and Kempton, 2017). One of the main characteristics of smart charging is that it is monitored by an external control system (ENTSO-E, 2021).

Smart Charging can be configured in different control architectures. Grid operators or electric vehicle owners can regulate charging if the owners receive price incentives (Flath, Ilg, and Weinhardt, 2012). A third option that has received increasing attention in recent years is for the process to be operated by so-called aggregators in hierarchical or intermediate control architectures (Schuller, Flath, & Gottwalt, 2015; Vaya & Andersson, 2012; Bessa et al, 2011). Moreover, electric vehicles and smart charging impose entirely new tasks on grid users. The battery of an electric vehicle can not only store energy to meet travel needs, but also ensure the stability of the power system. Electric vehicles can act as short-term storage for the grid and provide additional services, a concept known as vehicle-to-grid (V2G) (Kempton and Tomić, 2005a).

Research shows that technical goals can be achieved by making the charging process flexible. By shifting the charging time of an electric vehicle, smart charging can be used to balance peak loads (so-called peak demand trimming) and achieve other optimization goals. For charging flexibility, it is important to provide the required SoC in less than a certain time frame (Huber, Schaule, Jung, and Weinhardt, 2019). Smart charging allows grid operators to control the charging process to avoid grid congestion and costly grid expansion. Electric utilities can respond to price increases or reduce billing costs. Electric vehicle owners can respond to electricity prices to reduce their charging costs (Will and Schuller, 2016). Figure 7 shows an example of the impact of smart charging on electric vehicle load. In the case of uncoordinated charging of a typical owner of an electric vehicle, the peak load (green line) of electric vehicle charging is in the evening hours because that is when people are at home and plug in their electric vehicles. Evening hours are already a challenging period for the power grid, as the residual load increases during this time even without charging of electric vehicles. In the case of smart charging, electric vehicle load could, for example, be adjusted to the price of electricity (yellow dashed line) based on electricity consumption and generation (e.g., solar generation is highest in the middle of the day), so that charging of electric vehicles could be moved to less problematic times of the day (red line). Thus, most charging could be done in the middle of the day and late at night or very early in the morning, when there is relatively more electricity (ENTSO-E, 2021). The flexibility offered by smart charging could also enable charging when more renewables are available in the energy mix, reducing charging prices and CO_2 emissions (Huber & Weinhardt, 2018).

Figure 7. Smart changing effect on electric vehicle load (source: ENTSO-E, 2021)

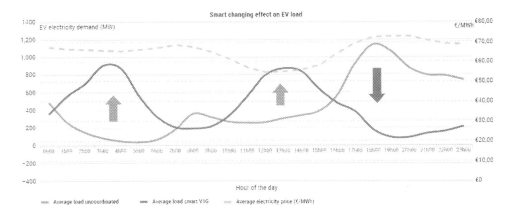

Vehicle-to-Grid Concept

As described in previous chapters (e.g., PV example), the power grid faces many challenges. Many of them could be overcome with energy savers that would help balance the electricity supply with consumption. At the local level, or even just at the household level, the most feasible and appropriate use of batteries at this time would be to feed electricity into the grid. This allows for short-term energy storage and rapid energy release when needed. In recent years, there has been a lot of investment in battery development for one reason: electric vehicles.

If we assume that electric vehicles will dominate passenger cars in the future and become the most common type of vehicle, this means that batteries will be in vehicles all around us. This represents a great potential for the use of vehicle batteries, not only for driving but also for services to the electric

The Role of Electromobility in the Energy-Related Smart Grids

grid. Nevertheless, studies have shown that private vehicles are parked on average for more than 90% of their lifetime (Kempton & Tomić, 2005a). Therefore, the concept of vehicle-to-grid (V2G) has emerged. V2G is an advanced form of smart charging with bidirectional energy flow capability (ENTSO-E, 2021). This means that the battery can draw power from or return power to the grid depending on the state of the grid (e.g., electricity price) and a set of predetermined conditions (e.g., minimum state of charge). V2G could help smooth electric vehicles' load and even some of the global residual load (ENTSO-E, 2021).

For a vehicle to be used for the V2G approach, it must meet at least three requirements. It must be connected to the power grid, it must have controls to connect and communicate with the grid operator, and it must have controls and metering equipment (Kempton & Tomić, 2005a). This approach is not only intended for use by households (private vehicles) but also holds great potential for use by fleet operators such as car rental companies (Kempton & Tomić, 2005b). V2G is particularly interesting for fleet operators, as they can fairly well predict when they will need a certain car (booking of rental cars). In this way, they can more easily decide to include the car in the V2G scheme, since they can predict the required SoC at a given time.

Probably the biggest barrier to the diffusion of the V2G concept from a user perspective is battery degradation due to cycle ageing. The V2G concept could accelerate the charge/discharge cycle of vehicle batteries, increasing battery ageing through use. Research shows this is also one of the major concerns of current electric vehicle users (Schmalfuss et al., 2015 & Huber, Schaule, Jung, & Weinhardt, 2019).

DISCUSSION

Increasing the share of distributed power generators from RES is promising, but careful planning and coordination are needed for grid stability. The same is true for electric vehicle charging infrastructure. Much research has been done in the field of electrical engineering on the impact of electric vehicles and RES on the power grid.

To analyse and predict the impact of electric vehicles on the power grid, researchers use various modelling approaches (Richardson, 2013). One promising area for future research is to better understand electric vehicle users' behaviour and their segmentation. Thus, there is a need to better understand when to what extent electric vehicle users are willing to give up fast, uncoordinated charging and join a smart charging system, and how factors such as the number of children and type of living unit (house vs. apartment) influence their habits and preferences. This data could then be used in grid modelling and improve its accuracy. When we talk about the electrification of mobility, concerns often arise about the impact of batteries on the environment and their limited lifespan and use. Researchers are already investigating how to better utilise used batteries from electric vehicles (Börner, et al., 2022). However, given the rapid and continuous development of battery technologies and the great need to make better use of them, there is a great need for further research in this area.

As we have seen, the smart grid presents a set of new technology applications in the power grid. This enables many opportunities to optimise and improve the system, but many solutions still need to be researched and developed. We have described two practical examples of integrating active energy consumers into the grid to improve grid stability and save costs. However, there are many other opportunities enabled by the smart grid that still need to be explored. Thus, there is still a lot of room for future research in this area.

CONCLUSION

As we can see, a lot is happening in the field of energy and mobility. Changes are inevitable due to several factors and trends, but at the same time, new solutions and concepts such as smart grid and electric vehicles are not without challenges. The main challenges are the integration of a larger share of volatile renewable energy sources, the increase in electricity consumption, and the inclusion of new types of consumers. The concept of the smart grid seeks to provide solutions to these challenges using new technologies. The grid aims to efficiently and cost-effectively integrate all components and actors with different characteristics.

The electrification of transport presents a very different challenge for the power grid. Integrating a large number of electric vehicles without any planning and control can be a very big problem for the grid. Electric vehicles can increase the daily peak demand. On the other hand, electromobility offers a new element in the electrical system that, if implemented in a planned and intelligent way, can enable the support of the future power grid.

REFERENCES

Aggarwal, S., & Kumar, N. (2021). *Advances in Computers, Smart grid*. Elsevier. doi:10.1016/bs.adcom.2020.08.023

Allen, M., Dube, O. P., Solecki, W., Aragón-Durand, F., Cramer, W., Humphreys, S., & Mulugetta, Y. (2018). *Global warming of 1.5° C. An IPCC Special Report on the impacts of global warming of 1.5° C above pre-industrial levels and related global greenhouse gas emission pathways, in the context of strengthening the global response to the threat of climate change, sustainable development, and efforts to eradicate poverty*. Sustainable Development, and Efforts to Eradicate Poverty.

Bessa, R. J., Matos, M. A., Soares, F. J., & Lopes, J. A. P. (2011). Optimized bidding of an EV aggregation agent in the electricity market. *IEEE Transactions on Smart Grid, 3*(1), 443–452. doi:10.1109/TSG.2011.2159632

Börner, M. F., Frieges, M. H., Späth, B., Spütz, K., Heimes, H. H., Sauer, D. U., & Li, W. (2022). Challenges of second-life concepts for retired electric vehicle batteries. *Cell Reports Physical Science, 101095*(10), 101095. doi:10.1016/j.xcrp.2022.101095

Botelho, D. F., Dias, B. H., de Oliveira, L. W., Soares, T. A., Rezende, I., & Sousa, T. (2021). Innovative business models as drivers for prosumers integration-Enablers and barriers. *Renewable & Sustainable Energy Reviews, 144*, 111057. doi:10.1016/j.rser.2021.111057

Clement-Nyns, K., Haesen, E., & Driesen, J. (2009). The impact of charging plug-in hybrid electric vehicles on a residential distribution grid. *IEEE Transactions on Power Systems, 25*(1), 371–380. doi:10.1109/TPWRS.2009.2036481

Clement-Nyns, K., Haesen, E., & Driesen, J. (2009). The impact of charging plug-in hybrid electric vehicles on a residential distribution grid. *IEEE Transactions on Power Systems, 25*(1), 371–380. doi:10.1109/TPWRS.2009.2036481

Colak, I., Sagiroglu, S., Fulli, G., Yesilbudak, M., & Covrig, C. F. (2016). A survey on the critical issues in smart grid technologies. *Renewable & Sustainable Energy Reviews, 54,* 396–405. doi:10.1016/j.rser.2015.10.036

Delmonte, E., Kinnear, N., Jenkins, B., & Skippon, S. (2020). What do consumers think of smart charging? Perceptions among actual and potential plug-in electric vehicle adopters in the United Kingdom. *Energy Research & Social Science, 60,* 101318. doi:10.1016/j.erss.2019.101318

Demirbaş, A. (2006). Global renewable energy resources. *Energy Sources, 28*(8), 779–792. doi:10.1080/00908310600718742

EasyPark AB. (2021). *The future of European parking – demand for electric cars and free parking spots.* EasyPark. https://www.easyparkgroup.com/news/the-future-of-european-parking-demand-for-electric-cars-and-free-parking-spots/

Energy Information Administration. (2022). *Electricity explained - U.S.* EIA. https://www.eia.gov/energy-explained/electricity/#:~:text=Electricity%20is%20a%20secondary%20energy%20source&text=The%20electricity%20that%20we%20use,wind%20energy%2C%20into%20electrical%20power

ENTSO-E. (2021). *ENTSO-E Position Paper: Electric Vehicle Integration into Power Grids.* ENTSO-E. https://eepublicdownloads.entsoe.eu/clean-documents/Publications/Position%20papers%20and%20reports/210331_Electric_Vehicles_integration.pdf

EU. (2014). Directive 2014/94/EU of the European Parliament and of the Council of 22 October 2014 on the deployment of alternative fuels infrastructure. *Official Journal of the European Union L, 307*(1). https://eur-lex.europa.eu/legal-content/en/TXT/?uri=CELEX%3A32014L0094

EU Parliament. (2018). Directive 2018/2001 of the European Parliament and of the Council on the promotion of the use of energy from renewable sources. *Official Journal of the European Union.* https://eur-lex.europa.eu/legal-content/EN/TXT/?uri=uriserv:OJ.L_.2018.328.01.0082.01.ENG

Eureletric (2015). *Prosumers: an integral part of the power system and the market.* Eureletric. https://www.eurelectric.org/media/1945/prosumers_an_integral_part_of_the_power_system_and_market_june_2015-2015-2110-0004-01-e.pdf (Accessed 1 August, 2021).

European Federation for Transport and Environment AISBL. (2020). *TE Infrastructure Report.* AISBL. https://www.transportenvironment.org/wp-content/uploads/2021/07/01%202020%20Draft%20TE%20Infrastructure%20Report%20Final.pdf

Fazeli, S. M., Zangeneh, A., & Kalantar, M. (2014). Optimal Operation of Smart Grids Based on Power Loss Minimization Using Distribution Optimal Power Flow Model. *International Journal of Scientific Engineering and Technology, 3*(7), 978–982.

Flath, C., Ilg, J., & Weinhardt, C. (2012). Decision support for electric vehicle charging. *AMCIS Proceedings.* AIS. https://aisel.aisnet.org/amcis2012/proceedings/GreenIS/14

Hozjan, V. (2022). GEN-I razbremenjuje omrežje z zamikom vklopa toplotnih črpalk [GEN-I relieves the grid by delaying the start-up of heat pumps]. *Energetika.* https://www.energetika.net/novice/en.vizija/gen-i-razbremenjuje-omrezje-z-zamikom-vklopa-toplotnih-crpal

Huber, J., Schaule, E., Jung, D., & Weinhardt, C. (2019). Quo vadis smart charging? A literature review and expert survey on technical potentials and user acceptance of smart charging systems. *World Electric Vehicle Journal, 10*(4), 85. doi:10.3390/wevj10040085

Huber, J., & Weinhardt, C. (2018). Waiting for the sun-can temporal flexibility in BEV charging avoid carbon emissions? *Energy Informatics, 1*(1), 115-126. https://energyinformatics.springeropen.com/articles/10.1186/s42162-018-0026-2

Carrasco, J. M., Franquelo, L. G., Bialasiewicz, J. T., Galvan, E., PortilloGuisado, R. C., Prats, M. A. M., & Moreno-Alfonso, N. (2006). Power-Electronic Systems for the Grid Integration of Renewable Energy Sources. *IEEE Transactions on Industrial Electronics, 53*(4), 1002–1016.

International Electrotechnical Commission. (2022). *Medium voltage.* Electropedia. https://www.electropedia.org/iev/iev.nsf/display?openform&ievref=601-01-28

International Energy Agency. (2022a). *Electricity.* IEA. https://www.iea.org/fuels-and-technologies/electricity

International Energy Agency. (2022b). *World Energy Investment 2022.* IEA. https://iea.blob.core.windows.net/assets/b0beda65-8a1d-46ae-87a2-f95947ec2714/WorldEnergyInvestment2022.pdf

Kaplan, S. M. (2009, April). *Electric power transmission: background and policy issues.* Library of Congress, Congressional Research Service. https://www.nosue.org/app/download/7244200729/2009-04-14-09+CRS+18743.pdf

Kaur, I. (2021). Metering architecture of smart grid. In Design, Analysis, and Applications of Renewable Energy Systems (pp. 687-704). Academic Press. doi:10.1016/B978-0-12-824555-2.00030-7

Kempton, W., & Tomić, J. (2005a). Vehicle-to-grid power fundamentals: Calculating capacity and net revenue. *Journal of Power Sources, 144*(1), 268–279. doi:10.1016/j.jpowsour.2004.12.025

Kempton, W., & Tomić, J. (2005b). Vehicle-to-grid power implementation: From stabilizing the grid to supporting large-scale renewable energy. *Journal of Power Sources, 144*(1), 280–294. doi:10.1016/j.jpowsour.2004.12.022

Kylili, A., & Fokaides, P. A. (2015). European smart cities: The role of zero energy buildings. *Sustainable Cities and Society, 15*, 86–95. doi:10.1016/j.scs.2014.12.003

Lambert, F. (August 22, 2022). Small Vermont utility quietly builds fleet of 4,000 Tesla Powerwalls. *Electrek.* https://electrek.co/2022/08/22/small-vermont-utility-builds-fleet-4000-tesla-powerwalls/

Li, S., Tong, L., Xing, J., & Zhou, Y. (2017). The market for electric vehicles: Indirect network effects and policy design. *Journal of the Association of Environmental and Resource Economists, 4*(1), 89–133. doi:10.1086/689702

Lopes, J. A. P., Soares, F. J., & Almeida, P. M. R. (2010). Integration of electric vehicles in the electric power system. *Proceedings of the IEEE, 99*(1), 168–183. doi:10.1109/JPROC.2010.2066250

Lund, H. (2009). *Renewable energy systems: the choice and modeling of 100% renewable solutions.* Academic Press.

Ma, H., Balthasar, F., Tait, N., Riera-Palou, X., & Harrison, A. (2012). A new comparison between the life cycle greenhouse gas emissions of battery electric vehicles and internal combustion vehicles. *Energy Policy, 44*, 160–173. doi:10.1016/j.enpol.2012.01.034

Molina-Markham, A., Shenoy, P., Fu, K., Cecchet, E., & Irwin, D. (2010, November). Private memoirs of a smart meter. In *Proceedings of the 2nd ACM workshop on embedded sensing systems for energy-efficiency in building* (pp. 61-66). ACM. 10.1145/1878431.1878446

Moshari, A., Yousefi, G. R., Ebrahimi, A., & Haghbin, S. (2010). *Demand-side behavior in the smart grid environment. In 2010 IEEE PES Innovative Smart Grid Technologies Conference Europe (ISGT Europe).* IEEE. doi:10.1109/ISGTEUROPE.2010.5638956

Murdock, H. E., Collier, U., Adib, R., Hawila, D., Bianco, E., Muller, S., & Frankl, P. (2018). *Renewable energy policies in a time of transition.* IRENA.

Øgaard, M. B., Riise, H. N., Haug, H., Sartori, S., & Selj, J. H. (2020). Photovoltaic system monitoring for high latitude locations. *Solar Energy, 207*, 1045–1054. doi:10.1016/j.solener.2020.07.043

Parag, Y., & Sovacool, B. K. (2016). Electricity market design for the prosumer era. *Nature Energy, 1*(4), 1–6. doi:10.1038/nenergy.2016.32

Pedersen, T. S., Andersen, P., Nielsen, K. M., Stærmose, H. L., & Pedersen, P. D. (2011). Using heat pump energy storages in the power grid. In *2011 IEEE International Conference on Control Applications (CCA)* (pp. 1106-1111). IEEE. 10.1109/CCA.2011.6044504

Pickerel, K. (May 14, 2021). Green Mountain Power will use 200 Tesla Powerwalls as virtual power plant. *Solar Power World.* https://www.solarpowerworldonline.com/2021/05/green-mountain-power-will-use-200-tesla-powerwalls-as-virtual-power-plant/

Richardson, D. B. (2013). Electric vehicles and the electric grid: A review of modeling approaches, Impacts, and renewable energy integration. *Renewable & Sustainable Energy Reviews, 19*, 247–254. doi:10.1016/j.rser.2012.11.042

Richter, M. (2013). Business model innovation for sustainable energy: German utilities and renewable energy. *Energy Policy, 62*, 1226–1237. doi:10.1016/j.enpol.2013.05.038

Rietmann, N., Hügler, B., & Lieven, T. (2020). Forecasting the trajectory of electric vehicle sales and the consequences for worldwide CO_2 emissions. *Journal of Cleaner Production, 261*, 121038. doi:10.1016/j.jclepro.2020.121038

Ritchie, A. G., Lakeman, B., Burr, P., Carter, P., Barnes, P. N., & Bowles, P. (2001). Battery degradation and ageing. In *Ageing Studies and Lifetime Extension of Materials* (pp. 523–527). Springer., doi:10.1007/978-1-4615-1215-8_58

Ritchie, H., & Roser, M. (2022b). Electricity Mix. *Our World in Data.* https://ourworldindata.org/electricity-mix#:~:text=In%202019%2C%20almost%20two%2Dthirds,and%20nuclear%20energy%20for%2010.4%25

Santos, G. (2017). Road transport and CO_2 emissions: What are the challenges? *Transport Policy, 59*, 71–74. doi:10.1016/j.tranpol.2017.06.007

Schmalfuss, F., Mair, C., Döbelt, S., Kaempfe, B., Wuestemann, R., Krems, J. F., & Keinath, A. (2015). User responses to a smart charging system in Germany: Battery electric vehicle driver motivation, attitudes and acceptance. *Energy Research & Social Science, 9*, 60–71. doi:10.1016/j.erss.2015.08.019

Schuller, A., Flath, C. M., & Gottwalt, S. (2015). Quantifying load flexibility of electric vehicles for renewable energy integration. *Applied Energy, 151*, 335–344. doi:10.1016/j.apenergy.2015.04.004

Shabanzadeh, M., & Moghaddam, M. P. (2013, November). What is the smart grid? Definitions, perspectives, and ultimate goals. In *28th International Power System Conference.*

Smith, R., Meng, K., Dong, Z., & Simpson, R. (2013). Demand response: A strategy to address residential air-conditioning peak load in Australia. *Journal of Modern Power Systems and Clean Energy, 1*(3), 219–226. doi:10.100740565-013-0032-0

Sovacool, B. K., Axsen, J., & Kempton, W. (2017). The future promise of vehicle-to-grid (V2G) integration: A sociotechnical review and research agenda. *Annual Review of Environment and Resources, 42*(1), 377–406. doi:10.1146/annurev-environ-030117-020220

Stikvoort, B., Bartusch, C., & Juslin, P. (2020). Different strokes for different folks? Comparing pro-environmental intentions between electricity consumers and solar prosumers in Sweden. *Energy Research & Social Science, 69*, 101552. doi:10.1016/j.erss.2020.101552

Store, J. (2022, June 29). *Fit for 55 package: Council reaches general approaches relating to emissions reductions and their social impacts.* Council of the EU. https://www.consilium.europa.eu/en/press/press-releases/2022/06/29/fit-for-55-council-reaches-general-approaches-relating-to-emissions-reductions-and-removals-and-their-social-impacts/

The European Automobile Manufacturers' Association. (2022a). *New Car Registrations by Fuel Type, European Union. ACEA.* https://www.acea.auto/files/20220202_PRPC-fuel_Q4-2021_FINAL.pdf (Accessed 1 August 2022).

The European Automobile Manufacturers' Association. (2022b). *Progress Report 2022. Making The Transition to Zero-Emission Mobility.* ACEA. https://www.acea.auto/files/ACEA_progress_report_2022.pdf

van den Akker, M., Blok, H., Budd, C., Eggermont, R., Gutermon, A., Lahaye, D., & Wadman, W. (2012). *A case study in the future challenges in electricity grid infrastructure.* Research Gate. https://www.researchgate.net/figure/Typical-daily-power-production-profile-from-solar-panels-1_fig7_325951690

Vaya, M. G., & Andersson, G. (2012). *Centralized and decentralized approaches to smart charging of plug-in vehicles. In 2012 IEEE power and energy society general meeting.* IEEE. doi:10.1109/TSG.2011.2159632

Will, C., & Schuller, A. (2016). Understanding user acceptance factors of electric vehicle smart charging. *Transportation Research Part C, Emerging Technologies, 71*, 198–214. doi:10.1016/j.trc.2016.07.006

KEY TERMS AND DEFINITIONS

Electric Vehicles: Electric vehicles (EVs) are vehicles that use electricity for their propulsion, using batteries and electric motors. Electric vehicles can be pure electric vehicles, also known as battery electric vehicles (BEVs), which draw all their energy from the power grid or so-called vehicles plug-in hybrid electric vehicles (PHEVs) which also use an alternative energy source to assist electric powertrain.

Electromobility: Electromobility refers to the concept of using electric vehicles and other means of transport which use electric power for their propulsion to transport people and goods.

Power Grid: The power grid, also known as the electrical grid, is a network of components which delivers electricity to consumers. The main components of the power grid are: generating plants, electrical substations, an electric power transmission network and an electric power distribution network.

Prosumer: Prosumer refers to a type of active energy consumer who consumes electricity from the power grid and also produces it for his own consumption or for sale in the grid. The term "prosumer" is a combination of the two words "producer" and "consumer".

Smart Charging: Smart charging refers to an advanced electric vehicle charging system which aims to manage the charging process in an intelligent way to achieve given objectives. Compared to uncoordinated charging, where vehicles start charging as soon as they are plugged, smart charging, also known as coordinated charging or directed charging, adjusts the time and power of charging. For example, such a system can optimise charging costs in a way that a vehicle is charged when the price and demand of electricity are the lowest.

Smart Grid: Smart grid refers to the power grid that uses advanced information and communication technologies that enable bidirectional communication in the grid, monitoring and intelligent management of the grid. The smart grid aims to better connect all components of the power grid and ensure a more stable and secure supply of electricity.

Vehicle-to-Grid: Vehicle-to-Grid (V2G): refers to the concept of electric vehicle charging where the vehicle draws electricity from the grid, stores it and returns electricity into the grid. Vehicle-to-Grid is an advanced form of electric vehicle smart (coordinated) charging with bidirectional energy flow capability. By discharging electricity from the battery back into the grid, electric vehicle contribution to the grid ancillary services.

Chapter 4
Information Systems and Technologies for Green Public Transportation

Ivana Ninčević Pašalić

https://orcid.org/0000-0002-4610-0344

Faculty of Economics, Business, and Tourism, University of Split, Croatia

Maja Ćukušić

Faculty of Economics, Business, and Tourism, University of Split, Croatia

Silvia Golem

Faculty of Economics, Business, and Tourism, University of Split, Croatia

Tea Jašić

Faculty of Economics, Business, and Tourism, University of Split, Croatia

ABSTRACT

Overloaded infrastructure is one of the main challenges cities are facing nowadays. Cities attempt to overcome these challenges by applying different innovative concepts and technologies, some of which are smart city initiatives. One of the elementary features of smart cities is the modernization of public transport and a well-designed transportation infrastructure. Modern information systems are used in public transportation in many ways, with the main purpose of facilitating and improving public transport for citizens. This chapter overviews the implementation of some standard information systems in public transportation and explains their purposes, way of functioning, and advantages for both users and providers. The aim of this chapter is to demonstrate relevant information systems used in public transport in several European cities - Rome, Paris, London, and Split. It is clearly shown that each city has its own version of a particular information system that achieves the goals of smart mobility.

DOI: 10.4018/978-1-6684-5996-6.ch004

Copyright © 2023, IGI Global. Copying or distributing in print or electronic forms without written permission of IGI Global is prohibited.

Information Systems and Technologies for Green Public Transportation

INTRODUCTION

Inefficient urban mobility in general, and overloaded urban infrastructure, in particular, are one of the main challenges cities are facing nowadays. Cities attempt to overcome these challenges by applying different innovative concepts and technologies, as a part of smart city initiatives. In a nutshell, a smart city is "a complex, long-term vision of a better urban area, aiming at reducing its environmental footprint and at creating a better quality of life for citizens" (Benevolo, Dameri & D'Auria, 2016). Smart urban mobility which entails the development and implementation of smart public transportation systems, inevitably supported by the application of IT solutions, is one of the elementary features of smart cities.

The concept of smart mobility is designed to offer an on-demand service to its users who are provided with instant access to a system of clean, green, efficient and flexible transport (Anable et al., 2018). Among other benefits, smart mobility solutions enable providing data to passengers in real-time, diverse logistics planning features, IT systems that match the supply and demand for mobility, etc. In addition, smart mobility includes new mobility services that optimize the use of existing capacities, renting and sharing vehicles, new cycling systems, using smartphones to facilitate mobility and similar (Scrudato, 2018).

Efficient urban mobility, as one of the primary goals in the modern urban planning system, requires efficient traffic flow and a reduction of passenger waiting times. This can be done by several approaches that use a combination of GPS tracking and mobile connectivity to transmit real-time data to passengers and allow precise travel planning. Some of the relevant solutions accelerate the payment of public transportation services and automate traffic lights to function depending on the traffic conditions. An additional system that could be introduced is a smart system for parking and locating vehicles, software reporting information on the desired route change depending on road conditions (GoDigital, 2020).

This chapter presents some of the standard information systems in public transport in (smart) cities and explains their purposes, way of functioning and advantages for both users and providers. The aim of this chapter is to classify relevant information systems used in public transport and to show examples of the use of modern information systems in public transport in several smart cities in Europe. Examples from four European cities - Rome, Paris, London and Split - show different practical implementations of modern infrastructure and transport information systems employed to improve public transport services.

UNDERLYING TECHNOLOGIES FOR SMART MOBILITY SECTOR

The smart cities concept is based, but not limited, to the following concepts:

a. Communication between devices, the M2M (Machine to Machine) concept is used to exchange data between machines, devices, or applications (e.g. between vehicles, between ATMs, various vending machines for goods and services). All systems can be controlled remotely in an easy way by using a mobile network, while the data is sent to a monitoring center (Sokač, 2017). The aim is to ensure that all information is available to those users who need it to make decisions.

b. Internet of Things, (IoT) signifies automation systems and processes put into a single, common intelligent network. IoT involves the installation of various sensors and their connection to local and city internet networks in order to obtain the function of recognizing, monitoring and managing objects.

69

c. ITS (Intelligent Transport System). As a large number of vehicles in cities cause high air pollution, greenhouse gas emissions, traffic accidents and traffic jams, the solution to resolve these problems is to introduce intelligent transportation systems. Information and communication (ICT) technologies are applied in the manufacturing process to improve the communication network between vehicles (Vehicle to Vehicle - V2V) and between vehicles and infrastructure networks (Vehicle to Infrastructure - V2I). This system optimizes traffic routes and traffic flow on the roads, enables easier and simpler choices between different transport means, has a positive effect on the vehicle production process and increases the flow capacity of goods and people in traffic.

CLASSIFICATION OF MODERN INFORMATION SYSTEMS IN PUBLIC TRANSPORTATION IN (SMART) CITIES

There are many classifications of modern information systems set in the urban mobility environment. Avril et al. (2007) recognize four main components of the urban mobility system where first two components belong to transport demand (the users' needs and behavior and the urban structure) while the other two components (integrated mobility services and integrated transport system) are components of transport supply. Haque, Chin & Debnath (2013) consider sustainability, safety and smartness as three key elements of a modern transportation system based on Singapore example. In this chapter, authors aimed to present the characteristics of underlying technologies and information systems important for public transportation, as well as management systems needed to manage this type of transportation, with a special focus on user-oriented systems important for higher rates of user acceptance of public transportation services.

Table 1. Classification of modern ISs in public transportation

Underlying technologies and information systems	Management systems	User-oriented systems
Automatic vehicle location system (AVLS) & Real-time vehicle monitoring	Fleet management system	Automated fare collection service
Internet of Things	Depot management system	Passenger information system (PIS)
Autonomous Vehicle public transportation system	Smart camera systems	Smart ticketing system
Vehicle sharing systems (car and bicycle)		

Source: Authors' work

Automatic Vehicle Location System (AVLS)

For many years, designers of urban communication systems have worked to develop devices and systems that can continuously monitor the position and status of vehicles located in an urban environment (Riter, 1977). The proliferation of cheap and compact GPS receivers has influenced the emergence of automatic vehicle location systems or AVLS that almost exclusively use satellite location systems. AVLS is a command and control system intended primarily for vehicle tracking, intending to obtain precise coordinates such as the time and place of a particular object of observation. In this way, data users can see and be in

Information Systems and Technologies for Green Public Transportation

contact with a specific vehicle at any time via the GPS station device (Ministry of the Interior, 2012). AVL systems have two main parts: GPS on each public transport vehicle that tracks the real-time location and software that displays the location of the vehicle on a map. GPS is usually transmitted first to the satellite and then to the end-user via various information systems in public transport (US Department of Homeland Security, 2009) as seen in Figure 1.

Figure 1. GPS based AVL system
Source: (RoseIndia, 2018)

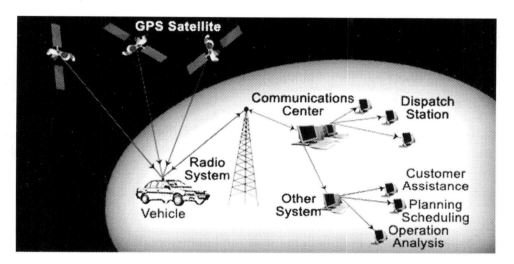

Formally, an AVL system is a collection of electronic or electromechanical devices used to collect vehicle position data in urban areas. The keyword in this definition is automatic as the system should not require (or only occasionally) action by the vehicle operator. These devices combine GPS technology, "street-level" mapping, and an intuitive user interface to improve fleet management and customer service (TechTarget, 2020). For example, a company using an AVL system can determine the length, width, speed, and direction of a particular vehicle. The location of the vehicle can be found quickly and the vehicle can be rerouted to provide timely service to the public transport user. AVL systems also allow public transport companies to create vehicle routes more efficiently by compiling a vehicle database, including the location of users in relation to established vehicle routes. All vehicle location information is sent to the central station where it is further processed, stored and used to make decisions about vehicle routes. Vehicle location information is used by a large number of transit staff, including dispatchers, vehicle operators, planners, maintenance staff, and customer support staff. Recent advances of the AVL system, based on the Global Positioning System (GPS), provide the transit industry and public transport companies' tools for monitoring and control of their vehicles and fleet management in a very efficient and cost-effective manner.

The most important advantages of the AVL systems are the following (Racca, 2004):

- Improving the optimal use of the fleet,
- Reduced fuel consumption,

Information Systems and Technologies for Green Public Transportation

- Reduced workforce,
- Reduced capital costs,
- Increase of available information,
- Efficiency and productivity increase,
- Improved customer service.

Information from AVL systems is necessary for the functioning of other information systems in public transport such as passenger information systems as passengers are provided with timely and accurate information about their journey. This information increases passenger satisfaction, attracts new public transport users and allows users to make better decisions related to planning their transport.

The cost of an AVL system includes the purchase, installation, and corresponding software for the embedded device and control center. Labor costs that should not be excluded from the calculation are related to maintenance and system management. Prices of AVL systems differ, and the price depends on the size, number of components and sophistication of the system. AVL systems are offered in a variety of models. There are models with basic features like GPS/DGPS AVL systems that have computerized shipping, mobile data terminals, and silent alarms (Khalifa, 2010). Other models have very sophisticated features. These are systems more convenient for a large fleet that needs similar features as the cost of the central monitoring system is deployed to multiple vehicles (RoseIndia, 2018).

Real-Time Vehicle Monitoring

Similar to ALV system explained above, a real-time vehicle tracking system allows real-time vehicle and driver tracking using any device connected to the internet (not only through GPS and radio system). This is a very simple system because it enables reliable real-time information for providers of public transport without the use of additional software. A real-time vehicle tracking system also records data on vehicle behavior in traffic (Figure 2). Each action in the trip is recorded with the start and end time, the distance the vehicle made, and the idle time.

Figure 2. An example of a real-time vehicle tracking system
Source: (Saad et al., 2018)

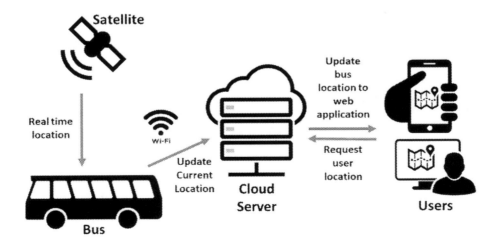

Internet of Things

The internet of things (IoT) is defined as a network of devices that communicate with each other and exchange data over the internet. The objects are equipped with various types of sensors, transmitters and receivers that are interconnected and form a network that can be analyzed.

Global transport is increasing every year and estimated numbers report an increase of 60% by 2050 despite the seen increase in awareness and willingness of individuals and businesses (Centlewski & Warchol, 2021). The impact of road transport on local air quality has become a major public policy concern. This problem inspired the research aimed at improving the technology for the management of vehicles and traffic in general (Figure 3). Recently, there is a growing body of research proving that real-time IoT systems that address real-time traffic behavior, vehicle emissions, pollutant dispersion, and passenger concentration could address this problem (Xhafka, 2015).

Improved navigation is one of the primary ways the IoT can help reduce emissions. IoT devices in the fleet, in real-time, transmit traffic and time information between vehicles. With this information, smart navigation systems can adjust the route to ensure as few delays as possible, and as the delay is reduced, vehicle travel will be reduced along with emissions.

Vehicle maintenance is an often overlooked aspect of green public transportation. Vehicle engines are more efficient when in good condition, so preventing malfunctions and resolving problems early can prevent higher CO_2 emissions. The IoT can help in this area by providing the data needed to deliver efficient vehicle maintenance practices. Many fleets today rely on preventive maintenance, and the IoT can assist in providing predictive maintenance to predict possible vehicle repair. This data-based approach prevents malfunctions and unnecessary repairs. In addition, for example, improperly maintained tires can increase rolling resistance which increases fuel consumption. IoT sensors can detect these problems in advance and thus help prevent excessive emissions of harmful gases.

To make transport truly sustainable, fossil-fueled vehicles should be replaced with zero-emission vehicles. Achieving this goal will take years, meanwhile, transportation must make other methods to reduce CO_2 emissions. Numerous IoT applications have already begun to have a significant positive impact on transportation. Since the adoption of IoT in traffic grows, the world will become "greener" (Marsh, 2021).

Autonomous Vehicle Public Transportation System

Autonomous vehicles (AV) are vehicles operating without the need for human intervention in a way that they sense the environment, detect and classify objects and identify the navigation paths.

The US Department of Transportation classified autonomous vehicles into six levels:

- Level 0 - no autonomy,
- Levels 1-3 - the driver has primary control over the vehicle and vehicle autonomy is partially used,
- Levels 4-5 - the vehicle is completely autonomous.

Figure 3. IoT sensor capabilities
Source: (Indiamart, 2021)

The AV concept first appeared in the 1920s and has been researched for more than 30 years. The AV system is equipped with a large number of sensors, including rangefinders, side and front radars, high-resolution cameras, GPS modules, gyroscopes and more. These systems give the vehicle full sensory capability to be able to adapt to the environment and have fully automated control. In 2007, the DARPA Urban Challenge raised awareness of the possibilities of AV systems in traffic and their performance in complex maneuvers. In 2010, ViSLAB conducted an experiment in which several vehicles without drivers successfully traveled 13,000 kilometers from Italy to China. Numerous studies have made it possible that by the end of 2013, several countries prepared legal frameworks that allowed AVs to operate on roads (Lam et al., 2014).

AVs offer an opportunity for governments, transport companies and agencies to improve the efficiency, competitiveness, safety, accessibility and reliability of current public transport services (Baxter, 2020). AVs improve traffic safety by avoiding bad driving and distracted drivers. Research has shown that autonomous public transport vehicles pose a lower risk of accidents compared to conventional vehicles (e.g. Portouli et al., 2017).

One of the major shortcomings of the emergence of autonomous vehicles in public transport is the reduction of drivers' jobs and it is estimated that in the future this reduction will increase to significantly (OECD, 2017). On the other hand, this loss can be offset by other jobs such as ones in engineering, management and vehicle maintenance. The reduction in the number of drivers leads to a reduction in total costs. Large savings are one of the most important advantages of autonomous public transport vehicles because they range between 50-60% of all operating costs. Travel time in an autonomous transit network can have a positive effect on waiting time, overall costs and system reliability. AVs in public transport generally have a positive impact on the environment. Research has shown that collective autonomous mobility can have a positive impact on emissions and energy consumption, specifically when compared with private AVs (Azad et al., 2019). Additionally, the research uncovered that electric and fully autonomous public transport vehicles are cost-competitive versus diesel-powered public transport vehicles (ibid).

Ensuring safe, green, accessible and equitable mobility for citizens is one of the main principles of every city and region. New technology should be used to help cities achieve these goals. Therefore, the role of the government should be to make a regulatory framework to ensure that AVs benefit the cities. Autonomous vehicles offer the opportunity to provide more public transport options to people and locations where it was previously difficult or impossible due to high operating costs. Shared autonomous "robo-taxis" and on-demand transport are very cost-effective as they are driver-free and they offer door-to-door mobility. AV integrates into a versatile and highly efficient public transport system where citizens can choose the best mobility option through an integrated multi-modal mobility platform that offers mobility as a service ("MaaS") (UITP, 2017). The following Figure 4 shows the autonomous bus architecture.

Figure 4. Autonomous bus architecture
Source: (Montes et al., 2017)

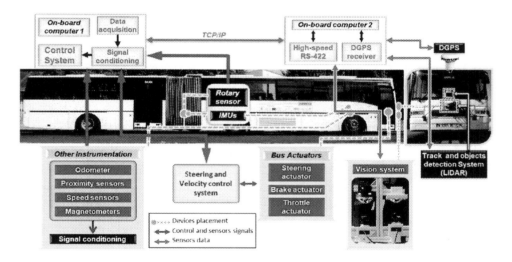

Car Sharing Systems

Car sharing is a subscription-based service that has a network of stations and vehicles that provide an alternative to traditional car use (Zheng, 2013). This is a service increasingly present in a globalized industry and is based on providing a car when needed by the user, without having to use their car. In the last 30 years, car-sharing has grown from a basic service provided by local organizations to a largely recognized, transforming the urban transportation industry.

The car sharing system makes vehicle usage easy and affordable. This service relieves citizens of the costs of purchase, registration, maintenance and insurance, loss of its value and additional work such

Information Systems and Technologies for Green Public Transportation

as refueling and finding a parking space. Although this is an innovative system, this system is easy to use as vehicle booking, unlocking and payment are done via a smartphone application (DuList, 2019).

The growth of car sharing services was initially initiated by private organizations such as Zipcar, and Car2Go. Modern car sharing originated in Switzerland and Germany in the 1980s and gained the greatest popularity in the first decade of the 21st century. In 2009, the number of cities offering car sharing services rose to 1,000 (Zheng, 2013).

The most popular car sharing model is a two-way model that requires users to borrow and return the car to the same station. This model showed positive social and environmental impacts, including the reduction of ownership of private vehicles. According to Jochem et al. (2020) study in European cities, one shared vehicle can replace up to 20 private vehicles in some cities. Recent studies show that car sharing vehicle "reduces the need for 4 to 10 privately owned cars in continental Europe, 6 to 23 cars in North America, and 7 to 10 vehicles in Australia" (Rydén and Morin, 2005 in Shaheen & Cohen, 2007). Also, shared vehicles can reduce the kilometers traveled from 28 to 45% in Europe (ibid). These advantages are the reason that the two-way model received great support from governments in Europe, North America and Australia, mostly through free or subsidized parking.

Peer-to-peer and one-way models are the latest advancements in the car sharing industry (Zheng, 2013). In peer-to-peer models, shared vehicles are owned by a private person, in this way, the existing stock of private vehicles is used. RentMyCar was the first to implement this model, and today peer-to-peer models use is growing as this model does not require an initial investment in buying a car. The one-way model is the latest model that allows the user to pick up the vehicle at one location and return it to another. This model has experienced great profit growth in recent years, and the most famous are the services offered by Car2Go and DriveNow (Lane et al., 2017).

Some of the advantages of car sharing system are (Make a wish, 2021):

- Savings by avoiding vehicle maintenance and purchase,
- Choice between different types of cars,
- Reduction of harmful gas emissions,
- Reduced need for free parking spaces,
- Fewer cars in traffic,
- Less restriction than when renting a car,
- Increased use of electric cars.

Bicycle Sharing Systems

A bicycle sharing system is a service of common carriage in which bikes are available to individuals on a short-term basis for common use with a specific fee or free of charge (Kittilaksanawong & Liu, 2021). Many bicycle sharing systems allow people to borrow a bicycle from a terminal and return it to another (same system) terminal. The terminals or docks are special bicycle racks that lock and release the bike with the help of computers. When the user provides payment information and requests a bicycle, the computer unlocks the bicycle at the terminal. After riding, the user returns the bicycle by placing it in the terminal that locks it.

For many bicycle sharing systems, there are applications designed to show nearby bicycles and open terminals on a map (see how it work in Figure 6). In July 2020, Google Maps has started to include bike sharing systems in its route recommendations.

Information Systems and Technologies for Green Public Transportation

Figure 5. How car sharing works
Source: (Edwin Conan, 2008)

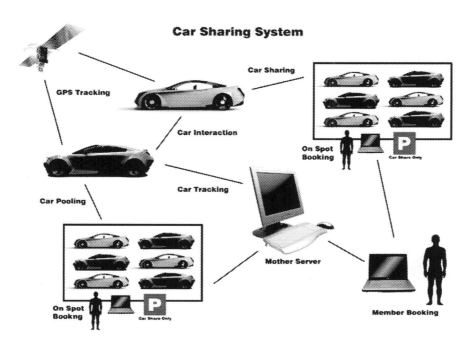

Most city bicycle sharing systems have multiple bicycle terminals and operate similarly to public transport systems, providing services to tourists and visitors as well as the local population. Their idea is to provide to bicycles for short journeys in urban areas at affordable prices or for free, thus reducing congestion, noise and air pollution (Kittilaksanawong & Liu, 2021).

Bicycle sharing systems generate both positive and negative. Positive effects include reduction of traffic congestion and pollution, while negative effects may include degradation of the urban environment and reduction of parking spaces. Some of the benefits of using a bike sharing system (Kass, 2020):

- Reduced traffic jams,
- Reduced environmental pollution,
- Healthier transport,
- Cheaper transport,
- Easy to use.

Fleet Management System

The fleet management system represents the organization and coordination of public transport vehicles with the help of modern technological solutions. Effective fleet management can help reduce costs and improve vehicle efficiency and typically consists of tracking vehicle location and mechanical information, as well as drivers' monitoring systems, all using a series of built-in sensors to collect data wirelessly (Samspon et al., 2019). The vehicle is connected to the operational base where all the necessary information is sent and then processed to achieve quality service for passengers.

Figure 6. How the bicycle sharing system works
Source: (MicroProgram, 2021)

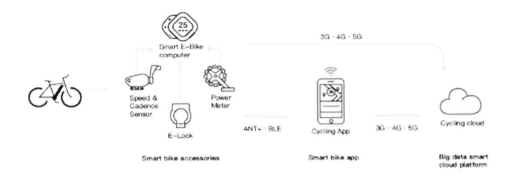

The most important functions of a fleet management system are (MixTelematics, 2021):

- Monitoring drivers' behavior to improve efficiency and reduce the number of traffic accidents,
- Providing safety to passengers,
- Locating vehicles and determining arrival times on predetermined routes at scheduled stops,
- Facilitation of service and license procedures,
- Monitoring the duration of vehicle travel,
- Monitoring driver working hours.

The purpose of fleet management and operating principles are the same regardless of the type of fleet (types see in Figure 7). However, tasks may vary depending on the size of the company that deals with public transport and depending on the volume of vehicles. For heavier vehicles, the system can monitor the driver's time at work to ensure compliance with international regulations. For lighter vehicles, the system can assess the performance of similar vehicles, as well as to measure the cost-effectiveness of drivers with similar vehicles and routes.

Some of the advantages of using a fleet management system are (Samspon et al., 2019):

- Overall improvement of public transport,
- Traffic jam prevention,
- Noise reduction,
- CO_2 reduction,
- Improved air quality.

Passenger safety and fleet management solution that ensures safety is essential in public transport. It is necessary to have a system that collects information about the drivers and the vehicle and with the help of this information effective management of vehicles on numerous routes can be organized. The fleet management system performs these tasks efficiently, saving both time and money.

Information Systems and Technologies for Green Public Transportation

Figure 7. Fleet management system modules
Source: (Tech Moukthika, 2016)

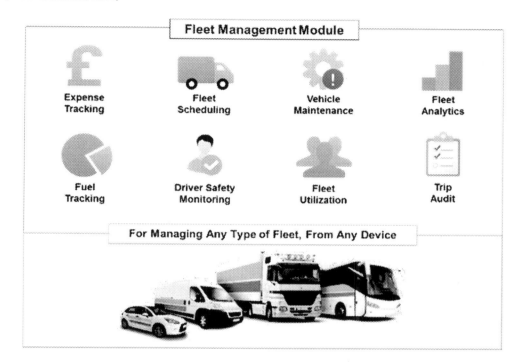

Depot Management System

A depot is a place where public transport vehicles are parked and maintained. Usually, this place has various facilities such as a place for washing vehicles, regular maintenance, services and refueling. Due to the increasing number of activities in depot, depot management software is increasingly used, with the primary purpose of facilitating and automating the regular maintenance of vehicles.

The depot management system (DMS) uses software to collect a range of data such as fleet data, office administration data and refueling data. In addition, this system allows users to make better decisions based on mentioned data, improve their performance and achieve selected goals. DMS allows public transport vehicles to be ready for daily operations and instructed to the right routes. The system monitors all processes that take place in depots, from the arrival of vehicles to their repair and parking - efficiently in a way that saves resources and prevents additional unforeseen costs (CEPT University, 2018).

Some of the DMS components are as seen in Figure 8 (PSItraffic, 2021):

- Vehicle tracking - with the help of GPS it is possible to collect data on vehicles to pre-determine the time of their arrival at the depot. The later arrival from the scheduled time is reported in the system to make necessary changes timely.
- Automatic allocation of parking spaces - once vehicles arrive at the depot, the driver automatically gets the information where to park the vehicle depending on the services needed (refuel, inspection, vehicle service, cleaning).

79

- Providing information to drivers - DMS informs drivers about their shift, vehicle location and vehicle condition with the help of terminals and mobile phones.
- Quality management - the system collects historical operational data which are then analyzed and graphically presented in reports which form the basis for analysis and process optimization.
- Automatic allocation of vehicles and routes - vehicles are parked in depots so that the appropriate vehicles are available for all subsequent routes. If the vehicle is not working, the new deployment is done in real-time. If a route cannot be met because there are not enough vehicles, the system automatically reports the lack of vehicles to act timely.

Some of the advantages of using a DMS are (PSItraffic, 2020):

- Greater transparency,
- Real-time parking and vehicle allocation,
- Increased vehicle availability,
- Optimized vehicle supply,
- Automatic vehicle dispatch,
- Use of standardized interfaces,
- Integration with other information systems,
- Integrated quality management system.

Figure 8. Depot management system modules
Source: (NEC, 2021)

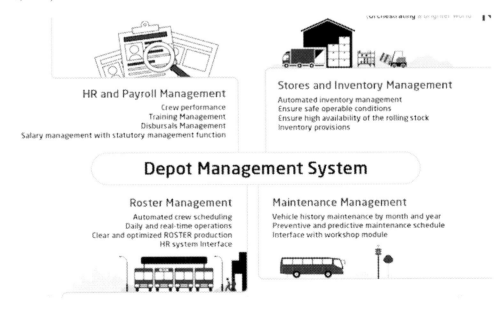

Information Systems and Technologies for Green Public Transportation

Smart Camera Systems

The privacy and safety of passengers are of great importance in public transport. The security camera system helps in securing safety in large cities. Today, more and more attention is being paid to the way the security camera system can be improved using modern technology to raise the safety and privacy of passengers to a higher level. There is increasing use of smart IoT cameras, equipped with powerful processors and video analysis software that can recognize objects and interpret events in the environment in the same way that people can. These cameras, if connected to other IoT devices, can respond in real-time to various events, such as sending emergency messages or stimulating the activities of other systems (Penfold, 2020).

There are many ways in which intelligent security cameras can make public transport safer and more efficient. First of all, smart cameras detect danger. For example, smart cameras are much more efficient in recognizing fire than conventional smoke detectors. In addition, they can be programmed to automatically call the fire department. Smart cameras are also effective in recognizing people in need. With the help of face recognition, without compromising their identity and private data, they can very easily recognize if a person has a heart attack or faints. In these cases, the system reacts very quickly and automatically calls for help. Video analysis based on IoT cameras can increase the safety of public transportation using smart vision. These cameras have high-resolution video technology and the ability to analyze video data, so they are very fast in detecting threats and help in intervention as soon as the danger arises. In addition, smart cameras can recognize different objects. For example, unsupervised luggage poses a major threat to the prevention of terrorism at public transport stations. Since these cameras easily recognize people and their movements, smart cameras are very effective in detecting and preventing criminal acts (Penfold, 2020).

In addition to improving passenger safety and satisfaction, smart cameras make it easy to plan and allocate resources in real-time. Since smart cameras are equipped with a video analytics system, they can interpret video data for statistical purposes. The processing of this data creates very useful information for public transport providers as it gives them clear guidelines for improving business processes.

Smart cameras improve public transportation in three main ways:

- They increase the quality of public transport,
- They allow for a timely response,
- They save resources.

Automated Fare Collection Service

Automated fare collection service or AFCS systems are systems that operate in a precise, reliable and contactless way when charging transportation services and in that way contribute to stable and productive public transport. AFCS consists of automatic ticket sales and ticket verification with the assistance of vending machines. Instead of paying the tickets to use public transport services in the traditional way, vending machines and internet services are used (World Bank, 2016). AFCS integrates different functionalities of control, monitoring and maintenance of different operations during the process of issuing, distributing, selling and validating a transport ticket. AFCS system needs to be adapted to the needs of public transport of the specific (smart) city.

Figure 9. How the security camera system works
Source: (Ashtopus Technologies, 2022)

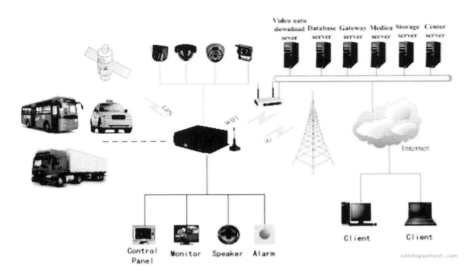

The main components of this system are (Sociedad Ibérica de Construcciones Eléctricas, 2016):

- Tickets (paper or electronic),
- Ticket vending machines or Internet services with various payment options,
- Connected card reader,
- Central management system.

AFCS works in a way that the user of the transport service makes the ticket purchase at the appropriate ticket vending machine or via the internet with a selected payment instrument. After purchasing tickets, in physical or digital form, the user scans the ticket on the ticket machine that checks the validity of the ticket and ultimately enables a user to use public transport service. All the above steps in this process are guided and controlled by the central management system (Figure 10).

AFCS is a key component of a sustainable, high-quality public transport service system and represents a high-tech solution designed to improve public transport. Such systems require integrated and stable platforms to maintain the easy passenger flow at prime time and to enable data collection. However, its implementation is complex and affects all parts of the transport organizations. In addition, it may take several years to be implemented. In summary, AFCS is a complex IT project that aims to improve public city transport services (European Bank for Reconstruction and Development, 2017). For AFCS to be successfully implemented, decision makers need to present a clear vision, taking into account that an integrated ticketing system should meet several key criteria such as (Rubiano & Darido, 2019):

- The system should be interoperable, flexible, secure and scalable,
- The city should develop and own the system and takeovers by private service providers should be prevented.

Figure 10. Components AFCS
Source: (Lotgroup, 2018)

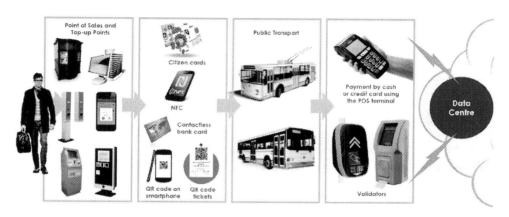

Automated fare collection services offer a higher level of transparency when purchasing the tickets, but also significantly reduce the level of abuse as the number of payments for transport services in cash is reduced.

The advantages of introducing such systems for transport service providers are:

- Reduction of cash payments thus reduced costs,
- A unified platform that provides access to various public services,
- Reduced infrastructure service costs,
- Reduced infrastructure support cost for ticket sales,
- Improved efficiency by encoding, processing and distributing tickets electronically,
- Cost reduction as a result of centralized management of the ticketing system,
- Reduced risks of fraud and ticket misuse,
- Effective control as a result of numerous reports,
- Low investment costs,
- Ability to obtain statistical data needed to analyze and manage operational activities.

The advantages of introducing a system for automated fare collection services for users of transport services are:

- Easy payment,
- Automatic access to the best prices and offers,
- Improved user experience,
- Access to multiple transportation services.

The development and implementation of AFCS is a critical step towards increasing the efficiency and accessibility of public transport. The key step is integration. AFCS today is compatible with a large number of payment options, such as smart cards, smartphones, debit and credit cards, e-commerce platforms (e.g. PayPal), Quick Response (QR) codes, SMS, and others (Rubiano & Darido, 2019).

AFCS technology considerably simplifies the access to various systems important to passengers. For example, it enables diversification of rates/fees to certain groups of the population (e.g. users with lower income, retired, students), differential pricing depending on the time of day, usage of weekly tickets, opening the front door for disabled users, restoring unused balance on a lost card, providing "credit" travel when card balance drops to zero, etc. The introduction of 5G (fifth-generation technology standard for broadband cellular networks), along with saturation in the smartphone market, has ensured that the majority of the population has technology that allows the AFCS system to function better in most countries (Grad View Research, 2019). AFCS, in addition to facilitating the sale of transport tickets, also generates substantial anonymous customer data, which can encourage innovation in service delivery and user experience sectors, as well as service integration and more efficient transaction processing. For example, AFCS data in combination with information on the Automatic Vehicle Location (AVL) are valuable resources that make it possible to better understand and recognize the patterns, mobility deficiencies, and the threats to public transportation system (Rubiano & Darido, 2019).

Passenger Information System (PIS)

Passenger Information System (PIS) is one of the main ways to improve the passenger experience and their main goal is to provide accurate information to public transport users and other participants promptly so that vehicle routes can be adapted according to this information. These systems can operate through a variety of computer terminals, mobile devices such as smartphones, and in-vehicle devices (example shown in Figure 11). These systems are important as passengers can be informed of any changes in real-time, and they can be informed about alternative options based on their preferences. Passengers can be informed about situations that may affect their traveling decisions (e.g. weather changes, prices changes, etc.). In smart cities, the passenger information system should be understood as a key element in the public transport strategy given that these systems supply passengers with direct information. These systems are important in planning the routes, but also in reducing uncertainty for passengers in case of possible delays or changes in routes.

Providing the correct information is essential in offering users a seamless and worry-free experience using public transportation. Active modes of public transport (such as cycling) are often forgotten when collecting the data but have one of the greatest impact on sustainable mobility (Samspon, 2019).

For the passenger information systems to be precise and efficient, it is necessary to connect all vehicles involved in the transport. Vehicles are most easily connected using computer-assisted data transmission systems and automatic vehicle locating systems. Ultimately, passengers are best informed when every vehicle in public transportation is connected via mentioned systems and connected to the internet.

When informing passengers, there are a large number of distribution channels through which passengers receive information about their journey. Different travelers have different preferences for the way they receive information. The following modern distribution channels are distinguished:

- Web pages,
- Mobile applications,
- Google map,
- SMS alerts/notifications,
- Information displays,
- Audio notification systems.

Information Systems and Technologies for Green Public Transportation

The ideal situation when informing passengers is represented via omnichannel that integrates all of the above distribution channels to ensure that passengers have access to information in real-time at all stages of their travel.

The information given to passengers depends on several factors, most commonly the stage of the trip. Travelers most often ask for information about routes, arrival time, travel time, connections, incidents, delays, prices and discounts. These are information often associated with other local information such as weather, events, news, services and similar. When informing passengers, the most important thing is the accuracy of information.

For information to be available to everyone at the right time, it is necessary to use appropriate technologies to inform passengers. The use of passenger information technology creates a feeling that the waiting time for transport is reduced and that the journey takes less time (Hribernik, 2020).

Figure 11. Possible forms of ISP
Source: (Saman control, 2018)

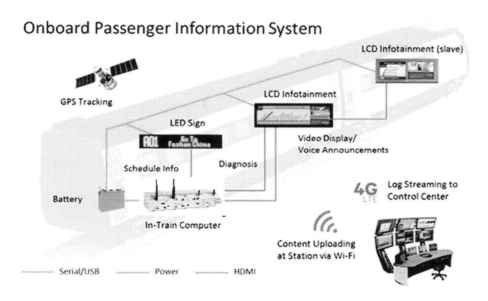

Smart Ticketing System

Traditionally, a transport ticket is a piece of paper or cardboard with information about the origin and destination of the trip paid for, and any related conditions such as a specific timeline or legal conditions applicable for the trip. To increase passengers' flexibility and reduce the printing of tickets, many public transportation providers offer a range of new types of tickets, including QR codes based that can be displayed and checked on smartphone screens (Samspon et al., 2019).

Innovations in ticket issuance coincided with innovations in payment technologies. Many cities today issue some form of smart card, i.e. a device the size of a credit card that has a small amount of processing power and storage on a microchip that is built into the smart card. The smart card gets electricity from communication with the infrastructure in the near field so battery power is not required. This kind of city card can be issued once per trip, but some cards can be charged with money depending on the wishes and needs of the users. Some cards serve as weekly, monthly, or yearly transportation tickets. Traditional banks and credit card companies have also emerged in the transportation services market by offering contactless payment cards in public transport at swipe in and swipe out terminals (Samspon et al., 2019).

Smart cards allow public transport users to get in and out of buses, trams, or trains without the need to use traditional payment systems such as cash or buying a paper ticket. Nowadays users can scan the contactless smart card at a static or manual ticket vending machine to validate their trip.

The smart card system is considered to be one of the most important factors that encourage people to use public transport because it has the following characteristics (ITSO, 2018):

- Convenience - eliminates the need for cash,
- Flexibility - tickets can be purchased in advance and online,
- Speed - reduces the time required for boarding and disembarking, and consequently increases the accuracy of public transport,
- Ease of use - can be used while traveling "door to door" with different modes of transportation.

There are many advantages of the smart card system, and they generally coincide with the AFCS system which integrates smart card systems. Some of the advantages of the smart cards system are (Figure 12):

- Reduced cash handling costs,
- Reduced risk of fraud,
- Real-time availability of business data,
- Greater flexibility in determining ticket prices,
- Easier implementation of changes in the transport system.

The design of a smart card system should be approached with great care. Many public transport providers have launched their e-schemes to encourage brand loyalty. City services should be planned to ensure that card issuers and account management companies do not have a monopoly and that future system upgrades and changes are guaranteed (Samspon et al., 2019).

Recent trends show that transport users want a "universal" card, not a wallet with a lot of cards. Therefore, many public transportation providers offer one ticket option for all trips or separate tickets in a single secure smart wallet. This reduces complexity, easy the handling of numerous data and other inconveniences for the user are avoided (World Bank, 2016).

PUBLIC TRANSPORT IN CITIES – CASE STUDIES FROM EUROPE

This subchapter describes the use of different public transportation systems and their local applications in the example of four European cities.

Information Systems and Technologies for Green Public Transportation

Figure 12. Smart ticketing system
Source: (Huajie, 2020)

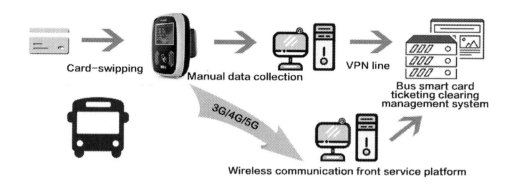

City of Rome

Integrated Mobile E-Ticketing Service and PIS

In 2015, a new service called BiPiù was launched in Rome which allowed the purchase of online bus and metro tickets via smartphones. Service BiPiù is available through a free application called myCicero that integrates into the application all the information about local mobility, schedules and calculated routes, information about the purchase of bus and metro tickets, as well as information about street parking. From 2015, MyCicero provides Rome with a new contactless ticketing service available through mobile devices. This system responds to the needs of new customer segments through media dematerialization, and on the other hand, responds to the needs of virtual sales networks i.e. new distribution channels that provide 24 hours coverage. Once a user is registered on myCicero, he/she can buy a ticket through the application and get the ticket to his smartphone. In order to use the transport service, the users must scan obtained tickets from a smart device using the QR code reader, which will then allow him/her to use the public transport service. A new ticket sales system required new management methods: controllers have a hand-held device with an application that checks if the ticket has been scanned (Samspon, 2019).

Trenitalia trains in Rome use a passenger information system (Figure 13) that displays all the information a passenger needs in one place. The information is displayed on screens placed in several places in the trains, and displays the following information:

- Current train location on the map,
- Stations where the train will stop,
- The estimated time when the train will arrive at each station,
- The speed at which the train is moving,
- Smart surveillance camera footage,
- Date, time and weather information.

Figure 13. PIS in Trenitalia trains
Source: authors

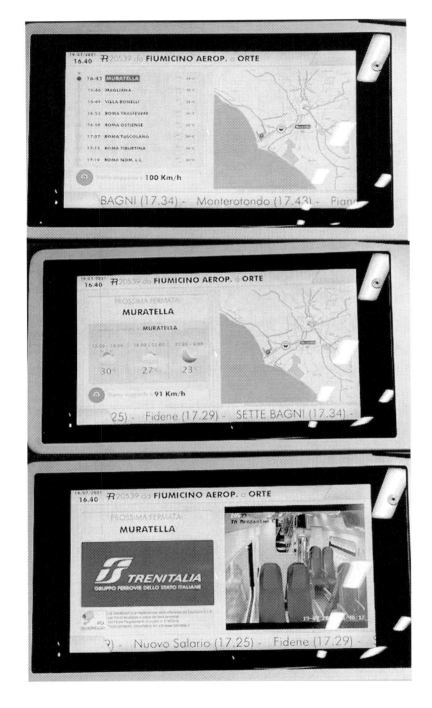

City of Paris

AV Metro Line 1

Since 2000, RATP, the Paris city transport operator, has undertaken an extensive program of automatic train control (ATC) on its metro network. The entire program aimed to increase safety and transport capacity and improve passenger comfort. The program aimed to automate trains (Paris lines 3, 5, 9, 10 and 12) while partnering with Siemens Transportation as part of the overall modernization plan of Paris transport (Braban & Charon, 2010). In addition to the benefits of improving passenger safety and comfort, the aim is to achieve substitutability in train management, i.e. to enable trains to run automatically, without drivers. In collaboration with program Ouragan, feasibility studies were carried out to upgrade existing high-demand lines to driverless lines, following the example of line 14, which has been operating since 1998 and is driverless since day one.

Great attention is paid to the automation of line 1, which is the busiest metro line in Paris. Line 1 automation achieves two goals:

- Upgrading PA BF (tag type of automatic train management solution designed by Siemens in the early 1970s) communication-based control of trains and
- A complete transfer to driverless train management.

Line 1 was opened to the public in 1900 and stretches through Paris from east to west over 17 km. It is the oldest metro line, and at the same time the most prestigious because its 25 stations are located in the most interesting tourist places in the capital of France, as well as numerous business districts and shops. The annual turnover on line 1 is 207 million passengers which is the highest in the network. These characteristics of line 1 lead to high demand for the flexibility of the transport offer, which is difficult to access if this line is operated by drivers.

Line 1 equipment for driverless traffic consists of:

- Operating Control Center that is installed on the Boulevard Bourdon,
- Track signals used to safely separate trains,
- PA BF.

Switching to the driverless lines enabled an increase in transport capacity because of a reduction in time progress from 105 to 85 seconds. The speed of trains with drivers is limited to 70 km/h, while one without drivers runs at the maximum speed of 80 km/h, which speeds up transport. 72% of delays are passengers related and among them, 69% can be controlled by placing doors on stations that separate the station from the rails. From an economic side, line 1 automation reduced operating costs by 10-15%, without taking into consideration accidents that are thus avoided. Finally, the automation of line 1 caused passenger satisfaction thus proving that this process was the best solution to the problems of this metro line (Braban & Charon, 2010).

City of London

Green Public Transport

Given the growing negative trends associated with transport, the City of London has developed a Transport Strategy that seeks to change the way passengers choose the mode of transport. By 2041, 80% of London residents are expected to travel on foot, by bicycle, or by public transport (Mayor's Transport Strategy, 2018). The emission of harmful gases from vehicles damages the streets, harms health and contributes to climate change. London aims to meet the legal limits of air quality as soon as possible, and the creation of streets and routes that encourage walking, cycling and the use of public transport will play a major role in achieving this goal (City of London, 2022).

Six priorities of the Transport for London (TfL) initiative are (Campbell, 2020):

- Accelerating the transition to public and active transport,
- Decarbonisation of road vehicles,
- Decarbonisation of the way goods and services reach their destination,
- Site-based emission reduction solutions,
- The UK as a hub of green technology and innovation,
- Carbon reduction in the global economy.

For vehicles remaining on the roads, it is important to reduce emissions as soon as possible and to switch to zero-emission technologies. TfL plans to realize its approach after widespread public consultation and by introducing an ultra-low emission zone and a toxicity charge (T- Charge). In the following years, most London double-decker buses are expected to be hybrid or electric so that only the greenest and cleanest buses take part in public transport. By 2037, all 9,200 buses across London are expected to have zero emissions. The success of London's transport system in the future will depend on the city becoming a place where people choose to walk and ride a bike.

TfL is also expanding its use of traffic sensors using artificial intelligence (AI) to detect traffic participants and decide on the mode of transportation they use. Sensors from the Vivacity Labs laboratory, whose production began in 2018, proved to be 98% more accurate than manual methods and can collect data 24 hours a day for a much more detailed picture of how to use roads. All videos recorded by the sensors are processed and discarded within seconds, which means that personal data is not stored. The collected data helps in assessing the demand for new cycling routes and helps TfL in planning how to manage the road network to achieve the objectives of the transport strategy (Smart Cities Connect, 2020).

City of Split

Bicycle Sharing System

Split parking company for communal services, in cooperation with the City of Split, introduced the public bicycle system as a new form of public city transport within the European project REMEDIO. This system was adopted as part of a new multimodal way of traffic functioning in Split, which enables a healthier and more mobile way of life and reduces traffic jams and the emission of harmful gases. The

Information Systems and Technologies for Green Public Transportation

system of public bicycles in Split has enabled better traffic connections in the city area and has responded positively to modern environmental challenges (Split Tourist Board, 2021).

The system of public bicycles Nextbike in Split consists of a total of 280 public bicycles (of whom 120 are electric) and 51 stations will that are situated all over the city (see example in Figure 14). The Nextbike system of public bicycles is currently present in 20 cities throughout Croatia, three cities in Bosnia and Herzegovina and eight cities in Slovenia. Registration on the Nextbike public bike system is valid worldwide. The system use is simple: after downloading the application and paying an annual subscription, the user has an unlimited number of half-hour rides between the marked stations. For users to use the public bicycle system, they must have the Nextbike application installed on their smart device, where they need to register. After registering and reaching the station from which they want to rent a bike, they must log in to their account on the application and enter their mobile number and the number of the bike they want to rent. After that, the bike is ready for rent and users can pull it off the stand at the station. The system also allows temporary parking of the bike with the help of an application and a lever on the bike. After using the bike, it can be returned to any station in the city k. If all the stands at the station are occupied, users are allowed to leave the bike between other bikes while lowering the lever on the lock. Payment for the service is also made via the application and a credit card or SMS can be used for payment.

The goal of the public bicycle system is not to make money, but to provide an alternative form of transport and a range of options from which each user can choose what suits them. The City of Split invests most of the funds generated through leases and subscriptions in the maintenance and expansion of the system.

The aforementioned examples from four cities show different and diverse uses of public transportation technologies and information systems customized according to the needs of specific cities.

CONCLUSION

Modern information systems are the foundation of all smart city initiatives, particularly in the field of public transportation. The main aim is to facilitate and improve the quality and efficiency of urban mobility, and ultimately to improve the satisfaction of public transport passengers. Using modern information systems in public transport has many advantages. This chapter presented the most important ones; fundamental technologies and information systems needed in general, as well as management systems and user-oriented systems. Modern information systems allow for greater flexibility as passengers are given multiple choices related to their journey. Some modern information systems make it easier to manage and plan travel routes, and other increase passenger safety and reduce gas emissions, thus promoting sustainable public transportation.

Given that modern information systems in public transport are of many purposes and types, through the examples of several (smart) cities it is shown that each city has its own version of a particular information system that achieves the goals of smart mobility.

Although very important, the topic of collecting personal data by different ISs discussed in the chapter, was not elaborated in the chapter which points to the limitation of the paper.

Figure 14. Station of the public bicycle system in Split
Source: authors

Although not explicitly explored in this chapter, it should be noted that pedestrian transportation is an important part of the smart transportation system in modern planning processes. While still underaddressed in the literature, smart pedestrian system planning represents an interesting avenue for further research.

ACKNOWLEDGMENT

This work has been supported by the Croatian Science Foundation [grant number UIP-2017-05-7625].

REFERENCES

Anable, J., Docherty, I., & Marsden, G. (2018). The governance of smart mobility. *Transportation Research Part A, Policy and Practice, 115*, 114–125. doi:10.1016/j.tra.2017.09.012

Ashtopus Technologies. (2022). Commercial Vehicle Onboard Video Systems. Pinterest. https://www.pinterest.com/pin/558164947544320947/

Avril, S., Bozzani-Franc, S., L'Hostis, A., & Pico, F. (2007). *Strategic Research Agenda for Urban Mobility*. Retrieved December 15, 2022 from https://hal.archives-ouvertes.fr/hal-00575525

Azad, M., Hoseinzadeh, N., Brakewood, C., Cherry, C. R., & Han, L. D. (2019). Fully Autonomous Buses: A Literature Review and Future Research Directions. *Journal of Advanced Transportation, 2019*, 4603548. doi:10.1155/2019/4603548

Baxter, B. (2020). Autonomous vehicles and public transport in Europe. *Eltis*. https://www.eltis.org/printpdf/participate/events/autonomous-vehicles-and-public-transport-europe

Benevolo, C., Dameri, R. P., & D'Auria, B. (2016). Smart Mobility in Smart City. In T. Torre, A. Braccini, & R. Spinelli (Eds.), *Empowering Organizations Lecture Notes in Information Systems and Organisation* (pp. 13–28). Springer.

BillyFlorian. (2019). *Metro Platform Screen Doors*. Youtube. https://www.youtube.com/watch?v=wIbLyaHhAkI

Campbell, M. (2020). UK announces an "ambitious" plan to become a hub for green transport. *Euronews*. https://www.euronews.com/green/2020/03/30/uk-announces-ambitious-plan-to-become-hub-for-green-transport

Centlewski, B., & Warchol, J. (2021). *IoT and its Role in Sustainable Transportation*. Lingaro Group. https://lingarogroup.com/blog/iot-and-its-role-in-sustainable-transportation/

CEPT University. (2018). *A bus transport management document*. ISSUU. https://issuu.com/monikagupta/docs/brts_final_book

City of London. (2022). Official web page. *Green Transport*. https://www.london.gov.uk/what-we-do/transport/green-transport

DuList. (2019). *Use car sharing and forget about caring*! DuList. https://dulist.hr/prvi-u-hrvatskoj-koritete-car-sharing-i-zaboravite-na-brigu-o-parkingu/613101/

Edwin Conan. (2008). *Muscle Car Sharing System*. Edwin Conan. https://edwinconan.wordpress.com/2008/10/29/muscle-car-sharing-system

European Bank for Reconstruction and Development (EBRD). (2017). *On the move: delivering automated fare collection*. EBRD. https://www.google.com/url?sa=t&rct=j&q=&esrc=s&source=web&cd=&ved=2ahUKEwiPgcHM6Lj2AhVxk_0HHRupAX0QFnoECAYQAQ&url=https%3A%2F%2Fwww.ebrd.com%2Fdocuments%2Fadmin%2Fon-the-move-delivering-automated-fare-collection.pdf&usg=AOvVaw0eN3cc-C-QU99j1bHITudv

GoDigital. (2020). Smart public transport the foundation of the smart city system. *Go Digital.* https://godigital.hrvatskitelekom.hr/pametni-javni-prijevoz-temelj-sustava-pametnog-grada/

Grand view research (2019). *Automated Fare Collection Market Size, Share & Trends Analysis Report By System (TVM, TOM), By Technology (Smart Card, NFC), By Application, By Component (Hardware, Software), And Segment Forecasts, 2019–2025.* Grand View Research. https://www.grandviewresearch.com/industry-analysis/automated-fare-collection-afc-system-market

Haque, M. M., Chin, H. C., & Debnath, A. K. (2013). Sustainable, safe, smart-three key elements of Singapore's evolving transport policies. *Transport Policy, 27,* 20–31. doi:10.1016/j.tranpol.2012.11.017

Hribernik, U. (2020). *Passenger Information Systems (PIS): Your top 8 questions answered.* Lit Transit. https://lit-transit.com/insights/passenger-information-systems-pis-your-top-8-questions-answered/

Huajie (2020). *Bus Smart Card Payment Ticketing System.* Sinalbolr. https://en.wxhjic.com/b070c208-ccfa-c7d3-c271-bb71a6e5df2a/9322782a-b69d-a348-6f6f-0a98f98aa9a4.shtml

Indiamart (2021). Iot Automation Projects. Retrieved March 9, 2022 from https://www.indiamart.com/proddetail/factory-iot-automation-project-21653851388.html

ITSO. (2018). *What is smart ticketing?* ITSO. https://www.itso.org.uk/about-us/what-is-smart-ticketing/#:~:text=ITSO%20Smart%20ticketing%20is%20a,usually%20embedded%20on%20a%20smartcard

Jašić, T. (2021). *Suvremeni informacijski sustavi u javnom prijevozu u pametnim gradovima [Modern Information Systems in Public Transport in Smart Cities].* [Unpublished master's dissertation, University of Split, Croatia].

Jochem, P., Frankenhauser, D., Ewald, L., Ensslen, A., & Fromm, H. (2020). Does free-floating carsharing reduce private vehicle ownership? The case of SHARE NOW in European cities. *Transportation Research Part A, Policy and Practice, 141,* 373–395. doi:10.1016/j.tra.2020.09.016 PMID:33052178

Kass, A. (2020). *Bike sharing benefits and disadvantages.* Kass and Moses. https://kassandmoses.com/bicycle/blog/bike-sharing-benefits-and-disadvantages

Khalifa, A. (2010). Vehicle tracking system for sugarcane. API. http://api.uofk.edu:8080/api/core/bitstreams/81315bda-39e5-4487-8a02-75867d444104/content

Kittilaksanawong, W. & Liu, H. (2021). Mobike China: competing through the giant's ecosystem. *Emerald Emerging Markets Case Studies, 11*(1).

Lam, A., Leung, Y., & Chu, X. (2016). Autonomous-Vehicle Public Transportation System: Scheduling and Admission Control. *IEEE Transactions on Intelligent Transportation Systems, 17*(5), 1210–1226. doi:10.1109/TITS.2015.2513071

Lane, C., Hidalgo, D., Schleeter, R., & Mackie, K. (2017). On the move: Car-sharing scales up. *Smart Cities Dive.* https://www.smartcitiesdive.com/ex/sustainablecitiescollective/move-car-sharing-scales/208451/

Lotgroup (2018). *Automated Fare Collection System.* Lot Group. https://lotgroup.eu/product/smart-city/afc/

Marsh, J. (2021). How IoT can make transportation more sustainable. The internet of all things web page. *The Internet of All Things.* https://www.theinternetofallthings.com/how-iot-can-make-transportation-more-sustainable/

Mayor of London. (2018). Mayor's Transport Strategy. London Assembly. https://www.london.gov.uk/what-we-do/transport/our-vision-transport/mayors-transport-strategy-2018?intcmp=46686

MicroProgram. (2021). *Smart Bike Solution.* MicroProblem. https://www.program.com.tw/en/solution/transportation/category/smart-bike-solution

Ministry of the Interior. (2012). *Videoconference with presentation of AVL system.* Ministarstco unutarnjih poslova. https://mup.gov.hr/vijesti-8/videokonferencija-s-prezentacijom-sustava-avl-a/130967

MixTelematics. (2021). *Fleet solutions for the public transport industry.* Mix Telematics. https://www.mixtelematics.com/industries/public-transport

Montes, H., Salinas, C., Fernández, R., & Armada, M. (2017). An Experimental Platform for Autonomous Bus Development. *Applied Sciences (Basel, Switzerland), 7*(11), 1131. doi:10.3390/app7111131

National Operations Center of Excellence. (2021*). Big Data and TSM & O.* National Operations Center of Excellence. https://transportationops.org/BigData/BigData-overview

NEC. (2021). *Transportation Solutions.* NEC. https://in.nec.com/en_IN/solutions_services/intelligent_transport_solutions/transportation.html

OECD & International Transport Forum. (2017). *Managing the Transition to Driveless Road Freight Transport.* OECD. https://www.itf-oecd.org/sites/default/files/docs/managing-transition-driverless-road-freight-transport.pdf

Paliaga, M., & Oliva, E. (2018). Trends in the application of the concept of smart cities. *Ekonomska Misao i Praksa, 2,* 565–583.

Penfold, A. (2020). 5 use cases for smart cameras to improve security in public transportation. *Azena.* https://www.securityandsafetythings.com/insights/5-ways-smart-cameras-improve-public-transport

Penfold, A. (2020). Why we should not underestimate the value of smart video cameras in public. *Azena.* https://www.securityandsafetythings.com/insights/not-underestimate-smart-cameras-public

Portouli, E., Karaseitanidis, G., Lytrivis, P., Amditis, A., Raptis, O., & Karaberi, C. (2017). Public attitudes towards autonomous mini buses operating in real conditions in a Hellenic city. *Intelligent Vehicles Symposium* (pp. 11-14). IEEE. 10.1109/IVS.2017.7995779

PSItraffic. (2020). *In 5 Steps to a Depot Management System for Transport Companies.* PSI. https://www.psi.de/en/blog/psi-blog/post/in-5-steps-to-a-depot-management-system-for-transport-companies/

PSItraffic. (2021). *Depot Management - A clear overview of all processes.* Retrieved March 10, 2022 from https://www.psitrans.de/en/solutions/depot-management/

Racca, D. (2004). Cost and Benefits of Advanced Public Transportation Systems at Dart First State. *Center for Applied Demography and Survey Research,* p. 20. https://udspace.udel.edu/handle/19716/1100

Riter, S., & McCoy, J. (1977). Automatic vehicle location - An overview. *IEEE Transactions on Vehicular Technology*, *26*(1), 7–11. doi:10.1109/T-VT.1977.23649

RoseIndia. (2018). Automatic Vehicle Location Advantage. *Rose India*. https://www.roseindia.net/technology/vehicle-tracking/automatic-vehicle-location-advantage.shtml

Rubiano, L. Canon, & Darido G. (2019*). The ticket to a better ride: How can Automated Fare Collection improve urban transport?* World Bank blogs. https://blogs.worldbank.org/transport/ticket-better-ride-how-can-automated-fare-collection-improve-urban-transport

Rydén, C., & Morin, E. (2005). *Mobility Services for Urban Sustainability: Environmental Assessment. Report WP 6.* Trivector TrafficAB.

Saad, S., Aisha Badrul Hisham, A., Ishak, M., Mohd, F., Mohd, H., Baharudin, M., & Idris, N. (2018). Real-time on-campus public transportation monitoring system. *2018 IEEE 14th International Colloquium on Signal Processing & Its Applications (CSPA),* (pp. 215-220).

Saman control (2018). *Passenger Information System.* Saman Control. https://samancontrol.com/solutions/passenger-information-system-onboard-pis/

Samspon, E., Signor, L., Flachi, M., Hemmings, E., Somma, G., Aifadopoulou, G., Mitsakis, E., & Sourlas, V. (2019). The role of Intelligent Transport Systems (ITS) in sustainable urban mobility planning. European platform on sustainable mobility plans.

Scrudato, M. (2018). Smart Mobility Reinventing insurance for the future of mobility. *Munichre.* https://www.munichre.com/content/dam/munichre/contentlounge/website-pieces/documents/SmartMobility_06-18-2019.pdf/_jcr_content/renditions/original.media_file.download_attachment.file/SmartMobility_06-18-2019.pdf

Shaheen, S. A., & Cohen, A. P. (2007). Growth in Worldwide Carsharing: An International Comparison. *Transportation Research Record: Journal of the Transportation Research Board*, *1992*(1), 81–89. doi:10.3141/1992-10

Smart Cities Connect. (2020). *Transport for London Expands Use of Traffic Sensors Using AI.* Smart Cities Connect. https://smartcitiesconnect.org/transport-for-london-expands-use-of-traffic-sensors-using-ai/#:~:text=Transport%20for%20London%20(TfL)%20is,of%20transport%20they%20are%20using.&Text=The%20sensors%20are%20also%20able, trucks%2C%20motorcyclists%2C%20and%20buses

Sociedad Ibérica de Construcciones Eléctricas. (2016). *AutomaticFare Collection (AFC)*. SICE. https://www.sice.com/sites/Sice/files/2016-12/TR_TICKETING_0.pdf

Sokač Š. (2017). *Perspectives for investments and realization of development projects based on the concept of "Smart Cities" in Croatia*, 15-30. Varaždin: University North, final paper.

Sokač, Š. (2017). Perspektive za ulaganja i realizacije razvojnih projekata baziranih na konceptu "Pametnih gradova" u Hrvatskoj [Perspectives for investments and implementation of development projects based on the concept of 'smart cities' in Croatia. [Doctoral Dissertation, Sveučilište Sjever, Croatia.].

Split Tourist Board. (2021). *Public bicycles.* Split. https://visitsplit.com/hr/4280/javni-bicikli

Tech Moukthika. (2016). Vehicle (fleet) management system. *Tech Moukthika*. https://techmoukthika. com/vms.html

TechTarget. (2020). Automatic vehicle locator (AVL). *Tech Target*. https://whatis.techtarget.com/definition/automatic-vehicle-locator-AVL#:~:text=An%20automatic%20vehicle%20locator%20(AVL,fleet%20 by%20using%20the%20Internet

The World Bank. (2016). *Public Transport Automatic Fare Collection Interoperability: Assessing Options for Poland*, p. 13. World Bank. https://openknowledge.worldbank.org/handle/10986/24931?show=full

UITP. (2017). *Autonomous vehicles: A potential game changer for urban mobility*. UITP. https://www. uitp.org/publications/autonomous-vehicles-a-potential-game-changer-for-urban-mobility/

US Department of Homeland Security. (2009). *Automatic Vehicle Locating Systems*. DHS. https://www. dhs.gov/sites/default/files/publications/AVLSys-TN_0609-508.pdf

Wheels for Wishes. (2021). *11 Car sharing benefits*. Wheels for Wishes. https://www.wheelsforwishes. org/11-car-sharing-benefits/

Xhafka, E., Teta, J., & Agastra, E. (2015). Mobile Environmental Sensing and Sustainable Public Transportation Using ICT Tools. *Acta Physica Polonica A*, *128*(2B), 128. doi:10.12693/APhysPolA.128.B-122

Yelloz, G., & Charon, P. (2008). Re-signaling the Paris line 1: From driver operated line to driverless line. *International Conference on Railway Engineering - Challenges for Railway Transportation in Information Age*, (pp. 1-4).

Zheng, H. (2013). On the move: Car-sharing scales up. *CityFix*. https://thecityfix.com/blog/on-the-move-car-sharing-scales-up-heshuang-zeng/

KEY TERMS AND DEFINITIONS

Automated Fare Collection Service: Combination of elements that automate a public transportation network's ticketing system.

Automatic Vehicle Location System: System that automatically determine and transmits the geographic location of a vehicle.

Depot Management System: System that automates operations at the depot stations.

Fleet Management System: System that may include wide range of functions such as vehicle maintenance, driver management, tracking and diagnostics of difference vehicles, safety management etc.

Internet of Things: network of connected devices and the technology that enables communication between the devices themselves and between the cloud and devices.

Passenger Information Systems: Systems that provide users/passengers with relevant information regarding the status of a public transportation service.

Vehicle Sharing Systems: System that offer users to rent vehicles (e.g. car or bicycle) for a period of time.

Chapter 5

Challenges in the Development of Urban Intermodal Mobility Systems

Dorinela Costescu
https://orcid.org/0000-0002-1562-5834
Polytechnic University of Bucharest, Romania

Eugenia Alina Roman
Polytechnic University of Bucharest, Romania

ABSTRACT

Technological progress and the economic and social environment dynamics lead to changing mobility needs. Modifying travel practices, increasing the pressures for fast and predictable services, and expanding the demands of users for individualized offers determine requirements for diversifying the mobility supply in an integrated framework that must meet sustainable development objectives. In this framework, intermodal public transport plays a significant role. The chapter introduces the definitions of multimodality and intermodality in urban mobility systems. Intermodal transportation accounts for the different capabilities of diverse modes, including their availability, speed, density, costs, limitations, and, therefore, their most appropriate operating. The functions of intermodal public transportation are discussed. It is emphasized that solutions for sustainable mobility can be developed through a better understanding of the opportunities and challenges of the new mobility services.

INTRODUCTION

Mobility requirements are changing all over the world. Urban travel behaviors are adjusting, and various travel modes and services are supplied. Innovative technologies have been developed to meet daily urban mobility needs according to current urban spatiality and temporality. The spread of cities, with direct effects on density, affecting the economic efficiency of public transportation, determined the development of more appropriate solutions for the reduced and dispersed travel flows. New mobility solutions

DOI: 10.4018/978-1-6684-5996-6.ch005

Challenges in the Development of Urban Intermodal Mobility Systems

can be stimulated both by adapting collective public transportation to individual requirements and by the shared use of personal vehicles. Transportation operators must satisfy the travel demand with ever more convenient, fast, and predictable services (Van Audenhove et al., 2014).

At the same time, users must become more concerned about the sustainability of their mode of travel because mobility brings many benefits for its users but with costs for our society. These include greenhouse gas emissions, air, noise, and water pollution, crashes, congestion, and biodiversity loss – all affecting people's health and well-being. Actions to ensure a more sustainable operation of all transportation modes and to provide available sustainable options in a multimodal transportation system are necessary to achieve the aspiring goals defined at European Union level (COM, 2020). The European Green Deal calls for a 90% reduction in greenhouse gas emissions from transportation. The EU will become a climate-neutral economy by 2050 while working towards a zero-pollution ambition.

According to these goals, cities with a high proportion of individual motorized travel need to (COM, 2020):

- **Redesign Their Mobility Systems** (defined by the set of infrastructures, travel patterns and related services, as well as the offer of parking spaces) **to become more orientated towards public transportation.**
- **Integrate the travel value chain to encourage smooth, intermodal mobility and increase public transportation's overall attractiveness by service extension.**

In this framework, this chapter highlights the advantages and challenges of intermodal public transportation and discusses the levels of integration required by intermodal services as sustainable mobility solutions. The first part discusses the objectives followed in the design of intermodal networks. It demonstrated how the main functions of intermodal mobility contribute to achieving the goals of sustainable development in cities. In many cases, the development of public transportation networks has been segmented by mode of transportation/travel, sometimes leading to complex and inflexible routes for passengers. Designing appropriate intermodal solutions correlated to local circumstances requires identifying correct competition and complementarities between different travel modes. In this regard, the main particularities of urban travel modes are reviewed, and key components of urban intermodal mobility systems are explained. The last part of the chapter analyzes the challenges related to the attractiveness of intermodal services. It presents the required levels of integration and the main problems in ensuring seamless transitions from one mode to another (continuity of the journey chain, compatibility between modes, consistency, readability, etc.).

PARTICULARITIES OF INTERMODAL URBAN MOBILITY

Multimodality vs Intermodality in Urban Mobility Systems

As a broad concept, mobility encompasses a set of individual and collective strategies to access opportunities and services. The mobility offering must be restructured according to the requirements of sustainable development and must adapt to supply (and not vice versa). The new individual and collective mobility offerings for urban trips, friendly to the environment, demonstrate that modal choice and competition are consequences of concerns to reduce generalized and/or social costs.

The Sustainable Urban Mobility Plan (SUMP) should seek to stimulate the balanced development of transportation modes while encouraging a shift towards more sustainable transportation modes (Rupprecht Consult, 2019). According to the SUMP principle, "develop all transportation modes in an integrated manner", the mobility solutions must encourage balanced and integrated development of all modes to improve the overall mobility system's quality, security, safety, accessibility, and cost-effectiveness. A particular concern is limiting car dependence.

Various documents and studies on the integration of transportation modes use terms such as intermodal, multimodal, and door-to-door mobility, with different meanings in passenger and freight transport sectors. This chapter uses the terms according to the definitions provided by Eltis (2019):

- **Multimodality** refers to selecting alternative transportation modes for different trips over a certain period (e.g., a day or week) (Figure 1.a). Multimodality is a critical term in sustainable mobility planning, allowing the assessment and promotion of options other than private cars (Eltis 2019). In the freight and logistics domain, multimodal often refers to transferring goods using several modes (e.g., ship, train, lorry etc.). It is the equivalent of intermodality for passenger transportation.
- **Intermodality** relates to improving the efficiency and attractiveness of a single trip made with more than one transportation mode (e.g., walking, metro, and bus) to offer travelers a seamless journey (Figure 1.b). It requires developing integrated transportation systems by harmonizing different transportation services and the design of organized connections between different transportation modes, such as park-and-ride (Eltis, 2019).

The term "integrated public transportation" is generally defined as a system that provides door-to-door public mobility services for passengers. Luk & Olszewski (2003) recommended using the term "integrated public transportation" instead of "intermodal transportation", which was commonly used to freight. But in this chapter, the term "intermodal mobility" is used.

Goals of Intermodal Mobility Networks

Intermodal mobility (IM) combines the essential elements of different mobility options in terms of accessibility, travel mode, and travel preferences to accomplish an optimal efficiency level. A transportation network must adapt to potential demand under the covered territory's financial, political and social constraints. For extended urban spaces, the public transportation network is far from ideal. Essentially, a trade-off between the two objectives must be found: maximizing the area coverage and increasing the effectiveness of the public transportation system. The planning and operating solutions always involve compromises (Raicu & Costescu, 2020). The reality has confirmed that an optimal network converges towards hub-and-spoke topologies based on corridors of the high-capacity technical infrastructures in a territorial system (Figure 2). Such topologies with reduced connectivity indexes and consolidations of flows in major nodes are appropriate for the development of intermodal technologies, in which the performances of different mobility and transportation modes (concerning speed, capacity, energy consumption, and space occupancy) are correlated in order to ensure the objectives of sustainable mobility (Costescu et al., 2021).

Challenges in the Development of Urban Intermodal Mobility Systems

Figure 1. Multimodal and intermodal mobility schemes

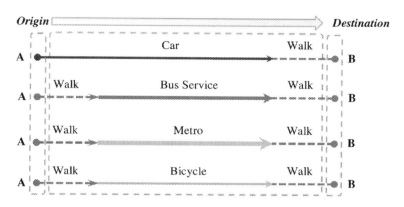

a) *Multimodal transport solutions for a trip from A to B*

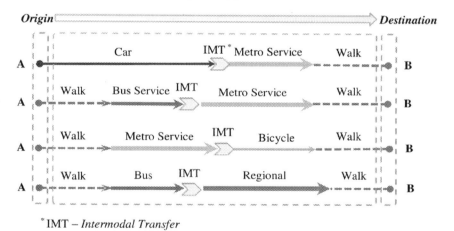

IMT – Intermodal Transfer

b) *Intermodal transport solutions for a trip from A to B*

Figure 2. Network configuration with flow concentration/distribution in major nodes

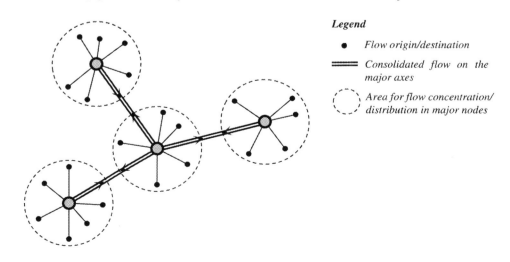

Intermodal networks are based on feeder services that can be provided along transportation corridors (Figure 3). Feeder services usually consist of low-capacity mobility or transportation services (e.g., scooters, cars, local buses). They supply passenger flow to fixed high-capacity service systems (tram, light rail, metro, rail). Trunk-and-feeder intermodal services could be appropriate to demand travel on medium to long distances.

Figure 3. Direct and feeder services
Source: after Bruun, 2014

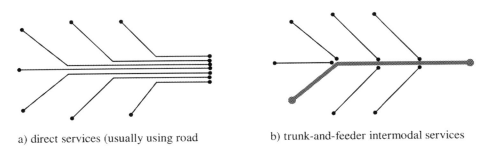

a) direct services (usually using road

b) trunk-and-feeder intermodal services

Feeder services contribute to a more integrated network with improved local benefits by reallocating operating costs from parallel trips (Figure 3.a) to a more judicious modal distribution (Figure 3.b). In addition, a feeder service can often deliver a more frequent and valuable local service and thus increase the service attractiveness (if there is potential in the covered urban area). Feeder service implementation could design a network where each mode achieves high performance. E.g., metro and rapid bus lines as trunk routes and micro-mobility services (or cars or local buses) as feeders. In this way, the high capacity of the rapid transit is more efficiently used, contributing to sustainable mobility targets (Figure 4) (Costescu et al., 2022).

Figure 4. Load diagram for a trunk-and-feeder intermodal line

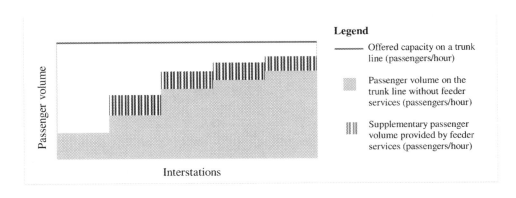

Challenges in the Development of Urban Intermodal Mobility Systems

Users of this kind of trunk-and-feeder intermodal service often encounter significant transfer disadvantages due to inappropriate physical and network integration (including deficiencies in timetable correlation). Nevertheless, if appropriate intermodal mobility solutions are developed according to travel requirements and urban patterns, the efficacy and efficiency of sustainable urban mobility can be significantly enhanced. Considering the functions of public transportation (Caywood et al., 2015; Faivre d'Arcier, 2012; Litman, 2015; Negre, 2008), intermodality has an essential role in (Figure 5):

- **Making public transportation more efficient**
- **Making non-motorized trips more competitive and attractive for users**
- **Enhance the quality of the urban environment.**

Integrating different transportation and mobility modes leads to increase spatial accessibility for public transportation, with significant benefits related to congestion and air pollution, the efficiency of public transit and urban economic environment, social cohesion and mobility affordability (Figure 5).

Figure 5. The role of intermodality in urban mobility systems

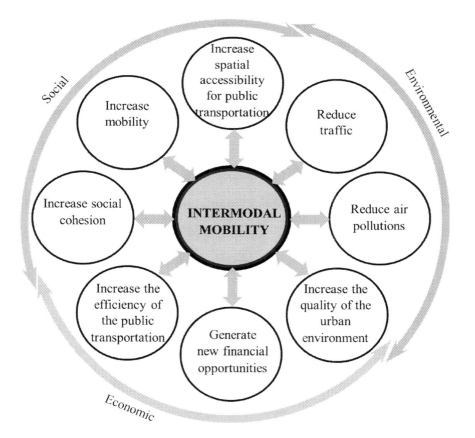

The main benefits start from increased spatial accessibility for public transportation. That means that circumstances for reducing car usage are created, with consequences on reducing congestion, air pollution and improving the quality of the urban environment. At the same time, increased spatial accessibility for public transportation leads to higher passenger volumes, with benefits on the efficiency of public transportation, social cohesion, and mobility affordability. In parallel, correlations between various mobility services and intermodal transfer facilities generate new financial opportunities. All these benefits correspond to the three pillars of sustainable development and emphasize the role of intermodal modality in sustainable urban mobility planning. But, to obtain such benefits, coordination of different transportation services and transfer facilities is required.

CHARACTERISTICS OF INTERMODAL URBAN MOBILITY SYSTEMS

Categories of Travel Modes

The structure of the areas where people live and work determines the origins and destinations of urban travel, the intensities and lengths of travel, and energy consumption. According to the objectives of sustainable urban mobility, public transportation systems must be improved to become an appealing option to private car usage. The role of the public transportation system usually varies from urban area attributes (distances, physical conditions), as well as its mobility policies and planning. Only one transportation mode cannot be appropriate for all urban journeys. Integrating several modes could lead to improved efficacy and efficiency of public transportation.

Corresponding to the urban morphology and structure, but also the specificities of the behavioral pattern of the urban population, the most appropriate modes must be identified in each context in terms of capacity and operating costs. Some studies (Lefevre, 2010; UN-Habitat, 2013) argue that investments in public transportation infrastructure are economically justified only for adequate housing and employment densities in the coverage area (Figure 6).

Figure 6. Relationships between urban structure and public transportation efficiency
Source: Lefevre, 2010

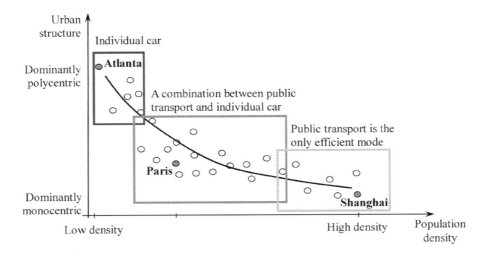

Challenges in the Development of Urban Intermodal Mobility Systems

Urban policies and traffic infrastructure planning focused on the satisfaction of auto travel have resulted in auto-dependent cities where walking is difficult, and public transportation mainly serves captive riders. Public transportation is not a solution for predominantly polycentric urban structures with low population densities (Bertaud 2004). Public transportation stops must be easily accessible from homes or points of interest. Accepted walking distances differ in terms of cultural environment and income, but people generally prefer to avoid using public transportation if a walking time of more than 10 minutes is required. As a result, the catchment areas of the stops have a maximum radius of 800 m for rapid services and 400 m for regular buses. In most circumstances, intermodal services can extend these areas, including secondary lines (feeder, minibus, taxi) or trips with two-wheeled vehicles. Nevertheless, these solutions must overcome problems associated with intermodal transfers: extra time, additional facilities and infrastructures for transfer.

Appropriate solutions for increasing the attractiveness of public transportation can be identified according to the particularities of the mobility needs of the urban population related to the interactions between the characteristics of the areas of the urban space served. Comprehensive knowledge of modal features and performance under different conditions is essential for selecting optimal modes and developing intermodal services.

Each urban travel mode is characterized by advantages and disadvantages and has a different task in satisfying various mobility demands (Figure 7). Based on the type of operation and usage, three basic categories of urban travel can be defined (Van Nes, 2002; Vuchic, 2007):

- **Private travel** – private vehicles operated by owners for their use, usually on publicly administrated streets.
- **Public individual** – services supplying individual passenger travel on-demand, provided by an operator, and available to all persons who meet the conditions of a contract for transportation (i.e., pay prescribed fares or rates).
- **Collective public transportation** - mass transportation or transit with fixed paths and schedules, available for everyone who pays the established fare. In the analysis of public transportation systems, three main categories are considered based on the travel ways (which strongly determine the operating performances) (Vuchic, 2007):
  - Street transit - for the public transportation modes operating on the road infrastructure shared by other vehicles (individual cars, goods vehicles, social service vehicles, etc.); operating and service reliability depend on the temporal and spatial non-uniformities of urban road traffic.
  - Semi-rapid transit – usually operating in congested areas on dedicated ways or dedicated road lanes.
  - Rapid transit - on the grade-separated or exclusive way, with traffic technologies based on guidance systems (rail or rubber-tired) which ensure high transportation capacity and operating speeds, high levels of safety and reliability.

In most cities (not including the small ones), a sustainable transportation system contains several complementary modes managed in an intermodal structure due to various constraints for urban travel. Travel modes can be generally found in their optimal roles in cities that have implemented a rational, long-term mobility policy toward all modes. In cities without such a policy, uncoordinated short-term decisions, unsatisfactory funding, the supporting of one mode over others, insufficiencies of industries, and various stakeholder interests often determine the misallocation of tasks to different modes.

Public individual services offer high levels of accessibility and flexibility. Their integration with collective public transportation (especially with semi-rapid and rapid transit, characterized by high transit capacity and higher operating speed than private cars) creates opportunities to increase the quality of intermodal mobility services and decrease the modal share of car usage. Sequences of low-capacity mobility services and high-capacity public transportation provide door-to-door mobility solutions.

Figure 7. Different types of travel modes
Source: Van Nes, 2002

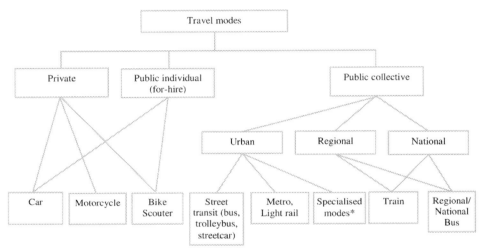

* *Ferryboat, Cable car, Cog railway, Aerial tramway, Hydrofoil*

New Mobility Technologies

New emerging mobility technologies, undoubtedly the results of advances in information and communication technology (Table 1), provide a substantial potential to increase public transportation accessibility. The urban mobility system incorporates interconnected infrastructure and services. Each mode plays a role in the integrated network according to its technical and operating characteristics (Gebhardt et al., 2017).

Offering solutions for first- and last-mile urban trips can contribute to changes in travel behavior. The shared mobility concept supports the development of new mobility services, such as bike, e-scooter, car sharing. Different models of bike and e-scooter sharing have been implemented according to the particularities of urban mobility patterns in worldwide cities (Cohen & Shaheen, 2016; Galatoulas et al., 2020; Shaheen & Martin, 2015). Two-wheel vehicles (e.g., bicycles, e-scooters) in shared mobility service systems facilitate access to high-capacity public transportation (Fazio et al., 2021; Kager et al., 2016; Oeschger et al., 2020; Shaheen et al., 2020).

Carsharing can encourage the usage of less-pollutant cars and improve the efficiency of urban road traffic systems (mainly in reducing car stand idle and road infrastructure occupancy).

Challenges in the Development of Urban Intermodal Mobility Systems

Table 1. New mobility services

Solutions		Usage characteristics	Particularities
Individual mobility	Bike sharing	• Symbol of environmentally friendly mobility • Automated access at locations next to public transportation stations or points of interest • Available at any time (24/24; 7/7)	• Cost-effective • Appropriate to intermodality • Secure Parking • Easy access in central areas
	E-scooters sharing	• Symbol of sustainable mobility • Automated access at different locations through smartphone applications • Available at any time (24/24; 7/7)	• Appropriate to intermodality • Low road safety due to shared use of traffic infrastructure (in many cities, with insufficient regulations) • Unprotected parking
	Car sharing	• Less-pollutant cars; electric cars may offer potential environmental benefits • Automated access at particular parking lots through smartphone applications • Available at any time (24/24; 7/7)	• Remote management by mobility centers • Mutual usage of a public car fleet
Individual transportation (agreed service)	Carpooling, On-demand ride service	• Usage of private cars driven by non-professional drivers accompanied by one or more passengers for a partial/full shared ride • Prior agreement and booking through smartphone or internet applications	• Remote management by mobility centers • Mutual usage of private cars
	Transportation on demand	• Coverage in less dense areas, poorly served by public transportation • Prior booking through smartphone or internet applications	• Schedules adapted to demands • Different carriage on a requested route • Appropriately to intermodality
Collective transportation (dedicated)	Bus rapid transit	• Operating on dedicated lanes with traffic priorities than other road vehicles • Fast and comfortable services • Performant vehicles	• High transit capacities • High operating speed
	Autonomous bus	• Driverless buses, a symbol of smart mobility • Flexible schedule and stop, according to passenger demand • Innovative, performant vehicles	• Providing first and last-mile transportation; appropriately to intermodality • High operating speed • Security risks • Potential social risks

Carpooling, organized in different systems (e.g., acquaintance-based, organization-based, or ad hoc), contribute to reducing single-occupancy vehicle trips, with consequences of road traffic intensity and road driver costs (Shaheen et al., 2020; Santi et al., 2014).

Transportation on demand (TOD) has been implemented in different ways (with fixed or dynamic routes and fixed schedules or dispatch operations), mainly in areas poorly served by public transportation (Shaheen et al., 2020; Vuchic, 2007). Through flexible routing and scheduling, complemented by information technologies facilitating booking, TOD provides opportunities to adapt services to dynamic travel demand. Being targeted to special population categories (i.e., disabled, older adults, and low-income groups), TOD services ensure the achievement of the social goals of public transportation.

Autonomous buses are implemented to increase public transportation attractiveness and efficiency (Ainsalu et al., 2018; Long & Axsen, 2022; Nenseth et al., 2019). Generally, they operate first and last-mile transportation (Ainsalu et al., 2018; Bösch et al., 2018). Even if they are considered environmentally friendly and are well-perceived by passengers (Goldbach et al., 2022; Litman, 2020; Mouratidis et al., 2021; Salonen et al., 2019), further efforts are necessary to solve technological and legislative issues.

Generally, the new travel technologies (Table 1) provide new opportunities to adapt mobility supply to the dynamic mobility needs of the urban population in economic, social and environmental circumstances. They may represent sustainable monomodal solutions, but most of all must be integrated into intermodal solutions to increase the overall efficacy and efficiency of the urban mobility system. A permanent improvement of solutions to meet specific urban mobility is essential. The mobility service network must continually adapt to potential demand under financial, political and social constraints.

Key Components of Intermodal Urban Mobility Systems in Smart Cities

The trunk-and-feeder intermodal services enhance the overall efficiency of the public transportation system (Figure 4). Nevertheless, from the user perspective, the transfer penalty involved in interchanging modes (which is added to the generalized cost of the trip) represents one of the main disadvantages in comparing intermodal and monomodal options (Figure 8).

Figure 8. Time/Cost-distance diagram for monomodal and intermodal trip
Source: after Van Nes, 2002

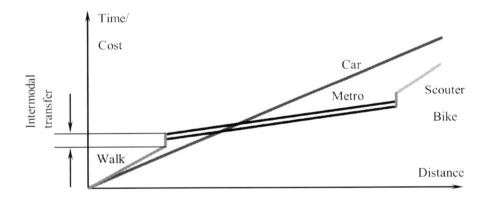

The impact of transfer discomfort could be minimized through the physical integration of networks of different modes and the design of seamless transfer facilities, fares integration, and additional value-added services complementary to basic mobility services. The characteristics of the integrated services should compensate for the disutility of transfers.

Mobility systems need to be developed to meet the increasing demand in cities and, in addition, match the dynamics of travel requirements (changes in travelling behavior, necessity for increased convenience, speed and predictability, expectations for service customization). The mobility service portfolio must be expanded, ensuring the transformation of business models based on multiple categories of stakeholders. Cities must develop intermodal urban mobility systems by extending their public transportation supply and adapting it from "delivering transportation" to "delivering solutions" (Van Audenhove et al., 2014). It is necessary to improve the travel experience by combining some high-quality attributes of public transportation and additional services offered based on partnerships with other stakeholders. Consequently, mobility supply should comprise three main categories of components, the first two representing part of the main mobility system (Figure 9):

- **Supply and operations of infrastructure and transportation modes.** The physical network (or the infrastructure network) includes both line features (such as railways, roads, and highways sections) and point features (stops. stations, gates) that ensure access to the line feature, i.e., to the traffic network.
- **Mobility services.** The physical network must provide specific services (characterized by quality, safety, security, convenience, sustainability, and affordability) to respond to the mobility/travel demand, which implies connections between different locations.
- **Additional value-added services next to core mobility services.** The attractiveness of intermodal mobility services can be increased with additional services (e.g., retail and food areas, business, convenience and leisure services) adapted to the demands of different target groups (local passengers, tourists, staff, nearby residents). Transportation operators can complement mobility supply with commercial offerings through partnerships and alliances with third parties.

Correlations of modes and complementary services are necessary to ensure the service characteristics of different types of travel. Linking private and public transportation in an integrated system generates possibilities to benefit from the strengths of some systems while preventing their disadvantages (Van Nes, 2002). The development of intermodal service networks requires correct categorization of the physical and service networks. The physical network characterizes the supply of spatial mobility for non-motorized and motorized individual trips, and the service network represents the mobility supply for public transportation.

Figure 9. Main components of public mobility services
Source: after Van Audenhove et al., 2014

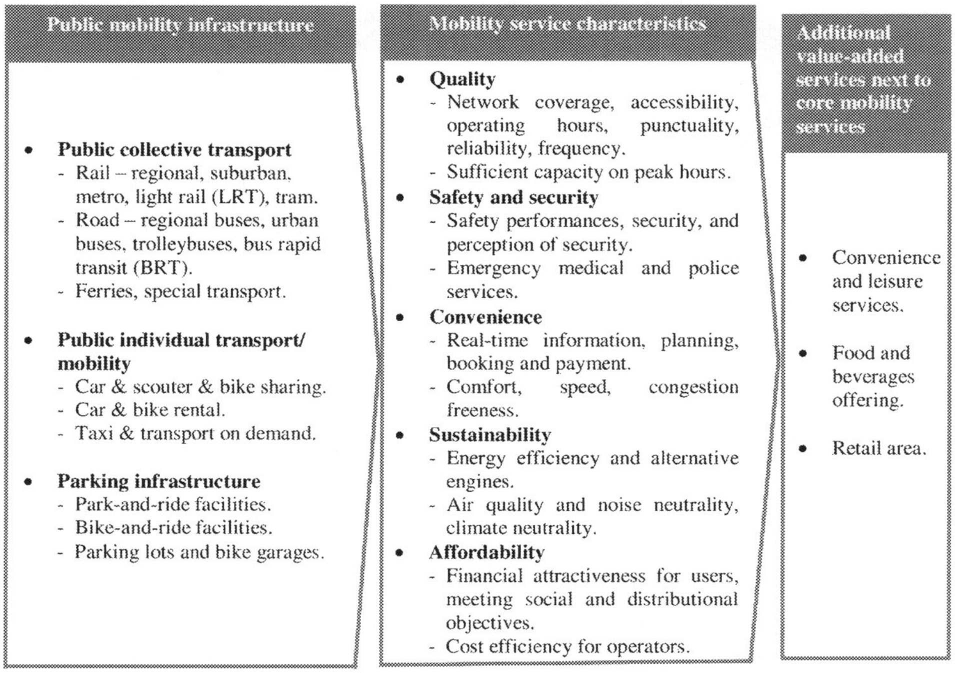

Depending on the decisions of the urban management and transportation operators, the same physical network can determine a specific service network and different service levels for travelers. Consequently, the characterization of the mobility supply for individual trips refers only to the physical network (especially to the coverage area of the access to the traffic infrastructure, spatial accessibility, and performances of the line infrastructure features – e.g., maximum permitted speeds and loads, gauges, technical and financial access requirements). For collective public transportation, the characterization of the service network is necessary. The service network is specific for a transportation mode characterized by (*i*) infrastructures, (*ii*) vehicles and (*iii*) operating technologies, all well adapted to the mobility demands of land use. There is a close dependency between the three components of the service network. Deficiencies in the operation of only one of the components may compromise the quality of service. Except for transportation modes with separate infrastructure (e.g., railways), the transportation modes that share the same infrastructure (buses, taxis) with personal cars, bicycles, and motorcycles are more sensitive to the quality of the supplied services.

The design of an intermodal service network aims to correlate the performances of different travel modes (in terms of speed, capacity, energy consumption, and space consumption) to ensure sustainable mobility objectives. Integrating individual mobility and public transportation, intermodal service network design reflects the antagonism between (Figure 10):

- **The economic optimum** - a network specific to large traffic infrastructures defined by major corridors for consolidated traffic flows that ensure the efficiency of construction and operation
- **The user optimum** - a network with multiple direct connections between nodes, like a "mesh" that almost uniformly covers the entire area to meet social equity requirements.

Harmonization of the objectives must be achieved by maintaining an acceptable efficiency of all the traffic infrastructures in a particular area. It leads to the differentiation of the infrastructures in relation to the design, construction, and operation costs, which must be consonant with the mobility demands of the served areas. Consequently, there are necessary solutions that mitigate and harmonize the antagonistic objectives regarding the economic efficiency and social equity that the functions of the traffic infrastructure for the entire socio-economic system must ensure.

The trade-off between comfortable access to public transportation (by walking or individual mobility services) and the highest possible average traffic speeds needs solutions for services with different performances.

DEVELOPMENT OF INTERMODAL URBAN MOBILITY SYSTEMS

Levels of Integrations

To be efficient, a transportation system must serve various mobility needs (Litman, 2020). The design of public transportation networks has long been segmented by mode of transportation/travel, sometimes leading to complex and inflexible routes for passengers. The complexity and densification of the spatial units involved diversification and a widening of the mobility areas. Thus, city authorities have developed measures to connect different transportation and mobility modes according to sustainable mobility goals. This approach aims to organize a mobility offer towards intermodality.

Challenges in the Development of Urban Intermodal Mobility Systems

Figure 10. Network configurations specific to antagonist objectives
Source: after Van Nes, 2002

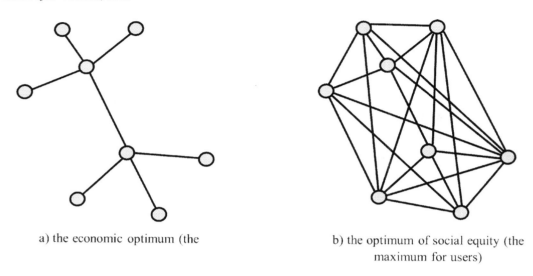

a) the economic optimum (the

b) the optimum of social equity (the maximum for users)

Travel demands, and thus the value of intermodal planning, can be evaluated from different perspectives. In an integrated approach, a crucial task consists in organizing an "integrated mobility platform operator", responsible for planning, booking, payment and billing, ensuring "one face to the traveler" (Van Audenhove et al., 2014). Developing an integrated mobility structure supposes a complex set of cooperation relationships and negotiations between public and private stakeholders (Figure 11).

Figure 11. Components operated by public and private stakeholders within the mobility system
Source: Van Audenhove et al., 2014

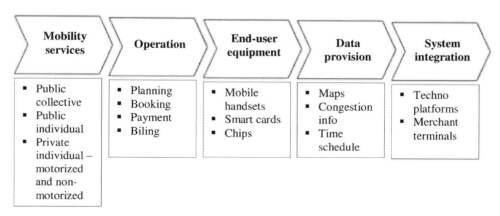

Intermodal integration involves five general levels (Bernal, 2016; Booz, 2012; Luk & Olsewski, 2003):

- **Physical integration** - is associated with a complex scheme of intermodal facilities ensuring easy access to modal interchanges; the design of pedestrian ways facilitating modal transfers and minimizing distances for access to stops.
- **Transportation network integration** – modal service networks (bus, tram, metro, etc.) should form an integrated network that is complementary in relation to their modal characteristics. Metro and tram services should be designed to ensure high-capacity corridors and rapid services.
- **Fare integration** involves developing a standard fare collection system for all modes through a single shared payment medium.
- **Information integration** – complete and easy-to-use information and guidance system is critical for encouraging intermodal travel. Signage at metro and bus stations should be designed to deliver passengers' information effectively. Intelligent Transportation Systems (ITS) have an essential role in transportation integration, in general, and information integration, in particular.
- **Institutional or administrative integration** - involves developing only one institutional scheme to plan, coordinate, manage and control a set of transportation networks (e.g., a common metropolitan entity).

As previous topics revealed, the main problem in developing an intermodal mobility system is ensuring seamless transitions from one mode to another: continuity of the journey chain, compatibility between modes, consistency, readability, etc. In fact, in the intermodal approach of the mobility system, more and more interchange points intervene to connect and correlate several types of services to widen users' options (national, regional, tram-train heavy rail transportation, urban rail transportation, bus, interurban road transportation, etc.).

Journey Chain and Urban Intermodal Hubs

Despite the demonstrated economic, environmental and social equity benefits, intermodal mobility solutions are commonly perceived by travelers as a constraint compared to individual trips (especially by cars). Besides the correlation of infrastructure and service networks at different levels, a coordinated approach is necessary for designing the transfer station and facilities.

Solutions for transfer comfort improvement are required. Generally, the multiplication of links between services diminishes the attractiveness of public transportation (Faivre, 2015; Keizer et al., 2015; Litman, 2012; Wardman & Hine, 2000). For users, intermodal transfers negatively influence the perceived time of public transportation. E.g., journey time increased by less than 10% due to the restructuring of the public transportation networks was perceived by users as a time increase of 40 to 50% (Dobruszkes et al., 2011). Walking or waiting time for public transportation access is typically perceived as two to five times longer or more "costly" than time spent in vehicles (Faivre, 2015). Therefore, the increase in the attractiveness of intermodal transportation supposes the reduction of the penalty (or disutility) implied by intermodal transfers. In this framework, the main functions of the intermodal terminals or hubs must be established.

The terms intermodal hub, mobility hub, or interchange pole are similar but often used differently. The term intermodal hub (IMH) is defined as a node that concentrates multimodal and intermodal flows, including facilities that enable access for all user categories to all modal service networks, allow physical transfers between different transportation modes, mobility service integration and additional

Challenges in the Development of Urban Intermodal Mobility Systems

value-added services (next to core mobility services). Consequently, three main function categories are assigned to the IMHs (Figure 12):

- **Mobility function** - organizing and facilitating connections between modes; it decisively influences the attractiveness of public transportation and intermodal solutions.
- **Urban function** - insertion into the urban environment through the architectural quality of the location and through the appropriateness of the integrated street facilities and furniture.
- **Service function** - improving the comfort of travelers and quality of information through the development of commercial spaces and integration into urban activities at the local level.

Figure 12. Role of the intermodal hub
Source: after Richer, 2008

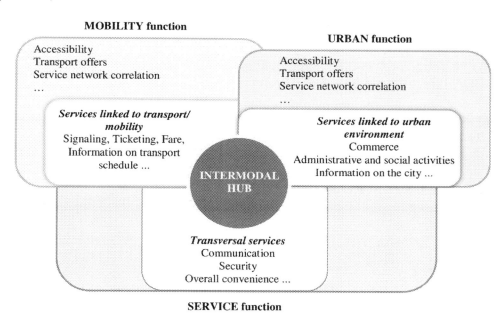

IMHs mainly aim to diminish the discomfort related to journey chain splitting, ensuring seamless access and intermodal transfers through efficient correspondence between different available transportation modes and maintaining the safety and comfort of travelers. Generally, the efficiency of IMHs depends on (Faivre, 2015; Pitsiava-Latinopoulou & Iordanopoulos, 2012):

- **Adequate reliability and service adapted to the capacities of the IMH components**
- **Good level of satisfaction in providing intermodal connections**
- **A reduced-cost intermodal connection**
- **Reduction of travel time**
- **Direct access to different transportation modes.**

IMHs are variable-sized, from the simple combination of two transportation modes, such as a key node in the suburbs, to large terminals with connections between multiple transportation modes and large-scale urban functionality (shopping centres, housing, offices etc.). Depending on their geographical location, available transportation modes, and passenger flow size, the following IMH classes can be distinguished (Faivre, 2015):

- **For long-distance trips (interzonal)** - ensuring long-distance travel between main cities. This category includes railway stations, bus stations, and airports. In general, waiting times are significant, and the frequency of trips varies more by the time of year than daily. Generally, railway stations are located in the city's centre, contributing to developing an IHM. Airports integrate many other transportation and mobility modes to connect travel in urban centers and peripheries.
- **For short-distance trips** - refers mainly to journeys connecting the outskirts and the city centers. The frequency of trips is regular and the flow of people may vary during the day. Waiting times are relatively short, and transfers between different modes of transportation must be efficient.
- **Park-and-ride** – refers to parking areas built next to a railway station or metro station; it aims to facilitate access to the urban network. They also contribute to helping the parking for travelers who come to the railway station and have no other satisfactory alternative to access the railway network.
- **Urban facilities** – include all urban layouts to facilitate travel between different transportation and mobility modes (bus, tram, metro, bicycles, scooters, etc.). Stops and stations are designed to facilitate interchanges (access to platforms, ramps, and bicycle and scooter parking). These urban interchange areas are generally inaccessible to private vehicles with their traffic routes, thus avoiding the densification of road flows.

Generally, in every country, the introduction and organization of regular and on-demand public transportation are assigned to transportation authorities. Usually, the decision levels are established according to land administration entities and transportation modes. The organization of urban transportation is the responsibility of the municipality, a public institution of inter-municipal cooperation or a mixed union. For interregional transportation, road links are managed by local departments, and rail transportation is mainly at the regional or national level. The operation of the service networks is done by the service delegation assigned to public or private companies.

The design and management of the IMHs (in an integrated manner with types of activities related to the transportation itself, the access infrastructure, and the circulation and connection paths between different transportation modes and networks) involves a diversity of decision-makers:

- **Infrastructure management companies** (railways, platforms, underground passages, etc.)
- **Transportation operators**
- **Administrative authorities** at different territorial levels (general councils - for bus stations, municipalities - for roads, etc.)
- **Users and local communities**
- **Private companies** (providing additional services)
- **Urban planners, architects.**

Challenges in the Development of Urban Intermodal Mobility Systems

The collaboration between the various players is beneficial for both the user and the community and is based on the complementarity of the implemented offers. In practice, the stakeholder involvement is reflected by identifying a functionality domain (e.g., railway company/regional administrative authority, metro/railway authorization authority). Thus, this variety of stakeholders defines areas of institutional competencies that often are not coherent but where institutional cooperation is essential to ensure the seamless functioning of IMHs. This state can concern both network design, improvement of service connections (timetable correlation, intermodal facilities development etc.) and access to passenger information.

CONCLUSION

In most cities, continuous dynamics are recorded in the planning and operations of different transportation modes. Often, controversial goals and competitive relationships intervene in the mobility system. The subjective preferences of users in choosing their travel modes, pressures from industrial groups promoting individual modes, and even limited focus of some transportation companies on a single mode, generate negative impact and poor efficiency of the overall mobility system. The most crucial controversy is related to "cars vs public transportation". Intermodal solutions can increase the weight of public transportation. But significant efforts are necessary to ensure seamless journeys in an integrated mobility system.

Each travel mode has assigned specific tasks in the integrated network according to its technical and operating characteristics. Rapid public transportation lines (rail, subway, light rail with grade-separated or exclusive right of way) are perceived as solutions to improve the attractiveness of public transportation. Nevertheless, rapid public transportation projects require substantial funds. Further, the high transportation capacities supplied by these lines must be appropriately used to justify the investments. The efficacy and efficiency of public transportation can be improved by using several modes of transportation. The development of an intermodal public transportation network can enlarge the area of accessibility to rapid transportation lines.

From the user perspective, an integrated mobility system has powerful advantages due to an extensive set of public transportation modes across various mobility operators. Such interoperability can be achieved through several levels of integration: physical, transportation network, fare, information, institutional or administrative.

Physical integration is strongly related to network integration. Both support the integration of infrastructure. Fare integration and information integration require intense cooperation between urban public transportation operators and other mobility operators (national and regional – e.g., rail companies, or local – e.g., taxi operators, sharing and rental companies). All levels of integration must be supported and stimulated by public authorities. Practice demonstrates that the strong support of city management is critical for establishing broad partnerships and, thus, the successful implementation of an integrated urban mobility system.

REFERENCES

Ainsalu, J., Arffman, V., Bellone, M., Ellner, M., Haapamäki, T., Haavisto, N., Josefson, E., Ismailogullari, A., Lee, B., Madland, O., Madžulis, R., Müür, J., Mäkinen, S., Nousiainen, V., Pilli-Sihvola, E., Rutanen, E., Sahala, S., Schønfeldt, B., Smolnicki, P. M., & Åman, M. (2018). State of the Art of Automated Buses. *Sustainability*, *10*(9), 3118. doi:10.3390u10093118

Bernal, L. M. M. D. (2016). Basic Parameters for the Design of Intermodal Public Transportation Infrastructures. *Transportation Research Procedia*, *14*, 499–508. doi:10.1016/j.trpro.2016.05.104

Bertaud, A. (2004). *The Spatial Organization of Cities: Deliberate Outcome or Unforeseen Consequence?* (Working Paper No. 2004-01). University of California, Institute of Urban and Regional Development.

Booz Allen. (2012). *Integrating Australia's Transportation Systems: A Strategy for An Efficient Transportation Future*. Infrastructure Partnership Australia.

Bösch, P. M., Becker, F., Becker, H., & Axhausen, K. W. (2018). Cost-based analysis of autonomous mobility services. *Transport Policy*, *64*, 76–91. doi:10.1016/j.tranpol.2017.09.005

Bruun, E. C. (2014). *Better Public Transit Systems. Analyzing Investments and Performance* (2nd ed.). Routledge.

Caywood, M., Cochran, A., & Schade, M. (2015). *Urban Mobility Score: Quantifying Multimodal Transportation Access*. Disrupting Mobility Summit, Cambridge MIT.

Cohen, A., & Shaheen, S. (2016). *Planning for shared mobility*. PAS Report 581. American Planning Association, pp. 1–106. https://www.planning.org/publications/report/9107556/

COM. (2020). Sustainable and Smart Mobility Strategy – putting European transportation on track for the future. European Commission.

Costescu, D., Olteanu, S., & Roman, E. A. (2022). Model for Bus Line Planning in an Intermodal Urban Transportation Network. In: Moldovan, L., Gligor, A. (Eds) *The 15th International Conference Interdisciplinarity in Engineering. Inter-Eng 2021. Lecture Notes in Networks and Systems*, (vol 386). Springer.

Costescu, D., Stere, A. S., & Serban, A. M. (2021). Network of Dedicated Bus Lanes: A Solution to Increase the Accessibility of the Urban Intermodal Transport. *Romanian Journal of Transport Infrastructure*, *10*(2), 1–15. doi:10.2478/rjti-2021-0008

Dobruszkes, F., Hubert, M., Laporte, F., & Veiders, C. (2011). Réorganisation d'un réseau de transportation collectif urbain, ruptures de charge et mobilités éprouvantes à Bruxelles [Reorganization of an urban collective transportation network, load breaks and stressful mobility in Brussels]. *Journal of Urban Research 7*. https://journals.openedition.org/articulo/1844

Eltis. (2019). *SUMP Glossary*. Eltis. https://www.eltis.org/mobility-plans/glossary#

Faivre C.G. (Coord.). (2015). *Chaine de déplacement et pôles d'échanges multimodaux: diagnostics de situations [Travel chain and multimodel exchange hubs: situation diagnosis]*. Projet TIMODEV, Programme PREDIT.

Faivre d'Arcier, B. (Coord.) (2012). *Measure de la performance des lignes de transportation public urbain [Measurement of the performance o furban public transportation lines]*. APEROL.

Fazio, M., Giuffrida, N., Le Pira, M., Inturri, G., & Ignaccolo, M. (2021). Planning Suitable Transportation Networks for E-Scooters to Foster Micromobility Spreading. *Sustainability, 13*(20), 11422. doi:10.3390u132011422

Galatoulas, N. F., Genikomsakis, K. N., & Ioakimidis, C. S. (2020). Spatio-temporal trends of e-bike sharing system deployment: A review in Europe, North America and Asia. *Sustainability, 12*(11), 4611. doi:10.3390u12114611

Gebhardt, L., Krajzewicz, D., & Oostendorp, R. (2017) Intermodality – key to a more efficient urban transportation system? *Proceedings of the 2017 ECEEE Summer Study Proceedings*, (pp. 759-769). ECEEE.

Goldbach, C., Sickmann, J., Pitz, T., & Zimasa, T. (2022). Towards autonomous public transportation: Attitudes and intentions of the local population. *Transportation Research Interdisciplinary Perspectives, 13*, 100504. doi:10.1016/j.trip.2021.100504

Kager, R., Bertolini, L., & Te Brömmelstroet, M. (2016). Characterization of and reflections on the synergy of bicycles and public transportation. *Transportation Research Part A, Policy and Practice, 85*, 208–219. doi:10.1016/j.tra.2016.01.015

Keizer, B., Kouwenhoven, M., & Hofker, F. (2015). New Insights in Resistance to Interchange. *Transportation Research Procedia, 8*, 72–79. doi:10.1016/j.trpro.2015.06.043

Lefevre, B. (2010). Urban Transportation Energy Consumption: Determinants and Strategies for its Reduction, *S.A.P.I.EN.S. 2*(3). https://journals.openedition.org/sapiens/914

Litman, T. (2012). *Toward More Comprehensive and Multimodal Transportation Evaluation*. Victoria Transportation Policy Institute. https://www.vtpi.org/comp_evaluation.pdf

Litman, T. (2015). *When Are Bus Lanes Warranted? Considering Economic Efficiency, Social Equity and Strategic Planning Goals*. Victoria Transportation Policy Institute. https://www.vtpi.org/blw.pdf

Litman, T. (2020). *Autonomous vehicle implementation predictions: Implications for transportation planning*. Victoria Transportation Policy Institute. https://www.vtpi.org/avip.pdf

Long, Z., & Axsen, J. (2022). Who will use new mobility technologies? Exploring demand for shared, electric, and automated vehicles in three Canadian metropolitan regions. *Energy Research & Social Science, 88*, 102506. doi:10.1016/j.erss.2022.102506

Luk, J., & Olszewski, P. (2003). Integrated public transportation in Singapore and Hong Kong. *Road and Transport Research, 12*(4), 41–51.

Mouratidis, K., & Cobeña Serrano, V. (2021). Autonomous buses: Intentions to use, passenger experiences, and suggestions for improvement. *Transportation Research Part F: Traffic Psychology and Behaviour, 76*, 321–335. doi:10.1016/j.trf.2020.12.007

Negre L. (Coord.) (2008). *Charte des services publics locaux. Indicateurs de performance des réseaux de transportation public [Charter of local public services, Performance indicators of public transportation networks]*. Institut de la Gestion Déléguée (IDG), Association des Maires de France.

Nenseth, V., Ciccone, A., & Kristensen, N. B. (2019). *Societal consequences of automated vehicles: Norwegian scenarios*. Institute of Transportation Economics. https://www.toi.no/getfile.php?mmfileid=50576

Oeschger, G., Carroll, P., & Caulfield, B. (2020). Micromobility and public transportation integration: The current state of knowledge. *Transportation Research Part D, Transport and Environment, 89*, 102628. doi:10.1016/j.trd.2020.102628

Pitsiava-Latinopoulou, M., & Iordanopoulos, P. (2012). Intermodal Passengers Terminals: Design standards for better level of service. *Procedia: Social and Behavioral Sciences, 48*, 3297–3306. doi:10.1016/j.sbspro.2012.06.1295

Raicu, S., & Costescu, D. (2020). *Mobility. Traffic Infrastructures*. AGIR Press. (*In Romanian*)

Richer, C. (2008). L'émergence de la notion de pôle d'échanges, entre interconnexion des réseaux et structuration des territoires [The emergence of the notion of exchange hub, between interconnection of netweks and structuring of territories]. *Les Cahiers scientifiques du transportation [The scientific papers of transportation]*, AFITL, 101-123.

Rupprecht Consult. (2019). *Guidelines for Developing and Implementing a Sustainable Urban Mobility Plan* (2nd ed.). Rupprecht Consult.

Salonen, A. O., & Haavisto, N. (2019). Towards autonomous transportation. Passengers' experiences, perceptions and feelings in a driverless shuttle bus in Finland. *Sustainability, 11*(3), 588. doi:10.3390u11030588

Santi, P., Resta, G., Szell, M., Sobolevsky, S., & Strogatz, S. H. & C. Ratti C. (2014). Quantifying the benefits of vehicle pooling with shareability networks. *Proceedings of the National Academy of Sciences of the United States of America (PNAS), 111*(37), 13290-13294. PNAS. 10.1073/pnas.1403657111

Shaheen, S., Cohen, A., Chan, N., & Bansal, A. (2020). Sharing strategies: Carsharing, shared micromobility (bikesharing and scooter sharing), transportation network companies, microtransit, and other innovative mobility modes. In E. Deakin (Ed.), *Transportation, Land Use, and Environmental Planning* (pp. 237–262). Elsevier. doi:10.1016/B978-0-12-815167-9.00013-X

Shaheen, S., & Martin, E. (2015). Unravelling the modal impacts of bikesharing. *Access, 47*, 8–15.

UN-Habitat. (2013). *Planning and Design for Sustainable Urban Mobility, Global Report on Human Settlements 2013*. United Nations Human Settlements Programme.

Van Audenhove, F. J., Korniichuk, O., Dauby, L., & Pourbaix, J. (2014). *The Future of Urban Mobility 2.0. Imperatives to shape extended mobility ecosystems of tomorrow*. Arthur D. Little & The International Association of Public Transportation (UITP). https://www.adlittle.com/en/insights/viewpoints/future-urban-mobility-20-%E2%80%93-full-study

Van Nes, R. (2002). *Design of multimodal transportation networks. A hierarchical approach*. [Doctoral Thesis, Delft University, The Netherlands].

Vuchic, V. (2007). *Urban Transit Systems and Technology*. Wiley. doi:10.1002/9780470168066

Wardman, M., & Hine, J. (2000). *Costs of Interchange: A Review of Literature*. (Working Paper 546). Institute of Transportation Studies, University of Leeds, Leeds, UK.

KEY TERMS AND DEFINITIONS

Accessibility: Capability of reaching destinations. It can be assessed at different levels of transport networks or systems based on various metrics (distances, time, money, other quality factors).

Feeder service: Low-capacity mobility or transportation services (e.g., scooters, cars, local buses) provided to supply passenger flow to fixed high-capacity service systems (tram, light rail, metro, rail).

Mode of Transportation: A variant of transportation provided by a specific ensemble of infrastructures, vehicles and technologies, characterized by a set of features in terms of accessibility, capacity, speed, reliability, safety, etc.

Shared mobility: Public individual travel services provided based on short-term hire payment vehicles (bikes, scooters, cars) operated by users, function on their needs, according to restrictions of urban authority and service provider operator.

Trunk-and-feeder service: A set of low-capacity travel or transport services connected to a transport corridor organized to feed flow to use the provided high-capacity efficiently.

Urban Intermodality: A Set of different travel modes and transportation services integrated to ensure a seamless trip made with more than one mode (e.g., walking, metro, and bus) to offer travelers a seamless journey. It combines the most robust features of different mobility options in terms of accessibility, travel mode, and travel preferences to increase urban mobility efficiency.

Urban Intermodal Hub: Transport node that concentrates multimodal and intermodal flows, including facilities that enable access for all user categories to all modal service networks, allow physical transfers between different transportation modes, mobility service integration and additional value-added services.

Urban Multimodality: A set of available alternative transportation and travel modes for different trips over a certain period (e.g., a day or week).

Urban Mobility System: Set of traffic and transport infrastructures, technologies for all modes of travel (walking, cycling, private car and scooter usage, public transportation offerings) and related services (including parking supply) satisfying the mobility demand at the urban level.

Chapter 6
Nudging Towards Sustainable Public Transportation

Anton Manfreda
https://orcid.org/0000-0003-0469-5201
School of Economics and Business, University of Ljubljana, Slovenia

Jure Erjavec
https://orcid.org/0000-0002-9923-7686
School of Economics and Business, University of Ljubljana, Slovenia

ABSTRACT

The chapter presents the importance of public transportation in coping with contemporary environmental issues. However, the aim is not to present public transportation as the only method of transportation leading towards a green future. New services and solutions should be carefully developed in cooperation with residents considering their needs, culture, habits, and existing procedures. Transforming the mindset of residents should be considered as well. Therefore, the authors present the readers with different theories, models, tools, and frameworks, illustrated with existing cases for promoting behavioral change amongst individuals, focusing specifically on nudging mechanisms. While the focus of the chapter is mainly on nudging towards sustainable public transportation, the authors illustrate nudging with examples from other areas as well and argue how such uses can also be applied to promote sustainable public transportation. This chapter is therefore aimed at policymakers and other stakeholders involved in promoting sustainable public transportation modes.

INTRODUCTION

The increasing population in urban areas is causing modern problems and is affecting the quality of individuals' life. It is notable to mention that more than half of the world's population live in cities and the share of people living in urban environments is constantly rising. It is expected that up to 68% of the world's population will leave in urban areas by 2050 ("68% of the world," 2018). Many places are already facing problems and challenges arising from quick urbanization and ageing infrastructure that

DOI: 10.4018/978-1-6684-5996-6.ch006

Copyright © 2023, IGI Global. Copying or distributing in print or electronic forms without written permission of IGI Global is prohibited.

Nudging Towards Sustainable Public Transportation

are hardly able to handle these issues. Existing procedures in cities have been ineffective in many areas. However, with the recent progress and the potential of digital technologies and relevant communication opportunities, cities are increasingly becoming smarter. The idea of a smart city or community as a way to improve an individual's quality of life is gaining the attention of policymakers, academic researchers and other relevant stakeholders.

Together with population growth also technological advancement is increasing and offering a way to cope with modern solutions. The diffusion of information technology is now noticeable everywhere, not only in organizations but also considering individuals and society. Digitalization is bringing new opportunities for cities and communities; however, the progress and new development must be considering sustainability issues as well. Namely, to ensure that the resources are well-maintained and well-kept-up (Nagode & Manfreda, 2022). After all, proper economic growth and respectable quality of life for individuals should be considered as well. Due to the anticipated growth of urban areas, it is important to simultaneously take care of the social, economic and environmental sustainability use of resources. Decision-makers in several cities are trying to implement different technologies into various aspects of their cities' operations. This includes public transport, urban mobility, solid waste management, water and power supply, citizen participation and many others.

However, similarly, as organizations need to change their way of operating in order to digitally transform or become more sustainability-oriented, the same applies to individuals. With respect to changing citizens' behaviors, the role that institutions have on individuals should not be neglected. Local government has an especially particular role as it is the institution geographically closest to citizens and has the authority to influence the local environment, services and civic infrastructure related to civil society (Cotterill & Richardson, 2009). However, human behavior can be modified by restructuring the flow of information and incentives, or through education (Ekins, 2004). Behavior change of individuals in urban areas and outside them needs should be considered as an important and well-thoughtful element for achieving defined sustainability goals.

Digital technologies may be used to promote sustainable mobility behaviors of the citizens (Kazhamiakin et al., 2016). The use of persuasive technologies offering data analytics and visualization can be used to inform and make the users aware of the consequences of their behavior. Lately the way of notifying people about their behavior through displays and applications has been proven to raise awareness and affect their behavior (Petersen et al., 2020). Digital technology can also engage with diverse stakeholders and increase knowledge among individuals, foster changes in public policy and behavioral change (Rajanen & Rajanen, 2019), and encourage citizens towards changing their behaviors to be more in line with the sustainable future of the whole society (Caroleo et al., 2019). That includes encouraging the use of public transportation, multimodal transport and offering micro-mobility solutions are the most user-oriented opportunities.

Therefore, the purpose of this chapter is twofold. Firstly, we present the importance of mobility and public transportation as a source for coping with contemporary environmental issues. Any transformational change should not be radically implemented, but transforming the mindset of residents should be considered as well. Therefore, the second objective of this chapter is to present the readers with different theories, models, tools and frameworks, illustrated with existing cases for promoting behavioral change amongst individuals, focusing specifically on nudging mechanisms. While the focus of the chapter is mainly on nudging towards sustainable public transportation, we illustrate nudging with examples from other areas as well and argue how such uses can also be applied to promoting sustainable public transportation. This chapter is therefore aimed at policy makers and other stakeholders involved in promoting sustainable public transportation modes.

Firstly, we present the current state and importance of public transport. Then we provide an overview of behavioral change field with a focus on definitions of the concepts and description of theories used. In the third part, we firstly present some general nudging examples towards sustainability, which are followed with nudging towards sustainable transportation examples. This is followed by a discussion where we argue which nudging approaches are most suitable for use in promoting sustainable public transportation. Concluding remarks include an overview of the chapter and suggestions for further research.

THE STATE AND IMPORTANCE OF PUBLIC TRANSPORTATION

Because of the growing population, it is expected that individuals will travel more and more. Figure 1 shows a projection of global urban mobility demand from 2010 through 2050. As it is evident from the figure, individuals will travel almost 50 trillion kilometers considering urban transportation networks only. With this huge increase, properly managing transportation is a necessity in efforts to maintain sustainable development goals. Thus, proper public transportation with supportive new methods of transportation and business models accepted by the residents will be crucial.

Considering the mobility service market only, the public transportation segment represents the main market within the global mobility services in terms of users. In 2021 more than 3.6 billion people used a public transportation, and the number is projected to increase to nearly 4.5 in 2026 (Arthur D. Little, 2018). Covid-19 pandemic caused an important decrease in the global usage of public transportation. Even higher decrease in the usage is evident in the flight segment, while contrary bike-sharing as a mobility service was faced with increased demand during the pandemic. All mobility services are projected to recover from the Covid-19 pandemic and continue with their growing rate that was observed before the pandemic.

Figure 1. Urban passenger mobility demand worldwide between 2010 and 2050 (in trillion passenger kilometers)
Source: Arthur D. Little (2018)

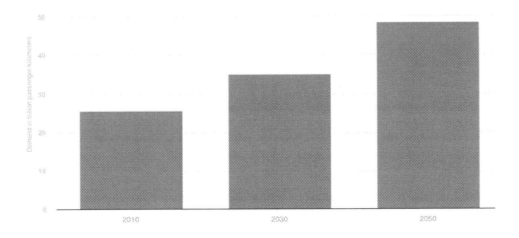

Figure 2. Users of selected segments of the mobility services market worldwide from 2017 to 2025 (in millions)
Source: Statista (2022)

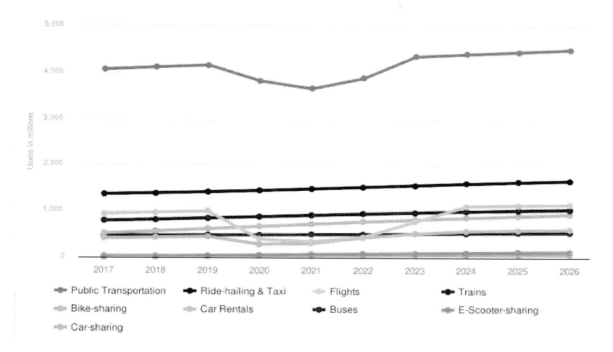

However, despite the fact that mobility services market is growing in the last years, including the public transportation, there is also a rising market of motor vehicle sales, as evident from Figure 3, indicating that car ownership is important for many individuals. Also, motor vehicle sales have increased again after the decline caused by Covid-19 pandemic. Yet, even after the first waves of Covid-19 pandemic crisis, production facilities in the motor vehicle segment remained restrained due to several bottlenecks in their supply chains, and consequently influencing the vehicles sales market as well.

It is hard to predict the future in this market, since there has been some decline before the Covid-19 pandemic. However, it is too soon to draw any conclusions if the decline before the Covid-19 pandemic is caused by the increased usage of public transportation or any other reason.

One may object that in Figure 3 also vehicles that are part of public transportation are included. Considering the structure of motor vehicle production, the majority of produced vehicles refer to passenger cars with a share of slightly more than 70%, quite constantly in the last three years. Light commercial vehicles represent slightly more than 20%, while heavy commercial vehicles and heavy buses and coaches represents around 5% (OICA, 2022a). The latter clearly indicates that increased demand in the mobility segment is covered both by the increased sales of motor vehicles and increased usage of public transportation. Contrarily, sharing business models and other new methods of mobility services and not following that demand with the same speed, signifies a potential in the mobility market by either integrating new services in the existing public transportation market or providing these services as supplements to the public transportation. However, micro-mobility services are relatively new, and not even well-developed in several regions.

Figure 3. Worldwide motor vehicle sales from 2005 to 2021 (in million units)
Source: OICA (2022b)

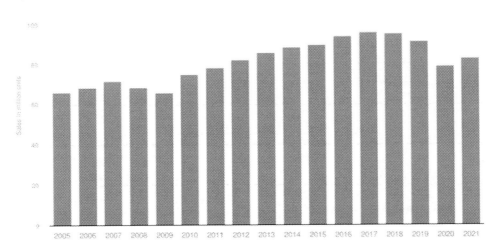

Public transportation in many regions also lacks modernization or offering digitally enabled services for the residents. One indicator of technological development is also the number of high-speed trains. Individuals when considering the mode of transportation consider the costs, own benefits, value and time. High-speed lines can present an important mode when value or time is considered.

Figure 4. Number of high-speed rail lines in operation worldwide as of 2020
Source: UIC (2020)

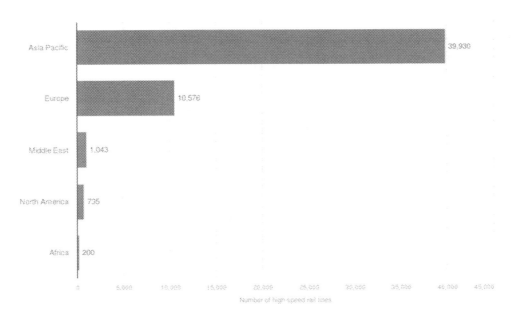

Nudging Towards Sustainable Public Transportation

As Figure 4 shows, Asia and Pacific are currently prevailing with the highest number of high-speed railway lines in the world. Europe has the second-highest number, while there were no high-speed rail lines in operation in Latin America in 2020 (UIC, 2020). High-speed rail services may not be related to public transportation in all regions; however, they present an important element when considering multimodality and connectivity between cities. The decision to use that type of transport would increase the likelihood to use public transportation in the final destination.

Although public transport presents one of the most important methods of transportation towards assuring a sustainable future, it is extremely difficult to make significant changes in the short term. It is also not possible to make unified policy decisions due to different settlements in different countries. Some countries are facing a population fragmented into several smaller towns and areas, perhaps even less accessible, while some countries consist of well-connected cities, and some countries are represented by a single city only. Due to the problems that cities are facing with the growing population, we are focusing also on public transportation in cities. The system in the cities must be offering efficient public transportation, including different mobility options; followed by developing an optimized multimodal transportation system connecting fragmented areas.

After all, in many cities, public transportation is highly accessible within cities (Figure 5). Cities provide high-frequency access to 56% of their population, while in cities with more than 1 million inhabitants, this share is larger than 80% (Poelman et al., 2020). That is another reason for emphasizing the importance of between-cities transportation to further increase the use of public transportation.

An example of a city where the growth of sustainable modes of transport is higher as the growth of population is London. Figure 6 presents the growth in journeys using core transport modes in London, in the period 2000-2020, together with the population growth. The effect of Covid-19 pandemic is clearly visible. For proper interpretation it should be overlooked; however, it may also present an important aspect dealing with resilience towards different crises. Overlooking the pandemic, linear growth of public transport daily usage throughout the year and growth of population is evident. Even more importantly, a constant decline in the use of privately-owned cars on London's streets is evident as well. Contrary, cycling seems to have the largest growth. The latter could be due to the extensive network of bikes in the city, the changed mindset of the culture and awareness of global climate change, internal happiness whenever individuals perform a type of physical activity or a combination of the mentioned factors.

That important increase in demand across all public transport modes in London that are growing faster than population can signify that with proper planning, communication and providing multimodal mobility services, changes over time are possible. However, once again it is notable to mention, that it is not possible to compare the cities due to significant characteristic differences.

BEHAVIORAL CHANGE AND NUDGING

Behavioral economics field has been the main proponent of explaining the phenomena of economic agents, especially individuals or households who not always behaving rationally and thus not following the classical economic theory. It helps us to understand why people make mistakes consistently either through loss aversion, power of defaults, confirmation biases etc.

Figure 5. Population with high level of access to public transport departures in urban centres
Source: Poelman et al. (2020)

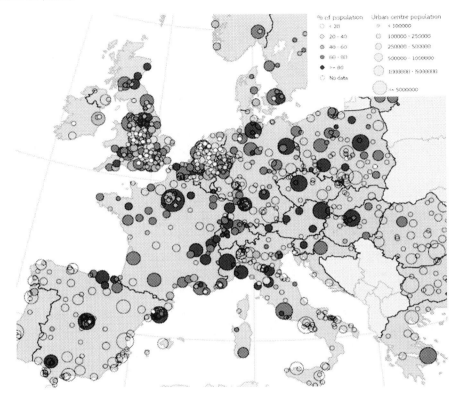

Figure 6. Growth in journeys using core transport modes in London
Source: Mayor of London (2021)

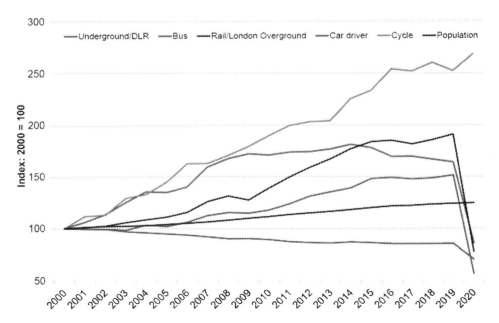

Nudging Towards Sustainable Public Transportation

One of the integral parts of behavioral economics is the research focused on how to drive human behavior or how to change human behavior. This deals with the question on how to alter habits and behavior of individuals either short or long term. Sources promoting behavioral change of individuals can include individuals themselves, organizations where they work or are involved with in any other way (for example as customers), governments and other policing bodies. The field has been extensively studied and is supported by various behavioral change theories such as theory of reasoned action (Ajzen & Fishbein, 1980) and theory of planned behavior (Ajzen, 1991), which mainly deal with explaining why individuals behave in a certain way. On the other hand, there are two widely used models that deal primarily with behavior change: transtheoretical behavior change model (Prochaska & Velicer, 1997) and Fogg behavior model (Fogg, 2009). As these models are highly applicable to promoting sustainable behavior, including the use of sustainable public transportation, we will briefly present each of the models.

The transtheoretical behavior change model was developed as a model to change individuals' behavior to a healthier one. It has since been used in various other contexts, including increasing sustainability awareness (Mair & Laing, 2013). The model consists of five stages of change: pre-contemplation, contemplation, preparation, action, and maintenance. There are different intervention strategies used in each of the phases, thus making each of the phases tailored to the individual, in order to help them reach the desired maintenance phase (Ferron & Massa, 2013). The model has proved to be one of the most effective ones when employed for actual behavior change technologies and approaches (Orji & Moffatt, 2018). Fogg's behavior model (Fogg, 2009) posits that behavior change is based on individuals' motivation and their ability to perform the target behavior. The behavior change must then be triggered with what the model refers to as prompts, that are usually of extrinsic nature. The level of motivation and ability define whether a specific prompt will succeed in changing behavior. There are three types of prompts: facilitator, signal and spark. The focus of the first model is the longitudinal approach of transitioning through several stages of behavior change, while the focus of the second model is focused on identifying the factors for behavior change. Both described models of behavior change emphasize the importance of individuals' motivation for change. When designing for behavior change, the designers need to take into consideration the level of individuals' motivation to change. The mechanism and tools used to promote behavior change consequentially have to be based on the level of that initial motivation.

There are different sources of motivation on why an individual, either as a consumer or as a part of an organization, would want to behave in a particular way. If the motivation is intrinsic, then the individual will usually work towards behaving a certain way by their own volition, because doing so is enjoyable by itself. An example of intrinsically motivated activity would be reading this chapter because the reader believes it is fun to learn something new and they do not have any other motive. However, more frequently, the individual might not have enough intrinsic motivation, therefore some sort of external motivators will have to be either present (extrinsic motivation) or actual rewards (external motivators) need to be used to ensure a certain behavior. An example of extrinsic motivation for reading this chapter might be because the reader is preparing a policy on sustainable public transportation and they need more information on how to incorporate some nudging mechanism into it. An example of external motivators for reading this chapter would be getting some sort a reward for doing it. It is important to note that intrinsic and extrinsic motivations are not exclusive. Often times both intrinsic and extrinsic motivation will be present. In this case extrinsic motivation is present to support and further encourage the intrinsic motivation. An example would be working hard at your job because you enjoy being good at it (intrinsic motivation) but also because you want to earn a bonus at the end of the month (extrinsic motivation). There are four separate types (Deci & Ryan, 1985) of the extrinsic motivation and how they correlate with intrinsic motivation. The main difference between the four types is the intensity of intrinsic motivation present next to the extrinsic motivation. For example, the most extreme stage (externally regulated behavior) involves no intrinsic motivation and is only performed because of some external reward or even potential punishment. The other end of the spectrum includes the integrated regulation stage where extrinsic motivation is in line with intrinsic motivation. More information can be found in a chapter by Deci & Ryan (2012).

We can conclude that motivation directs our behavior. I we want to change someone's behavior we need to understand their motivation and what sorts of external motivators can be used in order to promote the behavior we want to achieve. An example of such behavior change would be encouraging citizens use public transportation more frequently. This behavioral compliance can be achieved through various methods, such as education, legislation, active enforcement, persuasion etc.

With the advent of digitalization, one important aspect is also the design of information systems that encourage, support or otherwise effect behavior change. This is by no means a trivial process as it requires various techniques and strategies to ensure its success. One of the most widely used frameworks to support this process is persuasive system design framework (Oinas-Kukkonen & Harjumaa, 2009). The framework provides postulates behind persuasive systems, different ways to analyze the context, and offers several design principles. It identifies three potential successful outcomes: voluntary reinforcement, change of shaping attitudes, and change of shaping of behaviors. Its main purpose is to understand the strategies that influence the individual's behavior the most. The framework has been widely used in promoting sustainable consumption behavior (Kappel & Grechenig, 2009; Kuznetsov & Paulos, 2010) and sustainable mobility initiatives (Jylhä et al., 2013; Meloni & Teulada, 2015). Several mechanisms were identified as appropriate when developing technology-mediated nudging. The mechanisms are clustered in six categories: facilitate, confront, deceive, social influence, fear and reinforce (Caraban et al., 2019).

Nudging is one of the concepts that can be used when applying the described behavioral change models or when designing persuasive systems to promote behavior. Nudging is defined as a group of interventions in the choice architecture that influence people's choices in a predictable way, while not forbidding any of the options or making them costlier in terms of time, money, trouble, or social sanctions (Thaler & Sunstein, 2008). In other words, nudges are minor changes that influence decision making process, while not restricting choices or changing economic incentives. Therefore, nudging needs to be able to be easily avoided, and should not be costly for the implementation. Nudges should guide and enable choice by (Lehner et al., 2016):

- **Simplifying and Framing Information** such as providing clear information and maps to encourage cycling and walking, decluttering streets.
- **Change Physical Environment** such as road and lane planning and urban design.
- **Change the Default Policy** such as autopilot decisions in cars.
- **Using Social Norms** such as providing feedback information to consumers on their own progress and compare them with their peers (friends, family, neighbors etc.).

An example of a nudge to promote a healthier lifestyle would be placing more healthy food at the eye level in the grocery store, while not banning any of the unhealthy foods. Therefore, a consumer can still pick any choice of food they like, however the design of the shelves in the grocery stores nudges them towards a healthier option. An extensive overview of nudging is offered in aforementioned book by Thaler and Sunstein (2008), while a more recent overview of research on this field and avenues for

Nudging Towards Sustainable Public Transportation

future research is accessible in Marchiori et al. (2017). Nudging can be used by policy makers and other with responsibilities over a group of individuals to help them make decisions that are in line with the target behavior (Guthrie et al., 2015; Quigley, 2013). Nudging units have been formed on different national and even international levels, either as a standalone unit such as UK's Behavioral Insights Team or as a part of a larger behavioral units such as World Bank's Mind, Behavior and Development Unit. The basic steps that nudging units follow are identification of opportunities, measuring of outcomes, implementation of nudging, aligning stakeholders, compare effectiveness of the nudging approaches, and scaling up their findings (Patel et al., 2018).

The main focus of the remainder of this chapter is on presenting various nudging examples towards sustainable behavior. We start with an overview of applications on several different fields, and later focus more on how to nudge individuals to use sustainable public transportation more often.

NUDGING TOWARDS SUSTAINABLE BEHAVIOR

Overview of the Field and Implications for Sustainable Public Transportation

The pervasiveness of the nudge concept (Thaler & Sunstein, 2008) has been increasing since its inception. It has been applied in various domains such as health, safety, financial well-being, and climate, whereas in some fields such as education it is still underused (Weijers et al., 2021). While most of the research on nudging towards sustainable behavior is based on real life experiments, there have also been attempts that use controlled laboratory experiments (Permana & Sanjaya, 2022). The goal of this section is to provide an overview of the applications of nudging towards sustainable behavior. The focus will be on the applications that offer possible parallel approaches to promoting the use of sustainable public transportation. Byerly et al. (2018) propose six domains where decisions have major environmental impacts. According to their research, half of them (transportation choices, waste management and water use) have a wide array of research, while the other half (family planning, land management, meat consumption) still need to have more interventions tested.

Since smart cities already deploy technologies (i.e. internet of things, big data) that are often prerequisite for efficient persuasive systems, they represent an ideal environment for implementation of different technology enhanced nudging approaches. This can include real-time feedback on driving to increase road safety or using light sensors to successfully reduce crime and nighttime disturbance (Ranchordás, 2020). Klieber et al. (2020) provide an extensive SWOT analysis of nudging in smart cities. The main identified strengths are offering some lenience to government, low costs with significant effects, ability for opting out and high approval rates amongst citizens. Weaknesses include using nudging only as a superficial tool, decreasing citizens' trust in the government, inability for nudging to work without accompanying policies and little evidence for long-term effects of nudging. Web and mobile applications are considered as an opportunity to reach and involve more citizens. On the other hand, the possible threats are potential non-transparency by the public agencies, reducing citizens acceptance and support for such policies, and increasing unfairness.

Nudges have been successfully employed to promote sustainable electricity consumption. These nudges usually focus on either promoting "green" energy choices by changing the default choice (Momsen & Stoerk, 2014), or by using social norms to alter behavior (Kasperbauer, 2017). The latter are particularly interesting for potential application for nudging sustainable public transportation. Sending monthly letters to households, providing comparison of their household electricity consumption with the consumption of their neighbors and offering them plans to reduce their consumption, the overall energy consumption was reduced by 2.0% (Allcott, 2011). Similar approach was used in hospitality industry through a scenario-based experiment, where nudging hotel guests by providing them feedback on energy consumption of consumption conscientious guests led to reduced energy consumption (Chang et al., 2016).

Increasing visibility such as listing products at the top of the menu or placing them in more prominent positions in the stores has also proven to be an effective way of nudging towards a more sustainable consumer behavior (Vandenbroele et al., 2021). This concept can easily be adopted for promoting a more sustainable public transportation such as increasing information and visibility of the more sustainable transportation choices. For example, airports could provide more frequent and more visible signs for trains and buses connecting to other transportation hubs or city centers.

Another important issue are expectations versus reality of choice architects that use nudges. Fashion industry provides a good example as consumers often do not want to sacrifice their fashion needs and desires just for the sake of promoting sustainability. This can be attributed to the gap between their attitude toward sustainability and their actual behavior (Lee et al., 2020). Therefore, it is imperative for the choice architect to take this gap into consideration when developing nudging mechanism. If the gap is wide, then just nudges might not be able to achieve the desired effect and will have to be combined with other mechanism that we mention elsewhere in this subchapter. This coin does have two sides though. There have been proven discrepancies between what consumers think should influence their environmentally friendly behavior and what actually does it (Kristensson et al., 2017). This means that the choice architects should be wary when taking indirect consumer feedback into consideration.

Employing choice architecture can also be done on a meta level. Harris et al. (2017) suggest using choice architecture for developing sustainable infrastructure. In this case sustainable infrastructure is defined as the one that meets the overall community needs and enhances the quality of life, while also improving the performance of waste disposal, energy efficiency, water use reduction etc. Their research identifies social, organizational and individual levels of the infrastructure design process. Nudging in particular is suggested to be used at the organizational level, where it can nudge designers and constructors of the infrastructure towards a whole system design approach.

Another such approach studies interventions geared at leveraging more environmentally sustainable behaviors among the agents of the food chain, from the producers to the final consumers (Ferrari et al., 2019). The study concludes that while nudging towards more sustainable practices do work, they should complement and not potentially replace the actual food and environmental policies, which are usually stricter than nudges. This is further reinforced in study by Lehner et al. (2016), who also conclude that there seems to be a consensus among experts for the nudges to complement traditional coercive measures and economics tools, rather than replacing them.

In some cases, nudging might not be the best option. Such an example are restaurant food menus where nudging can be used to inform restaurant guests about the environmental and societal implications of their food choice and consequently promoting a more benign food option. However, the research has shown that this might not be the case when it comes to managerial decisions. This happens because of the lack of internal resources, inconsistent customer demand, organizational and operational complexities (Filimonau & Krivcova, 2017), while the consumers were more lenient for such nudges (Filimonau et al., 2017). This research offers an important insight for sustainable public transportation nudges by identifying the managerial issues that need to be taken into consideration.

Nudging Towards Sustainable Public Transportation

An important and often emphasized issue about choice architecture and nudging in particular are the ethics of the nudges. Does a nudge affect the individuals' autonomy when making a decision? Are nudges manipulative? A broad discussion on ethics of nudging is presented in Sunstein (2015). Reducing human autonomy in decision making process by using nudges is one of the major and most common ethical objections. However, Kasperbauer (2017) argues that the infrastructure and framework such as in the case of energy production and consumption are strongly influenced by factors external to individuals and largely determined prior to human decision making. This in turn diminishes the potential for reducing human autonomy by using nudges. A similar argument can be used for public transportation, where infrastructure is already in place and there is hardly any effect on diminishing individuals' autonomy on whether to select a sustainable public transportation or not.

The Use of Nudging in the Context of Sustainable Transportation

The motivating factors on travel mode choices can be conflicting between different consumers. Therefore, the nudging mechanism that are employed, need to be tailored to specific consumers in order to promote the use of more sustainable travel modes (Sivasubramaniyam et al., 2020). Not only can the citizens be the target of nudging mechanism, they can also participate in influencing decisions for mobility planning (Pourhashem et al., 2021). Previous studies on nudging towards sustainable transportation have focused mainly on nudging towards driving efficiency, driving behavior, and the use of public transportation (Byerly et al., 2018). This section of the chapter presents the overview of various nudging mechanisms for nudging towards sustainable transportation, with a special focus on public transportation.

In the first example, the customers of carsharing were nudged to inspect their vehicle before using it. The customers had to wait around 20 seconds for activation of their membership card before using the vehicle. In the meanwhile, they were nudged via a reminder card to inspect the vehicle before use (Namazu et al., 2018). Besides increasing safety by inspecting the vehicle, this example also shows us how to use nudging when a consumer has the time available to perform a certain action. In the described case, the time was very short, however a nudge provided the consumers with a reminder, that they can use that time for a specific activity (car inspection).

Another interesting example is using social norms as a nudge mechanism. This was implemented in a case of bus transport where card holders of bus lines received a social label that branded them as sustainable travelers because of the use of the public bus. This nudge let to an increase of more than one ride per day when compared to the control group which did not receive any social label (Franssens et al., 2021).

Some sustainable transportation modes such as cycling can raise the concern of safety (Pucher & Buehler, 2016). In some cases, nudges towards more sustainable transportation can also have positive externalities on safety. For example, coloring cycling lanes (physical environment change nudge) to provide nudges towards more frequent use of bicycles ended up also increasing safety for cyclists. There were fewer motorists that stopped in the cycle lane rather than elsewhere, the motorists also kept a greater distance from the cycle lanes and the cyclists themselves used the cycle lines more diligently (Fyhri et al., 2021).

Digital technology provides an opportunity for a more personalized approach to nudging. This can lead to smart nudging (Andersen et al., 2018) where nudging mechanism match the current situation of the user. This can be achieved through three step approach by deploying smart nudging architecture that consists of three components: sense, analyze, inform and nudge. Sensing includes gathering data from different sensing elements either based on public infrastructure and transport system or user devices (such as smart phones). The data sources for sensing can include internet of things sensors, crowdsensing, aggregated data, crowdsourcing, or static data. The gathered data can then be analyzed with various data mining and other statistical tools. The information will be extracted and will form the basis for the choice of actual nudging mechanism tailored to the specific user in order to nudge them towards the direction of choosing a sustainable transportation mode.

Being able to collect data about specific consumers enables us to better understand their motivations and behavior. For example, high penetration of mobile technology can help to segment the consumers through creating data-driven user profiles (Anagnostopoulou et al., 2020). The authors present how the users of mobile application are presented with multiple route options and then nudged towards selecting a more sustainable route. This is achieved through the use of personalized intervention mechanisms based on the previously collected consumer data. Through abundance of collected information smart cities also offer various opportunities for developing data-driven nudges to nudge citizens towards behaving and consuming public transportation in a more sustainable way (Gandy & Nemorin, 2019). These incentives can be typical nudges such as providing citizens with personalized route maps from their homes to work and informing them which private and public ones are more sustainable, or they can also include other mechanisms such as weekly rewards for safest drivers or rewarding good behavior (Ranchordás, 2020).

In some cases, behavior change can be a single event of nudging an individual to perform a certain activity which then becomes permanent. An example of such single event nudge is an annual event where commuters are encouraged to ride their bike to work. The research has shown that the retention rate of the commuters who used this sort of transportation is not negligible. More than one quarter of first-time participants are still using bicycles to work five months after the event (Rose & Marfurt, 2007). As already mentioned in the early sections of this chapter, behavioral change can also be a long-term process. We demonstrated this with two models: transtheoretical behavior change model and Fogg behavior model. For example, changing individuals' behavior to commute to work using a bicycle is a process that follows the five stages of the transtheoretical model of behavior change. In this case the nudges are complementing other actions such as positive feedback or social support (Gatersleben & Appleton, 2007).

Nudging towards promoting the use of public transportation can also be indirect. One such example is through interventions that trigger residential choices. Certain types of residential choice interventions, such as "focalism", can nudge residents towards reducing their commuting times and increasing their sustainable modes of travel (Bhattacharyya et al., 2019).

Nudging by itself is not always enough to promote permanent behavior change. When the cycle lanes in the city of Oslo got painted red in order to nudge commuters towards cycling, the results showed that there was a significant increase in cycling in the first streets that were painted, however this was not the case later in the project (Fyhri et al., 2021). Therefore, other mechanisms should be used together with nudging (Mauro et al., 2022).

DIFFERENT APPROACHES TOWARDS USING SUSTAINABLE PUBLIC TRANSPORTATION

As already mentioned, different cities are facing modern transportation problems differently. After all, there is no single approach for promoting sustainable public transportation or leading towards a green future. Besides, one solution may work well for a particular region, while the same solution may not be accepted in other regions. Thus, new solutions leading towards transformational or behavioral change

Nudging Towards Sustainable Public Transportation

should be prudently prepared considering the needs of residents, including the culture and existing habits. Therefore, we are presenting some possible approaches in different cities for promoting sustainable public transportation together with emphasizing the important steps that should be considered in the future.

The government of Oslo is encouraging citizens to use electric cars, public transport, and bicycles by cutting taxes, giving free parking spaces, plug-in charging etc. This resulted in increasing the purchase of electric cars up to 490 000 units in 2020, meaning that more than 70% of cars purchased were electric cars. Also, the parking spaces are reduced to a minimum so that students and residents start using electric car-sharing, bicycles, or public transport (Rote, 2017).

Amsterdam has solidified its position not only as a smart city but also in terms of innovation in the field of smart cities, with the move to make all its city data open-source, resulting that everyone could access it and adding their contribution to improving the services even further. This was done by using smart meters to remotely regulate house energy consumption in real-time, improvements to support public transport, electric vehicles and also by strengthening the already existing biking culture in Amsterdam and the Netherlands (Brokaw, 2016; Danielou, 2014).

The Helsinki model includes open data as well, an innovation ecosystem and public-private cooperation. Most of the operators and transportation companies have allowed access to their data. Helsinki Region Transport as a local public transportation authority has opened all the relevant data about the routing, maps, timetables and vehicle locations that can be used by everyone. Helsinki is highly ranked on the lists for air quality, congestion, bicycle use, mass transit use and cost of single-city public transport tickets as well. The ambitious target and vision of Helsinki Regional Transport is public transport to be the number one choice for travel. The plan by 2025 is that 30% of the buses should be running on electricity which would be generated in a sustainable manner using wind, hydro or solar energy sources. To complete that vision, the city set some goals like smooth journeys, clear services, compact and attractive regions, fewer emissions and others (Hämäläinen, 2020).

Lisbon is another European city that has made significant improvements in Smart Mobility in recent years. Lisbon is one of the top performers in modal diversity since the public transport options include bus, commuter rail, metro, tram, bike and ferry. However, based on data given by Deloitte City Mobility Index 2020 for Lisbon, one of the challenges that Lisbon faces is that private cars remain the most popular and widely used mode of transport (58%) aggravating the traffic congestion issues. Only 16% of Lisbon's citizens use public transportation, although more affordable monthly passes are available for them (Deloitte & Insights, 2020). It is claimed that improving mobility and replacing cars, taxes and buses with autonomous vehicles would be the solution to many mobility problems that Lisbon faces, such as congestion, and high CO_2 emissions (Witzel, 2018).

Although Lisbon is introducing several initiatives to improve the performance and resilience of its mobility, as well as its integration, the citizens seem not to share the enthusiasm. Lisbon citizens are namely not aware of several mobility applications' existence in the city. Besides, they are highly unhappy with the available mobility systems and use mainly the private car as a transport mode (Bernardo et al., 2019).

The latter is clearly demonstrating that implementing technology or improving services without changing the mindset or developing the services without proper citizens' participation is not driving towards reaching sustainable goals. It is therefore imperative to deploy behavior changing tools such as nudging in order to promote the change towards a more sustainable behavior.

As seen in the examples in the previous parts of the chapter, nudging towards sustainable public transportation has been most successfully achieved through simplifying and framing information, and changing the physical environment. Changing the default policy and use of social norms as a nudging mechanism is not as widely used in the context of promoting sustainable public transportation, however these two are the most promising nudging mechanisms (Byerly et al., 2018). While changing the default policy is more challenging to implement in the case of public transportation, there is still a great potential to deploy new nudging interventions that are focusing on the use of social norms. The latter can be achieved together with other behavioral interventions such as gamification, where various tools, such as social graphs, to support the use of social norms can also be deployed. There can also be lessons learned from other areas where nudging has been applied, such as food industry (increasing visibility) or electrical industry.

The reported cases of nudges towards the use of sustainable public transportation are usually examples of isolated nudging mechanisms (such as paved bike lines, annual biking event, personalized route maps etc.). Very few cities, some of which are mentioned at the beginning of this sections, are tackling the issues in a systematic way. Therefore, there is a great potential in many cities, where nudging has not been systematically deployed or not deployed at all. The policy makers should keep in mind that systematic use of nudge interventions holds a greater potential than just isolated examples. Therefore, nudging interventions that communicate the benefits of public transport, could help nudge behaviors towards more sustainable mobility choices (Acheampong et al., 2021). Lastly, the potential of mobile technologies as an enabler of nudging towards sustainable public transportation should not be neglected (van Lierop & Bahamonde-Birke, 2021).

CONCLUSION

There is no single method for ensuring a better green future; however, encouraging the use of public transportation, multimodal transport and offering micro-mobility solutions are the most user-oriented opportunities. Among them public transportation in any kind of its form presents an option that should be further enhanced by both the development and the use side.

The aim of this chapter was not to present public transportation as the only method of transportation leading towards a green future, but more to open a discussion on different arrangements in different regions. After all, there is no single solution that could work for every region and new services and solutions leading towards transformational change should be carefully developed in cooperation with residents considering their needs, their culture, their habits and existing procedures. This transformational change should include a gradual transformation of the mindset of residents as well, rather than implementing radical solutions or policies. Therefore, the chapter was focusing also on presenting different theories and frameworks for promoting behavioral change amongst individuals, focusing specifically on nudging mechanisms. After all, several improvements in public transportation are not sufficient for achieving a green future without a simultaneous change in residents' behavior.

ACKNOWLEDGMENT

This research was supported by Slovenian Research Agency: ARRS [grant number P2-0037]

REFERENCES

Acheampong, R. A., Cugurullo, F., Gueriau, M., & Dusparic, I. (2021). Can autonomous vehicles enable sustainable mobility in future cities? Insights and policy challenges from user preferences over different urban transport options. *Cities, 112*. doi:10.1016/j.cities.2021.103134

Ajzen, I. (1991). The theory of planned behavior. *Organizational Behavior and Human Decision Processes, 50*(2), 179–211. https://doi.org/10.1016/0749-5978(91)90020-T

Ajzen, I., & Fishbein, M. (1980). *Understanding Attitudes and Predicting Social Behavior*. Prentice Hall.

Allcott, H. (2011). Social norms and energy conservation. *Journal of Public Economics, 95*(9–10), 1082–1095. https://doi.org/10.1016/j.jpubeco.2011.03.003

Anagnostopoulou, E., Urbančič, J., Bothos, E., Magoutas, B., Bradesko, L., Schrammel, J., & Mentzas, G. (2020). From mobility patterns to behavioural change: Leveraging travel behaviour and personality profiles to nudge for sustainable transportation. *Journal of Intelligent Information Systems, 54*(1), 157–178. https://doi.org/10.1007/s10844-018-0528-1

Andersen, A., Karlsen, R., & Yu, W. (2018). Green Transportation Choices with IoT and Smart Nudging. In Handbook of Smart Cities (pp. 331–354). Springer International Publishing. https://doi.org/10.1007/978-3-319-97271-8_13.

Arthur, D. Little. (2018). *Urban passenger mobility demand worldwide between 2010 and 2050 (in trillion passenger kilometers)*. United Nations. https://www.statista.com/statistics/1013579/urban-passenger-mobility-demand-worldwide/

Bernardo, M. R., Neto, M. de C., & Aparicio, M. (2019). Smart Mobility: a multimodal services study in the metropolitan area of Lisbon. In Conferência da Associação Portuguesa de Sistemas de Informação (CAPSI 2019).

Bhattacharyya, A., Jin, W., le Floch, C., Chatman, D. G., & Walker, J. L. (2019). Nudging people towards more sustainable residential choice decisions: An intervention based on focalism and visualization. *Transportation, 46*(2), 373–393. https://doi.org/10.1007/s11116-018-9936-x

Brokaw, L. (2016). *Six Lessons From Amsterdam's Smart City Initiative*. Sloan Review.

Byerly, H., Balmford, A., Ferraro, P. J., Hammond Wagner, C., Palchak, E., Polasky, S., Ricketts, T. H., Schwartz, A. J., & Fisher, B. (2018). Nudging pro-environmental behavior: Evidence and opportunities. *Frontiers in Ecology and the Environment, 16*(3), 159–168.

Caraban, A., Karapanos, E., Gonçalves, D., & Campos, P. (2019, May 2). 23 Ways to Nudge: A review of technology-mediated nudging in human-computer interaction. *Conference on Human Factors in Computing Systems - Proceedings*. doi:10.1145/3290605.3300733

Caroleo, B., Morelli, N., Lissandrello, E., Vesco, A., di Dio, S., & Mauro, S. (2019). Measuring the change towards more sustainable mobility: MUV impact evaluation approach. *Systems, 7*(2), 30.

Chang, H., Huh, C., & Lee, M. J. (2016). Would an Energy Conservation Nudge in Hotels Encourage Hotel Guests to Conserve? *Cornell Hospitality Quarterly, 57*(2), 172–183. doi:10.1177/1938965515588132

Cotterill, S., & Richardson, L. (2009). Changing the nature of transactions between local state and citizens: an experiment to encourage civic behaviour. *Political Studies Association Conference.*

Danielou, J. (2014). *Smart city and sustainable city : the case of Amsterdam.* Citego. https://www.citego.org/bdf_fiche-document-2429_en.html

Deci, E. L., & Ryan, R. M. (1985). Conceptualizations of intrinsic motivation and self-determination. In *Intrinsic motivation and self-determination in human behavior* (pp. 11–40). Springer.

Deci, E. L., & Ryan, R. M. (2012). Self-Determination Theory. In Handbook of Theories of Social Psychology (Vol. 1, pp. 416–437). SAGE Publications Ltd., https://doi.org/10.4135/9781446249215.n21.

Deloitte, & Insights. (2020). *Deloitte City Mobility Index 2020.* Deloitte.

Ekins, P. (2004). *Environment and human behaviour: a new opportunities programme.* Springer.

Ferrari, L., Cavaliere, A., de Marchi, E., & Banterle, A. (2019). Can nudging improve the environmental impact of food supply chain? A systematic review. *Trends in Food Science & Technology, 91,* 184–192.

Ferron, M., & Massa, P. (2013). Transtheoretical model for designing technologies supporting an active lifestyle. *Proceedings of the Biannual Conference of the Italian Chapter of SIGCHI on - CHItaly '13,* 1–8. doi:10.1145/2499149.2499158

Filimonau, V., & Krivcova, M. (2017). Restaurant menu design and more responsible consumer food choice: An exploratory study of managerial perceptions. *Journal of Cleaner Production, 143,* 516–527. https://doi.org/10.1016/j.jclepro.2016.12.080

Filimonau, V., Lemmer, C., Marshall, D., & Bejjani, G. (2017). 'Nudging' as an architect of more responsible consumer choice in food service provision: The role of restaurant menu design. *Journal of Cleaner Production, 144,* 161–170. https://doi.org/10.1016/j.jclepro.2017.01.010

Fogg, B. (2009). A behavior model for persuasive design. *Proceedings of the 4th International Conference on Persuasive Technology - Persuasive '09, 1.* doi:10.1145/1541948.1541999

Franssens, S., Botchway, E., de Swart, W., & Dewitte, S. (2021). Nudging Commuters to Increase Public Transport Use: A Field Experiment in Rotterdam. *Frontiers in Psychology, 12.* doi:10.3389/fpsyg.2021.633865

Fyhri, A., Karlsen, K., & Sundfør, H. B. (2021). Paint It Red - A Multimethod Study of the Nudging Effect of Coloured Cycle Lanes. *Frontiers in Psychology, 12.* doi:10.3389/fpsyg.2021.662679

Gandy, O. H., & Nemorin, S. (2019). Toward a political economy of nudge: Smart city variations. *Information Communication and Society, 22*(14), 2112–2126. https://doi.org/10.1080/1369118X.2018.1477969

Gatersleben, B., & Appleton, K. M. (2007). Contemplating cycling to work: Attitudes and perceptions in different stages of change. *Transportation Research Part A, Policy and Practice, 41*(4), 302–312. https://doi.org/10.1016/j.tra.2006.09.002

Guthrie, J., Mancino, L., & Lin, C.-T. J. (2015). Nudging Consumers toward Better Food Choices: Policy Approaches to Changing Food Consumption Behaviors. *Psychology and Marketing, 32*(5), 501–511. https://doi.org/10.1002/mar.20795

Hämäläinen, M. (2020). A framework for a Smart City design: digital transformation in the Helsinki Smart City. In *Entrepreneurship and the Community* (pp. 63–86). Springer.

Harris, N., Shealy, T., & Klotz, L. (2017). Choice architecture as a way to encourage a whole systems design perspective for more sustainable infrastructure. In *Sustainability (Switzerland)* (*Vol. 9,* Issue 1). doi:10.3390/su9010054

Jylhä, A., Nurmi, P., Sirén, M., Hemminki, S., & Jacucci, G. (2013). MatkaHupi: a persuasive mobile application for sustainable mobility. *Proceedings of the 2013 ACM Conference on Pervasive and Ubiquitous Computing Adjunct Publication*, (pp. 227–230). ACM. https://doi.org/10.1145/2494091.2494164

Kappel, K., & Grechenig, T. (2009). "Show-Me": water consumption at a glance to promote water conservation in the shower. *Proceedings of the 4th International Conference on Persuasive Technology - Persuasive '09*, 1. ACM. doi:10.1145/1541948.1541984

Kasperbauer, T. J. (2017). The permissibility of nudging for sustainable energy consumption. *Energy Policy*, *111*, 52–57. https://doi.org/10.1016/j.enpol.2017.09.015

Kazhamiakin, R., Marconi, A., Martinelli, A., Pistore, M., & Valetto, G. (2016). A gamification framework for the long-term engagement of smart citizens. *2016 IEEE International Smart Cities Conference (ISC2)*, (pp. 1–7). IEEE.

Klieber, K., Luger-Bazinger, C., Hornung-Prähauser, V., Geser, G., Wieden-Bischof, D., Paraschivoiu, I., Layer-Wagner, T., Möstegl, N., Huemer, F., & Rosan, J. (2020). Nudging sustainable behaviour: Data-based nudges for smart city innovations. *The ISPIM Innovation Conference – Innovating in Times of Crisis*, (pp. 1–18). www.simplicity-project.eu

Kristensson, P., Wästlund, E., & Söderlund, M. (2017). Influencing consumers to choose environment friendly offerings: Evidence from field experiments. *Journal of Business Research*, *76*, 89–97. https://doi.org/10.1016/j.jbusres.2017.03.003

Kuznetsov, S., & Paulos, E. (2010). UpStream: motivating water conservation with low-cost water flow sensing and persuasive displays. *Proceedings of the 28th International Conference on Human Factors in Computing Systems - CHI '10*, 1851. ACM. doi:10.1145/1753326.1753604

Lee, E. J., Choi, H., Han, J., Kim, D. H., Ko, E., & Kim, K. H. (2020). How to "Nudge" your consumers toward sustainable fashion consumption: An fMRI investigation. *Journal of Business Research*, *117*, 642–651. https://doi.org/10.1016/j.jbusres.2019.09.050

Lehner, M., Mont, O., & Heiskanen, E. (2016). Nudging – A promising tool for sustainable consumption behaviour? *Journal of Cleaner Production*, *134*, 166–177. https://doi.org/10.1016/j.jclepro.2015.11.086

Mair, J., & Laing, J. H. (2013). Encouraging pro-environmental behaviour: The role of sustainability-focused events. *Journal of Sustainable Tourism*, *21*(8), 1113–1128. https://doi.org/10.1080/09669582.2012.756494

Marchiori, D. R., Adriaanse, M. A., & de Ridder, D. T. D. (2017). Unresolved questions in nudging research: Putting the psychology back in nudging. *Social and Personality Psychology Compass*, *11*(1), e12297. https://doi.org/10.1111/spc3.12297

Mauro, S., Shinde, S., Arnone, M., Zamith, V. M., de Rosa, G., & Pietroni, D. (2022). *The role of awareness of mobility offer and nudges in increasing sustainable mobility habits of citizens: a case study from the Munich region.* Springer. doi:10.1109/COMPSACS54236.2022.00267

Mayor of London. (2021). *Travel in London. Report 14.* Mayor of London.

Meloni, I., & di Teulada, B. S. (2015). I-Pet Individual Persuasive Eco-travel Technology: A Tool for VTBC Program Implementation. *Transportation Research Procedia, 11*, 422–433. https://doi.org/10.1016/j.trpro.2015.12.035

Momsen, K., & Stoerk, T. (2014). From intention to action: Can nudges help consumers to choose renewable energy? *Energy Policy, 74*(C), 376–382. https://doi.org/10.1016/j.enpol.2014.07.008

Nagode, K., & Manfreda, A. (2022). IT Diffusion in the Society: The Expansion of Smart Cities and Their Impact on the Sustainable Development. *International Working Conference on Transfer and Diffusion of IT*, (pp. 177–187). Springer. https://doi.org/10.1007/978-3-031-17968-6_14

Namazu, M., Zhao, J., & Dowlatabadi, H. (2018). Nudging for responsible carsharing: Using behavioral economics to change transportation behavior. *Transportation, 45*(1), 105–119. https://doi.org/10.1007/s11116-016-9727-1

OICA. (2022a). Estimated worldwide motor vehicle production between 2019 and 2021, by type (in 1,000 units). *Statista.* https://www.statista.com/statistics/1097293/worldwide-motor-vehicle-production-by-type/

OICA. (2022b). Worldwide motor vehicle sales from 2005 to 2021. *Statista.* https://www.statista.com/statistics/265859/vehicle-sales-worldwide/

Oinas-Kukkonen, H., & Harjumaa, M. (2009). Persuasive systems design: Key issues, process model, and system features. *Communications of the Association for Information Systems, 24*(1), 485–500. https://doi.org/10.17705/1cais.02428

Orji, R., & Moffatt, K. (2018). Persuasive technology for health and wellness: State-of-the-art and emerging trends. *Health Informatics Journal, 24*(1), 66–91. https://doi.org/10.1177/1460458216650979

Patel, M. S., Volpp, K. G., & Asch, D. A. (2018). Nudge Units to Improve the Delivery of Health Care. *The New England Journal of Medicine, 378*(3), 214–216. https://doi.org/10.1056/NEJMp1712984

Permana, Y. H., & Sanjaya, M. R. (2022). Nudging Green Preferences: Evidence from a Laboratory Experiment. *Journal of International Commerce. Economic Policy, 13*(02). https://doi.org/10.1142/S1793993322500119

Petersen, S. A., Petersen, I., & Ahcin, P. (2020). Smiling earth—raising awareness among citizens for behaviour change to reduce carbon footprint. *Energies, 13*(22), 5932.

Poelman, H., Dijkstra, L., & Ackermans, L. (2020). *How many people can you reach by public transport, bicycle or on foot in European cities? Measuring urban accessibility for low-carbon modes.* European Commission. doi:https://doi.org/10.2776/021137

Pourhashem, G., Malichova, E., & Kovacikova, T. (2021). The role of participation behavior and information in nudging citizens sustainable mobility behavior: A case study of Bratislava region. *ICETA 2021 - 19th IEEE International Conference on Emerging ELearning Technologies and Applications, Proceedings*, (pp. 300–306). IEEE. doi:10.1109/ICETA54173.2021.9726681

Prochaska, J. O., & Velicer, W. F. (1997). The Transtheoretical Model of Health Behavior Change. *American Journal of Health Promotion*, *12*(1), 38–48. https://doi.org/10.4278/0890-1171-12.1.38

Pucher, J., & Buehler, R. (2016). Safer cycling through improved infrastructure. *American Journal of Public Health*, *106*(12), 2089–2091.

Quigley, M. (2013). Nudging for health: On public policy and designing choice architecture. *Medical Law Review*, *21*(4), 588–621. https://doi.org/10.1093/medlaw/fwt022

Rajanen, D., & Rajanen, M. (2019). Climate change gamification: A literature review. *GamiFIN*, 253–264.

Ranchordás, S. (2020). Nudging citizens through technology in smart cities. *International Review of Law Computers & Technology*, *34*(3), 254–276. https://doi.org/10.1080/13600869.2019.1590928

Rose, G., & Marfurt, H. (2007). Travel behaviour change impacts of a major ride to work day event. *Transportation Research Part A, Policy and Practice*, *41*(4), 351–364. https://doi.org/10.1016/j.tra.2006.10.001

Rote, L. (2017). FutureBuilt is Changing the Way Buildings are Built in Oslo. *Gb&d*. https://gbdmagazine.com/futurebuilt/

Sivasubramaniyam, R. D., Charlton, S. G., & Sargisson, R. J. (2020). Mode choice and mode commitment in commuters. *Travel Behaviour and Society, 19*, 20–32. doi:10.1016/j.tbs.2019.10.007

Statista. (2022). Users of selected segments of the mobility services market worldwide from 2017 to 2025 (in millions). *Statista*. https://www.statista.com/forecasts/1182725/users-mobility-services-worldwide

Sunstein, C. R. (2015). The Ethics of Nudging. *Yale Journal on Regulation*, *32*, 413–450. https://www.cdc.gov/media/releases/2011/pO5

Thaler, R. H., & Sunstein, C. R. (2008). *Nudge: improving decisions about health, wealth and happiness*. Yale University Press.

UIC. (2020). *Number of high-speed rail lines in operation worldwide as of 2020. Statista*. https://www.statista.com/statistics/1126292/high-speed-rail-lines-in-the-world/

United Nations. (2018, May 16). *68% of the world population projected to live in urban areas by 2050*. UN. https://www.un.org/development/desa/en/news/population/2018-revision-of-world-urbanization-prospects.html

Van Lierop, D., & Bahamonde-Birke, F. J. (2021). Commuting to the future: Assessing the relationship between individuals' usage of information and communications technology, personal attitudes, characteristics and mode choice. *Networks and Spatial Economics*. doi:10.1007/s11067-021-09534-9

Vandenbroele, J., Slabbinck, H., van Kerckhove, A., & Vermeir, I. (2021). Mock meat in the butchery: Nudging consumers toward meat substitutes. *Organizational Behavior and Human Decision Processes*, *163*, 105–116. https://doi.org/10.1016/j.obhdp.2019.09.004

Weijers, R. J., de Koning, B. B., & Paas, F. (2021). Nudging in education: From theory towards guidelines for successful implementation. *European Journal of Psychology of Education*, *36*(3), 883–902. https://doi.org/10.1007/s10212-020-00495-0

Witzel, S. (2018). *MaaS in Europe Part 1: Helsinki, Lisbon, Paris*. SkedGo. https://skedgo.com/maas-in-europe-part-1-helsinki-lisbon-paris/

KEY TERMS AND DEFINITIONS

Behavioral Economics: The field that deals with explaining the phenomena of economic agents, especially individuals or households, not always behaving rationally and thus not following the classical economic theory.

Choice Architecture: Design that deals with how different choices are presented to decision makers.

External Motivation: The drive or desire to engage in a particular behavior or activity that is influenced by external factors, such as rewards or punishments. These external factors can be tangible (money, grades, recognition) or intangible (social approval, avoidance of negative consequences).

Internal Motivation: The drive or desire that comes from within an individual to engage in a particular behavior or activity. It is not influenced by external factors such as rewards or punishments, but rather by personal goals, values, and interests.

Nudge: A small change in the environment of the individual decision maker that affects their decision in a predictable way without removing any of the existing choices or changing their economic initiatives.

Sustainability: The concept that aims to prevent the overuse of limited resources and protect the environment.

Chapter 7
Use of Green Bonds to Promote Green Projects

Öykü Yücel

Faculty of Economics and Administrative Sciences, TED University, Turkey

ABSTRACT

With increasing concern in environment and sustainability and rising costs, the need for alternative financing mechanisms has arisen. Especially in developing countries, where financial resources are scarce, it is necessary to come up with new ways of financing options to cover for the upfront investment needs of green projects. Recently green bonds are commonly used to finance green projects. Like conventional bonds, green bonds are fixed income securities, however proceeds of green bonds can only be used in financing or re-financing new or existing green projects that have environmental benefits. In this chapter the author details the concept and types of green bonds, figures on how developed and integrated green bond market is, green bond principles and measurement of objectives, regulatory bodies, investment advantages and risks, investment alternatives, real-life examples as well as suggested greenium (green premium) and concept for investors.

INTRODUCTION

"Green bonds are a type of bond instrument where the proceeds or an equivalent amount will be exclusively applied to finance or re-finance, in part or in full, new and/or existing eligible green projects" (International Capital Market Association [ICMA], 2021, p.3). Green bonds make it possible to finance the shift to a low-carbon economy and spread out the cost of combating climate change across many generations (Flaherty et al., 2017; Monasterolo & Raberto, 2018). Bond instruments are fixed-income securities in the sense that they provide investors the principal amount they invested in an organization or a project, plus fixed interest payments until the maturity date depending on the type of the loan terms. Just like conventional bonds, investors lend their money to the government, and in return green bonds provide investors fixed income of interest and return. Green bonds are attractive to investors for two primary reasons;

DOI: 10.4018/978-1-6684-5996-6.ch007

Copyright © 2023, IGI Global. Copying or distributing in print or electronic forms without written permission of IGI Global is prohibited.

- Investors and society as a whole have become more conscious of the effects that investment choices have on society and the environment, and demand for investment alternatives that provide not only high financial returns but also positive environmental consequences has risen (Imberg et al., 2019).
- Institutional investors choose to include green bonds in their investment portfolios to raise their environmental, social, and governance (ESG) ratings.

This chapter aims to provide an overlook of green bonds used frequently to finance projects with sustainability and environmental benefits. The concept will be explained by focusing on types of green bonds, principles, rules, and regulations set by the International Capital Market Association (ICMA), and external reviewers on green bond markets and pricing.

BACKGROUND

Green bonds offer an alternative financing source for green projects. Environmentally sound initiatives or businesses that consider a green transformation mostly obtain the necessary funds from issuing green bonds (Azhgaliyeva et al., 2020; Banga, 2018). Therefore, green bonds enable large investors such as mutual funds, sovereign wealth funds, insurance companies and pension funds to invest sustainably (Akhtaruzzaman et al., 2022). In 2008, the World Bank issued the first green bond. The Intergovernmental Panel on Climate Change initiated the process in 2007. After the panel, some managers of Swedish pension funds reached out to World Bank wanting to invest in initiatives that assist the environment but unsure of which initiatives were truly green. The group collaborated with the World Bank and Norway's Center for International Climate Research, and the first official green bond was issued in 2008 (National Academies Sciences Engineering Medicine [NASEM], 2021). Currently, corporations, municipalities, public sector organizations, and supranational institutions are the primary green bond issuers (Jiang et al., 2022).

The inaugural edition of the Green Bond Principles (GBP), which is optional guidelines for green bond issuers, was released by the International Capital Market Association (ICMA) in 2014. Since giving false information and greenwashing is a great concern, it is essential to standardize which project metrics should be used to label a project as green, and how the measurement and reporting will be conducted. According to ICMA, green bond issuers should create an annual report that includes a concise summary of the projects to which proceeds from the bonds are going, how much is going there, and what the impact will be. GBP underlines the fact that reporting should be up-to-date, transparent, and informative. To be transparent, issuers are advised to get consultancy from a third party or an internal auditor (ICMA, 2021). All of this information is also advised to be disclosed in the voluntary nonfinancial disclosures attached to the green bond by the issuer organization.

By lowering investor concerns about unethical company practices, addressing climate policy and issues, and promoting transparency in day-to-day corporate operations, green bonds help to promote sustainability in the market (McGlade & Ekins, 2015).

Use of Green Bonds to Promote Green Projects

TYPES OF GREEN BONDS

Based on different issuer profiles, "the main types of green bonds can be listed as sovereign, loan, development bank, non-financial corporate, government-backed entity, asset-backed securities (ABS), local government, and financial corporate green bonds" (Climate Bond Initiative [CBI], 2021, p.10).

A sovereign green bond can be issued by a sovereign government. Countries use sovereign green bond issuance as a signal to global investors to show how committed the countries are to sustainability and the environment. Climate Bonds Initiative (CBI) describes the steps to issue sovereign green bonds as follows; "engaging governmental stakeholders, establishing a green bond framework, identifying eligible green budget items, arranging independent reviews, issuing the green bonds, and monitoring and reporting" (CBI, 2017, p.4). Engaging governmental stakeholders require coordination between different levels of governmental bodies. Establishing a framework for green bonds includes deciding on eligible sectors, eligible accounting, and reporting standards as well as measurement practices. Identifying eligible green budget items requires labeling green project assets such as energy-efficient equipment, certain rights, or patents (CBI, 2017).

A loan green bond is a type of green bond where investment comes from a bank instead of the investment market. Proceeds are anticipated to be invested in initiatives or resources that help the environment.

A development bank green bond is an ordinary green bond issued by a development bank for funding eligible projects and assets. Similar to how local government green bonds are issued by municipalities, financial corporate green bonds are issued by financial corporations, and government-backed entity green bonds are issued by organizations sponsored, chartered, or under the control of the federal governments. Non-financial corporate green bonds are regular green bonds issued by non-financial corporations.

Asset-backed securities (ABS) are green bonds collateralized by one or more green assets such as electric vehicle loans or leases, and solar leases. Proceeds of these bonds are mostly used in refinancing eligible environmentally friendly projects.

GLOBAL GREEN BOND MARKET

A significant milestone of USD 1 trillion in cumulative issuance since 2008 was reached in the global green bond market. According to the CBI's 2021 projection report, annual green bond issuance will surpass USD 522.7 billion in 2021 for the first time, representing a 75% increase over the volume issued in the previous year. As can be seen from Figure 1, cumulative investment for green bonds totals USD 1.6tn. Coming from 80 different countries with Europe region being the leader, the number of issuers in total is raised to 2045. Most green bond transactions occurred in September (USD 86bn). By the end of the year, financial corporations were the biggest issuers.

When it comes to regions, as of 2021, Europe is the leader followed by Asia-Pacific, North America, Supranational, and Latin America. It can be concluded that in 2021, half of the green bond volume (USD 265bn) was issued from Europe only, mostly from financial corporate and sovereign green bonds. In 2021, developed markets issued 73% of the green bond volume, followed by emerging markets with 21%, and supranational issuers with 4%.

143

Figure 1. Annual Green Bond Issuance (CBI, 2021)
Source: CBI, 2021

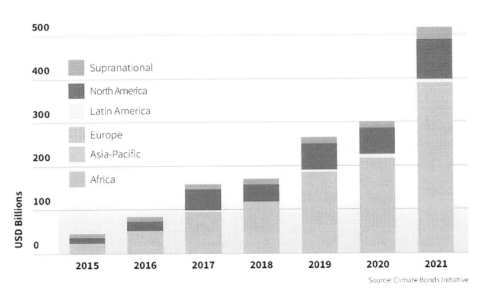

In time issuers of green bonds shifted from advanced economies to emerging markets. In 2014 and 2015 mainly issuers from Europe and the United States were the main players. Starting in 2016 emerging market economies began issuing green bonds. Compared to 2020, emerging markets' contribution increased the most with 17%, which results from increasing volumes of development banks (378%), financial (324%), and nonfinancial corporate (278%) issuers (CBI, 2021). The top five highest-growing emerging market countries since 2016 are China (68.4%), India (5.4%), Chile (4.2%), Brazil (3.1%), and Poland (2.2%).

As can be seen from Figure 2, country-wise, the USA is the leader in 2021. USA increased its green bond volume by 63% from USD 50.3bn to USD 81.9bn. The total cumulative amount is USD 304bn, which, with a total of USD 199 billion, is 50% more than China, the second-largest country to issue green bonds. China also succeeded in tripling its output compared to 2020. Third on the list, Germany increased their volume by 49% compared to 2020 (CBI, 2021).

Local currencies as well as US dollar and Euro currencies are used. Maturities of green bonds are usually around eight years. Both governments and corporate companies can issue green bonds to attract investors and collect funding for green projects.

For the corporation-specific ranking, the most influential top five issuers can be listed as China Three Gorges Corp, Iberdrola, CTP Group, Ardagh Group, and Engie SA.

In 2021, the private sector issued the majority of green bonds; compared to 2020, finance corporation green bonds climbed by 143% and non-financial corporate green bonds by 111%. As can be seen from Figure 3, together, these two issuer categories accounted for 44% of all green bond transactions at the end of 2021. Sovereign green bonds also grew by 111%, and contribute 10% to cumulative volumes. Use of proceeds was mostly used to fund green energy projects, followed by buildings and transport projects making up 81% of total investment in 2021.

Figure 2. Annual Green Bond Issuance by Countries (CBI, 2021)
Source: CBI, 2021

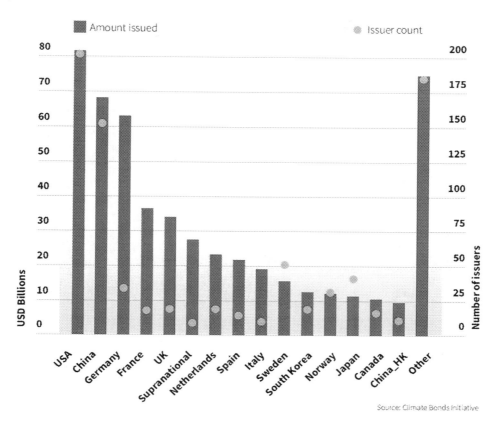

Building projects received the largest assistance from financial corporations (37.5%), while green energy and transportation projects were mostly financed by green bonds issued by non-financial corporate issuers, accounting for 40% and 27% of the total capital, respectively (CBI, 2021).

Projects with favorable ESG risk profiles are financed using green bonds. Companies that consistently issue green bonds show the capital markets that they understand the value of ESG risk management, and as a result, are regarded as desirable companies to invest in. Additionally, it is less likely that these firms will be impacted by future environmental rules (NASEM, 2021).

Green Bond Principles (GBP) and Regulatory Bodies

To avoid greenwashing which is thought to be the biggest concern for green bond market investors (Shishlov et al., 2016) it is essential to develop Green Bond Principles (GBP) that provide a general framework of which green projects are worth investing in. GBP were introduced by the International Capital Market Association (ICMA) in 2014 to facilitate the integration of the green bond market with an emphasis on measurement and reporting standards. GBP are voluntary procedure rules set to improve transparency and encourage integrity in the green bond market. As of June 2021, GBP are updated by ICMA. The use of procee, the mechanism for project appraisal and selection, the administration of proceeds, and reporting are the four essential factors for alignment with the GBP (ICMA, 2021).

Figure 3. Annual Green Bond Issuance by Categories (CBI, 2021)
Source: CBI, 2021

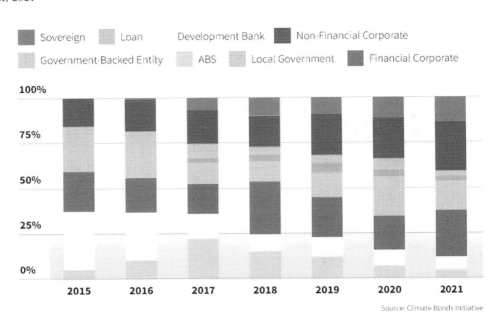

As the cornerstone of the green bond concept "use of proceeds should only be focused on financing or re-financing, in part or in full, new and/or existing eligible green projects. All designated eligible green projects should provide clear environmental benefits, which will be assessed and, where feasible, quantified by the issuer" (ICMA, 2021, p.4). The GBP concentrates on several categories when it comes to deciding if the project is contributing to environmental objectives or not. As of 2021, some of the qualified Green Project categories listed by ICMA include "clean transportation, green buildings, renewable energy, energy efficiency, climate change adaptation, pollution prevention, and control, circular economy adapted products, terrestrial and aquatic biodiversity, environmentally sustainable management of living and sustainable water management" (ICMA, 2021, p.5).

GBP suggests that the project appraisal and selection process should be formed upon transparent communication between the issuers and investors. Issuers should state based on which criterion they decided a certain project is eligible for green bond financing, which environmental objectives are opted to be fulfilled, and, if any, project-related social and environmental risks (ICMA, 2021). Some examples of green project metrics can be given as; reduction of annual greenhouse gas emissions, reduction of air pollutants (sulfur oxide, carbon monoxide, and nitrogen oxides), number of clean vehicles deployed, and estimated reduction in fossil fuel use.

Issuers must confirm how they will guarantee that the green bond revenues will only be applied to the designated project as part of the management of proceeds process. GBP demands that "the net proceeds of the green bond, or an amount equal to these net proceeds, should be credited to a sub-account, moved to a sub-portfolio or otherwise tracked by the issuer in an appropriate manner, and attested to by the issuer in a formal internal process linked to the issuer's lending and investment operations for eligible green projects" (ICMA, 2021, p.6). The ICMA advises working with a third party or external auditor to create an annual report that includes the projects to which proceeds from green bonds have

Use of Green Bonds to Promote Green Projects

been allocated, gives a short description of each project, counts the amounts dispersed, and calculates the impact of each project (ICMA, 2021). According to GBP, reporting should be up-to-date, transparent, and informative. All of these issues above can be disclosed in the voluntary nonfinancial disclosures attached to the issued green bond by the issuer organization.

Transparency is also essential when it comes to establishing green bond ratings rated by Moody's Green Bond Assessments, Standard & Poor's Green Evaluations, and indexes such as the Bloomberg Barclays MSCI Green Bond Index. Investors that wish to invest in green projects also keep track of these ratings and interpret them as how well the project is being managed and how well the proceeds have been used for financing as well as the possible impact the project has on the environment.

To scale up the green bond issuance, countries are advised to promote transparency, availability of information and know-how, increased use of green assets, providing political and financial stability as well as increased liquidity and decreased transaction costs (Amundi Asset Management & International Finance Corporation, 2021).

External Reviewers and Second-Party Opinions

GBP urges green bond issuers to seek outside reviewers and second-party viewpoints while putting together the yearly report to ensure transparency on the usage and management of proceeds. The ICMA advises working with a third party or external auditor to create an annual report that includes the projects to which proceeds from green bonds have been allocated, gives a short description of each project, counts the amounts dispersed, and calculates the impact of each project (ICMA, 2021). Since these external reviews are voluntary, issuers decide whether to get consultancy or not. However, these external reviews signal to the investors and the market that certain issuer is transparent and avoids greenwashing practices.

"Moody's Green Bond Assessments provides an evaluation of an issuer's approach to managing, administering, allocating proceeds to, and reporting on environmental projects financed with green bond proceeds" (Moody's Investors Service [Moody's], 2018, p.1). Moody's considers five categories each with unique weights to decide whether the green bond is worth investing in or not. 40% weight is given to how well the use of proceeds is channeled to environmental objectives, 20% weight is given to adequacy and transparency of reporting, 15% weight is given to organization and governance, 15% weight is given to the management of proceeds and auditing, and 10% weight is given to disclosure on the use of proceeds if an external report is generated or not. These assessments result in a green bond's rating, which ranges from poor (GB5) to exceptional (GB1) (Moody's, 2018).

Standard & Poor's Green Evaluations evaluate whether a green bond or any other particular financial instrument has an environmental impact throughout its life. The view takes into account the transaction's governance, transparency, and relative net environmental impact of the supported technology. The study assigns a score to the financial transaction between zero and a hundred. A higher rating denotes a greater overall net environmental impact over the funded assets' lifetime (Standard & Poor's Global, 2017).

Found in 2014, Bloomberg Barclays MSCI Green Bond Index evaluates whether a green bond can actually be classified as green based on four categories identical to the GBP framework which are listed in the previous section. At least one of the six environmental categories must be considered for the use of funding which includes climate adaptation, green buildings, pollution prevention and control, energy efficiency, alternative energy, and sustainable water. Bonds are deemed to be eligible if the issuer makes it apparent in the bond prospectus or any supporting materials, such as the green bond supplement, website, or investor presentation, how exactly they identified projects or investments that qualify the criteria.

One-year follow-up reporting and or any other valid auditing process to keep track of the management of proceeds are also a must (Bloomberg & Barclays, 2021). Prospective investors view the green bonds featured in the MSCI Green Bond Index as a trustworthy green bond investment opportunity.

Bonds designated as green by CBI are included in the Solactive Green Bond Index. Included green bonds must have a six-month minimum maturity date and an outstanding balance of at least USD 100 million. A total return index in USD is used to calculate the index (Solactive, 2021). Their green criterion matches with CBI's climate bonds taxonomy (Organisation for Economic Co-operation and Development [OECD], 2016). Climate bonds taxonomy identifies the assets and projects needed to be invested in to provide zero carbon emissions. As of 2021, "the main sectors are listed as energy, transport, water, buildings, land use and marine resources, industry, waste and pollution control, and information and communications technology" (CBI, 2021, p.11).

Grade agencies are urged to change their methods so that a green bond cannot receive a high grade only based on solid governance, proceeds management, and reporting practices if the bond is not supporting actual green initiatives (OECD, 2016).

Other than ICMA, there are also other entities to review green projects externally. Independent research institutions such as the Center for International Climate Research (CICERO), ISS-Oekom, Kestrel Verifiers, and Sustainalytics serve as external reviewers and provide second-party opinions. They function as an impartial third party between fundraisers and investors. They analyze how green bonds align with GBPs or rate greenness using their own unique standards and techniques (Dorfleitner et al., 2021).

CICERO is a center for climate research. They assess the methodology used by the green bond issuer to choose projects and make investments. The primary sections of a second-party opinion published by CICERO define and assess the issuer's green bond framework, standards, and procedures for operations including climate change. A SWOT analysis of the green bond framework is included in the report's assessment section (Dorfleitner et al., 2021). Three levels of assessment, or "shades of green," are provided by CICERO after evaluations, indicating the bond's commitment to a long-term vision for an environmentally benign, low-carbon society (Ehlers & Packer, 2017). Light green is given to initiatives that help the environment but don't have a long-term plan, like efficiency investments in fossil fuel technologies. Projects that support the environment and have a sort of mid-term outlook, such as hybrid buses, are given medium green color. Projects that fit within a vision of a low-carbon future over the long term, such as renewable energy infrastructure projects, are given the dark green color specification (CICERO, 2021).

ISS-oekom provides second-party opinion ratings on the ESG performance of projects. The environmental, social, and governance rating dimensions are weighted in accordance with an industry classification to determine the relevance of sectors. Higher relevance stands for higher performance on the rating scale. In addition, four to five industry-specific key issues are defined for every sector and are given a cumulated weighting. The rating scale ranges from D- being the worst to A+ being the best (ISS-oekom, 2021).

Kestrel Verifiers accredited by the Climate Bonds Initiative (CBI), provides independent external review on green bonds. Kestrel Verifiers state that they follow ICMA's five fundamental principles to maintain a basis for ethical and professional standards which can be listed as honesty, objectivity, professionalism, care, discretion, and appropriate conduct (Kestrel Verifiers, 2022).

Sustainalytics is a Morningstar company that evaluates ESG risks of financial securities and how they might affect the long-term performance of these securities including green bonds. ESG risk ratings are determined by taking into account both the company's exposure to ESG risks specific to its industry and

Use of Green Bonds to Promote Green Projects

the effectiveness with which it manages such risks. Sustainalytics ESG Risk Ratings places companies into five risk categories ranging from severe (being the riskiest) to negligible (being the safest). Exposure to ESG risk, how well it is managed, and how much risk is unmanaged; whether the unmanaged risk may be handled with alternative activities; as a result, the management gap concepts are taken into consideration when the rating is given (Sustainalytics, 2020).

Even though second-party opinions provide validity and comfort to investors, a lack of standardization among measures and reports increases the transaction cost of investors. Thus, second-party reviews are highly recommended to increase consistency and provide more detailed disclosures (OECD, 2016).

The Cost of Issuing Green Bonds

The cost of issuing a green bond does not vary greatly from the cost of issuing a traditional bond. However, some initial investment for developing and identifying the issuer organization's and project's sustainability goals and strategies is necessary. Some examples of the initial cost items can be given as costs related to internal decision-making, learning required to identify projects as green or not, accounting system adjustments, and reporting. There would be initial additional charges related to the verification process in the case of third-party external consultation (NASEM, 2021). Issuers may attach voluntary nonfinancial disclosures to the green bonds indicating how the proceeds will be used and according to which environmental criterion the project is decided to be worth funding. Thus, investors would be more informed, and the process would be more transparent. This would also have a positive impact on external second-party reviews and credit ratings.

In addition, from an economic perspective, green bonds are essential instruments to lower externalities related to adverse environmental decisions. An externality is a cost that interferes with the economic effectiveness of a market equilibrium which has an impact on people who are not directly involved in the production or consumption of a good or service. Conventional transportation means causes many negative externalities, notably air pollution, greenhouse gases, water pollution, and other impacts on ecosystems, especially with the use of fossil fuels (Santos et al., 2010). The promotion of green projects through green bonds such as infrastructure improvements for electrical buses would indirectly also lower these external costs in the long run for the economy.

The Investment Advantages and Risks

The issuance of green bonds offers a different source of funding for environmentally friendly projects. Without green bonds, bank loans are typically used to support green initiatives, which results in a maturity mismatch. Banks are willing to offer loans with maturities that are relatively shorter than those of green project maturities because there are no instruments for hedging duration risks. Finding a new loan to refinance is therefore required in order to move forward with the project. This issue of re-financing sources would be resolved by using green bonds with longer maturities (OECD, 2016).

Potential investors are more inclined to select green bond issuers as investments since projects with favorable ESG risk profiles are financed using green bonds. Thus, if green bond issuer organizations follow regulations set by ICMA; they will enhance their reputation for being sustainable and environmentally responsible. Additionally, it is less likely that these firms will be impacted by future environmental rules (NASEM, 2021).

From a financial standpoint, green property bonds and municipal bonds in some nations, like the USA, include benefits including tax breaks, interest subsidies, and credit guarantees that would also reduce the required funding costs. Governments can encourage the greening of formerly brown sectors with the help of these policies. In other words, by supporting the green bond issuance of organizations governments can back up their fiscal policies for carbon pricing, waste reduction and recycling targets, greenhouse gas reductions, etc. (OECD, 2016).

On the investor's side, both individual and institutional investors are becoming more conscious of the social and environmental effects of investment choices, and they are demanding investment alternatives that offer not only strong financial returns but also beneficial environmental effects (Imberg et al., 2019). In addition, investing in environmentally responsible sustainability projects would help institutional investors to increase their ESG ratings and reduce their risks through portfolio diversification. Diversification is a strategy to minimize portfolio risk by investing in different financial instruments. A recent study from China examines the benefits of green bonds and traditional bonds on diversification using various asset allocation schemes in various market scenarios. The key findings demonstrate that a portfolio of green bonds has a better risk-return profile than a portfolio of conventional bonds for the majority of asset allocation techniques (Han et al., 2020). Another recent study that focused on the US and European markets discovered a similar trend; risk-adjusted returns for portfolios with green bonds outperformed those for portfolios with conventional bonds on average in both markets. Green bond advantages frequently include higher returns and lower volatility (Han et al., 2022).

Regarding the financial return, the idea of "greenium," which is discussed in the following section, contends that green bonds are more expensive than traditional bonds, which pay investors a negative premium. This negative yield is thought to arise from increasing awareness of environmental issues which increases demand and thus supply fell short of the demand in the market (E. Agliardi & R. Agliardi, 2021). On the issuers' side, greenium suggests that issuers of green bonds can gather funding at lower interest rates compared to conventional bonds since potential investors' primary concern is not the rate of return but supporting green projects.

Just like traditional bonds, green bonds also have a default risk of the issuer which stands for the case where the issuer can't make the investors promised coupon payments. However, greenwashing is thought to be the biggest concern for the green bond market, not the default risk (Shishlov et al., 2016). Greenwashing is defined as "the act of disseminating disinformation to consumers regarding the environmental practices of a company or the environmental benefits of a product or service" (Baum, 2012, p.2). If the voluntary disclosures provided with the green bond exaggerate the environmental impact or if the benefit stated on the disclosure is incorrect then the issuer organization would be accused of greenwashing which can harm their reputation and credibility. Close monitoring of bond proceeds, compliance with GBP standards, transparent, and timely communication with the investors would help mitigate this risk (NASEM, 2021). In addition, yearly external reviews can also help diminish the risk.

If the issuer organization can't explain the environmental benefits of the funded project clearly this may be considered an attempt to greenwash. In this case, it might be beneficial to search for alternative investment methods. From the issuer organization's perspective, if the funds needed for the project are relatively small compared to the external review costs and the initial issuance costs of the green bond, then again searching for alternative financing methods might be better suited in terms of cost and benefit perspective. An example could be given as Hong Kong airport authorities issuing USD 1bn green bonds to finance a third airport runway. The opponents immediately started a debate stating building a new runway would not help reduce GHG emissions (International Financing Review, 2022).

Use of Green Bonds to Promote Green Projects

A sector-based analysis conducted for the period 2012-2020 by Baldi and Pandimiglio (2022) shows that the industrial sector has a larger risk of greenwashing than the services sector. The finance industry is where greenwashing is most noticeable overall, though. Compared to local governments, multinational or sovereign issuers can more easily pursue greenwashing methods when public sector-like governments issue green bonds (Baldi & Pandimiglio, 2022).

Greenium (Green Premium) Concept

The pricing of green bonds and so-called green premium is also a debated concept. "A green bond premium is defined as the difference between the yield of a green bond and a comparable conventional bond" (Dorfleitner et al., 2021, p.797).

Greenium suggests that green bonds are more expensively priced than traditional bonds, which provide investors a negative yield premium. This negative yield is thought to arise from increasing awareness of environmental issues which increases demand and thus supply fell short of the demand in the market (E. Agliardi & R. Agliardi, 2021). For the issuers' side, greenium suggests that issuers of green bonds can gather funding at lower interest rates compared to conventional bonds since potential investors' primary concern is not the rate of return but supporting green projects.

Like any financial asset, the price of the green bond is calculated by adding the present value of future cash flows (interest payments) related. Some studies examine the factors that affect the price of green bonds in the literature. Basic bond characteristics like the credit rating and issuer type have an impact on the green bond premium, as demonstrated by Hachenberg and Schiereck (2018) as well as Zerbib (2019). Along with green credentials (Baker et al., 2018; Bachelet et al., 2019; Li et al., 2019), liquidity is discovered to be a crucial component (Wulandari et al., 2018; Zerbib, 2019). Therefore, for green bond issuer organizations it is essential to prepare voluntary nonfinancial disclosures indicating how the proceeds will be used and according to which environmental criterion the project is decided to be worth funding. Consequently, this would create a positive impact on external second-party reviews and credit ratings.

In the literature, there is evidence for both cases and still, no consensus has been reached. Baker et al. (2018), Nanayakkara and Colombage (2018), Zerbib (2019) found evidence for the green premium that shows yields for green bonds are below yields paid by equivalent (in terms of maturity, issuer, liquidity, etc.) conventional bonds. A study conducted by Amundi Asset Management (2021) over the years 2016-2020 shows that on average green bonds have negative premiums. In other words, investors of green bonds earned less interest compared to similar conventional bond investors. For the issuer's side, this finding indicates that issuers of green bonds were able to gather funding at lower interest rates compared to conventional bonds.

The study by Amundi contrasts the yields of a benchmark conventional bond index (the Bloomberg Barclays Global Aggregate Bond Index) with those of the green index (Bloomberg Barclays MSCI Global Green Bond Index). To evaluate the performance of both portfolios, the benchmark is weighted to reflect the sector, credit grade, currency, and maturity characteristics of the green index (Amundi, 2021). The green premium is said to have a mean value of -4.7 basis points and a maximum value of -2.5 basis points. The first few weeks of the COVID-19 crisis saw the lowest premium, at -10.5 basis points (Amundi, 2021).

151

Figure 4. Annual Green Bond Premium (Amundi Asset Management, 2021)
Source: Amundi Asset Management, 2021

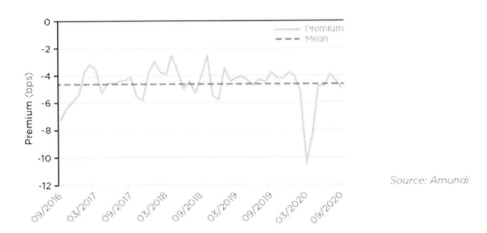

Hachenberg and Schiereck (2018), Karpf and Mandel (2017), Larcker and Watts (2020) discovered no discernible variation in yields between comparable conventional and green bonds. Östlund (2015) and Bachelat et al. (2019) found positive premiums for green bond investors which indicated green bonds bring higher yields than equivalent conventional bonds. In these studies, green bonds are compared with conventional bonds with similar issuing volume, coupon interest, maturity date, currency, rating, and coupon type (Bachelat et al., 2019). Baldi and Pandimiglio (2022) showed that the perceived greenwashing image of the issuer is also contributing to the yield expectations of investors. According to their research, investors are willing to accept lower returns in exchange for green initiatives that they believe will truly improve society's sustainability and the environment. On the contrary, when investors think a project is more likely to be subject to issuers' greenwashing, they frequently demand a greater premium as a kind of compensation (Baldi & Pandimiglio, 2022).

Alternative Investment Methods to Green Projects

Especially in developing countries, where financial resources are scarce, it is necessary to come up with new ways of financing options to cover the upfront investment needed for green projects. In such developing countries, revenue from their small-scale systems and other sources may not be sufficient to support the ongoing maintenance and operating costs of green initiatives. These high expenses and limited revenue generation causes an "underfunding trap" (World Bank Group, 2016, p.1). Therefore, in addition to conventional financing methods governments are seeking alternative ways to finance their green projects. Other than green bonds, crowdfunding, social impact investing, sustainability bonds, green funds from banks, and international grants are mostly used.

Crowdfunding and Social Impact Investing

Crowdfunding is raising funds from stakeholders to finance a project. Donation-based crowdfunding, passive investment crowdfunding, and active investment crowdfunding are the three basic types of crowdfunding discussed in the literature. In the donation-based model, investors make donations to the initiative without anticipating a payout. In the passive investment version, investors receive some kind of reward as a result of their contribution. This reward can be in form of a discount, honorary recognition, or a free sample. In the active investment version, investors get to have a chance to participate in the prototype, design, etc. of the project like a shareholder (Hörisch, 2015).

Usually, private companies or startups chose this kind of financing using online platforms. Modern crowdfunding initiatives started in 2003 in the US with the launch of the platform ArtistShare, followed by UK-based Zopa (2005), the US-based lending platform Lending Club (2006), the US-based Indiegogo (2008), the US-based Kickstarter (2009), and Finnish based Invesdor (2012).

The study by Hong, et al. (2019) shows that crowdfunding can also be an effective fundraising alternative for governments especially if the project is about sustainability and welfare of the society as a whole. In Korea, Crowdfunding Law was accepted in 2015, and the government started to raise money for public projects using Wadiz online platform. In this case, government primarily determines and announces areas for improvement. Then they request solutions from private sector organizations like NPOs. The government then evaluates crowdfunding submissions made by NPOs and individuals and chooses the most viable initiatives. Finally, feasible projects are published on the crowdfunding platform to attract investors (Hong et al., 2019). In their study Hong et al. (2019) finds that the success rate of crowdfunding roughly increased by 64% when there is government help.

Social impact investment is the use of money to generate both financial and social benefits. It serves as a tool to help nonprofits obtain the right funding and increase their ability to make a difference (Maduro et al., 2018). Social impact investing often differs from more traditional types of investment because it offers broader repayment flexibility, lower interest rates, and the acceptance of higher risk than commercial lenders would typically contemplate (European Parliament, 2014). Social change (impact) aimed at the project must be reliably measurable and monitored. With their limited financial budgets, governments may find social issues harder to address. Combining both financial and social outcomes, impact investing helps governments to raise investment for many projects.

Social impact bonds are the main source of funding for social impact investments. "Bond-issuing organizations or government raises funds from private-sector investors, charities, or foundations. These funds are distributed to service providers to cover their operating costs. If the measurable outcomes agreed upfront are achieved, the government or the commissioner proceeds with payments to the bond-issuing organization or the investors" (OECD, 2016, p.4). If the desired social impact or outcome is not received investors won't get any return back. Therefore unlike green bonds, default risk is higher. Also, unlike green bonds, there is a service provider intermediary.

Financial-first investors and impact-first investors are the two primary categories of investors prepared to take part in social impact investments. Financial first investors are typically institutional investors who anticipate enough financial returns for social impact projects that are similar to mainstream investments after taking into account sufficient risk. Instead, impact-first investors are willing to accept more risk or lower financial returns in order to accomplish social goals (Australian Government Discussion Paper, 2017).

Even though it has many benefits there are some obstacles in implementing social impact investing for governments. For the supply side, higher risks and transaction costs associated with the investment may cause low attractiveness for private investors. For the demand side, the lack of social enterprises or their unwillingness to pay social service providers creates an obstacle. However, the most important problem is the lack of a coherent standardized approach to impact measurement and the lack of guidance (Mackevičiūtė et al., 2020).

Sustainability Bonds, SDG Bonds, and Blue Bonds

Different types of bonds can also be used as alternative finance mechanisms. "Sustainability bonds are fixed-income securities where the proceeds or an equivalent amount will be exclusively applied to finance or re-finance, in part or in full, to a combination of new and/or existing eligible green and social projects" (ICMA, 2021, p.4). Sustainability bonds are also regulated by the Green Bond Principles (GBP), which were developed by ICMA. Municipalities, corporations, and government entities can all issue sustainability bonds.

SDG Bonds are fixed-income instruments whose proceeds are intended to finance initiatives that have an impact on the sustainable development goals of the United Nations (SDGs). There are presently 17 SDGs, which address issues including gender equality, a lack of access to quality education, poverty, a lack of access to clean water and sanitation, and sustainable cities and communities (United Nations [UN], 2022).

Blue Bonds are fixed-income instruments, the revenues of which are used to fund initiatives supporting the preservation of clean water and the ocean (NASEM, 2021).

Green Funds from Banks

Financial institutions, particularly banks, have a critical role to play in the process of decarbonizing economies. For green investors, banks offer products ranging from green mortgages and eco-loans to investment and pension funds linked to sustainable investments. Eco-loans support investments in energy-efficient materials and equipment such as the purchase of electric vehicles. A mortgage designed specifically for green assets is known as a green mortgage. To encourage the borrower to either buy a green building or modify an existing one to be more environmentally friendly, the bank would provide the borrower either a reduced interest rate or a higher loan amount.

Grants from International Organizations and Partnerships

National and international organizations, private organizations (such commercial banks), and foreign sources can all offer loans and grants to fund green initiatives. Clean technology fund and global environment facility funds are also available internationally. Grants frequently don't need to be paid back in the future, but they do include requirements that must be met, such as a set amount of local government or private sector involvement. Financial assistance from funding organizations lends legitimacy to a project and may draw in further sources of support (World Bank Group, 2016).

For green transportation projects, public-private partnerships are also considered as a financing alternative. Through a binding contract, public-private partnerships (PPPs) enable the government to access resources from the private sector. In this manner, the funding for a project is assured over its whole lifecycle starting from construction. Private partners get to use their expertise in a large-scale project guaranteed by the government, and in some contracts operate the new facility. The government on the other hand gets the funding needed without harming taxpayers. Long-term funding for the project comes

Use of Green Bonds to Promote Green Projects

from tickets and tolls paid by the general public, but short-term funding for its development comes from the corporate sector (World Bank Group, 2016).

Some Real-life Project Based Examples

Many governments and private organizations are issuing green bonds to finance green projects or assets. Some successful real-life examples from different countries located in Europe, North America, and Asia are shown below to illustrate the scope of funded projects in both emerging and developed markets, as well as the different investment amounts raised by green bond issuance. As these examples show, governments mostly issued green bonds to finance or refinance green projects categorized under renewable energy, green transportation, and smart city infrastructure.

Cases from Asia

China, Ganjiang New Area of Jiangxi Province issued its first municipal green bond in 2019, with a total of RMB 300m with a maturity of 30 years. In Rulehu's new town, an intelligent utility tunnel project called the Xingye Avenue Project is being built with some of the proceeds, while other portions of the proceeds are spent on smart utility pipelines overseen by the city government (Lin & Hong, 2022).

In order to fund the Rampur Hydropower Project in India, which planned to supply the energy grid in northern India with low-carbon hydroelectric power, the World Bank issued green bonds. Currently, it almost prevents 1.4 million tons of GHG emissions (Segal, 2022).

Moscow issued green bonds to finance an urban infrastructure improvement that aims to reduce greenhouse emissions of pollutants. With the funding from green bonds, a new metro line with more than 43 km of length and 18 new stations will be constructed (Intelligent Transport, 2021).

In 2021, the National Environment Agency of Singapore released green bonds to finance the Tuas Nexus Integrated Waste Management Facility which is one of the sustainable infrastructure development projects. In addition, Housing & Development Board also issued green bonds in 2021. The proceeds for this will be used to fund green building projects (Singapore Ministry of Finance, 2022).

In 2013, the Korea Export-Import Bank (KEXIM) of South Korea issued its first green bond for a total of USD 500 million. Renewable energy projects, water projects, energy-efficient lighting, and initiatives associated with the UN Clean Development Mechanism are all funded using the money raised. Hyundai Capital Services issued green bonds worth USD 500 million in 2016 to support the leasing of hybrid and electric automobiles (CBI, 2018).

Cases From Europe

French private company Électricité De France (EDF) issued EUR 1.4b worth of green bonds in 2013, followed by Engie EUR 2.5 b in 2014. Both companies stated to use the proceeds in the renewable energy sector and pledged not to develop new projects using fossil fuels (OECD, 2016).

Germany issued 10-year federal green bonds in 2020, worth EUR 6.5b, as well as 5-year federal green bonds in 2020 worth EUR 5b. The proceeds funded green projects that aim to increase rail track speed and capacity for public transport, reduce GHG emissions from ships, improve bicycle lanes, build a renewable power plant in India, and provide loans and grants to developing countries with particularly transformational projects for low-emission (The Federal Republic of Germany, 2021).

155

The Netherlands issued green bonds in 2019, and as of February 2021, they had a total outstanding value of USD 12.13 billion. The majority of the money raised will go toward paying for the government's Delta Plan, a scheme for managing floodplains. This mechanism will control both the distribution of freshwater and the nation's resistance to rising sea levels. The remaining funds will be used to fund and re-fund government subsidies for offshore wind development, solar energy development, and investments in the passenger rail network (CBI, 2022).

In 2021, Spain issued its first green bond, which had a EUR 5 billion face value and a 20-year maturity. The majority of the earnings will be utilized to fund clean transportation projects (NN Investment Partners, 2021).

Swiss Prime Site AG issued green bonds worth CHF 300 million to finance environmentally friendly real estate initiatives. The maturity date of the bonds is 2029, and they are externally reviewed by second-party reviewers (Standard & Poor's Global, 2020).

In 2021, the UK issued its first package of GBP 10 billion in green bonds. According to the UK government, the funds will be used to support projects promoting adaptation to climate change, energy-efficient living, renewable energy, clean transportation, pollution prevention and management, and conservation of living resources (HM Treasury and UK Debt Management Office, 2021).

Cases From North America

Canada's province of Ontario issued green bonds worth USD 80 million to fund sustainable transportation and eco-friendly infrastructure projects across the province (Ontario Newsroom, 2017).

The state of Los Angeles metro issued two US-approved climate bonds to encourage the creation and construction of electrified light and heavy rail transit networks. Both the first batch, which was released in 2017 for USD 471 million, and the second, which was released in 2019, both adhered to the CBI's green bond framework (NASEM, 2021).

DISCUSSION

The rapid transaction towards green economies and the need for new environmentally friendly smart city infrastructures cause the governments to seek funds to invest in green projects. As an alternative financing source allocated to only green projects, the green bond market has been evolving since 2008 globally. By integrating green bonds into their investment portfolios, institutional investors can enhance their environmental, social, and governance (ESG) ratings. Green bonds are issued by businesses, municipalities, public sector organizations, and supranational agencies. By investing in green bonds, institutional investors can also diversify their portfolio risks.

International Capital Market Association (ICMA) released the first edition of the voluntary Green Bond Principles (GBP) in 2014. GBP is a guideline both for issuers and investors since it is crucial to specify which project metrics should be used to classify a project as green, as well as how the measurement and reporting will be carried out. ICMA advises issuers of green bonds to submit an annual report with a brief synopsis of the projects, and an analysis of the effects of those initiatives.

As of 2021, Europe has the highest green bond issuance volume, followed by Asia-Pacific, North America, Supranational, and Latin America. In 2021, developed markets issued 73% of the total of green bonds, followed by emerging markets with 21%, and supranational issuers with 4%. Green bonds were mostly used to fund green energy projects, followed by buildings and transport projects making up 81% of total investment in 2021.

"A green bond premium is defined as the difference between the yield of a green bond and a comparable conventional bond" (Dorfleitner et al., 2021, p.797). Greenium concept states that the price of green bonds is greater than the price of conventional bonds, which gives investors a negative return on investment. This negative yield is thought to arise from increasing awareness of environmental issues which increases demand and thus supply fell short of the demand in the market (E. Agliardi & R. Agliardi, 2021). For the issuers' side, greenium suggests that issuers of green bonds can gather funding at lower interest rates compared to conventional bonds since potential investors' primary concern is not the rate of return but supporting green projects.

The main criticism for the use of green bonds derives from which projects should be considered green. The broad definition of "green" can allow organizations to take advantage of environmentally concerned investors. An organization can issue green bonds to fund a project that supports sustainability such as the installment of renewable energy panels; however, that particular organization might harm the environment by adopting manufacturing practices that increase the level of greenhouse gas emissions. For instance, to support wind energy projects in Europe, green bonds worth $840 million were issued by the company that runs China's Three Gorges Dam. These bonds initially appeared to be a responsible way to raise money for climate-conscious initiatives. However, the Three Gorges Dam has frequently come under fire for contaminating the surrounding waterways and damaging the ecosystem. Repsol, an oil and gas firm with headquarters in Madrid, issued green bonds to fund the improvement of its oil refineries. These initiatives, despite theoretically still aiming for energy efficiency, do not considerably improve the environment, despite what issuers frequently say (Rajwanshi, 2019). Investors purchased green bonds while ignoring any potential deeper environmental effects.

Solutions and Recommendations

The criticism toward green bonds mostly arises from the broad definition of green and the lack of proper "green" indicators. To narrow the definition of "green" and avoid greenwashing, it is essential to develop and extend the application of Green Bond Principles (GBP) introduced by ICMA. Governmental bodies, regulators, market groups, financial institutions, development agencies, rating agencies, and second-opinion providers should all work to raise public awareness of GBP and the need for proper disclosure (OECD, 2016). Since each country has its own local rules, regulations, and economic conditions, custom-made local rules for green bond markets may be beneficial for some countries (such as having tax benefits or not, etc.). In these cases, international organizations such as ICMA and CBI may provide technical support for creating regional green bond regulations (OECD, 2016). In order to achieve uniformity in the concept of "green," auditing, and reporting processes, it would also be beneficial to encourage international collaboration between governments and private sector entities. Some of the green indicators developed to measure whether a project is green or not can be listed as the decline of GHG emissions, increased number of clean vehicles, annual renewable energy generation, reduction of air pollutants, etc. (ICMA, 2021). Correct measurement of green indicators is as essential as developing them. Organizations should provide possible measures to evaluate how green their fundraising project is.

Green bond issuer organizations should be asked to provide additional information on their disclosures. The general scope of their other projects, their ESG ratings, and their sustainable green practices should be clearly stated. In this case, a potential investor can keep track of the organization's environmental policies and won't be misguided by the promised outcomes of one project.

Investors that wish to invest in green projects keep track of green bond ratings prepared by second-party reviewers and interpret them as how well the project is being managed and how well the proceeds have been used for financing as well as the possible impact the project has on the environment. Thus, proper management of these ratings is a must to guide investors on the right path. Even though second-party opinions provide validity and comfort to investors, a lack of standardization among measures and reports increases the transaction cost of investors. Thus, second-party reviews are highly recommended to increase consistency and provide more detailed disclosures (OECD, 2016).

Although the cost of issuing a green bond is not significantly more than the price of issuing a conventional bond, some initial investment for developing and identifying the issuer organization's and project's sustainability goals and strategies is necessary such as costs related to internal decision-making, learning required to identify projects as green or not, accounting system adjustments, and reporting. There would be initial additional charges related to the verification process in the case of third-party external consultation to ascertain the project's green benefits (NASEM, 2021). Establishing standardization of methodologies may help reduce the costs of green bond issuance and reporting costs. Therefore, it is recommended that international organizations, governments, and non-governmental groups subsidize the creation and distribution of standardized GBPs (OECD, 2016)

FUTURE RESEARCH DIRECTIONS

The green bond market is still very new and growing, thus future research can contribute to the integration and standardization of regulations applied by countries. Ideas for future research include but are not limited to integrated analysis of challenges faced by developed and developing countries while preparing green bond market framework and standards, quantitative comparison of the advantages of taxable versus tax-exempt green bond issuances, cost-benefit analysis of obtaining second-party opinions and external reviews before green bond issuance, and analysis of green premium concept separately in developed and developing countries.

In addition, the interaction between the stock market and the green bonds, supply-side analysis of green bonds, relations between the bond issuer and investor characteristics, green bond indexes, and green bond index making by using artificial intelligence and deep learning models can be studied.

CONCLUSION

With global environmental and sustainability consciousness growing, especially in developing nations with limited financial resources, it is essential to establish new financing strategies to meet the initial investment requirements of green initiatives. This chapter discusses types of green bonds, figures on how developed and integrated the green bond market is, green bond principles and measurement of objectives, regulatory bodies, investment advantages and risks, alternative investment options as well as suggested greenium (green premium) concept for investors. It can be concluded that when provided with necessary standardized rules and regulations, green bond investments are viable options to fund green projects and assets operated both globally and locally.

REFERENCES

Agliardi, E., & Agliardi, R. (2021). Corporate green bonds: Understanding the greenium in a two-factor structural model. *Environmental and Resource Economics, 80*(2), 257–278. doi:10.100710640-021-00585-7 PMID:34366567

Akhtaruzzaman, M., Banerjee, A. K., Ghardallou, W., & Umar, Z. (2022). Is greenness an optimal hedge for sectoral stock indices. *Economic Modelling, 117*, 106030. doi:10.1016/j.econmod.2022.106030

Amundi Asset Management & International Finance Corporation. (2021). *Emerging market green bonds report 2020.* Amundi. https://research-center.amundi.com/article/emerging-market-green-bonds-report-2020

Australian Government. (2017). Social impact investing discussion paper. Commonwealth of Australia.

Azhgaliyeva, D., Liu, Y., & Liddle, B. (2020). An empirical analysis of energy intensity and the role of policy instruments. *Energy Policy, 145*, 111773. doi:10.1016/j.enpol.2020.111773

Bachelet, M. J., Becchetti, L., & Manfredonia, S. (2019). The green bonds premium puzzle: The role of issuer characteristics and third-party verification. *Sustainability, 11*(4), 1098. doi:10.3390u11041098

Baker, M., Bergstresser, D., Serafeim, G., & Wurgler, J. (2018). *Financing the Response to Climate Change: The Pricing and Ownership of US Green Bonds. No. w25194.* National Bureau of Economic Research. doi:10.3386/w25194

Baldi, F., & Pandimiglio, A. (2022). The role of ESG scoring and greenwashing risk in explaining the yields of green bonds: A conceptual framework and an econometric analysis. *Global Finance Journal, 52*, 1–16. doi:10.1016/j.gfj.2022.100711

Banga, J. (2018). The green bond market: A potential source of climate finance for developing countries. *Journal of Sustainable Finance & Investment, 9*(1), 17–32. doi:10.1080/20430795.2018.1498617

Baum, M.L. (2012). It's not easy being green ... or is it? A content analysis of environmental claims in magazine advertisements from the United States and United Kingdom. *Environmental Communication: A Journal of Nature and Culture, 6*(4), 423-440.

Bloomberg & Barclays. (2021). *Bloomberg Barclays MSCI Global Green Bond Index.* Bloomberg Barclays Indices. https://www.msci.com/documents/10199/242721/Barclays_MSCI_Green_Bond_Index.pdf/6e4d942a-0ce4-4e70-9aff-d7643e1bde96

California Debt and Investment Advisory Commission. (2019). *Green bonds in the golden state: A practical path for issuers.* University of California Berkeley. https://www.treasurer.ca.gov/cdiac/webinars/2019/greenbonds/presentation.pdf

CICERO. (2021). *Freddie Mac multifamily green bond second opinion.* CICERO. https://mf.freddiemac.com/docs/2nd_opinion_from_CICERO.pdf

Climate Bond Initiative. (2017). *Sovereign green bonds briefing.* CBI. https://www.climatebonds.net/files/files/Sovereign_Briefing2017.pdf

Climate Bond Initiative. (2018). *Korea climate bond market overview and opportunities*. CBI. https://www.climatebonds.net/files/files/CBI-Korea_Market-Final-01A.pdf

Climate Bond Initiative. (2021). *Sustainable debt global state of the market 2021*. CBI. https://www.climatebonds.net/files/reports/cbi_global_sotm_2021_02h_0.pdf

Climate Bond Initiative. (2022). *Netherlands sovereign green bond*. CBI. https://www.climatebonds.net/certification/netherlands_sovereign

Dorfleitner, G., Utz, S., & Zhang, G. (2021). The pricing of green bonds: External reviews and the shades of green. *Review of Managerial Science, 16*(3), 797–834. doi:10.100711846-021-00458-9

Ehlers, T., & Packer, P. (2017). Green bond finance and certification. *BIS Quarterly Review*, 89-104.

European Parliament. (2014), *Social impact bonds: private finance that generates social returns*. European Parliament. https://www.europarl.europa.eu/EPRS/538223-Social-impact-bonds-FINAL.pdf

Federal Republic of Germany. (2021). *Green bond investor presentation*. BDF GmbH. https://www.deutsche-finanzagentur.de/fileadmin/user_upload/institutionelle-investoren/pdf/Green_Bond_Investor_Presentation_2021.pdf

Flaherty, M., Gevorkyan, S., Radpour, S., & Semmler, W. (2017). Financing climate policies through climate bonds – A three stage model and empirics. *Research in International Business and Finance, 42*(C), 468–479. doi:10.1016/j.ribaf.2016.06.001

Hachenberg, B., & Schiereck, D. (2018). Are green bonds priced differently from conventional bonds? *Journal of Asset Management, 19*(6), 371–383. doi:10.105741260-018-0088-5

HanY.LiP.WuS. (2020). Does Green Bond Improve Portfolio Diversification? Evidence from China. Retrieved from doi:10.2139/ssrn.3639753

HM Treasury and UK Debt Management Office. (2021). Green gilts investor presentation. HM Treasury and UK Debt Management Office. https://assets.publishing.service.gov.uk/government/uploads/system/uploads/attachment_data/file/1033194/Green_Gilt_Investor_Presentation.pdf

Hong, S., & Ryu, J. (2019). Crowdfunding public projects: Collaborative governance for achieving citizen co-funding of public goods. *Government Information Quarterly, 36*(1), 145–153. doi:10.1016/j.giq.2018.11.009

Hörisch, J. (2015). Crowdfunding for environmental ventures: An empirical analysis of the influence of environmental orientation on the success of crowdfunding initiatives. *Journal of Cleaner Production, 107*, 636–645. doi:10.1016/j.jclepro.2015.05.046

Imberg, M., & Shaban, M. (2019). *A generational shift: Family wealth transfer report 2019*. Wealth-X. https://thehometrust.com/wp-content/uploads/2019/11/Wealth-X_Family-Wealth-Transfer-Report_2019.pdf

Intelligent Transport. (2021). *Moscow using green bonds to finance sustainable transport projects*. Intelligent Transport. https://www.intelligenttransport.com/transport-news/128394/moscow-green-bonds/

International Capital Market Association. (2021). *Green bond principles voluntary process guidelines for issuing green bonds june 2021.* ICMA. https://www.icmagroup.org/assets/documents/Sustainable-finance/2021-updates/Green-Bond-Principles-June-2021-100621.pdf

International Financing Review. (2022). *Airport authority HK sells controversial green bond.* IFR. https://www.ifre.com/story/3196600/airport-authority-hk-prices-us4bn-144areg-s-four-tranche-senior-bond-tnp3jy9rns

Investment Partners, N. N. (2021). *Spain's first green bond to pay for clean transport and climate change plan.* NNIP. https://www.nnip.com/en-INT/professional/insights/articles/spains-first-green-bond-to-pay-for-clean-transport-and-climate-change-plan

ISS-oekom. (2021). *Methodology: ISS-oekom corporate rating.* ISS-oekom. https://www.deka-etf.de/documents/iss_oekom_47_latest_de.pdf

Jiang, Y., Wang, J., Ao, Z., & Wang, Y. (2022). The relationship between green bonds and conventional financial markets: Evidence from quantile-on-quantile and quantile coherence approaches. *Economic Modelling, 116*, 106038. doi:10.1016/j.econmod.2022.106038

KarpfA.MandelA. (2017). Does it pay to be green? A comparative study of the yield term structure of green and brown bonds in the US municipal bonds market. https://ssrn.com/abstract=2923484

Kestrel Verifiers. (2022). *Second party opinions on green, social and sustainability bonds.* Kestrel Verifiers. https://kestrelverifiers.com/second-party-opinions/

Knoch, M., & Van der Plasken, C. (2020). *The green finance market emerging in Brazil leading players, products, and main challenges.* GmbH. https://www.giz.de/en/downloads/the-green-finance-market-emerging-in-brazil-oct-2020-final.pdf

Larcker, D. F., & Watts, E. M. (2020). Where's the greenium? *Journal of Accounting and Economics, 69*(2-3), 101312. doi:10.1016/j.jacceco.2020.101312

Li, Z., Tang, Y., Wu, J., Zhang, J., & Lv, Q. (2019). The interest costs of green bonds: Credit ratings, corporate social responsibility, and certification. *Emerging Markets Finance & Trade, 56*(12), 2679–2692. doi:10.1080/1540496X.2018.1548350

Lin, L., & Hong, Y. (2022). Developing a green bonds market: Lessons from China. *European Business Organization Law Review, 23*(1), 143–185. doi:10.100740804-021-00231-1

Mackevičiūtė, R., Martinaitis, Z., Lipparini, F., Scheck, B. C., & Styczyńska, I. (2020). *Social impact investment. Best practices and recommendations for the next generation.* EMPL. https://www.europarl.europa.eu/RegData/etudes/STUD/2020/658185/IPOL_STU(2020)658185_EN.pdf

Maduro, M., Pasi, G., & Misuraca, G. (2018). Social impact investment in the EU. Financing strategies and outcome oriented approaches for social policy innovation: narratives, experiences, and recommendations. Publications Office of the European Union. .. doi:10.2760/159402

McGlade, C. E., & Ekins, P. (2015). The geographical distribution of fossil fuels unused when limiting global warming to 2°C. *Nature, 517*(7533), 187–190. doi:10.1038/nature14016 PMID:25567285

Mona, I., & Raberto, M. (2018). The EIRIN flow-of-funds behavioural model of green fiscal policies and green sovereign bonds. *Ecological Economics*, *144*, 228–243. doi:10.1016/j.ecolecon.2017.07.029

Moody's Investors Service. (2018). *A greener approach to financing: green bond assessment overview.* Moody's https://www.moodys.com/sites/products/ProductAttachments/MIS_Green_Bonds_Assessment. pdf?WT.z_referringsource=TB~ESGhub~GREENBONDS

Nanayakkara, M., & Colombage, S. (2019). Do investors in green bond market pay a premium? Global evidence. *Applied Economics*, *51*(40), 1–13. doi:10.1080/00036846.2019.1591611

National Academies Sciences Engineering Medicine. (2021). *Analysis of green bond financing in the public transportation industry.* The National Academies Press.

Ontario Newsroom. (2017). Green bond proceeds to fund environmentally friendly infrastructure projects. *Ontario Newsroom.* https://news.ontario.ca/en/release/43595/green-bond-proceeds-to-fund-environmentally-friendly-infrastructure-projects

Organisation for Economic Co-operation and Development. (2016). *Green bonds: country experiences, barriers and options.* OECD. https://www.oecd.org/environment/cc/Green_Bonds_Country_Experiences_Barriers_and_Options.pdf

Rajwanshi, Y. (2019). Are green bonds as good as they sound? *Econ Review.* https://econreview.berkeley.edu/are-green-bonds-as-good-as-they-sound/

Santos, G., Behrendt, H., Maconi, L., Shirvani, T., & Teytelboym, A. (2010). Part I: Externalities and economic policies in road transport. *Research in Transportation Economics*, *28*(1), 2–45. doi:10.1016/j.retrec.2009.11.002

Segal, T. (2022). Green Bond. *Investopedia.* https://www.investopedia.com/terms/g/green-bond.asp

Shishlov, I., Morel, R., & Cochran, I. (2016). *Beyond transparency: Unlocking the full potential of green bonds.* Institute for Climate Economics Report. https://www.i4ce.org/wp-content/uploads/2022/07/I4CE_Green_Bonds-1-1.pdf

Singapore Ministry of Finance. (2022). *Green bonds.* MOF. https://www.mof.gov.sg/policies/fiscal/greenbonds#:~:text=Examples%20of%20eligible%20green%20SINGA,the%20greenest%20ways%20to%20move

Solactive. (2021). Shining green: bonds to tackle climate change. *Solactive.* https://www.solactive.com/wp-content/uploads/2021/09/Solactive-Green-Bonds-September-2021.pdf

Standard&Poor's Global. (2017). *Frequently Asked Questions: S&P Global Ratings' Analytical Approach In Evaluating Green Transactions.* S&P Global. https://www.maalot.co.il/Publications/GRB20171207111217.pdf

Standard&Poor's Global. (2020). *Swiss prime site issues chf 300m green bond.* S&P Global. https://www.spglobal.com/marketintelligence/en/news-insights/latest-news-headlines/swiss-prime-site-issues-chf-300m-green-bond-61504351

Sustainalytics. (2020). *The ESG risk rating: frequently asked questions for companies.* Sustainalytics. https://connect.sustainalytics.com/hubfs/SFS/Sustainalytics%20ESG%20Risk%20Rating%20-%20FAQs%20for%20Corporations.pdf

United Nations. (2022). *Do you know all 17 SDGs?* UN. https://sdgs.un.org/goals

World Bank Group. (2016). *Sustainable Urban Transport Financing from the Sidewalk to the Subway: Capital, Operations, and Maintenance Financing.* World Bank. doi:10.1596/978-1-4648-0756-5

Wulandari, F., Schäfer, D., Stephan, A., & Sun, C. (2018). *Liquidity risk and yield spreads of green bonds, DIW Discussion Papers, No. 1728, Deutsches Institut für Wirtschaftsforschung.* DIW.

Zerbib, O. D. (2019). The effect of pro-environmental preferences on bond prices: Evidence from green bonds. *Journal of Banking & Finance, 98*(C), 39–60.

KEY TERMS AND DEFINITIONS

Bond: A loan agreement issued by public authorities or private businesses. Typically includes coupon payments until maturity.

Bond Yield: Total annual return to the bondholder.

Coupon payment: Bond's yearly interest rate, calculated as a percentage of face value.

Face value: The sum given to the bondholder at maturity.

Green Bond: A special type of bond specifically issued to finance green projects.

Greenium: The ongoing debated concept stating green bonds are priced higher than conventional bonds.

Maturity: The date at which the face value is paid by the issuer to the bondholder.

Social Impact Bond: A special type of bond specifically issued to finance social impact projects.

Chapter 8

An Overview of Sustainable Public Transportation in Higher Education

Pelin Irgin

ⓘD https://orcid.org/0000-0001-5222-5648

Independent Researcher, Canada

ABSTRACT

Very few engineering and business/management education programs emphasize the importance of sustainable public transportation in urban environments, even though agencies and practitioners recognize it. Many undergraduate and graduate students have little training on how a sustainable public transport system is planned, designed, and operationalized, which is critical for a better understanding of sustainability and equity in public transportation. Content and instructional materials in sustainable public transportation education are still not readily available for practitioners. Therefore, this chapter aims to examine the public content and instructional materials on the websites of various universities in North America and Europe and to understand their commitment to education in sustainable public transportation, specifically to "sustainable public transportation" courses offered in the programs. It addresses how sustainability and equity in public transportation are integrated with textual and visual materials used in engineering and business/management education programs.

INTRODUCTION

Currently, there is growing evidence that sustainability and equity as a ground for innovative purposes have been discussed in the field of education, economy, environment, etc (Kim et al., 2016; Liu et al., 2020; Rid, 2017). The US Environmental Protection Agencies (USEPA) declared its partnership with other communities: The US Department of Housing and Urban Development (USHUD) and the US Department of Transportation (USDOT) in 2009, which is an immense growth to afford transportation and housing while protecting the environment. Nowadays, stakeholders of various transportation

DOI: 10.4018/978-1-6684-5996-6.ch008

Copyright © 2023, IGI Global. Copying or distributing in print or electronic forms without written permission of IGI Global is prohibited.

An Overview of Sustainable Public Transportation in Higher Education

companies plan and operate transportation systems to support environmental, economical, and social purposes such as protecting natural sources, improving the health system, controlling energy security, and providing opportunities for disadvantaged people. In order to reveal these goals, human activities have caused continuous change and development in the environment. As people have over-exploited the existing natural sources and caused global crises by endangering the environment for the sake of economic growth (Liu et al., 2020), they have become aware of problems and strived against worldwide threats. Global attention to the environmental crisis first appeared in 1980 as "sustainable development" proposed by the World Conservation Organization (Sachs, 2015). UNESCO (2005) defined sustainable development as being more aware of global needs and keeping a balance among economic, social, and environmental concerns. With the emergence of sustainable development goals, United Nations (2022) provided the blueprint for the acceleration of growth and changes as a universal call to promote sustainability, equity, prosperity, and justice.

Today, there is continuous momentum around sustainability concerning innovation and business goals. The sustainable development goals reported in 2022 pictured an overview of universal development on the implementation of the 2030 Agenda for sustainable development, and it shared the currently available data and global and local estimates towards 17 goals as indicators of in-depth analysis of these goals. According to the United Nation's report (2022), the combination of crises after COVID-19 prevails over the global economy and ecology and affects sustainable development goals. Therefore, there is an urgent need for global action not to jeopardize the environment, health, peace, and people's needs. The report points out how people have progressed in eradicating hunger, poverty, and disease, and improving the education system in order to rescue sustainable development goals. The world has started to create a sustainability agenda on a global scale to pursue these sustainable development goals and to achieve a sustainable future with a good quality education. According to Kioupi and Voulvoulis (2019), "the road to sustainability is paved by education" (p. 13). The emphasis of education on the notion of sustainability and sustainable development goals has been recognized in the global agenda to reach more sustainable futures (UNESCO, 2005).

BACKGROUND

Sustainability is the use of resources by considering the well-being of people and protecting the environment (UNCED, 1992). Sustainability is also described as an attempt to satisfy the needs of the future generation (Rauch, 2002). In our current world, the role of education is not only to adapt people to a changing world but also to satisfy their needs and improve their perspectives to protect the environment (UNCED, 1992). In other words, transforming education to have a more sustainable world is an attempt of creating an ecologically, economically, and socially safe system (Greene & Wegener, 1997). According to the Transportation Research Board, "sustainability is not about threat analysis; sustainability is about systems analysis. Specifically, it is about how environmental, economic, and social systems interact to their mutual advantage or disadvantage at various space-based scales of operation." (Toutanji, Anderson, & Leonard, 2013, p. 7). Rauch (2002) explains the concept of sustainability in three fundamental components: (i) ecological, (ii) economic, and (iii) social sustainability, all of which denote global preservation and development.

Table 1. Triple bottom lines in sustainability

Ecological sustainability	Economic sustainability	Social sustainability
Pollution prevention	Affordability	Equity
Climate protection	Resource efficiency	Human health
Biodiversity	Cost internalization	Education
Precautionary action	Trade and business activity	Community
Avoidance of irreversibility	Employment	Quality of life
Habitat preservation	Productivity	Public participation
Aesthetics	Tax burden	

Ecological sustainability stands on long-term perspectives and developments to maintain the natural balance and survival of the ecosystem (Callicott & Mumford, 1998). To reduce the negative impact on nature, energy sources, agriculture, and industry, the ecosystem is conserved regarding the natural cycles such as raw materials, biological diversity, pollination, emissions, wastes, food production, cleaning processes, etc. Economical sustainability implies the optimal use, safeguarding, and sustaining of resources so as to preserve the life quality of individuals over the long term (Ikerd, 2012). The present and future value of resources and the global economy regarding investments, debts, consumption, and marketing are considered to cater next generations' needs. Many business companies incorporate different aspects of economic sustainability in their strategic goals to monitor their operations and cooperate with their customers. The most widespread issues discussed can be listed as climate change, harmful $CO2$ emissions, recycling, urban agriculture, and urban transportation (United Nations, 2022).

Social (and cultural) sustainability covers internal and external unity and solidarity. It implies people are ready to fulfill their potential and be in relationships with other people, cultures, and communities in a global environment (Tumlin, 2012). People's needs and demands look different even if they live in the same world. So, social sustainability aims to deal with supplying freedom and peace and keeping balance among communities and regions at large. It may also concern freedom of education, religion, and providing opportunities to disadvantaged individuals and groups in the global agenda. Overall, a set of sustainability indicators is required to deal with the negative impacts on ecological, economic, and social (cultural) issues. As "the industry would exploit nature and the environment for its purposes and postulate solutions to problems" (Rauch, 2002, p. 47), sustainability with triple bottom lines, environmental, economical, and social, for global growth stands for a long-term safeguard.

Public transportation is a system of vehicles that operates at regular times and takes people from one place to another. Public transportation, simply public transport, is currently under the scope of various research because of the high proportion of gas emissions (Kim et al., 2017). According to the American Public Transportation Association (APTA, 2021), there are plenty of benefits of public transportation in a new mobility era for travelers and communities. These can be listed as enlarging opportunities, building thriving communities, controlling, and decreasing traffic congestion, etc. To establish sustainable transportation systems, governments are expected to put efforts to increase the use of public transportation (dell'Olio et al., 2010) and follow transportation planning policies and strategies.

Public transport is available in both urban and rural areas in the US and Europe. From commuter rail to high-speed systems, public transportation includes bus systems in both urban and rural areas, bus-rapid transits, subways, railways, and streetcars (APTA, 2021). Public transport also provides almost 10 billion commuter, leisure, medical and special trips annually. In the US, approximately 6,800 organizations provided transportation in various modes, and Federal Transit Administration financially supported transportation systems operating in both urban and local areas. As reported in the US National Transit Database, 1,159 of the 2,202 transport systems were in rural areas while 1,043 of them were in urban areas, which demonstrates many urban transport systems were in rural areas.

Several studies (Ceder, 2015; Kim et al., 2017) have revealed the necessity of investigations on public transportation facilities and public transport users' needs. For instance, what public transportation users/passengers want and need, and what operational requirements are to attract the needs and satisfaction of the users/passengers are among some matters to have a better understanding of transportation services. Many developing countries do not have policies and strategies for public transport and do not provide enough investment as they are restrained by the scarcity of energy and capital sources (Replogle, 1991). Even if public transport is relatively reasonable and efficient, it is still difficult to afford it because of economic problems. According to Raicu, Popa, and Dorinela (2022), there is a need for agreement on a long-term adaptive policy to deal with the scientific, social, and economic uncertainties in the design and operation of transportation systems. Notably, it is plausible first to identify the level and quality of public transport and second to meet the needs of public transport users and satisfy them sufficiently.

THE NECESSITY OF SUSTAINABLE PUBLIC TRANSPORTATION IN HIGHER EDUCATION

The Commission of the European Communities simply defines sustainable transportation, also called sustainable mobility, as "satisfying current transport and mobility needs without compromising the ability of future generations to meet these needs" (Black, 1996, p. 151). According to the European Conference of Ministers of Transport's (ECMT) (2001) report, a sustainable transport system is an accessible, safe, environmentally friendly, and affordable system. A sustainable transport system meets the needs of society and companies in many countries safely as well as promotes environmental, economic, and social equity from generation to generation (Black, 1996; Black, 1997). In 2009, USHUD, USDOT, and USEPA had an agreement to coordinate, transportation, housing, and ecological policies and investments framed with six principles, all of which guide the decision-making in public transportation. It is comprised of these six principles: (1) providing reliable, safe, and affordable transportations choices to promote the well-being of the public, (2) expanding locations and housing and increasing mobility with public transportation, (3) enhancing competitiveness in the economy and expanding business marketing, (4) supporting transportation oriented public works of communities and companies, (5) coordinating with federal policies for sustainable public transportation and leveraging funding for renewable energy, and lastly, (6) enhancing the value of communities and urban and rural neighbourhoods (ICF International, 2010). The USHUD, USDOT, and USEPA use performance measures in decision-making toward sustainable transportation objectives and planning and support the livability of these principles. Performance measures in transportation provide information for decision-making and public transportation agencies. Implementation of performance measures in the long term is deemed to be critical to addressing sustainable environmental requirements and the necessary investment. As well as professionals, academics and practitioners can deliver education on sustainable public transportation and influence planning, and programming by providing evidence and information to decision-makers about sustainable transportation in urban and rural areas.

Concurrently, the American Society of Civil Engineering (ASCE) issued Vision for Civil Engineering 2025, a guidebook for professionals and civil engineers worldwide. It clearly describes new features of leadership and professionalism and civil engineers as "(1) planners, designers, and constructors; (2) stewards of the natural environment; (3) innovators and integrators of technology; (4) managers of risk; and (5) leaders in shaping public policy, where master implies leader in both role and knowledge" (ASCE, p. 5). So, Kim, Schmöcker, and Fujii (2016) explained that if this description is for future engineers in general, it is particularly acceptable to describe this role for students in other fields focusing on sustainable public transportation systems in urban environments. Planners of sustainable public transportation are intended to set up a relationship between society and nature and to work on infrastructural changes and the impact of the changes on the economy and ecology. Therefore, in the field of sustainable transportation, there are a bunch of publications changing the way of thinking and research purposes. The direction is on discussing the short-term and long-term impact of education and the sustainable transport attitudes of university students. However, it is required to give education to students to gain a deeper understanding of the complexity of environmental problems and sustainable transportation systems in different environments. To serve their understanding, undergraduate and graduate courses should be designed to prepare future planners and decision-makers to take active roles in dealing with various environmental matters. At that point, Hyde and Karney's (2001) report on engineering and environmental education in different faculties of universities explains how urgent and essential it is.

Moreover, apart from environmental education in higher education, more specifically education in public transportation systems should be recognized as a very critical component of the courses at faculties. It may address urban and rural environments, and mobility challenges such as traffic congestion, air pollution, and lack of accessibility from the surrounding areas. Truly, the USHUD, USDOT, and USEPA have partnerships with sustainable communities and provide more options for public transportation with the livability principles to guide interagency cooperation among agencies and communities (ICF International, 2010). Interestingly, the USEPA names transit accessibility and transit productivity among the twelve performance measures in transportation (USEPA, 2011). According to the Southeastern Transportation Research, Innovation, Development and Education (STRIDE) center's report on public transportation education published in 2015, even though the practitioners recognize this, many engineering and environment education programs still do not give emphasis to sustainable public transportation in urban environments and transportation systems. Therefore, most of the graduates from universities have very limited knowledge of sustainable public transportation and little understanding of increasing transit accessibility and productivity.

Besides the concepts of social, ecological, and economic sustainability which have already been configured in engineering education, the notion of sustainability in public transportation in urban environments and how it is embedded in courses in higher education is becoming a trailblazer (Kim et al., 2016; Kim et al., 2017; Rid, 2017). Hence, students' consciousness of sustainable public transportation in urban areas can be increased through education at universities. They can play increasingly an important role to develop a sustainable transport system and policies.

Transit Cooperative Research Program (TCRP) supported by the Federal Transit Administration published Report 77 entitled "managing transit's workforce in the new millennium (McGlothin, 2002). This report pinpoints the necessity of academic research and training to find innovative solutions to operating problems and to introduce new technologies and innovations into the public transportation system. It recognizes the need to broaden qualified labour and various positions in engineering through higher education programs. TCRP has three objectives: "1. Assess the transit industry's workforce needs

An Overview of Sustainable Public Transportation in Higher Education

and prospects for the twenty-first century; 2. Develop strategies to attract, develop, and retain a qualified workforce; and 3. Develop a tool and guidelines to enable employers to assess their workforces and monitor continually their workforce needs" (p. 8). In 2008, a report by the APTA provided important information about the civil engineering workforce and the necessity for professionals to build a strong background in the public transportation systems in urban and rural environments and to solve problems. The objectives of TCRP and the main aim of APTA align with the development goals of STRIDE, which is to come up with innovative programs in higher education and to support advanced transit planning and sustainable transportation education. For instance, STRIDE (2015) reported that there is a need for renewal in transportation education especially in civil engineering programs because of the increased need for professionals with a very strong educational background in public transportation systems in both rural and urban environments to address congestion, CO_2 emission, and mobility challenges.

In 2005, public transportation reduced CO_2 emissions by 6.9 million metric tons, and 340 million gallons of gasoline were saved (SAIC, 2007). So, it means that travelling collectively uses less gas and reduces emissions. Even though public transportation in urban and rural environments reduces CO_2 emissions (Davis & Hale, 2007) and hybrid electric vehicles considerably lower carbon emissions, it is still not enough to combat traffic congestion, air pollution, and mobility, and to develop sustainable communities and environments. For this reason, students in transportation-related programs and departments such as civil and environmental engineering in higher education should be trained on how to meet the needs of communities by bringing sustainability to transportation systems with up-to-date planning, design, and operation systems. They also should be engaged in collaborative work to meet new development goals.

In academic research done by Turochy (2006), mass transit was listed as the 14th topic among 31 transportation topics ranked in transportation education. With the growing interest and awareness in transportation livability, education may change the understanding of the new generation on transportation behaviour and promote their interest in sustainable and livable transportation. In 2009, a group of researchers and practitioners teaching at various universities' transportation programs met at a transportation research conference, and decide on transportation courses in higher education, mostly civil engineering programs (Beyerlein et al., 2010). After the conference, some educators developed learning outcomes of introduction to transportation courses covered in undergraduate programs and composed a knowledge table including public transportation (system design, system modes, system operating characteristics, etc.), public transportation modes, radial, linear, and collector-distributor system designs, service analysis, integration of transportation systems (Bill et al., 2011). However, there still appears limited evidence about the materials used for planning, design, and system operations in public transportation even if it has been issued and discussed to carry it from theory to practice. In 2015, STRIDE reported that many young people still seek better opportunities to take education to understand the efficient use of the public transportation system and move people sustainably. According to the findings of the Transportation Research Center in 2015, 74% of universities have undergraduate-level transportation planning courses which are on the list of elective courses. Even, very few universities have a course in their programs related to sustainable public transportation systems.

It is clearly seen that the students who graduated from engineering and transportation-related programs and/or departments most probably will seldom explain the significance of sustainable public transportation in transit systems planning and designing. Besides this, course time and lack of course materials are other points that are ignored in undergraduate and graduate programs (STRIDE, 2015). Therefore, given the importance of focusing on sustainability in transportation courses, there has not been a detailed overview of undergraduate and graduate programs' sustainable public transportation-related courses.

There is also no other paper and/or study in my knowledge that addresses how sustainability and equity in public transportation are integrated with textual and visual materials used in engineering and business/management education programs. So, when students graduate from their universities, they can be hired to plan, design, and operate transportation systems for diverse companies' and governments' public transportation services. However, students can only demonstrate their mastery of program goals if they have an education in a well-designed program that helps them become qualified and knowledgeable engineers and managers in their future careers.

All in all, public transportation education for sustainability and equity can become an innovation for many education reforms with its ecological, economic, and social outlook (Rauch, 2002). The idea of a sustainable and equitable environment would address the constructivist approach to sustainable public transportation education. Also, its principles and objectives would motivate and coordinate individuals to deal with environmental matters. Additionally, it would consider national and international sustainability, equity, and well-being as core elements of education. Finally, it would imply recognizing the needs of individuals in various societies.

SUSTAINABLE TRANSPORTATION CURRICULA IN THE US AND EUROPE

As the global urban population tripled between 1950 and 2015, the number of vehicles used in urban life increased tremendously and gave rise to traffic congestion in these areas (OECD, 2018). In 2019, Victoria Transport Policy Institution reported there had been an increase in more automobile-oriented and/or dependent travel as a self-reinforcing cycle instead of public transportation use in urban and rural environments. It also added that there was a high-level automobile dependency in most communities. Currently, there is a growing dependence on automobile driving rather than public transportation use because of its various advantages such as comfort, speed, mobility, and convenience. Rodrigue (2020) claims that 70% of the global population could be urbanized by 2050, which reminds the importance of ongoing attempts to cope with future congestion in public transportation, urban transport planning, and public transport management. However, when the prior generation is compared with the younger one, it is seen that they prefer living in urban areas with a high population and find automobile driving less attractive than public transit options (Rodrigue, 2020). Recently discussed topics such as sustainability, equity, ecosystem, and global warming, might be one factor affecting their understanding and preferences about mass transit.

According to APTA (2021) and Transportation Research Board (TRB) (2022) reports, major transportation programs in universities in the various regions of the US and Europe have started to offer sustainability-related curricula. Both APTA and TRB have been the US initiative in organizing annual meetings and conferences to discuss major transportation-related topics with the researchers and practitioners. Also, they are oftentimes with the European Transport Board and many European academicians at their meetings. Therefore, most of the attendees on executive and research boards of North American and European organizations and universities contribute to the expansion of the understanding in the field of sustainable public transportation. To understand their commitment to education in sustainable public transportation, specifically to "sustainable public transportation" courses offered in undergraduate and graduate programs, public content, and instructional materials on the websites of various universities in North America and Europe were examined in this chapter.

An Overview of Sustainable Public Transportation in Higher Education

To increase the awareness and preference of future generations, universities, companies, and associations in the broad area of sustainable public transportation can benefit from cooperation and research efforts. Recent global actions undertaken in the US and European contexts and steps for designing sustainable transport-related courses can achieve a high yield. The US Transportation Research Board (TRB), American Public Transportation Association (APTA), and the Transportation Cooperative Research Program have undertaken many actions and provided leadership in public transportation developments and research. At the same time, European members of the Organization for Economic Co-operation and Development (OECD) and European Community Ministers of Transport (ECMT) members have taken action to promote innovations and sustainability and to progress in the transportation industry. At that point, researchers' and practitioners' cooperative and collaborative work can become mutually beneficial to all partners interested in the future of sustainable public transportation area.

Public transit systems provide lots of opportunities for sustainability and mobility, and 21st-century innovation in technology encourages mobility sustainably in urban areas. Hence, the innovation in the field of the public transportation system, and transportation education in higher education should be adapted to the university-level sustainable transportation curricula to train engineers and sustainable smart city planners in the future. In the review of the transportation curricula, in the US and European contexts, it is seen that the US and European transportation education curricula on transit systems focus on public transportation system planning (Meyer & Miller, 2000; TRB, 2012) but design and operation in transit systems are undervalued course materials though it provides opportunities for sustainable and efficient public transportation. Most frequently offered elective and compulsory courses in the field of sustainable transportation in both undergraduate and graduate programs can be listed as transportation engineering, environmental engineering, urban transportation planning, transportation planning, water resources engineering, transportation system analysis, and hazardous waste management.

There is very limited research (Kim et al., 2016; Rid, 2017; Wu et al., 2014; Wu et al., 2015) and research projects (EUGPUT, 2021) on the university level university course design except for the reports of various associations and companies. However, the ones that have been currently searched highlights the importance of providing public transportation course in higher education. For example, in Beiler's (2018) study, existing public transportation courses in engineering departments in the US, including 145 schools, were investigated to provide pedagogical recommendations to other departments and programs during the course development process for the future academic years. It was found that almost 30% of civil engineering programs have at least one undergraduate-level public transportation course. 98% of the courses in the programs in the curricula are offered to graduate-level students. Research findings recommended the integration of some topics such as high-speed rails and connections to automated vehicles to expand the public transportation systems and transportation facilities. Bhattacharjee et al. (2011) had a systematic course review and sustainability in construction engineering and reported that there was a lack of consensus regarding the course objectives, the learning outcomes, the course design, and the delivery of the sustainability concepts. They found that one-third of 128 universities, members of the associated schools of construction, have at least one course in sustainable construction and transportation at the undergraduate level. Sustainable construction topics were categorized into eight groups which are environment/ eco-system, health, sustainable construction, sustainable rating systems, the role of stakeholders, lifecycle cost, ethics, and community. The contents of the courses and the course materials can lend some ideas about what can be included in public transportation education.

COURSE TOPICS AND MATERIALS AVAILABLE IN PUBLIC TRANSPORTATION EDUCATION

This chapter addresses how sustainability in public transportation is integrated with textual and visual materials used in engineering and business/management education programs and how they position and shape students' understanding. There are several top-notch universities in the US and European countries having professionals and educators creating technical and educational materials consisting of transportation systems, sustainability in public transportation, etc. According to the report of the transportation research and education center, many public transportation course topics have been covered in higher education since 2005. Public transportation courses are the common three or four credits and students take public transportation courses in fall and spring terms as an elective and/or compulsory course of 14 or 15 weeks in length. Public transportation course topics in some programs have been led over a period of 12 weeks. North American and European public transportation course credits are equivalent regardless of the course level in undergraduate and graduate programs.

Common topics in sustainable public transportation education can be listed as mentioned below:

1. Bus transit (route design, scheduling, station design)
2. Rail transit (route design, scheduling, station design)
3. Paratransit (route design, scheduling, station design)
4. Pedestrians and cyclists (Sidewalk design, intersection design, regulations)
5. Management (organizations, companies, labour organizations, institutions)
6. Conducting surveys on public transportation and sustainability
7. Coordinating transportation systems
8. Planning in public transportation systems (planning process, forecasting, decision making, evaluating, transit system management)
9. Transport policy and law (legislation and lawmaking, fare structuring policies, land use policies, environmental policies)
10. Finance transit systems (financing public transportation, funding, grants, funds, contracts)
11. Safety in public transportation
12. Transit technologies
13. Design of public transportation vehicles and networks
14. Marketing in the public transit environment
15. Public transport projects (Mini-projects, class projects)

As one of the components of a course syllabus, textbooks and supplementary readings are recommended and professors use their class notes, booklets, and research papers in common. Here are the recommended readings among public transportation courses:

1. Transit Cooperative Research Program (TCRP) Report 30 Scheduling
2. Transit Cooperative Research Program (TCRP) Report 88 Performance Measurements
3. Transit Cooperative Research Program (TCRP) Report 12
4. Urban Transportation System, written by Grava in 2002
5. Urban Transit: Operations, Planning, and Economics, written by V. Vuchic in 2005
6. Urban Transit Systems and Technology, written by V. Vuchic in 2007

An Overview of Sustainable Public Transportation in Higher Education

7. Public Transit Planning and Operation: Theory, Modelling, and Practice, written by A. Ceder in 2007
8. America Public Transportation Association (APTA) Fact Book issued in 2011
9. Track Design Handbook for Light Rail Transit, National Academies of Sciences, Engineering, and Medicine, issued in 2012
10. Transit Capacity and Quality of Service Manual (TCQSM), Third Edition, issued in 2013
11. Public Transportation: Planning, Operations, and Management, written by G. Gray and L. Hoel in 1992
12. Public Transit Economics and Deregulation Policy: A Volume in Studies in Regional Science and Urban Economics, written by J. Berechman in 1993
13. Understanding and Diagnosing Compulsive Buying, written by H. Dittmar in 2004
14. The New Transit Town, written by H. Dittmar and G. Ohland in 2004
15. Managing Public Transit Strategically: A Comprehensive Approach to Strengthening Service and Monitoring Performance, written by G. Fielding in 1987
16. Transit Performance Evaluation in the U.S.A., written by G. Fielding in 1992
17. Cash, Tokens, and Transfers: A History of Urban Mass Transit in North America, written by B. J. Cudahy in 2002
18. Advanced Modeling for Transit Operations and Service Planning, written by W. H. K. Lam in 2003
19. Better Public Transit Systems: Analyzing Investments and Performance, written by E. Bruun in 2007
20. Moving Cooler: An Analysis of Transportation Strategies for Reducing Greenhouse Gas Emissions, written by Cambridge Systematics in 2009
21. Human Transit, written by J. Walker in 2011
22. My Kind of Transit: Rethinking Public Transportation, written by D. Nordahl in 2009
23. Public Transportation Systems: Basic Principles of System Design, Operations Planning, and Real-Time Control, written by C. Daganzo in 2010
24. Urban Public Transportation Systems: Implementing Efficient Urban Transit Systems and Enhancing Transit Usage, edited by M. Bondada in 2000
25. Public Transport: Its Planning, Management, and Operation, written by P. White in 2008
26. Sustainable Transportation Systems Engineering, written by F. Vanek, L. Angenent, J. Banks, R. Daziano and M.A. Turnquist in 2014

Practitioners and professors may encourage students' technical skill development in their courses for public transportation in higher education. There is a number of critical software for professionals in the field of public transportation education such as Microsoft Excel, AutoCAD, Microstation, ArcGIS (a geospatial software), RouteMatch, PTV VISSIM Multimodal Traffic Simulation Software, JMP Statistical Discovery Software from SAS, Minitab Statistical Software, JPSS, TransCAD Transportation Planning Software, Visual Basic, C++, Java, and so forth. Besides the software that can be used in public transportation education, there is a set of software that can help mass transit recover as well as make services more sustainable, inclusive, and efficient for all communities, agencies, passengers, operators, and professionals.

Public transportation is necessarily an inevitable part of students' and professionals' daily routines. Even though social distancing measures are taken during and after the COVID-19 pandemic (Fumagalli, Rezende, & Guimaraes, 2021), many people have faced lots of problems related to transportation planning, safety concerns, and health issues. At this point, improving public transportation demand in current years has been challenging. In addition to health issues, the world population in urban environments has emerged as a big problem waiting for solutions in the public transportation systems. Today, the utilization of various public transportation-related software might be handy to serve the possible problems occurring because of transportation operation systems and public transit infrastructure. Here, professionals may find some helpful public transportation software on the global market that may be pedagogically integrated into sustainable public transportation education at universities. These are recommended software links: Ecolane, Optibus, Remix, TripSpark, QRyde for Public Transportation, TripMaster NEMT Software, Moovit, Spare, Amadeus RAILyourWAY, Conduent Transportation, Trapeze, Via, AMCONSOFT, Ncryped, Swarco, TSO Mobile, EZTransport, CODICE PT, Actionfigure, and Pantonium. The use of software would contribute to helping transit agencies operate efficiently and meet the demands of the public to increase their quality of life.

In addition to the software recommendations, professors covering public transportation courses at universities use some supplementary materials and/or sources chosen from education blogs, journals, conference proceedings, and reports of some associations and companies on sustainable public transportation and its goals. The most commonly used materials can be listed in four categories as (a) reports, (b) conference proceedings, (c) magazines, and (d) books.

a. Reports are:
   ◦ American Public Transportation Association (APTA) Reports,
   ◦ Center of Transit-oriented Development (CTOD) Reports,
   ◦ Minority Transportation Officials (MTO) Reports,
   ◦ Federal Transit Administration (FTA) Reports,
   ◦ Transportation Research Board (TRB) Reports,
   ◦ Transportation Cooperative Research Program (TCRP) Reports,
   ◦ Urbanrail.net Reports,
   ◦ Women's Transportation Seminar (WTS) Reports.
b. Conference Proceedings are:
   ◦ Conference of Minority Transportation Officials (COMTO) Proceedings,
   ◦ Federal Transit Administration (FTA) Conferences Proceedings,
   ◦ Transportation Research Board (TRB) Conference Proceedings,
   ◦ Women's Transportation Seminar (WTS) Conference Proceedings.
c. Magazines are:
   ◦ Mass Transit Magazine,
   ◦ Progressive Railroading Magazine,
   ◦ Trafficware University Newsletter.
d. Books are:
   ◦ Urban Transit: Operations, Planning, Economics, written by V. Vuchic in 2005,
   ◦ Urban Transit Systems and Technology, written by V. Vuchic in 2007,
   ◦ The Geography of Urban Transportation, written by S. Hanson in 2004.

Furthermore, there appears skill development of students taking public transportation education at a higher education level to make their future jobs. Nowadays multiple programs in engineering, technology, and science faculties at universities execute sustainability and equity issues and support university

An Overview of Sustainable Public Transportation in Higher Education

students' skill development regarding these aspects of public transportation. Therefore, students can develop their communication and technical skills, and have enough knowledge of funding and legislation. Communication skills include students' skill development in social and political aspects of sustainable public transportation, policy writing, public administration, project management, community and customer services, public speaking, public presentations, problem-solving, and coordination. Technical skills like critical thinking, dealing with operations and transit systems, planning and scheduling, modelling software, financial analysis of projects, performance management, analysis of trade-offs in operations management, transport demand forecasting, and quality management of transport services. The last important skill to improve is understanding funding regulations and legislation, more specifically, new legislation, collective bargaining, labour relations, grant management, transportation funding and finance, public transportation partnership, and transportation benefits.

Finally, practitioners and professionals might provide in-service training for engineers and planners about public transportation systems and sustainable development. The scope of training may depend on the categories of target groups to be trained. Universities and companies in US and European contexts provide specific training courses such as BRT workshops and seminars, apprenticeships, project management systems, FTA courses, transit construction projects, project management systems, transit planning training, etc. These types of training would provide engineers and planners to gain technical and practical knowledge and develop their skills in public transit planning, designing, and management. So, they would become efficient engineers and planners at providing consistent work and projects as well as following the current trends in sustainable public transportation in different environments.

CONCLUSION

Public transportation is an efficient option for policymakers and governments to develop sustainability of urban systems as it would supply more sustainability to public transportation users, satisfy them with the desired quality, and meet their needs. Changes are needed in sustainable transportation policies to overcome ecological and economic problems such as environmental pollution, global climate change, capital shortages, and debts, and to increase the quality of life and standards. By promoting sustainability in public transportation and covering courses in higher education, it is possible to witness a transition to more aware communities and an economically and ecologically developed world that is based on sustainable production and consumption. As long as professors, researchers, and educators continue to refine their teaching materials in public transportation education and keep their pedagogical sources consistent with the up-to-date versions and latest innovations.

National and international academies of engineering, science, and technology for sustainability in public transportation can organize workshops and training on sustainable public transportation in urban environments by focusing on sustainable urban health and climate change. The professional can review the current situation of sustainable public transportation policies and strategies periodically. Also, professionals can design materials and activities at the higher education level to promote sustainable public transportation in urban environments. Lastly, they can do a needs analysis and bring out the gaps in the field of transportation in urban environments and sustainable urbanization widespread in many countries. Collaboration with professionals and stakeholders might be essential to making decisions on planning and project development regarding all aspects of sustainable public transportation goals.

ACKNOWLEDGMENT

I would like to acknowledge my gratitude to the editors and the reviewers for their insightful and constructive comments in improving the quality of my manuscript.

REFERENCES

APTA. (2021). *Public transportation fact book.* APTA.

ASCE. (2009). Vision for civil engineering in 2025: A roadmap for the profession. *ASCE Library.* https://ascelibrary.org/doi/epdf/10.1061/9780784478868.002

Beiler, M. R. O. (2017). Sustainable mobility for the future: Development and Implementation of a Sustainable Transportation Planning Course. *Journal of Professional Issues in Engineering Education and Practice, 143*(1). https://ascelibrary.org/doi/10.1061/%28ASCE%29EI.1943-5541.0000298

Beiler, M. R. O. (2018). Public transportation education: Inventory and recommendations on curricula. *Journal of Professional Issues in Engineering Education and Practice, 144*(3). https://ascelibrary.org/doi/full/10.1061/%28ASCE%29EI.1943-5541.0000369

Beyerlein, S., Bill, A., van Schalkwyk, I., Bernhardt, K., Young, R., Nambisan, S., & Torochy, R. (2010). Formulating learning outcomes based on core concepts for the introductory transportation engineering course. *Proceedings of the 2010 Transportation Research Board Annual Meeting,* (pp. 10-3946). TRB.

Bhattacharjee, S. S. (2011). Sustainability education in the United States: Analyses of the curricula used in construction programs. *Proceedings of ICSDC 2011: Integrating Sustainability Practices in the Construction Industry,* (pp. 172–179). ASCE.

Bill, A., Beyerlain, S., Heaslip, K., Hurwitz, S., Sanford Bernhardt, K., Kyte, M., & Young, R. (2011). *Development of knowledge tables and learning outcomes for an introductory course in transportation engineering. Transportation research record no 22211,* 27–35. Transportation Research Board. doi:10.3141/2211-04

Black, W. R. (1996). Sustainable transportation: A US perspective. *Journal of Transport Geography, 4*(3), 151–159. doi:10.1016/0966-6923(96)00020-8

Black, W. R. (1997). North American transportation: Perspectives on research needs and sustainable transportation. *Journal of Transport Geography, 5*(1), 12–19. doi:10.1016/S0966-6923(96)00042-7

Callicott, J. B., & Mumford, K. (1998). Ecological sustainability as a conservation concept. In J. Lemons, L. Westra, & R. Goodland (Eds.), *Ecological sustainability and integrity: Concepts and approaches. Environmental Science and Technology Library, 13.* Springer. doi:10.1007/978-94-017-1337-5_3

Cambridge Systematics. (2009). *Moving Cooler: An Analysis of Transportation Strategies for Reducing Greenhouse Gas Emissions.* Urban Land Institute.

Ceder, A. (2015). *Public transit planning and operation: Modeling, practice, and behaviour.* CRC Press. doi:10.1201/b18689

Christensen, T. B., & Kjær, T. (2011). Planning for sustainable transport: The case of Copenhagen. In W. Gronau, K. Reiter, & R. Pressl (Eds.), *Transport and Health Issues: Studies on Mobility and Transport Research, 3*, 119–140. MetaGIS-Systems. https://www.eltis.org/docs/tools/Transpot_health_issues_complete-book.pdf

Davis, T., & Hale, M. (2007). *Public transportation's contribution to US greenhouse gas reduction.* APTA. https://www.apta.com/wp-content/uploads/Resources/resources/reportsandpublications/Documents/climate_change.pdf

dell'Olio, L., Ibeas, A., & Cecin, P. (2010). Modelling user perception of bus transit quality. *Transport Policy, 17*(6), 388–397. doi:10.1016/j.tranpol.2010.04.006

ECMT. (2001). *European conference of ministers of transport.* OECD Library. https://www.oecd-ilibrary.org/transport/european-conference-of-ministers-of-transport-annual-report_23099488

EPA. (2011). Guide to sustainable transportation performance measures. EPA 231-K-10-004. https://www.epa.gov/sites/default/files/2014-01/documents/sustainable_transpo_performance.pdf

EUGPUT. (2021). *Energy usage and green public transportation in future smart cities: An innovative teaching program for students, stakeholders and entrepreneurs.* EUGPUT. https://upb.ro/wp-content/uploads/2020/03/Comunicat-EUGPUT.pdf

Fumagalli, L. A. W., Rezende, D. A., & Guimaraes, T. A. (2021). Challenges for public transportation: Consequences and possible alternatives for the Covid-19 pandemic through strategic digital city application. *Journal of Urban Management, 10*(2), 97–109. doi:10.1016/j.jum.2021.04.002

Greene, D. L., & Wegener, M. (1997). Sustainable transport. *Journal of Transport Geography, 5*(3), 177–190. doi:10.1016/S0966-6923(97)00013-6

Hanson, S. (2004). *The Geography of Urban Transportation.* Guilford Press.

Hyde, R. A., & Karney, B. W. (2001). Environmental education research: Implications for engineering education. *Journal of Engineering Education, 90*(2), 267–275. doi:10.1002/j.2168-9830.2001.tb00602.x

Ikerd, J. (2012). *The essentials of economic sustainability.* Kumarian Press.

International, I. C. F. (2010). Livability in transportation guidebook. FHWA-HEP-10-028. https://www.recpro.org/assets/Library/Livability/livability_in_transportation_guide_072910_lowres.pdf

Kim, J., Schmöcker, J. D., & Fujii, S. (2016). Exploring the relationship between undergraduate education and sustainable transport attitudes. *International Journal of Sustainable Transportation, 10*(4), 385–392. doi:10.1080/15568318.2014.961108

Kim, S. H., Chung, J.-H., Park, S., & Choi, K. (2017). Analysis of user satisfaction to promote public transportation: A pattern-recognition approach focusing on out-of-vehicle time. *International Journal of Sustainable Transportation, 11*(8), 582–592. doi:10.1080/15568318.2017.1280715

Kioupi, V., & Voulvoulis, N. (2019). Education for sustainable development: A systemic framework for connecting the SDGs to educational outcomes. *Sustainability, 11*(21), 6104. doi:10.3390u11216104

Liu, Z., Yang, H.-C., & Shiau, Y.-C. (2020). Investigation on evaluation framework of elementary school teaching materials for sustainable development. *Sustainability*, *12*(9), 3736. doi:10.3390u12093736

McGlothin, D. (2002). Managing transit's workforce in the new millennium. *Transit Cooperative Research Program Report 77*. https://trb.org/publications/tcrp/tcrp_rpt_77.pdf

Meyer, M. D., & Miller, E. J. (2000). *Urban transportation planning: A decision-oriented approach*. McGraw-Hill.

OECD. (2018). *The shared-use city: Managing the curb, international transportation forum*. OECD. https://www.itf-oecd.org/sites/default/files/docs/shared-use-city-managing-curb_5.pdf

Potter, S. (2007). Exploring approaches towards a sustainable transport system. *International Journal of Sustainable Transportation*, *1*(2), 115–131. doi:10.1080/15568310601091999

Raicu, S., Popa, M., & Costescu, D. (2022). Uncertainties influencing transportation system performances. *Sustainability*, *14*(13), 7660. doi:10.3390u14137660

Rauch, F. (2002). The potential of education for sustainable development for reform in schools. *Environmental Education Research*, *8*(1), 43–51. doi:10.1080/13504620120109646

Replogle, M. A. (1991). Sustainable transportation strategies for third-world development. *Transportation Research Record: Journal of the Transportation Research Board*, 1294. https://onlinepubs.trb.org/Onlinepubs/trr/1991/1294/1294-001.pdf

Rid, W. (2017). Human dimensions approach towards integrating sustainable transportation and urban planning policies: A decision support system (DSS) based on stated preferences data. *Theoretical Economics Letters*, *7*(04), 814–833. doi:10.4236/tel.2017.74059

Rodrigue, J. P. (2020). *The geography of transport systems*. Routledge. doi:10.4324/9780429346323

Sachs, D. D. (2015). *The age of sustainable development*. Columbia University Press. doi:10.7312ach17314

SAIC (2007). Public transportation's contribution to US greenhouse gas reduction. *Growing Cooler*.

Toutanji, H. A., Anderson, M., & Leonard, K. M. (2013). *Developing sustainable transportation performance measures for ALDOT. UTCA theme: Management and safety of transportation systems*. UTCA Report Number 12302.

Tumlin, J. (2011). *Sustainable transportation planning: Tools for creating vibrant, healthy, and resilient communities*. John Wiley & Sons.

Turochy, R. E. (2006). Determining the content of the first course in transportation engineering. *Journal of Professional Issues in Engineering Education and Practice*, *132*(3), 200–203. doi:10.1061/(ASCE)1052-3928(2006)132:3(200)

UNCED. (1992). Agenda 21, New York. UNCED. https://sustainabledevelopment.un.org/content/documents/Agenda21.pdf

UNESCO. (2005). United nations decade of education for sustainable development: Draft international implementation scheme (2005-2014): International implementation scheme. UNESCO. https://unesdoc.unesco.org/ark:/48223/pf0000148654

United Nations. (2022). Sustainable development goals report. UN. https://unstats.un.org/sdgs/report/2022/The-Sustainable-Development-Goals-Report-2022.pdf

USDOT. (2022). *The US Department of Transportation*. US DOT. https://www.transportation.gov/

USEPA. (2011). *Guide to Sustainable Transportation Performance Measures*. USEPA. https://www.epa.gov/sites/default/files/2014-01/documents/sustainable_transpo_performance.pdf

USEPA. (2022). *US HUD-DOT-EPA Partnership for Sustainable Communities*. USEPA. https://19january2017snapshot.epa.gov/smartgrowth/hud-dot-epa-partnership-sustainable-communities_.html

USHUD. (2022). *The US Department of Housing and Urban Development*. USHUD. https://ushud.com/

Vanek, F., Angenent, L., Banks, J., Daziano, R., & Turnquist, M. A. (2014). *Sustainable transportation systems engineering*. McGraw-Hill Education.

Victoria Transport Policy Institute. (2019). Public Transit Improvements. *Transport Demand Management Encyclopedia.* VTPI. https://www.vtpi.org/tdm/tdm100.htm

Vuchic, V. (2005). *Urban transit: Operations, planning, and economics*. John Wiley & Sons Inc.

Vuchic, V. (2007). *Urban transit systems and technology*. John Wiley & Sons Inc. doi:10.1002/9780470168066

Watkins, K., La Mondia, J., & Brakewood, C. (2015). Developing a new course for public transportation education. *Southeastern Transportation Research, Innovation, Development, and Education Center Final Report.* https://rosap.ntl.bts.gov/view/dot/29100

Wu, Y. C. J., Lu, C. C. J., Lirn, T. C., & Yuan, C. H. (2014). An overview of university-level sustainable transportation in North America and Europe. *Transportation Research Part D, Transport and Environment, 26*, 27–31. doi:10.1016/j.trd.2013.10.006

Wu, Y. C. J., Shen, J. P., & Kuo, T. (2015). An overview of management education for sustainability in Asia. *International Journal of Sustainability in Higher Education, 16*(3), 341–353. doi:10.1108/IJSHE-10-2013-0136

ADDITIONAL READING

UNESCO. (2022). Education for sustainable development: A roadmap. *Education, 2030.* https://unesdoc.unesco.org/ark:/48223/pf0000374802

United Nations. (2022). *Transforming our world: the 2030 agenda for sustainable development*. UN. https://sdgs.un.org/2030agenda

Urban Transportation Council. (2007). *Strategies for sustainable transportation planning.* Transportation Association of Canada. https://www.tac-atc.ca/sites/tac-atc.ca/files/site/doc/resources/briefing-sustain-trans-prac_0.pdf

KEY TERMS AND DEFINITIONS

Ecological Sustainability: Long-term perspectives and developments to maintain the natural balance and survival of the ecosystem.

Economic Sustainability: The optimal use, safeguarding, and sustaining of resources to preserve the life quality of individuals over the long term.

Public Transportation: A system of vehicles that operates at regular times on fixed routes for getting people from one place to another.

Social Sustainability: Internal and external unity and solidarity of people (and/or cultures) in a global environment.

Sustainability: The use of resources by considering the well-being of people and protecting the environment.

Sustainable Transportation System: A system promoting the current transport and mobility needs of communities by addressing ecologic, economic, and social concerns.

Urban Transportation: A movement of people within urban areas using group travel technologies (mass transportation) such as buses, trains, and streetcars.

Section 2
Case Studies and Empirical Research Findings

Chapter 9

The Use of Information and Communication Technologies and Renewable Energy in Europe:
Implications for Public Transportation

Ivana Nincevic Pasalic

https://orcid.org/0000-0002-4610-0344

Faculty of Economics, Business, and Tourism, University of Split, Croatia

ABSTRACT

Information and communication technologies (ICTs) can help in cutting up to 20% of global carbon emissions by assisting consumers, different industries, and the public sector in energy savings and energy efficiency improvement. This chapter explores the relationship between ICTs and the development of renewable energy in European countries. In the first part of the research, the author conducted a cluster analysis to measure the differences in the use of ICTs in Europe through information society indicators. The results of the clustering (hierarchical and K-means) showed the existence of four clusters, and the increased differences between clusters from 2015 to 2020. The second part of the research confirms the existence of differences between clusters in the share of energy consumption from renewable sources, and the differences proved to be statistically significant. The results are discussed in terms of implications for public transportation, concluding that local governments must start and/or keep using ICTs for urban solutions for the future to be greener and sustainable.

DOI: 10.4018/978-1-6684-5996-6.ch009

Copyright © 2023, IGI Global. Copying or distributing in print or electronic forms without written permission of IGI Global is prohibited.

The Use of Information and Communication Technologies and Renewable Energy in Europe

INTRODUCTION

Information and communication technologies (ICTs) can help reduce up to 20% of global carbon emissions by 2030 as a result of assisting consumers, different industries, and the public sector in energy savings and energy efficiency improvement. This potential is based on the use of smart and innovative ICTs to reach energy efficiency in transport, energy, real estate and other sectors. It is important to mention the smart cities development that is based on integrated ICT infrastructure that creates efficient solutions for supplying systems for transport, water, energy and other infrastructure. Implementing the comprehensive global sustainability action plan requires ICTs, which can help in a reach to fulfill the UN Sustainable Development Goals (SDGs) (Heuberger, 2017).

Advances in ICTs and their increasing prevalence are changing the way users use services. Innovative digital technologies such as robotics, cloud computing, the Internet of Things, open and big data, artificial intelligence and other technologies require organizations to continually evaluate and adjust their way of working in terms of changes in strategies, organizational processes, operational models, products and services (Berman, 2012; Ross et al., 2016). Analyzing the impact of ICT on public and private sectors, Gatautis et al. (2015) conclude that ICT enables better quality of service delivery, increased business efficiency, reduces costs and leads to greater business transparency. The great ICTs contribution is that it assists in its own energy efficiency improvement (as the work of ICT also generates gas emissions), but it also helps other sectors and industries to become energy and green-efficient.

The development and use of ICT and consequently e-government varies considerably among the EU Member States. In 2020, the highest share of users who used the websites of public authorities to obtain information was recorded in Denmark (89%) and Finland (85%), in contrast to Romania where only 10% of citizens received information from public authorities through their websites (Eurostat, 2021). Looking only at this indicator, it is clear that there are large differences between countries within the European Union. According to many studies, the digital divide is present in European countries (e.g. Cruz-Jesus, Oliveira & Bacao, 2012; Zoroja & Pejic Bach, 2016; Yera et al., 2020) which negatively affects the overall development of the information society (Vu, 2020; Toader et al., 2018). This mainly refers to the "digital divide" between the north and the rest of the EU, or north and south and west and east (Van Dijk, 2009; European Parliament, 2015), i.e. between more developed economies and those that entered the transition somewhat later (e.g. Zoroja (2011) in her research works on the division into developed and post-communist countries of Europe).

By introducing the Green Deal, part of the EU's strategy to achieve zero greenhouse gas (GHG) emissions, the European Union has set ambitious goals to improve overall energy efficiency and reduce its negative effects on the environment. According to Pakere et al. (2021), not all of the EU 27 member states made equally significant contributions to the overall EU green strategy. If each EU member states do not take action to lessen climate change, there is a major danger that the common objectives will not be met. This risk arises from each EU member state's strategy to the Green Deal as they have the freedom to set their own criteria for CO_2 cutback (Pakere et al., 2021). A similar situation in the EU concerns the Renewable Energy Directive where the share of renewable energy in total energy consumption is being set differently for each EU member state.

A study by Azam et al. (2021b) recommends implementing ICT-related policies to promote sustainable growth through renewable energy as ICT has the potential to significantly improve technological limitations and support the phenomena of renewable energy at the same time (Azam et al, 2021a). The aforementioned relationship between ICT and renewable energy is the focal point of this study. The literature on the subject is scarce because other research usually focuses on the relationship between ICT and economic growth (e.g. Fernández-Portillo, Almodóvar-González, Hernández-Mogollón, 2020) and the relationship between renewable energy and economic growth (e.g. Inglesi-Lotz, 2016). The relationship between ICTs and renewable energy development will be explored in the context of European countries while noting and expecting that there might be differences between them as they have different approaches to achieving energy efficiency.

As transportation is one of the largest energy consumers, the findings of the study will be discussed in terms of public transportation possibilities in the local government context. The overall aim of the chapter is to explore the relationship between ICTs and the development of renewable energy in European countries. Cluster analysis will be used to determine/group European countries based on information society (e-government) indicators, and to find similarities and differences between countries.

Therefore, the objectives of this study are to:

- Classify 32 European countries (members of the European Union and five non-members) into groups based on the homogeneity of the use of e-government services by their citizens;
- Given that the discourse of digital transformation of public administrations has been discussed for years, cluster analysis will be conducted for years 2015 and 2020 to determine whether there are shifts in the use of e-government services, i.e. whether they decrease or increase among countries considering the trends related to digital transition.
- Based on the results of clustering, the objective is to determine the common features of newly formed groups.
- Compare the countries in the clusters and determine whether there are differences according to the level of use of renewable energy consumption (in 2020) to see whether the development of ICTs is related to the green energy transition.
- Discuss the results of the research in scaling the practical implications for local government's efforts in creating more sustainable public transportation systems.

The initial part of the chapter, background, gives a literature overview on three topics: the use of ICTs in the public sector, renewable energy in Europe and transportation and its renewable energy ratio. The second part describes the methodology used in the study while the fourth part shows the results. Afterward, the results are discussed in general with a special focus on the implications for public transportation in cities/municipalities. The conclusion is given at the end listing the limitations and future research propositions.

BACKGROUND

The use of ICTs in the public sector will be observed using information society indicators delivered by Eurostat. The following subchapters describe the literature review background for ICTs and energy consumption themes as a part of the digital and green transition efforts.

Use of ICTs in the Public Sector

Citizens and businesses are increasingly using the internet to perform their daily tasks. Recently, the use of e-government services has become increasingly popular because it allows information to be obtained at any time, in addition to performing administrative tasks remotely. In 2020, 47% of EU citizens aged 16-74 used the websites of public authorities to obtain the necessary information (Eurostat, 2021), which is a significant increase compared to 2008 when 33% used them.

Although it has many definitions, e-government refers to the use of ICT to provide better services to stakeholders (citizens, businesses, etc.). In addition to administrative services, public administrations today provide a variety of user-oriented electronic services: 1) providing information to stakeholders (sharing information known as e-information), 2) interacting with stakeholders (e-consultation), and 3) engaging in decision-making processes (e-decision-making). These three levels of services are also known as e-participation based on the OECD Model and the UN biennial survey (e.g. UNDESA, 2018). The goal of e-government is to provide citizens with an environment where services and information are offered electronically. For e-government to be successful in implementation and use, public administrations must understand citizens' needs and main concerns (Dudley et al., 2015). Every e-government program must have a clear idea of the benefits to be given to citizens, it needs to identify and understand the obstacles that must be addressed and the extent of institutional transformation required for e-government to be successful in a given context (Dwivedi, Weerakkody & Janssen, 2012).

Energy Consumption from Renewable Sources in Europe

According to the EU Renewable Energy Directive 2009/28/EC, EU member states had to reach at least a 20% share of RES in total energy consumption by 2020 (European Commission, 2009) and the new Renewable Energy Directive (2018/2001/EK) set a new objective at 32% renewable energy by 2030, with a provision for a potential increase by 2023 (European Commission, 2018). According to the latest European Green Deal (COM(2019) 640 final), Europe's objective and plan is to become the world's first climate-neutral continent by 2050. A comprehensive set of measures known as the European Green Deal should make it possible for businesses and citizens in Europe to profit from a sustainable green transition. (Eurostat, 2022).

When discussing renewable sources, the following are examples of renewable energy sources: wind energy, solar energy, hydropower, tidal power, geothermal energy, ambient heat absorbed by heat pumps, biofuels, and the renewable portion of trash. Table 1 below presents current data on the proportion of energy derived from renewable sources in the EU's three major consumption sectors: transport, heating and cooling, and electricity.

According to numbers from Eurostat, the EU met its stated goal (20%) for 2020 by consuming 22.1% of its energy from renewable sources, which is an increase from 2019 (19.9%). The countries with particularly high percentages of using renewable energy are Sweden (part of the EU) and Norway and Iceland (not part of the EU). The current aim of 27 EU member states of reaching 32% renewable energy set for 2030, will still require an enormous change in the energy infrastructure (see Figure 1).

Numerous advantages of using renewable energy and expanding the renewable energy sources in the EU include a decrease in greenhouse gas emissions, an increase in the diversity of energy sources, and a decreased dependence on the markets for fossil fuels (oil and gas). Another benefit includes increased employment in new "green" technology in manufacturing and installation (EPA, 2022).

Table 1. Renewable energy in 2020 – country analysis

COUNTRIES OVERACHIEVING THEIR TARGETS (% of energy from renewable sources)			
Sweden	60.1	Slovakia	17.3
Finland	43.8	Czechia	17.3
Latvia	42.1	Cyprus	16.9
Austria	36.5	Ireland	16.2
Portugal	34	Poland	16.1
Denmark	31.6	Hungary	13.9
Croatia	31	Luxemburg	11.7
Estonia	30.2	Malta	10.7
Lithuania	26.8	*Norway*	*77.4*
Romania	24.5	*Iceland*	*83.7*
Bulgaria	23.3	COUNTRIES MEETING THEIR TARGETS	
EU	22.1	Slovenia	25
Greece	21.7	Netherlands	14
Spain	21.2	Belgium	13
Italy	20.4	COUNTRY UNDER ITS TARGETS	
Germany	19.3	France	19.1

Source: (Eurostat, 2022)

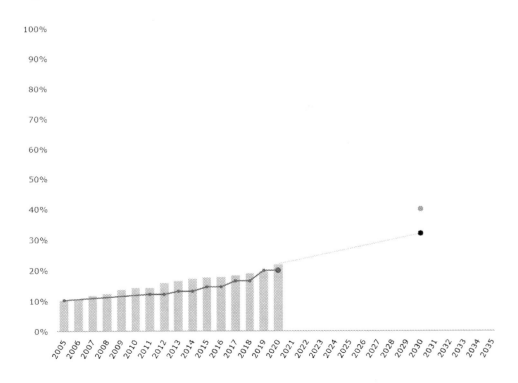

Figure 1. Progress toward renewable energy source targets for EU-27 Source: (EEA, 2022)

The Use of Information and Communication Technologies and Renewable Energy in Europe

In a scenario study that aimed 100% renewable energy system in Europe by 2050, Connolly, Lund & Mathiesen (2016) showed that a 100% renewable energy system in Europe is theoretically feasible utilizing the Smart Energy System concept without requiring an excessive amount of biomass. The reason is that interconnecting the sectors of transportation, heating, and cooling creates additional flexibility and permits a sporadic renewable diffusion of more than 80% in the energy sector. The findings include that the cost of the Smart Energy Europe scenario is 10-15% higher than the cost of the "business-as-usual scenario", but because the final scenario relies on domestic investments rather than foreign fuel imports, it will add almost 10 million direct jobs within the EU.

Renewable Energy in Transport

The following numbers describe the great influence of transportation worldwide; one-third of final energy consumption and one-quarter of worldwide energy-related CO_2 emissions are produced by the transportation industry (Turner et al., 2021). Even though the use of renewable energy is increasing in the electricity sector, only 3.4% of demand is met by it in the transportation sector (ibid).

Many authors agree that transport is the most challenging sector to decarbonise (e.g. Ruoso & Ribeiro, 2022) as it still heavily relies on fossil fuels and is predominately car-oriented (Siebenhofer, Ajanovic & Haas, 2022). This is the reason why many countries and cities are considering different ways of tackling the problem of non-renewable energy consumption. Nasiri et al. (2022) concluded that European directives, which serve as legal frameworks for promoting the development and use of renewable energy sources, are less successful than anticipated in encouraging renewable energy adoption. Their study confirmed that the 10% proportion of energy produced from renewable sources for the transportation sector was not reached by observed countries Denmark, Ireland, the Netherlands, Estonia, Latvia and Lithuania.

When considering renewable energy strategies, Danielis, Scoranno & Giansoldati (2022) concluded that EU countries rely on two strategies: 1) promoting the adoption of electric vehicles and 2) boosting the production and consumption of biofuels, particularly those made with innovative materials. Their calculation showed that the biofuel approach can result in a GHG reduction of up to 3.6%, while the electrification strategy can result in a GHG reduction of up to 8.3%, taking into account the intended policies and goals stated in the National Energy and Climate Plans (NECPs) for 2020–2030. When utilized together, the GHG reduction might be up to 11.9%.

The aforementioned three topics are meant to offer a better understanding of the research. The first two topics, ICT in form of e-government indicators in European countries and renewable energy ratio will be correlated in order to understand their possible relation and the third one is related to the implications in terms of transportation.

METHODOLOGY

This chapter explains the methodological approach to the research, which is divided into two parts. The first part of the research is related to measuring the use of ICT (in this case the internet) in the use of e-government services by citizens. In the following text, only the term "use of e-government services" will be used. The following indicators were used to measure e-government use: 1) use of the internet to interact with public administration authorities, 2) use of the internet to obtain information from public authorities websites, 3) use of the internet to download official online forms, and 4) use of the internet

The Use of Information and Communication Technologies and Renewable Energy in Europe

to submit completed online forms. All four indicators refer to data obtained from citizens aged 16 to 74 (expressed as a percentage) and refer to the use of the internet in the last 12 months.

The second part of the research is related to measuring the share of energy from renewable sources in selected European countries (clusters) conducting the ANOVA analysis, analysis of variance. Data for 2020 (last available in June 2022) was compiled by Eurostat's the International Energy Agency's annual joint questionnaires. Per EEA's definition renewable energy consumption "is the amount of renewable energy consumed for electricity, heating and cooling, and transport in the 27 EU Member States using actual and normalised hydropower and wind power generation and is expressed as a share of gross final energy consumption" (2022).

ICT data was collected for 32 European countries (all 27 EU member states and Norway, United Kingdom, North Macedonia, Serbia and Turkey) from the publicly available database Eurostat, Information Society section (Eurostat - Information society, 2021). Since data for 2020 was not available for France, data for 2019 was used. Data for other European countries (e.g. Albania, Bosnia and Herzegovina, Montenegro) were not analysed because they were not available/recorded for both reference years (in most cases they exist for 2020, but not for 2015).

Cluster analysis, as one of the multivariate methods, seeks to classify selected European countries depending on the similarities, i.e. differences in the observed characteristics of the use of e-government services. Since this is an exploratory analysis, hierarchical cluster analysis was conducted as the first step of research, to determine the number of clusters that started with 32 clusters (n) and finished up with one. As a measure of diversity between groups, a squared Euclidean distance between each observed pair was used, and the Ward method was used to group similar objects. This is one of the most commonly used methods, especially given the small number of observations in this study. It is characteristic that it uses cluster variance to calculate distances within a cluster. In addition, Ward was chosen because the results of the method are approximately equal to clusters which facilitates the interpretation of cluster characteristics. After analysing the results of hierarchical cluster analysis (explained in more detail in Chapter 3), the author decided to use four clusters in further research. Although it is a subjective assessment (as suggested for example by Datanovia (2018)), hierarchical analysis was chosen to determine the number of clusters as an input to the second step of the research.

As a second step, non-hierarchical clustering of k-means (K-means clustering) was performed, a method that does not require the calculation of all possible distances between all pairs of values (Rozga, 2015). Since this method requires a predetermined number of clusters that we want to have, we used a previously determined number that is further confirmed by empirical calculation, the formula (as done by Zoroja & Pejić Bach (2016)), $K = \ddot{O} (n / 2) = \ddot{O} (32/2) = 4$ clusters.

IBM SPSS Statistics 23.0 was used for all analyses.

RESULTS

Cluster analysis

European countries were classified according to the indicators of the use of e-government services by citizens (described in the subchapter above). In addition, the examination has been done on whether (and how) the situation has changed over the years, which is why the cluster analysis was conducted for 2015 and 2020, and the results will be presented for both reference years.

The Use of Information and Communication Technologies and Renewable Energy in Europe

Descriptive statistics for both analysed years are shown in Tables 2 and Table 3. A significant improvement by all countries in the use of e-government services in various activities of interaction with public administration bodies is seen when comparing the tables.

Table 2. Descriptive statistics for 2015

Descriptive statistics - internet use for 2015					
	N	Min	Max	Mean	Std. Dev.
Interaction with public authorities	32	11.00	88.00	48.28	20.01
Obtaining information from public authorities web sites	32	9.00	86.00	42.84	18.68
Downloading official forms	32	5.00	62.00	29.78	14.49
Submitting completed forms	32	5.00	71.00	28.91	18.19

Source: Author's work

Table 3. Descriptive statistics for 2020

Descriptive statistics - internet use for 2020					
	N	Min	Max	Mean	Std. Dev.
Interaction with public authorities	32	13.00	92.00	58.94	20.31
Obtaining information from public authorities web sites	32	10.00	89.00	49.59	19.55
Downloading official forms	32	8.00	84.00	35.88	16.16
Submitting completed forms	32	7.00	81.00	41.25	20.99

Source: Author's work

Table 4 shows the list of analysed countries and each country indicates the (non)membership to the European Union and additional geographical information for easier analysis of the results.

Hierarchical Clustering

As indicated in the second subchapter, Ward's method was used in the analysis of European countries, and the robustness of the estimate was made using the squared Euclidean distance. Standardization of variables was not required as all variables used were expressed as a percentage. Figure 2 and Figure 3 that follow show the dendrograms - a graphical representation of the results of cluster analysis for the two reference years.

According to selected e-government indicators, European countries can be divided into four groups according to the results of the 2015 cluster analysis. In the case of grouping into two groups only, the first group would consist of the northern European countries Denmark, Estonia, Finland, Norway, Netherlands and Sweden (at the bottom of the dendrogram), and the second from all other countries. This does not provide sufficient space for further research on the scale of the digital divide in Europe.

Table 4. List of European countries analysed

No.	EU member state	Year entered in EU	Geo info
1	Austria	1995.	Central Europe
2	Belgium	1958.	West Europe
3	Bulgaria	2007.	East Europe
4	Cyprus	2004.	Mediterranean country
5	Czech Republic	2004.	Central Europe
6	Denmark	1973.	North Europe
7	Estonia	2004.	North Europe
8	Finland	1995.	North Europe
9	France	1958.	West Europe
10	Greece	1981.	Mediterranean country
11	Croatia	2013.	Southeast Europe
12	Ireland	1973.	North Europe
13	Italy	1958.	Mediterranean country
14	Latvia	2004.	North Europe
15	Lithuania	2004.	North Europe
16	Luxemburg	1958.	West Europe
17	Hungary	2004.	Central Europe
18	Malta	2004.	Mediterranean country
19	Netherland	1958.	West Europe
20	Norway	Not EU member state, within EEA	North Europe
21	Germany	1958.	Central Europe
22	Poland	2004.	Central Europe
23	Portugal	1986.	Mediterranean country
24	Romania	2007.	East Europe
25	North Macedonia	Not EU member state	East Europe
26	Slovakia	2004.	Central Europe
27	Slovenia	2004.	Central Europe
28	Serbia	Not EU member state	East Europe
29	Spain	1986.	Mediterranean country
30	Sweden	1995.	North Europe
31	Turkey	Not EU member state	East Europe / Mediterranean country
32	United Kingdom*	1973. Left EU in January 2020	North Europe

EEA = European Economic Area

Source: Author's work

Figure 2. Dendrogram of cluster analysis results for 2015
Source: export from SPSS (author's work)

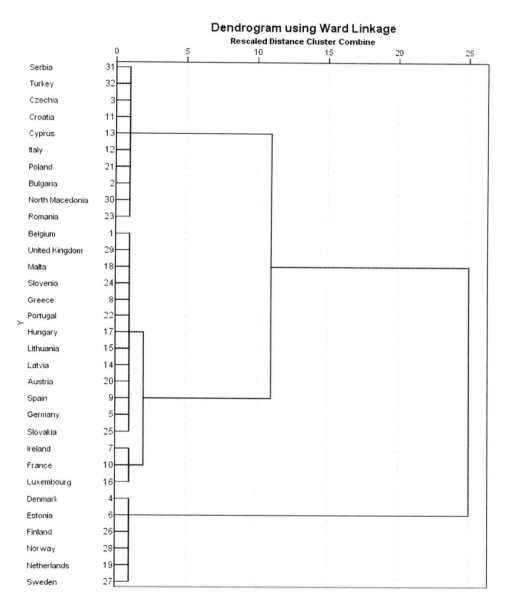

Based on selected e-government indicators, European countries can be divided into six groups according to the results of the cluster analysis for 2020. However, according to the author's decision, this number will be set to four clusters as an ideal number for further analysis. The decision was made based on the analysis of the dendrogram shown above (clusters marked in bold red) and the formula shown in the second subchapter.

Figure 3. Dendrogram of cluster analysis results for 2020
Source: export from SPSS with author's processing

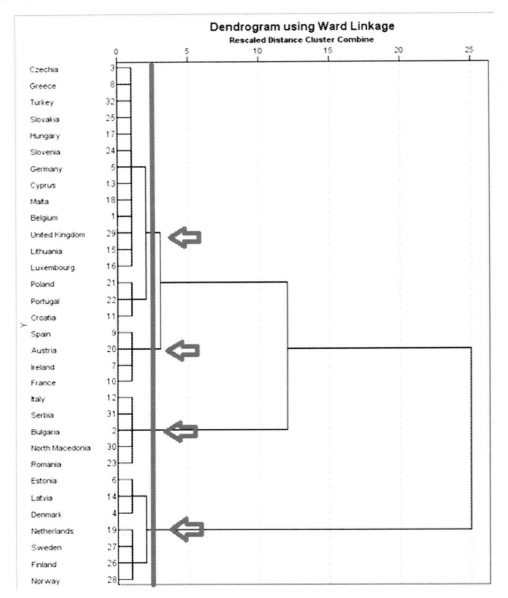

K-Means Clustering

According to the K-means method, 32 selected European countries are grouped into four clusters as shown in Table 5. The clusters are named A, B, C and D. The countries in cluster A have the highest average value of using e-government services, and those in cluster D have the lowest. Detailed average values of e-government usage indicators for different clusters are provided in Table 6 and Table 7.

The Use of Information and Communication Technologies and Renewable Energy in Europe

Table 5. Grouping of European countries by clusters for 2015 and 2020

Clusters in 2015			
A	**B**	**C**	**D**
Denmark, Estonia, Netherlands, Finland, Sweden, Norway	Ireland, France, Luxemburg, Austria	Belgium, Germany, Greece, Spain, Croatia, Cyprus, Latvia, Lithuania, Hungary, Malta, Portugal, Slovenia, Slovakia, UK	Bulgaria, Czech Republic, Italy, Poland, Romania, North Macedonia, Serbia, Turkey
Clusters in 2020			
A	**B**	**C**	**D**
Denmark, Netherlands, Finland, Sweden, Norway	**Estonia**, Ireland, *Spain*, France, Latvia, Austria	Belgium, *Czech Republic*, Germany, Greece, Croatia, Cyprus, Lithuania, **Luxemburg**, Hungary, Malta, *Poland*, Portugal, Slovenia, Slovakia, UK, *Turkey*	Bulgaria, Italy, Romania, North Macedonia, Serbia

Source: Author's work (Eurostat, 2021)

The results for 2020 indicate that cluster A includes northern European countries, and Scandinavian countries, except for the Netherlands. Their citizens show the highest level of use of e-government services. They are followed by the countries of Central and Northern Europe except for Spain (cluster B). In cluster C there are as many as 16 countries of different geographical locations with one non-EU member (Turkey). Although this is a relatively large number of countries, increasing the number of clusters to 5, it turned out that only 3 countries (Poland, Croatia and Portugal) would stand out, which does not make a significant contribution to the research. The presence of Turkey as the only non-EU member is interesting. Cluster D includes two non-EU member countries from Eastern Europe (Serbia and North Macedonia), Bulgaria and Romania, and Italy.

Table 6. Average values of e-government indicators for 2015

Indicators/Clusters	A	B	C	D
Interaction with public authorities	79.50	60.00	45.50	23.88
Obtaining information from public authorities web sites	74.00	45.75	41.21	20.88
Downloading official forms	49.83	41.50	27.64	12.63
Submitting completed forms	59.00	38.50	23.93	10.25

Source: Author's work (adapted SPSS export)

Table 7. Average values of e-government indicators for 2020

Indicators/Clusters	A	B	C	D
Interaction with public authorities	88.60	71.33	55.75	24.60
Obtaining information from public authorities web sites	78.40	56.00	47.38	20.20
Downloading official forms	62.00	39.17	32.88	15.40
Submitting completed forms	74.00	59.17	33.00	13.40

Source: Author's work (adapted SPSS export)

As can be seen from Table 4, there have been several changes in cluster groupings over five years. Thus, Spain, the Czech Republic, Poland and Turkey recorded a jump to a "better" cluster (in italic), while Estonia and Luxembourg recorded a decline to a "weaker" cluster.

Tables 6 and 7 show an improvement in the average values of e-government indicators in 2020 for all four clusters (compared to 2015 values). This improvement is more significant in A, B and C clusters, and is minimal in D cluster. For example, interaction with authorities increased from 2015 to 2020 by 9.1 percentage points (pp) in cluster A, 11.33 pp in cluster B, 10.25 in cluster C, and 0.72 in cluster D. Similarly submitting completed forms increased by 15 percentage points in cluster A, 20.67 pp in cluster B, 9.07 pp in cluster C and 3.15 pp in cluster D. The results show deepening the gap between the best (A) and the worst cluster (D).

Results of ANOVA Analysis

The results of the analysis of variance are shown in Table 8 including mean values, standard deviation (SD) and F value along with the significance level. It shows a comparison of the renewable energy consumption of countries within the previously described four clusters A, B, C and D for 2020. The consumption of energy from renewable sources was tested through the indicator share of energy consumption from renewable sources in Europe. The average values of the renewable energy proportion are the highest in cluster A, followed by clusters B and D, and the lowest values are in cluster C. Turkey was not included in the analysis as data was not available for it.

Differences in renewable energy consumption in clusters exist and are statistically significant (level of significance 1%), so it can be concluded that there is a relation between the use of ICTs (through the use of e-government services used by citizens) and the use of renewable energy by EU countries.

Table 8. Development of e-government on the supply side

Index / Clusters	A	B	C	D	å		
% of renewable energy	Mean (SD)	Mean (SD)	Mean (SD)	Mean (SD)	Total Mean (SD)	F value	Sig
	45.4 (14.6)	27.5 (10.4)	19.2 (7.2)	22.7 (2.8)	25.6 (14.6)	6.434*	0.002

Source: Author's work (adapted SPSS export)

DISCUSSION

Per research results, the cluster with the best results of information society indicators includes the most developed countries in the Scandinavian region (Sweden, Norway, Finland and Denmark) and the Netherlands. Previously mentioned countries are followed by Estonia, Ireland, Spain, France, Latvia, and Austria in cluster B. Cluster C consists of countries of different geographical locations with moderate results: Belgium, Czech Republic, Germany, Greece, Croatia, Cyprus, Lithuania, Luxembourg, Hungary, Malta, Poland, Portugal, Slovenia, Slovakia, United Kingdom, and Turkey. The worst-rated countries (members of cluster D) are Bulgaria, Romania, Italy, Northern Macedonia and Serbia, a combination of non-EU countries or EU member countries that were among the last to join the EU, except for Italy.

The Use of Information and Communication Technologies and Renewable Energy in Europe

Comparing the results of the two cluster methods (Table 9), it can be concluded that there are no major deviations in results. The only difference is noted to Estonia and Latvia (noted in blue), which, according to the hierarchical analysis, belong to cluster A, in contrast to the results of clustering k-means where they belong to a slightly worse cluster B.

Table 9. Clusters according to two cluster methods

A	B	C	D
K-means clustering			
Denmark, Netherlands, Finland, Sweden, Norway	**Estonia**, Ireland, Spain, France, **Latvia**, Austria	Belgium, Czech Republic, Germany, Greece, Croatia, Cyprus, Lithuania, Luxemburg, Hungary, Malta, Poland, Portugal, Slovenia, Slovakia, UK, Turkey	Bulgaria, Italy, Romania, North Macedonia, Serbia
Hierarchical clustering			
Denmark, Netherlands, Finland, Sweden, Norway, **Estonia**, **Latvia**	Ireland, Spain, France, Latvia, Austria	Belgium, Czech Republic, Germany, Greece, Croatia, Cyprus, Lithuania, Luxemburg, Hungary, Malta, Poland, Portugal, Slovenia, Slovakia, UK, Turkey	Bulgaria, Italy, Romania, North Macedonia, Serbia

Source: Author's work

The results obtained by the cluster analysis, in general, indicate the existence of four clusters of European countries concerning the use of e-government services by citizens. The results confirm the existence of the digital divide and indicate that the divide has been deepening for the last five years. This is in line with the results of previous research from an earlier period. Grbavec et al. (2019) researched and grouped EU member states in the somewhat broader context of the digital economy and society according to the DESI index (The Digital Economy and Society Index) and identified a gap among EU members. Banhidi, Dobos & Nemeslaki (2020), using the components of the DESI index as well, got five clusters, taking into account EU members only. Zoroja and Pejić Bach (2016) observed several dimensions of the digital society, such as e-business (commerce), e-government, and e-learning, and identified a gap between European countries. Cluster membership in the previously mentioned research differs from this research, except for the common members of the best and worst clusters. Thus, it could be determined that members of A and D clusters are the most and least developed countries in the digital transition.

Mucunska Palevska and Novkovska (2021) made recommendations for non-EU/EU candidate countries, in this case, cluster D countries (Northern Macedonia and Serbia). They suggest to these countries to start creating policies that will shape their digital single market, and improve digital infrastructure to close the digital divide between their urban and rural regions.

The research supports the existence of a relationship between the use of ICTs/e-government services by citizens and the share of renewable energy consumption. The share of renewable energy shows the country's development of renewable sources and ability to influence gas emissions, and the results of the one-way ANOVA analysis indicate significant differences among the observed clusters where leading information societies are also leading in the share of renewable energy consumption.

Smart grids, smart buildings, and smart logistics are implemented using ICTs. The potential advantages of renewable energy sources are understood by the ICT sector and their application in large-scale systems such as telecom base stations, as well as smaller-scale systems such as computer peripherals and electric vehicles (Ahmed, Naeem, & Iqbal, 2017).

The results of a study conducted by Jayaprakash & Radhakrishna Pillai (2022) indicate that ICT has a significant positive influence on the economic, social and environmental dimensions of sustainable development of a country. To reduce the influence or avoid the influence on the environment and to confirm ICT as a facilitator for sustainable development, policymakers need to have their focus on the environmental component and adopt regulations that encourage the use of green technologies (ibid).

Pakere et al. (2021) used their multidimensional energy and climate policy indicator to rank the performance of EU countries and several similarities for the highest score can be found when compared to the results of this study. Out of three groups, their results show that Sweden, Denmark, Latvia, Austria, Finland, Ireland, and Lithuania obtained the highest score in climate and energy indicator values, but it is worth mentioning that in addition to the number of groups, their research did not include countries outside EU.

On the example of South Asian countries, Murshed (2020) showed that ICT trade increases renewable energy consumption, and increases renewable energy shares while indirectly lessening CO2 emissions through advancing RE consumption levels.

Implications for Public Transportation in Urban Environment

The findings discussed in the previous subchapter show the existence of a relationship between the development of ICT and renewable energy. Knowing that cities are responsible for 80% of the world's s energy consumption and 75% of global CO_2 emissions, and the largest contributors are transport and buildings (Turner et al., 2021), this section will focus on public transportation changes needed in terms of green energy consumption in an urban environment.

As transportation is one of the largest energy consumers and gas emitters worldwide (as shown in Figure 4), it can be concluded that one of the quickest and most economical methods to cut emissions and improve local air quality is to encourage people to use public transportation that relies on renewable energy (Turner et al., 2021). To achieve this goal, the first step is to build a public transportation system that leverages renewable energy sources and makes sure users can afford it and prefer it to owning a car. Sustainable energy use will not only increase the effectiveness of transit services, but over time, it might also enable cities to lower commuting expenses without compromising the quality of the service (Marsh, 2022).

The local and central governments can help promote and amplify initiatives to use renewable energy in public transportation by taking the following seven steps. These action steps are detailed in the policy brief developed by the International Association of Public Transport and REN21 - international renewable energy community with contributors from academia, governments, NGOs and industry (Turner et al., 2021):

- Setting targets for public transport along with support policies,
- Participating and leading pilot and demonstration projects,
- Creating support tax and regulatory environment at all levels,
- Leveraging public transport's purchasing power and developing new business models,
- Using green Covid-19 recovery funds to develop further,
- Integrating renewables in "urban carbon-neutral planning",
- Build capacity and skills of people.

Figure 4. Share of renewable energy in total energy consumption for 2018
Source: (Turner et al., 2021)

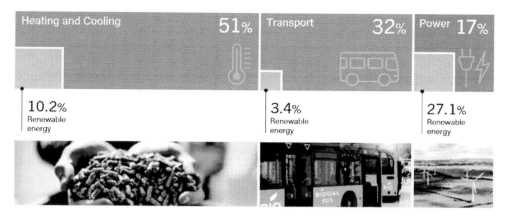

Plans tailored to the local resources, governance, and market circumstances must be developed by local governments and public transportation authorities. Countries and cities may make significant contributions to combating climate change while also enhancing local air quality and public health by utilizing renewable energy to power public transportation (UITP, 2021).

According to SLOCAT Foundation (2021), he primary points of entry for renewable energy in the transportation sector include:

- "The use of biofuels combined with conventional fuels, including higher blends containing 100% liquid biofuels;
- Natural gas vehicles and infrastructure converted to run on upgraded biomethane; and
- The electrification of transport modes, including the use of battery electric and plug-in hybrid vehicles or of hydrogen, synthetic fuels, and electro-fuels, where the electricity is itself renewable".

Another way for local governments to significantly reduce their gas emissions is to purchase or generate electricity directly from renewable sources (EPA, 2022). Local governments can generate energy locally. Buying green power or renewable energy, and using different combinations of energy options can help in meeting city/municipal targets, particularly in regions that face variability in the availability and quality of renewable resources (ibid).

To avoid and lessen the demand for motorized transportation, city governments should upgrade pedestrian and cycling infrastructure in addition to public transportation technological and other upgrades. The acceptance of policy initiatives could be improved with better stakeholder involvement techniques and planning tools for pedestrians and cyclists (Bardal, Gjertsen & Reinar, 2020).

In addition, city governments should promote electric vehicles powered by renewable energy and renewable fuels to advance vehicle technology and transportation system effectiveness. According to the analysis of D'Adamo, Gastaldi & Ozturk (2022), there are three requirements for the transition to electric vehicles to be sustainable: 1) the use of renewable energy sources, 2) local industrial development of the sector, and 3) battery recycling. Ruoso & Ribeiro (2022) agree with the argument that renewable energy consumption is correlated with the adoption of electric vehicles in various countries.

Better solutions for supplying enhanced transportation systems will be produced by the shift to smart cities with integrated ICT infrastructure. Smart cities can bring green technologies specialized in green and smart mobility solutions such as real-time processing of data (e.g. for trams or buses), GPS technology, sensors as part of the Internet of Things (IoT) solutions, online journey planners, etc.

In general, the most crucial tactic to implement policy packages is one using a mix of "push" and "pull" approaches where success factors include the strategic use of communication, allowing for experiments, and introducing policy changes sequentially (Bardal, Gjertsen & Reinar, 2020).

CONCLUSION

One of the main drivers of the socioeconomic development of the nations' economies is technological development. For this reason, ICTs indicators of digital society have been used to group the European countries depending on their ICT development stage. The results of the clustering (hierarchical and K-means) showed the existence of four clusters and the increased differences from 2015 to 2020. Scandinavian countries showed the highest rate of ICT development (cluster A) while countries in cluster D had the lowest development of ICT and belonged to European countries outside of the EU and ones that joined the EU last.

The objective of this exploratory research was to investigate the relationship between ICTs and renewable energy and to set guidelines for public transportation in urban settings. The findings showed the existence of a relationship between clusters (European countries) in the share of energy consumption from renewable sources, and the differences between groups of European countries proved to be statistically significant. This finding contributes to the literature as explains the existence of a relationship between the efficiency of using ICTs in e-government and renewable energy shares in ICT more efficient countries. The results may help in tackling the challenges in advancing green energy implementation, as well as in tackling transportation challenges. Local governments must start and/or keep using ICTs in public transportation solutions for the future to be greener and more sustainable.

The concluding remarks include an emphasis on the importance of ICTs as they help in delivering ambitious, shared action plans for reaching sustainability. ICTs are required in the sustainable development of cities, regions, and countries and the ICT sector not only makes it possible for other industries to go green but also works to reduce its ecological footprint.

The limitations of this research consist of the subjective assessment of the number of clusters (this is also a limitation of the method), and the selection of information society indicators focusing on citizens only.

Future research can use the results of this research as a basis for researching the reasons why countries are in a certain cluster, by analysing for example GDP per capita, R&D investments, internet access, checking for differences between urban and rural areas, etc., and can use other ways of obtaining cluster numbers (e.g., Elbow method). Future research can expand the relationship research between ICT and other "green" indicators besides renewable energy.

ACKNOWLEDGMENT

This research has been supported by the Croatian Science Foundation [grant number UIP-2017-05-7625].

REFERENCES

Ahmed, F., Naeem, M., & Iqbal, M. (2017). ICT and renewable energy: A way forward to the next generation telecom base stations. *Telecommunication Systems, 64*(1), 43–56. doi:10.100711235-016-0156-4

Azam, A., Rafiq, M., Shafique, M., Ateeq, M., & Yuan, J. (2021a). Investigating the Impact of Renewable Electricity Consumption on Sustainable Economic Development: A Panel ARDL Approach. *International Journal of Green Energy, 18*(11), 1185–1192. doi:10.1080/15435075.2021.1897825

Azam, A., Rafiq, M., Shafique, M., Yuan, J., & Salem, S. (2021b). Human Development Index, ICT, and Renewable Energy-Growth Nexus for Sustainable Development: A Novel PVAR Analysis. *Frontiers in Energy Research, 9*, 760758. doi:10.3389/fenrg.2021.760758

Banhidi, Z., Dobos, I., & Nemeslaki, A. (2020). What the overall Digital Economy and Society Index reveals: A statistical analysis of the DESI EU28 dimensions. *Regional Statistics, 10*(2), 42–62. doi:10.15196/RS100209

Bardal, K. G., Gjertsen, A., & Mathias Brynildsen Reinar, M. B. (2020). Sustainable mobility: Policy design and implementation in three Norwegian cities. *Transportation Research Part D, Transport and Environment, 82*, 102330. doi:10.1016/j.trd.2020.102330

Berman, S. J. (2012). Digital transformation: Opportunities to create new business models. *Strategy and Leadership, 40*(2), 16–24. doi:10.1108/10878571211209314

Connolly, D., Lund, H., & Mathiesen, B. V. (2016). Smart Energy Europe: The technical and economic impact of one potential 100% renewable energy scenario for the European Union. *Renewable & Sustainable Energy Reviews, 60*, 1634–1653. doi:10.1016/j.rser.2016.02.025

Cruz-Jesus, F., Oliveira, T., & Bacao, F. (2012). Digital divide across the European Union. *Information & Management, 49*(6), 278–291. doi:10.1016/j.im.2012.09.003

D'Adamo, I., Gastaldi, M., & Ozturk, I. (2022). The sustainable development of mobility in the green transition: Renewable energy, local industrial chain, and battery recycling. *Sustainable Development*, 1–13. doi:10.1002d.2424

Danielis, R., Scoranno, M., & Giansoldati, M. (2022). Decarbonising transport in Europe: Trends, goals, policies and passenger car scenarios. *Research in Transportation Economics, 91*, 101068. doi:10.1016/j.retrec.2021.101068

Datanovia (2018). *Determining The Optimal Number Of Clusters: 3 Must Know Methods*. Data Novia. https://www.datanovia.com/en/lessons/determining-the-optimal-number-of-clusters-3-must-know-methods/

Dudley, E., Lin, D. Y., Mancini, M., & Ng, J. (2015). *Implementing a citizen-centric approach to delivering government services*. McKinsey & Company. www.mckinsey.com/industries/public-sector/our-insights/implementing-a-citizen-centric-approach-to-delivering-government-services

Dwivedi, Y., Weerakkody, V., & Janssen, M. (2012). Moving towards maturity: Challenges to successful e-government implementation and diffusion. *Advanced Information Systems, 42*(4), 11–22.

EPA (United States Environmental Protection Agency). (2022). *Local Renewable Energy Benefits and Resources*. Retreived June 20, 2022 from https://www.epa.gov/statelocalenergy/local-renewable-energy-benefits-and-resources

European Commission. (2009). Directive 2009/28/EC of the European Parliament and of the Council of 23 April 2009 on the promotion of the use of energy from renewable sources and amending and subsequently repealing Directives 2001/77/EC and 2003/30/EC. *Official Journal of the European Union, L, 140*, 1–148.

European Commission. (2018). Directive (EU) 2018/2001 of the European Parliament and of the Council on the promotion of the use of energy from renewable sources. Official Journal of European Union, 328.

European Environmental Agency (EEA). (2022). *Share of energy consumption from renewable sources in Europe*. EEA. https://www.eea.europa.eu/ims/share-of-energy-consumption-from

European Parliament. (2015). *Bridging the digital divide in the EU*. European Parliamnet. https://www.europarl.europa.eu/RegData/etudes/BRIE/2015/573884/EPRS_BRI(2015)573884_EN.pdf

Eurostat (2022). *Renewable energy statistics*. Eurostat. https://ec.europa.eu/eurostat/statistics-explained/index.php?title=Renewable_energy_statistics

Eurostat - Information society. (2021). *E-government activities of individuals via websites*. Eurostat. https://appsso.eurostat.ec.europa.eu/nui/show.do?dataset=isoc_ciegi_ac&lang=en

Fernández-Portillo, A., Almodóvar-González, M., & Hernández-Mogollón, R. (2020). Impact of ICT development on economic growth. A study of OECD European union countries. *Technology in Society, 63*, 101420.

Gatautis, R., Medziausiene, A., Tarute, A., & Vaiciukynaite, E. (2015). Towards ICT Impact Framework: Private and Public Sectors Perspective. *Journal of Economics. Business and Management, 3*(4), 465–469.

Grbavec, P., Pejic Bach, M., Zoroja, J., Strugar, I., & Jaković, B. (2019). Digital economy and society index as the indicator of digital divide in European countries: preliminary cluster analysis. *Conference proceedings of the 8th International scientific conference, Kovač, Tatjana; Cingula, Marijan – Celje* (pp. 29-36). Slovenia: Fakulteta za komercialne in poslovne vede.

Heuberger, R. (2017). Achieving the shared sustainable development goals: How the ICT sector can drive the renewable energy revolution. *Connect World Magazine*. https://connect-world.com/achieving-shared-sustainable-development-goals-ict-sector-can-drive-renewable-energy-revolution/

Inglesi-Lotz, R. (2016). The Impact of Renewable Energy Consumption to Economic Growth: A Panel Data Application. *Energy Economics, 53*, 58–63.

Jayaprakash, P., & Radhakrishna Pillai, R. (2022). The Role of ICT for Sustainable Development: A Cross-Country Analysis. *European Journal of Development Research, 34*, 225–247.

Marsh, J. (2022). Will Renewables Make Public Transportation More Affordable? *Renewable Energy Magazine*. https://www.renewableenergymagazine.com/jane-marsh/will-renewables-make-public-transportation-more-affordable-20220518

Mucunska Palevska, V., & Novkovska, B. (2021). Increasing use of digital technologies in function of economic growth in European countries. *UTMS Journal of Economics (Skopje)*, *12*(1), 84–94.

Murshed, M. (2020). An empirical analysis of the non-linear impacts of ICT-trade openness on renewable energy transition, energy efficiency, clean cooking fuel access and environmental sustainability in South Asia. *Environmental Science and Pollution Research International*, *27*(29), 36254–36281.

Nasiri, E., Rocha-Meneses, L., Inayat, A., & Kikas, T. (2022). Impact of Policy Instruments in the Implementation of Renewable Sources of Energy in Selected European Countries. *Sustainability*, *14*(10), 6314.

Pakere, I., Prodanuks, T., Kamenders, A., Veidenbergs, I., Holler, S., Villere, A., & Blumberga, D. (2021). Ranking EU Climate and Energy Policies. *Environmental and Climate Technologies*, *25*(1), 367–381.

Rozga, A. (2015). *Multiavariate anaylsis (authorised lectures)*. Faculty of Economics, Business and Tourism.

Ruoso, A. C., & Ribeiro, J. L. D. (2022). The influence of countries' socioeconomic characteristics on the adoption of electric vehicle. *Energy for Sustainable Development*, *71*, 251–262.

Siebenhofer, M., Ajanovic, A., & Haas, R. (2022). On the Future of Passenger Mobility and its Greenhouse Gas Emissions in Cities: Scenarios for Different Types of Policies. *Journal of Sustainable Development of Energy. Water and Environment Systems*, *10*(4), 1100424.

SLOCAT Foundation. (2021). *Partnership on Sustainable, Low carbon transport. Renewable Energy in Transport*. SLOCAT Foundation. https://tcc-gsr.com/responses-to-policies/renewable-energy-in-transport/

Toader, E., Firtescu, B. N., & Roman, A., Anton, & S. G. (2018). Impact of Information and Communication Technology Infrastructure on Economic Growth: An Empirical Assessment for the EU Countries. *Sustainability*, *10*, 3750.

Turner, P., Dommergues, E., Mayer, T., Murdock, H. E., & Ranalder, L. *A smooth ride to renewable energy*. Policy brief. https://www.ren21.net/wp-content/uploads/2019/05/Policy-Brief-A-Smooth-Ride-to-Renewable-Energy-REN21-UITP.pdf

UITP (Union Internationale des Transports Publics). (2021). *A smooth ride to renewable energy: 7 actions for public transport to address emissions and air pollution by advancing renewables*. Advancing Public Transportation. https://www.uitp.org/publications/a-smooth-ride-to-renewable-energy-7-actions-for-public-transport-to-address-emissions-and-air-pollution-by-advancing-renewables/

United Nations Department of Economic and Social Affairs (UNDESA). (2018). *E-government survey 2018: gearing e-government to support transformation towards sustainable and resilient societies*. UNDESA. https://publicadministration.un.org/egovkb/portals/egovkb/documents/un/2018-survey/e-government%20survey%202018_final%20for%20web.pdf

United Nations Department of Economic and Social Affairs (UNDESA). (2020). *E-Government Survey 2020: Digital Government in the Decade of Action for Sustainable Development*. UNDESA. https://publicadministration.un.org/egovkb/Portals/egovkb/Documents/un/2020-Survey/2020%20UN%20E-Government%20Survey%20(Full%20Report).pdf van Dijk, J. (2009). The Digital Divide in Europe. *The Handbook of Internet Politics, Routledge, London and New York.* https://www.researchgate.net/publication/265074677_The_Digital_Divide_in_Europe

Vu, K., Hanafizadeh, P., & Bohlin, E. (2020). ICT as a driver of economic growth: A survey of the literature and directions for future research. *Telecommunications Policy*, *44*(2), 101922-1–101922-20.

Yera, A., Arbelaitz, O., Jauregui, O., & Muguerza, J. (2020). Characterization of e-Government adoption in Europe. *PLoS One*, *15*(4), e0231585.

Zoroja, J. (2011). Internet, E-commerce and E-government: Measuring the Gap between European Developed and Post-Communist Countries. *Interdisciplinary Description of Complex Systems*, *9*(2), 119–133.

Zoroja, J., & Pejić-Bach, M. (2016). Impact of Information and Communication Technology to the Competitiveness of European Countries - Cluster Analysis Approach. *Journal of Theoretical and Applied Electronic Commerce Research*, *11*(1), 1–10.

KEY TERMS AND DEFINITIONS

Cluster analysis: A type of analysis that groups similar objects together in a cluster, away from other objects not similar to them.

Digital divide: Signifies disparities in access to digital technologies.

E-government: The practice of providing public services to different stakeholders on a central, regional or local level using the internet.

Information and communication technologies (ICTS): Broad range of technological resources and techniques that are used to create, transfer, store, share, and exchange information.

Public transportation: A form of transportation that is available to the general public.

Renewable energy: The type of energy that comes from natural sources that replace themselves, its use doesn't produce greenhouse gas emissions.

Urban environment: This signifies an urban area that may consist of cities, towns, and suburbs.

Chapter 10

Comparison of Traditional and Green Public Transportation Vehicles in Terms of CO$_2$ Emissions

Gizem Çelik
TED University, Turkey

Zafer Yılmaz
ⓘ https://orcid.org/0000-0001-5839-5381
TED University, Turkey

ABSTRACT

There is a high demand in energy consumption of cities due to growth in population, and more pollution due to high CO2 emissions. Effective methods for increasing energy efficiency include the adoption of green vehicles to the transportation systems. The chapter aims to evaluate traditional public transportation technologies, introduce alternative future green transportation technologies in smart and sustainable cities, and make comparison between traditional and green public transportation systems. Istanbul is chosen to apply a case study to explain the importance of using green transportation ways in terms of CO2 emissions. The results of different transportation modes in different routes are compared. The results found for different scenarios on the routes in this case study ensure that the most eco-friendly options would be the walking, cycling, and public transportation ways for the passengers, although they may not provide the optimal solutions in terms of total duration and distance traveled.

INTRODUCTION

The world has limited resources, and the excess use of resources directly or indirectly influences the other sources because there is a balance between them. There is an increasing awareness about sustainable development due to taking global action about these limited resources. The United Nations (2021)

DOI: 10.4018/978-1-6684-5996-6.ch010

specifies 17 Sustainable Development Goals (SDGs) in the scope of the 2030 Agenda for sustainable development, and these are urgent calls for action by all countries (UN, 2021). In the current economic, political, and social context, the Agenda promotes global peace, eradicates poverty in all its forms and dimensions, and is an essential requirement for sustainable development (Firoiu et al., 2019). It is essential to take action about green and sustainable transportation. With global developments and the increasing importance of global warming, most municipalities and transportation service companies focus on intelligent and green public transportation systems.

This chapter aims to evaluate traditional public transportation vehicles, introduce alternative future green transportation technologies in smart and sustainable cities and compare traditional and green public transportation vehicles. The rest of the chapter is structured as follows. The first section presents a review of the relevant literature on traditional public transportation and discusses air pollution caused by the vehicles used in current public transportation. The following section reviews the literature on green and sustainable public transportation and the future projected green and sustainable public transportation vehicles. Section 3 defines the integration of green public transportation. Section 4 presents a case study comparing traditional and green public transportation vehicles regarding CO_2 emissions.

BACKGROUND

Recently, there has been increasing migration to urban areas because of social and economic conditions. Some %56 of the world's population lives in cities, and there is a rapid urbanization process in the world. After 2005, the urban population in the world exceed the rural population and the growing trend in urban population continues (UN, 2018).

Transportation has become a common problem in urban areas, and there are deficiencies in strategy and planning. Due to the inaccessibility of urban transportation systems and the limitations on time management, people living in urban areas prefer the single-occupant-vehicle mode. This mode causes transportation and traffic-related problems such as traffic congestion, air and noise pollution, and high energy consumption. However, the design of the single-occupant-vehicle mode is not efficient for a sustainable, safe, and equal transportation system (Watkins, 2018). Therefore, governments or authorized service providers encourage citizens to use public transportation to eliminate these externalities and reduce reliance on single-occupant-vehicle, saving them time, money, and stress while lowering CO_2 emissions.

1. Traditional Public Transportation Vehicles

Public transportation is "collective transport accessible by the general public, often provided on fixed routes" (Mulley et al., 2021). Public transportation is a system that enables the mobility of individuals within the urban area without the use of individual vehicles. Public transportation systems provides the opportunity to travel long distances with relatively low costs, while not bringing initial investment and operating costs to the user.

The public transportation system varies according to the mode of transportation, type of vehicle and transportation characteristics. Public transport services can be rendered by road vehicles (such as buses and trolleybus), rail vehicles (heavy rail, tram, and underground), vehicles using other fixed guideways (cable car, monorail) and water-borne vehicles (water taxis) (Jagiello et al., 2018). Traditional public vehicles

Comparison of Traditional and Green Public Transportation Vehicles in Terms of CO2 Emissions

can be differentiated by fuel type. Fossil fuel public vehicles like minibus, bus, bus rapid transit, light rail, subway, tram, passenger-only and vehicle ferries are examples of traditional public transportation. These vehicles differ in capacity, trip distance, energy consumption and CO_2 emissions (Table 1). The data for the below table includes information for buses by several urban bus companies in the UK, the light rail data for the modern tram operations in Manchester and the metro for the London Underground.

Table 1. Comparison of traditional public transportation vehicles

Mode	Capacity (Seats)	Corridor Capacity (passengers per hour per direction)	Trip distance (average)	Energy Consumption (MJ/V-km)	CO2 emissions (g/V-km)
Minibus	20	-	-	7.10	0.8
Single deck bus	49	1200-1400	>500m	14.2	1.6
Double deck bus	74	1900-2100	>1 km	16.2	1.9
Light rail	265	3600	>1 km	47	10.1
Metro	555	25000	>1 km	122	26

Source: (Potter, 2003), (Carpenter, 1994)

Road vehicles are the most preferred type of transportation due to the direct door-to-door mobility advantage in urban areas. Improving accessibility and increasing the quality of road transport to meet the needs of passengers have positive effects on passengers. However, the increase in accessibility causes many problems related to traffic and the environment in an irregular and unmonitored transportation system, such as an increase in congestion and road accidents in urban areas and a growing amount of CO_2 emissions.

The rise in CO_2 emissions from human activities is the primary cause of global warming. European Commission (2020) stated that there are growing environmental concerns about the increasing CO_2 emissions and air pollution from all sectors. While transportation demand in cities is increasing, there is difficulty in reducing emissions in the transport sector.

Many factors increase CO_2 emissions in urban areas. Transportation is an essential factor that triggers this increase considering all these factors. Also, it has the largest share, with 27% in the United States. CO_2 emissions by sector in the EU are given in Figure 1. As seen in Figure 1, the transportation sector has the second biggest share, considering CO_2 emissions. CO_2 emissions from transportation are anticipated to contribute to global warming in the next few decades significantly. Recently, the population of the cities has increased every year; hence, people need more transportation means in addition to private car usage. More vehicles in the traffic will cause more pollution due to CO_2 emissions. Therefore, the transport sector is critical in ensuring environmentally friendly and sustainable economic growth for Europe.

Rapid population growth in urban areas, extensive use of road transport and high carbon dioxide emissions lead to adverse environmental consequences related to energy consumption and climate change. Transportation is a critical factor in taking precautions to eliminate these negative consequences. European Environment Agency (EEA) conducted research about the change in GHG emissions in the EU-27 countries, Iceland and UK, between 2019 and 2020. Source categories that increased or decreased by more than 3 million tonnes of CO_2 equivalent in the period are included in Figure 2. Total GHG emissions decreased by 346 million tonnes in 2020, and there is a drastic reduction of 123 million tonnes in road transportation compared to other source categories (see Figure 2). It is stated that mobility and transport activities decreased in 2020 due to lockdown measures during the Covid-19 pandemic (EEA, 2022).

Figure 1. Distribution of carbon dioxide emissions in the EU-27 in 2020, by sector (Tiseo, 2022)
Source: Tiseo, 2022

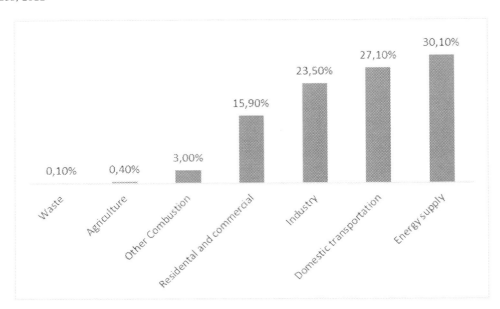

Figure 2. Distribution of the source categories making the largest contribution to GHG emissions reduction in the EU between 2019 and 2020 (EEA, 2022)
Source: EEA, 2022

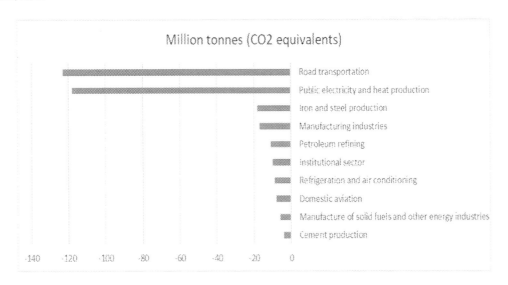

It is expected to be a downward trend in emissions from transportation until 2030, with the policies implemented globally to reduce the negative effects of global warming, energy consumption and CO_2 emissions being specified as priority issues by the European Union. Different strategies supported by the European Union are determined to achieve this declining trend. Increasing fuel efficiency and promoting alternative fuel vehicles are proposed to reduce CO_2 emissions in road transportation. The implemented strategies for decreasing the trend of CO_2 emissions show positive effects gradually. However, this expected reduction is seen in some years due to congestion and increasing demand for road transportation. For example, the European Environment Agency stated that between 2013 and 2016, greenhouse gas emissions from road transport increased by 5% (EEA, 2022). The results of policies and strategies, particularly in road transportation, demonstrate fluctuations each year, and there is no stable declining trend. Therefore, there is a debate about the sustainability of the current transport system.

2. Green and Sustainable Public Transportation Vehicles

European Union published White Paper to establish a competitive, sustainable and resource-efficient public transport system. The EU also agreed to reduce greenhouse gas emissions by 20% (relative to 1990) by 2020 and 80-95% by 2050. Road transport is responsible for more than 70% of total energy use in transport. However, this share is projected to significantly decline over time, to 68% by 2030 and 59% by 2050, thanks to the progressive electrification of the sector and greater use of more sustainable transport modes (EC, 2020).

Increasing pollution caused by the transportation sector due to CO_2 emissions raises the importance of green vehicle use worldwide. There are different definitions of the green vehicle in the literature. A green or clean vehicle is that produces less harmful impacts on the environment than the equivalent conventional internal combustion engine vehicles that run on gasoline or diesel (Senin et al., 2021). Also, Li (2016) defined green vehicles as low-pollution vehicles, emphasizing the side effects of high CO2 emissions. Battery Electric Vehicles (BEV), Compressed Natural Gas (CNG) vehicles, Plug-in Hybrid Vehicles (PHEV) and Hydrogen Vehicles (H2) are commonly used alternative fuels for low-pollution vehicles in Europe (EAFO, 2021). Low-pollution vehicles consume energy sources that have a less negative impact on the environment, and these vehicles gain priority with the growing global environmental consciousness. Municipalities and transport companies prefer to use powered vehicles with LNG and CNG gas, biogas and hydrogen (Jagiello et al., 2018).

Kaldellis et al. (2017) stated that promoting alternative fuel vehicles, eco-driving and green public transportation support citizens and transport companies to prefer energy-efficient methods and reduce CO_2 emissions. Vehicles in use Europe 2021 report (ACEA, 2021) proposed that 55.7% of all public transportation in the European Union (EU) is made by urban and sub-urban buses, and 8.5% of passengers on road transportation in the EU use buses and coaches. The number of compressed natural gas (CNG) buses is the highest every year. The reason behind the popularity of CNG is the availability of natural gas resources and the more straightforward conversion from diesel and gasoline engines to CNG engines. However, Choi et al. (2012) conducted a study in Seoul, South Korea, about transforming public vehicles to CNG and electric vehicles. The study found that electric vehicles created %21.6 more advantageous to the environment and economical than CNG vehicles. Also, there is an increasing demand for greener fuel types in public road transport in the EU. For example, there was a 170.5% increase in new registered electric buses in the EU from 2018 to 2019, and only eight petrol buses were sold in 2019 across EU countries (ACEA, 2020).

Electric vehicles such as buses are effective green vehicle alternatives in public transportation. Electric Vehicles (EVs) are more energy efficient than other types of vehicles, and they cause a lower level of CO_2 emission (EEA, 2020). The world, China is one of the successful countries in the production and usage of electric buses, and cities in China such as Shanghai and Shenzhen constitute a new law about providing public transportation services with only electric buses.

In theory, electric vehicles (BEVs) are CO_2-free power sources but always depend on the energy mix of the charging system. Fuel Cell Electric Vehicles (FCEVs) running on hydrogen produced emit 45% fewer emissions than vehicles with internal combustion engines (Cell & Undertaking, 2019). Furthermore, hydrogen fuel cells are more energy-efficient to produce than charging systems and require significantly fewer materials. Hydrogen is a source of energy from natural gas, coal, wind, biomass, or solar energy. In addition to being a less polluting and energy-saving fuel type, hydrogen provides fast and convenient replenishment time and has a high fuel conversion rate when used in vehicles (Chang et al., 2019). Even though the production process of hydrogen is relatively simple, it has disadvantages in the transportation, storage and distribution stages as a transportation fuel when compared to other alternative fuels (Zhao & Melaina, 2006). The International Renewable Energy Agency (IRENA) proposed that 8 percent of global energy consumption will be transformed from hydrogen by 2050. This proposal was supported by encouraging the use of hydrogen as a fuel and emphasizing the advantages of hydrogen-fueled vehicles at global events such as the 2008 Beijing Olympic Games and the 2010 Shanghai World Expo in China. In addition, The Hydrogen Roadmap Europe report published in 2019 (Cell and Undertaking, 2019) stated that there would be an increase in hydrogen energy demand in 2050 in several industries, especially in the transportation industry and approximately 250000 buses and more than 5500 trains would fuel with hydrogen.

Green public vehicles are actively used in many cities worldwide, and there is an increase in the number of agreements signed to make public transportation greener. For example, in 2019, Barcelona signed an agreement worth €73.5 million with the European Investment Bank (EIB) to purchase new CNG, electric and hybrid buses for the public transportation service. Also, De Lijn, a company that provides public transportation services in Belgium, allocated €93 million of the EU Covid recovery budget to purchase green public transportation vehicles such as electric vehicles and their charging systems.

The energy demand for public transportation has been increasing year by year, and there are different projected scenarios to meet this demand. However, authorities are more careful about a greener and more sustainable options due to several side effects of climate change and pollution.

New approaches to transportation planning are required to overcome the complicated problems of urban transportation, which include the integration of emerging technologies, such as electrification, digital support systems, and new mobility services like shared solutions and micro-mobility. The demand for new and innovative solutions to improve the efficiency of urban transportation has grown due to increasing CO_2 emissions, environmental pollution and traffic congestion.

A strategic combination of different transportation technologies can support green transportation and sustainable urban development. Abduljabbar et al. (2021) define micro-mobility as environmentally friendly and innovative transportation options for short-distance travel. Bicycles, scooters, skateboards, segways, and hoverboards are micro-mobility vehicles that can be either privately owned or shared. These vehicles can be updated to be compatible with the developing technology and can be integrated into public transportation systems (Esztergár-Kiss & Lizarraga, 2021). McQueen et al. (2021) offer three different elements which are applied in the integration process of micro-mobility to the transportation system:1) Micro-mobility has the potential to reduce greenhouse gas emissions, so municipalities and transportation companies pursue and encourage citizens to use micro-mobility vehicles; 2) Micro-mobility is reliable and equitable by providing adequate access to data; 3) Micro-mobility improves the human experience, lowering transportation barriers and emphasizing rider safety. Therefore, the use of micromobility vehicles in public transportation systems increases the quality of transportation and reduces the use of individual vehicles.

Shared mobility services are another approach to be used for green and sustainable transportation. The advantages of shared mobility include reducing vehicle ownership and user travel expenses. People can obtain a comparable service by sharing with others instead of buying a vehicle or renting a parking place. There are different shared mobility modes, some of which are bike-sharing, car-sharing, ridesharing, ride-sourcing and scooter-sharing. Also, this service is more effective when combined with public transportation so that different modes of transport, such as autonomous vehicles and micro-mobility vehicles, can work together to replace private vehicles.

Under the sustainable transportation concept, people should be placed at the centre position, and the perspectives focus on them. In the planning process of transportation systems, Ogryzek et al. (2020) proposed the hierarchy of participants. The most privileged group should be pedestrians because they are the most vulnerable and endangered group (Ogryzek et al., 2020). The second group is cyclists, then the public transport network. The last one is car users, which cause more dangerous situations for society and the environment than other transportation types. Incorporating bikes in the planning process of transportation systems is a promising approach that may lead to changes in urban transport (Gössling, 2013).

3. Integration of Green Public Transportation

Traditional transport solutions are becoming mostly insufficient in achieving and maintaining sustainable road and transport systems (Nkoro & Vershinin, 2014). Therefore, developing a sustainable, intelligent transportation system requires better infrastructure usage and seamless integration of information and communication technologies (ICT) into green transportation systems (Guerrero-Ibanez et al., 2015). However, because of the various disturbances and uncertainties such as extreme weather, unstable demand of passengers, traffic conditions, and environmental problems, there is a challenging situation for municipalities and private companies in managing, controlling and scheduling of public transportation system.

Nkoro and Vershinin (2014) defined intelligent transportation systems (ITS) as a controlled system that provides communication between vehicles and highways using advanced road and telecommunications infrastructure. Integrating emerging technologies into the transportation system helps to reduce CO_2 emissions, improve traffic efficiency and road safety, and decrease vehicle wear, transportation times, and fuel consumption (Guerrero-Ibanez et al., 2015). ITS provide communication and information exchange between each transportation unit, such as people, vehicle, infrastructure and the centre which controls transportation. There are four fundamental principles in integrating and adapting intelligent systems to the transportation process. These are safety and personal security, access and mobility, environmental sustainability and economic development (Guerrero-Ibanez et al., 2015).

In the literature, various applications and methods exist to integrate intelligent technology elements into the public transportation system. Although this topic has gained importance in the last decade, several examples worldwide have applied intelligent transportation systems (ITS) since the 1990s. Different transportation-related technologies have emerged over the years since the mid-1990s. Starting from melody roads to the emergence of vehicle-to-vehicle communications, vehicular ad hoc networks, electriðed roads, harvesting of energy from roads, self-weighing roads, ITS cooperative emergency rescue, methods to capture driving behaviour, smart street lights and wireless digital trafðc signs (Toh et al., 2020). Also, Erokhina and Brega (2020) propose smart cameras, traffic intensity and navigation sensors, and smart roads as components of the intelligent transport system.

Improved communication and connectivity contribute to the efficiency of the transportation process. The Internet of things (IoT) is an information technology based on the Internet and wireless telecommunication. It is a helpful tool to reduce the uncertainty of the system and increase the ability to control and manage the system (Luo et al., 2019). For example, an automatic passenger counter provides data about the total number of passengers on the bus. The data used to forecast demand and schedule buses, and based on these improvements, public transportation is much more technology oriented. The automated system appeared with big data gathered from this technology-based system. Automated buses and minibuses in public transportation will be implemented with trials by 2025 and become commonplace (40% of those in service) by 2035 in the UK Transport Vision 2050 report (Innovate, 2021).

Recently, the European Commission has focused on applying more ITS solutions to achieve more efficient management of the transport network for passengers and businesses. One of the top concerns of decision-makers and transportation authorities is integrating various transport modes and offering seamless mobility. "Mobility as a Service" (MaaS) is a concept that builds on these shared modes and advancements in information and communication technology. MaaS combined vehicles with both public and private transportation services. MaaS is based on three components: ticket and payment integration, mobility package and ICT integration (Kamargianni et al.,2016).

Several intelligent transportation system tools can be used to integrate green vehicles into the urban transportation system effectively. Integrating shared mobility services, autonomous and connected vehicles, micro-mobility vehicles, intelligent transportation systems like smart parking, and real-time traffic management decrease the congestion in traffic in urban transportation. Fishman (2012) explained future mobility in the digital age transportation report based on these elements:

- Integrated fare management
- Car sharing, ride sharing, bike sharing
- Autonomous vehicles, connected vehicles
- Smart parking
- Real-time traffic management
- Multi-modal transportation solutions

ITS provides real-time data about the road, passengers and traffic. The data collected from mobile operators integrated with public vehicles and combined city fare systems are used in determining new routes and optimizing existing routes (Erokhina & Brega, 2020). In addition to that, passengers have been involved in the green transportation process thanks to the integration of intelligent systems. This contributes to increase participation and consciousness among passengers. The study by Olaverri-Monreal (2016) stated that mobile applications as a communication platform are useful for encouraging passengers about green, efficient and safer road transportation.

Comparison of Traditional and Green Public Transportation Vehicles in Terms of CO2 Emissions

Gamification is one of the best ways to increase the popularity and awareness among passengers about green public transportation. For example, local authorities in Sofia introduced a new mobile application called Sofia Coin to promote green mobility and healthier lifestyles. The app collects data about the distance taken by green vehicles or modes and trip routes and automatically calculates the carbon emissions saved. After specified periods, there is a reward for people who have saved the highest carbon emissions. In this example, there is a collaboration between the municipality, local businesses and citizens. Applying these new technologies to public transportation services is insufficient for effective results.

Beyond specific ITS use cases, using various information and communication technologies for mobility brings many advantages, such as safer transportation for elderly or disabled people and more efficient and sustainable mobility options, such as making car sharing much easier (EC, 2020). Coordination of public transportation services through regional and local stakeholders is also crucial. Therefore, Buehler (2018) stated that public transportation agencies and governments would endeavour to coordinate with each other about more sustainable and effective services in the region. The data gathered from this collaboration is a valuable tool to improve services, ticketing, and marketing regionally.

4. CASE STUDY: Comparison of Traditional and Green Public Transportation Vehicles

This section presents a case study in Istanbul to explain the importance of using green vehicles in terms of CO_2 emissions. The results of different scenarios are compared for each route based on the CO_2 emissions. First, there is a description of the data used and then the presentation of the results.

Description and data

Istanbul is selected to apply our case study since Istanbul has the highest population in Turkey, and accordingly, there are various problems related to urbanization and traffic congestion. The municipality of Istanbul and private transport companies have several projects to handle these problems and make transportation greener and more sustainable. The case study has four different routes (Figure 3), and each route has scenarios to apply for origin-destination (OD) points. Those OD pairs are selected considering the most popular regions of Istanbul. Distance, duration, and vehicle data are obtained for a specific time on the Google maps application. The vehicles used are metro, tram, bus, bike, average car (Diesel), average car (Petrol), average car (Hybrid), average car (CNG), average car (LPG), average car (Plug-in HEV), small motorbike, medium motorbike, large motorbike, average motorbike, regular taxi, black cab. The scenarios for each route are the optimal scenarios within this specified time.

The CO_2 emissions of different transport modes have been published previously by UK Government. We employ the same approach as in the UK Government GHG Emission Conversion Factor Report (UK, 2022) for the calculation of GHG emissions (Table 2). According to this model, activity data which is the distance traveled by vehicle is multiplied by an estimated kg CO_2 emissions for the distance traveled by individual passengers per transport mode, and total GHG emissions are calculated as follows:

GHG emissions = activity data x emission conversion factor

Figure 3. Routes that specified for the case study application in İstanbul

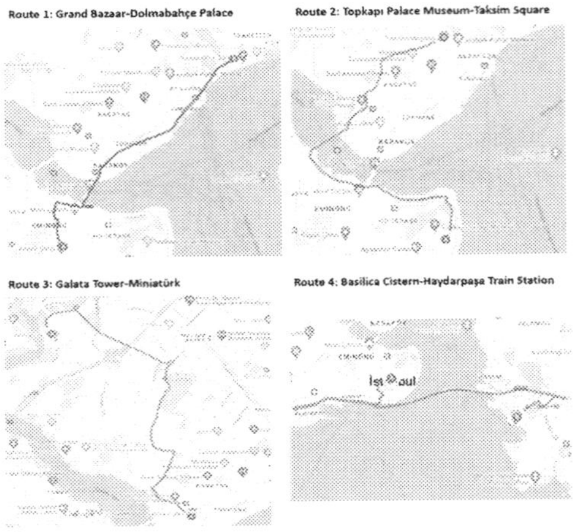

Table 2. CO_2 Emission conversion factor for each vehicle type

Vehicle	Unit	CO_2 emission (kg CO_2)
Walking	km	0
Tram	passenger.km	0.0348
Bus (IETT)	passenger.km	0.10391
Metro	passenger.km	0.03059
Average car (Diesel)	km	0.17152
Average car (Petrol)	km	0.18014
Average car (Hybrid)	km	0.11346
Average car (CNG)	km	0.17599
Average car (LPG)	km	0.19851
Average car (Plug-in HEV)	km	0.07033
Small motorbike	km	0.08241
Medium motorbike	km	0.10004
Large motorbike	km	0.13308
Average motorbike	km	0.11314
Regular taxi	passenger.km	0.14886
Black cab	passenger.km	0.21053

Source: UK, 2022

Analysis and Discussion

Tables 3-6 show the emission calculations of four routes based on different scenarios. Google maps is used to find the optimal routes between OD pairs. Those optimal routes include multiple scenarios in which multiple transportation ways are applied. For example, on Route 1, five scenarios are applied. For the first scenario on Route 1, the passenger must start the journey by walking 0.12 km, take the tram and

Comparison of Traditional and Green Public Transportation Vehicles in Terms of CO2 Emissions

go 4.7 kilometres, and finally walk 0.35 km more to reach the destination (see Scenario 1 in Table 3). For Route 1, the passenger has four more options indicated in Scenario 2, 3, 4 and 5 in Table 3. Scenarios 1, 2 and 3 require walking and public transportation; however, in scenarios 4 and 5, the passenger uses a private car, motorbike or taxi with different fuel types instead. The total distance travelled in route 1 for scenarios 1 to 5 is 5.17, 5.99, 7.4, 4.7 and 6.4 kilometres, respectively. Duration for different scenarios and the corresponding CO_2 emissions are also given in Table 3. The best scenarios for route one, which gives the optimal routes with respect to distance, duration and CO_2 emissions, are scenarios 4, 5, and 1, respectively. It is concluded that scenario 1 is the optimal one in terms of the lowest CO_2 emissions for route one, which promotes walking and tram. A similar approach is applied for routes 2, 3, and 4. Different scenarios are applied, which include a mixture of transportation ways. The results are given in Tables 4, 5, and 6.

Table 3. CO_2 Emission calculation of Route 1 (Grand Bazaar - Dolmabahçe Palace) based on different scenarios

Route 1: Grand Bazaar-Dolmabahçe Palace				
Scenario 1	Distance (km)	Duration (min)	Vehicle	CO_2 emission (kg CO_2)
	0.12	2	Walking	0
	4.7	20	Tram	0.16356
	0.35	4	Walking	0
Total	5.17	26		**0.16356**
Scenario 2	1	12	Walking	0
	4.7	12	Bus (IETT)	0.488377
	0.29	4	Walking	0
Total	5.99	28		**0.488377**
Scenario 3	0.75	10	Walking	0
	4	6	metro	0.12236
	0.3	3	Walking	0
	1.7	5	Bus (IETT)	0.176647
	0.29	4	Walking	0
Total	7.04	28		**0.299007**
Scenario 4	Distance (km)	Duration (min)	Vehicle	CO_2 emission (kg CO_2)
	4.7	23	Average car (Diesel)	0.806144
			Average car (Petrol)	0.846658
			Average car (Hybrid)	0.533262
			Average car (CNG)	0.827153
			Average car (LPG)	0.932997
			Average car (Plug-in HEV)	0.330551
			Small motorbike	0.387327
			Medium motorbike	0.470188
			Large motorbike	0.625476

continues on following page

Comparison of Traditional and Green Public Transportation Vehicles in Terms of CO2 Emissions

Table 3. Continued

Route 1: Grand Bazaar-Dolmabahçe Palace				
			Average motorbike	0.531758
			Regular taxi	0.699642
			Black cab	0.989491
Scenario 5	**Distance (km)**	**Duration (min)**	**Vehicle**	**CO_2 emission (kg CO_2)**
	6.4	20	Average car (Diesel)	1.097728
			Average car (Petrol)	1.152896
			Average car (Hybrid)	0.726144
			Average car (CNG)	1.126336
			Average car (LPG)	1.270464
			Average car (Plug-in HEV)	0.450112
			Small motorbike	0.527424
			Medium motorbike	0.640256
			Large motorbike	0.851712
			Average motorbike	0.724096
			Regular taxi	0.952704

Table 4. CO_2 Emission calculation of Route 2 (Topkapı Palace Museum – Taksim Square) based on different scenarios

Route 2: Topkapı Palace Museum-Taksim Square				
Scenario 1	**Distance (km)**	**Duration (min)**	**Vehicle**	**CO_2 emission (kg CO_2)**
	0.65	9	Walking	0
	2	6	Tram	0.0696
	0.35	4	Walking	0
	5.5	6	metro	0.168245
Total	8.5	25		**0.237845**
Scenario 2	1.8	21	Walking	0
	3.8	11	Bus (IETT)	0.394858
	0.1	2	Walking	0
Total	5.7	34		**0.394858**
Scenario 3	0.65	8	Walking	0
	3.8	14	Tram	0.13224
	0.1	2	Walking	0
	1.7	8	Cycling	0.034833
	0.1	2	Walking	0
Total	6.35	34		**0.167073**

continues on following page

Comparison of Traditional and Green Public Transportation Vehicles in Terms of CO2 Emissions

Table 4. Continued

Route 2: Topkapı Palace Museum-Taksim Square				
Scenario 4	Distance (km)	Duration (min)	Vehicle	CO_2 emission (kg CO_2)
	6.9	27	Average car (Diesel)	1.183488
			Average car (Petrol)	1.242966
			Average car (Hybrid)	0.782874
			Average car (CNG)	1.214331
			Average car (LPG)	1.369719
			Average car (Plug-in HEV)	0.485277
			Small motorbike	0.568629
			Medium motorbike	0.690276
			Large motorbike	0.918252
			Average motorbike	0.780666
			Regular taxi	1.027134
			Black cab	1.452657
Scenario 5	Distance (km)	Duration (min)	Vehicle	CO_2 emission (kg CO_2)
	8.8	28	Average car (Diesel)	1.509376
			Average car (Petrol)	1.585232
			Average car (Hybrid)	0.998448
			Average car (CNG)	1.548712
			Average car (LPG)	1.746888
			Average car (Plug-in HEV)	0.618904
			Small motorbike	0.725208
			Medium motorbike	0.880352
			Large motorbike	1.171104
			Average motorbike	0.995632
			Regular taxi	1.309968

Table 5. CO_2 Emission calculation of Route 3 (Galata Tower – Miniatürk) based on different scenarios

Route 3: Galata Tower-Miniatürk				
Scenario 1	Distance (km)	Duration (min)	Vehicle	CO_2 emission (kg CO_2)
	0.5	7	Walking	0
	7.4	27	Bus	0.768934
	0.2	2	Walking	0
Total	8.1	36		**0.768934**
Scenario 2	1	12	Walking	0
	5.9	6	Bus	0.613069
	0.2	3	Walking	0
Total	7.1	21		**0.613069**

continues on following page

Comparison of Traditional and Green Public Transportation Vehicles in Terms of CO2 Emissions

Table 5. Continued

Route 3: Galata Tower-Miniatürk				
Scenario 3	**Distance (km)**	**Duration (min)**	**Vehicle**	**CO_2 emission (kg CO_2)**
	7.8	19	Average car (Diesel)	1.337856
			Average car (Petrol)	1.405092
			Average car (Hybrid)	0.884988
			Average car (CNG)	1.372722
			Average car (LPG)	1.548378
			Average car (Plug-in HEV)	0.548574
			Small motorbike	0.642798
			Medium motorbike	0.780312
			Large motorbike	1.038024
			Average motorbike	0.882492
			Regular taxi	1.161108
			Black cab	1.642134
Scenario 4	**Distance (km)**	**Duration (min)**	**Vehicle**	**CO_2 emission (kg CO_2)**
	6.9	20	Average car (Diesel)	1.183488
			Average car (Petrol)	1.242966
			Average car (Hybrid)	0.782874
			Average car (CNG)	1.214331
			Average car (LPG)	1.369719
			Average car (Plug-in HEV)	0.485277
			Small motorbike	0.568629
			Medium motorbike	0.690276
			Large motorbike	0.918252
			Average motorbike	0.780666
			Regular taxi	1.027134

Table 6. CO_2 Emission calculation of Route 4 (Basilica Cistern-Haydarpaşa Train Station) based on different scenarios

Route 4: Basilica Cistern-Haydarpaşa Train Station				
Scenario 1	**Distance (km)**	**Duration (min)**	**Vehicle**	**CO_2 emission (kg CO_2)**
	0.9	11	Walking	0
	6	8	metro	0.18354
	1.3	17	Walking	0
Total	8.2	36		**0.18354**
Scenario 2	1.3	16	Walking	0
	4.52	11	Ferry	0.0835296
	0.9	11	Walking	0
Total	6.72	38		**0.0835296**

continues on following page

Comparison of Traditional and Green Public Transportation Vehicles in Terms of CO2 Emissions

Table 6. Continued

			Route 4: Basilica Cistern-Haydarpaşa Train Station	
Scenario 3	0.24	4	Walking	0
	2.3	9	Tram	0.08004
	0.15	3	Walking	0
	4	20	Ferry	0.07392
	0.75	9	Walking	0
Total	7.44	45		**0.15396**
Scenario 4	**Distance (km)**	**Duration (min)**	**Vehicle**	**CO_2 emission (kg CO_2)**
	14.4	27	Average car (Diesel)	2.469888
			Average car (Petrol)	2.594016
			Average car (Hybrid)	1.633824
			Average car (CNG)	2.534256
			Average car (LPG)	2.858544
			Average car (Plug-in HEV)	1.012752
			Small motorbike	1.186704
			Medium motorbike	1.440576
			Large motorbike	1.916352
			Average motorbike	1.629216
			Regular taxi	2,143584
			Black cab	3,031632
Scenario 5	**Distance (km)**	**Duration (min)**	**Vehicle**	**CO_2 emission (kg CO_2)**
	8.8	28	Average car (Diesel)	1,509376
			Average car (Petrol)	1,585232
			Average car (Hybrid)	0,998448
			Average car (CNG)	1,548712
			Average car (LPG)	1,746888
			Average car (Plug-in HEV)	0,618904
			Small motorbike	0,725208
			Medium motorbike	0,880352
			Large motorbike	1,171104
			Average motorbike	0,995632
			Regular taxi	1,309968

We can conclude that although it may not be the optimal way in terms of distance travelled and time of travel, we should promote the transportation options (walking, cycling and public transportation) which include optimal ways with respect to CO_2 emissions in order to contribute vision zero and cause less air pollution.

SOLUTIONS AND RECOMMENDATIONS

The summary of the case study, which includes all the values of the scenarios for routes 1 to 4, is given in Table 7 to compare findings with respect to distance, duration and CO_2 emission. In Table 7, the best solutions considering distance, duration and CO_2 emission for each route are shaded in grey colour and written in bold numbers. For example, for the first route, the best solution according to distance is 4.7 km found in scenario 4. Hence, if a traveller wants to travel the minimum distance, she should select scenario 4. Percentage changes in distance are also given for the other scenarios to indicate with which percentages the distances will be increased if the traveller selects the other scenarios. Considering the duration, the best option for route 1 is selecting scenario 5 with a value of 20 minutes. The traveller should select scenario 1 if she would like to minimize CO_2 emissions while travelling. The percentage changes in duration and CO_2 emission are given in Table 7 to show the increases in duration and CO_2 emission if the traveller selects other scenarios.

Table 7. Comparison of routes and scenarios by percentage change in terms of distance, duration and CO_2 Emission

		Distance (km)	Percentage change in distance (%)	Duration (min)	Percentage change in duration (%)	CO_2 emission (kg CO_2)	Percentage change in CO_2 emission (kg CO_2) (%)
Route 1	Scenario 1	5.17	10.00	26.00	30.00	**0.163560**	0.00
	Scenario 2	5.99	27.45	28.00	40.00	0.488377	198.59
	Scenario 3	7.04	49.79	28.00	40.00	0.299007	82.81
	Scenario 4	**4.70**	0.00	23.00	15.00	0.330551	102.10
	Scenario 5	6.40	36.17	**20.00**	0.00	0.450112	175.20
Route 2	Scenario 1	8.50	49.12	**25.00**	0.00	0.237845	42.36
	Scenario 2	**5.70**	0.00	34.00	36.00	0.394858	136.34
	Scenario 3	6.35	11.40	34.00	36.00	**0.167073**	0.00
	Scenario 4	6.90	21.05	27.00	8.00	0.485277	190.46
	Scenario 5	8.80	54.39	28.00	12.00	0.618904	270.44
Route 3	Scenario 1	8.10	17.39	36.00	89.47	0.768934	58.45
	Scenario 2	7.10	2.90	21.00	10.53	0.613069	26.33
	Scenario 3	7.80	13.04	**19.00**	0.00	0.548574	13.04
	Scenario 4	**6.90**	0.00	20.00	5.26	**0.485277**	0.00
Route 4	Scenario 1	8.20	22.02	36.00	33.33	0.183540	119.73
	Scenario 2	**6.72**	0.00	38.00	40.74	**0.083530**	0.00
	Scenario 3	7.44	10.71	45.00	66.67	0.153960	84.32
	Scenario 4	14.40	114.29	**27.00**	0.00	1.012752	1112.45
	Scenario 5	8.80	30.95	28.00	3.70	0.618904	640.94

Comparison of Traditional and Green Public Transportation Vehicles in Terms of CO2 Emissions

All values of the scenarios for routes 2, 3, and 4 are depicted in Table 7. Again, the best values regarding distance, time, and CO_2 emission are shaded in grey and written in bold numbers. Eventually, we advise the travellers to select scenarios 1, 3, 4, and 2, respectively, for routes 1 to 4 to minimize CO_2 emission while travelling, although those scenarios are not optimal with respect to distance and duration. To explain it, if the traveller selects scenario 3 to minimize CO_2 emission, the distance that will travel becomes 6.35 km rather than the optimal distance of 5.7 km found in scenario 2, causing an 11.40% increase in distance.

FUTURE RESEARCH DIRECTIONS

In this study, the focus is on green transportation vehicles and observing CO_2 emissions of these vehicles compering with traditional transportation vehicles. The chapter reviews traditional public transportation, green and sustainable public transportation vehicles and the integration of green public transportation. Finally, a case study is applied to compare CO_2 emissions for the scenarios in which different transportation modes are used. The authors select Istanbul to apply the case study. Different locations in other countries and continents can be selected in future studies to compare CO_2 emissions for different transportation modes so that the authorities can use the results to motivate the residents to use optimal transportation modes in terms of CO_2 emissions. Other methodologies and applications can also be used in future studies to compare the results of this study to ensure to propose optimal scenarios considering energy consumption and less air-polluting options.

Vehicle providers are introducing shared transportation vehicles to replace with traditional ones. Future studies should also consider those options to focus on recent technologies and their possible solutions for less CO_2 emissions.

CONCLUSION

The chapter aims to review traditional public transportation, explain green and sustainable public transportation ways and promote the integration of green public transportation in an effort to show the importance of micro-mobility (walking, cycling, e-scooters etc.) and public transportation ways considering CO_2 emissions. Different scenarios are applied for four routes which are given in the case study section. İstanbul is selected, one of the most crowded cities in the world, to apply the case study and analyze the results. Findings encourage the public authorities to motivate their citizens to use micro-mobility options and public transportation to cause less CO_2 emissions, which will result in less air pollution.

The results found for different scenarios on the routes in the case study ensure that the most eco-friendly options would be the walking, cycling and public transportation ways for the passengers. However, they may not provide the optimal solutions regarding total duration and distance travelled.

The transportation providers in the cities now focus on more eco-friendly public transportation ways. Electric buses, as well as buses which use natural gas, have been in action for public transportation in those cities.

It can be concluded that eco-friendly public transportation ways should be used to contribute zero emissions and vision zero actions. People should also be encouraged to replace their cars with more eco-friendly cars such as electric and hybrid cars for the regions where private car usage is inevitable.

REFERENCES

Abduljabbar, R. L., Liyanage, S., & Dia, H. (2021). The role of micro-mobility in shaping sustainable cities: A systematic literature review. *Transportation Research Part D, Transport and Environment*, *92*, 102734. doi:10.1016/j.trd.2021.102734

ACEA. (2020). *Fuel types of new buses: diesel 85%, hybrid 4.8%, electric 4%, alternative fuels 6.2% share in 2019*. ACEA. https://www.acea.auto/fuel-cv/fuel-types-of-new-buses-diesel-85-hybrid-4-8-electric-4-alternative-fuels-6-2-share-in-2019-2/.

ACEA. (2021). *Fuel types of new buses: Electric 6.1%, hybrids 9.5%, Diesel 72.9% market share in 2020*. ACEA. https://www.acea.auto/fuel-cv/fuel-types-of-new-buses-electric-6-1-hybrids-9-5-diesel-72-9-market-share-in-2020/.

Buehler, R. (2018). Can Public Transportation Compete with Automated and Connected Cars? *Journal of Public Transportation*, *21*(1), 7–18. https://digitalcommons.usf.edu/jpt/vol21/iss1/2. doi:10.5038/2375-0901.21.1.2

Carpenter, T. G. (1994). *The environmental impact of railways*. Wiley.

Cell, F., & Undertaking, H. J. (2019). *Hydrogen Roadmap Europe: A Sustainable Pathway for the European Energy Transition*. EU Publications.

Chang, X., Ma, T., & Wu, R. (2019). Impact of urban development on residents' public transportation travel energy consumption in China: An analysis of hydrogen fuel cell vehicles alternatives. *International Journal of Hydrogen Energy*, *44*(30), 16015–16027. doi:10.1016/j.ijhydene.2018.09.099

Choi, U. D., Jeong, H. K., & Jeong, S. K. (2012). *Commercial operation of ultra low floor electric bus for Seoul city route. In 2012 IEEE vehicle power and propulsion conference*. IEEE.

Erokhina, O. V., & Brega, A. V. (2020). Intelligent transport technologies in "smart" cities. In 2020 Systems of Signals Generating and Processing in the Field of on Board Communications. IEEE.

Esztergár-Kiss, D., & Lizarraga, J. C. L. (2021). Exploring user requirements and service features of e-micromobility in five European cities. *Case Studies on Transport Policy*, *9*(4), 1531–1541. doi:10.1016/j.cstp.2021.08.003

European Alternative Fuels Observatory (EAFO). (2021). *Country detail vehicles and fleet*. EAFO. https://www.eafo.eu/countries/european-union-efta-turkey/23682/vehicles-and-fleet

European Commission (EC). (2020). *Sustainable and Smart Mobility Strategy–putting European transport on track for the future*. EC.

European Environment Agency (EEA). (2022). *Annual European Union greenhouse gas inventory 1990–2020 and inventory report 2022. Submission to the UNFCCC Secretariat, May 2022*. EU NIR.

Firoiu, D., Ionescu, G. H., Băndoi, A., Florea, N. M., & Jianu, E. (2019). Achieving sustainable development goals (SDG): Implementation of the 2030 Agenda in Romania. *Sustainability*, *11*(7), 2156. doi:10.3390u11072156

Fishman, T. D. (2012). *Digital-Age Transportation: The Future of Urban Mobility*. Deloitte University Press.

Gössling, S. (2013). Urban transport transitions: Copenhagen, city of cyclists. *Journal of Transport Geography, 33*, 196–206. doi:10.1016/j.jtrangeo.2013.10.013

Guerrero-Ibanez, J. A., Zeadally, S., & Contreras-Castillo, J. (2015). Integration challenges of intelligent transportation systems with connected vehicle, cloud computing, and internet of things technologies. *IEEE Wireless Communications, 22*(6), 122–128. doi:10.1109/MWC.2015.7368833

Innovate U. K. (2021). *UK TRANSPORT VISION 2050: investing in the future of mobility*. Innovate UK. https://www.ukri.org/wp-content/uploads/2022/01/IUK-110122-UK-Transport-Vision-2050.pdf

Jagiello, A., Wojtach, A., & Łuczak, A. (2018). *Report benchmarks for the current public transport systems*. Inno Baltica. http://interconnect.one/images/PDFs/report-Interconect-4-2.pdf

Kaldellis, J. K., Spyropoulos, G., & Liaros, St. (2017). Supporting electromobility in smart cities using solar electric vehicle charging stations. Mediterranean green buildings and renewable energy: Selected papers from *the world renewable energy network's med green forum* (pp. 501-513). Springer. doi:10.1007/978-3-319-30746-6_37

Kamargianni, M., Li, W., Matyas, M., & Schäfer, A. (2016). A critical review of new mobility services for urban transport. *Transportation Research Procedia, 14*, 3294–3303. doi:10.1016/j.trpro.2016.05.277

Li, H. (2016). Study on green transportation system of international metropolises. Paper presented at *the Procedia Engineering, 137*, (pp. 762-771). Procedia Engineering. 10.1016/j.proeng.2016.01.314

Luo, X. G., Zhang, H. B., Zhang, Z. L., Yu, Y., & Li, K. (2019). A new framework of intelligent public transportation system based on the internet of things. *IEEE Access: Practical Innovations, Open Solutions, 7*, 55290–55304. doi:10.1109/ACCESS.2019.2913288

McQueen, M., Abou-Zeid, G., MacArthur, J., & Clifton, K. (2021). Transportation transformation: Is micromobility making a macro impact on sustainability? *Journal of Planning Literature, 36*(1), 46–61. doi:10.1177/0885412220972696

Mulley, C., Nelson, J., & Ison, S. (Eds.). (2021). *The Routledge handbook of public transport*. Routledge. doi:10.4324/9780367816698

Nkoro, A. B., & Vershinin, Y. A. (2014). Current and future trends in applications of Intelligent Transport Systems on cars and infrastructure. In *17th International IEEE Conference on Intelligent Transportation Systems (ITSC)* (pp. 514-519). IEEE. 10.1109/ITSC.2014.6957741

Ogryzek, M., Adamska-Kmieć, D., & Klimach, A. (2020). Sustainable transport: An efficient transportation network—case study. *Sustainability, 12*(19), 8274. doi:10.3390u12198274

Olaverri-Monreal, C. (2016). Intelligent technologies for mobility in smart cities. *Hiradastechnika Journal, 71*, 29–34.

Potter, S. (2003). Transport energy and emissions: urban public transport. In *Handbook of Transport and the Environment* (Vol. 4, pp. 247–262). Emerald Group Publishing Limited. doi:10.1108/9781786359513-013

Senin, S. N., Fahmy-Abdullah, M., & Masrom, M. A. N. (2021). The implementation of green transportation towards low carbon city. Paper presented at the *IOP Conference Series: Earth and Environmental Science, 736*(1).IOP Science. doi:10.1088/1755-1315/736/1/012063

Tiseo, I. (2022). *EU-27: CO2 emissions shares by sector 2020*. Statista. https://www.statista.com/statistics/1240108/road-transportation-greenhouse-gas-emissions-eu/

Toh, C. K., Sanguesa, J. A., Cano, J. C., & Martinez, F. J. (2020). Advances in smart roads for future smart cities. *Proceedings of the Royal Society of London. Series A, 476*(2233), 20190439. doi:10.1098/rspa.2019.0439 PMID:32082053

UK. G. (2022). Greenhouse gas reporting: conversion factors 2019. UK Government. https://www.gov.uk/government/publications/greenhouse-gas-reporting-conversion-factors-2022

United Nations. (2021). Sustainable Transport, Sustainable Development. *Interagency Report for Second Global Sustainable Transport Conference*, (pp. 59-68).

United Nations (UN). (2018). *World Urbanization Prospects: The 2018 Revision-Highlights*. UN.

Watkins, K. (2018). Does the future of mobility depend on public transportation? *Journal of Public Transportation, 21*(1), 6. doi:10.5038/2375-0901.21.1.6

Zhao, J., & Melaina, M. W. (2006). Transition to hydrogen-based transportation in china: Lessons learned from alternative fuel vehicle programs in the United States and china. *Energy Policy, 34*(11), 1299–1309. doi:10.1016/j.enpol.2005.12.014

KEY TERMS AND DEFINITIONS

CO_2 emission: Carbon dioxide is produced during the consumption of solid, liquid, and gas fuels and gas flaring.

Energy Consumption: The amount of energy used to travel between OD pairs.

Green transportation: It refers to travel from an origin to a destination (OD) using eco-friendly vehicles.

Green vehicle: A vehicle that causes less environmental damage than other traditional transportation vehicles.

Micro-mobility vehicle: It is an environmentally friendly and innovative transportation option for short-distance travel which work with human power or an electric motor.

Mobility as a Service (MaaS): It is a concept that builds on these shared modes and advancements in information and communication technology.

Traditional transportation vehicle: It refers to a vehicle that uses fossil fuels like diesel and petrol, which cause high CO_2 emissions and energy consumption.

Chapter 11

Attractiveness of Urban Public Transport From the Point of View of Young Passengers:
Experience From the Czech Republic

Zdenek Kresa
https://orcid.org/0000-0003-4431-0839
Faculty of Economics, University of West Bohemia, Czech Republic

Jan Tluchor
https://orcid.org/0000-0003-0779-1792
Faculty of Economics, University of West Bohemia, Czech Republic

Adam Heyes
Faculty of Economics, University of West Bohemia, Czech Republic

ABSTRACT

This chapter uses the customer-oriented approach to help enhance understanding of the use of sustainable public transportation (PT) systems in urban areas to support climate change actions. It studies the views and experiences of young passengers (Generation Z) in a heavily used Central European PT system. Three surveys were conducted to study the effect of the coronavirus epidemic on the behavior of passengers. Additionally, automated passenger counting data were utilized. The surveys identified that despite the epidemic, the most important factors of customer experience were those that related to the total travel time. Findings further included the fact that the PT is starting to be used more frequently in 2022 after decline in 2020 and 2021. The decline was not caused by a massive outflow of regular passengers, but in general by passengers having fewer reasons to travel. Discussions are underway as to how to increase the attractiveness of PT systems.

DOI: 10.4018/978-1-6684-5996-6.ch011

Copyright © 2023, IGI Global. Copying or distributing in print or electronic forms without written permission of IGI Global is prohibited.

INTRODUCTION

Urban public transport (UPT) is an essential symbol of every large city. Every day, buses, trolleybuses, trams, and underground transport large numbers of passengers. In Central Europe, just as in other countries, UPT has been competing against personal transport by passenger vehicles. Extensive development of modern public transport (PT) in the late 19th and early 20th century was gradually replaced with the "automobile era" (Schaeffer & Sclar, 2002), particularly in the latter half of the 20th century. Its effects, both positive and negative ones, are felt daily. These days, increased awareness, sustainable thinking as well as the perception of the negative state of public space have led to the renaissance of public transport. Which was originally perceived as a "necessary evil for the poor" is now considered "a modern solution for urban mobility". The need for more intensive use of UPT is becoming ever more topical in the context of climate change.

In the past, UPT in the Czech Republic (CR) faced a long-term decrease in the number of users, but since 2011 data have indicated an upward trend. During this period, PT operators have modernized their fleets, placed growing importance on the role of marketing and generally strived to improve the parameters of UPT services. Public transport in Prague ranked among the best in Europe, respectively world (Arcadis, 2017; Biazzo et al., 2019; Praha.eu, 2010). CR had the highest use of public transport per capita among the countries of the European Union (Enerdata, 2019). However, this promising trend received a blow in March 2020 in the form of the coronavirus epidemic (CE). The unprecedented decline in human activity led to a significant drop in the number of PT users. Over the next two years there was some reluctance to respect the current epidemiological measures (particularly enforced wearing of face masks in public transport vehicles). The list of potential negatives of UPT has grown by several further items. UPT operators cannot merely rely on the social responsibility of people or their poor financial situation (could become relevant shortly given rising energy prices and increasing inflation in 2022), which would force them to use UPT. Instead, they must actively "fight" for passengers. Creating a sustainably functional and reliable UPT system requires a comprehensive strategic approach.

Formulating strategies for sustainable transport and their implementation is a must topic for virtually every large, developed city. The emphasis on sustainability, "greenification", planning further development of systems and the implementation of smart city principles must also be accompanied by a customer-oriented approach. This approach will be represented in this chapter. The opinions of young passengers – representatives of Generation Z (Dolot, 2018; Seemiller & Grace, 2016) – in the heavily used PT system in Pilsen will be investigated. At the beginning of their professional life, the young generation is faced with a decision of what means of transport to use. This decision often affects their choice of means of transport for the rest of their lives, thus forming the future customer base and demand for transportation. Therefore, when designing strategies for transportation systems, it is advisable to consider the views (and deciding factors) of this new generation, now represented by Generation Z. Generally speaking, the specifics of this generation are many (Berkup, 2014), while in transport field, there is a higher interest in PT services and a preference for PT instead of the car. The beginning of these tendencies, especially the lower usage of cars, began to be observed already among Generation Y (Chatterjee et al., 2018; Hopkins, 2016). For Generation Z, shift from cars to PT was mainly attributed to the efforts for environmentally friendly travel (Chen et al., 2021; Parzonko et al., 2021), although it is worth noting that: *"Generation Z is not always more environmentally friendly than people of the same age in previous decades"* (Chen et al., 2021, p. 21). As another motive, the aspect of social interactions and doing other activities (multi-task) while riding is described (Larkin et al., 2018). Even with these aspects, another

Attractiveness of Urban Public Transport From the Point of View of Young Passengers

demand of Generation Z must not be forgotten - requirement for convenient service (Johnson & Sveen, 2020). Just the convenience of using UPT services may have been significantly affected by CE. How is the UPT service perceived by those for whom it is important to be environmentally friendly, have their comfort, and also have a choice of their means of transport? If they will be satisfied, it can be assumed that other generations of passengers will be satisfied as well.

The aim of this chapter is to provide information that will help to make UPT systems more attractive for young generation in the period following the coronavirus epidemic and to achieve a better understanding of this segment of passengers. This information will be based on the authors' own research conducted among young UPT users in an advanced and heavily used Central-European UPT system. For the purpose of this research, young (generation Z) passengers are defined as people aged between 15 and 26 who at least occasionally use the UPT system in Pilsen.

The Main Objective: To provide information aimed at making UPT systems more attractive for young people after the coronavirus epidemic and at achieving a better understanding of this segment of passengers.

- Subobjective 1: Examine possible changes in the significance of various factors of customer experience among young passengers (in using UPT) resulting from the coronavirus epidemic.
- Subobjective 2: Describe tendencies in the use of UPT in Pilsen by young people during and after the coronavirus epidemic.

From the stated objectives, followed research questions were derived:

- RQ_1: Did the customer experience factors of young UPT passengers in Pilsen remain the same during the coronavirus epidemic?
- RQ_2: Did the frequency of UPT use in Pilsen (represented by defined frequency groups) by young passengers remained the same during the coronavirus epidemic?

A synthesis of the results of individual research studies will lead to a description of key aspects in increasing the attractiveness of urban public transport systems.

BACKGROUND

Public Transport

The Czech Republic is a country with high-quality and widely used UPT. Mass transit means of transport are operated by companies, which are typically owned by the city (municipality). PT companies collaborate with municipal and regional transport organizers – institutions with an integrating role in the spirit of the Mobility as a Service (MaaS) concept – (Smith et al., 2018). At both the national as well as European level, PT companies are incentivized to implement strategies of sustainable urban mobility to increase the share of UPT at the expense of less sustainable transport options (Office of the Government of the Czech Republic, 2017). Marketing management is essential in increasing the attractiveness of UPT systems. PT companies in Central Europe are well aware of the necessity of customer-oriented communication; however, in practice they encounter limitations in terms of the resources allocated by their owner. The meager funds allocated to the marketing communication of the various PT companies contrast starkly with the large sums invested in marketing communication by large automobile manufacturers. For example, in 2012 the annual advertising expenses of automaker Škoda amounted to CZK 429 million, more than one-third of the total annual costs of the Pilsen Municipal Public Transportation (CZK 1.161 billion) (E15, 2013; PMDP, 2013). General problems of UPT marketing (Ibraeva & Sousa, 2014) in CR also include *"lack of funds, fear of failure, non-specific goals, a conservative environment, and the perceived monopoly"* (Dolejš, 2015). Particularly the lack of finances in public services in general is also noted by Slavík (2014).

The presented research was conducted in the UPT operation in Pilsen. The system is operated by the company called "Plzeňské městské dopravní podniky" (hereinafter referred to as PMDP). Electrification of PT in Pilsen dates back to 1899. Now, two-thirds of the transport service is provided by eco-friendly trams and trolleybuses. In 2017, the Pilsen Sustainable Mobility Plan was approved (Mobility Pilsen, 2022). PMDP is bringing new innovations to passengers (e. g. pay fares using a contactless credit card). Vehicles operated by PMDP are equipped with data collection systems (for monitoring current location, delays, and in an increasing number of vehicles also their current occupancy). According to customer satisfaction survey results, Pilsen's UPT is perceived as a high-quality, cost-effective and reliable form of transport. Responses from the last several surveys indicate that 65% of respondents consider Pilsen's UPT better than those in other cities and 65% of respondents agree with the statement that using public transport is "in" (PMDP internal documents). Apart from organizing the city's PT, is PMDP also responsible for the parking systems in the city, for city lighting and traffic lights and launched a car sharing service (which was an unprecedented move among Czech PT companies).

From 1950, numbers of transported passengers rose steadily; however, from the early 1990s numbers dropped. Over the past 20 years, passenger transport outputs have fluctuated, as seen in Figure 1 (fare increases – 2004, 2008 and 2012; economic recession – after 2008; onset of CE – 2020). PMDP's transport performance expressed in vehicle-kilometers stagnated or slightly rose during the reference period. Figure 2 indicates the trend in the number of transported passengers among members of Czech Public Transportation Association (SDP ČR). The trend in Pilsen does not significantly differ from the nationwide trend. The second graph also shows a drop due the onset of CE (only 60% compared to the year prior).

Figure 1. Development of Pilsen's UPT transport performance in terms of vehicle-kilometers (in columns) and transported passengers (by the line)
Source: (own elaboration, 2022 according to SDP ČR (n. d.))

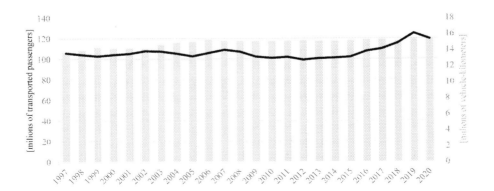

Figure 2. Development of SDP ČR members' transport performance in terms of transported passengers
Source: (own elaboration, 2022 according to SDP ČR (n. d.))
Note: In 2004 and 2005, the methodology for determining transport performance changed, which makes direct comparisons impossible.

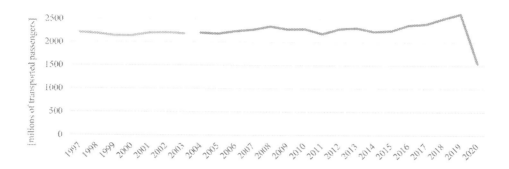

In 2019 PMDP transported close to 125 million passengers (static indicator) covering 15.46 million vehicle-kilometers (PMDP, 2020). In this period, UPT had the highest share of passenger transport output expressed in vehicle-kilometers covered of all forms of transport (Mott MacDonald, 2021).

According to Marada (2003), Pilsen belongs to the centers with greater specialization in long-distance or railway transport. According to the right-of-way classification (Vuchic, 2011) could be described as type C (urban streets with mixed traffic) with certain aspects of type B (partially separated tracks/lanes, usually in street medians). Looking at the organization of the system the city PT system could be described, in reference to Shibayama (2011), as an "all-in-one governmental service for the majority of services in cooperation with other operators run by the city-owned transportation company".

Customer Experience

Customer experience (CX) represents the concept customer-oriented approach. This concept has increasingly drawn the attention of both researchers and managers in the past decade, although customers have acted on their experience, intuitively for much longer. The first mention of CX aspects in scientific literature dates back to the early 1980s (Holbrook & Hirschman, 1982). The work of Pine II & Gilmore (1999) is considered to be key research, in which experience is considered to be a new subject of economic transactions – apart from commodities, products and services. The publication by Shaw & Ivens (2002) largely contributed to its practical application. In this publication, CX is defined as a *"blend of a company's physical performance and the emotions evoked, intuitively measured against customer expectations across all moments of contact"* (Shaw & Ivens, 2002, p. 21). A comprehensive definition of the CX concept was put forth by Gentile et al. (2007, p. 397).

Quite recently, Klaus et al. (2015) stated that despite the growing practical application, research into the phenomenon of CX is fragmented and there is still a relatively small amount of information about concept. Research at that time focused primarily on the moments of truth and service blueprints (Stickdorn & Schneider, 2011, p. 204). Bueno et al. (2019) state that there is no general consensus among authors on the subject in terms of how to measure and understand CX. The heterogeneity in defining the concept of CX is also manifested in CX components. Typically, these comprise the physical and emotional components, but they can also include psychological, rational and subconscious components (Beyond Philosophy, n. d.). There is also disunity among researchers as to which is the more comprehensive concept – customer experience or customer satisfaction (CS). The authors of this research article more closely identify with the view that CX is the more comprehensive concept (including CS), which is in line with publications Chatzopoulos & Weber (2018), CXcentral (2019) and Lemon & Verhoef (2016). Regardless of which one is perceived as the superordinate concept, there is no doubt that both concepts are closely connected and mutually related. Empirical data have confirmed the effect of CX on CS, and the impact of CX on customer loyalty as well as CS on customer loyalty – for example, Allen et al. (2019), Klaus & Maklan (2013), Shankar et al. (2003), and in the area of transportation Biesok & Wyród-Wróbel (2012) and Pratiwi et al. (2018). Klaus & Maklan (2013) note that the correlation between loyalty and CX and is statistically more significant than with CS. The heterogeneity in the understanding of these concepts is not ideal from the academic standpoint, though their practical implications are similar. Both quantitative and qualitative research methods are recommended for practical monitoring of CX, and the use of service design tools also appears suitable.

In the context of UPT, passengers' views are most frequently acquired by monitoring passenger satisfaction. Research in the context of CX and service design is not as common – exceptions are e.g. Accenture (2014), Kwon et al. (2015) and Thoughtfull Design Limited (2013). Broader generalization of the results is prevented primarily by differences in the geographical characteristics, passenger mentality, the economic conditions in different countries and the resulting differences between systems. The perception and use of UPT systems in general also play a role UPT systems also feature many local specifics. It is also necessary to consider the integration of UPT systems into other systems transport. The specifics of UPT are also influenced by the interaction with individual transport (e. g. the degree of preference of public transport).

Based on extensive research, Dell´Olio et al. (2018, p. 55) state that the most frequent attributes affecting CS include: *"access to the stops/stations, behavior/attitude of the staff and drivers, transfer time, journey time, waiting time, service reliability, available information, cleanliness of the vehicle and the stations/stops, safety on board, payment methods"*. In countries with high per capita income (including CR), the most common factors (for city buses) include: *"travel time (speed), frequency (waiting time), punctuality, safety and driver kindness"* (pp. 75-76). A more up-to-date study, De Oña (2021, p. 129) mentions the following main attributes contributing to the evaluation of UPT service quality: *"frequency, punctuality, speed and intermodality"*. In the context of excellent CX, Mallet (International Association of Public Transport, 2018) further states that the most essential customer needs are: *"seamless travel, safety, punctual and productive journey time"*. The aforementioned factors affecting CX can be viewed using the optics of the Kano Model of Customer Satisfaction (Berger et al., 1993). The must-be requirements in the context of UPT include *"punctuality, direct connections and ease of interchanges"* (Dienel & Schiefelbusch, 2009, p. 23). According to the authors of this article, one-dimensional (performance related) requirements include, for example, the behavior of the driver and passengers (which the operator can affect only partly). Given the type of service, attractive requirements are more difficult to implement. Dienel and Schiefelbusch (2009) consider the availability of daily newspapers or TV broadcast on board UPT vehicles to be examples of attractive requirements. In the current context, should be included wireless Internet connection, USB charging ports, etc. According to the authors of this research, attractive requirements may also include acts or benefits on top of the usual expectations (i.e., outside the scope of

Attractiveness of Urban Public Transport From the Point of View of Young Passengers

standard performance-related requirements) – for example, giving flowers to female passengers (DPMCB, 2016). In general, it can be assumed that what is key for the customer is the fulfillment of the essential factors, which over time comprise more attributes (including some that were originally considered attractive requirements – a Wi-Fi connection, USB charging ports, air-conditioning, informing passengers of any disruptions in service in real time). If these attributes which passengers take for granted are not provided, it causes a high degree of dissatisfaction. UPT is exposed to a lot of pressure in meeting basic requirements that mainly prevent dissatisfaction rather than ensure satisfaction. UPT operators are faced with a relatively difficult task, as the nature of their service may easily lead to passengers feeling unhappy, but it is relatively difficult to delight them. The issue of measuring service quality in UPT is also addressed in industry standards (e. g. ČSN EN 13816 in the Czech Republic).

According to authors of this research, CS in the area of UPT focuses particularly on the evaluation of how the key attributes of the service are fulfilled. The concept of CX can be perceived in broader terms – apart from mapping a wide range of service touchpoints (Stickdorn & Schneider, 2011) also referred as points of contact (POCs), there may be stronger emphasis on interactions with other passengers, which affect passengers' overall perception and impression. This chapter will cover factors of customer experience related to the core service provided as part of UPT, i.e., transport by UPT vehicles (and related aspects). The fact is that UPT vehicles are the key and most frequent POCs between the customer and the UPT operator (Kresa, 2019).

CUSTOMER EXPERIENCE OF YOUNG PASSENGERS

The customer experience of traveling by UPT vehicles is a complex and multi-factorial issue. It can be expected that the coronavirus epidemic (which affected CR particularly in 2020 and 2021) affected CX of traveling by UPT. Did the epidemic change the significance of CX factors? Was the reduction in passenger numbers as a result of the epidemic only temporary? How can the recovery be accelerated and UPT made more attractive in the post-COVID period? These are the principal questions that the authors will seek answers to.

To meet the set objectives, research was conducted among young passengers in a highly developed and heavily used UPT system in Central Europe (in Pilsen, Czech Republic). First, the design of both sections of the research will be described in detail, followed by key findings.

Methods

In order to achieve the set research objectives, a mostly exploratory sequential design was used. Its key component is made up of three conducted surveys (presented in Table 1). The overall design of the research is explained in Figure 3. The homogeneity of the target segment (corresponding to Generation Z) was assumed, which with the same methodology allows data from individual surveys to be compared with each other and further analyzed. The presentation of the results comes in the form of a case study. The authors assume that the findings will be applicable even to other, at least Central European UPT operations.

Table 1. Overview of conducted research surveys

	Survey A	Survey B	Survey C
Achievement of objective	Subobjective 1 (CX factors)	Subobjective 1 (CX factors)	Subobjective 2 (Use of UPT)
Date of survey	12/2018-01/2019 (before the epidemic)	04-10/2021 (during the epidemic)	03-04/2022 (after the epidemic)
Target group	UPT users aged 15–26	UPT users aged 15–26	UPT users aged 15–30
Method	Personal interviewing/on-line questionnaire	Personal interviewing/on-line questionnaire	On-line questionnaire
Sampling	n = 45 stratified sampling	n = 114 stratified sampling	n = 215 stratified sampling

Source: (own elaboration, 2022)

Figure 3. Design of the conducted research
Source: (own elaboration, 2022)

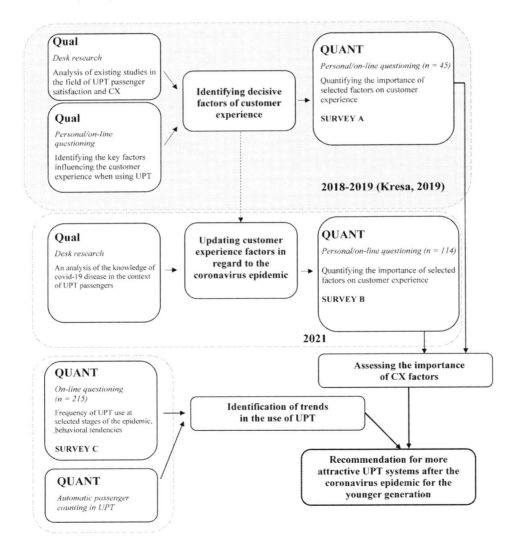

Attractiveness of Urban Public Transport From the Point of View of Young Passengers

The subobjective 1 (identification of a change in the importance of individual CX factors for young passengers as a result of the coronavirus epidemic) will be achieved by comparing the results of surveys A and B. Identification of factors in the first wave and determining the importance of factors took place within a wider survey of CX of young UPT passengers conducted by one of the authors before the outbreak of CE (Kresa, 2019). Identified factors were expanded in 2021 in the context of CE by other prospective significant factors, and using another sample of respondents their importance was studied (the respondents in the two waves of the survey are not identical, therefore it is not a before-and-after study; however, in both waves respondents were selected from the same segment of young UPT passengers, which can be viewed as homogeneous).

The results of Survey C (conducted during a period without any major CE-related restrictions) will serve the purpose of achieving the subobjective 2 (describing tendencies in using UPT in Pilsen by young people during and after CE). In this part, the frequency of use of UPT by young passengers in the selected time periods with respect to CE is studied. In this respect, the research further examines the reasons that led respondents to any changes in their transport behavior. For output verification purposes, data from automated passenger counting systems in Pilsen's UPT are further examined.

The synthesis of the results of both parts of the research will lead to identifying the key trends related to changes in CX among young passengers, and it will be possible to make recommendations.

Stratified sampling is used to ensure that the samples of respondents are representative in all research phases. The target group consisted of young people aged between 15 and 26 (and 16–30 years of age in the second part of the research due to the later data collection) who at least occasionally use UPT in Pilsen (at least in one of the survey periods). Having filled the set minimum quota, the demographic criteria were studied, namely: gender, frequency of use of UPT in Pilsen (following the subject's journey to his or her destination, including any transfers along the way); and "social status" (student, full-time employee, unemployed...). Equal quotas were set for each segment. Data collection was conducted in collaboration with PMDP.

Factors of Customer Experience

The first part of the research focuses on CX factors among young passengers. Based on an earlier, initial qualitative survey carried out among young users of Pilsen's UPT (Kresa, 2019), a total of 38 factors of CX were identified. From among these, ten main factors were identified based on the frequency of responses as well as research of earlier studies (mentioned in the "Customer Experience" section). These include the following areas: *adherence to the timetable (punctuality), transport speed, frequency of connections, vehicle occupancy rate (i.e., the number of passengers on board), the (good or bad) smell of other passengers, the behavior of passengers, temperature inside the vehicle (thermal comfort), easy transfers between routes, the driver's driving style, cleanliness of the vehicle (interior).* The identified CX factors are similar to factors studied in CS research. Specifically, the factors *punctuality, travel speed, frequency* are consistent with review by Dell´Olio et al. (2018), factor *vehicle cleanliness* has been identified e. g. by Tyrinopoulos & Antoniou (2008), factor *easy transfers between routes* suggests, e. g. Christopher et al. (1999), and it is also consistent with *intermodality* described by De Oña (2021). Also, in line with Christopher et al. (1999, p. 106) is the *temperature inside the vehicle.* The results are also in line with Sinha, et al. (2020, p. 3313) identifying among others "*drive quality of bus ride, cleanliness inside the bus, ease of transfer or crowding levels on bus*". However, it is clear that identified factors focus not only on the evaluation of the carrier's "performance", but also on areas that the transport company has very little influence over. Factors describing employee behavior and safety on board (behavior of passengers) are also common, but the exact focus varies between authors - mapped extensively by Dell´Olio et al. (2018).

The factors were further sorted by respondents according to importance. For the purpose of this research, the importance of factors was viewed as ordinal data, although in the first wave of research the so-called Fuller's triangle method (Friebelová & Klicnarová, 2007) was used, which also provides a cardinal view. A total of 149 young UPT users took part in this stage of the research (45 in the first phase and 114 in the second). The conducted analysis revealed differences in the perception of factors between genders, which is why their importance will be presented separately for men and women (see Table 2). In general, emphasis was put on sticking to the route schedule (punctuality), transport speed and the frequency of connections. The Intraclass correlation coefficient (2, k) – in short ICC, according to Koo & Li (2016) – exhibited between good and satisfactory reliability of the results. The calculated coefficients indicate that while there is a high degree of agreement among men in terms of the importance of factors, for women all the factors play a role and some women may find different factors more important than others, which is reflected in the much lower value of the ICC – although still fair (Cicchetti, 1994). It is clear that the sample as a whole shows a fair amount of agreement, although there are differences between respondents.

Table 2. The importance of factors according to the respondents' gender (2018-2019)

Factor importance	Order	Factor (n=21, men)	Factor importance	Order	Factor (n=24, women)
13.54%	1	punctuality	12.31%	1	vehicle occupancy rate
12.49%	2	transport speed	12.04%	2	punctuality
11.96%	3	frequency of connections	11.02%	3	transport speed
11.75%	4	(good/bad) smell of passengers	10.46%	4	passenger behavior
9.84%	5	easy transfer between routes	10.28%	5	frequency of connections
9.63%	6	vehicle occupancy rate	10.19%	6	driver's driving style
9.63%	6	passenger behavior	9.63%	7	(good/bad) smell of passengers
8.68%	8	temperature inside the vehicle	8.89%	8	temperature inside the vehicle
7.62%	9	vehicle cleanliness	7.59%	9	easy transfer between routes
4.87%	10	driver's driving style	7.59%	9	vehicle cleanliness
ICC (2, k) = 0.7719			ICC (2, k) = 0.4781		

Source: (Kresa, 2019)

To map out the effect of the coronavirus epidemic, it was first necessary to update the original list of factors. Given the dynamic nature of the situation, the number of earlier studies was very small. Based on research conducted among passengers in Chinese UPT, Dong et al., (2021) assumed a change in the original CS factors among passengers and an increase in the effect of the perceived safety of UPT. He found that passengers are feeling more anxious, which negatively affects their satisfaction (and CX). His findings indicate that UPT is perceived to be less safe. The increase in the importance of safety is also stated in study by McKinsey (2021). Similar tendencies were also generally seen in CR. The gathering of

Attractiveness of Urban Public Transport From the Point of View of Young Passengers

large numbers of people (typical for UPT) can lead to increased concerns about infection and the perception of lower safety. As a result, safety measures are implemented in the form of obligatory wearing of face masks on PT, with UPT carriers disinfecting the vehicles more thoroughly. Based on the authors' own observation on UPT in Pilsen, customer experience may be affected by passengers (not) observing the mask obligation, or by the staff not enforcing these measures and the ensuing conflicts. Failure to observe the mask obligation was a common violation and led to a number of conflicts, which in extreme cases led to passenger being removed from the vehicle (with the assistance of the Police and resulting in a major delay). Situations like these may affect passengers' customer experience. As a result, another two factors affecting CX from using UPT include *regular disinfection of UPT vehicles* and *enforcing (or failure to enforce) the mask obligation in UPT vehicles* (i.e., passengers masking up or not while traveling by UPT). These factors were added to the original ten questioned factors.

The evaluation of the importance of the various factors, including the comparison against 2018/2019, is shown in Table 3. The factors are sorted from the most important (1) to the least important (12), plus there is an indication of any change in the rank (a positive number meaning an increase in the importance of the given factor). To determine reliability, Kendall's coefficient of concordance was used in this case – as per Kraska-Miller (2014). For men, its value reached 0. 6519 and for women 0. 5212, which according to Schmidt (1997) can be viewed as moderate agreement (bordering on strong agreement for men). There is a clear trend of a generally lower degree of concordance among female respondents, which can be attributed to the individual character of CX.

Table 3. The importance of factors according to the respondents' gender (comparison)

Men			Individual factors	Women		
2018-19	2021	Change		2018-19	2021	Change
1	2	- 1	punctuality	2	1	+ 1
3	1	+ 2	frequency of connections	5	2	+ 3
5	4	+ 1	easy transfer between routes	9	3	+ 6
2	3	- 1	transport speed	3	4	- 1
9	5	+ 4	vehicle cleanliness	9	5	+ 4
6	6	0	vehicle occupancy rate	1	6	- 5
6	7	- 1	passenger behavior	4	7	- 3
4	8	- 4	(good/bad) smell of passengers	7	9	- 2
8	9	- 1	temperature inside the vehicle	8	10	- 2
10	10	0	driver's driving style	6	8	- 2
-	11		regular disinfection	-	11	
-	12		enforcing (or failure to enforce) safety measures	-	12	

Source: (own elaboration, 2022)

Table 3 clearly shows that in both periods the key factors of CX among young passengers was the punctuality of connections (adhering to the timetable) as well as their sufficient frequency and reasonable transport speed. In 2021, there is an apparent increase in the importance of the frequency of connections and easy transfer between routes (the increase is clearly noticeable particularly among women, for whom transfer between routes saw the largest increase in its effect on customer experience). This can be seen as the direct consequence of the prolongation of intervals between UPT connections in Pilsen. During CE, PMDP limited its services on a number of routes (the lines were carefully selected so that the reduction in the number of connections would present the lowest impact possible on people's regular commute to work during rush hour). The reasons for reducing the number of connections included lower demand as well as the need to cut costs. It can be assumed that passengers view as more important those factors that present a problem. Passengers thus respond to the longer intervals between connections, and the lower number of connections also affects the transfer between various routes.

Relatively surprising is the very low effect of the newly included factors, particularly in the context of the fact that the importance of vehicle cleanliness saw a significant increase in both sexes. This may be explained in the sense that young passengers care about the overall cleanliness of the vehicle interior, though they do not take much notice of other adopted safety measures and neither do they find the mask obligation too restrictive. Another possible explanation is the fact that as COVID does not present a high risk for young people, they are not as concerned about spread of the disease if safety measures are not enforced. It can also be argued that passengers who were afraid of getting infected had switched to a different means of transport.

The decrease in the importance of factors concerning other passengers (i.e., the occupancy rate, passengers' behavior and odor) can be attributed to the lower number of passengers during CE (due to a pronounced drop in demand). There is a marked decrease in the effect of the factor occupancy rate, which prior to the epidemic was viewed as the most important factor among women, while at this time it is perceived as equally important by both sexes (sixth most important factor). With respect to the lower importance of passengers' odors, this is perhaps caused by passengers wearing protective face masks.

The conducted analysis indicates that importance of the factors has not remained same (answer to question RQ_1). A detailed analysis of the importance of factors in 2021 was conducted. The effect of respondents' "social status" on the importance of factors was not detected. There were differences with respect to the frequency of connections. Men who use UPT only occasionally (on average less than three rides a week) find vehicle cleanliness more important compared to regular passengers (ten or more rides a week). Regular disinfection and the number of passengers on board have a relatively higher importance for women who use UPT occasionally. Women who use UPT "moderately" (three to nine rides a week) find the temperature inside the vehicle and other passengers' behavior relatively more important. Other demographic factors have not been surveyed.

The main identified factors can also be important in the context of sustainability and the smart approach. Ease of finding connections, ease of transfers (and frequent connection frequency) is a major challenge in the future smart system. From a sustainability perspective, preference measures can be discussed. This is discussed more in the "Solutions and recommendations" section. Furthermore, it is necessary to focus on the sustainability of the whole system (and the set standard) under increasing travel demands.

The earlier mentioned degree of concordance between the respondents was satisfactory to good for the analyzed data. In terms of reliability, what is positive is the concordance between the "pre-COVID" phase of research and the CS survey conducted among Pilsen UPT users in 2018 (PMDP internal documents). In both cases, the most important factors included *sufficient frequency of connections, transport speed, enough room in the vehicle* (equivalent to *vehicle occupancy rate*) and *punctuality* (any slight variations in the order may be attributable mainly to differences in the structure of the sample of respondents in the two surveys – the PMDP's survey included passengers of all age groups). Pawlasová (2015) dealt with the identification of factors affecting CS among UPT users (of all age groups) in the Czech city Ostrava. She identified as most important: *proximity and accessibility of stations/stops, seamless transport (easy transfers) and the frequency of connections* (p. 30). The high importance of the aspect of proximity and accessibility of stations/stops can be explained by the specific geographic characteristics of Ostrava. Apart from the concordance in terms of the frequency of connections, there is a higher importance of easy transfers in Ostrava, which can be attributed to the way PT operation is organized. No published research has so far focused on updating the importance of factors affecting Czech UPT passengers in the post-COVID period. Data from metropolises around the world (McKinsey, 2021) confirm the increase in the importance of factors associated with transport speed (time spent on route). The high importance of journey time is also illustrated by Ulahannan & Birrell (2022). The identified high importance of the factors *transport speed* and *scope of connections* (in this chapter) are in line even with the more generally focused work by De Oña (2021), as mentioned earlier.

Travelling During the Epidemic

The second part of the research (Survey C) focuses on tendencies in the use of UPT during the period of the coronavirus epidemic, and the possible reasons for the changes in behavior. The data acquired in the survey will provide a wider context of information about the number of passengers transported by UPT in Pilsen.

The frequency of use of UPT in Pilsen during CE is very well documented thanks to the system of automated passenger counting (APC). A growing number of vehicles are equipped with this system and the acquired data are extrapolated to make up 100% of the operation. These data provide an overview of the total number of transported passengers (without any distinction) – for the purpose of this research it is assumed that the trend in the number of young passengers roughly corresponds to the overall trend of transported passengers. The development of the daily numbers of transported passengers in the period

Figure 4. Development in the number of transported passengers by UPT in Pilsen on weekdays between January 2020 and May 2022 (with the key events related to the epidemic highlighted)
Source: (PMDP internal documents, 2022, modified)
Note: Introduction of epidemiological restrictions (lockdowns, restrictions on school attendance, store closures, etc.) – red (darker grey) vertical lines, relaxation of restrictions – green (lighter grey) vertical lines. "Classic" school holidays in a lighter shade of grey (lower chart area).

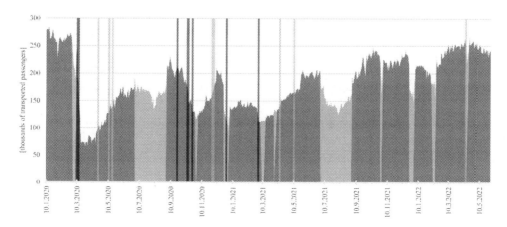

between 10 January 2020 – 31 May 2022 is shown in Figure 4. The key moments of the epidemic are highlighted (as vertical lines).

At the beginning of the epidemic, following the announcement of the first lockdown (March 2020), the number of passengers transported by UPT in Pilsen dropped by about 75% to approx. 60 thousand people daily. Subsequently, in 2020 and 2021 the number of transported passengers saw dynamic changes based on the situation at the time (lockdowns, relaxed measures, school closures, etc.). The year 2022, without any major epidemiological measures, has seen an increase in the number of transported passengers. Their numbers are closely approaching the pre-COVID level. So far, the highest number of transported passengers after the epidemic was in the second half of April 2022, a total of 267,317 people in a single day. For comparison purposes, the highest number of passengers transported in a single day in January 2020 was 283,313, and in February 2020 272,065 people/day. However, seasonal differences need to be taken into consideration (demand in winter is lower). In February 2022, the highest volume of passengers transported in a single day was 238,194 people, which is 87% of the maximum daily number in February 2020. Although the earlier values were not exceeded, the equalizing tendency in their levels is a positive trend – there is no massive outflow of regular passengers (moving to cars) after the epidemic.

For the sake of better interpretation of the development of the numbers of transported passengers, another research study focusing on young passengers was conducted in 2022. Respondents were asked about their frequency of use of UPT in three selected time periods - February 2020 (shortly before the outbreak of the coronavirus pandemic in CR); May 2021 (in this year was CR affected the most by the pandemic) and March-April 2022 (time without any CE-related travel restrictions; the only obligation was to wear a face mask on board UPT vehicles until 13 April 2022) (Ministry of Health, 2022). It is logical that in 2021, during the period of the toughest restrictions on the movement of people and the implementation of remote instead of in-person learning for schoolchildren, etc., the number of passengers using UPT will be much lower. That is why the spring following the relaxation of epidemiological measures after the second wave of the pandemic and with ongoing COVID vaccinations was chosen deliberately. At that time some students also returned to regular in-person learning. The research results included data from respondents who in at least one of the reference time periods used the Pilsen UPT at least occasionally. Respondents may not have remembered the exact frequency of travel, which is why a scale was chosen.

The frequency of use of UPT in the individual time periods, including the transitions between the various groups, is shown in Figure 5, the absolute frequencies are summarized in Table 4.

It is apparent that a certain number of passengers (less than half of each group) did not change their frequency of travel (FOT). The largest change occurred between March 2020 and May 2021 when there was a pronounced decrease. The relatively largest decrease is seen in the group of regular passengers (approximately half of respondents reporting 10 or more rides a week). In the last research period, among some of the passengers there is a noticeable increase in the FOT. In general, this frequency is not the same (high) as it was before the epidemic. In a more detailed analysis, it was observed that the shift of passengers takes place across all groups, the dominant trend being stagnation or a decrease in the FOT. In general, the FOT by UPT after the coronavirus pandemic is slightly lower, which is caused primarily by the not so frequent use by formerly regular UPT users. The analysis shows that the frequency of use of UPT has not remained the same (RQ_2).

Figure 5. Changes in the frequency of use of UPT
Source: (own elaboration, 2022)

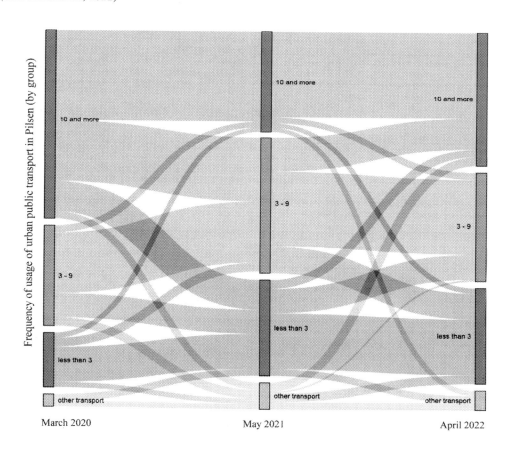

Table 4. Frequencies of UPT use by respondents [number of respondents]

Average weekly number of UPT journeys (in groups)	February 2020	May 2021	April 2022
10 and more	119	67	88
3 - 9	57	78	61
less than 3	31	55	55
not use UPT (other transport)	8	15	11
Total	215	215	215

Source: (own elaboration, 2022)

Also were investigated the main reasons that led respondents to change the frequency of use of UPT before and after CE. A total of 150 respondents (70% of all respondents) stated that their FOT had changed (due to the definition of the categories of responses based on the average weekly number of rides, some changes in the FOT are not shown in the previous graph). When answering the multiple-choice question, these respondents stated a total of 230 reasons, which are represented in Figure 6.

Figure 6. Reasons for changes in the frequency of use of UPT [number of responses]
Source: (own elaboration, 2022)

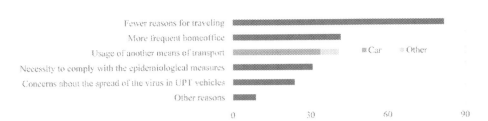

There is a noticeable decrease in the number of reasons for traveling (commuting) by UPT (as stated by 82 of 150 respondents). Respondents in general traveled by UPT less than before the pandemic with the exception of two respondents. One of them said that after the pandemic he uses UPT more often and drives his car less, and the other started to use UPT during the pandemic. Respondents who reported a decrease in the FOT by PT most often reported a switch to using their car (34x), walking (2x), cycling (1x) and traveling by train (1x). One of the respondents replied: *"I prefer walking; it is better for my health and often faster, and I don't have to breathe through a respirator and share space with an ever-rising number of inconsiderate passengers."* Another respondent stated that *"due to the high cost of the annual pass, I stopped using UPT and started commuting on my bike instead."* Other reasons that respondents listed as the reason for a change in their FOT by UPT included mainly personal reasons (moving out of the region). One respondent pointed out the fact that *"UPT vehicles, particularly trams, are fuller than they were before the epidemic."*

The frequency analysis of responses indicates that the majority of passengers commuting to work by UPT do not work from home. A total of 144 working people took part in the research, though only 42 of them used UPT less due to a home office arrangement with their employer. The mask obligation and concerns about the spread of the disease led a total of 46 respondents to use UPT less, eleven of whom started to use their passenger car instead of UPT, two started to walk and one biked to work. Reasons associated with the coronavirus pandemic thus directly affected the FOT of 20% of all respondents. An additional decrease in the frequency of UPT use is caused primarily by indirect factors connected with less common reasons to travel (e.g. fewer cultural events). More detailed frequency analysis did not identify any major differences.

The research also studied the young generation's satisfaction with the implementation of epidemiological measures to prevent the spread of the coronavirus disease (particularly the mask obligation). One positive finding was the fact that 47% of respondents were satisfied with them (7% of them actually very satisfied). Another 38% expressed a neutral stance. Dissatisfaction was reported by 16% of respondents (of whom 7% very dissatisfied). It is thus clear that by a large these safety measures are not too restrictive (this is in line with the observation of the low importance of these factors in first part of the research).

The varied positions on epidemiological measures are represented by the following selected responses:

- *The mask obligation makes it very unpleasant for me to travel by UPT* (male passenger, 3–9 rides per week)

Attractiveness of Urban Public Transport From the Point of View of Young Passengers

- *You cannot image what it is like to have a respirator on when traveling by UPT after a workout; it makes it difficult to breathe. What is particularly unpleasant is the fogging up of glasses, the hot air around my mouth and the ensuing eczema* (female passenger, 10 or more rides a week)
- *I am glad that people are masking up on UPT* (female passenger, 3–9 rides per week)
- *It would be desirable to check whether people wear respirators on UPT. Many passengers do not respect this rule and lower their respirator below their nose (…) This is unfair to other passengers who do follow this measure* (male passenger, 10 or more rides a week)
- *What's great is the regular morning disinfection of vehicles* (male passenger, 10 and more rides a week)

The issue of epidemiological measures is generally very complex, and for the carrier it is an external obligation which they must respect. This issue became quite controversial in CR. A certain degree of discomfort for passengers caused by wearing a face mask is understandable. Passengers may also fear the high concentration of people and the increased risk of infection. These concerns significantly affect the image of UPT, which is why Czech mass transit authorities tried to dispel these apprehensions. After conducting research in mass transit vehicles of the Prague UPT system, the Czech Academy of Sciences (2021) confirmed that it was safe to travel by UPT. The report specifically said: *"Out of the total of 558 samples, only 6 (i.e., roughly 1%) showed any detectable presence of viral material. Subsequent tests (using the standard qRT-PCR test method) showed, in each case, at each of the different timing intervals, that the viral particulate matter found was inanimate and non-infectious."*

SOLUTIONS AND RECOMMENDATIONS

The three conducted surveys led to a better understanding of the behavior of young UPT passengers in Pilsen.

The principal finding of the first part of the research is that despite the coronavirus epidemic, the most important CX factors for young passengers remained those factors that relate to the total amount of time spent on route – the punctuality, i.e., delays, of the connections, their frequency and the travel speed. In connection with CE, the cleanliness of the vehicle interior is paid more attention to; on the other hand, young passengers' CX was not affected much by the safety measures.

The findings from the second part of the research indicate the decrease in the number of young passengers using UPT in Pilsen is not caused by regular passengers opting en masse to shift away from PT, but generally by fewer reasons to travel. Fewer reasons for travel are an external effect, the consequence of society-wide developments, which the UPT carrier can hardly affect.

The results can be interpreted using the following points:

- A high-quality and sustainable UPT system must offer sufficient frequency and transport speed on its routes even during times of crises, such as CE. The amount of time spent en route is the most important criterion for an attractive UPT system, which would be the users' "first choice".
- The decrease in the number of passengers using UPT during the epidemic was caused mainly by fewer reasons to travel rather than a negative perception of UPT. Even regular passengers reported less frequent use of UPT during the epidemic. People are starting to use (Pilsen's) UPT more; the number of passengers in spring of 2022 was roughly 85–90% of pre-epidemic levels. It can be

assumed that within a few years the figure will in fact reach pre-COVID levels. UPT operators should be prepared to increase their capacity following the recent cost-reduction periods.

- The young generation is mostly responsible and had no problems with respecting and abiding by the imposed epidemiological measures. Generally speaking, the responsible and sustainable behavior of young passengers has its limits in the form of the required service quality (expectations in terms of travel time). In formulating its strategy, the priority for UPT operators should be to reduce passengers' travel time as much as possible (particularly in comparison with other modes of transport).

The key recommendation is to build up high-quality punctual UPT systems with frequent connections and acceptable transport speed. CE showed that social crises also negatively impact transportation. Reduced demand for transport, the loss of revenue from fares as well as the expected increase in costs (disinfecting, etc.) led PT companies to reduce service and prolong the intervals between connections. However, such reduction must be done thoughtfully and selectively, but with comprehensive approach – prolonging intervals can have a significant impact on transfers between UPT lines and other modes of transport. Longer intervals and a limited service offering lead to a drop in the popularity of UPT and the level of passengers' satisfaction (McKinsey, 2021).

The lesson learned from CE is the fact that a crisis may come at any time. It would be advisable for UPT operators to have several emergency service reductions plans ready to prevent service reduction being implemented in a hasty and chaotic ad-hoc manner. Preparing such scenarios in advance allows a sufficient amount of time to design the scope of operation in such a way as to preserve the key factors of operation performance and CX (transfer between routes, travel time). If reduced UPT operation were to render the UPT service in certain locations "insufficient", new, more flexible and less traditional forms of mobility could come into play, for example, on-demand public transport or the engagement of shared mobility services such as carsharing, carpooling and bikesharing (all integrated in spirit of the MaaS).

Pilsen can be viewed as an example of best practice in terms of reducing UPT operation during the epidemic. UPT was reduced selectively: due to lower demand, the service on the most heavily used lines was reduced, while operation on lines servicing industrial areas (which stayed operational) remained intact, and even increased as needed in order to enable social distancing inside UPT vehicles. Vehicles equipped with APC alternated on the different lines in order for the UPT company to have actual current data available pertaining to occupancy, according to which UPT operation was adjusted as needed.

The results of the conducted survey also identified transfers between connections as the weak spots of the organization of UPT operation during the COVID period. In Pilsen, transfers between lines are monitored particularly during the night. PMDP has had experience with the integration of flexible forms of mobility since before the epidemic. Apart from operating its own car sharing service, also integrated into the city's UPT system the "Scootbike sharing" service (shared scooters). In 2022, operation of the first full-fledged P+R parking lot was launched.

In general, it is better to look for savings not by limiting transportation services, but by streamlining current operations. A well-known general recommendation is giving priority, i.e., the right of way, to UPT in traffic, which can shorten travel time, speed up vehicle circulation and also contribute to improving other important factors – punctuality and travel speed. In formulating strategies for sustainable transportation, the highest priority should be given to the factor of travel time. Managers must take into account the factors, but at the same time they must pay attention to "sustainability" - the challenge will be to balance customer requirements (including growing demand) and sustainable issues of the whole system.

In CR, implementing UPT priority measures in practice is rather difficult. Particularly controversial is UPT having priority over individual car traffic. Despite all the above, Pilsen has managed to implement selected priority measures (UPT has priority at a number of intersections; several dedicated bus lanes were created). What has proven to be beneficial was presenting best practice examples from other cities as well as thorough presentation of the potential benefits of certain measures thanks to large amounts of operational data. PMDP actively searches for problematic spots and thanks to operational data it is possible to see the benefits of already implemented measures.

FUTURE RESEARCH DIRECTIONS

The conducted research and the authors' recommendations naturally have their limitations. The focus on the segment of young UPT passengers enables the characteristics of the particular group to be described in detail (however, even here it would be possible to observe even more detailed information such as income level, occupation...), but the UPT operator should also consider the needs of other segments of passengers. However, it can be assumed that fulfilling the demanding requirements of Generation Z representatives will improve the attractiveness of the service for other generations of passengers. Also limiting may be the information value of the descriptive statistical methods used and the ordinal manner of expressing the importance of factors (more advanced methods can be considered in the future). Another limitation may also be the size of the research sample (particularly in the first part of research). Due to the possible local specifics, ability of other UPT operators to apply findings may be questionable (although these specifics were not significantly seen in the UPT system in Pilsen). In this respect, the UPT system in Pilsen can be viewed as heavily used and very positively evaluated, and it can definitely be used as a best practice example for other municipalities, at least in Central Europe.

Further surveys may study the importance of CX factors using more advanced statistical methods or in the segment of young passengers in other UPT systems. What also suggests itself is studying CX factors for other segments of UPT users in Pilsen and other locations. Even within the surveyed segment of young passengers in Pilsen, the survey may be expanded, or may be made more precise and specific (e. g. may focus on factors of even more specific groups of young passengers such as pregnant women or disabled persons). In the second branch of the survey, the limitation may lie in the retrospective questioning and the respondents' inaccurate memory. What would be interesting is observing the traffic behavior of a selected group of passengers using a longitudinal study.

A new issue in general is the transport behavior of Generation Z, particularly with respect to smart cities, sustainability and their relationship toward UPT. It would be desirable to study the role of accessibility by UPT in deciding on the purchase of one's own housing. It would also be interesting to understand the main factors affecting the choice of means of transport at the start of young people's professional career and the main motivations of regular passengers for using UPT. Earlier research investigated Generation Z's approach to free time travel (Rončák et al., 2021). Another relevant contribution (Wawer et al., 2022, p. 1) states that the *"conscious approach of Generation Z to sustainability has a significant and positive impact on their evaluation of actions taken in the field of smart mobility for a smart city"*.

There are a number of challenges to be investigated in the field of strategic UPT management. For example, objective evaluation of the effectiveness of newly emerging, forcibly implemented forms of electromobility in UPT fleets – previously conducted studies by Grigorieva & Nikulshin (2022), Rzędowski & Sendek-Matysiak (2021) and Wołek et al. (2021) can be viewed as up-to-date and beneficial. Another challenge may be to enumerate the total costs of UPT operation in various predictable situations or scenarios and assess the effect of various factors on these costs (e.g. greater unification of vehicles used). Very desirable in formulating sustainability strategies are findings from the implementation of more flexible forms of operating UPT – e. g. Flexible Mobility on Demand concept, or experience with the integration of shared forms of mobility into UPT services. Studies by Atasoy et al. (2015), Campisi et al. (2021), Patel et al. (2022) and Torrisi et al. (2021) represent an interesting contribution. In the area of attractiveness of UPT, it would be desirable to acquire comprehensive knowledge from the integration of UPT fares in collaboration with educational institutions and large employers (transferable pre-paid UPT cards). In the more distant future, a big topic is the effect of autonomous vehicles used in surface PT on transport systems (Pigeon et al., 2021; Trubia et al., 2021).

The current challenge for UPT operators in CR is to learn to effectively process and utilize the big data acquired from UPT vehicles (Kohout, 2019).

CONCLUSION

The presented chapter used a customer-oriented approach in order to improve understanding of the use of sustainable PT systems in urban areas to support climate change actions. The conducted surveys focused on the behavior of Generation Z with respect to using UPT in a heavily used Central European UPT system. Young people's views may be considered crucial in formulating strategies for sustainable UPT systems. The key factor turned out to be the total travel time, more specifically the punctuality (delays) of connections, their frequency and journey time. If a UPT strategy is "green" and "smart", but the system fails in the attribute of travel time, UPT authorities cannot expect passengers to be interested. A system which is not attractive enough to be the "first choice" for passengers is not sustainable in the long run. Competitive travel time is primarily the result of a broad offering of connections, priority for UPT in traffic, but also smooth transfers between various routes and modes of transport.

The challenge for UPT operators is to provide an attractive service in times of crises, such as the coronavirus pandemic. Passengers had fewer reasons to travel, their demand for PT declined and so did the revenue from fares, which resulted in UPT operators having to cut costs and look for savings. The service offering is reduced as a result the total travel time spent by passengers en route is usually extended.

The experience from Pilsen further shows that CE caused Generation Z, just as other segments of passengers, to use UPT less. The APC systems for monitoring vehicle occupancy rates have proven themselves useful, and not only during the coronavirus crisis. These data, along with those on connection delays, provide a very good basis for UPT system management.

The acquired knowledge can certainly be applied even to other UPT operations, and not only in Central Europe. The steps with which no UPT operator can go wrong include optimizing the system with the aim of minimizing passengers' travel time, utilizing actual collected data for operation management as well as proposals of UPT priority measures, as well as trying to understand "their" passengers. The qualitative approach represented by understanding passengers along with quantitative data collected from UPT operation are deemed by the team of authors to be the ideal combination, which is why it was also used in this chapter.

ACKNOWLEDGMENT

This research was supported by the University of West Bohemia [SGS-2021-022].

REFERENCES

E15. (2013, February 27). *Automobilky loni snížily výdaje do reklamy o šest procent [Car Companies reduced advertising spending by six per cent last year]*. E15. https://www.e15.cz/byznys/ostatni/automobilky-loni-snizily-vydaje-do-reklamy-o-sest-procent-960867

Accenture. (2014). Transforming the Transit Passenger Experience. *Accenture.* https://www.accenture.com/gb-en/~/media/Accenture/Conversion-Assets/DotCom/Documents/Global/PDF/Dualpub_1/Accenture-Transforming-Transit-Passenger-Experience.pdf

Allen, J., Eboli, L., Forciniti, C., Mazzulla, G., & Ortúzar, J. de D. (2019). The role of critical incidents and involvement in transit satisfaction and loyalty. *Transport Policy, 75,* 57–69. doi:10.1016/j.tranpol.2019.01.005

Arcadis. (2017, November). Sustainable Cities Mobility Index 2017. *Arcadis.* https://www.arcadis.com/campaigns/scmi/images/sustainable-cities-mobility-index_spreads.pdf

Atasoy, B., Ikeda, T., Song, X., & Ben-Akiva, M. E. (2015). The concept and impact analysis of a flexible mobility on demand system. *Transportation Research Part C, Emerging Technologies, 56,* 373–392. doi:10.1016/j.trc.2015.04.009

Berger, C., Blauth, R., & Boger, D. (1993). Kano's methods for understanding customer-defined quality. Kano's methods for understanding customer-defined quality. *Center for Quality Management Journal, 2*(4), 3–35. https://www.academia.edu/29830721/Kano_s_method_for_understanding_customer_defined_quality

Berkup, S. B. (2014). Working with generations X and Y in generation Z period: Management of different generations in business life. *Mediterranean Journal of Social Sciences, 5*(19), 218–218. doi:10.5901/mjss.2014.v5n19p218

Beyond Philosophy. (n. d.). Understanding the True Definition of Customer Experience. *Beyond Philosophy.* https://beyondphilosophy.com/customer-experience/

Biazzo, I., Monechi, B., & Loreto, V. (2019). General scores for accessibility and inequality measures in urban areas. *Royal Society Open Science, 6*(8), 190979. doi:10.1098/rsos.190979 PMID:31598261

Biesok, G., & Wyród-Wróbel, J. (2012, September 6). *Indicative methods of customer satisfaction surveys in public transport services* [Conference presentation]. QMOD Conference, Poznan, Poland. https://www.academia.edu/33285555/Indicative_methods_of_customer_satisfaction_surveys_in_public_transport_services

Bueno, E. V., Weber, T. B. B., Bomfim, E. L., & Kato, H. T. (2019). Measuring customer experience in service: A systematic review. *Service Industries Journal, 39*(7-8), 779–798. Advance online publication. doi:10.1080/02642069.2018.1561873

Campisi, T., Garau, C., Acampa, G., Maltinti, F., Canale, A., & Coni, M. (2021, September). *Developing Flexible Mobility On-Demand in the Era of Mobility as a Service: An Overview of the Italian Context Before and After Pandemic* [Conference presentation]. International Conference on Computational Science and Its Applications. Cagliari, Italy. 10.1007/978-3-030-86979-3_24

Chatterjee, K., Goodwin, P., Schwanen, T., Clark, B., Jain, J., Melia, S., Middleton, J., Plyushteva, A., Ricci, M., Santos, G., & Stokes, G. (2018). *Young People's Travel – What's Changed and Why? Review and Analysis*. Report to Department for Transport. UWE. https://core.ac.uk/download/pdf/323892995.pdf

Chatzopoulos, Ch. G., & Weber, M. (2018). Challenges of Total Customer Experience (TCX): Measurement beyond Touchpoints. *International Journal of Industrial Engineering and Management*, *9*(4), 187–196. doi:10.24867/IJIEM-2018-4-187

Chen, X., Li, T., & Yuan, Q. (2021). Impacts of built environment on travel behaviors of Generation Z: A longitudinal perspective. *Transportation*, 1–30. doi:10.100711116-021-10249-6

Christopher, M. K., Stuart, D., & Foote, P. J. (1999). Structuring and assessing transit management response to customer satisfaction surveys. *Transportation Research Record: Journal of the Transportation Research Board*, *1669*(1), 99–108. doi:10.3141/1669-12

Cicchetti, D. V. (1994). Guidelines, Criteria, and Rules of Thumb for Evaluating Normed and Standardized Assessment Instrument in Psychology. *Psychological Assessment*, *6*(4), 284–290. doi:10.1037/1040-3590.6.4.284

CXCentral. (2019, July 5). What's the difference between customer satisfaction and customer experience? *CXCentral*. https://cxcentral.com.au/executives/customer-satisfaction-different-to-customer-experience/

Czech Academy of Sciences. (2021, June 10). *Covid-19: The safety of Prague's public transportation system confirmed*. AVCR. https://www.avcr.cz/en/media/press-releases/Covid-19-The-safety-of-Pragues-public-transportation-system-confirmed/

De Oña, J. (2021). Understanding the mediator role of satisfaction in public transport: Across-country analysis. *Transport Policy*, *100*, 129–149. doi:10.1016/j.tranpol.2020.09.011

Dell'Olio, L., Ibeas, A., de Oña, J., & de Oña, R. (2018). *Public Transportation Quality of Service*. Elsevier Ltd.

Dienel, H.-L., & Schiefelbusch, M. (2009). *Public Transport and its Users: The Passenger's Perspective in Planning and Customer Care*. Ashgate Publishing, Ltd.

Dolejš, S. (2015, April 10). *Marketing – Dopravní podnik města České Budějovice* [Conference presentation]. Smart and Healthy Transport in Cities 2019, Pilsen, Czech republic. https://konference.pmdp.cz/uploads/_web/prezentace2015/Slavoj_Dolejs.pdf

Dolot, A. (2018). The characteristics of Generation Z. *e-mentor, 2*(74), 44-50. doi:10.15219/em74.1351

Dong, H., Ma, S., Jia, N., & Tian, J. (2021). Understanding public transport satisfaction in post COVID-19 pandemic. *Transport Policy*, *101*, 81–88. doi:10.1016/j.tranpol.2020.12.004

Attractiveness of Urban Public Transport From the Point of View of Young Passengers

DPMCB. (2016, March 5). *Ženy dostanou v autobusech a trolejbusech tisíc růží [Women receive a thousand roses on buses and trolleys]*. DPMCB. E15. https://www.dpmcb.cz/o-nas/novinky/zeny-dostanou-v-autobusech-a-trolejbusech-tisic-ruzi-48.html

Enerdata. (2019). *Odyssee-Mure - Sectoral Profile – Transport*. Enerdata. https://www.odyssee-mure.eu/publications/efficiency-by-sector/transport/passenger-mobility-per-capita.html

Friebelová, J., & Klicnarová, J. (2007). *Rozhodovací modely pro economy [Decision models for economists]*. Jihočeská univerzita.

Gentile, Ch., Spiller, N., & Noci, G. (2007). How to Sustain the Customer Experience: An Overview of Experience Components that Co-create Value With the Customer. *European Management Journal, 25*(5), 395–410. doi:10.1016/j.emj.2007.08.005

Grigorieva, O., & Nikulshin, A. (2022). Electric buses on the streets of Moscow: Experience, problems, prospects. *Transportation Research Procedia, 63*, 670–675. doi:10.1016/j.trpro.2022.06.061

Holbrook, M. B., & Hirschman, E. C. (1982). The experiential aspects of consumption: Consumer fantasy, feelings and fun. *The Journal of Consumer Research, 9*(2), 132–140. doi:10.1086/208906

Hopkins, D. (2016). Can environmental awareness explain declining preference for car-based mobility amongst generation Y? A qualitative examination of learn to drive behaviours. *Transportation Research Part A, Policy and Practice, 94*, 149–163. doi:10.1016/j.tra.2016.08.028

Ibraeva, A., & de Sousa, J. F. (2014). Marketing of public transport and public transport information provision. *Procedia: Social and Behavioral Sciences, 162*, 121–128. doi:10.1016/j.sbspro.2014.12.192

International Association of Public Transport. (2018, July 18). *Customer Service Excellence: A word from our members* [Video]. YouTube. https://www.youtube.com/watch?v=4EZvb-kSllE&

Johnson, D. B., & Sveen, L. W. (2020). Three key values of Generation Z: Equitably serving the next generation of students. *College and University, 95*(1), 37–40. https://www.proquest.com/scholarly-journals/three-key-values-generation-z-equitably-serving/docview/2369316081/se-2?accountid=14965

Klaus, P., Jaakkola, E., Gustafsson, A., & McColl-Kennedy, J. R. (2015). Fresh perspectives on customer experience. *Journal of Services Marketing, 29*(6/7), 430–435. doi:10.1108/JSM-01-2015-0054

Klaus, P., & Maklan, S. (2013). Towards a better measure of customer experience. *International Journal of Market Research, 55*(2), 227–246. doi:10.2501/IJMR-2013-021

Kohout, J. (2019, 25 November). *Automatické počítání cestujících – nový kontinent příležitostí [[Automatic passenger counting- a new contineny of opportunity*. [Conference presentation]. Veřejná doprava, Prague, Czech Republic. http://www.telematika.cz/download/doc/10_Kohout_PMDP_APC.pdf

Koo, T. K., & Li, M. Y. (2016). A Guideline of Selecting and Reporting Intraclass Correlation Coefficients for Reliability Research. *Journal of Chiropractic Medicine, 15*(2), 155–163. doi:10.1016/j.jcm.2016.02.012 PMID:27330520

Kraska-Miller, M. (2014). *Nonparametric Statistics for Social and Behavioral Sciences*. CRC Press.

Kresa, Z. (2019). *Comparison of customer experience among selected transport companies* [Master's thesis, University of West Bohemia, Czech Republic.]. https://dspace5.zcu.cz/bitstream/11025/39300/1/DP-Kresa.pdf

Kwon, Y.-I., Kyun-Kim, Ch., Kim, T., Hagen, J., Barone, R., & Joaquin, D. (2015, June). *Improving the Customer Experience* [White paper]. Transit Leadership Summit. https://s3.us-east-1.amazonaws.com/rpa-org/pdfs/TLS-WP-Improving-the-Customer-Experience.pdf

Larkin, C. M., Jancourt, M., & Hendrix, W. H. (2018). The Generation Z world: Shifts in urban design, architecture and the corporate workplace. *Corporate Real Estate Journal, 7*(3), 230-242. https://www.ingentaconnect.com/content/hsp/crej/2018/00000007/00000003/art00005

Lemon, K. N., & Verhoef, P. C. (2016). Understanding Customer Experience Throughout the Customer Journey. *Journal of Marketing, 80*(6), 69–96. doi:10.1509/jm.15.0420

Marada, M. (2003). Transport typology of settlement centres of Czechia from public passenger transport point of view. *Acta Universitatis Carolinae. Geographica. Universita Karlova, 38*(1), 259–269. http://hdl.handle.net/20.500.11956/160824

McKinsey. (2021, July). *Urban transportation systems of 25 global cities. Elements of success.* McKinsey. https://www.mckinsey.com/~/media/mckinsey/business%20functions/operations/our%20insights/building%20a%20transport%20system%20that%20works%20new%20charts%20five%20insights%20from%20our%2025%20city%20report%20new/elements-of-success-urban-transportation-systems-of-25-global-cities-july-2021.pdf

Ministry of Health. (2022, April 13). *Mimořádné opatření, č. j.: 8789/2022-2/MIN/KAN.* Ministry of health. https://www.mzcr.cz/wp-content/uploads/2022/04/Mimoradne-opatreni-ochrana-dychacich-cest-ve-zdravotnickych-zarizenich-a-zarizenich-socialnich-sluzeb-s-ucinnosti-od-14-4-2022.pdf

Mobility Pilsen. (2022). *Pilsen Sustainable Mobility Plan – Overview of measures.* Mibillity Pilsen. https://www.mobilita-plzen.cz/prehled_opatreni

Mott MacDonald. (2021, October 31). *Analysis - Sustainable Mobility Strategy of the Pilsen Metropolitan ITI Area.* Plzeň v pohybu. https://sump-iti.plzen.eu/wp-content/uploads/2022/05/oprava_ka01_sumpplzen-iti-analyza_2021-12-20.pdf

Office of the Government of the Czech Republic. (2017). *Strategic Framework Czech Republic 2030.* OGCR. https://www.cr2030.cz/strategie/wp-content/uploads/sites/2/2018/05/Strategic_Framework_CZ2030_graphic2.compressed.pdf

Parzonko, A. J., Balińska, A., & Sieczko, A. (2021). Pro-Environmental Behaviors of Generation Z in the Context of the Concept of Homo Socio-Oeconomicus. *Energies, 14*(6), 1597. doi:10.3390/en14061597

Patel, R. K., Etminani-Ghasrodashti, R., Kermanshachi, S., Rosenberger, J. M., & Foss, A. (2022). Mobility-on-demand (MOD) Projects: A study of the best practices adopted in United States. *Transportation Research Interdisciplinary Perspectives, 14*, 100601. doi:10.1016/j.trip.2022.100601

Pawlasová, P. (2015). The Factors Influencing Satisfaction with Public City Transport: A Structural Equation Modelling Approach. *Journal of Competitiveness, 7*(4), 18–32. doi:10.7441/joc.2015.04.02

Pigeon, C., Alauzet, A., & Paire-Ficout, L. (2021). Factors of acceptability, acceptance and usage for non-rail autonomous public transport vehicles: A systematic literature review. *Transportation Research Part F: Traffic Psychology and Behaviour, 81,* 251–270. doi:10.1016/j.trf.2021.06.008

Pine, B. J. II, & Gilmore, J. H. (1999). *The Experience Economy.* Harvard Business School Press.

PMDP. (2013). *Annual Report of PMDP - 2012.* PMDP. https://www.pmdp.cz/WD_FileDownload.ashx?wd_systemtypeid=34&wd_pk=WzE5ODAsWzQ0XV0%3d

PMDP. (2020). *Annual Report of PMDP - 2019.* PMDP. https://www.pmdp.cz/WD_FileDownload.ashx?wd_systemtypeid=34&wd_pk=WzI3MTYsWzQ0XV0%3d

PMDP. (2022). *Annual Report of PMDP - 2021.* PMDT. https://www.pmdp.cz/WD_FileDownload.ashx?wd_systemtypeid=34&wd_pk=WzI5MDEsWzQ0XV0%3d

Praha.eu. (2010, February 18). *Prague Public Transport Stands Shoulder to Shoulder with the Best in Europe.* Praha eu. https://www.praha.eu/jnp/en/transport/getting_around/prague_public_transport_stands_shoulder.html

Pratiwi, P. U. D., Landra, N., & Kusuma, G. A. T. (2018). The Construction of Public Transport Service Model to Influence the Loyalty of Customer. *Scientific Research Journal, 6*(2), 56-63. http://www.scirj.org/feb-2018-paper.php?rp=P0218502

Rončák, M., Scholz, P., & Linderová, I. (2021). Safety concerns and travel behavior of generation Z: Case study from the Czech Republic. *Sustainability, 13*(23), 13439. doi:10.3390u132313439

Rzędowski, H., & Sendek-Matysiak, E. (2021, September). *Evaluation of BEV and FCHEV Electric Vehicles in the Creation of a Sustainable Transport System* [Conference presentation]. Scientific And Technical Conference Transport Systems Theory And Practice. Katowice, Poland. doi:10.1007/978-3-030-93370-8_4

Schaeffer, K. H., & Sclar, E. (2002). The automobile era: a cultural analysis. In A. Root (Ed.), *Delivering Sustainable Transport* (pp. 116–126). Emerald Group Publishing Limited., doi:10.1108/9780585473956-007

Schmidt, R. C. (1997). Managing Delphi surveys using nonparametric statistical techniques. *Decision Sciences, 28*(3), 763–774. doi:10.1111/j.1540-5915.1997.tb01330.x

SDP ČR. (n. d.). *Annual Reports of the Association of Transport Companies of the Czech Republic 2001-2021.* SDP CR. http://www.sdp-cr.cz/o -nas/vyrocni-zpravy/

Seemiller, C., & Grace, M. (2016). *Generation Z goes to college.* John Wiley & Sons.

Shankar, V., Smith, A. K., & Rangaswamy, A. (2003). Customer satisfaction and loyalty in online and offline environments. *International Journal of Research in Marketing, 20*(2), 153–175. doi:10.1016/S0167-8116(03)00016-8

Shaw, C., & Ivens, J. (2002). *Building great customer experiences.* Palgrave. doi:10.1057/9780230554719

Shibayama, T. (2011). Organizational Structures of Urban Public Transport-A Diagrammatic Comparison and a Typology. *Journal of the Eastern Asia Society for Transportation Studies, 9*, 126–141. doi:10.11175/easts.9.126

Sinha, S., Swamy, H. S., & Modi, K. (2020). User perceptions of public transport service quality. *Transportation Research Procedia, 48*, 3310–3323. doi:10.1016/j.trpro.2020.08.121

Slavík, J. (2014). *Marketing a strategické řízení ve veřejných službách. Jak poskytovat zákaznicky orientované veřejné služby*. Grada Publishing.

Smith, G., Sochor, J., & Karlsson, I. M. (2018). Mobility as a Service: Development scenarios and implications for public transport. *Research in Transportation Economics, 69*, 592–599. doi:10.1016/j.retrec.2018.04.001

Stickdorn, M., & Schneider, J. (2011). *This is service design thinking: basics, tools, cases*. John Wiley & Sons.

Thoughtfull Design Limited. (2013, November 21). *PT Customer Experience Project - Update. Mission to close the gap*. https://at.govt.nz/media/311248/Item-no-9i-PT-Customer-Experience-Project-Update-final.pdf

Torrisi, V., Inturri, G., & Ignaccolo, M. (2021). Introducing a mobility on demand system beyond COVID-19: Evidences from users' perspective. *AIP Conference Proceedings, 2343*(1), 090007. doi:10.1063/5.0047889

Trubia, S., Curto, S., Severino, A., Arena, F., & Zuccalà, Y. (2021). Autonomous vehicles effects on public transport systems. *AIP Conference Proceedings, 2343*(1), 110014. doi:10.1063/5.0048036

Tyrinopoulos, Y., & Antoniou, C. (2008). Public transit user satisfaction: Variability and policy implications. *Transport Policy, 15*(4), 260–272. doi:10.1016/j.tranpol.2008.06.002

Ulahannan, A., & Birrell, S. (2022). Designing better public transport: Understanding mode choice preferences following the COVID-19 pandemic. *Sustainability, 14*(10), 5952. doi:10.3390u14105952

Vuchic, V. R. (2002). Urban public transportation systems. *University of Pennsylvania, 5*, 2532-2558. https://citeseerx.ist.psu.edu/viewdoc/download?doi=10.1.1.362.6956&rep=rep1&type=pdf

Wawer, M., Grzesiuk, K., & Jegorow, D. (2022). Smart Mobility in a Smart City in the Context of Generation Z Sustainability, Use of ICT, and Participation. *Energies, 15*(13), 4651. doi:10.3390/en15134651

Wołek, M., Jagiełło, A., & Wolański, M. (2021). Multi-criteria analysis in the decision-making process on the electrification of public transport in cities in Poland: A case study analysis. *Energies, 14*(19), 6391. doi:10.3390/en14196391

KEY TERMS AND DEFINITIONS

Automated Passenger Counting (APC): A system for automatic tracking of the movement of passengers through the doors of a UPT vehicle. In Pilsen, the APC system is based on infrared sensors or cameras placed above each door of the UPT vehicle.

Coronavirus Epidemic (CE): The spread of the infectious disease caused by the SARS-CoV-2 virus. In the Czech Republic, the epidemic began in March 2020. Czech society was most affected by the epidemic in the first half of 2021.

Customer Experience (CX): A mixture of a customer's internal reactions (of various kinds) resulting from the comparison between the customer's expectations and the stimuli from the interaction with the organization (service) at all points of contact throughout the customer's life. A crucial component of a positive customer experience is the customer's satisfaction, both contributing toward the customer's loyalty. For the purpose of this research, the focus was on the CX during the ride on a UPT vehicle.

Epidemiological Measures: Measures implemented with the aim of preventing further spread of the coronavirus epidemic. In the context of UPT in the Czech Republic, these measures primarily included the obligation to wear face masks on board UPT vehicles (face masks and later respirators), and social distancing rules. On their own initiative, UPT operators also started to thoroughly disinfect the interiors of UPT vehicles.

Generation Z: A designation for people born roughly between 1995 and 2010 (there is no agreement on the precise dates delimiting this time period).

On-demand Transport: A regular public transport connection operated only based on a prior request by telephone. Alternatively, it may be a transportation model where the UPT vehicle is ready to service a particular location in a given time period based on telephone requests.

Passenger-Kilometer / Person-Kilometer: A measure expressing the transportation of one person over the distance of one kilometer.

Rush Hour: A time period with the highest demand for UPT services. In Pilsen, the rush hour is between 5–8 a.m., between 1:30–4:00 p.m., and at times also around 10 p.m.

Vehicle-Kilometer: A measure of the distance of one kilometer traveled by one standard vehicle (regardless of occupancy).

Chapter 12
Social Big Data for Improving Urban Mobility Services:
The Case of Douala, Cameroon

Sévérin Bertand Etémé Bessala
University Institute of Technology, University of Douala, Cameroon

Justin Moskolai Ngossaha
https://orcid.org/0000-0002-9228-4543
Faculty of Science, University of Douala, Cameroon

Jean Gaston Tamba
University Institute of Technology, University of Douala, Cameroon

Jacques Etamé
University Institute of Technology, University of Douala, Cameroon

ABSTRACT

In the context of developing countries such as Cameroon, which is the case study, urban mobility is still mainly based on the traditional model, and the major tools of urban mobility governance are practically not in place. Only the main cities have an urban development plan. These cities are marked by poor knowledge of urban mobility issues due to lack of data and studies on the continuous monitoring of the performance of urban mobility. In this context, how can innovative solutions based on big data technologies and sophisticated approaches be integrated to address the challenges of sustainable urban mobility? In this study, a methodological framework based on a system engineering approach has been proposed to guide mobility decision makers and users in the implementation and use of urban mobility services. The result of this study helps to extract knowledge and massive data for a better decision making in the context of developing countries and proposes a model of urban mobility system to be deployed as a recommendation to decision makers.

DOI: 10.4018/978-1-6684-5996-6.ch012

Copyright © 2023, IGI Global. Copying or distributing in print or electronic forms without written permission of IGI Global is prohibited.

Social Big Data for Improving Urban Mobility Services

INTRODUCTION

Modern cities are crucial components in sustainable strategic development; this is clearly reflected in the Sustainable Development Goals (SDGs), in particular SDG 11 of the United Nations 2030 Agenda for Sustainable Development. The agenda aims to make cities more sustainable, resilient, inclusive and safe. According to the Agenda, Information and Communication Technologies (ICTs) are seen as a way to promote socio-economic development, protect the environment, achieve human progress and knowledge in societies, and modernize existing infrastructure industries on sustainable design principles (Bibri, 2019a). Thus, integrating innovative data-driven solutions and sophisticated approaches to overcome the challenges of sustainability and urbanization using Big Data ecosystems becomes a key challenge.

Although there are different definitions of big data in the context of smart and sustainable cities, the term can be used to describe a massive volume of urban data. Big data is used for processing, analysis, management and communication to solve computational, analytical, logistical and coordination problems. (Sivarajah, et al. 2017). There are now billions of cell phone subscribers worldwide and millions of Internet users who generate terabytes of heterogeneous data with a variety of information daily and at high speed (Lepri et al., 2015). Data from human behavior through social networks and the physical world through location constitute Big Data. These large amounts of data are nowadays a lever for improving urban mobility systems in the context of developed countries, providing relevant indicators in decision-making (Olshannikova et al., 2017).

In the context of developing countries in general and Cameroon in particular (considered the study area), urban mobility has become a challenge for the population. In most emerging countries, urban growth has decreased over the decades and is now between 2 and 2.5% per year. In Cameroon, however, urban development remains very rapid, with an estimated 55% of the country's population now living in cities. These statistics correspond to an average of 500,000 new inhabitants per year in urban areas, which is the equivalent of the city of Douala every six years. The main governance tools for urban mobility are practically not in place in Cameroon's urban communities. Only the cities of Douala (the economic capital) and Yaoundé (the political capital) have urban development plans (PNMU Cameroon, 2019). These cities are characterized by a lack of information on urban mobility issues due to the absence of data and studies on the permanent monitoring of urban mobility performance in the agglomeration. There is no existing mechanism for consultation and participation of civil society in the formulation and monitoring of public actions in this sector (Eteme & Ngossaha, 2020). There are currently no good guidelines or best practice guides available to ensure the quality of decisions, especially those taken at the local level to find practical and cost-effective solutions to urban mobility problems. Finally, the use of digital tools is still insignificant, whether for data collection, user information, or matching demand with transport supply. However, according to the Hootsuite report, as of January 31, 2021, Cameroon had approximately 9.15 million Internet users, representing an Internet penetration rate of approximately 34% and the number of social media users equivalent to 16% of the total population. However, on the other hand, the rate of mobile connections has increased to 99% of the total population in the same period, stating that many people in Cameroon have more than one mobile connection.

In terms of mobility or flow management, there is a problem with managing the exponentially growing population in Douala. This population growth is closely linked to the absence of socio-economic and environmental observatories. This study aims to set up a database to help understand urban changes through the daily use of ICTs by mobility users to have a real-time overview of transport and mobility behaviors. Data is collected in real-time regardless of traditional surveys, cultural values and political

251

preferences. This issue aims to sensitize city authorities on the central role of social Big Data for intelligent urban planning. Through a system engineering approach, the result of this study is the proposal of a methodological framework and an innovative decision support system in the context of developing countries that facilitates the analysis of people flow, adaptable and based on "social Big data". The system predicts the daily flow of travelers by mode according to periods and times in order to better stimulate traveler demand and thus consolidate the transport offer. The following section presents the context of sustainable urban mobility and Big Data. Next, the social Big Data as a factor in the development of sustainable urban mobility is presented. A methodological framework is then proposed to carry out this study, followed by the results and the discussion and perspectives in the section. A conclusion and perspectives end the chapter.

URBAN MOBILITY CHALLENGES IN DEVELOPING COUNTRIES

Current Situation Of Mobility Performance In Cities In Developing Countries

World population growth continues to follow an exponential trajectory, with 6 billion people registered in 1999, an estimated 7.7 billion in 2020, and a projected number of about 9 billion expected by 2040 (Paiva et al., 2021), and by 2050, two-thirds of the population will reside in metropolises. However, in most developed countries, urban growth has declined significantly over the past decade (or two) to about 2-2.5% or less per year. Still, it remains very rapid in some developing countries, as shown in Figure 1.

Based on Figure 1 above, it can be noted that sub-Saharan African countries are all facing an increase in the rate of urbanization. In West African countries, such as Nigeria, half the population lives in metropolitan areas. In Ghana, the proportion is even higher, at 55%; Benin, Mali and Togo have urbanization rates of over 40% of the total population. In contrast, East African countries are relatively less urbanized, with urbanization rates of 20% in Kenya and 30% in Rwanda. These countries, however, have high urban growth rates. These results confirm the prediction of the World Bank (World Bank, 2022) that all developing countries will experience high urban growth, regardless of their starting point.

Today, travel in developing countries relies much more on individual motorized vehicles (Silva and Teles, 2020). Moreover, cities such as Lagos, Douala and Nairobi encourage motorization and are in contradiction with the objectives of sustainable development. Although congestion problems are not solely the result of high levels of motorization, mobility management has failed due to institutional weakness, lack of planning, poor public transport and lack of technical capacity and funds for the preparation and implementation of measures to improve urban mobility (Guzman et al., 2020).

For example, congestion generated by cars has increased greenhouse gas (GHG) emissions in São Paulo. There is unequal access to transport and a lack of infrastructure in non-motorized modes in Bangalore and Mumbai. And there is a lack of a modern multimodal transport system and road safety problems in several cities in Pakistan (Silva and Teles, 2020). However, such infrastructure is needed in particular to provide efficient public transport to help manage all these flows of people. The lack of efficiency in public transport is likely to accentuate the trend towards an increase in the number of individual motorized modes in developing countries. These modes of transport contribute significantly to greenhouse gas emissions and indirectly to climate change.

Social Big Data for Improving Urban Mobility Services

Figure 1. Urban population growth in selected African countries (Helluin, 2018)

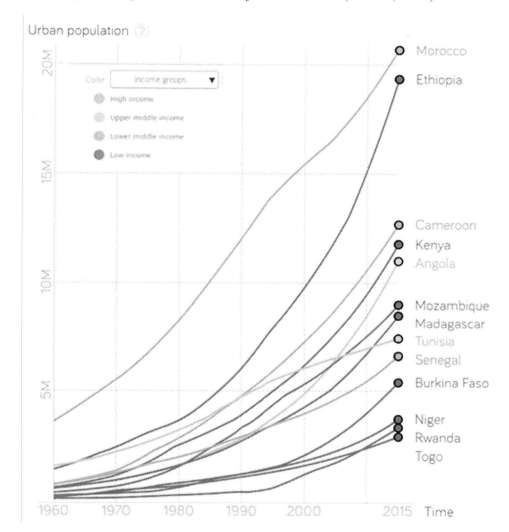

Urban Mobility Challenges in Cameroon

Cameroon has not been left aside in this urban growth scenario, having passed the 50% urbanization threshold rate in 2007-2008. It is estimated that about 55% of the country's population is now living in cities (Table 1).

Urban mobility is one of the major challenges of Cameroonian cities. City dwellers need to move around to get to markets, schools, job places and all other activities in a city. However, the sprawl of the city leading to the proliferation of small-scale transport and its limited road infrastructure are often unable to cope. The consequences are traffic jams, forcing the population to spend a lot of time travelling every day, often in crowded conditions or using dangerous means of transport. These conditions expose people to air pollution affecting their health and safety. In the context of developing countries, the problem has been intensified by the rapid increase in motorization, the growing number of people using private transport modes, the rise of informal motorcycle-based transport and, above all, the absence of a fundamental regulator of mobility services. Therefore, it is difficult for urban managers to assess the sustainability of urban mobility in order to propose solutions. Butler et al. (2020) identify five criteria for assessing sustainability, namely safety, accessibility, congestion, energy consumption and environmental impact.

Table 1. Characteristics of the urban mobility system in Cameroon (PNMU Cameroon, 2019)

Component	Characteristics
Cameroonian cities	- Rapid urbanization - Urbanization rate of around 55% (i.e. 65% by 2035) - The GDP of cities is approximately 65% of the national GDP - 45% and 22% of permanent jobs (respectively, Douala and Yaounde) - Urban sprawl
Travel Demand	- 50% of trips represent journeys - home-work and home-school/university (Yaounde and Douala) - motorbike taxi trips to Yaoundé and Douala, about 2-3km - about 4 km for taxis, - 4.5 km for private vehicles, and - 7.5-8 km for large buses (Stécy or Socatur)
The transport offer	- Urban transport system: private transportation: 42.5%; public transportation: 57.5% - Modes of public transport: formal transportation: 3%; artisanal transport: 54.5% - Artisanal modes of transport: midi and minibus: 2.5%; taxis and motorcycle taxis: 52%
Urban mobility infrastructures	- Low density and uneven distribution of paved roads, i.e., about 1.5 km per 100 ha - No clear hierarchy of the network - The rugged terrain imposes long detours due to the lack of crossing structures - Weaknesses in bypassing city centers - Poorly managed intersections - Pedestrian traffic largely constrained - Non-existent facilities for two-wheelers
Travek usage in Douala	- Walking: 33%. - Collective cab: 13%. - Personal motorcycle: 4%. - Moto taxi: 40%. - Private vehicle: 5%. - Formal public transport: 3%. - Other: 2%.

For Butler et al. (2020), for the safety factor of transport systems, the key strengths of smart urban mobility innovations are improvements in the way mobility systems can monitor and respond to incidents. Implementing cyber-physical systems and advances in in-vehicle assistance systems can also reduce human error (Samalna et al., 2023). In the Cameroonian context, the reality is quite different with about 20.1 deaths per 100,000 inhabitants per year. The country still has a higher mortality rate than the African average (which is between 17 and 18 deaths per 100 000 inhabitants). Most of these accidents (71%) take place on urban roads, which highlights the fact that this problem must be taken into account in mobility planning in Cameroonian cities such as Douala, where insecurity is the problem that most characterizes traffic (PNMU Cameroon, 2019).

Social Big Data for Improving Urban Mobility Services

Concerning accessibility, the main assets related to smart urban mobility include reducing transport costs, improving physical access to the vehicle and improving accessibility to employment and services. It must be acknowledged that public transport services are indeed available in a variety of forms in Cameroonian cities. However, it should be noted that public transport services are generally relatively slow, expensive, of low comfort, and sometimes dangerous in all Cameroonian cities (PNMU Cameroon, 2019). In this context, in cities such as Douala, preferential public pricing is non-existent. There are no preferential fares for the elderly, young, disabled, unemployed or large families.

Regarding congestion problems, the way transport systems respond to incidents and redirect traffic, the promotion of shared mobility as a means of reducing the number of vehicles per passenger, and operational improvements leading to increased road capacity are innovative assets to urban mobility. Developing countries must consider these improvements, as congestion remains a significant problem in metropolises. In Douala, for example, congestion is highly variable in intensity and duration, and largely unpredictable, due to very poor road use, the lack of traffic plans and real traffic organization through the establishment of a hierarchy of the road network, and the poor, or even very poor, condition of certain sections of road, which considerably reduces vehicle speeds and the flow of traffic in the affected areas.

When considering issues related to energy consumption and the environmental impacts of smart mobility innovations, it is essential to note the significant overlap between the above criteria. Increased road congestion can lead to increased energy consumption, which in turn can lead to increased environmental impact through direct vehicle emissions. In this context, Cameroonian cities have no reliable measurement of air quality. The contribution of urban mobility to pollution is also unknown. Given the state of the taxi fleet, the fact that most motorbikes have two-stroke engines, the age and general lack of maintenance of the vehicle fleet, and congestion, it is certain that urban mobility substantially affects air quality, especially in central areas dense with commerce and other activities.

Urban mobility has therefore become a significant issue for Cameroonian populations, yet the quality, efficiency and performance of urban mobility systems are not satisfactory. In this respect, the major tools for governance of urban mobility are practically not in place in Cameroon's urban communities. Only Douala and Yaoundé have Urban Development Plan (UDP)/Sustainable Urban Mobility Plans (SUMP), knowledge of mobility issues is poor due to lack of data and studies, and even in Douala and Yaoundé, relevant data on the performance of mobility systems is scarce and limited in scope, with no continuous monitoring of urban mobility performance in the agglomeration. There is currently no mechanism for consultation and participation of civil society in the formulation and monitoring of public actions in this sector. Good benchmarks, or good practice guides, are not currently available to ensure the quality of decisions, especially those taken at the local level, aiming to find concrete and cost-effective solutions to urban mobility problems. Finally, the use of digital tools remains insignificant, whether for data collection, user information, or matching demand with transport supply (PNMU Cameroon, 2019).

In the context of the United Nations 2030 Agenda for Sustainable Development, information and communication technologies (ICTs) are seen as a means to promote socio-economic development and protect the environment. It, therefore, becomes necessary for countries aspiring to such development to ensure the integration of innovative data-driven solutions and sophisticated approaches. These societies will be able to overcome the challenges of sustainability and urbanization by using Big Data ecosystems.

Social Big Data

The term 'Big Data' refers to a data set that is too large for traditional data processing systems. In the context of smart and sustainable cities, there are different definitions of Big Data. Mazhar Rathore et al. (2017) define as the diesel of social physics as according to (Pentland, 2008), social physics is the "quantitative social science that describes reliable mathematical links between the flow of information and ideas on the one hand and the behavior of people on the other". The term can be used to describe a large volume of urban data, usually to the extent that its processing, analysis, management and communication present significant computational, analytical, logistical and coordination challenges (Bibri and Krogstie, 2017). Big Data helps to assess different urban dynamics such as event detection, planning, design, urban mobility and city governance, coastal flooding and emergency response risks, natural disaster management, etc.

In this same context, (Olshannikova et al., 2017a) define Social Big Data as "high-volume, high-velocity, high-variety and/or highly semantic data that are generated from technology-mediated social interactions and actions in the digital domain, and can be collected and analyzed to model social interactions and behaviours". Based on this definition, data from human behaviour through social networks and from the physical world via user location constitute geosocial Big Data (Olshannikova et al., 2017b). According to Abu-Salih et al. (2021), Big Data and social Big Data have similar properties. The definition of social Big Data addresses in this concept the description of the characteristics of social data, its sources and origins as well as the purpose of its use.

In summary, volume refers to the rapid growth of social data, the enormous size of the data. Variety refers to the different types and forms of social data sources, which can be semi-structured, structured or unstructured. Variety can also mean different formats (e.g. text, image, sound, video). Velocity refers to the fact that social data is generated and distributed at a phenomenal speed. One can simply count one's activity in online services per hour to imagine how often billions of people are creating or sharing information online at this very moment. These characteristics define the size of social data available for analysis as well as the real-time and dynamic nature of social Big Data. Velocity, volume and variety are traditional characteristics of all Big Data (Abu-Salih et al., 2021; Emmanuel and Stanier, 2016; Sun et al., 2018), while semantics (Olshannikova et al., 2017a) is a more unique characteristic of social Big Data. It refers to the fact that all manually created content is highly symbolic with various, often subjective meanings, which need to be analyzed with intelligent solutions.

Wang et al. (2019) define two categories of data: traditional research data and popular urban data. Traditional research data refers to survey data, Call Detail Records (CDR) and bank data transactions. In the context of urban mobility, survey data can be data from a population census to collect information (age, gender, household and salary). These data help to answer specific socio-demographic and economic questions or to collect data on journeys such as home to work, place of leisure, etc. However, survey data are valuable for analyzing human movements. These data are not always reliable, and their acquisition requires high collection costs. In the case of detailed telephone call records, various information is obtained, such as time, duration, base station location and origin and destination numbers, base station positions and source and destination numbers. We have access to the real-time trajectories of a single individual, the similarity between users can also be deduced by helping a more in-depth study on the spatio-temporal evolution, characteristic of human mobility. CDR data provide an important source for inferring mobility but pose many challenges in processing the data to obtain a quality result. In urban areas, for example, the coverage areas of cell towers vary from a few tens of meters to several

Social Big Data for Improving Urban Mobility Services

kilometers. The position of the cell towers approximates the geographic location of the user making a call, hence the complexity of the accuracy of the geographic coordinate.

In contrast to traditional research data, popular urban data follows datasets such as GPS data, social network data, physical sensor data or the internet of things. This type of data provides a detailed view of urban mobility patterns and contributes to a better understanding of people's movements. In metropolises, smartphones and vehicles equipped with GPS receivers are the primary data source on individuals' movement trajectories with a high degree of accuracy and continuous spatio-temporal resolution. In terms of positioning accuracy, the error of GPS data is much lower than CDR data, which provides more accurate location information for GPS-enabled mobile devices. In addition to GPS data, social network logging data is also a valuable source of data collection. Social networking platforms such as Flickr, Twitter, Instagram or Foursquare offer the possibility to geo-reference content shared by users. Thus, they are a timely source of high-resolution disaggregated spatio-temporal data on human mobility. The advantage of social media traces over other digital information sources is that they can be accessed publicly and at a very low cost. Figure 2 below by Wang et al. (2019) summarizes the primary sources of social Big Data.

Figure 2. Sources of social Big Data (Wang et al., 2019)

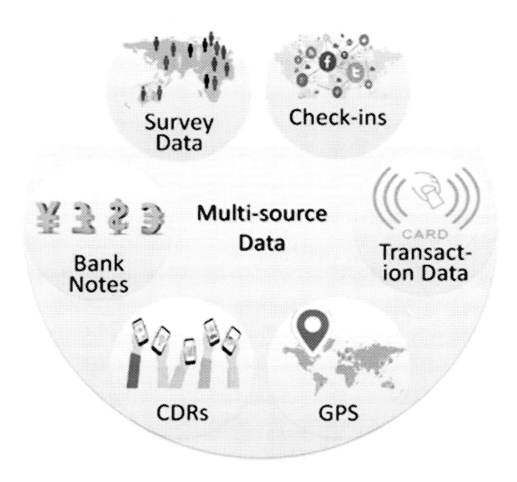

Depending on the data sources, it can be concluded that the Big Data, considered valuable by researchers, offer a major advance to research on specific urban aspects. Through their representation and interpretation, Big Data provide a means to assess different urban dynamics such as event detection, city planning, design and governance (Bribri, 2019b; Martí et al., 2019), urban mobility (Bibri, 2019b; Huang and Wong, 2015; Lepri et al., 2015; Maeda et al., 2019; Martí et al., 2019; Thakuriah et al., 2020), coastal flood risk assessment and emergency response. Other applications can also be considered, such as natural disaster management (Mazhar Rathore et al., 2017; Pollard et al., 2018; Sangameswar et al., 2017), surveillance, disease control and life-threatening infections (Ed-daoudy and Maalmi, 2019; Mavragani and Ochoa, 2018; Mazhar Rathore et al., 2017) and sentiment or behavioural analysis (El Alaoui et al., 2018).

Recent technological advances and the availability of non-traditional datasets have helped to study urban phenomena at spatio-temporal granularities that traditional methods cannot. Mobile phone data, for example, offers a cost-effective way to explore urban human mobility, as mobile operators already generate, store and analyze the data for billing and marketing purposes. The aggregation of digital traces of the age of mobile phone use has been used to uncover data gaps on mobility.

Can and Alatas (2017) presented the use of social Big Data as an important factor in social, environmental and economic sustainability. Sustainable development is defined as "the planning of present and future life and development in a way that helps to meet the needs of future generations by maintaining a balance between humans and nature without exploiting natural resources to the point of exhaustion". The notion of social Big Data is very useful because it offers opportunities for the world's population to communicate with each other, and to present solutions quickly in real-time by evaluating immediate data flows through information and communication technologies. The application of this technology helps to make predictions and suggestions by exploiting the results to contribute to sustainable development strategies.

SOCIAL BIG DATA IN SUPPORTING THE DEVELOPMENT OF SUSTAINABLE MOBILITY SOLUTIONS

Big Data, the masses of data that are constantly being produced, are the source of considerable advances in decision-making for governments. Many stakeholders consider the exploitation of Big Data as a lever for development and poverty reduction (Hader et al., 2022). Accelerating access to education and health services, facilitating agricultural productivity, optimizing the management of essential services, reducing urban traffic or responding to crises; solutions are available in all sectors. It is, therefore a real opportunity for development; data can be put at the service of sustainable development, even though the question of personal data protection looms large.

Based on the literature on the different aspects of Big Data from the perspective of analytics and their specific application in the public sector, there are several opportunities to improve governance processes. Also, several other challenges remain unexploited especially in the context of developing countries (Ngos-saha, et al., 2020). With over 7 billion unique mobile phone subscribers today, the majority of whom are in emerging economies, access to phones in Africa is easier than access to clean water or energy. "The penetration rate of mobile phones in Africa reaches 80%, compared to only 30% for drinking water" (Akad, 2022). The mobile phone is therefore the most widely used technology today, even though half of the world's population does not have access to the internet.

Social Big Data for Improving Urban Mobility Services

Currently, citizens are more demanding and connected than ever due to the proliferation of multiple services offered through emerging technologies and new needs. Moreover, at every point of contact or connection, the citizen leaves a 'digital footprint on the sand of devices' (Malhotra et al., 2018). It is up to the service delivery agents/organizations to collect these digital footprints and build an integrated, holistic map of their needs and aspirations. Big Data helps to 'collect' this data, and data analytics helps to 'mine' it to satisfy the needs of sustainable development economically, socially and environmentally

In the field of urban mobility, which is of interest in this study, analysis of this massive data helps to improve the decision-making process in the choice of infrastructures and sustainable solutions to be deployed. It is not a question of deploying reference solutions or solutions that have been tried and tested elsewhere but rather personalized solutions that best meet local needs. In Senegal, for example, a GSMA project helped identify the most relevant paths for road construction based on data on the routes taken by mobile phone users. The same applies to Ebola, where the mobility of citizens is analyzed to anticipate population movements; "We are building an algorithm by looking at the uses of customers, the duration of calls, their transactions, to be able to differentiate the teenager from the small businessman and better meet their professional needs"(Malhotra et al., 2018). Data analysis is important for industrialization; whether it is to define policies or to satisfy essential needs. But operators and other digital actors need to be able to build a model that helps access data in a secure way. They need to be able to capitalize on this important information source while protecting it.

Data analysis can be used to make intelligent decisions in a dynamic and constantly changing context. A lot of data is generated from different sources, i.e. social media, sensors, RFID devices, government services, etc. The following figure (Figure 3) shows how through the use of ICT in everyday life and in particular Big Data by mobility users, it is possible to build up a database that helps to get a real-time overview of transport and mobility behavior in order to make the best decisions.

Suppose the data generated is properly analyzed using various Big Data analysis techniques. In that case, it can be a valuable aid to effective decision-making for the sustainable governance of urban mobility services in the context of developing countries. However, it is important to propose a methodological framework considering the local context and specificities for its implementation.

Figure 3. Big data analytics and sustainable urban mobility (adapted after Malhotra et al., 2018)

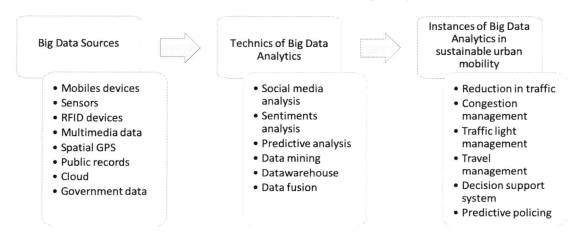

METHODOLOGICAL FRAMEWORK PROPOSED

Understanding the mobility pattern and characteristics of users in the context of developing countries can inform decision-making by city managers to provide mobility users with more intelligent and personalized services. The objective of this study is to model urban mobility systems based on data acquired on the daily use of ICT by mobility users, in order to build a database that gives a real-time overview of transport and mobility behaviors to better understand urban changes and anticipate actions to be taken. In this work, our analysis is based on a set of mobile phone data, also called Call Detail Record (CDR), provided by Cameroonian telecommunication operators such as Camtel, Orange or MTN.

Basically, CDR is defined by two types of information, namely: information related to the phone itself, such as the mobile phone identifier, the international mobile equipment identity (IMEI), the roaming and the city identifier, and on the other hand, information related to calls such as call type identifier, start time, call duration, the recipient's mobile phone identifier, its city and the location resulting from the coupling with radio base stations. In order to better exploit this information to improve the services offered in the context of developing countries, the following methodological framework (Figure 4) has been proposed.

Figure 4. The methodological framework for Big Data analysis for sustainable urban mobility

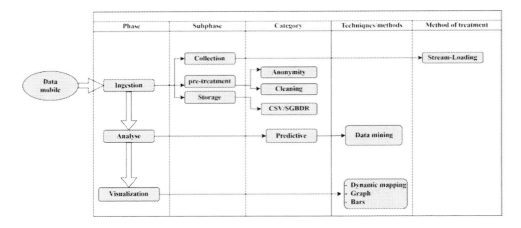

Its process of processing mobility data is carried out in three phases:

- **Step 1: Ingestion** - This consists of the collection, pre-treatment, and storage of data from mobility users (Alaoui, 2019). Regarding data collection, a stream-loading mode is used to record data when telecommunication traffic occurs. It helps to collect and aggregate data from different sources in real-time. This raw data collected from different sources is highly redundant and consumes storage capacity by keeping insignificant data. It is necessary to perform a data cleaning process by combining different data sources to resolve value conflicts (redundancy) and manage noise. In the context of Cameroon's legislation, data must be protected by operators and regulatory authorities to ensure integrity and confidentiality. Before any data extraction by external parties,

Social Big Data for Improving Urban Mobility Services

telecommunication operators implement rigorous data anonymization procedures to preserve confidentiality so that anonymous records cannot be linked to subscribers.

- **Step 2: Data analysis -** This consists of extrapolating new information from the existing data in order to predict the mobility system. In our context, we chose to model the data following two extensions: TrajDataFrame and FlowDataFrame, implemented in the Python Dataframe data analysis library in order to simulate the spatio-temporal patterns of human mobility realistically through scikit-mobility (Pappalardo et al., 2021; Bessala et al., 2022), a Python library that analyses mobility data using indicators characterizing mobility and prediction patterns (Table 2).

- **Step 3: Data Visualization -** This involves representing relationships within the data and universally conveying information with artistic visual representation such as dynamic mapping, bars, graphs and dashboards. When the results of an analysis are clearly illustrated, decision-making becomes more efficient and manageable. Thus, the combination of visualization and data analysis helps identify areas requiring attention or improvement, spot trends, identify the best opportunities, understand risks, and determine the factors driving a trend.

Table 2. Summary of measures for data analysis

Measures	Types	Descriptions
jump_length	Individual	The distance of a path travelled by a person (Wang et al., 2019)
distance_maximal		The maximum distance travelled by an individual
right_line_distance		The sum of the distances travelled by an individual
temps_d'attente		The interval between the movements of an individual or the interval is the time elapsed between two consecutive journeys
number_of_locations		Number of separate locations visited by an individual
radius_of_gyration		Characteristic distance travelled by an individual (Wang et al., 2019)
k_radius_of_gyration		Characteristic distance travelled by an individual between its k most frequent locations
random_entropy		Degree of predictability of an individual's whereabouts if each location is visited with equal probability (Wang et al., 2019)
uncorrelated_entropy		The historical probability that a place has been visited by an individual
real_entropy		The mobility entropy of an individual also considering the order in which sites are visited
home_location		Place most visited by an individual at night
number_of_locations		Number of separate locations visited by an individual
emplacement_fréquence		Frequency of visits to each location of an individual
matrice_origine_destination	Collective	Origin-destination matrix based on individuals' trajectories
visites_per_time_unit		Number of visits to any one location per unit of time
visites_per_location		Number of visits per location

The methodological framework helps to set up a decision support tool to improve urban mobility services in the context of developing countries by using data engineering and system engineering tools.

FURTHER WORK DIRECTIONS

The implementation of the proposed methodological framework is based on the architecture of the urban mobility information system presented in Figure 5.

Figure 5. Architecture of the information system of urban mobility system

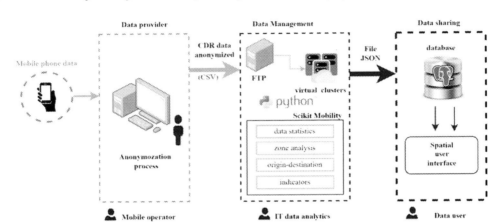

The architecture of the urban mobility information system proposed in this chapter is structured in three units: (i) data users, (ii) data managers and (iii) data providers. In this work, the architecture of the mobility system is structured into three units, namely data users, data managers and data providers. Telecommunications operators such as Camtel, Orange or Mtn will be the main data providers. The "Agence de Régulation des Telecommunication "(ART) has mobile data access and is, therefore, the main data manager. Finally, the user (public authorities, mobility service providers, etc.) exploits the analyzed data for better decision-making and consequently to improve the various mobility services such as traffic management, traveler information management, à la carte services, and so on.

The telecommunication operators prepare the data from the different sources in real-time, according to a well-defined structure and save it in a file in CSV format. The data is then subjected to an anonymization process that uses an encryption algorithm to hash out the key identifiers. Finally, the anonymized data is transferred via a secure channel to the FTP server. The transfer action is required by the mobile operator. From there, the data manager then imports the new data to an online server, using a script based on the Scikit mobility Python library for pre-processing, calculation of data statistics and calculation of mobility indicators. The computing is required by the IT Data analysis. The result of the processing is transferred via a Json file to the PostGres/PostGis database for further exploitation and visualization of the data users.

The most reasonable assumption is that the difficulty of accessing raw data has so far hampered scientific research. Furthermore, in most cases, simple data is insufficient, and the development of ad hoc software and systems in partnership with mobile phone companies is necessary. In the Cameroonian context, legislation on mobile data access remains almost non-existent. Data must be protected by operators and regulatory authorities, who ensure its integrity and confidentiality. The data should not be used for commercial purposes. The database must be accessible to regulatory authorities. The lack of availability of data is a real obstacle to the development of urban mobility services

Therefore, the volume of human mobility data helps predict migration flows between origins and destinations, as well as the next locations of people in their daily lives. However, due to material (inaccuracy) and human errors, the travel trajectory data are not fully reliable. For these reasons, we need to use an appropriate map matching algorithm to transform latitude and longitude coordinates into appropriate geographical locations and to deal with uncertainties. These insights will help urban decision-makers to improve people's daily lives by deploying targeted and specific solutions.

CONCLUSION

In the context of developing countries, urban mobility has become a challenge for the population. Its implementation and design are of concern to urban policymakers. In this context, the proposed chapter aimed to show the interest in using urban social data to improve mobility services in developing countries. An overview of the current mobility conditions in cities in developing countries was presented, followed by a discussion of how the use of urban information technology can improve services to users and help the organizations involved to improve their efficiency. The city of Douala in Cameroon was taken as a case study. This study considers that CDR data from mobile phone providers represent data sources. The delivered data represent valuable information for urban traffic management in Douala. The resulting data analysis help highlight, for example, the most used roads in the city, as well as the peak hours. These results constitute a decision-making tool for the city managers in order to propose specific solutions for each area. These efforts by decision-makers will thus contribute to the sustainable improvement of mobility systems and, consequently, of the quality of life of the population.

This preliminary study, marked by the proposal of a methodological framework, will constitute a decision-making tool that helps users to organize themselves according to the days and times of traffic peaks and decision-makers to anticipate solutions in congested areas. However, the difficulty of accessing raw data and the lack of regulation in the mobility sector in the context of developing countries are major obstacles in acquiring data to validate the proposed models. Also, numerous biases, such as areas not covered by the telephone network in urban peripheries, and the inaccuracy of the geolocation positions generated, could produce results or service models that are not totally reliable. To this end, a global study to characterize the mobility system in the context of developing countries is envisaged, as well as evaluation models considering uncertainties and uncertainties and modern data analysis tools such as artificial intelligence.

REFERENCES

Abu-Salih, B., Wongthongtham, P., Zhu, D., Chan, K. Y., & Rudra, A. (2021). Social Big Data: An Overview and Applications. In Social Big Data Analytics. Springer Singapore. doi:10.1007/978-981-33-6652-7_1

Akad, İ. (2022). Assessing the impact of information and communication technologies on human development: a regional analysis for Africa. In *Digital Innovations, Business and Society in Africa* (pp. 363–385). Springer. doi:10.1007/978-3-030-77987-0_16

Alaoui, I.E., (2019). Transformer les big social data en prévisions - méthodes et technologies. *Application à l'analyse de sentiments, 150*.

Bessala, E. S. B., Moskolaï, N. J., Tamba, J. G., & Etame, J. (2022). Urban computing for traffic prediction in the context of developing countries. *Journal Sciences. Technologies et Développement, 24*, 87–96.

Bibri, S. E. (2019a). On the sustainability of smart and smarter cities in the era of big data: An interdisciplinary and transdisciplinary literature review. *Journal of Big Data, 6*, 25. doi:10.1186/s40537-019-0182-7

Bibri, S. E. (2019b). The anatomy of the data-driven smart sustainable city: Instrumentation, datafication, computerization and related applications. *Journal of Big Data, 6*(1), 59. doi:10.118640537-019-0221-4

Bibri, S. E., & Krogstie, J. (2017). The core enabling technologies of big data analytics and context-aware computing for smart sustainable cities: A review and synthesis. *Journal of Big Data, 4*(1), 38. doi:10.118640537-017-0091-6

Butler, L., Yigitcanlar, T., & Paz, A. (2020). Smart Urban Mobility Innovations: A Comprehensive Review and Evaluation. *IEEE Access: Practical Innovations, Open Solutions, 8*, 196034–196049. doi:10.1109/ACCESS.2020.3034596

Can, U., & Alatas, B. (2017). Big Social Network Data and Sustainable Economic Development. *Sustainability, 9*(11), 2027. doi:10.3390u9112027

Ed-daoudy, A., & Maalmi, K. (2019). A new Internet of Things architecture for real-time prediction of various diseases using machine learning on big data environment. *Journal of Big Data, 6*(1), 104. doi:10.118640537-019-0271-7

El Alaoui, I., Gahi, Y., Messoussi, R., Chaabi, Y., Todoskoff, A., & Kobi, A. (2018). A novel adaptable approach for sentiment analysis on big social data. *Journal of Big Data, 5*(1), 12. doi:10.118640537-018-0120-0

Emmanuel, I., & Stanier, C. (2016). Defining Big Data. In *Proceedings of the International Conference on Big Data and Advanced Wireless Technologies - BDAW '16*. ACM Press. 10.1145/3010089.3010090

Eteme, A. A., & Ngossaha, J. M. (2020). The contribution of ICTs to sustainable urbanization and health in urban areas in Cameroon. In Waste Management: Concepts, Methodologies, Tools, and Applications (pp. 624-641). IGI Global. doi:10.4018/978-1-7998-1210-4.ch030

Graells-Garrido, E., Meta, I., Serra-Buriel, F., Reyes, P., & Cucchietti, F. M. (2020). Measuring Spatial Subdivisions in Urban Mobility with Mobile Phone Data. In *Companion Proceedings of the Web Conference 2020. Presented at the WWW '20: The Web Conference 2020*. ACM. 10.1145/3366424.3384370

Guzman, L. A., Arellana, J., & Alvarez, V. (2020). Confronting congestion in urban areas: Developing Sustainable Mobility Plans for public and private organizations in Bogotá. *Transportation Research Part A, Policy and Practice, 134*, 321–335. doi:10.1016/j.tra.2020.02.019

Hader, M., Tchoffa, D., El Mhamedi, A., Ghodous, P., Dolgui, A., & Abouabdellah, A. (2022). Applying integrated Blockchain and Big Data technologies to improve supply chain traceability and information sharing in the textile sector. *Journal of Industrial Information Integration, 28,* 100345. doi:10.1016/j.jii.2022.100345

Helluin, J.-J., (2018). *La planification de la mobilité urbaine dans les pays en développement pour des villes plus économes en énergie : la nécessaire alliance entre objectifs globaux et besoins locaux.* Academic Press.

Huang, Q., & Wong, D. W. S. (2015). Modeling and Visualizing Regular Human Mobility Patterns with Uncertainty: An Example Using Twitter Data. *Annals of the Association of American Geographers, 105*(6), 1179–1197. doi:10.1080/00045608.2015.1081120

Lepri, B., Antonelli, F., Pianesi, F., Pentland, A., (2015). Making big data work: smart, sustainable, and safe cities. *EPJ Data Sci., 4,* 16. doi:10.1140/epjds/s13688-015-0050-4

Maeda, T. N., Shiode, N., Zhong, C., Mori, J., & Sakimoto, T. (2019). Detecting and understanding urban changes through decomposing the numbers of visitors' arrivals using human mobility data. *Journal of Big Data, 6*(1), 4. doi:10.118640537-019-0168-5

Malhotra, C., Anand, R., & Singh, S. (2018). Applying Big Data Analytics in Governance to Achieve Sustainable Development Goals (SDGs) in India. In U. Munshi & N. Verma (Eds.), *Data Science Landscape. Studies in Big Data* (Vol. 38). Springer. doi:10.1007/978-981-10-7515-5_19

Martí, P., Serrano-Estrada, L., & Nolasco-Cirugeda, A. (2019). Social Media data: Challenges, opportunities and limitations in urban studies. *Computers, Environment and Urban Systems, 74,* 161–174. doi:10.1016/j.compenvurbsys.2018.11.001

Mavragani, A., & Ochoa, G. (2018). Infoveillance of infectious diseases in USA: STDs, tuberculosis, and hepatitis. *Journal of Big Data, 5*(1), 30. doi:10.118640537-018-0140-9

Mazhar Rathore, M., Ahmad, A., Paul, A., Hong, W.-H., & Seo, H. (2017). Advanced computing model for geosocial media using big data analytics. *Multimedia Tools and Applications, 76*(23), 24767–24787. doi:10.100711042-017-4644-7

Ngossaha, J. M., Ngouna, R. H., Archimède, B., Patrascu, R. G., Petrisor, A. I., & Ndjodo, M. F. (2020). Methodological Framework for Defining the Sustainability Management Process for Urban Mobility Systems Based on System Engineering. *International Journal of Digital Innovation in the Built Environment, 9*(1), 1–21. doi:10.4018/IJDIBE.2020010101

Olshannikova, E., Olsson, T., Huhtamäki, J., & Kärkkäinen, H. (2017). Conceptualizing Big Social Data. *Journal of Big Data, 4*(1), 3. doi:10.118640537-017-0063-x

Paiva, S., Ahad, M. A., Tripathi, G., Feroz, N., & Casalino, G. (2021). Enabling Technologies for Urban Smart Mobility: Recent Trends, Opportunities and Challenges. *Sensors (Basel), 21*(6), 2143. doi:10.339021062143 PMID:33803903

Pappalardo, L., Simini, F., Barlacchi, G., & Pellungrini, R. (2021). *Scikit-mobility: A Python library for the analysis, generation and risk assessment of mobility data.* Academic Press.

Pentland, A. (2008). *Honest Signals: How They Shape Our World*. The MIT Press. doi:10.7551/mit-press/8022.001.0001

PNMU Cameroun - Septembre. (2019). https://www.mobiliseyourcity.net/fr/pnmu-cameroun

Pollard, J. A., Spencer, T., & Jude, S. (2018). Big Data Approaches for coastal flood risk assessment and emergency response. *Wiley Interdisciplinary Reviews: Climate Change, 9*(5), e543. doi:10.1002/wcc.543

Samalna, D. A., Ngossaha, J. M., Ari, A. A., & Kolyang. (2023). Cyber-Physical Urban Mobility Systems: Opportunities and Challenges in Developing Countries. *International Journal of Software Innovation, 11*(1), 1–21. doi:10.4018/IJSI.315662

Sangameswar, M. V., Nagabhushana Rao, M., & Satyanarayana, S. (2017). An algorithm for identification of natural disaster affected area. *Journal of Big Data, 4*(1), 39. doi:10.118640537-017-0096-1

Silva, B. V. F., & Teles, M. P. R. (2020). Pathways to sustainable urban mobility planning: A case study applied in São Luís, Brazil. *Transportation Research Interdisciplinary Perspectives, 4*, 100102. doi:10.1016/j.trip.2020.100102

Sivarajah, U., Kamal, M. M., Irani, Z., & Weerakkody, V. (2017). Critical analysis of Big Data challenges and analytical methods. *Journal of Business Research, 70*, 263–286. doi:10.1016/j.jbusres.2016.08.001

Sun, Z., Strang, K., & Li, R. (2018). Big Data with Ten Big Characteristics. In *Proceedings of the 2nd International Conference on Big Data Research - ICBDR 2018*. ACM Press. 10.1145/3291801.3291822

Thakuriah, P., Sila-Nowicka, K., Hong, J., Boididou, C., Osborne, M., Lido, C., & McHugh, A. (2020). Integrated Multimedia City Data (iMCD): A composite survey and sensing approach to understanding urban living and mobility. *Computers, Environment and Urban Systems, 80*, 101427. doi:10.1016/j.compenvurbsys.2019.101427

Wang, J., Kong, X., Xia, F., & Sun, L. (2019). Urban Human Mobility: Data-Driven Modeling and Prediction. *SIGKDD Explorations, 21*(1), 1–19. doi:10.1145/3331651.3331653

World Bank. (2022). *Mobilité urbaine dans les villes africaines: Élaboration d'une politique nationale de mobilité urbaine et mise en œuvre au niveau de la ville - Rapport de synthèse*. World Bank.

Chapter 13
The Development and Significance of Bengaluru Suburban Rail Project

Aditya Singh

https://orcid.org/0000-0001-9347-5627

Lovely Professional University, India

ABSTRACT

The suburban rail project in Bengaluru city in the Karnataka state of India will address the local mass travel needs from Bengaluru city to nearby towns or satellite cities. The chapter discusses the development stages of the Bengaluru Suburban Rail Project. The necessity, essential features, and significant advantages of the suburban rail project are presented. The project is expected to reduce traffic congestion problems in Bengaluru city and its nearby towns. Supplementary benefits related to time savings and increased passenger comfort are also estimated. Further, the challenges and risks faced by the project are discussed. Some future potential extensions of the project are considered.

INTRODUCTION

Bengaluru Suburban Rail project is also known as Bengaluru Commuter Rail and it consists of railway network which is supposed to run through the Bengaluru city and connecting the nearby suburban areas around the city. Initially in the year of 1983, commuter rail system was 1st proposed for the capital of the Karnataka state in the country- India. From that time onwards, there were various routes were proposed running through different places in and around the Bengaluru city. However, there was no real progress observed over the several decades. The Railway Budget in the year 2019 at last approved the proposal. This led to India's finance minister, Nirmala Sitharaman, to mention about the above mentioned Bengaluru Suburban rail project, to be executed at the cost of eighteen thousand six hundred crore Rupees or about $2.232 billion USD, while presenting the budget for the country on 1st Feb, 2020. The contribution of the central government with the cost of this project will be twenty percent and the Karnataka state

DOI: 10.4018/978-1-6684-5996-6.ch013

Copyright © 2023, IGI Global. Copying or distributing in print or electronic forms without written permission of IGI Global is prohibited.

government will also bear twenty percent of this project cost. The rest upto sixty percent of the project cost will be covered up by the central government in the form of external support. This rail project will be a unique one and a novel one in its kind in India. After completion, there will be rolling stock as well as facilities similar to what is available in the metros. Compared to the already established trains throughout the country, the Bengaluru Suburban Rail will be comparable to other suburban rails in India. The owner of this rail project will be Indian Railways and it will have four railway lines. The operator of this suburban rail will be Bengaluru Suburban Rail Company Ltd., and it will have Broad Gauge type of railway track. The total running length of the system is supposed to between 148 Km to 150 Km. as well as this project will serve as one of the advanced form of public transportation system in the future. Not only people living in the suburb areas of Bengaluru city will benefit from this project, but also the people living in the nearby towns or satellite towns and neighbouring villages, will also benefit from this project in the future. The project is expected to be completed by the year 2026 and the initial expected cost of the project was estimated at fifteen thousand seven hundred sixty seven crore Rupees or 157.67 billion Rupees or about $1.89204 billion USD, which is now expected to be over eighteen thousand crores or over 180 billion of Rupees or over $2.16 billion USD. This project is also called as the most integrated rail project of the country. This project is being handled and executed by the Rail Infrastructure Development Company, Karnataka, also known as K-RIDE, which is a combined project of the Karnataka state government as well as the Union Ministry of Railways. It is said that there will be 4 corridors and fifty seven stations will be connected, in such a way that the state capital will be able connect the outskirt areas in 6 different directions, Devanahalli (Kolar side), Kengeri (Mysuru side), Heelalige, Rajanukunte (Doddaballapura side), Whitefield (Bangarapet side), and Chikkabanavara (Tumakuru side). As mentioned earlier that there will be four corridors in this project, where they are called after the names of some commonly found local flowers which are generally found in the state capital and around its surrounding areas, like Parijata corridor was named after Prajakta flower, Sampige corridor was named after Champa flower, Kanaka corridor was named after Priyardarsha flower or after Kanak Champa flower, and Mallige corridor was named after Chameli flower. Taking out Sa from the name of Sampige corridor, M from the name of Mallige corridor, Par from the name of Parijata corridor, and Ka from the name of Kanaka corridor, after combining these letters in this order, they can form the word Samparka, which means connectivity in the state's official language, Kannada. According to the official statements of K-RIDE, the project after completion will make sure in providing proper connectivity, convergence, economical travelling, and a form of sustainable mobility, suitability and marketable inducement. Since, a considerable amount of the costs of the project will be written off, as it was being raised with the help of land monetization as well as innovative project financing, so the charges are anticipated to economical. Additionally, this project in the state capital is planned in such a way, that it can assimilate with numerous modes of transportation services. According to the officials, at more than three-fifths of the stations of the project will provide facility to the passengers to switch to other forms of transportation services, like the passengers from these stations can switch to the local metro nearby services or nearby Indian Railways services. It is expected that the Bengaluru Suburban rail after completion, will be able carry ten lakhs or one million passengers on a day to day basis, also being a sustainable mobility sol, it will decrease the carbon footprint of the industrial city as well as putting an end to the city's worrisome traffic problems. Plus, K-RIDE is also working on transformation of the stations involved in the project into an integrated commercial hubs, in order indorse Make in India initiative of PM Modi. According to the plan, these facilities will be termed as Smart Station Hubs. Hence, all the fifty seven stations involved in the project will be transformed into Smart Station Hubs, where general public will be able

The Development and Significance of Bengaluru Suburban Rail Project

to do shopping, trade, work, as well as eating facilities available, and so on. Since, they will be multi-storey, so they will be easily able to assist in numerous different types of businesses, using air space for commercial events; allowing people to switch from rail to air, from rail to metro, as well as from rail to rail; land parcels in as well as around these stations to monetize. These Smart Station Hubs are also anticipated to be able to support retail in addition to shopping facilities, convention spaces, plug as well as play workspaces, hospitality, in addition to parking amenities within them.

Figure 1. Image of Champa (Plumeria) flower, Chameli (Jasmine) flower, Prajakta or Paarijaata or Harsingar (Coral Jasmine) flower, and Kanak Champa flower (Maple-leaved Bayur Tree).
Source: Wikimedia

The above image (Figure 1.) shows the picture of Champa flower which is shown in the top left part, it is also called as Plumeria flower. The Sampige corridor in the Bengaluru Suburban Rail Project was named after the Champa flower. The top right part of the above figure shows the picture of Chameli flower, which is also called as Jasmine flower. The Mallige corridor in the Bengaluru Suburban Rail Project was named after the Chameli flower. The bottom left part of the above figure shows the picture of Prajakta or Paarijaata flower, which is also called as Harsingar flower or Coral Jasmine flower. The Parijata corridor in the Bengaluru Suburban Rail Project was named after the Prajakta or Paarijaata flower. The bottom right part of the above image shows the picture of Kanak Champa flower, which is also called as Maple-leaved Bayur Tree flower. The Kanak corridor in the Bengaluru Suburban Rail Project was named after the Kanak Champa flower.

What are the features of the Bengaluru Suburban Rail Project?

There are some important features of Bengaluru Suburban Rail Project, which are as follows:

- The stations in this project will have Platform Screen Doors in addition to Automated Fare Collection.
- Numerous stations in this project will serve as integrated commercial hubs.

- The Detailed Project Report points out that in Delhi Metro, Metro Train Sets (EMU) – RS 13 series was used, which was manufactured at M/s BEML, in Bengaluru, which also the most appropriate one to be used for Bengaluru Suburban Rail Project.
- Various stations will constructed as Intermodal Integration Hubs, which will help people in switching to other modes of transportation services, such as metro, etc.
- The traffic congestion problem in and around Bengaluru city will be greatly reduced after the completion of this project.
- The connectivity of places in Bengaluru city with the suburbs, nearby villages and satellite towns will be increased drastically.
- Public transportation service will also improve considerably in and around the Karnataka state capital.
- The mass transit system will make the journey of passengers travelling in as well as around Bengaluru city, will be way more comfortable.

Objectives

There are several major objectives of this book chapter, which are as follows:

- The chapter explains briefly about Bengaluru Suburban Rail Project.
- It explains the working of the suburban rail in brief.
- The book chapter also highlights the need and benefits of Bengaluru Suburban Rail Project in the state of Karnataka, in India.
- The chapter further highlights the development of Bengaluru Suburban Rail Project and its current status.

Motivation and Main Focus of the Chapter

The author performed this study because Bengaluru Suburban Rail Project was proposed many times in the last four decades, but due to some reasons the proposed routes were being rejected. It all started from the year 1983, but in the recent years this project came into limelight again. Additionally, the proposed routes were finally accepted by the concerned authorities and recently the current Prime Minister of India, Modi, laid the foundation of this project earlier this year. Even, proper budget was allocated for the project by the Central Government of India, in the recent years. Bengaluru city being the Karnataka state capital as well as a major industrial city, is highly populated with traffic congestion problems. Also, the state capital is famous by the name of India's Silicon Valley, which attracts more and more talented IT sector professionals and with the growing traffic in the city, it was important to proceed with this project, as it was the best possible solution in the current times. The author being a Civil Engineer, felt the need to study this ongoing major suburban rail project in his home country, India. Plus, the author felt responsible to highlight the importance and the way this major suburban rail project is developing in India. This book chapter introduces Bengaluru Suburban Rail Project briefly and it focused on the development of this project, in the state of Karnataka. The author also highlighted the need of the Suburban Rail Project in and around the industrial city and the state capital – Bengaluru, in the Karnataka state of India. It also describes the history and the way the current project was first proposed in the year 1983, as well as the way it came into existence at present. The chapter also briefly explains the construc-

The Development and Significance of Bengaluru Suburban Rail Project

tion phases of the current ongoing suburban rail project in Bengaluru city. Further, it points towards the ways, Bengaluru city and its surrounding suburban areas, villages as well as its satellite towns will be transformed in the future due to the project. The traffic congestion problems in and around Bengaluru city will also be solved with this project in the growing industrial city. Additionally, the book chapter mentions the decrease in air pollution in and around the state capital after the current ongoing project will be completed in the future.

Figure 2. Map of Karnataka state of India
Source: Google Earth

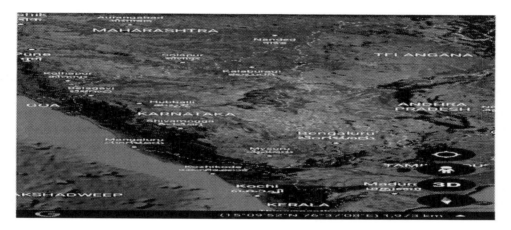

The above image (Figure 2.) is the map of southern state of India, which is Karnataka whose capital is Bengaluru city and it is highlighted with the help of Google Earth, to give a better understanding of the location of Karnataka state and its capital Bengaluru.

Figure 3. Map of Bengaluru city located in Karnataka state.
Source: Google Earth

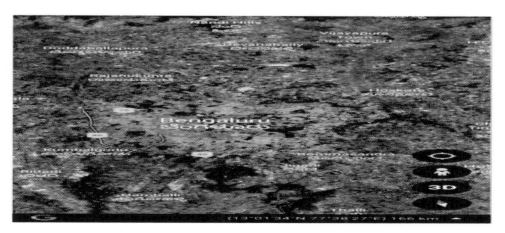

The above image (Figure 3.) is the map of Bengaluru city, which is the capital of Karnataka state in the country India. The readers can get understand the map of Bengaluru city and understand the location of nearby areas situated around the Bengaluru city.

BACKGROUND

In this section, we need to understand that the context of this project is in regards to public transport system project which is in being constructed at present, in order to promote not only public transportation system, but Intermodal Passenger Transportation system especially in the Silicon Valley of India.

Necessity of the Project

This section will help to understand the importance of Bengaluru Suburban Rail Project and the way it promotes sustainable transport practices and other related concepts. In order to understand these concepts, the following subsections have discussed them in detail.

What is the need of Bengaluru Suburban Rail Project?

The Bengaluru Suburban Rail Project will be a suburban commuter rail, it will connect Bengaluru city with the surrounding suburban areas, nearby villages as well as satellite towns of Bengaluru city. The project was almost being proposed almost from the last four decades. The Bengaluru city is a major IT sector industrial area, as well as being the state capital, it is still being growing with the population of people in addition to the number of automobiles. This is making the current city with huge traffic problems, like traffic congestions, parking issues, road accidents, and wastage of time of passengers while travelling in and around the Bengaluru city. There are huge number of people who daily moves from Bengaluru city to the nearby suburban areas or villages or satellite towns and vice versa. However, these traffic problems will keep on increasing as the time passes by, in the future. This further leads to air pollution, sound pollution, and release of greenhouse gas and in the direction of unsustainable development. This further negatively affects the health of humans and animals, as well as decreases the life expectancy of the people. People develop more and more stress, the health of the patients also worsen, happiness index decreases, and life quality as well as quality in work of the people decreases. Bengaluru Suburban Rail Project is expected to solve all these problems greatly after its completion, in the future, similar to the way the existing suburban rails in Delhi, Kolkata, Chennai and Mumbai reduced the above mentioned problems greatly. Similarly it is expected to decrease air pollution, traffic congestions, noise pollution as well as lead to sustainability development and to sustainable transport, etc., just like other major suburban rails did in the cities like Mumbai, Kolkata, Chennai and Delhi in the past.

Will the Bengaluru Suburban Rail Project be Able to Promote Sustainable Transport Practices?

The Bengaluru Suburban Rail Project is still under construction and to know will it really be able to promote sustainable transport practices or not, will at least take five to six years, meaning by 2027 or 2028, which is a long period of time. However, as per the government claims the Bengaluru Suburban

The Development and Significance of Bengaluru Suburban Rail Project

Rail will use electricity to run from origin to its destination stations. Plus, the cost of passenger ticket will be cheap according to the distance it will cover, which will be affordable by general public. It is expected to reduce the emission of noise and air pollution while running from one station to another. It is safe to say that it will act as a type of green vehicle, similar to Delhi Suburban Rail which promotes sustainable transport practices. Hence, with the use of latest technology, cheap fare and clean fuel, Bengaluru Suburban Rail can be considered a sustainable transportation service in the future, which should be able to promote sustainable transport practices in the future, after its completion, according to the information provided by the Indian Government.

Is it Really Possible to Promote and Encourage People to Use Public Transportation And Intermodal Passenger Transportation Through The Completion Of Bengaluru Suburban Rail Project?

Since, the Bengaluru Suburban Rail Project will take at least four years to complete and be open for public, it's not definite that suddenly the general public will start using the suburban rail in Bengaluru on a daily basis and they will leave their usual habit of using personal transportation services. However, with lucrative facilities, finest service and quality, along with affordable prices, it has the ability to attract most of the people to at least use it for once for their journey, on the basis of their satisfaction level, it can attract the passengers to slowly and steadily to use it for their journey on the daily basis. This way it will also attract more passengers to use the suburban rail for their journey, but of course government incentives and media support will also play a huge part in its success, as encouragement and motivation are also needed for people to change their habits. It is safe to say that Delhi has focussed on Public Transportation and Intermodal Passenger Transportation services greatly, in the last two decades. The Delhi Metro and Delhi Suburban Rail along with DTC Busses had played a huge part in encouraging people as well as in promoting the use of Public Transportation and Intermodal Passenger Transportation within Delhi as well as its satellite cities, suburban areas and nearby villages. People in Delhi are using the Metro routes and suburban rail routes like usual in addition to they are using DTC Busses or autos or cabs for pickups or reach the nearest stations to catch metro or suburban rail. With this process, Delhi was able to control air pollution, personal vehicle population as well as reduce congestion on the roads considerably. Bengaluru is also supposed to use similar approach like Delhi to promote and encourage people to use such transportation services. Of course Smart Station Hubs and the interconnecting routes as well facility to switch to other means of transportation at the stations or nearby, will help people to rely more on using Public Transportation and Intermodal Passenger Transportation services.

HISTORY OF BENGALURU SUBURBAN RAIL PROJECT

In the year 1963, in Bengaluru city, there existed a commuter rail service to carry HAL employees from KSR Bengaluru to Vimanapura Railway Station. By the year 1983, an official commuter rail system for the city was 1st time proposed by the Southern Railway's team, which was under that time Railway Minister, C.K. Jaffer Sharief as well as MP representing Bangalore. Based on that recommendation, it was required to invest in three commuter rail lines as well as a fifty eight Km ring railway. According to that time's term (1983), the estimated cost was 6.5 billion Rupees or US $ six hundred twenty eight million six hundred thousand, spread over the time period of a quarter of a century. Mr. Jaffer again brought this proposal ten years later and he convinced the Karnataka state to form another committee in order to look into the matters related to Mass Rapid Transit system. This new committee also put forward the same proposal what was proposed in the year 1983. Both of these proposals were rejected by that time's PM of the country India. By the year 2007, the Karnataka state government commissioned Rail Indian Technical and Economic Services or RITES, to create a Comprehensive Traffic and Transportation Plan for the state capital. Based on the report submitted by RITES, ten commuter rail routes were needed with total distance of two hundred four Km. Further, according to the report, the project (including the existing routes) would be much cheaper than a Mass Rapid Transit system. Three years later, in the month of July, Praja Bangalore proposed a report, named as Call To Action, which received support as well as presented at CisTup or Centre for Infrastructure, Sustainable Transportation and Urban Planning; IISc Bangalore. According to it, three hundred seventy six Km around 3 hubs with forty two novel stations were required. The next year, in the month of November, RITES performed a feasibility study solely for the commuter rail services in state capital as well as submitted it one year later to DULT or Directorate of Urban Land Transport. Their study consisted of one hundred seventy nine pages report including four hundred forty eight Km long present routes at that time, along with the mentioned 3 phases. The next year in the month of July, the Karnataka state government gave their approval on the proposed commuter rail system. The following year, in the 2013-2014 Karnataka state budget, CM Siddaramaiah gave his approval to the proposed system, which was presented by him on July 9, 2013. This led to the formation of the Bengaluru Suburban Rail Corporation Ltd., like a SPV to execute the project with an anticipated cost of eighty seven billion five hundred ninety million Rupees or about one billion one hundred million USD. Similarly, the proposals were also made in the year 2016, but it didn't proceed further. RITES was again appointed by the concerned state government to perform a feasibility study of the project, where RITES found it feasible. However, later on Railways stated that the Phase 2 of the project is unfeasible. In the year 2018, in the month of Nov, RITES again submitted a revised plan for one hundred sixty one Km, which was again modified in the next year, in the month of August. Like the twenty nine stations were removed out of the initial list of eighty two stations, the length of the route was also decreased to over 148 Km as well as cost was dropped to around one hundred sixty billion Rupees or about $1.92 billion USD. Later on, the Central Government of India finally approved it.

Figure 4. Route Map of Bengaluru Suburban Rail with Namma Metro
Source: Wikimedia

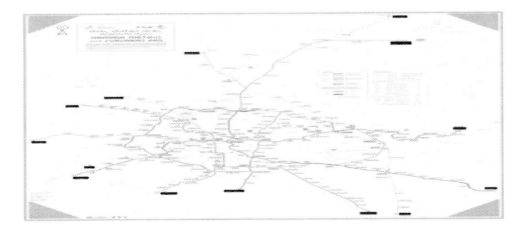

The Development and Significance of Bengaluru Suburban Rail Project

In the above image (Figure 4.) the route map of Bengaluru Suburban Rail is shown along with Namma Metro, just to make the readers understand that after the completion of both of them, their routes are supposed to look like the way it is represented in the above map.

Figure 5. Proposed CRS route map of Bengaluru Suburban Rail in 2010
Source: Wikimedia

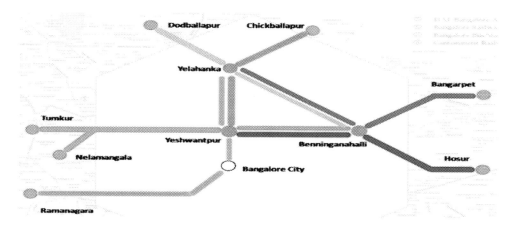

In the above image (Figure 5.) the CRS route map of Bengaluru Suburban Rail which was proposed in the year 2010, is shown, which is almost a decade and a quarter ago.

Figure 6. Route map of Bengaluru Suburban Rail Project in 2014
Source: Wikimedia

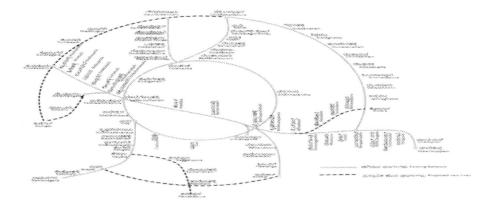

The above image (Figure 6.) is the route map of Bengaluru Suburban Rail Project, which was proposed in the year 2014. It shows the existing rail network through orange colour line and the proposed new lines with dotted red colour lines.

Figure 7. Route map of Bengaluru Suburban Rail with Namma Metro planned phase 3 expansion
Source: Wikimedia

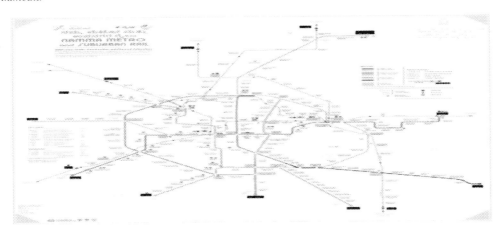

The above image (Figure 7.) shows the route map of Bengaluru Suburban Rail project along with Namma Metro based on the phase 3 expansion plan.

Table 1. Showing the summarised history and evolution of the Bengaluru Suburban Rail Project

Type	Year	Location	For	Proposed By	Recommendation	Cost	Time	Status
Commuter Rail Service	1963	Bengaluru (KSR Bengaluru to Vimanapura Railway Station)	HAL Employees	NA	NA	NA	NA	NA
1st Proposal of formal Commuter Rail System	1983	Bengaluru City	Public	Southern Railway Team under Railway Minister C.K. Jaffer Sharief (also MP from Bangalore)	3 Commuter rail lines and 58 Km ring railway.	$628.6 Million USD according to 1983 terms.	25 years period	Rejected by India's PM.
2nd Proposal: For Mass Rapid Transit	1993	Bengaluru City	Public	Another Committee made by Railway Minister of India – C.K. Jaffer	Similar to 1st proposal	Similar to 1st proposal	Similar to 1st proposal	Rejected by India's PM.
Report on Comprehensive Traffic and Transportation Plan	2007	Bengaluru City	Public	RITES commissioned by Government of Karnataka state	10 commuter rail routes of length upto 204 Km along with existing rail	Much cheaper than Mass Rapid Transit Systems.	NA	NA

continues on following page

The Development and Significance of Bengaluru Suburban Rail Project

Table 1. Continued

Type	Year	Location	For	Proposed By	Recommendation	Cost	Time	Status
Proposal: Call to Action Report	2010	Bengaluru City	Public	Praja Bangalore's proposal which was supported and presented at CisTup along with IISc Bangalore.	376 Km network 3 hubs with 42 novel stations.	NA	NA	NA
Feasibility Study and Report on Commuter Rail Services	Nov 2011-12	Bengaluru City	Public	Feasibility Study conducted by RITES and they submitted their report to DULT.	179 pages report covered the existing routes which were upto 440.8 Km of rail network in and around the city. Commuter Rail was planned to be developed in 3 phases.	$1.1 Billion USD around.	NA	The State Government approved it, followed by Karnataka state's CM Siddaramaiah in 2013 during the state budget, followed by the announcement of partnership by Union Railway Minister Prabhu with the State Government during 2016-17 Railway budget, but no funds were allotted.
Proposal: Modified Version of RITES' s original plan	2016	Bengaluru City (Mandya with Kengeri, Whitefield with Baiyappanahalli and Tumakuru with Yeshwanthpura Junction).	Public	RITES was appointed by the State Government to study the feasibility of the project.	Modified Version of the earlier one.	$120 Million USD investment to start the project.	NA	RITES approved the feasibility of the project. However, Railways specified the 2nd phase of the project as unfeasible.
Revised Plan	2018	Bengaluru City	Public	RITES prepared a Revised Plan.	161 Km network for Commuter Rail was prepared.	NA	NA	Due to high cost it wasn't agreed to implement it.
Amended Plan: Final	2019	Bengaluru City	Public	RITES earlier Revised Plan was amended.	Around 29 stations were removed. The route length was 148-150 Km.	Initially thought to br $1.92 Billion USD but it reached $2.232 Billion USD	Deadline is 2026	Approved by Government of India. Foundation was laid by India's PM in 2022 and currently the project is under construction.

LITERATURE REVIEW

This section of literature review is divided into following subsections, based on the study of different researchers from all over the world in the recent years.

Mumbai Suburban Railway

Shinde et al. (2018) studied the Mumbai Suburban railway present in the country India, in order to analyse the life cycle on the basis of the evaluation done on the broad environ performance of it. They stated that on the basis of their obtained results, for the total environ impact, the operation phase contributes heavily, between eighty seven percent to ninety four percent. Plus, the left out life cycle phases have a minor contribution comparatively, like six percent to thirteen percent.

Air Quality and Land Value Analysis in the Bengaluru Region

Guttikunda et al. (2019) studied the Greater Bengaluru region present in the Karnataka state, of the country India and they performed an analysis on source contributions, emissions in addition to air quality. They mainly focus on the decreasing air quality in region and they found out the exhaust of the automobiles contributes the most towards it.

Sharma and Newman (2018) worked on finding out whether land value can be increased through urban rail or not, particularly in the cities which are still emerging. They took the case of Bangalore metro and they used panel data hedonic price model as well as a cross sectional data hedonic price model, to perform an analysis, which gave them the desired results.

Service Quality, Scheduling Process and Operational Schemes Optimization of Suburban Rails

Romero et al. (2021) worked on rail infrastructure in order to find out the supposed service quality in regards to suburban trains. To carry on their research, they took the case of Madrid (Cercanias), in Spain in order to get a rough idea about European countries. They also collected the data from the annual traveller satisfaction survey of Cercanias of the year 2019, to obtain the desired study results.

Tang et al. (2021) studied the suburban transit lines and they worked on the scheduling process of the express as well as local trains running on it. They also used adaptive genetic algorithm in addition to mixed integer nonlinear programming to conduct their research. They also conducted their study focussed on Shanghai Metro Line 16, as well as they carried out a sensitive analysis on the main parameters of their mathematical formulations, to obtain the desired study outcomes.

Tang et al. (2022) studied the suburban rail transit lines and they worked on the way to optimize the operational schemes of local as well as express trains running on it. Their study was based on the classification of the stations and passenger flow assignment as well as they proposed a bi-level programming model to perform their research. They took the case of Shanghai Metro Line 16, to perform their study.

Suburban Areas with BRTS and Light Rail Introduction

McGreevy (2021) studied the suburban areas of Adelaide, located in the south part of Australia and he worked on highlighting the supporting as well as negative points of introducing bus rapid transit system in addition to light rail in the middle as well as inner part of the earlier mentioned areas. He used literature review, physical as well as statistical analysis to support his study.

Specific Analysis of Suburban Rails

Shen et al. (2020) studied suburban elevated rail transit line and they worked on integrating the photovoltaic power near trackside into the DC traction power system of their studied area. They took the case of Metro Line 11 in suburban Shanghai for the study and they claimed that their study result will help in enhancing the safety as well as the quality of the traction power.

He et al. (2022) studied the suburban concrete box girder bridges and they worked on the way the resilient wheels affects the acoustics radiation as well as vibration characteristics of it. They took the case of China to conduct their research. They also used finite element method as well as boundary element method to perform their study and obtain the desired results.

Alimo et al. (2022) studied suburban train and worked on finding out the factors behind the its low demand. They considered Sekondi-Takoradi suburban train service as the case for their research and worked in Ghana, located in the western part of African continent. They conducted a survey involving six hundred people residing near it and present in fourteen different communities, in order to find out the decreasing ridership of it.

Negative Effect on People Living in the Suburban Areas

Michaud et al. (2022) studied the urban as well as rural suburban regions present in Canada and they worked towards irritation in regards of construction as well as transportation noise in these areas. They conducted a survey involving twenty six questions and six thousand six hundred forty seven adults participants were randomly made to participate in it, in order to obtain the required study results.

Tao et al. (2022) studied the physical activity, surrounding environ in addition to public health and they performed a multilevel analysis in order to understand the surrounding effects on people's health, especially in suburban Shanghai area in China. They stated that their study results will be urban planners as well as public health policymakers in their decisions in addition to their plans in the future.

Impact of Improvement of Public Transport System Especially Railways in and Around Urban Areas

Sahu and Verma (2022) studied the Karnataka high speed rail and they worked in the direction to quantify the broader economic impacts of it in regards to accessibility as well as connectivity. They stated that for uniform as well as sustainable development high speed rails are important and they focused on in order to increase productivity with the help of appropriate decision making ability, after considering a given inter regional connectivity level as well as investment.

Singh and Gupta (2020) studied urban rail system in order to work on freight distribution in Delhi, which is a mega city. They found that eco-friendly modes are needed for urban freight distribution to work effectively and also in the direction of sustainability. They focussed on the prospective of metro rail as well as ring rail systems in the mega city.

Gadepalli et al. (2022) studied metro rail systems and they worked on impact due to its introduction on bus services in a given area. They conducted a comprehensive analysis on the patterns related to travel demands as well as service supply, after the intro of metro rail in Bengaluru city in India, and how it affected the bus services in the industrial city.

Yin et al. (2022) studied the rail transit systems and they worked in the direction to maximize network utility as well as considering relative impartiality for such systems. They also focussed on equally optimize schedules of the automobiles as well as allocation of the passengers. They used Newton iteration algorithm to obtain the desired study results.

Yu et al. (2022) studied high speed rail and they worked on its ripple effects in Chinese cities in terms of arable land, land conversion as well as urbanization. They used structural equation modelling estimation to get the desired results. They also stated that the land conversion is highly possible to occur in less developed areas in China, due to high speed rail.

Hiramatsu (2022) studied high speed rail and he worked in the direction of stimulated migration happening because of it, in an inter-metropolitan region. He took the case of Japan, where he focused on Linear Chuo Shinkansen line and he performed a simulation analysis to obtain the preferred study results.

RESEARCH GAPS

The author thoroughly reviewed various scientific as well as research papers, especially the ones published in the recent years, but he couldn't find any direct research paper published on Bengaluru Suburban Rail Project. He observed that there was lack of direct research done on the current ongoing project in the recent years. Maybe in the future, as the ongoing Bengaluru Suburban Rail Project proceeds, it is expected that the researchers will do more and more direct research in this area. Further, there was not enough research done on suburban rails especially in India, in the recent years.

ISSUES, CONTROVERSIES, PROBLEMS

In this book chapter, the author has briefly explained some major issues and problems, which can't be ignored. The project was being proposed from the last four decades almost, but some of the concerned authorities were not convinced with the past proposals of the project. The project also faced funding issues in the past and there was also problem with the high cost of the project. There were also some problems with the proposed routes and stations in the project in the past. Feasibility of the project was also in question by some of the concerned authorities. Land acquisition of the project was also obstacle on the path of development of this project. Plus, there are unnecessary current delays in the project, by the concerned company which is handling the project. Such issues and problems are discussed in this book chapter in brief.

METHODOLOGY

In this section the major defined issues which were observed during the course of almost last four decades of the suburban rail project are discussed, which are as follows:

- A total of eight proposals were made in almost last four decades but except the current one all of them were rejected by some of the concerned authorities.
- Feasibility of the project was also in question by some of the concerned authorities in the past.
- Excessive number of stations in the past proposals also delayed the project.
- The overall cost of the project was significantly high which also made the concerned authorities to hesitate or reject the past proposals.
- Land acquisition was also a major obstacle, so far around 85% land is acquisitioned for the project.
- Unnecessary delays are also being caused by the concerned company for the project, as no progress has been observed after PM Modi laid the foundation of the project, earlier this year.

RESULTS AND DISCUSSION

In this section, data from various sources are collected by the author in order to plot graphs. The author further performed a graphical analysis in order to support the study.

Table 2. Decrease in the number of non-suburban passengers from the year 2009 to 2021

Year	Number of Non-suburban Passengers
2009	3,120,000,000
2021	330,000,000

Source: Statista

In the above table (Table 2.), it shows the decrease in the number of non-suburban passengers from the year 2009, where over 3 billion passengers were there, to year 2021, where over 300 million passengers were only there. Over the decade and a quarter almost, the non-suburban passengers are decreasing sharply in India.

Table 3. The number of suburban passengers carried by Central Railway and Western Railway in a financial year (2016-17).

Suburban Passengers Being Carried By CR and WR	Financial Year 2016-17
Central Railway	1,484,900,000
Western Railway	1,234,470,000

Source: DNA

The Development and Significance of Bengaluru Suburban Rail Project

In the above table (Table 3.), it shows the comparison of suburban passengers carried by Central Railway and Western Railway in the financial year 2016-17. The Central Railway and Western Railway are only two of the eighteen zones of the Indian Railway. The Central Railway carried the suburban passengers higher than the Western Railway, in the same year. The number of suburban passengers are clearly higher and similarly the same can happen in Bengaluru city, suburban areas and nearby villages, in the future after the completion of Bengaluru Suburban Rail Project.

Table 4. Decrease in number of non-suburban passengers carried by Central Railway and Western Railway as well as increase in number of suburban as well as long distance passengers carried by Central Railway and Western Railway

Financial Year	Number of Non-suburban Passengers Carried By CR	Number of Non-suburban Passengers Carried By WR	Suburban As Well As Long Distance Passengers Carried By CR	Suburban As Well As Long Distance Passengers Carried By WR
2015-16	227,900,000	334,700,000	1,658,540,000	1,541,200,000
2016-17	225,700,000	327,060,000	1,710,600,000	1,561,530,000

Source: DNA

In the above table (Table 4.), it shows the decrease in number of non-suburban passengers carried by Central Railway and Western Railway. It also shows the increase in number of suburban as well as long distance passengers carried by Central Railway and Western Railway. The Central Railway and Western Railway are only two of the eighteen zones of the Indian Railway. It is easily noticeable that the non-suburban passengers are reducing and suburban as well as passengers travelling long distances are increasing, which shows us the trend of the passengers and similarly this can be taken into consideration in the Bengaluru city, suburban areas and nearby villages, in the future after the completion of Bengaluru Suburban Rail Project.

Table 5. Percentage of types of vehicles out of 67.22 lakh or 6.722 million vehicles in Bengaluru city by March 2017

Vehicle Type in Bengaluru	Vehicle Population by March 2017 (In %) out of 67.22 Lakh or 6.722 million
Two Wheelers	69.24
Personal Vehicle	88.6

Source: DriveU Blog

In the above table (Table 5.), it shows the percentage of vehicles which are two wheelers and personal vehicles out of all the registered vehicles by the March of the year 2017, in Bengaluru. Of course there must be unregistered vehicles also in Bengaluru, but it won't be considered here. It is clear, that there is a need to control the personal vehicles particularly in Bengaluru, because with the increase in people's population, the vehicle population will also increase in the future which will increase congestion and other related problems in the city and nearby areas. Hence, new Public Transport and Intermodal Passenger Transport models are required like Bengaluru Suburban Rail to control or reduce it in the future.

The Development and Significance of Bengaluru Suburban Rail Project

Table 6. Average percentage of congestion in two major cities of India in 2019

Major Cities of India	Average Percent of Congestion (%)
Bengaluru	71
New Delhi	56

Source: TomTom Report, India Today, Mint and Business Today

In the above table (Table 6.), it shows that the average percentage of congestion in Bengaluru city is way higher than in Delhi in the year 2019. Bengaluru had the highest average percentage of congestion in the world based on the report, which means that people in Bengaluru were spending unnecessary a lot of time in traffic congestion while travelling on a daily basis. This clearly shows that new Public Transport and Intermodal Passenger Transport models are required like Bengaluru city.

Table 7. Increase in the number of total registered vehicles in Bengaluru from the year 2015 to year 2019

Year	Total Number of Registered Vehicles in Bengaluru
2015	5,949,816
2019	8,253,218

Source: GoMechanic Blog

In the above table (Table 7.), it shows the rapid increase of total registered vehicles in Bengaluru city within the span of a few years. Of course, there must be unregistered vehicles in Bengaluru, but it won't be considered here. This trend of rapid increase in the vehicle population is not good for the city and suburban areas. Hence, there is a need of new Public Transport and Intermodal Passenger Transport models are required like Bengaluru city.

Table 8. Increase in Bengaluru's population over the years

Year	Bengaluru's Population
2011	8,636,000
2022	13,193,000

Source: macrotrends

In the above table (Table 8.), drastic increase in the population of Bengaluru city within 11 years, is shown. This trend will make the city more congested in the future, which is not good, as well as increase the traffic and transportation problems along with the load on transport service. This shows that there is a need of new Public Transport and Intermodal Passenger Transport models are required like Bengaluru city.

In the table (Table 9.), the top operating speed of some of the major already existing suburban rails in India, are compared along with the upcoming Bengaluru Suburban Rail. Their top operating speed are almost comparable.

Table 9. Top Operating speed of major Suburban rails in India (Km/Hr)

Name of Suburban Rails	Top Operating Speed (Km/Hr)
Chennai Suburban Railway	100
Mumbai Suburban Railway	110
Kolkata Suburban Railway	100
Bengaluru Suburban Rail (Expected)	90

Source: The Indian Express, Financial Express, Times Now, and The Metro Rail Guy

Table 10. Years of operation of major suburban rails in India

Name of Suburban Rails	Year of Operation
Chennai Suburban Railway	1931
Mumbai Suburban Railway	1853
Kolkata Suburban Railway	1854
Bengaluru Suburban Rail (Expected)	2026

Source: The Hindu, Culture Trip, Frontline (The Hindu), and Times of India

In the above table (Table 10.), the year of operation of some of the major already existing suburban rails in India, are compared along with the upcoming Bengaluru Suburban Rail.

Figure 8. The decrease in the number of non-suburban passengers from the year 2009 to 2021
Source: Statista

In the above graph (Figure 8.) shows the decrease in the number of non-suburban passengers from the year 2009, where over 3 billion passengers were there, to year 2021, where over 300 million passengers were only there. Over the decade and a quarter almost, the non-suburban passengers are decreasing sharply in India.

The Development and Significance of Bengaluru Suburban Rail Project

Figure 9. The number of suburban passengers carried by Central Railway and Western Railway in a financial year (2016-17)
Source: DNA

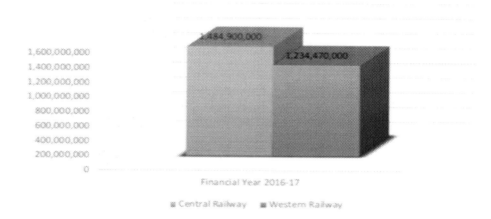

In the above graph (Figure 9.), it shows the comparison of suburban passengers carried by Central Railway and Western Railway in the financial year 2016-17. The Central Railway and Western Railway are only two of the eighteen zones of the Indian Railway. The Central Railway carried the suburban passengers higher than the Western Railway, in the same year. The number of suburban passengers are clearly higher and similarly the same can happen in Bengaluru city, suburban areas and nearby villages, in the future after the completion of Bengaluru Suburban Rail Project.

Figure 10. Decrease in number of non-suburban passengers carried by Central Railway and Western Railway as well as increase in number of suburban as well as long distance passengers carried by Central Railway and Western Railway
Source: DNA

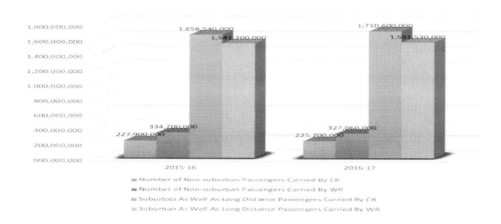

285

In the above graph (Figure 10.), it shows the decrease in number of non-suburban passengers carried by Central Railway and Western Railway. It also shows the increase in number of suburban as well as long distance passengers carried by Central Railway and Western Railway. The Central Railway and Western Railway are only two of the eighteen zones of the Indian Railway. It is easily noticeable that the non-suburban passengers are reducing and suburban as well as passengers travelling long distances are increasing, which shows us the trend of the passengers and similarly this can be taken into consideration in the Bengaluru city, suburban areas and nearby villages, in the future after the completion of Bengaluru Suburban Rail Project.

Figure 11. Percentage of types of vehicles out of 67.22 lakh or 6.722 million vehicles in Bengaluru city by March 2017
Source: DriveU Blog

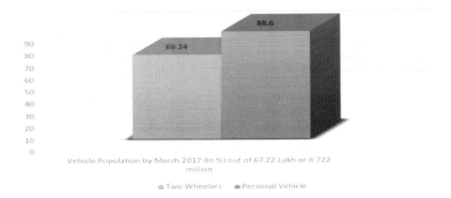

In the above graph (Figure 11.), it shows the percentage of vehicles which are two wheelers and personal vehicles out of all the registered vehicles by the March of the year 2017, in Bengaluru. Of course there must be unregistered vehicles also in Bengaluru, but it won't be considered here. It is clear, that there is a need to control the personal vehicles particularly in Bengaluru, because with the increase in people's population, the vehicle population will also increase in the future which will increase congestion and other related problems in the city and nearby areas. Hence, new Public Transport and Intermodal Passenger Transport models are required like Bengaluru Suburban Rail to control or reduce it in the future.

In the graph (Figure 12.), it shows that the average percentage of congestion in Bengaluru city is way higher than in Delhi in the year 2019. Bengaluru had the highest average percentage of congestion in the world based on the report, which means that people in Bengaluru were spending unnecessary a lot of time in traffic congestion while travelling on a daily basis. This clearly shows that new Public Transport and Intermodal Passenger Transport models are required like Bengaluru city.

In the graph (Figure 13.), it shows the rapid increase of total registered vehicles in Bengaluru city within the span of a few years. Of course, there must be unregistered vehicles in Bengaluru, but it won't be considered here. This trend of rapid increase in the vehicle population is not good for the city and suburban areas. Hence, there is a need of new Public Transport and Intermodal Passenger Transport models are required like Bengaluru city.

The Development and Significance of Bengaluru Suburban Rail Project

Figure 12. Average percentage of congestion in two major cities of India in 2019
Source: TomTom Report, India Today, Mint and Business Today

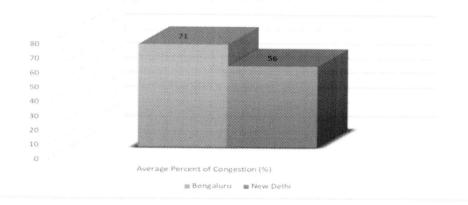

Figure 13. Increase in the number of total registered vehicles in Bengaluru from the year 2015 to year 2019
Source: GoMechanic Blog

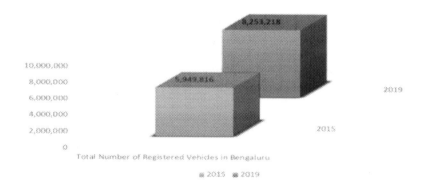

Figure 14. Increase in Bengaluru's population over the years
Source: macrotrends

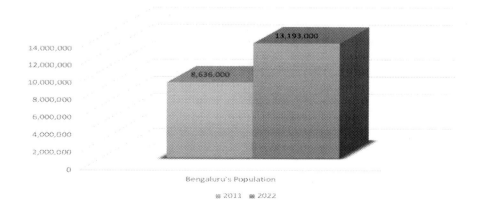

In the above graph (Figure 14.), drastic increase in the population of Bengaluru city within 11 years, is shown. This trend will make the city more congested in the future, which is not good, as well as increase the traffic and transportation problems along with the load on transport service. This shows that there is a need of new Public Transport and Intermodal Passenger Transport models are required like Bengaluru city.

Figure 15. The top operating speed of some major suburban rails in India
Source: The Indian Express, Financial Express, Times Now, and The Metro Rail Guy

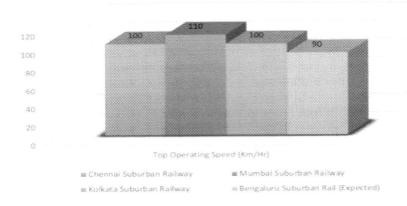

In the above graph (Figure 15.), the top operating speed of some of the major already existing suburban rails in India, are compared along with the upcoming Bengaluru Suburban Rail. Their top operating speed are almost comparable.

Figure 16. Year of operation of some major suburban rails in India
Source: The Hindu, Culture Trip, Frontline (The Hindu), and Times of India

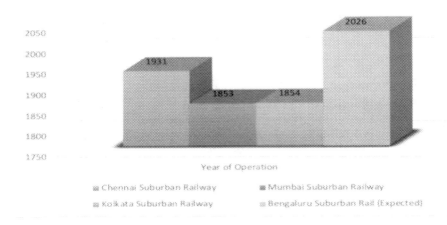

The Development and Significance of Bengaluru Suburban Rail Project

In the above graph (Figure 16.), the year of operation of some of the major already existing suburban rails in India, are compared along with the upcoming Bengaluru Suburban Rail.

Advantages of Bengaluru Suburban Rail Project

In this subsection, some major advantages of Bengaluru Suburban Rail Project are discussed, which are as follows:

- According to Fig 8, the number of non-suburban passengers are decreased almost near to ten times in the recent decade in the country, the suburban passengers are increasing as more people are shifting to suburban areas in the country. The same goes for the mega city Bengaluru, with this suburban rail project, it is possible for the people settling down to suburban areas, towns and near-by villages to use suburban rail and depend upon public transport according to their convenience.
- According to Fig 9, the number of suburban passengers carried by 2 out of 18 Indian Railway zones in the recent years in India is huge, it is safe to say that in the future with the development it will increase more and more. Such suburban rail projects are indeed essential in mega cities like Bengaluru.
- According to Fig 10, the trend is shown for 2 out of 18 Indian Railway zones that the number of non-suburban passengers are decreasing whereas suburban and long distance passengers are increasing in the country over the years. Plus, latter is preferred by the public comparatively higher than the former. The suburban rain project in Bengaluru city after completion might also have similar impact in the mega city and nearby areas.
- According to Fig 12, the average traffic congestion of Bengaluru city is higher than the country's capital and highest average percent of congestion in the world in 2019. The project might solve or reduce this traffic congestion problem, to avoid this problem becoming worse in the future.
- According to Fig 14, Bengaluru's population is drastically increasing in the recent decade, with this trend the population might significantly increase by the coming decades. Hence, the suburban rail project might improve the public transport system in the megacity and nearby areas in order to support the transportation facility of the increasing population of the region.

Major Challenges

In this subsection, the major challenges faced in the development of the project are:

- According to Fig 11, majority of the people have two wheelers and personal vehicles which are registered in the city. This is a major challenge which the project needs to solve and overcome after its completion in the future.
- According to Fig 13, the trend is shown that the number of registered vehicles rapidly increased in Bengaluru city in the recent years, along with Fig 18, this shows the people's preference to the tremendous increase of personal vehicles over the current existing public transport facility, which is bad for the megacity's future.

SOLUTIONS AND RECOMMENDATIONS

This suburban rail project which is ongoing in the Bengaluru city and around, is an innovative project, which is expected to solve traffic problems in including congestions and road fatalities and so on in the future. However, there are certain problems which exist in the project like unnecessary delay in the start of the project PM Modi laid the foundation of this project, earlier this year. The concerned company has to make sure that there shouldn't be unnecessary delays in the project and the state government of Karnataka as well as central government of the country India, need to monitor the progress of the current project on a timely basis frequently as well as solve the causes of the unnecessary delays as soon as possible, in order to complete the project within the time frame. Around 15% of the land for the project still needs to be acquisitioned, which the concerned authorities must make sure that it can be done as soon as possible, in order to cause further delays in the project in the future. Once, the project completes and the suburban rail becomes operational in and around the state capital of Karnataka state, the concerned authorities have to adjust the charges of the other public transportation services accordingly if needed in the future.

FUTURE RESEARCH DIRECTIONS

The current suburban rail project in and around Bengaluru city, will definitely improve the future transportation of not only Bengaluru city but also the Karnataka state of India, along with the development in the sustainable direction. However, there are still some major challenges observed in this project, which needs to be overcome with the help of more and more direct research done on this project in the future. There might be rise in future problems later on, which can again be assisted with direct research done on the project, which will help in overcoming such challenges and limitations.

CONCLUSION

The book chapter explained the concept of suburban rail or commuter rail as well as introduced the Bengaluru Suburban Rail Project in brief. The author performed a comprehensive review of scientific and research papers, particularly published in the recent years, to support the study. There was lack of direct research done on the current ongoing project, found by the author based on the comprehensive review of those scientific and research papers. The book chapter highlighted the numerous major advantages of the current suburban rail project going on in and around Bengaluru city. Additionally, some major challenges faced throughout the project from almost last four decades, are also mentioned in this book chapter. The development and history of the project is also explained briefly in the chapter. Further, the working of a suburban rail is also mentioned in brief. The author also collected data from various sources to support his study in this book chapter. The book chapter also supports sustainability, sustainable development, sustainable transport practices, public transportation and Intermodal Passenger Transportation, through the ongoing Bengaluru Suburban Rail Project, which in a way also supports the main theme of the book in regards to Sustainable Public Transport practices, upto certain extent. The limitations of this book chapter has also been discussed in this section. The book chapter doesn't explain Bengaluru Suburban Rail Project in much detail. It highlighted the development process of the current ongoing project but it only covered it briefly. Some major benefits or advantages of this ongoing project was discussed but that wasn't discussed in detail. It further mentioned about the past numerous proposals of this project in the last almost four decades, but it didn't explain all of them in detail to the reader. Some major challenges were also only focussed briefly in the chapter. Further the details of the project weren't mentioned in depth in the book chapter.

ACKNOWLEDGMENT

This research received no specific grant from any funding agency in the public, commercial, or not-for-profit sectors.

REFERENCES

Alimo, A., & Zankawah, Y. (2022). Factors causing low demand for a suburban passenger train in Sekondi-Takoradi. *Journal of Transport Geography*, *98*.

Gadepalli, G., Gumireddy, S., Bhamidipati, S., & Cats, O. (2022). Impact of introducing a metro line on urban bus services. *Case Studies on Transport Policy*, *10*(2), 940–947. doi:10.1016/j.cstp.2022.03.007

Guttikunda, N., Gota, S., & Chanda, J. (2019). Air quality, emissions, and source contributions analysis for the Greater Bengaluru region of India. *Atmospheric Pollution Research*, *10*(3), 941–953. doi:10.1016/j.apr.2019.01.002

He, W., Wang, X., Han, J., Xiao, X., & Sheng, X. (2022). Study on the influence of resilient wheels on vibration and acoustic radiation characteristics of suburban railway concrete box girder bridges. *Applied Acoustics*, *187*(February), 108529. doi:10.1016/j.apacoust.2021.108529

Hiramatsu. (2022). Inter-metropolitan regional migration galvanized by high-speed rail: A simulation analysis of the Linear Chuo Shinkansen line in Japan. *Socio-Economic Planning Sciences*, 101268.

McGreevy. (2021). Cost, reliability, convenience, equity or image? The cases for and against the introduction of light rail and bus rapid transit in inners suburban Adelaide, South Australia. *Case Studies on Transport Policy*, *9*(1), 271–279.

Michaud, Marro, & Denning, Shackleton, Toutant, & McNamee. (2022). Annoyance toward transportation and construction noise in rural suburban and urban regions across Canada. *Environmental Impact Assessment Review*, *97*, 106881.

Romero, Zamorano, & Monzon. (2021). Can rail infrastructure determine perceived quality of service of suburban trains? Insights from Cercanias Madrid. *Transportation Research Procedia*, *58*, 567–574.

Sahu & Verma. (2022). Quantifying wider economic impacts of high-speed connectivity and accessibility: The case of the Karnataka high-speed rail. *Transportation Research Part A, Policy and Practice*, *158*, 141–155.

Sharma & Newman. (2018). Does urban rail increase land value in emerging cities? Value uplift from Bangalore Metro. *Transportation Research Part A, Policy and Practice, 117*, 70–86.

Shen, Wei, & Wei. (2020). Study of trackside photovoltaic power integration into the traction power system of suburban elevated urban rail transit line. *Applied Energy, 260*, 114177.

Shinde, Dikshit, Singh, & Campana. (2018). Life cycle analysis based comprehensive environmental performance evaluation of Mumbai Suburban Railway, India. *Journal of Cleaner Production, 188*, 989–1003.

Singh & Gupta. (2020). Urban rail system for freight distribution in a mega city: Case study of Delhi, India. *Transportation Research Procedia, 48*, 452–466.

Tang, Ariano, & Xu, Li, Ding, & Sama. (2021). Scheduling local and express trains in suburban rail transit lines: Mixed–integer nonlinear programming and adaptive genetic algorithm. *Computers & Operations Research, 135*, 105436.

Tang & Xu. (2022). Optimization for operation scheme of express and local trains in suburban rail transit lines based on station classification and bi-level programming. *Journal of Rail Transport Planning & Management, 21*, 100283.

Tao, Ma, Shen, & Chai. (2022). Neighborhood effects on health: A multilevel analysis of neighborhood environment, physical activity and public health in suburban Shanghai. *Cities (London, England), 129*, 103847.

Yin, Li, & Han, Dong, & Liu. (2022). Maximizing network utility while considering proportional fairness for rail transit systems: Jointly optimizing passenger allocation and vehicle schedules. *Transportation Research Part C, Emerging Technologies, 143*, 103812.

Yu, Chen, Long, & Mansury. (2022). Urbanization, land conversion, and arable land in Chinese cities: The ripple effects of high-speed rail. *Applied Geography (Sevenoaks, England), 146*, 102756.

Chapter 14

Evaluation of the Barriers to the Use of Sustainable Transportation Systems in City Logistics With an Integrated Grey DEMATEL–ANP Approach

Nida Durmaz
Gebze Technical University, Turkey

Aysenur Budak
Gebze Technical University, Turkey

ABSTRACT

The rapid increase in journeys, freight transport, and the use of private vehicles in cities causes environmental problems such as the decrease in urban environmental quality as well as economic and social problems in transportation. In this context, the concept of the city logistics shows up to improve and maintain logistics activities in settlements. It is necessary to define the barriers to the use of sustainable transportation systems in city logistics and to plan strategic steps by prioritizing these barriers according to their importance. In this study, an integrated approach of Grey DEMATEL-ANP is proposed to model these barriers in the city logistics for Istanbul. The proposed method determines the cause-effect relationships and relative weights of the key barriers. The results of this study may help decision makers and practitioners to address the key barriers highlighted and provide the theoretical guideline to use the sustainable transport systems across city logistics successfully.

DOI: 10.4018/978-1-6684-5996-6.ch014

Copyright © 2023, IGI Global. Copying or distributing in print or electronic forms without written permission of IGI Global is prohibited.

INTRODUCTION

Today, the majority of the world's population prefers to live in cities in order to reach better living, working and educational opportunities. As a result, problems such as increase in urban population, unplanned urbanization, traffic density, air and noise pollution arise (Savrun and Mutlu, 2019). The concept of city logistics gains importance in order to avoid these problems or to solve them easily. In this context, urban logistics focuses on the planning, coordination and control of the logistics processes taking place in settlements, and deals with the physical movement of materials (raw materials, products, waste, etc.), people and information in a way that optimizes costs, reduces congestion and increases the quality of life (Witkowski and Kiba-Janiak, 2014).

In addition to economic and social objectives, the biggest factor that ensures successful results in city logistics is to consider sustainable objectives such as energy saving, increasing efficiency in transportation, and protecting the environment. For this reason, besides supporting social and economic development in city logistics, freight transportation and transportation systems, it offers a sustainable life by increasing environmental efficiency (Yıldız et al., 2021). Activities such as advanced information systems, cooperative freight transport systems, general logistics terminals, load-based controls, underground freight transport systems are some of the urban logistics initiatives to achieve sustainable goals. Thus, logistics companies carrying freight in urban freight transportation, which is an important part of city planning, are expected to provide higher quality service levels with just-in-time transportation systems at lower costs (Taniguchi and Der Heijden, 2000; Akben, 2020).

Transportation and mobility are one of the basic components of urban life as well as human life. Consequently, transportation services in urban areas cause various urban problems such as traffic congestion, air pollution, accessibility and noise pollution (Akben, 2020). Making urban transportation sustainable in terms of energy, traffic, health and economic dimensions is one of the main goals in transportation systems. In this context, the use of sustainable transportation systems in city logistics gains more importance.

Sustainable transportation is defined as meeting the need for mobility in order to protect and improve human and ecosystem health, economic development and social justice, continuously (Deakin, 2001; Cirit, 2014). Within the scope of sustainable transportation, issues such as reducing private vehicle ownership, facilitating pedestrian transportation, increasing the use of bicycles, and implementing accessible public transportation systems are discussed (Altıntaş and Eyigün, 2020). For this reason, the preference of natural gas or electric vehicles, the usage of public transportation systems such as tramway and metro in the planning of cities, especially in transportation regulations, paves the way for sustainable practices. In addition, companies engaged in urban transportation activities, benefiting from information technologies and minimizing load transportation times also contribute to the increase in air quality (Akben, 2020).

Use of sustainable transportation systems in city logistics; privacy and security threats, regulations, public perception and psychological difficulties, environmental problems, economic problems, technical problems and operational problems such as some difficulties and risks. In this chapter, an integrated approach of Grey Decision-Making Trial and Evaluation Laboratory (DEMATEL) – Analytic Network Process (ANP) is proposed to model the use barriers of the sustainable transportation systems in the city logistics.

In the presented, a case study for Istanbul is taken into account. Istanbul has a large population, a significant part of the qualified workforce, an intercontinental transit, narrow and historical streets and a variety of harbours. This city is one of the cultural and commercial centers of the world. Essential part

Evaluation of the Barriers to the Use of Sustainable Transportation Systems in City Logistics

of Turkey's annual logistics activities take place in Istanbul. These urban features have made the city an important international logistics supply and distribution center on a global scale. City logistics in Istanbul also causes economic, social and environmental effects such as traffic jams, access restrictions, parking problems, emissions of freight movements in the city. Although daily logistics movements in the city are essential for the people living in the city to continue their daily lives, the social and environmental effects caused by these movements play an important role in the decrease in the quality of life of the city residents. On the other hand, the increasing demands of the logistics service areas for the shortening of the supply times and the growing population increase the importance of city logistics even more (Aydın, 2017; Savrun and Mutlu, 2019). In this respect, the implementation of sustainable transportation systems in city logistics for Istanbul is a key element in achieving high-level logistics goals. The application of the integrated model proposed in this study to the case of Istanbul provides a comprehensive analysis to achieve sustainability goals in transportation in city logistics. Evaluating the main barriers to the use of transportation systems in city logistics in terms of sustainability and prioritizing these barriers by weighting according to their importance will make significant contributions to improving the current logistics situation within the scope of Istanbul. Many advantages such as the productive use of resources for the most important main barriers, saving time, money and labour in the implementation process, the right logistics strategies applied at the right time, and the effective decision-making process can be provided with the case study carried out in this study.

The aim of this study is to examine the barriers encountered in the use of sustainable transportation systems in city logistics within the scope of the environmental, economic and social dimensions comprehensively. Moreover, it is aimed to identify the most important key barriers and overcome them by analysing both the interaction of these barriers with each other and the relative weight of each barrier with this study. Figure 1 depicts the proposed framework for analyzing key barriers to the use of sustainable transportation systems in city logistics.

The rest of the chapter is organized as follows. The literature review on city logistics and sustainable transportation systems is presented. The key barriers in using sustainable transportation systems in city logistics are explained. After that, the proposed integrated Grey DEMATEL-ANP method is explained and the details of the methodology and data used are presented. The findings of the case study in Istanbul are presented. Finally, conclusions and recommendations are drawn.

LITERATURE REVIEW

In the current literature, it is seen that studies are generally carried out on urban transportation policies, solution suggestions for barriers in transportation systems and comparisons of transportation systems. İnaç and Tanyaş (2012) examined the urban logistics solutions proposed by various institutions for Istanbul and evaluated the priorities of this solution suggestions using the Analytical Hierarchy Process (AHP) method in their study. Kaplan and Ulukavak (2013) adopted an approach that includes the sustainable and integrated transportation and evaluated the transportation problems and opportunities of cities together. Cirit (2014) has conceptually discussed sustainable urban transportation policies and evaluated the current situation of cities within the framework of basic transportation data and sustainable transportation projects. In addition, the author has made comparative analysis for the selection of public transport systems according to changed travel demands and route lengths. Deveci et al. (2015) handled the integration of public transportation systems for the solution of urban transportation problems in sustainable urban transportation planning and presented the advantages of integration in public transportation. Hamurcu and Eren (2017) presented the selection of public transportation type by using AHP and ANP methods in order to evaluate urban transportation in line with sustainable purposes. The authors made recommendations for public transportation by comparing the results of both methods.

Ağaoğlu and Başdemir (2019) listed the problems of urban transportation and offered solutions for the improvement of urban public transportation in their study. Masoumi (2019) conducted a Discrete Choice Analysis for the causality of transportation mode selection and barriers to sustainable mobility in the Middle East and North Africa region. The author outlined the main barriers to the selection of sustainable modes such as active mobility and public transport and compared the transport mode determinants he obtained with those in Western societies. Öztürk and Gündüz (2020) examined the obstacle factors to ride bicycle in the city of Manisa with statistical analysis and determined that the main factors are deficiencies in holistic planning, physical condition and infrastructure deficiencies, security and cultural values and habits. Morel et al. (2020) identified barriers to cooperation by examining management models for sustainable urban construction logistics and categorized them as formal/informal barriers.

The authors also proposed governance strategies to better deal with existing barriers to cooperation in urban construction logistics. Shah et al. (2021) identified the barriers and challenges that need to be considered when implementing green transport for global sustainability in their study. In addition, they proposed strategies and innovative technologies to overcome these identified barriers. Rodrigues and Seixas (2022) used the Causal Loop Diagram to identify barriers to the global adoption of battery electric buses in cities by considering the dimensions of sustainability. The authors made recommendations to deal with these barriers to the successful use of electric buses in cities.

In this study, an integrated approach of Grey DEMATEL - ANP is used to model the barriers to the use of sustainable transportation systems in city logistics for Istanbul. The DEMATEL can consider uncertain information. Moreover, it can determine the cause-effect relationship among barriers and their weight coefficient (Stevic et al., 2017; Chen et al., 2019). Since the classical DEMATEL method does not include the uncertainties in human judgments, the Grey-DEMATEL method is used to examine the causal relationship in this study. (Xia et al., 2015; Ren et al., 2017; Sarkar et al., 2018; Si et al., 2018; Luthra et al., 2019). Then, ANP method is employed in order to determine the relative weight of key barriers considering the results of Grey-DEMATEL.ANP method is more practical in the real-life conditions due to that in comparison to AHP method. (Al-Hawari et al., 2014; Mangla et al., 2018).

In recent years, with the increasing importance given to sustainable transportation systems and their use in city logistics, studies in the literature have also increased. There are studies on the separate evaluation of the use of sustainable transportation systems in city logistics. However, in the current literature, no study has been found in which the barriers to the usage of all sustainable transportation systems in city logistics are evaluated as a whole, the relationship between these barriers is examined, and the importance of the barriers is revealed by weighting them. This study deals with transportation systems and city logistics holistically within the framework of sustainability and analyses the cause-effect relationship between the barriers, the relative weights of the barriers and the interaction power by evaluating the barriers identified as a result of the literature review with the Grey DEMATEL-ANP method. In this respect, this study fills an important gap in the literature.

Evaluation of the Barriers to the Use of Sustainable Transportation Systems in City Logistics

Figure 1. Flowchart of the methodological framework

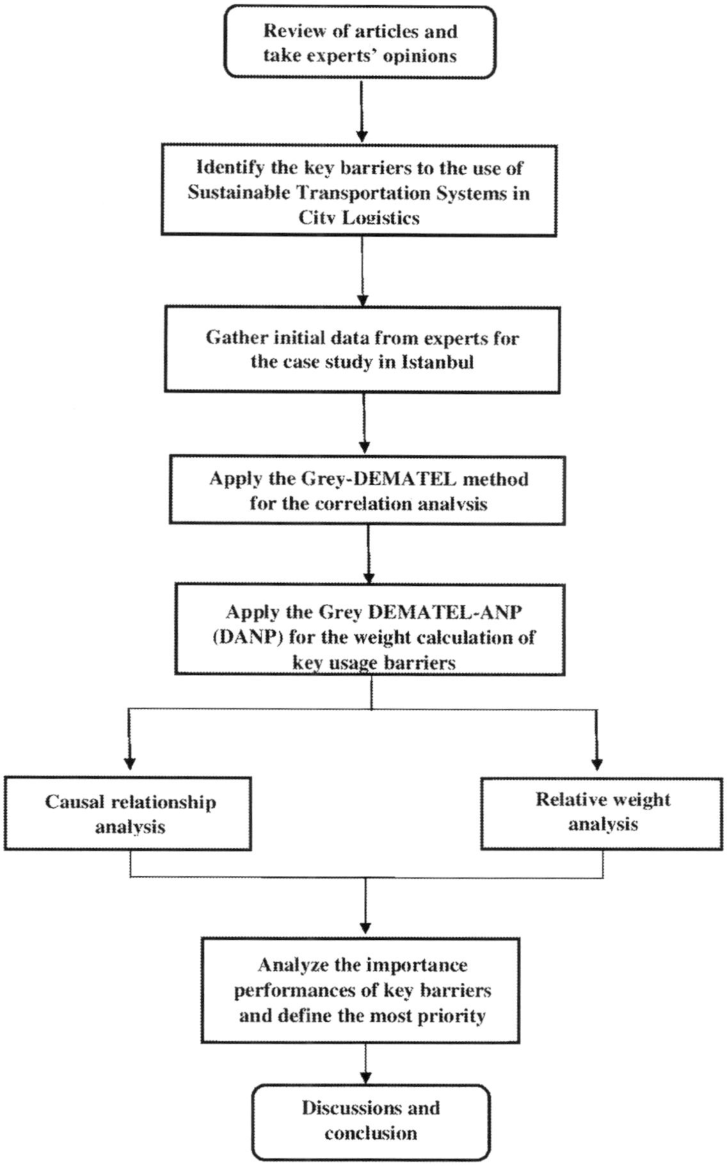

KEY BARRIERS TO THE USE OF SUSTAINABLE TRANSPORTATION SYSTEMS IN CITY LOGISTICS

Based on the literature review and expert opinions, this section presents 14 key barriers to the use of sustainable transport systems in city logistics in Istanbul. The identified key barriers in the study were evaluated within the scope of 3 dimensions consist of economic, social and environmental. The dimensions and the key barriers of these dimensions are presented in Table 1.

Table 1. Key barriers to the use of sustainable transportation systems in city logistics in Istanbul

Dimension	Symbol	Barrier
Social	ISM	Inadequate security measures
	LSP	Lack of public support and policy
	LIS	Lack of information systems
	II	Insufficient infrastructure
	ITC	Inadequate transportation capacity
	CZ	Comfort zone
	LA	Low accessibility
Economic	HIC	High investment costs
	UPM	Unwillingness to payoff more
Environmental	EC	Energy consumption
	NP	Noise pollution
	CC	Climate change
	TS	Traffic congestion
	PUP	Poor urban planning

The concept of sustainability includes three dimensions as economic, social and environmental (Cirit, 2014). For this reason, the key barriers identified in the study are evaluated within the scope of these 3 dimensions. Social dimension is based on meeting individual and social needs and creating a better quality of life. In this context, inadequate security measures (ISM), lack of public support and policy (LSP), lack of information systems (LIS), insufficient infrastructure (II), inadequate transportation capacity (ITC), comfort zone (CZ) and low accessibility (LA) are the main barriers evaluated within the scope of social dimension (Cirit, 2014; Morel et al., 2020; Öztürk and Gündüz., 2020).

Public transportation gathers passengers in confined spaces to be able to drive between regions. This situation causes adversarial targeting and threats. Road traffic accidents are still a major cause of deaths and injuries. For these reasons, inadequate security measures (ISM) become an important barrier in the presence of mobility system. An understanding of security planning is necessary effectively manage the risks of this environment. Lack of public support and policy (LSP) is a barrier that indicates the government may not have revealed the protocol for the development of sustainable transport systems, including energy-efficient multimodal transport systems, notably public mass transportation systems, and clean fuels and vehicles. This situation can be caused to legal and collaboration issues and unavailability of financial subsidies and incentives. Lack of public support and policy (LSP) is a barrier that indicates the government may not have revealed the protocol for the development of sustainable transport systems, including energy-efficient multimodal transport systems, notably public mass transportation systems, and clean fuels and vehicles. This situation can be caused to legal and collaboration issues and unavailability of financial subsidies and incentives. Inadequate infrastructure (II) is a barrier related to different types of public transport systems, and the lack of sustainable conditions for cyclists and pedestrians. Significant investments are needed to make infrastructure physically robust and to ensure transport systems maintain functionality. The inadequate transportation capacity (ITC) is the limited capacity for the sustainable transportation system to be preferred. This situation can be an important

Evaluation of the Barriers to the Use of Sustainable Transportation Systems in City Logistics

barrier to the public transportation preference of the women, children, older person, pregnant and persons with disabilities passengers. Comfort Zone (CR) indicates a situation where one feels safe or at ease in the mobility system. This barrier is one of the top criteria that affect passengers' satisfaction with public transportation systems. Private car can be preferred by people to stay in their comfort area. A poorly developed transport network may not provide easy access to all residents in urban or regional system in a safe. For this reason, Low accessibility (LA) is a barrier related to improving accessibility for underserved populations.

Secondly, economic dimension aims at growth and development and meeting human needs. For this reason, barriers to high investment costs (HIC) and unwillingness to payoff more (UPM) are considered in this dimension (Cirit, 2014; Shah et al., 2021; Rodrigues and Seixas, 2022).

Transitioning to a more efficient fleet like electric vehicles in city logistics requires extremely high investment including various costs for higher fuel efficiency. Beyond the environmental and social benefits, High investment costs (HIC) is an important barrier that reflects the economical aspect of smart city transportation system. Unwillingness to pay more (UPM) refers to the cost incurred by the passenger. Accordingly, a passenger may refuse to use some public transport systems, considering that it does not provide a good benefit compared to the cost incurred.

Finally, the environmental dimension is based on reducing the negative effects on the environment and the efficient use of natural resources. In this direction, the barriers to energy consumption (EC), noise pollution (NP), climate change (CC), traffic congestion (TS) and poor urban planning (PUP) have been evaluated within the scope of environmental dimension (Öncü and Öncü Yıldız, 2011; Cirit, 2014; Rodrigues and Seixas, 2022).

The road transportation is the primary mode that causes environmental problems like greenhouse gas (GHG) emissions, CO_2 emissions, fuel consumption etc. in city logistics. At this juncture, energy consumption (EC) is one of the most important barrier within the scope of environmental sustainability. Noise pollution (NP) is a crucial barrier indicates high decibel that damage hearing. The preferred transportation system may cause health problem such as Noise Induced Hearing Loss (NIHL) for the people exposed to noise pollution. Climate change (CC) is related to extreme weather events and natural disasters. This barrier has an impact on the choices of passengers significantly and infrastructure of the transportation system. For this reason, climate change adoption is urgently required in the city logistics activities. The congestion rate that represents the heaviness of the traffic peak travel times in the city is very high because of the overpopulation for Istanbul. This situation causes the environmental issues such as traffic accidents, scarcity of urban land and pollution. So, traffic congestion (TC) is a crucial barrier to the use of sustainable transportation systems. Poor urban planning (PUP) is a barrier that indicates the absence of environmentally friendly urban design, which promotes energy-efficient and low-carbon cities for sustainable transportation systems. Poor urban planning (PUP) effects infrastructure, technological development and urban sprawl directly for all different modes of travel.

METHODOLOGY

Grey DEMATEL Method

In this study, the integrated Grey DEMATEL-AAS method is used to analyse and prioritize the key barriers in the use of sustainable transportation systems in city logistics at various levels. Grey DEMA-

TEL is used to examine causal relationship in an unpredictable environment. Then, the ANP method is applied to calculate the relative weight of the barriers based on the relationship obtained with the Grey DEMATEL method. Each step of the integrated Grey DEMATEL-ANP methodology adopted in this study is described below.

Grey Theory was integrated with the traditional DEMATEL method to evaluate the relationships of barriers to the use of sustainable transport systems in city logistics. The steps of the Grey DEMATEL method are summarized as follows (Bai and Sarkis, 2013; Rajesh and Ravi, 2015; Raj et al., 2020).

1. Computation of the Initial Relation Matrices

Number of barriers to the use of sustainable transport systems in city logistics can be denoted by n. From k experts, directly interconnected relationships between these barriers are requested on an integer scale: where a score of 0 signifies no influence, 1 - very low influence, 2 - low influence, 3 - medium influence, 4 - high influence and 5 indicates a very high influence. As a result, k initial relationship matrices are formed.

2. Computation of the Grey Relation Matrix

Verbal evaluations from experts are converted to grey values using Table 2 (Raj et al., 2020).

Table 2. Gray scale for verbal evaluations

Verbal Variables	Grey Numbers
Very High Influence	[4,5]
High Influence	[3,4]
Medium Influence	[2,3]
Low Influence	[1,2]
Very Low Influence	[0,1]
No Influence	[0,0]

Grey relation matrix can be computed as follows.

$$\otimes \tilde{x}_{ij}^{k} = \left(\underline{\otimes} \tilde{x}_{ij}^{k}, \overline{\otimes} \tilde{x}_{ij}^{k} \right) \tag{1}$$

where "$1 \leq k \leq K$"; "$1 \leq i \leq n$"; "$1 \leq j \leq n$"; and $\underline{\otimes} \tilde{x}_{ij}^{k}$ represents the lower limit of grey values whereas $\overline{\otimes} \tilde{x}_{ij}^{k}$ represents the upper limit of grey values for expert k in terms of the relationship evaluation between barrier i and barrier j.

Evaluation of the Barriers to the Use of Sustainable Transportation Systems in City Logistics

3. Calculation of the Average Grey Relation Matrix (A)

A, the average grey relation matrix $\left[\otimes x_{ij}^{k} \right]$, is obtained from K grey relation matrices as shown below (Rajesh and Ravi, 2015; Raj et al., 2020):

$$\otimes x_{ij}^{k} = \left(\frac{\sum_{k} \underline{\otimes} \tilde{x}_{ij}^{k}}{K}, \frac{\sum_{k} \overline{\otimes} \tilde{x}_{ij}^{k}}{K} \right) \tag{2}$$

$$A = \left[\otimes x_{ij}^{k} \right] \tag{3}$$

4. Computation of the Crisp Relation Matrix (Z)

The crisp values of the grey number, $\otimes x_{ij}^{k} = \left(\underline{\otimes} x_{ij}^{k}, \overline{\otimes} x_{ij}^{k} \right)$, are obtained as shown below (Xia et al., 2015; Rajesh and Ravi, 2015; Raj et al., 2020):

Step 1. Normalization:

$$\underline{\otimes} \overline{x}_{ij}^{k} = \left. \left(\underline{\otimes} x_{ij}^{k} - \min_{j} \otimes x_{ij}^{k} \right) \middle/ \triangle_{\min}^{\max} \right. \tag{4}$$

$$\overline{\otimes} \overline{x}_{ij}^{k} = \left. \left(\overline{\otimes} x_{ij}^{k} - \min_{j} \overline{\otimes} x_{ij}^{k} \right) \middle/ \triangle_{\min}^{\max} \right. \tag{5}$$

where

$$\triangle_{\min}^{\max} = \max_{j} \overline{\otimes} x_{ij}^{k} - \min_{j} \underline{\otimes} x_{ij}^{k} \tag{6}$$

Step 2. Computation of a total normalized crisp value:

$$Y_{ij}^{k} = \left(\frac{\underline{\otimes} \overline{x}_{ij}^{k} \left(1 - \underline{\otimes} \overline{x}_{ij}^{k} \right) + \left(\overline{\otimes} \overline{x}_{ij}^{k} \times \overline{\otimes} \overline{x}_{ij}^{k} \right)}{\left(1 - \underline{\otimes} \overline{x}_{ij}^{k} + \overline{\otimes} \overline{x}_{ij}^{k} \right)} \right) \tag{7}$$

Step 3. Calculation of final crisp values:

$$Z_{ij}^{k} = \left(\min_{j} \underline{\otimes} x_{ij}^{k} + \left(Y_{ij}^{k} \times \triangle_{\min}^{\max} \right) \right) \tag{8}$$

$$Z = \left[Z_{ij}^{k} \right] \tag{9}$$

5. Calculation of the Normalized Direct Crisp Relation Matrix (X)

Each element in this matrix lies between 0 and 1 (Raj et al., 2020).

$$S = \frac{1}{\max\limits_{1 \le i \le n} \sum_{j=1}^{n} Z_{ij}} \tag{10}$$

where S is a normalization factor.

$$X = S \times Z \tag{11}$$

6. Computation of the Total Relation Matrix $(T=[t_{ij}])$

$$T = X \times (I - X)^{-1} \tag{12}$$

where I represents the identity matrix. t_{ij} denotes the overall effect of barrier i onto the barrier j (Liu et al., 2022).

7. Computation of the Overall Prominence and Net Effect (X)

The sum of the rows and columns in the total relation matrix is calculated as follows (Liu et al., 2021):

$$R = \left(R_i \right)_{n \times 1} = \left(\sum_{i=1}^{n} t_{ij} \right)_{n \times 1} \tag{13}$$

$$D = \left(D_j \right)_{1 \times n}^{'} = \left(\sum_{i=1}^{n} t_{ij} \right)_{1 \times n}^{'} \tag{14}$$

When i=j, $(R_i + D_j)$ is called "overall importance" and indicates the total interaction intensity of the barrier i with others. $(R_i - D_j)$ is called "net effect" and indicates the degree of net effect of barrier i on others. In addition, barriers with positive (R-D) values are mainly cause barriers that influence others; Barriers with negative (R-D) values are influencers based on other barriers and are known as effect barriers (Liu et al., 2021).

Analytic Network Process (ANP)

Grey DEMATEL-ANP (DANP) method are applied with the Grey DEMATEL results as follows (Liou et al., 2015; Çelikbilek and Tüysüz 2016; Sarkar et al., 2018; Hsu et al., 2018, Liu et al., 2021).

Evaluation of the Barriers to the Use of Sustainable Transportation Systems in City Logistics

8. Construction of the Unweighted Super Matrix

The total relationship matrix T is divided into sub-matrices according to the size of the barriers and is expressed as Tc in Equation (15).

$$
T_c = \begin{array}{c} V_1 \\ \vdots \\ V_i \\ \vdots \\ V_n \end{array}
\begin{array}{c}
\\ v_{11} \\ v_{12} \\ \vdots \\ v_{1m_1} \\ \vdots \\ v_{i1} \\ v_{i2} \\ \vdots \\ v_{im_i} \\ \vdots \\ v_{n1} \\ v_{n2} \\ \vdots \\ v_{nm_n}
\end{array}
\begin{bmatrix}
T_c^{11} & & T_c^{1j} & & T_c^{1jn} \\
\vdots & & \vdots & & \vdots \\
T_c^{i1} & & T_c^{ij} & & T_c^{in} \\
\vdots & & \vdots & & \vdots \\
T_c^{n1} & & T_c^{nj} & & T_c^{nn}
\end{bmatrix}
\tag{15}
$$

The sub matrix T_c^{ij} is normalized as $T_c^{\alpha ij}$. $T_c^{\alpha 12}$ is given as an example in Equation (16) below, where $d_i^{12} = \sum_{j=1}^{m_2} t_{ij}^{12}$, $i=1,2,\ldots,m_1$ (Liu et al., 2021).

$$
T_c^{\alpha 12} = V_1
\begin{array}{c} v_{11} \\ \vdots \\ v_{1i} \\ \vdots \\ v_{1m_1} \end{array}
\begin{bmatrix}
t_{11}^{12}/d_1^{12} & & t_{1j}^{12}/d_1^{12} & & t_{1m_2}^{12}/d_1^{12} \\
\vdots & & \vdots & & \vdots \\
t_{i1}^{12}/d_i^{12} & & t_{ij}^{12}/d_i^{12} & & t_{im_2}^{12}/d_i^{12} \\
\vdots & & \vdots & & \vdots \\
t_{m_1 1}^{12}/d_{m_1}^{12} & & t_{m_1 j}^{12}/d_{m_1}^{12} & & t_{m_1 m_2}^{12}/d_{m_1}^{12}
\end{bmatrix}
= V_1
\begin{array}{c} v_{11} \\ \vdots \\ v_{1i} \\ \vdots \\ v_{1m_1} \end{array}
\begin{bmatrix}
t_{11}^{\alpha 12} & & t_{1j}^{\alpha 12} & & t_{1m_2}^{\alpha 12} \\
\vdots & & \vdots & & \vdots \\
t_{i1}^{\alpha 12} & & t_{ij}^{\alpha 12} & & t_{im_2}^{\alpha 12} \\
\vdots & & \vdots & & \vdots \\
t_{m_1 1}^{\alpha 12} & & t_{m_1 j}^{\alpha 12} & & t_{m_1 m_2}^{\alpha 12}
\end{bmatrix}
\tag{16}
$$

Then, in the unweighted super matrix (W), $T_c^{\alpha ij}$ is transposed ($W=[W_{ij}]_{nxm}$, $W_{ij} = \left(T_c^{\alpha ij} \right)'$, $i=1,2,\ldots,n$; $j=1,2,\ldots,n$).

9. Construction of the Weighted Super Matrix

To construct the weighted super matrix, the total relationship matrix of dimensions $T_D=[t_{ij}^{D}]_{nxm}$ is calculated by repeating the same steps. Then, using Equation (17), the normalized matrix T_D^{α} is obtained where $d_i = \sum_{j=1}^{n} t_{ij}^{D}$, I=1,2,..,n.

$$
T_D^{\alpha} = \begin{matrix} & \begin{matrix} V_1 & \cdots & V_j & \cdots & V_n \end{matrix} \\ \begin{matrix} V_1 \\ \vdots \\ V_i \\ \vdots \\ V_n \end{matrix} & \begin{bmatrix} t_{11}^{D}/d_1 & & t_{1j}^{D}/d_1 & & t_{1n}^{D}/d_1 \\ \vdots & & \vdots & & \vdots \\ t_{i1}^{D}/d_i & & t_{ij}^{D}/d_i & & t_{in}^{D}/d_i \\ \vdots & & \vdots & & \vdots \\ t_{n1}^{D}/d_n & & t_{nj}^{D}/d_n & & t_{nn}^{D}/d_n \end{bmatrix} \end{matrix} = \begin{matrix} & \begin{matrix} V_1 & \cdots & V_j & \cdots & V_n \end{matrix} \\ \begin{matrix} V_1 \\ \vdots \\ V_i \\ \vdots \\ V_n \end{matrix} & \begin{bmatrix} t_{11}^{\alpha D} & & t_{1j}^{\alpha D} & & t_{1n}^{\alpha D} \\ \vdots & & \vdots & & \vdots \\ t_{i1}^{\alpha D} & & t_{ij}^{\alpha D} & & t_{in}^{\alpha D} \\ \vdots & & \vdots & & \vdots \\ t_{n1}^{\alpha D} & & t_{nj}^{\alpha D} & & t_{nn}^{\alpha D} \end{bmatrix} \end{matrix}
$$

(17)

The weighted super matrix W_w is formed as follows (Yang et al., 2008; Gölcük and Baykasoğlu, 2016).

$$
W_w = \begin{bmatrix} t_{11}^{\alpha D}xW_{11} & t_{21}^{\alpha D}xW_{12} & t_{n1}^{\alpha D}xW_{1n} \\ \vdots & \vdots & \vdots \\ t_{i2}^{\alpha D}xW_{21} & t_{22}^{\alpha D}xW_{22} & t_{n2}^{\alpha D}xW_{2n} \\ \vdots & \vdots & \vdots \\ t_{1n}^{\alpha D}xW_{n1} & t_{2n}^{\alpha D}xW_{n2} & t_{nn}^{\alpha D}xW_{nn} \end{bmatrix}
$$

(18)

10. Acquiring the Priority of Barriers through Limit Super Matrix

The limit super matrix W^* is obtained using Equation (19). The weight of each barrier is the element corresponding to each row in the W^* matrix.

$$
W^* = \lim_{k \to \infty} W_w^{k}
$$

(19)

Data Collection

The first stage of the study is to identify the barriers to the use of sustainable transportation systems in city logistics. In order to identify these barriers, first of all, a literature review was made on the research databases and expert opinions were taken. Accordingly, 14 usage barriers were determined. To apply the Integrated Grey DEMATEL-ANP method, qualitative evaluations by experts are needed as data input. For this reason, 2 experts who have fund of knowledge and deep understanding of key barriers to the use

Evaluation of the Barriers to the Use of Sustainable Transportation Systems in City Logistics

of sustainable transportation systems in city logistics from the academia were included in this research to assess these defined barriers. The experts measured the direct interdependent relationships between these barriers with the five levelled scales of 0–5, representing "no influence," "very low influence," "low influence," "medium influence," "high influence" and "very high influence" respectively. Likewise, relationships of dimensions were also evaluated to each other. In this way, the results were obtained by applying the relevant steps of the integrated method to the initial matrices.

RESULTS

Results of the Grey DEMATEL Method

In order to determine the interrelationship between the barriers to use of sustainable transportation systems in city logistics for Istanbul, the main barriers were evaluated with the Grey DEMATEL approach. Two direct grey relation matrices (14 x 14) were created based on the ratings obtained from the experts for 14 key barriers. Based on these matrices, the total relation matrix was obtained as shown in Table 3. Using this total relation matrix, overall importance and net effect values were determined for each barrier. Table 4 details the overall importance and net effect values.

Prominent barriers are also known as causal barriers and have a higher score with a higher correlation with other barriers. These barriers have significant effects on other barriers. Therefore it is very important to identify and analyse these barriers in planning for the use of sustainable transportation systems in city logistics (Bai and Sarkis, 2013; Raj et al., 2020).

As shown in Table 4, II (Insufficient infrastructure) has the strongest influence with the highest R+D value of 5.06864. That is, he has the highest interaction with others. This barrier is followed by TS (Traffic congestion) with a value of 4.95094, PUP (Poor urban planning) with a value of 4.64921, and LA (Low accessibility) with a value of 4.61463.

The most important cause barriers, which have very important effects on the use of sustainable transportation systems in city logistics, are determined according to the highest net effect or (R-D) value. These barriers are also called influencing barriers. As can be seen in Table 4, II (Insufficient infrastructure) has the highest (R-D) value with a value of 0.911088 and is the most important barrier to the use of sustainable transportation systems in city logistics in Istanbul. This barrier is followed by PUP (poor urban planning) and LSP (Lack of public support and policy) respectively.

Resulting barriers are also known as effect barriers and are those most affected by other barriers. As shown in Table 4, NP (Noise pollution) has the smallest negative (R-D) value of -1.18796. Therefore, it is most easily affected by other barriers. This barrier is followed by CZ (Comfort zone) and EC (Energy consumption), respectively.

According to the results; NP, CZ, and EC have both low (R+D) values and three largest negative (R-D) values, therefore they have low effects and relations. Therefore, these barriers have a limited impact on city logistics. In addition, II and PUP are defined as prominent barriers. Since (R- D) values are the largest positive values and (R+ D) values are greater than their averages, they are push indicators with high impact power. TS barrier is one of the important barriers since it ranks second according to the (R+D) value and has one of the smallest negative (R-D) values. According to the results of Grey DEMATEL, the most important barriers to the use of sustainable transportation systems in city logistics for Istanbul are II, TS and PUP.

Evaluation of the Barriers to the Use of Sustainable Transportation Systems in City Logistics

Table 3. Total relation matrix for key barriers

	ISM LSP LIS II ITC CZ LA HIC UPM EC NP CC TS PUP
ISM	0.0586 0.0690 0.0723 0.1236 0.0896 0.1858 0.0830 0.0859 0.1592 0.1284 0.1447 0.0477 0.1837 0.1229
LSP	0.1533 0.0830 0.1605 0.1788 0.1335 0.1858 0.1842 0.1663 0.2051 0.2011 0.1471 0.0817 0.2165 0.1807
LIS	0.0586 0.0901 0.0477 0.1104 0.0841 0.1285 0.1362 0.1130 0.1280 0.1114 0.1044 0.0440 0.1485 0.0833
II	0.2151 0.1898 0.1592 0.1545 0.2031 0.2674 0.2510 0.2148 0.2727 0.2145 0.2323 0.1264 0.2751 0.2139
ITC	0.1153 0.0697 0.0726 0.1671 0.0769 0.2005 0.1722 0.1101 0.1944 0.1377 0.1425 0.1200 0.1830 0.1276
CZ	0.0722 0.1041 0.0487 0.0786 0.0850 0.1047 0.0835 0.1212 0.1815 0.2033 0.1913 0.0785 0.1934 0.0897
LA	0.1460 0.1278 0.1360 0.2121 0.1149 0.2540 0.1265 0.1496 0.2364 0.2173 0.2172 0.1349 0.2188 0.1629
HIC	0.1829 0.1598 0.1662 0.2090 0.1739 0.1740 0.1923 0.1123 0.2249 0.2169 0.1636 0.0743 0.2042 0.1777
UPM	0.1099 0.0934 0.0585 0.1288 0.1029 0.2029 0.1637 0.1090 0.1152 0.2021 0.1715 0.0827 0.1460 0.1552
EC	0.0762 0.0673 0.0638 0.0966 0.1510 0.1401 0.1098 0.1513 0.1376 0.1000 0.1505 0.1116 0.1273 0.0987
NP	0.0448 0.0773 0.0354 0.0706 0.0671 0.1372 0.0621 0.0696 0.0901 0.1510 0.0721 0.0877 0.1466 0.0696
CC	0.1230 0.0675 0.0553 0.1424 0.1412 0.2136 0.1576 0.1013 0.1837 0.2075 0.1798 0.0641 0.1954 0.1122
TS	0.1156 0.0970 0.0962 0.1732 0.1320 0.2450 0.2002 0.1332 0.2264 0.2319 0.2327 0.0901 0.1472 0.1878
PUP	0.1723 0.1618 0.1418 0.2331 0.1534 0.2377 0.2378 0.2088 0.2342 0.2531 0.2195 0.0959 0.2568 0.1305

Table 4. Overall importance and net effect values of barriers

Symbol	R	D	Overall Importance (R+D)	Net Effect (R-D)	Type
ISM	1.55404	1.64379	3.19783	-0.089755	Effect
LSP	2.27729	1.45769	3.73498	0.819601	Cause
LIS	1.38835	1.31411	2.70246	0.0742394	Cause
II	2.98986	2.07877	5.06864	0.911088	Cause
ITC	1.88975	1.70871	3.59846	0.181044	Cause
CZ	1.63561	2.67716	4.31277	-1.04155	Effect
LA	2.45449	2.16015	4.61463	0.294341	Cause
HIC	2.43198	1.8464	4.27838	0.585576	Cause
UPM	1.84191	2.58931	4.43122	-0.7474	Effect
EC	1.58179	2.57636	4.15815	-0.994566	Effect
NP	1.18113	2.36908	3.55021	-1.18796	Effect
CC	1.94441	1.23942	3.18383	0.704994	Cause
TS	2.30864	2.6423	4.95094	-0.333656	Effect
PUP	2.7366	1.9126	4.64921	0.824001	Cause

Evaluation of the Barriers to the Use of Sustainable Transportation Systems in City Logistics

Results of the ANP Method

In this study, the ANP method was used to determine the weight of the barriers. First, the total relation matrix was calculated for all three main dimensions: social, economic and environmental, using the steps of the Grey DEMATEL method. Afterwards, the unweighted super matrix and the weighted super matrix were computed, respectively. Finally, the limit super matrix is obtained. The weight of a barrier is the corresponding element of each row in the limit matrix (Liu et al., 2021). According to the calculations and the limit super matrix, the final priorities of the barriers were obtained on a weight basis, as shown in Table 5.

Table 5. Relative weights of key barriers to use of sustainable transportation systems in city logistics for Istanbul

Barrier	Symbol	Weight	Rank
Unwillingness to payoff more	UPM	0.1983	1
High investment costs	HIC	0.1435	2
Comfort zone	CZ	0.0779	3
Energy consumption	EC	0.0695	4
Traffic congestion	TS	0.0675	5
Noise pollution	NP	0.0623	6
Low accessibility	LA	0.0619	7
Insufficient infrastructure	II	0.0587	8
Poor urban planning	PUP	0.0521	9
Inadequate transportation capacity	ITC	0.0501	10
Inadequate security measures	ISM	0.0465	11
Lack of public support and policy	LSP	0.0435	12
Lack of information systems	LIS	0.0355	13
Climate change	CC	0.0327	14

Table 5 shows that UPM (Unwillingness to payoff more) is the first priority with the highest weight of 0.1983, while CC (Climate change) is the least important barrier with the lowest weight of 0.0327. The seven most important barriers are UPM, HIC, CZ, EC, TS, NP and LA, respectively, and these barriers affect the sustainability of transport systems with greater weight in city logistics.

IMPLICATIONS TO THEORY AND PRACTICE

In this chapter, a framework for key barriers to use of the sustainable transportation systems in city logistics is created with a literature review and experts. The proposed Grey DEMATEL-ANP model serves as a more realistic and effective decision-making process to identify these key barriers. The crucial barriers of city logistics are determined by analysing in detail the cause-effect interrelationships, influential weights,

Evaluation of the Barriers to the Use of Sustainable Transportation Systems in City Logistics

and dimensions. Thus, this study allows logistics managers to make decisions by eliminating inaccuracy results. This will increase the performance in logistics systems. Efficient and effective systems will be established in city logistics. Some important practical implications can be obtained.

- It is crucial to consider all aspects of the decision-making process to identify key barriers to the use of transportation systems in city logistics in terms of sustainability.
- Implementation solutions must be included to overcome II (Insufficient infrastructure), TS (Traffic congestion) and UPM (Unwillingness to payoff more) barriers in the sustainable transportation strategy. In this way, a practical and useful decision-making process can be obtained in terms of both passengers, drivers and transportation modes considering social, economic and environmental priorities.
- A roadmap that gives better control of every aspect of the transportation operations is presented to managers with this process. This roadmap provides advantages such as time saving, economic benefit, national and international competitive advantage about the most efficient use of existing resources.
- This chapter may help to improve tactical or operational performance of city logistics with identified highly prioritized usage barriers and to increase the strategic performance by classifying these barriers as cause-and-effect groups.

DISCUSSION AND CONCLUSION

Thanks to the increasing awareness on sustainability, it is becoming more and more important to consider environmental dimensions such as reducing the negative effects on the environment and efficient use of natural resources, as well as economic and social dimensions in the use of transportation systems in city logistics. This situation not only facilitates the transition to sustainable transportation systems in city logistics, but also causes some difficulties and barriers. In this context, it is necessary for the sustainability of the use of transportation systems in city logistics to clearly define the key barriers encountered in the process and to plan strategic steps by prioritizing these barriers according to their importance levels.

In this study, an integrated Grey DEMATEL-ANP model was proposed to prioritize key barriers. First, the causality relation and interaction density were established by creating grey relation matrices and following the steps of the method according to the evaluations of the experts. Along with the relative weight, the effects of each barrier on city logistics for the city of Istanbul have been determined. In the literature, no study has been found in which the barriers to the use of all sustainable transportation systems in city logistics are evaluated as a whole, the relation of these barriers with each other is examined, and the importance of the barriers is revealed by weighting them. In this respect, this study sheds light on this deficiency in the literature.

According to the Grey DEMATEL results, II (Insufficient infrastructure), TS (Traffic congestion) and PUP (Poor urban planning) were determined as the most important barriers to the use of sustainable transportation systems in city logistics for Istanbul. When the results of the ANP method are examined, it is seen that the II and TS are among the top 7 most important barriers. In addition, UPM (Unwillingness to payoff more) is the barrier with the highest weight, ranking first according to the ANP results. Moreover, UPM has a relatively high (R+ D) value and one of the lowest negative (R- D) values according to the Grey DEMATEL results.

308

The results of the comprehensive analysis show that II (Insufficient infrastructure), TS (Traffic congestion) and UPM (Unwillingness to payoff more) barriers are the most important barriers with higher priority in city logistics for Istanbul. Thus, it has been concluded that the existing resources should be used to overcome especially the II, TS and UPM barriers to achieve the sustainability goals in the use of transportation systems in city logistics.

Evaluating the usage barriers of sustainable transportation systems by considering environmental and social dimensions as well as economic benefits has brought a sustainable solution to urban logistics problems. Accordingly, the key barriers identified as crucial have included each dimension, including social, economic and environmental. The positive relationship of the insufficient infrastructure (II) barrier with the social dimension has revealed that the individual and social needs of transportation problems should be met with priority. In addition, the traffic congestion (TS) barrier, which is evaluated within the scope of the environmental dimension, has shown that environmental impacts should also be minimized in order to overcome various city logistics issues. The unwillingness to payoff more (UPM) barrier has emphasized that economic benefits also should be considered. These positive relations between selected crucial barriers and the main dimensions has provided that the sustainable implementation for the city logistics.

As mentioned before, the proposed method has determined the cause-effect relationships and relative weights of key barriers to the sustainable transportation systems in the city logistics for Istanbul. This study provides the theoretical guideline them to use the sustainable transport systems across city logistics successfully.

In the future studies, other frequently used MCDM techniques such as Technique for Order of Preference by Similarity to Ideal Solution (TOPSIS), Linear Programming Technique for Multidimensional Analysis of Preference (LINMAP) or Preference Ranking Organization Method for Enrichment of Evaluations (PROMETHEE) can be applied to the model in order to measure the objectivity of the results. Sensitivity analysis can be performed to evaluate the determined barriers by considering different weights or different conditions, and their adaptability to real-life applications can be tested. Evaluation of subjective judgments in the decision-making process can be broadly analysed by involving more experts from academia and industry. On the other hand, fuzzy logic can be applied to enable decision making under uncertainty and various enabling factors and indicators can be analysed to help overcome identified barriers.

REFERENCES

Ağaoğlu, M. N., & Başdemir, H. (2019). Şehir içi ulaşım sorunları ve çözüm önerileri. *Gaziosmanpaşa Bilimsel Araştırma Dergisi, 8*(1), 27–36.

Akben, İ. (2020). Şehir Lojistiği: Tedarik Zinciri Ve Lojistikte Güncel Konular Ve Stratejik Yaklaşımlar, Ankara. *Sonçağ Yayıncılık, 2020,* 73–88.

Al-Hawari, T., Mumani, A., & Momani, A. (2014). Application of the Analytic Network Process to facility layout selection. *International Journal of Industrial and Manufacturing Systems Engineering, 33,* 488–497.

Altıntaş, S. T., & Eyigün, Y. (2020). Sürdürülebilir Kent İçi Ulaşım Politikaları Raylı Sistemler Örneği. *İstanbul Ticaret Üniversitesi Teknoloji ve Uygulamalı Bilimler Dergisi, 3*(2), 217-233.

Aydın, G. T. (2017). *Kent İçi Lojistik İstanbul İçin Bir Uygulama. Yüksek Lisans Tezi.* İstanbul Teknik Üniversitesi, Fen Bilimleri Enstitüsü.

Bai, C., & Sarkis, J. (2013). A grey-based DEMATEL model for evaluating business process management critical success factors. *International Journal of Production Economics, 146*(1), 281–292. doi:10.1016/j.ijpe.2013.07.011

Çelikbilek, Y., & Tüysüz, F. (2016). An integrated grey based multi-criteria decision making approach for the evaluation of renewable energy sources. *Energy, 115*, 1246–1258. doi:10.1016/j.energy.2016.09.091

Chen, Z., Ming, X., Zhang, X., Yin, D., & Sun, Z. (2019). A rough-fuzzy DEMATEL-ANP method for evaluating sustainable value requirement of product service system. *Journal of Cleaner Production, 228*, 485–508. doi:10.1016/j.jclepro.2019.04.145

Cirit, F. (2014). *Sürdürülebilir Kentiçi Ulaşım Politikaları Ve Toplu Taşıma Sistemlerinin Karşılaştırılması.* Planlama Uzmanlığı Tezi, İktisadi Sektörler ve Koordinasyon Genel Müdürlüğü, T.C. Kalkınma Bakanlığı, 2891.

Deakin, E. (2001). Sustainable development and sustainable transportation: strategies for economic prosperity, environmental quality, and equity. University of California, Berkeley Institute of Urban and Regional Development.

Deveci, M., Canıtez, F., & Çetin Demirel, N. (2015). *Toplu Ulaşımda Entegrasyon Basamakları: Kavramsal Bir İnceleme.* TRANSİST 8. Uluslararası Ulaşım Teknolojileri Sempozyumu ve Fuarı, 21-25, İstanbul, Türkiye.

Gölcük, I., & Baykasoğlu, A. (2016). An analysis of DEMATEL approaches for criteria interaction handling within ANP. *Expert Systems with Applications, 46*, 346–366. doi:10.1016/j.eswa.2015.10.041

Hamurcu, M., & Eren, T. (2017). *Toplu Taşıma Türünün Seçiminde Çok Kriterli Karar Verme Uygulaması. International Conference on Advanced Engineering Technologies, Bayburt, Türkiye.*

Hsu, C.-C., Liou, J. J. H., Lo, H.-W., & Wang, Y.-C. (2018). Using a hybrid method for evaluating and improving the service quality of public bike-sharing systems. *Journal of Cleaner Production, 202*, 1131–1144. doi:10.1016/j.jclepro.2018.08.193

İnaç, H., & Tanyaş, M. (2012). *İstanbul'un kentsel lojistik analizi ve çözüm önerilerinin AHP ile değerlendirilmesi.* Ulusal Lojistik ve Tedarik Zinciri Kongresi, Konya, Türkiye.

Kaplan, H., & Ulukavak, H. G. (2013). Kentlerimizde sürdürülebilir bütünleşik ulaşıma doğru: Sorun ve olanakların irdelenmesi. *TRANSİST 6. Ulaşım Sempozyumu ve Fuarı*, 181-195.

Liou, J. J. H., Tamosaitiene, J., Zavadskas, E. K., & Tzeng, G.-H. (2015). New hybrid COPRAS-G MADM Model for improving and selecting suppliers in green supply chain management. *International Journal of Production Research, 54*(1), 114–134. doi:10.1080/00207543.2015.1010747

Evaluation of the Barriers to the Use of Sustainable Transportation Systems in City Logistics

Liu, X., Deng, Q., Gong, G., Zhao, X., & Li, K. (2021). Evaluating the interactions of multi-dimensional value for sustainable product-service system with grey DEMATEL-ANP approach. *Journal of Manufacturing Systems*, *60*, 449–458. doi:10.1016/j.jmsy.2021.07.006

Luthra, S., Kumar, A., Zavadskas, E. K., Mangla, S. K., & Garza-Reyes, J. A. (2019). Industry 4.0 as an enabler of sustainability diffusion in supply chain: An analysis of influential strength of drivers in an emerging economy. *International Journal of Production Research*, *58*(5), 1505–1521. doi:10.1080/00207543.2019.1660828

Mangla, S. K., Luthra, S., Rich, N., Kumar, D., Rana, N. P., & Dwivedi, Y. K. (2018). Enablers to implement sustainable initiatives in agri-food supply chains. *International Journal of Production Economics*, *203*, 379–393. doi:10.1016/j.ijpe.2018.07.012

Masoumi, H. E. (2019). A discrete choice analysis of transport mode choice causality and perceived barriers of sustainable mobility in the MENA region. *Transport Policy*, *79*, 37–53. doi:10.1016/j.tranpol.2019.04.005

Morel, M., Balm, S., Berden, M., & Ploos van Amstel, V. (2020). Governance models for sustainable urban construction logistics: Barriers for collaboration. *Transportation Research Procedia*, *46*, 173–180. doi:10.1016/j.trpro.2020.03.178

Öncü, E., & Öncü Yildiz, A. (2011). *Sürdürülebilir Ulaşım: Devlet Bunun Neresinde?* TMMOB İnşaat Mühendisleri Odası İstanbul Şubesi.

Öztürk, S., & Gündüz, E. (2020). Sürdürülebilir Ulaşımda Bisiklet Kullanımını Engelleyen Sebepler: Manisa Örneği. *Düzce Üniversitesi Bilim ve Teknoloji Dergisi*, *8*, 2164–2182.

Raj, A., Dwivedi, G., Sharma, A., Lopes De Sousa Jabbour, A. B., & Rajak, S. (2020). Barriers to the adoption of industry 4.0 technologies in the manufacturing sector: An inter-country comparative perspective. *International Journal of Production Economics*, *224*, 107546. doi:10.1016/j.ijpe.2019.107546

Rajesh, R., & Ravi, V. (2015). Modeling enablers of supply chain risk mitigation in electronic supply chains: A Grey–DEMATEL approach. *Computers & Industrial Engineering*, *87*, 126–139. doi:10.1016/j.cie.2015.04.028

Ren, J., Liang, H., Dong, L., Gao, Z., He, C., Pan, M., & Sun, L. (2017). Sustainable development of sewage sludge-to-energy in China: Barriers identification and technologies prioritization. *Renewable & Sustainable Energy Reviews*, *67*, 384–396. doi:10.1016/j.rser.2016.09.024

Rodrigues, A. L. P., & Seixas, S. R. C. (2022). Battery-electric buses and their implementation barriers: Analysis and prospects for sustainability. *Sustainable Energy Technologies and Assessments*, *51*, 101896. doi:10.1016/j.seta.2021.101896

Sarkar, S., Pratihar, D. K., & Sarkar, B. (2018). An integrated fuzzy multiple criteria supplier selection approach and its application in a welding company. *International Journal of Industrial and Manufacturing Systems Engineering*, *46*, 163–178.

Savrun, B., & Mutlu, H. M. (2019). Kent Lojistiği Üzerine Bibliyometrik Analiz. *Kent Akademisi*, *12*(2), 364–386. doi:10.35674/kent.534729

Shah, K. J., Pan, S.-Y., Lee, I., Kim, H., You, Z., Zheng, J.-M., & Ciang, P.-C. (2021). Green transportation for sustainability: Review of current barriers, strategies, and innovative Technologies. *Journal of Cleaner Production*, *326*, 129392. doi:10.1016/j.jclepro.2021.129392

Si, S. L., You, X. Y., Liu, H. C., & Zhang, P. (2018). DEMATEL technique: A systematic review of the state-of-the-art literature on methodologies and applications. *Mathematical Problems in Engineering*, *2018*, 2018. doi:10.1155/2018/3696457

Stevic, Z., Pamucar, D., Vasiljevic, M., Stojic, G., & Korica, S. (2017). Novel Integrated Multi-Criteria Model for Supplier Selection: Case Study Construction Company. *Symmetry*, *9*(11), 279. doi:10.3390ym9110279

Taniguchi, E., & Van Der Heijden, R. E. C. M. (2000). An Evaluation Methodology for City Logistics. *Transport Reviews*, *20*(1), 65–90. doi:10.1080/014416400295347

Witkowski, J., & Kiba-Janiak, M. (2014). The role of local governments in the development of city logistics. *Procedia: Social and Behavioral Sciences*, *125*, 373–385. doi:10.1016/j.sbspro.2014.01.1481

Xia, X., Govindan, K., & Zhu, Q. (2015). Analyzing internal barriers for automotive parts remanufacturers in China using grey-DEMATEL approach. *Journal of Cleaner Production*, *87*, 811–825. doi:10.1016/j.jclepro.2014.09.044

Yang, Y.-P. O., Shieh, H.-M., Leu, J.-D., & Tzeng, G.-H. (2008). A Novel Hybrid MCDM Model Combined with DEMATEL and ANP with Applications. *International Journal of Operations Research*, *5*(3), 160–168.

Yıldız, B., Kütahyalı, D. B., & Çavdar, E. (2021). Şehir Lojistiği: Nicel Bir Araştırma. *Van Yüzüncü Yıl Üniversitesi Sosyal Bilimler Enstitüsü Dergisi*, *53*, 303–334.

Chapter 15
Relationship Between Intellectual Property Rights and Entrepreneurial Ecosystems

Seda Damla Yücel
TED University, Turkey

ABSTRACT

Intellectual property rights (IPR) are critical for developing new inventions and creations, transforming them into social and economic value, and increasing inventors' and creators' competitiveness. The main functions of IPR are preventing competitors from owning, using, selling, and monetizing related inventions and creations, access to markets and networks, and obtaining venture capital. Entrepreneurship contributes significantly to economic growth and is crucial to creating opportunities and improving the performance of new businesses. Its impact varies from economy to economy based on its outputs, a nation's industrial and technological prowess, and its legislative framework for developing entrepreneurs. Technological development is inevitable considering the increasing population, existing infrastructure, services offered to society, limited resources, the expected quality of life, and the city's ecological imprint. Therefore, creative and technological solutions will be essential, especially in building dynamic approaches while creating smart cities for the future.

INTRODUCTION

Although there are many different definitions of innovation, it can be said that innovation refers to something new or a change made in an existing product, idea, or field. So, although innovation is defined with different words, it can be said that innovation includes keywords such as new, changing, creating, and development.

Countries, governmental bodies, and private sectors focus on interdisciplinary research activities, innovation studies, and strategic collaborations to increase their competitiveness in the global market. In this process, the protection of products/services developed from these studies creates new demands

DOI: 10.4018/978-1-6684-5996-6.ch015

Copyright © 2023, IGI Global. Copying or distributing in print or electronic forms without written permission of IGI Global is prohibited.

and/or addresses new needs. At this point, the importance of intellectual property rights in protecting outputs emerges.

Intellectual Property is one of the most important key drivers of economic prosperity for companies and countries for growth, development, and competitiveness in the twenty-first century. As technology develops, the level of welfare rises and the interest of people in science, art, and research increases. While this situation is creating opportunities for research in different fields, it has opened doors to innovation. Because it is known that innovation is one of the most important key drivers of economic growth. At this stage, Intellectual Property Rights get involved.

Smart cities contain many software applications and hardware devices that connect city's physical and social spaces, forming complex ecosystems in various fields of knowledge and activities such as local communities, transportation, social care, etc. As a result, smart cities can be multi-layered complex systems, with universal access to services, applications, platforms, and infrastructures. Providing all of these structures and accessibility will require the use of new technologies and the development and use of new products and services. When it comes to generating, developing, and transforming new ideas into economic and social value, entrepreneurship and intellectual property rights come into play.

This chapter aims to provide an overlook of Intellectual Property Rights, their role in the entrepreneurial ecosystem, the relationship between intellectual property rights and the entrepreneurial ecosystem, and a general overview of relationship among intellectual property rights, entrepreneurship and smart cities. The structure of this chapter is organized as follows: The first section provides a piece of general knowledge about intellectual property rights and its types; in second section, commercialization instruments and valuation methods of intellectual property will be introduced, in the third section, a general perspective will be presented about the entrepreneurial ecosystem and the relationship between intellectual property rights and entrepreneurship, and in the final section, entrepreneurial ecosystem and intellectual property rights for smart cities will be considered.

BACKGROUND

Intellectual Property (IP), which is an output of intellectual capability and labour, is another class of property based on human intelligence activities. Intellectual Property Rights (IPR) can be defined as the rights to use and sell "the output of the creations of the mind such as inventions, literary and artistic works, etc." IPR is a policy tool that protects the rights of people who invent new products/services from their competitors and ensures a monopoly right for using, producing, and selling to gain economic power. In addition to providing a monopoly right to the owners of these new products/services (called "invention"), IPR also serves as an important resource in developing new knowledge.

IP is a tool which provides to establish a balance between the rights and interests of many actors, including creators, customers, their competitors, and to preserve the rights of all parties.

IP is categorized into three groups:

- **Industrial Property** includes trademarks, industrial designs, geographic signs, integrated circuit layout designs (topographies), as well as patents and utility models.
- **Copyright and Related Rights** include authors' and related rights such as novels, poems, films, etc.
- **Other Rights** which are about trade names, unfair competition, domain names, etc.

Relationship Between Intellectual Property Rights and Entrepreneurial Ecosystems

There are numerous legal reasons why a person should be aware of IPR. One of the most important reasons is to prevent potential competitors from copying their unique creations. The absence of such legal protections may create an environment for anyone to copy, produce, use and generate revenue by selling that creation/invention that belongs to another person/corporation. Additionally, this situation severely limits the ability of corporations such as SMEs, start-ups, entrepreneurs, etc., and also creators make profit from their creations/inventions invented by them. IP provides legal protection to prevent people/corporations which develop/invent new outputs from issues like this.

INTELLECTUAL PROPERTY RIGHTS AND ITS TYPES

IP is becoming an increasingly important business asset for corporations of all sizes, particularly for start-ups, SMEs, entrepreneurs, and creators. Although IP may appear to be a significant cost item, it plays an important role in gaining traction, generating revenue, gaining a competitive advantage, and attracting potential investors/creators. IP, positioned as a "profit center," is an important intangible asset in determining company business strategies.

Innovations and developed technologies protected by Intellectual Property Rights (IPR) are the engines and key drivers of the modern world economy. The main role of IPR, which is an intangible asset (it means that personal property that cannot be moved and touched, includes something such as negotiable instruments, knowledge, securities, etc.), is to transfer the know-how into society by generating the profit and create opportunities in order to be developed the new knowledge. Each IP type is unique and protects specific features of the company's/people's product/process developed and also provides the opportunity to observe the basic capabilities by protecting its identity.

Therefore, obtaining the proper balance of IPR protection requires not only evaluating the level of protection offered to IP owners by the institutional context, but also choosing the combination of IPR that best suits the businesses. People/corporations should tailor their strategy to each product/process in their portfolios. IP management considers the value of IP to the business and the kind of IP that best advances its corporate strategy.

IP enables companies to exercise a legal monopoly to create a niche market and exclude rivals. The companies are guaranteed an exclusive strategic position due to this monopoly at a specific point in developing products/processes. This exclusivity translates into a competitive edge that can stop rivals from gaining a crucial foothold in the market for the ground-breaking technology. The market assigns the IPR as a specific value to quantify these "valuable" ends. Due to its worth, IP owners can profit from their commercialization. Thus, they can create an opportunity to gain exclusivity over resources that can provide an advantage over competitors in the industry's technological evolution by utilizing IP. As mentioned before, IP is a tool which provides to establish a balance between the rights and interests of many actors, including creators, customers, their competitors, and to preserve the rights of all parties.

IP is categorized into three groups:

- Industrial property includes trademarks, industrial designs, geographic signs, integrated circuit layout designs (topographies), as well as patents and utility models.
- Copyright and Related Rights include authors' and related rights such as novels, poems, films, etc.
- Other rights which are about trade names, unfair competition, domain names, etc.

The following sections will provide information about industrial property, including trademarks, industrial designs, geographic signs, integrated circuit layout designs (topographies), as well as patents and utility models.

Patent/Utility Model

A patent provides an exclusive right to the inventor/owner to make, use, sell or offer to sell the inventions protected within the scope of the law (EC, 2019). According to Article 27.1 of the TRIPS Agreement, products or processes in all technology fields can be patented if they are new, involve an inventive step, and are capable of industrial application. The requirements for patent registration are:

- **Novelty:** For an invention to be patentable, it must be new, it must not be known anywhere in the world, and it must not be in use and printed anywhere; in short, the invention must not have been disclosed anywhere before the patent application date. It means that the invention must be new when compared with the existing knowledge in the relevant technical field.
- **Inventive step (Non-Obviousness):** It should not be inferred by a person who has an average technical knowledge in the relevant field.
- **Industrial Applicability:** It should have the possibility of making, manufacturing and using in practice.

Utility Models are much cheaper than patents and not available in all countries. Utility Models are valid for Austria, China, Germany, Japan, Spain, Taiwan, etc. Utility model systems have fewer stringent requirements (for example, a lower level of inventive step), more straightforward procedures, and shorter terms of protection.

Utility model systems have less stringent requirements in comparison with patents. The eligibilities and rules of utility model application vary from country to country. The utility model generally can be preferred for the products, not for chemical and biological processes.

The main differences between utility model and patent are as follows (EC, 2019) (Your Guide to IP in Europe):

- The requirements for a patent need to be more stringent than those of utility models. Because of this, for an invention which cannot meet the inventive step or has a limited inventive step, or cannot meet the patentability criteria, the utility model can be preferred instead of patent
- The protection duration of utility models is shorter than for patents and differs from country to country.
- The process for registration for utility models is generally simpler and faster than patents.
- The fees of utility models, including the application process and also maintenance, are generally cheaper than patents
- Utility models are valid in some countries.

Patents and Utility Models are territorial, which means that in which country to be protected, it is necessary to apply for protection for that country. In this way, the patent will be enforceable on using, producing, and selling in the country/region in which the patent rights are granted within the geographical boundaries.

Relationship Between Intellectual Property Rights and Entrepreneurial Ecosystems

Trademark, which is a sign used for distinguishing the products/services of an undertaking from others, provides an exclusive right. According to Article 15.1 of TRIPS Agreement, *"Such signs, in particular words including personal names, letters, numerals, figurative elements and combinations of colors as well as any combination of such signs, must be eligible for registration as trademarks"*. Any word, letter, or number combination, illustrations, symbols, three-dimensional aspects such as product packaging and shape, audible or smelly indications, or color hues used as distinguishing characteristics can be used as a trademark. The possibilities are virtually endless. Trademark protection is also territorial, but it is possible to obtain trademark protection in many countries in the scope of the Madrid System by a single application. The duration of protection varies but is typically ten years. It can also be renewed indefinitely beyond the time limit for an additional fee.

Industrial design provides protection rights for 'any new, original, and ornamental design for the outward appearance or a part of a product. Industrial design just protects the appearance of a product. For a product's technical and functional features to be protected by a patent, it must meet the standard protection requirements detailed above.

The main requirements for design registration can be listed as follows (EC, 2019):

- **Novelty:** It must not have been previously made public in order to be considered novelty.
- **Individual character** means different from previously produced designs, their combinations, and their overall impression; in short, it is not a copy of an existing design.
- **Non-functionality:** Those features of the design that are dictated solely by a technical function, do not provide protection

Industrial design provides a limited period of protection. In most countries, industrial design protection lasts five years from filing a design application and can be renewed for another five years, for a total term of 25 years. If the renewal fees are not paid, the design may expire sooner (EC, 2019). Industrial design protection is also territorial, but it is possible to obtain it in many countries in "Hague System" scope by filing a single international application.

As can be seen from Table 1, the content that each IP type focuses on, vary in terms of protection it offers, the duration of protection and the requirements to be met at the stage of applying for protection.. For this reason, choosing the necessary and appropriate IP type of protection according to the need, taking into account the developed output, is of great importance in terms of the best protection of the rights of the investor/creator/owner.

A geographical indicator is a label applied to goods with a particular geographic origin that has characteristics or a reputation resulting from that origin. A product's place of origin must be stated on a sign. Additionally, the origin of the product should largely account for its traits, attributes, or reputation. Generally, a geographical indication includes the name of the place of origin of the goods.

A layout design of an integrated circuit can be protected if it is original in the sense that it is the result of the creator's intellectual effort and not commonplace among creators of layout-designs and manufacturers of integrated circuits at the time of the creation.

Any confidential business information such as formula, manufacturing process, method of business, technical know-how, etc., which provides any competitive advantage against the competitors, can be accepted as a trade secret. A trade secret offers protection for an endless amount of time. It implies that its monopoly will continue unless the knowledge is released and made public.

Table 1. Differences Between Patent, Trademark and Industrial Design

IPR	Patent	Trademark	Industrial design
Subject Matter	Inventions (Processes, machines, articles of manufacture, compositions of matter, etc.)	Distinctive signs to identify the goods and services of a particular enterprise and distinguish them from others	Original ornamental and non-functional elements of a product or its parts
Requirements for Protection	Absolute Novelty Inventive Step Industrial Applicability	Distinctive	Novelty (new) Originality criteria
Scope of rights	Limited monopoly/Exclusive rights to produce, use and sell the patented inventions	Exclusive rights to use the mark in trade	Exclusive rights to use the design and prevent the third parties from using without permission
Duration	20 years from filling	Usually 10 years, can be renewed indefinitely on payment of fees.	At least 5 years, can be renewed every few years in many countries

Original works of authorship fixed in a physical medium of expression are protected by copyrights. Films, photos, paintings, sculptures, musical compositions, computer programs, and other media are some examples of copyrighted works. The owner (authors, artists, designers, dramatists, musicians, architects, and producers) is the sole authority to alter, distribute, perform, create, display, and copy the associated work, thanks to copyright protection.

COMMERCIALIZATION INSTRUMENTS OF IPR

Each IP category differs in subject matter, duration, and protection. For example, patents forbid unauthorized use and/or generation of the goods and services manufactured, while trademarks protect a start-up's name, logo, etc., copyrights protect the ideas behind the start-ups' artwork, marketing materials, etc. Trade secrets might be utilized to secure private "know-how" such as client lists, formulas, strategic plans, etc., if they were handled properly in high-stakes scenarios. In order to defend and expand the product/ service range in the market and to maintain a competitive advantage, all types of businesses need to have a solid IP management plan which can be defined as the organized processes for transformation of IP into valuable intellectual assets. The main aim of IP management is to turn the output of the research activities into utilizable, applicable, producible assets as products/services with economic benefit. During IP Management, the engagement of IP management to the strategy of the company should be made in a way to create economic value at the top of the level through portfolio management. Protecting the product/process with the right method does not mean that IP Management is implemented effectively. Effective IP portfolio management includes the development of the right IP protection strategy for the right product/process, as well as the use of the right commercialization method (Halt et al., 2014). Organizations that cannot utilize IP strategy effectively are inevitably faced with increased competition, decreased revenue, and a lack of leading innovation in the relevant sector.

A sound IP strategy enables a company to identify its intellectual property and offers a plan for its protection, optimization, and monetization. IP rights can be monetized in various ways and act as significant corporate assets. In this sense, IP, especially patents, provides corporations like start-ups, SMEs, and entrepreneurs with opportunities such as dominating the market by gaining an advantage over their competitors and strengthening their hands, especially against investors in the search for financing sources. Investors can utilize pending patent filings to determine whether a startup company will be able to fend off potential rivals successfully (Halt et al., 2017). The choice of different IP strategies may be made with the goal of improving a company's control over its assets, whether by enhancing its legal defenses, expanding its patent portfolios to protect entire industries from potential competitors, or simply by developing new technologies first. Additionally, businesses employ defensive tactics against rivals who can undermine their competitive advantage by gaining control over related technology or denying others the exclusive right to use their research. The decision balances the expenses of keeping an innovation a secret vs. the costs of releasing it and acquiring a legal right to disclosure, as is the case with other economic trade-offs. As a result, the best technique should take into account whether the disclosure is adequate to transmit knowledge or whether the innovation may be easily reverse engineered. As a result, the best IP strategy, and in particular the act of revealing innovation through IP protection, is thus influenced by several aspects. When deciding whether to apply Intellectual Property Rights, one should be taken into account many different aspects, including disclosure, definition, and description of the invention, the potential costs of reverse engineering, the duration of protection, and the costs associated with acquiring and enforcing the IPR.

The goal of IP management should be to create a patent-protected thicket around core innovations. Building a patent portfolio specifically around core competencies enables firms to control target technological areas, boosting value by introducing new products/services related to it. Additionally, this tactic stops rivals from creating similar technologies. IP management plans patent filing as a tactic to gauge the market. Companies can anticipate new threats and spot trends by keeping an eye on and examining files that could have an impact on their industry. This might allow effective blocking tactics like defense patenting, in which businesses pursue IP in uncharted territory where alternatives might appear, or the competition might be moving. Where the most significant future innovations will be judged can be determined by analyzing patent filing activity. This might make it easier for IP management strategists to predict where their rivals might go. As can be seen from Figure 3, in the scope of "Your Guide to IP Commercialization" prepared by the European IPR Helpdesk, IP commercialization is divided into three categorizations (EC, 2019).

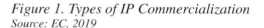

Figure 1. Types of IP Commercialization
Source: EC, 2019

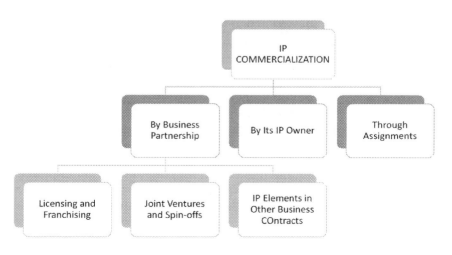

IP can be monetized by using various strategies to generate cash while taking advantage of its assets. These are the significant ways to monetize intellectual property:

- **Creating and selling goods and services that are covered by related IP:** Making money from the sale of goods and services that are created with or protected by IP.
- **IP Assigning (Selling):** IP assignment refers to the sale of IP assets to outside parties for the purpose of product development, production, and sale.
- **Licensing:** One of the most popular ways to profit from IP assets is through licensing. It grants consent to another party to use all or a portion of IP assets in exchange for payment within the parameters specified in the contract's scope.
- **Establishing a new legal entity (start-up, spin-off, or spin-out):** This step is used to commercialize IP assets by transforming them into goods or services.
- **Litigation**: Taking legal action against infringers to generate revenue.

VALUATION OF IPR

The quality of the intellectual assets and the commercialization strategy, which may involve transfer pricing, can both be decided upon through valuation. Potential investors and licensees could utilize this value to determine whether corporations such as start-ups and entrepreneurs have more valuable and long-lasting competitive advantages. It is more difficult than one might think to assign value to IP. It can be determined the worth of a company's inventory can be determined using accounting standards, which are typically defined and agreed upon internationally. Furthermore, there is a wealth of market information that may be used to determine the value of such tangible assets. In contrast, due to the variety of approaches available, intangible assets like intellectual assets are far more difficult to value. The calculation of value is not easy. While determining the value, it is expected that value consideration should embrace all necessary economic and technical aspects and risks.

Depending on the individual characteristics of the technology or its stage of development, these methods have diverse applications. Different valuation techniques used to estimate the value of IP are unavoidable, given various circumstances. Estimating the future economic value of IP in light of factors like the benefit period, market conditions, potential dangers, etc., is the primary goal of valuation. There are numerous approaches to valuing businesses and intellectual property. As shown in Figure 2, IP valuation techniques are divided into 2 main groups (ASEAN, 2019).

The most common approaches are:

- **Cost-Based Approach:** This approach analyzes and values every money spent on developing an IP asset. These expenses include direct costs that have an immediate impact on the IP asset, such as those related to consumables, infrastructure, capital, labor, and patent applications. This strategy could also take into account indirect costs like lost investment possibilities, potential profits, and the creation of similar IP assets. This method must take into account the IP asset's lifecycle while determining its value.
- **Income-Based Approach:** This approach is based on the idea that an IP asset's worth derives from the revenue it can create for its owner; the asset's value is equal to the estimated earnings it can provide (in the form of increased income or avoided costs) throughout its productive life.

The meaning of the productive life of the IP asset is the timing, and earnings are estimated. Using a rate that reflects the cost of capital return that has been modified for the riskiness of the future earnings stream, these earnings are discounted back to the asset acquisition date (ICC, 2019).

- **Market-Based Approach:** This approach is based on analyzing and contrasting commercialized IP that is related. It means that this approach compares the proposed price to the actual price paid for the transfer of rights to an equivalent intellectual property asset in a comparable setting (EC, 2020). This approach has the benefit of being straightforward and data-driven.

Figure 2. Types of Intellectual Property Valuation
Source: ASEAN, 2019

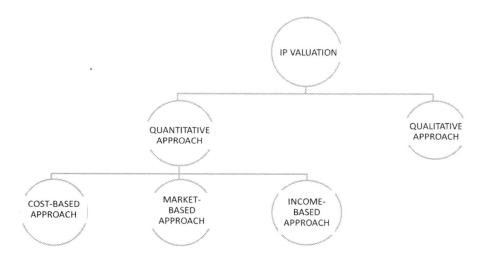

Choosing the best valuation strategy is challenging. However, by taking into account the following elements, the best course of action could be identified:

- The type of IPR
- Technology Readiness Level (TRL) of IPR
- IP development duration
- Target market knowledge
- Existing technologies/products/services in the target market
- Possible risks for IPR and target market
- The development of competitors' IPR portfolio
- Legal issues.

ENTREPRENEURIAL ECOSYSTEM AND THE RELATIONSHIP BETWEEN IPR AND ENTREPRENEURSHIP

The French term "entreprendre," which is the root of the English word "entrepreneur," meaning "to undertake." The entrepreneur has been defined differently by many people up until this point. For instance, Richard Contillon (1620–1734) places a strong emphasis on "risk" and characterizes the entrepreneur as someone who accepts the dangers in exchange for a particular sum of money. Entrepreneurship is defined by Joseph Schumpeter (1883–1955) as "innovation," with an emphasis on "innovation". An "entrepreneur" is a dynamic person who starts their own business to create economic value through expansion by spotting a fresh opportunity and taking any necessary risks.

Entrepreneurs do not develop services to solve only current problems and respond to current needs. Moreover, entrepreneurs anticipate the potential needs/problems of the future and act in the present with the expectation of future results. In this way, they invest in future results today by associating their current activities with potential future market expectations.

Entrepreneurship is the act or process of using talents to launch new enterprises, find business possibilities, ascertain current and/or potential problems/necessities, assemble the necessary resources, and establish a commercial activity while taking measured risks. Entrepreneurship contributes significantly to economic growth and is crucial for creating opportunities and improving the performance of new businesses. Entrepreneurship's impact varies from economy to economy and country to country based on its outputs, a nation's industrial and technological prowess, and its legislative framework for the development of entrepreneurs. Entrepreneurship is typically seen as a major force in advancing international markets. In order to produce jobs and spur economic growth - the foundation of a stable and civil society- entrepreneurship is important in national and global economies. As a result, several nations are attempting to encourage entrepreneurship by creating various support structures and tools.

The current entrepreneurial ecosystems vary greatly from one district to the next. Each entrepreneurial ecosystem has pillars in various locations worldwide; the functions, accessibility, and impacts of these pillars might vary depending on what the entrepreneurs, system, and government expect. There are no particular, one-to-one adaptive models of the entrepreneurial ecosystem that contain standards for success that apply to all structures. These pillars can be used to describe how each entrepreneurial ecosystem in the globe differs in terms of culture, politics, and depth. Building a successful entrepreneurial ecosystem requires a special process based on the region's structure, expectations, needs, and key skills.

As mentioned before, the term "property" has a fairly broad definition that encompasses both intangible rights that are viewed as a source or component of income or wealth as well as tangible things with a certain worth in monetary terms. Stuff like furniture, vehicles, clothing, products and other items that can be handled or moved are considered tangible property. Negotiable instruments, knowledge, securities, and other types of non-movable and non-touchable personal property are examples of intangible property. The scope of intellectual property law now includes intangible rights, which are protected and guaranteed by it. As a result, owners of intangible assets like books, discoveries, inventions, musical works, and designs, among others, now enjoy exclusive rights to those assets. Thus, the creation of inventions depends greatly on the success of intellectual property management.

Entrepreneurs with limited financial resources typically prefer to spend their limited resources on other activities instead of IPR, such as product/service development, human resources, etc. They frequently overlook the significance and impact of IP assets for entering the market, generating revenue from their ideas, and capturing a larger market share. Given that Intellectual Property (IP) is an intangible asset managing IP is one of the most important processes for all businesses, from small startups to established multinational corporations, in order to protect and/or increase the value of the organization, gain a competitive edge over rivals, and attract investment opportunities. IP management is concerned with the kinds of IP that help institutions maximize their plans. Patents cannot always be the best sort of protection, depending on the nature of the technology involved and the needs of the organizations.

Choosing the appropriate types of IP in accordance with the entrepreneur's needs and the nature of the technology involved is part of setting up a proper IP protection plan. The effects of developing strategic IP management by creating an IP portfolio for entrepreneurs could be summed up as below:

- having a legal monopoly.
- preventing competitors from entering the market.
- enabling owners to control target sectors by creating an exclusive market (market power).
- excluding competitors.
- adding value through new products and services linked to related technologies.
- preventing competition

Entrepreneurs use IP to organize their commercialization strategy, which may include entering the target market, granting licenses to third parties, and/or selling (through patent sales) their intellectual property. Businesses should use a variety of IPs to create the best possible portfolio while designing their strategy. For instance, an entrepreneur may decide to apply for a patent for protection depending on the nature of the developed technology and the costs associated with protection, or they may choose to protect the technology's know-how as a trade secret while taking into account potential issues with the trade secret protection.

In conclusion, some business owners prefer to protect their know-how through patent applications. In contrast, others prefer to keep the information a trade secret to avoid the fees and/or lack of knowledge associated with patents.

The following points can be used to explain which instances affect the preference of patent or trade secret protection:

- Cost-benefit analysis (cost of patent application versus income from commercialization)
- Technology basis (know-how-based or technology-based)
- Market positioning, commercialization, and/or investment plans.

There is not a single IP model that applies to all business owners. Entrepreneurs should integrate several kinds of IP into an ideal portfolio, which they continuously examine, given their capacity to consider their dynamic capabilities to compete in the target sector, rather than basing their IP competitive strategy on a single form of IP. Entrepreneurs should design their IP management strategy considering the lifecycle of the technology and the position it has in the company's IP stock. When determining the IP strategy, advantages and the approximate cost of the spectrum of IP should both be taken into account. Entrepreneurs should diversify their intellectual property portfolios to increase their market share. The IP portfolio is viewed as a "basket" of instruments that can be tailored to the specific technologies intended to commercialize by selling, licensing, etc.

If the technology is easily replicable, making a patent application can be counterproductive because it provides the technical details of the invention to copycats. There is always a risk that competitors will reverse engineer or re-adapt the invention and, in the worst-case scenario, reach the technical details of the patent, in which case the original inventor will face patent infringement. The patent application can be unappealing to innovators to protect intellectual assets due to high litigation costs and the uncertainty of effective enforcement (Leon & Donoso, 2018). The advantages of the patent, legal rights, and the technological status of the invention sought patent protection, and the entrepreneur's commercialization strategy should all be considered while establishing the best IP management strategy for the entrepreneur. A strong patent portfolio helps avoid litigation because a broader area of protection will reveal the infringement of others clearer. It also strengthens the patentee's negotiating position and increases the variety of the technology offered.

In a nutshell, each IP type plays a unique role and offers entrepreneurs unique chances to safeguard their intellectual property. It is thought that applying IP protection is important to take advantage of the laws in situations involving imitation, infringement, etc., as well as to evaluate the commercial value of the IP assets accurately.

ENTREPRENEURIAL ECOSYSTEM IN SMART CITIES

According to the United Nations (UN) report "*The World's Cities in 2018*", urban areas are expected to house 60% of the world's population by 2030, and one in three people will reside in cities with at least 500,000 residents (United Nations Digital Library, n.d.). When cities' resources and possibilities are considered, these numbers mean more demands, more needs, and more problems to be solved.

With the technological development and innovation, cities all over the world are staring to become "smart" (Manjon et al., 2021) which has many diverse definitions such as digital cities, intelligent cities, knowledge cities, sustainable cities, and ubiquitous cities are other names for smart cities (Ratten, 2017). For example, Achaerrondo et al. (2011, p. 1) defined smart cities as local entities with a comprehensive approach to the use of information and communication technologies, while European Commission (2014) defined smart cities as a place where traditional structures and services are made more efficient by using technology. However, while AMETIC (2012) includes the concept of "sustainable city" in addition to the expression technology in the definition of smart city, Richter et al. (2015, p. 214) used the keywords "creative citizens and institutions," "economic growth," "a high quality of life" in the definition of the smart city (Barba-Sánchez et al., 2019).

This situation shows that technological development and innovation is inevitable considering the increasing population, existing infrastructure, services offered to society, limited resources, the expected quality of life, and the city's ecological imprint. Although it differs from territory to territory, the existence of the concept of smart city and studies in this area are increasing day by day. The concept of smart cities covers existing and potential problems, developing technologies, and new demands. Therefore, creative thinking and high-tech solutions will play a crucial role, especially in building dynamic approaches while creating smart cities for the future, including all these issues. IoT (Internet of Things)-based solutions, goods, and services, as well as Information Technologies (IT), Artificial Intelligence (AI), block chain, and other next-generation technologies, will be crucial for the development of future smart cities as well as alternative revenue streams. Considering the financial and human resources available, the engagement of all these technologies will be possible not only with the knowledge, products, and services of existing companies but also with the start-ups established and to be established by today's creative and innovative people and potential entrepreneurs. Considering the important and critical problems faced by

Relationship Between Intellectual Property Rights and Entrepreneurial Ecosystems

cities such as ecological degradation, climate change, resource management, increasing population, and transportation, development and integration of innovative and disruptive solutions should be accelerated (Kuo et al., 2022) in the scope of "Smart Cities".

Although it varies from region to region with the effect of today's technological developments, interest in smart cities, research, and studies in this field are increasing day by day. The concept of smart cities includes many different disciplines. From this point of view, there will inevitably be different indicators that measure the performance of a smart city. Although various studies on indicators measure the performance of smart cities, these indicators can be grouped under eight main headings (Adiyarta et al., 2020):

- Smart Governance
- Smart Mobility
- Smart Economy
- Smart Infrastructure/Technology
- Smart Environment
- Smart People
- Smart Living
- Smart Energy

Smart mobility is one of the primary performance indicators of smart cities, which provides many advantages to users, stakeholders, and the environment. Mobility can be defined as the transfer of both people and things from one point to another point. Technological developments show themselves in the mobility sector as well as in many other industries. Mobility, which is changing cities daily, is open to engaging with technological development, such as IoT, big data, AI, etc., to create sustainable solutions within smart cities.

New and innovative solutions developed with new technologies are expected to meet the needs of citizens in the field of mobility, such as; assisting cars/motors in finding available parking spaces quickly without spending more time, establishing availability infrastructure for bike lanes, developing safe, walkable areas for pedestrians with digital applications, etc.

Technological developments in the field of mobility not only limit themselves to offering creative solutions and meeting needs but also create positive effects by reducing greenhouse gas emissions, ecological footprint and reducing damage to the environment and nature caused by mobility (Kuo et al., 2022). Considering the problems such as increasing population and consequently increasing the number of vehicles, limited infrastructure opportunities, inadequacy of transportation alternatives, etc., development of permanent and sustainable solutions in mobility is inevitable.

However, as future contributions are anticipated to offer distinctive and novel solutions, smart mobility blows past addressing current issues. In the upcoming years, smart mobility should emphasize the sustainability of the solutions created, active transportation, ecologically friendly fuels, and involvement of citizens. As a result, a wide range of affected characteristics, such as sustainability, economy, and living, directly affect people and government organizations (Paiva et al., 2021).

Start-ups and entrepreneurs are significant forces behind innovation and the advancement of technologies. The main goal of an entrepreneurial ecosystem in a smart cities should be to promote entrepreneurship and assist early-stage businesses through knowledge sharing and a comprehensive hand-holding procedure that includes services and infrastructure for knowledge for start-ups in smart cities.

One opportunity to unleash innovation and entrepreneurship is through smart city programs, which can be used in both wealthy and developing nations. In smart cities, the emergence of the entrepreneurial ecosystem is still in its infancy (Mitra et al., 2022). Entrepreneurs should be encouraged to:

- Recognize impactful and sustainable opportunities within smart cities.
- Develop new framework in order to address current city policies and future challenges for smart cities.
- Enhance creative solutions for smart cities through knowledge of the city and digital framework.

Additionally, the entrepreneurial ecosystem in smart cities should assist and direct entrepreneurs to concentrate on creative solutions that will be transformed into prosperous, long-lasting and economically viable outputs. The development of smart cities depends on the utilization of technology and entrepreneurial ecosystems. Entrepreneurs create innovative solutions/products/services to build a social, economic, and environmental future of a smart city that has well-planned connectivity, technology setups, electric vehicles, bicycles, a multimodal transportation system, urban laboratories, renewable energy resources, and public-private partnerships. While digital technologies play a transformational role in facilitating new business opportunities for entrepreneurs (Mitra et al., 2022). According to ABI Research named *"Role of Smart Cities for Economic Development"*, it is estimated that global Gross Domestic Product (GDP) is expected to reach US\$100 trillion by 2026, and 68% of GDP will be generated by cities (Bonte, 2018). Considering the GDP that smart cities can create, it is very clear that entrepreneurship and the impact of entrepreneurship should not be ignored.

For the cities that offer the opportunity to produce knowledge, transform the produced knowledge into a product/service, test and use this output for people; companies, NGOs, and government organizations act as a bridge that brings different disciplines and structures together. The influence of these actors is inevitable in transforming cities into smart ones. Therefore, cities are crucial structures that host a nation's innovation capability for creating and meeting demands. They accumulate the expected scientific level, investment knowledge abilities, and capacities of technological improvements of the nation (Wong et al., 2017). From this point of view, cities serve as both the final beneficiaries of the generated result and essential source providers of information, particularly for entrepreneurs and start-ups engaged in the development of new technologies.

Some examples of start-ups listed within the EIT Urban Mobility Start-up portfolio develop solutions in mobility sectors. EIT Urban Mobility, established in 2019, is an initiative of the European Institute of Innovation and Technology (EIT). The aim of EIT Urban Mobility is to create positive changes in cities by changing people's behaviors to build more livable places:

- Auvetech is an Estonian company that aims to create an autonomous shuttle from scratch. After completing the prototype in just a year, they continued to develop the shuttles. They have demonstrated their functionality in a variety of use cases for providing secure and environmentally friendly last-mile transportation solution (https://auve.tech/).
- ZenParking has put into place a smart reservation system with automatic payment through a smartphone app and an on-site hardware device that they created (https://zenparking.ro/).
- A Turkish company called Optiyol created a B2B software system that assists carriers and retailers in optimizing logistics from planning with cutting-edge algorithms through execution with driver apps (https://www.optiyol.com/).

IPR IN SMART CITIES

Every day, the movement of both people and things increases exponentially. Given the rise in global population, rapid technological advancement, and resource depletion, this growth brings challenges that jeopardize social and economic improvement as well as long-term development. Consequently, cities face increased population growth and must implement smart solutions to become more resilient to ongoing urbanization's economic, environmental, and social challenges.

As previously stated, according to the United Nations (UN) report *"The World's Cities in 2018"*, urban areas are expected to house 60% of the world's population by 2030, and one in three people will reside in cities with at least 500,000 residents (United Nations Digital Library, n.d.). When cities' resources and possibilities are considered, these numbers mean more demands, more needs, and more problems to be solved. Given the increase in population, migration from rural to urban areas, mobility of people and goods, existing city structures, and the inadequacy of cities to meet expected needs draws attention.

At this point, it is critical to use emerging technologies such as innovative information and communication technologies (ICT) and the Internet of Things (IoT) in the development of future smart cities. The first steps to be taken at this stage are to encourage people to contribute to the creation of smart cities of the future, to enable them to play an active role in the development and use of technology, and to ensure their integration into the process.

IPR has a central role as the regulatory backbone of modern innovation policies since the beginning of the digital revolution. One of the primary reasons for its growing importance is to address issues of knowledge and information protection in all forms, as well as risky investments.

For economic expansion and development, as well as industry competitiveness, innovation and technical progress are essential. It can be agreed that technological advancement and innovation promote productivity, one of the primary drivers of growth in both developed and developing countries, by enabling more effective use of labor and capital inputs. Regions and nations compete with one another to entice and keep those parts of the global value chains that generate the most wealth and employment. Policies aimed at boosting the scientific and technological competitiveness of economies must rely on a wide range of science, technology, and innovation indicators reflecting increasingly complex innovation systems in an era of growing globalization and interdependence of knowledge generation and its exploitation.

Indeed, historically, the global landscape of investment in science and technology, as well as education and human capital, has seen significant positive shifts. Carrying out R&D activities and having a large budget for these activities has become a common goal for all countries today. The process of transforming the outputs obtained as a result of all these efforts into economic and social value also marks intellectual rights.

The development of smart cities and the conversion of current cities into smart cities depend heavily on the presence of a strong innovation culture, a population that is technologically literate, and the presence of systems that promote original thought and sustainability. In the report titled "Smart Cities: Digital Solutions for a More Livable Future," McKinsey Global Institute (MGI) (Woetzel et al., 2022) prepared a matrix which has been designed by considering all technologies and application areas to make future Smart cities a reality. This framework states that by 2025, it is expected to focus on more than 50 smart applications under the headings of Security, Healthcare, Mobility, Energy, Water, Waste, Economic Development and Housing, and Engagement and Community. As mentioned in every title, it is expected that many smart applications, such as Real-time public transit information, digital public transit payment, smart parking, integrated multimodal information, etc., will be developed in the field of

Mobility. There are many products/services that are expected to be developed for the smart cities of the future, and also for engagement of technology needs with newly-developed outputs. In this context, the development of a robust entrepreneurial ecosystem and IP policy will play a critical role in the development and implementation of these innovative solutions that smart cities will need.

. A comfortable and smart transportation alternative that will make people to give up driving, will improve people's living conditions while minimizing environmental harm. This necessitates having access to a wide range of affordable, easily accessible alternative transportation options. Future smart cities will only be able to promote green public transportation if technology infrastructure is in place to enable it.

Because of this, growing the number of entrepreneurs and established businesses in this industry would help it produce fresh concepts and solutions. At this point, IPR is also a crucial tool for generating the dedication, cooperation, and finance necessary to fuel ideas, invention, and innovation in building future smart cities and integrating technology into daily life.

According to EPO Patent Index 2021, total patent applications at the European Patent Office increased by 4.5% when compared with previous year. The "transport" section includes vehicles, and more specifically, vehicle tyres, wheels, windows and roofs, and railway systems.

The data provided by the "*Global Innovation Index 2018*" regarding the total number of patent families in green energy technologies between 2005 and 2015 is shown in Figure 3 (Dutta, et. al, 2018). Figure 4 also shows the patent applications made for each subject within the scope of green transportation technologies (Leon, et. al, 2017).

Figure 3. Total Number of Patent Families in Green Energy Technologies, 2005–2015
Source: Global innovation index 2018

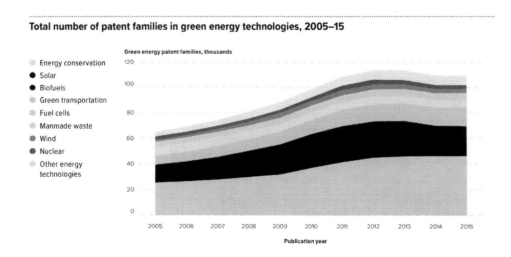

Figure 4. Patent filings in green transportation technologies
Source: Leon et al., 2017

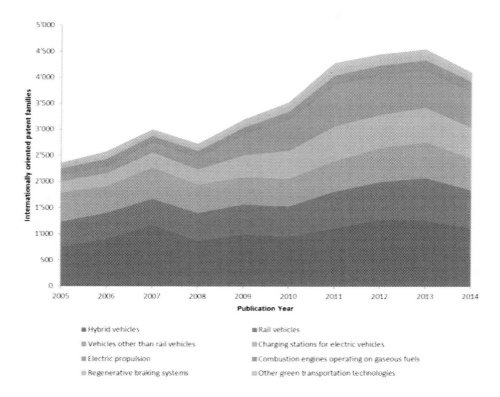

DISCUSSION AND CONCLUSION

The rapid technological changes in our age force people, companies, governmental bodies, non-governmental organizations, and even the areas we live in, to change. This change and the adaptation process to this change not only offer solutions to existing problems but also cause different problems to arise. Existing issues and solutions to new situations and needs that may occur are also hidden in technological developments. To develop solutions and offer products and services that can meet needs, not only the knowledge and experience of existing structures are sufficient, but also new structures and people who will produce creative outputs are needed.

Cities with different disciplines and structures together take their place in this journey and take steps to become "smart" by leaving their traditional forms. At this point, the existence of IPR will play an active role in the protection of entrepreneurship, the entrepreneurship ecosystem, and the outputs produced and to be produced in this ecosystem.

It is only possible for people, companies, governmental bodies, and even countries to gain an advantage in today's economic conditions and to open the doors of development only by following technological developments and even being a pioneer in this field.

It is necessary to establish common platforms for developing new products and services using technology and to encourage people and institutions to participate in this system. Strengthening the entrepreneurial ecosystem, whose impact is increasing rapidly, especially in today's economy, plays a key role. One of the many mechanisms necessary to maintain this ecosystem is IPR and the policies to be developed accordingly. In particular, a robust IPR system and procedure are essential in transforming inventors' and creators' innovative and creative solutions into economic value and social benefit. Although IPR offer an exclusive right to the owner, they also form the basis for accelerating technological developments by inspiring new products and services.

REFERENCES

Adiyarta, K., Napitupulu, D., Syafrullah, M., Mahdiana, D., & Rusdah, R. (2020). Analysis of smart city indicators based on prisma: Systematic review. *IOP Conference Series. Materials Science and Engineering*, *725*(1), 012113.

Barba-Sánchez, V., Arias-Antúnez, E., & Orozco-Barbosa, L. (2019). Smart cities as a source for entrepreneurial opportunities: Evidence for Spain. *Technological Forecasting and Social Change*, *148*, 119713. doi:10.1016/j.techfore.2019.119713

Bonte, D. (2018). *Role of smart cities for economic development*. ABI Research.

Dutta, S., Lanvin, B., & Wunsch-Vincent, S. (Eds.). (2018). *The global innovation index 2018: Energizing the world with innovation*. WIPO.

European Commission (EC). (2019). *Your guide to IP commercialisation*. Executive Agency for Small and Medium-sized Enterprises. Retrieved December 6, 2022, from https://op.europa.eu/en/publication-detail/-/publication/a75b3213-ebf4-11e9-9c4e-01aa75ed71a1/language-en/format-PDF/source-search

European Commission (EC). (2019). *Your Guide to IP in Europe*. Executive Agency for Small and Medium-sized Enterprises. Retrieved December 6, 2022, from https://op.europa.eu/en/publication-detail/-/publication/ddf8fb93-ec0e-11e9-9c4e-01aa75ed71a1/language-en/format-PDF/source-164620483

European Commission (EC). (2020). *European IP Helpdesk: Your guide to IP management in International Business*. Executive Agency for Small and Medium-sized Enterprises. Retrieved December 6, 2022, from https://op.europa.eu/en/publication-detail/-/publication/bb7327c0-12a2-11eb-9a54-01aa75ed71a1/language-en/format-PDF/source-188386935

Halt, G. B., Donch, J. C., Stiles, A. R., & Fesnak, R. (2017). *Intellectual property and financing strategies for technology startups*. Springer.

Halt, G. B., Donch, J. C., Stiles, A. R., & Robert, F. (2014). *Intellectual property in consumer electronics, software and technology startups*. Springer. doi:10.1007/978-1-4614-7912-3

International Chamber of Commerce (ICC). (2019). *Handbook on Valuation of Intellectual Property Assets*. Retrieved December 6, 2022, from https://iccwbo.org/publication/icc-handbook-valuation-intellectual-property-assets/

Kuo, N.-W., Sharifi, A., & Li, C.-E. (2022). Smart Cities and Urban Resilience: Insights from a delphi survey. *The Urban Book Series*, 119–138. doi:10.1007/978-3-030-95037-8_6

Leon, I. D., & Donoso, J. F. (2018). *Innovation, startups and Intellectual Property Management Strategies and evidence from Latin America and other regions*. Springer International Publishing.

León, L. R., Bergquist, K., Wunsch-Vincent, S., Xu, N., & Fushimi, K. (2017). *Measuring innovation in energy technologies: green patents as captured by WIPO's IPC green inventory* (Vol. 44). WIPO.

Manjon, M., Aouni, Z., & Crutzen, N. (2021). Green and Digital Entrepreneurship in smart cities. *The Annals of Regional Science*, *68*(2), 429–462. doi:10.100700168-021-01080-z

Mitra, S., Kumar, H., Gupta, M. P., & Bhattacharya, J. (2022). Entrepreneurship in smart cities: Elements of start-up Ecosystem. *Journal of Science and Technology Policy Management*. doi:10.1108/JSTPM-06-2021-0078

Paiva, S., Ahad, M., Tripathi, G., Feroz, N., & Casalino, G. (2021). Enabling Technologies for Urban Smart Mobility: Recent trends, opportunities and challenges. *Sensors (Basel)*, *21*(6), 2143. doi:10.339021062143 PMID:33803903

Ratten, V. (2017). *Entrepreneurship, innovation and smart cities*. Routledge.

The Association of Southeast Asian Nations (ASEAN). (2019). *Handbook on IP Commercialisation Strategies for Managing IPRS and Maximising Value*. Retrieved December 4, 2022, from https://aanzfta.asean.org/uploads/2020/12/IPPEA-FINAL-HANDBOOK-ON-IP-COMMERCIALISATION.pdf

United Nations digital Library. (n.d.). *The World's cities in 2018*. Retrieved December 4, 2022, from https://digitallibrary.un.org/record/3799524

Woetzel, J., Remes, J., Boland, B., Lv, K., Sinha, S., Strube, G., Means, J., Law, J., Cadena, A., & von der Tann, V. (2022, September 7). *Smart cities: Digital Solutions for a more Livable Future*. McKinsey & Company. Retrieved December 4, 2022, from https://www.mckinsey.com/capabilities/operations/our-insights/smart-cities-digital-solutions-for-a-more-livable-future

Wong, C.-Y., Ng, B.-K., Azizan, S. A., & Hasbullah, M. (2017). Knowledge structures of City Innovation Systems: Singapore and Hong Kong. *Journal of Urban Technology*, *25*(1), 47–73. https://doi.org/10.1080/10630732.2017.1348882

World Intellectual Property Organization (WIPO). (n.d.). Retrieved December 4, 2022, from https://www.wipo.int/patents/en/topics/integrated_circuits.html

World Trade Organization (WTO). (n.d.). Retrieved December 4, 2022, from https://www.wto.org/english/tratop_e/trips_e/intel2_e.htm#patents

KEY TERMS AND DEFINITIONS

European Patent Office (EPO): People, who discover new products/processes, can apply for a patent to protect their idea in up to 44 nations using a unified application process provided by the European Patent Office.

European Institute of Innovation and Technology (EIT): EIT, an independent organization, aims to improve Europe's potential for innovation by encouraging entrepreneurial talent and advancing new ideas.

International Patent Classification (IPC): IPC, which is a hierarchical system of language-independent symbols, provides to classify patents and utility models according to technological areas to which they relate.

Intellectual Property (IP): IP, which is an output of intellectual capability and labour, is another class of property based on human intellect's activities.

Intellectual Property Rights (IPR): IPR is the rights to use, sell and produce the output of the creations of the mind such as inventions, literary and artistic works, etc.

Small and Medium-Sized Enterprises (SMEs): SMEs have less than 250 employees, a balance sheet total under €43 million, and a turnover under €50 million.

Technology Readiness Level (TRL): Technology readiness level (TRL) is a method of measuring the maturity of technologies.

Chapter 16
A Walking–Friendly Environment?
How to Measure It

Silvia Golem

(iD) https://orcid.org/0000-0002-1635-1302

Faculty of Economics, Business, and Tourism, University of Split, Croatia

ABSTRACT

One of the main aims of the smart city paradigm is to reduce the environmental footprint of urban growth by managing the urban mobility in a citizen-friendly way. Facilitating and encouraging citizens to walk is a way to make the modern form of urban mobility greener and safer. Evidence of the benefits of walking and walkable urban forms has appeared in different strands of literature, suggesting the multidisciplinary nature of it. The main aim of this chapter is to document and review the existing measures of urban walkability, along with the relevant cases where the attempts to measure walkability were made, thereby contributing a wider literature which aims to identify and understand factors that are most relevant for urban walkers.

INTRODUCTION

In the last decade, there has been a significant paradigm shift in the area of urban planning and urban mobility from car-oriented towards pedestrian- or people-oriented urban design. In the last half of the twenty century cities were planned and design around motorized vehicular modes of mobility, with cars dominating many urban landscapes. Automobility as a trend, particularly in the period after World War II, as pointed out by Jamei et al. (2021), was promoted by a rapid population growth, and increasing urbanisation rates. In addition, necessity of a car in people's daily lives and a consequential "car-oriented" urban design was accelerated by the process of urban sprawl, that is, decentralization of urban services and housing at the edge of cities. On the other hand, urban planners and decision-makers disregarded the importance of sustainable and active modes of urban transportation (Hynes, 2022). The pervasive

DOI: 10.4018/978-1-6684-5996-6.ch016

usage of private cars has many obvious negative impacts on the environmental, social and economic levels for the society (Dobesova & Krivka, 2012); it contributes to urban traffic congestion, noise and air pollution; consumes disproportionate amounts of scarce public space (Gehl, 2010), that could have otherwise been allocated to pedestrians and public activities, and requires high investments in infrastructure for motorised vehicles. It also leads to "a disconnection in and between local communities and an increase in urban decay" (Kay 1998, in Hynes, 2022). The most profound negative consequences of such persistent automotive use are related to reduction of physical activity in general, and walking in particular. With the proliferation and globalisation of car-oriented urban design, many cities around the world have experienced a significant decrease in walking activities of their citizens. Recent developments and practices, however, show that urban planners and local governments throughout the world make active efforts to reverse such trends, drawing on the literature that widely acknowledges the benefits of low-intensity physical activity, such as walking. Walking not only has a direct positive effect on people's health and welfare, but also, indirectly, through the external effects, it reduces greenhouse gas emissions, noise, traffic congestion, etc. On a personal level, as pointed out by Hollenstein & Bleisch (2016), walking contributes to longevity and good health. Additionally, as pointed out by Singh (2016), walking may increase "individual peace of mind, community trust and decrease crime rates by supporting face-to-face contacts and community networks". According to Liu et al. (2022), people who make 9994.3 and more steps per day have a 75% lower risk of all-cause death than those who walk less than 1895 steps per day. On a societal level, walkability contributes to environmental sustainability by reducing the greenhouse gas emissions, air and noise pollution. In addition, walking improves social equity by benefiting low-income residents who depend on this type of urban mobility for their daily trips (Jamei et al., 2021). A great share of people, particularly in densely populated and underdeveloped countries and cities, still depend on walking and cycling. Across African cities, for instance, 50% of daily trips are made on foot (Wood, 2022). As pointed out by Kang (2018), walking is "the most democratic method of mobility", as it allows access to essential services and, consequently, greater equality in the use of these services. Among other benefits related to promoting active modes of urban mobility such as walking and cycling, Pérez et al. (2017) point to significant economic benefits resulting from the prevented deaths due to changes in the amount of walking and cycling in the case of Barcelona. Namely, by employing the Health Economic Assessment Tool (HEAT), they demonstrate that changes in transport policies in Barcelona introduced to increase pedestrian-friendly areas, and to reduce car usage have contributed to health and environment wellbeing, while not increasing the number of pedestrian nor cyclist traffic injuries.

To emphasise the economic benefits related to active modes of mobility in comparison to automobility, Gössling et al. (2019) calculate total, that is, both the external and private costs of automobility, cycling and walking in the European Union. Their findings show that the annual cost of automobility is about €500 billion. On the other hand, due to positive health effects related to it, cycling produces an external annual benefit of €24 billion and walking €66 billion, respectively. Given that transport investment projects in the EU commonly fail to include the full extent of the negative externalities related to automobility, they systematically underestimate the cost of it, leading to biased cost-benefit project assessments.

Local governments and urban planners can improve the quality of urban life through active efforts, public policies and instruments that increase and facilitate the walking-related amenities. The actual changes in peoples' mobility choices and behaviours, can be achieved not only by the pedestrian-oriented infrastructure investments, but also by the active programs and initiatives oriented towards changing the prevalent mentality of car-dependence and encouraging a culture of walking. Within that context, it is

A Walking-Friendly Environment?

not surprising that many modern cities nowadays go through a transformation that puts active modes of mobility - walking and cycling - at the centre of urban design. The alternation of the predominate car-oriented paradigm in the context of urban mobility, however, is a complex issue (Dobesova & Krivka, 2012). Given that the urban mobility has been highly dependent on the private cars for such a long time it is a challenging task for decision-makers and urban designers to produce a shift in trend from the car-oriented towards pedestrian-oriented urban mobility design. In addition, some factors that are crucial for walkability, such as pedestrian-related infrastructure, neighbourhood design and morphological conditions which are products of urban design, are highly resistant and require a long time to change.

METRICS FOR WALKABILITY

As to motivate citizens to engage more in the active modes of urban mobility and to create pedestrian-friendly spaces and mobility networks, for urban planners and local governments it is essential to identify, understand and assess the most significant factors that affect people's mobility choices. In that light, it is important to understand how the concept of walkability is defined. Given the inherent multidimensionality, the concept of walkability is rather difficult to define and measure (Dovey and Pafka, 2020). Most researchers agree that the concept of walkability is closely related to the built environment characteristics which shape the pedestrian space and influence people's mobility choices. An inadequate and underdeveloped pedestrian infrastructure may discourage people from undertaking walking activities. On the other hand, by providing safety, connectivity to main urban services and destinations, as well as comfort and pleasure, the built environment directly affects citizens' walking activities. In that regard, walkability can be defined as "the extent to which the built environment supports and encourages safe, comfortable and interesting urban walking trips" (Tsiompras & Photis, 2017), offering a high level of accessibility and connectivity to destinations, and visual interest within walking distance (Forsyth, 2015). In simple terms, walkability is "the measure of how walking-friendly an area is" (Hynes, 2022). There have been various attempts in the literature to identify the most important pedestrian-related factors of walkability, including physical features, urban design qualities and subjective perceptions.

Using a meta-analysis, Anapakula & Eranki (2021) identify the overlapping dimensions of pedestrian environment factors that have been marked as important for the walking behaviour in the relevant literature over the years. Most studies recognise safety and security as the most important pedestrian-related factors, which is quite reasonable given that pedestrians are most vulnerable road users. Other identified factors considered to affect the walking activities are convenience, comfort, system coherence and attractiveness. Lo (2009) summarises factors of different walkability indices that are commonly identified in the literature as "the most important for the quality of the pedestrian environment, and consequently the frequency of the walking activities:

- Presence of continuous and well-maintained sidewalks
- Universal access characteristics
- Path directness and street network connectivity
- Safety of at-grade crossing treatments
- Absence of heavy and high-speed traffic
- Pedestrian separation or buffering from traffic
- Land-use density

- Building and land-use diversity or mix
- Street trees and landscaping
- Visual interest and a sense of place as defined under local conditions
- Perceived or actual security".

Over the last years two decades, different approaches and methods have been developed to objectively assess and compare walkability levels. Different measures of the built environment and/or perceived levels of walkability are constructed and combined into composite indices that is, various walkability indicators (Hollenstein & Bleisch, 2016). Since there is no agreement on a standardized set of measures to be included in those indices (Weiss et al., 2010) it still remains, however, quite challenging to objectively measure all characteristics of the built environment and of other elements that affect walkability and, more importantly, walking. Nonetheless, as pointed by Jardim & de Castro Neto (2022), walkability indicators are an efficient supportive tool used by decision-makers and urban planners.

Rooted in the writings of Jane Jacobs, Dovey and Pafka (2020) start from the proposition that the concept of walkability should not be derived from the actual levels of walking, but from the long-term morphological conditions of a given neighbourhood. The underlying idea is that the urban DMA - density, mix, access - are key factors in determining walkability. Namely, density concentrates more people and attractions within walkable distances, mix produces a greater range of functional amenities within walkable destinations, while access networks facilitate flows of people. While density and land-use mix are important factors of the built that affect the walking behaviour, Vale et al. (2016) focus on measuring accessibility, or active accessibility - "the ability of a person to reach a place by walking or cycling". In general terms, accessibility is "the ability to reach relevant activities, individuals or opportunities, which might require traveling to the place where those opportunities are located" (Handy, 2005). If a person is not able to reach a desired place by the active modes of mobility within a reasonable time frame, that will reduce the likelihood of walking or cycling. Of all the distracting features of the walking environment, "places being too far away" has the most discouraging effect on walking (Ariffin & Zahari, 2013). In the same light, De Vos et al. (2022) emphasize the importance of accessibility; in fact, they define walkability as "a mode-specific type of accessibility referring to how easy it is to walk (to destinations)".

Given that spatiality is one of the defining dimensions of the above mentioned elements of walkability, a relatively widely used approach to develop walkability indices is to employ Geographic Information Systems (GIS). Based on the available data, as described by Hollenstein & Bleisch (2016), GIS-based walkability indices are directed mostly towards measuring the urban DMA elements - network design, density, land use mix diversity, and access to various destinations - and are computed mainly at the granularity of neighbourhoods or census blocks. Among the indices that measure walkable access to amenities within walking distance, Walk Score index has been widely used in the walkability studies. In fact, according to Koschinsky et al. (2016), Walk Score index "has gained enormous popularity as the main indicator of how walkable a neighbourhood is since the Walkscore.com was founded in 2007". The Walk Score index assesses the "walking potential" of a place by connecting distance accessibility (a gravity-based measure) with topological accessibility (street connectivity). It ranges from 0 to 100, where scores from 0 to 24 indicate highly car-dependent area, from 25 to 49 somewhat car-dependent area with some amenities within walking distance, from 50 to 69 somewhat walkable area, from 70 to 89 very walkable area with many amenities within walking distance, and from 90 to 100 area that do not require use of cars for daily errands. Hall & Ram (2018) provide a thorough review of the studies that use the Walk Score index to measure walkability and conclude that the index is used rather inconsistently in

A Walking-Friendly Environment?

the literature and should be taken only as "a surrogate measure of the density of the built environment of a specific neighbourhood that indicates utilitarian walking potential". By comparing Walk Scores to qualitative dimensions of walkability for several neighbourhoods in the Washington, DC., Koschinsky et al. (2016) test how good a proxy for the quality of the walking environment Walk Score really is and whether the proxy's effectiveness varies between richer and poorer neighbourhoods. They conclude that Walk Score's walkable access measure is not equally strong across all neighbourhoods, rendering the issue of different quality of the walking environment in high- and low-income neighbourhoods untreated. As for the future venues for the quantitative evaluation of walkability, new and promising technologies, such as deep convolutional neural networks in training datasets of georeferenced street-level images, deep-learning, sensor-network in combination with GIS, have been developed (Li et al., 2023). It should be emphasised, however, that the physical features of walkability or the spatial factors alone do not capture people's overall perceptions of the walkable environment. In that light, Shields et al. (2021) point out that the term walkability embraces more than the mere pedestrian accessibility and physical morphology. It also includes intangibles and subjective perceptions, such as a person's sense of the traffic safety and preference of certain routes or streets. Undertaking a qualitative approach to investigate the perceived walkability, Fonseca et al. (2022) highlight that the qualitative studies are an important input into resolving the walkability puzzle. It may be the case that an area with high objective walkability is not perceived as pedestrian-friendly by people. As pointed by Koschinsky et al. (2016), "walkable access to amenities, walkability and walking do not always align". In the same light, De Vos et al. (2022) point out that the perceived walkability rather than the objective features, such as the built environment, might have a stronger influence of the (non)walking decisions and behaviours. Even if there are many, easily accessible amenities within the walking distance, due to some negative perceived features of the walking environment, such as unsafe sidewalks and traffic, unpleasant weather, or air pollution and alike, people may restrain from walking. In the recent study, De Vos et al. (2022) propose a new, user-friendly indicator of perceived walkability; namely, perceived walkability scale (SPWS) - a simple scale that asks respondents to indicate how strongly they resonate with the statements that in their neighbourhood, it is feasible/convenient/comfortable/pleasant/ to walk to their destinations/to public transport stops/ recreationally, and whether their neighbourhood stimulates them to walk to their destinations/ to public transport stops/recreationally. Arellana et al. (2020) label the variables that are drawn from pedestrians' perceptions as subjective "micro-scale" factors. Those micro-scale variables, such as "zebra crossings, quality of sidewalks, benches, presence of green, etc." remain mainly unmeasured and underexplored as elements of walkability (De Vos et al., 2022). Those intangible, subjective elements, however, are still inadequately measured and taken into account in walkability studies. Blečić et al. (2016) summarise five "direct, on-street survey methods that have been use in the literature to collect data on the peoples' perceptions of walkability:

- observational method, evaluating the pedestrian level of service (LOS) based on in-situ observation of pedestrian behaviour (pedestrian density, pedestrian flow rate, walking speed, etc.);
- intercept survey, interviewing pedestrians after they have traversed a crosswalk at intersection or a street segment and asking them to grade the crossing or the segment;
- contingent field survey (CFS), involves subjects walking along routes and instructed to grade each crosswalk or street segments immediately after they have traversed the intersection or the street;

- controlled field valuation (CFV) involves taking subjects to different intersections and letting surveyors observe and then grade the crosswalk without actually undertake the crossing; usually used for intersections, this method can also be adapted for the street segments;
- laboratory/simulation studies (LSS) involve subjects observing and evaluating a representation of the pedestrian environment; simulations may comprise various techniques to describe, represent and visualize the walking environment, from 3D renderings, to photographs and photomontages, to video clips".

As pointed out by Tsiompras & Photis (2017), it seems that walkability mostly remains a relative composite measure - composed of both objective/quantifiable/built environment characteristics which can be geo-visualized and measured mainly by the GIS-based tools, and subjective perceptions of pedestrians that are extracted through audits and surveys. Employing a mixed qualitative and quantitative research design, for instance, Ewing & Handy (2009) identify the five urban design qualities and corresponding physical features of the streetscape that are important for explaining the walking behaviour; namely, imageability, enclosure, human scale, transparency and complexity. In the first part of the study, in a laboratory setting, they recruited a panel of ten urban design and planning experts. Video clips of streetscape were used to help the experts to define and rate the urban design qualities that, according to their specialised expertise, might have an influence on the walkability activities. In the second part of the study, employing a statistical analysis, they test the actual level of significance of the identified physical features of streetscape in affecting the walking behaviour.

It should be noted that, while the main focus in the literature on walkability is on how pedestrian-friendly the built environment is and how pedestrians perceive walkable-friendly routes and neighbourhoods, walkability has been addressed from various perspectives in the literature. There is also a strand of literature that focuses on macro-level features of the urban form (Shields et al., 2021). Forsyth (2015) also mentions the studies which focus on the outcomes of walkable environments, such as making places lively and sociable, enhancing transportation options, or inducing exercise, and those which use the term walkability as a proxy for better urban places. From that perspective, the literature on the future cities quite often includes and refers to walkable cities, with the focus being placed on slow and active modalities of urban mobility, public spaces, creativity, liveable neighbourhoods, face-to-face contacts and accessible amenities. Hynes (2022), for instance, uses an autoethnography approach to investigate urban walkability in the context of Galway, Ireland. By "experiencing" his own walk to work, Hynes (2022) looks through the eyes, or metaphorically, shoes of the city residents and comments on the crucial features of walkability that policy-makers could improve to encourage and increase the walking activates.

LITERATURE REVIEW

Literature review first starts with an overview of the studies that mainly use qualitative approaches to focus on subjective elements of walkability, and proceeds with the studies that use a mixed method approach to construct/use a composite indicator of walkability.

Drawing on policies and projects related to walkability in Johannesburg, Wood (2022) conducts interviews with architects, consultants, politicians, and urban planners between 2012 and 2020, to explain why, despite the local government's efforts, walkability in this city still fails to take root. The main findings of the study show that the main problem is in the fact that the focus is on "the glitzy infrastructure", and

A Walking-Friendly Environment?

not on the pedestrians who actually use the infrastructure. Fonseca et al. (2022) also employ a qualitative approach to evaluate perceived walkability in the cities of Bologna and Porto. Using a questionnaire, they investigate the respondents' perceptions of 19 built environment and streetscape attributes. The results obtained by the exploratory factor analysis revealed the four significant walkability determinants: urban ambiance (land use and street design attributes: land use mix, enclosure, transparency, and architectural and landscape diversity); pedestrian infrastructure (sidewalk conditions, street connectivity, and proximity to community facilities); and access to other modes of transport. Interestingly, some attributes that are considered important in literature, such as traffic safety and security, were not correlated with perceived walkability in both cities. Using a combination of walkability audits and a survey-based questionnaire, Ariffin & Zahari (2013) investigate the residents' perceptions of urban walking environment in several neighbourhoods in the Klang Valley, Malesia. Their findings suggest that the most important elements of the walking environment, as perceived by the respondents, are proximity of destinations, good weather condition, safety and well-designed pedestrian facilities. In order to identify the factors that contribute to increased urban walkability in Mehrauli in New Delhi, India, Sigh (2015) uses a combination of mostly qualitative methods, that is, the observation method, activity mapping and the anthropological approach to collect and analyse the data related to walking behaviour and walkability perception. The findings indicate that the most important factors that influence pedestrians' perception of a walkable neighbourhood are the built envelop on either side of the streets, enclosure, block length and edge conditions.

Tsiompras & Photis (2017) construct a weighted GIS-based composite walkability index, through two phases. The initial value of their index includes population density, pathway network connectivity, land use mix and proximity to basic land uses, while in the second phase, the authors take account of pathway characteristics (width, obstacles and condition). To arrive to the appropriate weights allocated to different parameters of the index, the author conducted a survey on 871 people who used walking and cycling as a preferred modality of mobility to reach their daily destinations. The respondents were asked to indicate the perceived significance of each of the walkability index's parameters and sub-parameters. Proximity to basic urban destinations proved to have the highest weight, while population density was assigned the lowest. In terms of the policy implications, this finding suggests that the diversity of land uses is a prerequisite for a high walkable urban districts.

In three Norwegian cities, Knapskog et al. (2019) assess walkability using a mixed method approach to measure walkability at neighbourhood-scale in four nodes. To assess walkability without the GIS support, they use data from the existing data sources, fieldwork, and interviews. Arellana et al. (2020) develop a composite walkability index for a medium-size Latin American city - Barranquilla, Colombia. Their walkability index is composed of both meso-scale variables/objective attributes such as: sidewalk conditions, traffic safety and security from crime, comfort, and attractiveness, as well as micro-scale variables/pedestrians' perceptions. A rank perception survey with 340 residents was used to construct the latter variables. In addition, their walkability index is a weighted one, that is, the authors used discrete choice models to obtain different weights for each of the above mentioned components. The results indicate that security and traffic safety are the most important factors that influence walkability, which in contrast to many studies that find sidewalk conditions and attractiveness to be the most important influencing factors.

Xia et al. (2018) develop and implement an integrated walkability measurement model that takes into consideration residents' usage characteristics of amenities in the city of Nanjing, China. In particular, using a questionnaire on the usage of public amenities in their everyday life, the authors focused on the walk travel characteristics of residents, divided into usage frequency, selection diversity and distance decay effect. Employing an exploratory spatial data analysis, they further analysed the spatial patterns of the walkability score. In general, their findings indicate great spatial inequalities in the walkability score between different residential areas in Nanjing. Namely; the walkability scores between different residential areas differs greatly, while residential areas with highest walkability scores are clustered mostly in the central regions. In addition, the authors employ the hedonic price model to demonstrate that "thigh walkability communities generally have concentrated rich amenity resources, and consequently have high property values" (Xia et al., 2018).

In the city of Alghero, Italy Blečić et al. (2016), use a contingent field survey and a simple regression analysis, to assess whether and how peoples' subjective perceptions of walkability are influenced by the objective street attributes. Their findings suggest that some elements of the built physical environment, such as "useful sidewalk width, architectural, urban and environmental attractions, density of shops, bars, services, economic activities, vehicles-pedestrians separation, cyclability, opportunities to sit, shelters and shades, car roadway width and street lighting" are significant determinants of perceived walkability.

Aiming to better understand the role of the built environment on physical activity of older adults in two New York City neighbourhoods, Weiss et al. (2010) undertake a pilot project and create an Objective Walkability Index (OWI), combing a GIS-based approach and a survey-based exploration of residents' perceptions. To quantify life quality as a function of walkability, Orozco et al. (2019) construct a life quality index (LQI) based on pedestrian accessibility to amenities and services, safety and environmental variables. The authors employ the open data sources for the city of Budapest and use a data-driven, network-based methods. In particular, they use three different data sources: networks, points of interest (that were acquired using OSMnx, a python library to download and construct networks from OpenStreetMap (OSM) and district-level attributes (specifically, population and crimes, population data and the air pollution).

Using participatory observation, Google street view and photography techniques, Shuaib & Rana (2021) examine the quality of the street facilities, with the special attention placed on the quality of the sidewalks in Rajshahi city, Bangladesh and its relation to the walking activities. They demonstrate that the unusable sidewalks in particular disrupt and reduce the walking activities.

Within the IPEN (International Physical Activity and the Environment Network) project, Dobesova & Krivka (2012) develop a Walkability index that consists of four partial indexes: Connectivity index, Entropy Index, Floor area ratio index and Household density index. They employ an indirect method of measuring the physical activity of inhabitants using the GIS in urban units. In particular, to obtain the data and tmeasures a frequency of steps, a step distance, number of steps and the intensity of movement, respondents were asked to wear the ActiGraph sensor for one week.

In their review of the literature on walkability indices published in the period 2009-2018, Arellana et al. (2020) find certain biases in the reviewed studies, in terms of the geographical coverage, size of cities and construction of walkability indices. As for the geographical coverage, the majority of studies refers to North American cities (45%), European cities (22.5%) and to Asian cities (15%). In addition, as a basis for investigation, larger cities are preferred over smaller cities. A bias is also noticeable in the approach used by various researcher to construct walkability indices. The majority of walkability indices is constructed on the basis of objective "meso-scale" factors, mostly referring to the quality and quantity of the built environment, while only a few studies also utilise subjective micro-scale factors, even though, as mentioned in the previous paragraph, such factors are important elements of walkability. In addition, walkability indices differ in terms of how different factors/variables are weighted. For instance, some

A Walking-Friendly Environment?

studies weigh all factors equally in the composite index while some other studies employ differential weighting to better capture the differential contributions of different variables.

CONCLUSION

A predominant car-oriented paradigm has underestimated and marginalised walking and other active modalities of urban mobility for a long time. The recent literature in the field of urban planning and transportation, however, seems to be placing slow, active and environment-friendly modalities of urban transportation at the pedestal of modern urban mobility. Within the new urbanism philosophy, the active modalities of urban mobility, along with the pedestrian-friendly designed neighbourhoods, have become an important part of the smart transportation system in modern planning processes.

At the same time, the concept of walkability still remains vaguely defined. In a simple format, walkability is the degree to which urban design and the built environment is walkable-friendly, referring to street conditions, the proximity, distribution and type of key amenities within walkable distances. Within that context, the GIS-based indicators, and the Walk Score® index in particular, have been increasing used to assess the walkability levels of an area. However, as recommended by Hall & Ram (2018), as well as Carr et al. (2010), the Walk Score® index should "be used simply as a proxy for estimating neighbourhood density and access to amenities rather than a global measure of neighbourhood walkability". In other words, the walkability concept is not just about physical features of the built environment; it is multidimensional and, as such, difficult to operationalise and measure. An ideal indicator of walkability requires a multidisciplinary approach to metrics for walkability. In order to understand and objectively measure the degree of walkability, it is important to identify and take into account all influential factors that shape the walkable-friendly areas, including the subjective pedestrians' perceptions of walkability of a certain area. An enormous effort has been place in the literature to construct an acceptable, if not perfect, measure of walkability of a place, that include both qualitative and/or quantitative approach to assessing the degree of walkability. In addition, to take into account some factors beyond the built environment, some studies investigate the broader social, cultural and historical context within which people make choices about their preferred mode of mobility. Nonetheless, despite all the effort, it seems that the concept of walkability still remains vague, both in terms of its definitions and measurements, and calls for a more multidisciplinary approach.

Despite the difficulties related to defining and measuring, the concept of walkability plays a fundamental role in promoting smart, carbon-neutral, sustainable, and inclusive cities. Local governments and decision-makers throughout the world promote active and green modalities of mobility - daily walking and cycling activities in particular - as a way of sustainable and healthy urban living. Urban planners and designers aim to optimise space for pedestrians and to tailor certain characteristics of the built environment so that it better resonates with pedestrian preferences. In order to do that, they need qualitative, but even more importantly, the quantified data and research-based studies in the field of walkability. A case-study of Santiago, Chile by Herrmann-Lunecke et al. (2020) is quite informative in this context, as it can offer some lessons to other cities that aim to promote walking activities. The authors summarise the reasons why this Chilean city has a high share of walking and cycling trips in total trips undertaken by city residents (64%) and why it has not experienced a significant reduction of the walking activities in the era of car-oriented urban paradigm. The authors believe that the prevalence of walking is attributable to a combination of factors, such as "cultural norms (active street life, street markets, and street fairs); the prevalence of low-income households; built environment characteristics (short blocks, mixed uses, and high densities that result in accessible and connected pedestrian networks); and a series of pedestrian initiatives promoted by local municipalities".

As to increase the active modes of urban mobility, local governments and urban planners focus their efforts at the neighbourhood-level settings. The walking choices and behaviours of the residents are most directly influenced by the environment elements of the neighbourhood. Community facilities - "the services or amenities utilized by local communities for various purposes, which may include food retail, transport, education, recreation, social and cultural, financial and health" (Xia et al., 2018) - should be safely and easily accessible on foot within the walking distance from a residential area. It seems that, from the residents' perspective, there is an increasing demand for the walkable communities characterised by the pedestrian-friendly and vivid streets, mix land uses, accessible community facilities and destinations (Koschinsky et al., 2016), and this has become more evident with the COVID-19 outbreak. Jardim & de Castro Neto (2022) argue that the concept of walkability has gained a particular attention with the CO-VID-19 crisis. During the population lockdowns and social distancing, people were spending more time in their residential area and were mostly choosing active modes of transportation. Among other things, this crisis has contributed to raise the awareness among general population and governing institutions, of how the built environment and urban design can facilitate people's mobility, and ultimately, the quality of urban life. In that light, recently, within the smart city paradigm, there has been a re-emergence of the 15-minute city concept, as an attempt to create self-sufficient neighbourhoods with the decentralised essential functions easily accessible by the residents. The concept was originally developed in 2016 by Moreno (Moreno et al., 2021) as an urban design response for combating greenhouse gas emissions in urban settings. The-15 min city concept is a holistic urban design approach to planning liveable, sustainable, inclusive and diverse neighbourhoods. The concept follows a proximity-based planning design and human-scale urban design, where the main idea is to ensure the proximity of basic urban community facilities within a 15-min walking or cycling distance, so as to decrease the necessity of the car usage in everyday life, to facilitate walkability and sustainable urban mobility in general, and ultimately, to increase the quality of urban life. In the aftermath of COVID-19, based on the challenges it has brought to city planning, the concept of 15-min city has been transformed into "modified 15-minute city" framework (Moreno et al., 2021). Apart from accessibility and proximity, the focus is on promoting density, diversity and digitalisation - three main pillars of the modified 15-min city concept. The emphasis is on the optimal density, so that the area comfortably and sustainably accommodates an optimal number of people and services per square kilometre. The diversity dimension is twofold and directed towards promoting vibrant urban fabrics, community participation and interaction; it refers to ensuring a mixed - residential, commercial and entertainment - components in neighbourhoods as well as multiculturality in terms of diversity in culture and people. Within the smart city concept, digitalisation is the most pronounced dimension that ensures the realisation and progress of all other dimensions of the modified 15-min city concept. As explained by Moreno et al. (2021), digital technologies and platforms are essential for facilitating inclusivity, community participation and real-time delivery of services. In addition to proximity, density, diversity and digitalisation, Khavarian-Garmsir et al. (2023) add three more constitutive dimensions of the 15-min city concept: human scale urban design, flexibility and connectivity. Human scale urban design refers to urban planning in accordance with human needs and characteristics, so that the public spaces and residential areas are pedestrian- rather than car-friendly. Flexibility is directed towards creating multi-purpose and multi-functional public and semi-public amenities and spaces. Finally, connectivity refers to inter-neighbourhood connections via public transportation as to avoid neighbourhood

A Walking-Friendly Environment?

isolation. As already mentioned, the (modified) 15-min city concept has gained particular popularity during and after the COVID-19 crisis; moreover, the Cities Climate Leadership Group recommended it as a vital strategy for post-COVID recovery (Khavarian-Garmsir et al., 2023). Despite the multiple positive economic, social and ecological aspects of the 15-min city concept, Khavarian-Garmsir et al. (2023) warn that the 15-minute city can also been criticized for "being physically deterministic, failing to take into account the needs of different social groups, biodiversity, energy-efficiency, clean energies, and culture and heritage".

REFERENCES

Arellana, J., Saltarín, M., Larrañaga, A. M., Alvarez, V., & Henao, C. A. (2020). Urban walkability considering pedestrians' perceptions of the built environment: A 10-year review and a case study in a medium-sized city in Latin America. *Transport Reviews, 40*(2), 183–203. doi:10.1080/01441647.2019.1703842

Ariffin, R. N. R., & Zahari, R. K. (2013). Perceptions of the Urban Walking Environments. *Procedia: Social and Behavioral Sciences, 105*, 589–597. doi:10.1016/j.sbspro.2013.11.062

Blečić, I., Canu, D., Cecchini, A., Congiu, T., & Fancello, G. (2016). Factors of Perceived Walkability: A Pilot Empirical Study. *9th International Conference on Innovation in Urban and Regional Planning. Lecture Notes in Computer Science.*

Boongaling, C. G. K., Luna, D. A., & Samantela, S. S. (2022). Developing a street level walkability index in the Philippines using 3D photogrammetry modeling from drone surveys. *GeoJournal, 87*(4), 3341–3364. doi:10.100710708-021-10441-2

Carr, L. J., Dunsiger, S. I., & Marcus, B. H. (2010). Walk score™ as a global estimate of neighborhood walkability. *American Journal of Preventive Medicine, 39*(5), 460–463. doi:10.1016/j.amepre.2010.07.007 PMID:20965384

De Vos, J., Lättman, K., van der Vlugt, A.-L., Welsch, J., & Otsuka, N. (2022). Determinants and effects of perceived walkability: A literature review, conceptual model and research agenda. *Transport Reviews*, 1–22. doi:10.1080/01441647.2022.2101072

Dobesova, Z. & Krivka, T. (2012). Walkability index in the Urban Planning: A case stud in Olomouc City. *Advances in Spatial Planning*, 179 - 196.

Dovey, K., & Pafka, E. (2020). What is walkability? The urban DMA. *Urban Studies (Edinburgh, Scotland), 57*(1), 93–108. doi:10.1177/0042098018819727

Ewing, R., & Handy, S. (2009). Measuring the Unmeasurable: Urban Design Qualities Related to Walkability. *Journal of Urban Design, 14*(1), 65–84. doi:10.1080/13574800802451155

Fonesca, F., Papageorgiou, G., Tondelli, S., Ribeiro, P., Conticelli, E., Jabbari, M., & Ramos, R. (2022). Perceived Walkability and Respective Urban Determinants: Insights from Bologna and Porto. *Sustainability, 4*(15), 1–19. doi:10.3390u14159089

Forsyth, A. (2015). What is a walkable place? The walkability debate in urban design. *URBAN DESIGN International, 20*(4), 274–292. doi:10.1057/udi.2015.22

Gehl, J. (2010). *Cities for People*. Island Press.

Gössling, S., Choi, A., Dekker, K., & Metzler, D. (2019). The Social Cost of Automobility, Cycling and Walking in the European Union. *Ecological Economics, 158*, 65–74. doi:10.1016/j.ecolecon.2018.12.016

Hall, C. M., & Ram, Y. (2018). *Walk score® and its potential contribution to the study of active transport and walkability: A critical and systematic review. Transportation Research Part D*, 61(B).

Handy. (2005). Planning for accessibility: In theory and in practice. In *Access to Destinations*. Elsevier.

Herrmann-Lunecke, M. G., Mora, R., & Sagaris, L. (2020). Persistence of walking in Chile: Lessons for urban sustainability. *Transport Reviews, 40*(2), 135–159. doi:10.1080/01441647.2020.1712494

Hollenstein, D., & Bleischa, S. (2016). Walkability for Different Urban Granularities. *The International Archives of the Photogrammetry, Remote Sensing and Spatial Information Sciences, Volume XLI-B2, 2016 XXIII ISPRS Congress*.

Hynes. (2022). Walk a Mile in My Shoes! An Autoethnographical Perspective of Urban Walkability in Galway. *Journal of Contemporary Ethnography, 51*(5), 619-644.

Jamei, E., Ahmadi, K., Chau, H. W., Seyedmahmoudian, M., Horan, B., & Stojcevski, A. (2021). Urban Design and Walkability: Lessons Learnt from Iranian Traditional Cities. *Sustainability, 13*(10), 1–14. doi:10.3390u13105731

Jardim, B., & de Castro Neto, M. (2022). Walkability Indicators in the Aftermath of the COVID-19 Pandemic: A Systematic Review. *Sustainability, 14*(17), 1–24. doi:10.3390u141710933

Kang, C.-D. (2018). The S + 5Ds: Spatial access to pedestrian environments and walking in Seoul, Korea. *Cities (London, England), 77*, 130–141. doi:10.1016/j.cities.2018.01.019

Kato, H. (2020). Effect of Walkability on Urban Sustainability in the Osaka Metropolitan Fringe Area. *Sustainability, 12*(21), 1–17. doi:10.3390u12219248

Khavarian-Garmsir, A. R., Sharifi, A., & Sadeghi, A. (2023). The 15-minute city: Urban planning and design efforts toward creating sustainable neighborhoods. *Cities (London, England), 132*.

Knapskog, M., Hagen, O. H., Tennøy, A., & Rynning, M. K. (2019). Exploring ways of measuring walkability. *Transportation Research Procedia, 41*, 264–282. doi:10.1016/j.trpro.2019.09.047

Koschinsky, J., Emily Talen, E., & Alfonso, M. (2016). How walkable is Walker's paradise? *Environment and Planning. B, Planning & Design*, 1–21.

Li, Y., Yabuki, N., & Fukuda, T. (2023). Integrating GIS, deep learning, and environmental sensors for multicriteria evaluation of urban street walkability. *Landscape and Urban Planning, 230*, 104603. doi:10.1016/j.landurbplan.2022.104603

Liu, Y., Sun, Z., Wang, X., Chen, T., & Yang, C. (2022). Dose-response association between the daily step count and all-cause mortality: A systematic review and meta-analysis. *Journal of Sports Sciences*, *40*(5), 1678–1687. doi:10.1080/02640414.2022.2099186 PMID:35819337

Lo, H. R. (2009). Walkability: What is it? *Journal of Urbanism*, *2*(2), 145–166. doi:10.1080/17549170903092867

Loo. (2021). Walking towards a happy city. *Journal of Transport Geography*, *93*, 1-11.

Moreno, C., Allam, Z., Chabaud, D., Gall, C., & Pratlong, F. (2021). Introducing the "15-Minute City": Sustainability, Resilience and Place Identity in Future Post-Pandemic Cities. *Smart Cities*, *4*(1), 93–111. doi:10.3390martcities4010006

Orozco, L. G. N., Deritei, D., Vancso, A., & Vasarhelyi, O. (2019). Quantifying Life Quality as Walkability on Urban Networks: The Case of Budapest. *International Conference on Complex Networks and Their Applications*, 905-918.

Pérez, K., Olabarria, M., Rojas-Rueda, D., Santamariña-Rubio, E., Borrell, C., & Nieuwenhuijsen, M. (2017). The health and economic benefits of active transport policies in Barcelona. *Journal of Transport & Health*, 1–9.

Shields, R., da Silva, E. J. G., Lima, T. L., & Osorio, N. (2021). Walkability: A review of trends. *Journal of Urbanism*, 1–24.

Singh, R. (2016). Factors Affecting Walkability of Neighborhoods. *Procedia: Social and Behavioral Sciences*, *216*, 643–654.

Tsiompras, A. B., & Photis, Y. N. (2017). What matters when it comes to "Walk and the city"? Defining a weighted GIS-based walkability index. *Transportation Research Procedia*, *24*, 523–530.

Vale, D. S., Saraiva, M., & Pereira, M. (2016). Active accessibility: A review of operational measures of walking and cycling accessibility. *Journal of Transport and Land Use*, *9*(1), 209–235.

Weiss, R. L., Maantay, J. A., & Fahs, M. (2010). Promoting Active Urban Aging: A Measurement Approach to Neighborhood Walkability for Older Adults. *Cities and the Environment*, *3*(1), 1–12.

Wood, A. (2022). Problematizing the concept of walkability in Johannesburg. *Journal of Urban Affairs*.

Xia, Z., Li, H., & Chen, Y. (2018). Assessing Neighborhood Walkability Based on Usage Characteristics of Amenities under Chinese Metropolises Context. *Sustainability*, *10*, 1–18.

KEY TERMS AND DEFINITIONS

15-Min City: A holistic urban design approach to planning liveable, sustainable, inclusive, and diverse neighbourhoods. The concept follows a proximity-based planning design and human-scale urban design, where the main idea is to ensure the proximity of basic urban community facilities within a 15-min walking or cycling distance, so as to decrease the necessity of the car usage in everyday life, to facilitate walkability and sustainable urban mobility in general, and ultimately, to increase the quality of urban life.

Car-Oriented Urban Design: Planning and design of cities and neighbourhoods that is characterised primarily by traffic planning, large urban blocks, low street connectivity, separation of facilities by driving distance, roadside parking, etc. (Loo, 2021)

Micro-Scale Factors of Walkability: The subjective variables related to pedestrians' perceptions, such as "zebra crossings, quality of sidewalks, benches, presence of green, etc." that remain mainly unmeasured and underexplored as elements of walkability (Arellana et al., 2020; De Vos et al., 2022).

Pedestrian-Oriented Urban Design: Planning and design of cities and neighbourhoods that is characterised primarily by pedestrian planning, human-scale urban blocks, high street connectivity, proximity of facilities by walking distance, street activities by pedestrians, integration of public transport and non-car modes, streets as public space, etc. (Loo, 2021)

Walkability: The extent to which the built environment supports and encourages safe, comfortable, and interesting urban walking trips (Tsiompras & Photis, 2017), offering a high level of accessibility and connectivity to destinations, and visual interest within a reasonable span of time (Forsyth, 2015).

WalkScore: One of the main indicators of how walkable a neighbourhood is. It assesses the "walking potential" of a place by connecting distance accessibility (a gravity-based measure) with topological accessibility (street connectivity).

Compilation of References

Abduljabbar, R. L., Liyanage, S., & Dia, H. (2021). The role of micro-mobility in shaping sustainable cities: A systematic literature review. *Transportation Research Part D, Transport and Environment, 92*, 102734. doi:10.1016/j.trd.2021.102734

Abu-Salih, B., Wongthongtham, P., Zhu, D., Chan, K. Y., & Rudra, A. (2021). Social Big Data: An Overview and Applications. In Social Big Data Analytics. Springer Singapore. doi:10.1007/978-981-33-6652-7_1

Accenture. (2014). Transforming the Transit Passenger Experience. *Accenture.* https://www.accenture.com/gb-en/~/media/Accenture/Conversion-Assets/DotCom/Documents/Global/PDF/Dualpub_1/Accenture-Transforming-Transit-Passenger-Experience.pdf

ACEA. (2020). *Fuel types of new buses: diesel 85%, hybrid 4.8%, electric 4%, alternative fuels 6.2% share in 2019.* ACEA. https://www.acea.auto/fuel-cv/fuel-types-of-new-buses-diesel-85-hybrid-4-8-electric-4-alternative-fuels-6-2-share-in-2019-2/.

ACEA. (2021). *Fuel types of new buses: Electric 6.1%, hybrids 9.5%, Diesel 72.9% market share in 2020.* ACEA. https://www.acea.auto/fuel-cv/fuel-types-of-new-buses-electric-6-1-hybrids-9-5-diesel-72-9-market-share-in-2020/.

Acheampong, R. A., Cugurullo, F., Gueriau, M., & Dusparic, I. (2021). Can autonomous vehicles enable sustainable mobility in future cities? Insights and policy challenges from user preferences over different urban transport options. *Cities, 112.* doi:10.1016/j.cities.2021.103134

Adiyarta, K., Napitupulu, D., Syafrullah, M., Mahdiana, D., & Rusdah, R. (2020). Analysis of smart city indicators based on prisma: Systematic review. *IOP Conference Series. Materials Science and Engineering, 725*(1), 012113.

Ağaoğlu, M. N., & Başdemir, H. (2019). Şehir içi ulaşım sorunları ve çözüm önerileri. *Gaziosmanpaşa Bilimsel Araştırma Dergisi, 8*(1), 27–36.

Aggarwal, S., & Kumar, N. (2021). *Advances in Computers, Smart grid.* Elsevier. doi:10.1016/bs.adcom.2020.08.023

Agliardi, E., & Agliardi, R. (2021). Corporate green bonds: Understanding the greenium in a two-factor structural model. *Environmental and Resource Economics, 80*(2), 257–278. doi:10.100710640-021-00585-7 PMID:34366567

Ahmed, F., Naeem, M., & Iqbal, M. (2017). ICT and renewable energy: A way forward to the next generation telecom base stations. *Telecommunication Systems, 64*(1), 43–56. doi:10.100711235-016-0156-4

Ainsalu, J., Arffman, V., Bellone, M., Ellner, M., Haapamäki, T., Haavisto, N., Josefson, E., Ismailogullari, A., Lee, B., Madland, O., Madžulis, R., Müür, J., Mäkinen, S., Nousiainen, V., Pilli-Sihvola, E., Rutanen, E., Sahala, S., Schønfeldt, B., Smolnicki, P. M., & Åman, M. (2018). State of the Art of Automated Buses. *Sustainability, 10*(9), 3118. doi:10.3390u10093118

Ajzen, I. (1991). The theory of planned behavior. *Organizational Behavior and Human Decision Processes, 50*(2), 179–211. https://doi.org/10.1016/0749-5978(91)90020-T

Ajzen, I., & Fishbein, M. (1980). *Understanding Attitudes and Predicting Social Behavior*. Prentice Hall.

Akad, İ. (2022). Assessing the impact of information and communication technologies on human development: a regional analysis for Africa. In *Digital Innovations, Business and Society in Africa* (pp. 363–385). Springer. doi:10.1007/978-3-030-77987-0_16

Akben, İ. (2020). Şehir Lojistiği: Tedarik Zinciri Ve Lojistikte Güncel Konular Ve Stratejik Yaklaşımlar, Ankara. *Sonçağ Yayıncılık, 2020*, 73–88.

Akhtaruzzaman, M., Banerjee, A. K., Ghardallou, W., & Umar, Z. (2022). Is greenness an optimal hedge for sectoral stock indices. *Economic Modelling, 117*, 106030. doi:10.1016/j.econmod.2022.106030

Alaoui, I.E., (2019). Transformer les big social data en prévisions - méthodes et technologies. *Application à l'analyse de sentiments, 150*.

Al-Hawari, T., Mumani, A., & Momani, A. (2014). Application of the Analytic Network Process to facility layout selection. *International Journal of Industrial and Manufacturing Systems Engineering, 33*, 488–497.

Alimo, A., & Zankawah, Y. (2022). Factors causing low demand for a suburban passenger train in Sekondi-Takoradi. *Journal of Transport Geography, 98*.

Allcott, H. (2011). Social norms and energy conservation. *Journal of Public Economics, 95*(9–10), 1082–1095. https://doi.org/10.1016/j.jpubeco.2011.03.003

Allen, J., Eboli, L., Forciniti, C., Mazzulla, G., & Ortúzar, J. de D. (2019). The role of critical incidents and involvement in transit satisfaction and loyalty. *Transport Policy, 75*, 57–69. doi:10.1016/j.tranpol.2019.01.005

Allen, M., Dube, O. P., Solecki, W., Aragón-Durand, F., Cramer, W., Humphreys, S., & Mulugetta, Y. (2018). *Global warming of 1.5° C. An IPCC Special Report on the impacts of global warming of 1.5° C above pre-industrial levels and related global greenhouse gas emission pathways, in the context of strengthening the global response to the threat of climate change, sustainable development, and efforts to eradicate poverty*. Sustainable Development, and Efforts to Eradicate Poverty.

Altıntaş, S. T., & Eyigün, Y. (2020). Sürdürülebilir Kent İçi Ulaşım Politikaları Raylı Sistemler Örneği. *İstanbul Ticaret Üniversitesi Teknoloji ve Uygulamalı Bilimler Dergisi, 3*(2), 217-233.

Amundi Asset Management & International Finance Corporation. (2021). *Emerging market green bonds report 2020*. Amundi. https://research-center.amundi.com/article/emerging-market-green-bonds-report-2020

Anable, J., Docherty, I., & Marsden, G. (2018). The governance of smart mobility. *Transportation Research Part A, Policy and Practice, 115*, 114–125. doi:10.1016/j.tra.2017.09.012

Anagnostopoulou, E., Urbančič, J., Bothos, E., Magoutas, B., Bradesko, L., Schrammel, J., & Mentzas, G. (2020). From mobility patterns to behavioural change: Leveraging travel behaviour and personality profiles to nudge for sustainable transportation. *Journal of Intelligent Information Systems, 54*(1), 157–178. https://doi.org/10.1007/s10844-018-0528-1

Anciaes, P., Jones, P., Mindell, J. S., & Scholes, S. (2022). The cost of the wider impacts of road traffic on local communities: 1.6% of Great Britain's GDP. *Transportation Research Part A, Policy and Practice, 163*, 266–287. doi:10.1016/j.tra.2022.05.016

Compilation of References

Andersen, A., Karlsen, R., & Yu, W. (2018). Green Transportation Choices with IoT and Smart Nudging. In Handbook of Smart Cities (pp. 331–354). Springer International Publishing. https://doi.org/10.1007/978-3-319-97271-8_13.

APTA. (2021). *Public transportation fact book*. APTA.

Arcadis. (2017, November). Sustainable Cities Mobility Index 2017. *Arcadis*. https://www.arcadis.com/campaigns/scmi/images/sustainable-cities-mobility-index_spreads.pdf

Arellana, J., Saltarín, M., Larrañaga, A. M., Alvarez, V., & Henao, C. A. (2020). Urban walkability considering pedestrians' perceptions of the built environment: A 10-year review and a case study in a medium-sized city in Latin America. *Transport Reviews*, *40*(2), 183–203. doi:10.1080/01441647.2019.1703842

Ariffin, R. N. R., & Zahari, R. K. (2013). Perceptions of the Urban Walking Environments. *Procedia: Social and Behavioral Sciences*, *105*, 589–597. doi:10.1016/j.sbspro.2013.11.062

Arthur, D. Little. (2018). *Urban passenger mobility demand worldwide between 2010 and 2050 (in trillion passenger kilometers)*. United Nations. https://www.statista.com/statistics/1013579/urban-passenger-mobility-demand-worldwide/

ASCE. (2009). Vision for civil engineering in 2025: A roadmap for the profession. *ASCE Library*. https://ascelibrary.org/doi/epdf/10.1061/9780784478868.002

Ashtopus Technologies. (2022). Commercial Vehicle Onboard Video Systems. Pinterest. https://www.pinterest.com/pin/558164947544320947/

Atasoy, B., Ikeda, T., Song, X., & Ben-Akiva, M. E. (2015). The concept and impact analysis of a flexible mobility on demand system. *Transportation Research Part C, Emerging Technologies*, *56*, 373–392. doi:10.1016/j.trc.2015.04.009

Australian Government. (2017). Social impact investing discussion paper. Commonwealth of Australia.

Avril, S., Bozzani-Franc, S., L'Hostis, A., & Pico, F. (2007). *Strategic Research Agenda for Urban Mobility*. Retrieved December 15, 2022 from https://hal.archives-ouvertes.fr/hal-00575525

Aydın, G. T. (2017). *Kent İçi Lojistik İstanbul İçin Bir Uygulama. Yüksek Lisans Tezi*. İstanbul Teknik Üniversitesi, Fen Bilimleri Enstitüsü.

Azad, M., Hoseinzadeh, N., Brakewood, C., Cherry, C. R., & Han, L. D. (2019). Fully Autonomous Buses: A Literature Review and Future Research Directions. *Journal of Advanced Transportation*, *2019*, 4603548. doi:10.1155/2019/4603548

Azam, A., Rafiq, M., Shafique, M., Ateeq, M., & Yuan, J. (2021a). Investigating the Impact of Renewable Electricity Consumption on Sustainable Economic Development: A Panel ARDL Approach. *International Journal of Green Energy*, *18*(11), 1185–1192. doi:10.1080/15435075.2021.1897825

Azam, A., Rafiq, M., Shafique, M., Yuan, J., & Salem, S. (2021b). Human Development Index, ICT, and Renewable Energy-Growth Nexus for Sustainable Development: A Novel PVAR Analysis. *Frontiers in Energy Research*, *9*, 760758. doi:10.3389/fenrg.2021.760758

Azhgaliyeva, D., Liu, Y., & Liddle, B. (2020). An empirical analysis of energy intensity and the role of policy instruments. *Energy Policy*, *145*, 111773. doi:10.1016/j.enpol.2020.111773

Bachelet, M. J., Becchetti, L., & Manfredonia, S. (2019). The green bonds premium puzzle: The role of issuer characteristics and third-party verification. *Sustainability*, *11*(4), 1098. doi:10.3390u11041098

Bai, C., & Sarkis, J. (2013). A grey-based DEMATEL model for evaluating business process management critical success factors. *International Journal of Production Economics*, *146*(1), 281–292. doi:10.1016/j.ijpe.2013.07.011

349

Baker, M., Bergstresser, D., Serafeim, G., & Wurgler, J. (2018). *Financing the Response to Climate Change: The Pricing and Ownership of US Green Bonds. No. w25194*. National Bureau of Economic Research. doi:10.3386/w25194

Baldi, F., & Pandimiglio, A. (2022). The role of ESG scoring and greenwashing risk in explaining the yields of green bonds: A conceptual framework and an econometric analysis. *Global Finance Journal, 52*, 1–16. doi:10.1016/j.gfj.2022.100711

Bamwesigye, D., & Hlavackova, P. (2019). Analysis of Sustainable Transport for Smart Cities. *Sustainability, 11*(7), 2140. doi:10.3390u11072140

Banga, J. (2018). The green bond market: A potential source of climate finance for developing countries. *Journal of Sustainable Finance & Investment, 9*(1), 17–32. doi:10.1080/20430795.2018.1498617

Banhidi, Z., Dobos, I., & Nemeslaki, A. (2020). What the overall Digital Economy and Society Index reveals: A statistical analysis of the DESI EU28 dimensions. *Regional Statistics, 10*(2), 42–62. doi:10.15196/RS100209

Banister, D., & Hickman, R. (2013). Transport futures: Thinking the unthinkable. *Transport Policy, 29*, 283–293. doi:10.1016/j.tranpol.2012.07.005

Barba-Sánchez, V., Arias-Antúnez, E., & Orozco-Barbosa, L. (2019). Smart cities as a source for entrepreneurial opportunities: Evidence for Spain. *Technological Forecasting and Social Change, 148*, 119713. doi:10.1016/j.techfore.2019.119713

Bardal, K. G., Gjertsen, A., & Mathias Brynildsen Reinar, M. B. (2020). Sustainable mobility: Policy design and implementation in three Norwegian cities. *Transportation Research Part D, Transport and Environment, 82*, 102330. doi:10.1016/j.trd.2020.102330

Bauer, J. (2002). Rural America and the Digital Transformation of Health Care: New Perspectives on the Future. *Journal of Legal Medicine, 23*(1), 73–83. doi:10.1080/019476402317276678 PMID:11957332

Bauer, J., & Brown, W. (2001). The digital transformation of oral health care: Teledentistry and electronic commerce. *The Journal of the American Dental Association, 132*(2), 204–209. doi:10.14219/jada.archive.2001.0156 PMID:11217594

Baum, M.L. (2012). It's not easy being green … or is it? A content analysis of environmental claims in magazine advertisements from the United States and United Kingdom. *Environmental Communication: A Journal of Nature and Culture, 6*(4), 423-440.

Baumstark, L., Ménard, C., Roy, W., & Yvrande-Billon, A. (2005). *Modes de gestion et efficience des opérateurs dans le secteur des transports urbains de personnes [Management methods and efficiency of operators in the urban passenger transport sector]*. Mobilité, territoires et développement durable [Mobility, territories and sustainable development].

Baxter, B. (2020). Autonomous vehicles and public transport in Europe. *Eltis*. https://www.eltis.org/printpdf/participate/events/autonomous-vehicles-and-public-transport-europe

Beck, D. E., & Cowan, C. C. (1996). *Spiral dynamics: mastering values, leadership and change*. Blackwell Publishing.

Beiler, M. R. O. (2017). Sustainable mobility for the future: Development and Implementation of a Sustainable Transportation Planning Course. *Journal of Professional Issues in Engineering Education and Practice, 143*(1). https://ascelibrary.org/doi/10.1061/%28ASCE%29EI.1943-5541.0000298

Beiler, M. R. O. (2018). Public transportation education: Inventory and recommendations on curricula. *Journal of Professional Issues in Engineering Education and Practice, 144*(3). https://ascelibrary.org/doi/full/10.1061/%28ASCE%29EI.1943-5541.0000369

Benevolo, C., Dameri, R. P., & D'Auria, B. (2016). Smart Mobility in Smart City. In T. Torre, A. Braccini, & R. Spinelli (Eds.), *Empowering Organizations Lecture Notes in Information Systems and Organisation* (pp. 13–28). Springer.

Compilation of References

Berger, C., Blauth, R., & Boger, D. (1993). Kano's methods for understanding customer-defined quality. Kano's methods for understanding customer-defined quality. *Center for Quality Management Journal, 2*(4), 3–35. https://www.academia. edu/29830721/Kano_s_method_for_understanding_customer_defined_quality

Berkup, S. B. (2014). Working with generations X and Y in generation Z period: Management of different generations in business life. *Mediterranean Journal of Social Sciences, 5*(19), 218–218. doi:10.5901/mjss.2014.v5n19p218

Berman, S. J. (2012). Digital transformation: Opportunities to create new business models. *Strategy and Leadership, 40*(2), 16–24. doi:10.1108/10878571211209314

Bernal, L. M. M. D. (2016). Basic Parameters for the Design of Intermodal Public Transportation Infrastructures. *Transportation Research Procedia, 14*, 499–508. doi:10.1016/j.trpro.2016.05.104

Bernardo, M. R., Neto, M. de C., & Aparicio, M. (2019). Smart Mobility: a multimodal services study in the metropolitan area of Lisbon. In Conferência da Associação Portuguesa de Sistemas de Informação (CAPSI 2019).

Bertaud, A. (2004). *The Spatial Organization of Cities: Deliberate Outcome or Unforeseen Consequence?* (Working Paper No. 2004-01). University of California, Institute of Urban and Regional Development.

Bessala, E. S. B., Moskolaï, N. J., Tamba, J. G., & Etame, J. (2022). Urban computing for traffic prediction in the context of developing countries. *Journal Sciences. Technologies et Développement, 24*, 87–96.

Bessa, R. J., Matos, M. A., Soares, F. J., & Lopes, J. A. P. (2011). Optimized bidding of an EV aggregation agent in the electricity market. *IEEE Transactions on Smart Grid, 3*(1), 443–452. doi:10.1109/TSG.2011.2159632

Beyerlein, S., Bill, A., van Schalkwyk, I., Bernhardt, K., Young, R., Nambisan, S., & Torochy, R. (2010). Formulating learning outcomes based on core concepts for the introductory transportation engineering course. *Proceedings of the 2010 Transportation Research Board Annual Meeting*, (pp. 10-3946). TRB.

Beyond Philosophy. (n. d.). Understanding the True Definition of Customer Experience. *Beyond Philosophy*. https://beyondphilosophy.com/customer-experience/

Bharadwaj, A. (2000). A resource-based perspective on information technology capability and firm performance: An empirical investigation. *Management Information Systems Quarterly, 24*(1), 169–196. doi:10.2307/3250983

Bhattacharjee, S. S. (2011). Sustainability education in the United States: Analyses of the curricula used in construction programs. *Proceedings of ICSDC 2011: Integrating Sustainability Practices in the Construction Industry*, (pp. 172–179). ASCE.

Bhattacharyya, A., Jin, W., le Floch, C., Chatman, D. G., & Walker, J. L. (2019). Nudging people towards more sustainable residential choice decisions: An intervention based on focalism and visualization. *Transportation, 46*(2), 373–393. https://doi.org/10.1007/s11116-018-9936-x

Biazzo, I., Monechi, B., & Loreto, V. (2019). General scores for accessibility and inequality measures in urban areas. *Royal Society Open Science, 6*(8), 190979. doi:10.1098/rsos.190979 PMID:31598261

Bibri, S. E. (2019a). On the sustainability of smart and smarter cities in the era of big data: An interdisciplinary and transdisciplinary literature review. *Journal of Big Data, 6*, 25. doi:10.1186/s40537-019-0182-7

Bibri, S. E. (2019b). The anatomy of the data-driven smart sustainable city: Instrumentation, datafication, computerization and related applications. *Journal of Big Data, 6*(1), 59. doi:10.118640537-019-0221-4

Bibri, S. E., & Krogstie, J. (2017). The core enabling technologies of big data analytics and context-aware computing for smart sustainable cities: A review and synthesis. *Journal of Big Data, 4*(1), 38. doi:10.118640537-017-0091-6

351

Biesok, G., & Wyród-Wróbel, J. (2012, September 6). *Indicative methods of customer satisfaction surveys in public transport services* [Conference presentation]. QMOD Conference, Poznan, Poland. https://www.academia.edu/33285555/Indicative_methods_of_customer_satisfaction_surveys_in_public_transport_services

Bill, A., Beyerlain, S., Heaslip, K., Hurwitz, S., Sanford Bernhardt, K., Kyte, M., & Young, R. (2011). *Development of knowledge tables and learning outcomes for an introductory course in transportation engineering. Transportation research record no 22211*, 27–35. Transportation Research Board. doi:10.3141/2211-04

BillyFlorian. (2019). *Metro Platform Screen Doors*. Youtube. https://www.youtube.com/watch?v=wIbLyaHhAkI

Black, W. R. (1996). Sustainable transportation: A US perspective. *Journal of Transport Geography*, *4*(3), 151–159. doi:10.1016/0966-6923(96)00020-8

Black, W. R. (1997). North American transportation: Perspectives on research needs and sustainable transportation. *Journal of Transport Geography*, *5*(1), 12–19. doi:10.1016/S0966-6923(96)00042-7

Blečić, I., Canu, D., Cecchini, A., Congiu, T., & Fancello, G. (2016). Factors of Perceived Walkability: A Pilot Empirical Study. *9th International Conference on Innovation in Urban and Regional Planning. Lecture Notes in Computer Science*.

Bloomberg & Barclays. (2021). *Bloomberg Barclays MSCI Global Green Bond Index*. Bloomberg Barclays Indices. https://www.msci.com/documents/10199/242721/Barclays_MSCI_Green_Bond_Index.pdf/6e4d942a-0ce4-4e70-9aff-d7643e1bde96

Bly, P. H. (1987). Managing public transport: Commercial profitability and social service. *Transportation Research Part A, General*, *21*(2), 109–125. doi:10.1016/0191-2607(87)90004-5

Bonte, D. (2018). *Role of smart cities for economic development*. ABI Research.

Boongaling, C. G. K., Luna, D. A., & Samantela, S. S. (2022). Developing a street level walkability index in the Philippines using 3D photogrammetry modeling from drone surveys. *GeoJournal*, *87*(4), 3341–3364. doi:10.100710708-021-10441-2

Booz Allen. (2012). *Integrating Australia's Transportation Systems: A Strategy for An Efficient Transportation Future*. Infrastructure Partnership Australia.

Börner, M. F., Frieges, M. H., Späth, B., Spütz, K., Heimes, H. H., Sauer, D. U., & Li, W. (2022). Challenges of second-life concepts for retired electric vehicle batteries. *Cell Reports Physical Science*, *101095*(10), 101095. doi:10.1016/j.xcrp.2022.101095

Bösch, P. M., Becker, F., Becker, H., & Axhausen, K. W. (2018). Cost-based analysis of autonomous mobility services. *Transport Policy*, *64*, 76–91. doi:10.1016/j.tranpol.2017.09.005

Botelho, D. F., Dias, B. H., de Oliveira, L. W., Soares, T. A., Rezende, I., & Sousa, T. (2021). Innovative business models as drivers for prosumers integration-Enablers and barriers. *Renewable & Sustainable Energy Reviews*, *144*, 111057. doi:10.1016/j.rser.2021.111057

Bouskela, M. (2016). *The Road toward Smart Cities: Migrating from Traditional City Management to the Smart City*. Inter-American Development Bank. doi:10.18235/0000377

Boyack, K. W., Klavans, R., & Börner, K. (2005). Mapping the backbone of science. *Scientometrics*, *64*(3), 351–374. doi:10.100711192-005-0255-6

Breque, M., De Nul, L., & Petridis, A. (2021). *Industry 5.0, towards a sustainable, human-centric and resilient European industry*. European Commission, Directorate-General for Research and Innovation. https://op.europa.eu/en/publication-detail/-/publication/468a892a-5097-11eb-b59f-01aa75ed71a1/

Compilation of References

Brokaw, L. (2016). *Six Lessons From Amsterdam's Smart City Initiative.* Sloan Review.

Brundtland, G. H. (1987). *Our Common Future: From One Earth to One World.* UN. http://www.un-documents.net/ocf-ov.htm

Bruun, E. C. (2014). *Better Public Transit Systems. Analyzing Investments and Performance* (2nd ed.). Routledge.

Buehler, R. (2018). Can Public Transportation Compete with Automated and Connected Cars? *Journal of Public Transportation, 21*(1), 7–18. https://digitalcommons.usf.edu/jpt/vol21/iss1/2. doi:10.5038/2375-0901.21.1.2

Bueno, E. V., Weber, T. B. B., Bomfim, E. L., & Kato, H. T. (2019). Measuring customer experience in service: A systematic review. *Service Industries Journal, 39*(7-8), 779–798. Advance online publication. doi:10.1080/02642069.2018.1561873

Butler, L., Yigitcanlar, T., & Paz, A. (2020). Smart Urban Mobility Innovations: A Comprehensive Review and Evaluation. *IEEE Access: Practical Innovations, Open Solutions, 8,* 196034–196049. doi:10.1109/ACCESS.2020.3034596

Byerly, H., Balmford, A., Ferraro, P. J., Hammond Wagner, C., Palchak, E., Polasky, S., Ricketts, T. H., Schwartz, A. J., & Fisher, B. (2018). Nudging pro-environmental behavior: Evidence and opportunities. *Frontiers in Ecology and the Environment, 16*(3), 159–168.

Cairns, S., Atkins, S., & Goodwin, P. (2002). Disappearing traffic: The story so far. *Municipal Engineer, 15*(1), 13–22. doi:10.1680/muen.2002.151.1.13

California Debt and Investment Advisory Commission. (2019). *Green bonds in the golden state: A practical path for issuers.* University of California Berkeley. https://www.treasurer.ca.gov/cdiac/webinars/2019/greenbonds/presentation.pdf

Callicott, J. B., & Mumford, K. (1998). Ecological sustainability as a conservation concept. In J. Lemons, L. Westra, & R. Goodland (Eds.), *Ecological sustainability and integrity: Concepts and approaches. Environmental Science and Technology Library, 13.* Springer. doi:10.1007/978-94-017-1337-5_3

Cambridge Systematics. (2009). *Moving Cooler: An Analysis of Transportation Strategies for Reducing Greenhouse Gas Emissions.* Urban Land Institute.

Campbell, M. (2020). UK announces an "ambitious" plan to become a hub for green transport. *Euronews.* https://www.euronews.com/green/2020/03/30/uk-announces-ambitious-plan-to-become-hub-for-green-transport

Campisi, T., Garau, C., Acampa, G., Maltinti, F., Canale, A., & Coni, M. (2021, September). *Developing Flexible Mobility On-Demand in the Era of Mobility as a Service: An Overview of the Italian Context Before and After Pandemic* [Conference presentation]. International Conference on Computational Science and Its Applications. Cagliari, Italy. 10.1007/978-3-030-86979-3_24

Can, U., & Alatas, B. (2017). Big Social Network Data and Sustainable Economic Development. *Sustainability, 9*(11), 2027. doi:10.3390u9112027

Căpușneanu, S., Mateș, D., Tűrkeș, M. C., Barbu, C. M., Staraș, A. I., Topor, D. I., Stoenica, L., & Fűlöp, M. T. (2021). The impact of force factors on the benefits of digital transformation in Romania. *Applied Sciences (Basel, Switzerland), 11*(5), 2365. doi:10.3390/app11052365

Caraban, A., Karapanos, E., Gonçalves, D., & Campos, P. (2019, May 2). 23 Ways to Nudge: A review of technology-mediated nudging in human-computer interaction. *Conference on Human Factors in Computing Systems - Proceedings.* doi:10.1145/3290605.3300733

353

Carayanis, E. G., & Morawska-Jancelewicz, J. (2022). The futures of Europe: Society 5.0 and Industry 5.0 as driving forces of future universities. *Journal of the Knowledge Economy*, *13*(4), 3445–3471. doi:10.100713132-021-00854-2

Caroleo, B., Morelli, N., Lissandrello, E., Vesco, A., di Dio, S., & Mauro, S. (2019). Measuring the change towards more sustainable mobility: MUV impact evaluation approach. *Systems*, *7*(2), 30.

Carpenter, T. G. (1994). *The environmental impact of railways*. Wiley.

Carrasco, J. M., Franquelo, L. G., Bialasiewicz, J. T., Galvan, E., PortilloGuisado, R. C., Prats, M. A. M., & Moreno-Alfonso, N. (2006). Power-Electronic Systems for the Grid Integration of Renewable Energy Sources. *IEEE Transactions on Industrial Electronics*, *53*(4), 1002–1016.

Carr, L. J., Dunsiger, S. I., & Marcus, B. H. (2010). Walk score™ as a global estimate of neighborhood walkability. *American Journal of Preventive Medicine*, *39*(5), 460–463. doi:10.1016/j.amepre.2010.07.007 PMID:20965384

Carvalho, M., Syguiy, T., & Nithack e Silva, D. (2015). Efficiency and Effectiveness Analysis of Public Transport of Brazilian Cities. *Journal of Transport Literature*, *9*(3), 40–44. doi:10.1590/2238-1031.jtl.v9n3a8

Caywood, M., Cochran, A., & Schade, M. (2015). *Urban Mobility Score: Quantifying Multimodal Transportation Access*. Disrupting Mobility Summit, Cambridge MIT.

Ceder, A. (2015). *Public transit planning and operation: Modeling, practice, and behaviour*. CRC Press. doi:10.1201/b18689

Çelikbilek, Y., & Tüysüz, F. (2016). An integrated grey based multi-criteria decision making approach for the evaluation of renewable energy sources. *Energy*, *115*, 1246–1258. doi:10.1016/j.energy.2016.09.091

Cell, F., & Undertaking, H. J. (2019). *Hydrogen Roadmap Europe: A Sustainable Pathway for the European Energy Transition*. EU Publications.

Centlewski, B., & Warchol, J. (2021). *IoT and its Role in Sustainable Transportation*. Lingaro Group. https://lingarogroup.com/blog/iot-and-its-role-in-sustainable-transportation/

CEPT University. (2018). *A bus transport management document*. ISSUU. https://issuu.com/monikagupta/docs/brts_final_book

Chakravorti, B., Chaturvedi, R. S., & Troein, C. (2017). *Building smart societies – A blueprint for action*. Tufts: The Fletcher School. https://sites.tufts.edu/digitalplanet/files/2020/06/Building-Smart-Societies.pdf

Chang, H., Huh, C., & Lee, M. J. (2016). Would an Energy Conservation Nudge in Hotels Encourage Hotel Guests to Conserve? *Cornell Hospitality Quarterly*, *57*(2), 172–183. doi:10.1177/1938965515588132

Chang, X., Ma, T., & Wu, R. (2019). Impact of urban development on residents' public transportation travel energy consumption in China: An analysis of hydrogen fuel cell vehicles alternatives. *International Journal of Hydrogen Energy*, *44*(30), 16015–16027. doi:10.1016/j.ijhydene.2018.09.099

Chatterjee, K., Goodwin, P., Schwanen, T., Clark, B., Jain, J., Melia, S., Middleton, J., Plyushteva, A., Ricci, M., Santos, G., & Stokes, G. (2018). *Young People's Travel – What's Changed and Why? Review and Analysis*. Report to Department for Transport. UWE. https://core.ac.uk/download/pdf/323892995.pdf

Chatzopoulos, Ch. G., & Weber, M. (2018). Challenges of Total Customer Experience (TCX): Measurement beyond Touchpoints. *International Journal of Industrial Engineering and Management*, *9*(4), 187–196. doi:10.24867/IJIEM-2018-4-187

Chen, X., Li, T., & Yuan, Q. (2021). Impacts of built environment on travel behaviors of Generation Z: A longitudinal perspective. *Transportation*, 1–30. doi:10.100711116-021-10249-6

Compilation of References

Chen, Z., Ming, X., Zhang, X., Yin, D., & Sun, Z. (2019). A rough-fuzzy DEMATEL-ANP method for evaluating sustainable value requirement of product service system. *Journal of Cleaner Production, 228*, 485–508. doi:10.1016/j.jclepro.2019.04.145

Choi, U. D., Jeong, H. K., & Jeong, S. K. (2012). *Commercial operation of ultra low floor electric bus for Seoul city route. In 2012 IEEE vehicle power and propulsion conference.* IEEE.

Christensen, T. B., & Kjær, T. (2011). Planning for sustainable transport: The case of Copenhagen. In W. Gronau, K. Reiter, & R. Pressl (Eds.), *Transport and Health Issues: Studies on Mobility and Transport Research, 3*, 119–140. MetaGIS-Systems. https://www.eltis.org/docs/tools/Transpot_health_issues_complete-book.pdf

Christopher, M. K., Stuart, D., & Foote, P. J. (1999). Structuring and assessing transit management response to customer satisfaction surveys. *Transportation Research Record: Journal of the Transportation Research Board, 1669*(1), 99–108. doi:10.3141/1669-12

Cicchetti, D. V. (1994). Guidelines, Criteria, and Rules of Thumb for Evaluating Normed and Standardized Assessment Instrument in Psychology. *Psychological Assessment, 6*(4), 284–290. doi:10.1037/1040-3590.6.4.284

CICERO. (2021). *Freddie Mac multifamily green bond second opinion.* CICERO. https://mf.freddiemac.com/docs/2nd_opinion_from_CICERO.pdf

Cirit, F. (2014). *Sürdürülebilir Kentiçi Ulaşım Politikaları Ve Toplu Taşıma Sistemlerinin Karşılaştırılması.* Planlama Uzmanlığı Tezi, İktisadi Sektörler ve Koordinasyon Genel Müdürlüğü, T.C. Kalkınma Bakanlığı, 2891.

City of London. (2022). Official web page. *Green Transport.* https://www.london.gov.uk/what-we-do/transport/green-transport

Clement-Nyns, K., Haesen, E., & Driesen, J. (2009). The impact of charging plug-in hybrid electric vehicles on a residential distribution grid. *IEEE Transactions on Power Systems, 25*(1), 371–380. doi:10.1109/TPWRS.2009.2036481

Climate Bond Initiative. (2017). *Sovereign green bonds briefing.* CBI. https://www.climatebonds.net/files/files/Sovereign_Briefing2017.pdf

Climate Bond Initiative. (2018). *Korea climate bond market overview and opportunities.* CBI. https://www.climatebonds.net/files/files/CBI-Korea_Market-Final-01A.pdf

Climate Bond Initiative. (2021). *Sustainable debt global state of the market 2021.* CBI. https://www.climatebonds.net/files/reports/cbi_global_sotm_2021_02h_0.pdf

Climate Bond Initiative. (2022). *Netherlands sovereign green bond.* CBI. https://www.climatebonds.net/certification/netherlands_sovereign

Cohen, A., & Shaheen, S. (2016). *Planning for shared mobility.* PAS Report 581. American Planning Association, pp. 1–106. https://www.planning.org/publications/report/9107556/

Colak, I., Sagiroglu, S., Fulli, G., Yesilbudak, M., & Covrig, C. F. (2016). A survey on the critical issues in smart grid technologies. *Renewable & Sustainable Energy Reviews, 54*, 396–405. doi:10.1016/j.rser.2015.10.036

Collins, J., & Porras, J. I. (1994). *Built to Last: Successful Habits of Visionary Companies.* HarperCollins Publishers.

COM. (2020). Sustainable and Smart Mobility Strategy – putting European transport on track for the future. Communication from the Commission to the European Parliament, the Council, the European Economic and Social Committee and The Committee of the Regions. European Commission.

COM. (2020). Sustainable and Smart Mobility Strategy – putting European transportation on track for the future. European Commission.

Commission of the European Communities. (2001). *Green Paper: Promoting a European framework for Corporate Social Responsibility.* Europa. https://ec.europa.eu/commission/presscorner/detail/en/DOC_01_9

Commission of the European Communities. (2002). *Corporate Social Responsibility: A business contribution to Sustainable Development.* Eurofound. https://www.eurofound.europa.eu/observatories/emcc/articles/business/corporate-social-responsibility-a-business-contribution-to-sustainable-development

Connolly, D., Lund, H., & Mathiesen, B. V. (2016). Smart Energy Europe: The technical and economic impact of one potential 100% renewable energy scenario for the European Union. *Renewable & Sustainable Energy Reviews, 60,* 1634–1653. doi:10.1016/j.rser.2016.02.025

Costescu, D., Olteanu, S., & Roman, E. A. (2022). Model for Bus Line Planning in an Intermodal Urban Transportation Network. In: Moldovan, L., Gligor, A. (Eds) *The 15th International Conference Interdisciplinarity in Engineering. Inter-Eng 2021. Lecture Notes in Networks and Systems,* (vol 386). Springer.

Costescu, D., Stere, A. S., & Serban, A. M. (2021). Network of Dedicated Bus Lanes: A Solution to Increase the Accessibility of the Urban Intermodal Transport. *Romanian Journal of Transport Infrastructure, 10*(2), 1–15. doi:10.2478/rjti-2021-0008

Cotterill, S., & Richardson, L. (2009). Changing the nature of transactions between local state and citizens: an experiment to encourage civic behaviour. *Political Studies Association Conference.*

Cruz-Jesus, F., Oliveira, T., & Bacao, F. (2012). Digital divide across the European Union. *Information & Management, 49*(6), 278–291. doi:10.1016/j.im.2012.09.003

Curtis, C., & Scheurer, J. (2017). Performance measures for public transport accessibility: Learning from international practice. *Journal of Transport and Land Use, 10*(1), 93–118.

CXCentral. (2019, July 5). What's the difference between customer satisfaction and customer experience? *CXCentral.* https://cxcentral.com.au/executives/customer-satisfaction-different-to-customer-experience/

Czech Academy of Sciences. (2021, June 10). *Covid-19: The safety of Prague's public transportation system confirmed.* AVCR. https://www.avcr.cz/en/media/press-releases/Covid-19-The-safety-of-Pragues-public-transportation-system-confirmed/

D'Adamo, I., Gastaldi, M., & Ozturk, I. (2022). The sustainable development of mobility in the green transition: Renewable energy, local industrial chain, and battery recycling. *Sustainable Development,* 1–13. doi:10.1002d.2424

D'Arcier, B.F. (2010). La situation financière des transports publics urbains est-elle "durable "? [The financial situation of public city transportation- is it durable?] *Les Cahiers scientifiques du transport [Journal of Scientific Transportation], 58,* 3-28.

D'Arcier, B.F. (Coord.) (2012). *Measure de la performance des lignes de transport public urbain [Measure of the performance of city public transport lines].* APEROL: Amélioration de la Performance Economique des Réseaux par l'Optimisation des Lignes [Improving the Economic Performance of Networks by Line Optimization].

Danielis, R., Scoranno, M., & Giansoldati, M. (2022). Decarbonising transport in Europe: Trends, goals, policies and passenger car scenarios. *Research in Transportation Economics, 91,* 101068. doi:10.1016/j.retrec.2021.101068

Danielou, J. (2014). *Smart city and sustainable city : the case of Amsterdam.* Citego. https://www.citego.org/bdf_fiche-document-2429_en.html

Compilation of References

Das, S., Boruah, A., Banerjee, A., Raoniar, R., Nama, S., & Maurya, A. K. (2021). Impact of COVID-19: A radical modal shift from public to private transport mode. *Transport Policy, 109*, 1–11. doi:10.1016/j.tranpol.2021.05.005 PMID:36570699

Datanovia (2018). *Determining The Optimal Number Of Clusters: 3 Must Know Methods.* Data Novia. https://www.datanovia.com/en/lessons/determining-the-optimal-number-of-clusters-3-must-know-methods/

Davis, T., & Hale, M. (2007). *Public transportation's contribution to US greenhouse gas reduction.* APTA. https://www.apta.com/wp-content/uploads/Resources/resources/reportsandpublications/Documents/climate_change.pdf

De Borger, B., Kerstens, K., & Costa, Á. (2002). Public transit performance: What does one learn from frontier studies? *Transport Reviews, 22*(1), 1–38. doi:10.1080/01441640010020313

De Borger, B., Proost, S., & Van Dender, K. (2005). Congestion and tax competition in a parallel network. *European Economic Review, 49*(8), 2013–2040. doi:10.1016/j.euroecorev.2004.06.005

De Oña, J. (2021). Understanding the mediator role of satisfaction in public transport: Across-country analysis. *Transport Policy, 100*, 129–149. doi:10.1016/j.tranpol.2020.09.011

De Vos, J., Lättman, K., van der Vlugt, A.-L., Welsch, J., & Otsuka, N. (2022). Determinants and effects of perceived walkability: A literature review, conceptual model and research agenda. *Transport Reviews*, 1–22. doi:10.1080/01441647.2022.2101072

Deakin, E. (2001). Sustainable development and sustainable transportation: strategies for economic prosperity, environmental quality, and equity. University of California, Berkeley Institute of Urban and Regional Development.

Deboosere, R., El-Geneidy, A. M., & Levinson, D. (2018). Accessibility-oriented development. *Journal of Transport Geography, 70*, 11–20. doi:10.1016/j.jtrangeo.2018.05.015

Deci, E. L., & Ryan, R. M. (2012). Self-Determination Theory. In Handbook of Theories of Social Psychology (Vol. 1, pp. 416–437). SAGE Publications Ltd., https://doi.org/10.4135/9781446249215.n21.

Deci, E. L., & Ryan, R. M. (1985). Conceptualizations of intrinsic motivation and self-determination. In *Intrinsic motivation and self-determination in human behavior* (pp. 11–40). Springer.

dell'Olio, L., Ibeas, A., & Cecin, P. (2010). Modelling user perception of bus transit quality. *Transport Policy, 17*(6), 388–397. doi:10.1016/j.tranpol.2010.04.006

Dell'Olio, L., Ibeas, A., de Oña, J., & de Oña, R. (2018). *Public Transportation Quality of Service.* Elsevier Ltd.

Delmonte, E., Kinnear, N., Jenkins, B., & Skippon, S. (2020). What do consumers think of smart charging? Perceptions among actual and potential plug-in electric vehicle adopters in the United Kingdom. *Energy Research & Social Science, 60*, 101318. doi:10.1016/j.erss.2019.101318

Deloitte, & Insights. (2020). *Deloitte City Mobility Index 2020.* Deloitte.

Demirbaş, A. (2006). Global renewable energy resources. *Energy Sources, 28*(8), 779–792. doi:10.1080/00908310600718742

Deveci, M., Canıtez, F., & Çetin Demirel, N. (2015). *Toplu Ulaşımda Entegrasyon Basamakları: Kavramsal Bir İnceleme.* TRANSİST 8. Uluslararası Ulaşım Teknolojileri Sempozyumu ve Fuarı, 21-25, İstanbul, Türkiye.

Dienel, H.-L., & Schiefelbusch, M. (2009). *Public Transport and its Users: The Passenger's Perspective in Planning and Customer Care.* Ashgate Publishing, Ltd.

Dobesova, Z. & Krivka, T. (2012). Walkability index in the Urban Planning: A case stud in Olomouc City. *Advances in Spatial Planning*, 179 - 196.

Dobruszkes, F., Hubert, M., Laporte, F., & Veiders, C. (2011). Réorganisation d'un réseau de transportation collectif urbain, ruptures de charge et mobilités éprouvantes à Bruxelles [Reorganization of an urban collective transportation network, load breaks and stressful mobility in Brussels]. *Journal of Urban Research 7.* https://journals.openedition.org/articulo/1844

Dolejš, S. (2015, April 10). *Marketing – Dopravní podnik města České Budějovice* [Conference presentation]. Smart and Healthy Transport in Cities 2019, Pilsen, Czech republic. https://konference.pmdp.cz/uploads/_web/prezentace2015/Slavoj_Dolejs.pdf

Dolot, A. (2018). The characteristics of Generation Z. *e-mentor, 2*(74), 44-50. doi:10.15219/em74.1351

Dong, H., Ma, S., Jia, N., & Tian, J. (2021). Understanding public transport satisfaction in post COVID-19 pandemic. *Transport Policy, 101,* 81–88. doi:10.1016/j.tranpol.2020.12.004

Dorfleitner, G., Utz, S., & Zhang, G. (2021). The pricing of green bonds: External reviews and the shades of green. *Review of Managerial Science, 16*(3), 797–834. doi:10.100711846-021-00458-9

Dovey, K., & Pafka, E. (2020). What is walkability? The urban DMA. *Urban Studies (Edinburgh, Scotland), 57*(1), 93–108. doi:10.1177/0042098018819727

DPMCB. (2016, March 5). *Ženy dostanou v autobusech a trolejbusech tisíc růží [Women receive a thousand roses on buses and trolleys].* DPMCB. E15. https://www.dpmcb.cz/o-nas/novinky/zeny-dostanou-v-autobusech-a-trolejbusech-tisic-ruzi-48.html

Dudley, E., Lin, D. Y., Mancini, M., & Ng, J. (2015). *Implementing a citizen-centric approach to delivering government services.* McKinsey & Company. www.mckinsey.com/industries/public-sector/our-insights/implementing-a-citizen-centric-approach-to-delivering-government-services

DuList. (2019). *Use car sharing and forget about caring!* DuList. https://dulist.hr/prvi-u-hrvatskoj-koritete-car-sharing-i-zaboravite-na-brigu-o-parkingu/613101/

Dutta, S., Lanvin, B., & Wunsch-Vincent, S. (Eds.). (2018). *The global innovation index 2018: Energizing the world with innovation.* WIPO.

Dwivedi, Y., Weerakkody, V., & Janssen, M. (2012). Moving towards maturity: Challenges to successful e-government implementation and diffusion. *Advanced Information Systems, 42*(4), 11–22.

E15. (2013, February 27). *Automobilky loni snížily výdaje do reklamy o šest procent [Car Companies reduced advertising spending by six per cent last year].* E15. https://www.e15.cz/byznys/ostatni/automobilky-loni-snizily-vydaje-do-reklamy-o-sest-procent-960867

EasyPark AB. (2021). *The future of European parking – demand for electric cars and free parking spots.* EasyPark. https://www.easyparkgroup.com/news/the-future-of-european-parking-demand-for-electric-cars-and-free-parking-spots/

Ebert, C., & Duarte, C. H. C. (2018). Digital transformation. *IEEE Software, 35*(4), 16–21. doi:10.1109/MS.2018.2801537

EC. (2016). Quality of Life in European Cities. 2015. Flash Eurobarometer 419, Directorate-General for Regional and Urban Policy, European Commission, Publications Office of the European Union.

ECMT. (2001). *European conference of ministers of transport.* OECD Library. https://www.oecd-ilibrary.org/transport/european-conference-of-ministers-of-transport-annual-report_23099488

Compilation of References

Ed-daoudy, A., & Maalmi, K. (2019). A new Internet of Things architecture for real-time prediction of various diseases using machine learning on big data environment. *Journal of Big Data*, 6(1), 104. doi:10.118640537-019-0271-7

Edwin Conan. (2008). *Muscle Car Sharing System*. Edwin Conan. https://edwinconan.wordpress.com/2008/10/29/muscle-car-sharing-system

Ehlers, T., & Packer, P. (2017). Green bond finance and certification. *BIS Quarterly Review*, 89-104.

Ekins, P. (2004). *Environment and human behaviour: a new opportunities programme*. Springer.

El Alaoui, I., Gahi, Y., Messoussi, R., Chaabi, Y., Todoskoff, A., & Kobi, A. (2018). A novel adaptable approach for sentiment analysis on big social data. *Journal of Big Data*, 5(1), 12. doi:10.118640537-018-0120-0

Elkington, J. (2018). *25 Years Ago I Coined the Phrase "Triple Bottom Line." Here's Why It's Time to Rethink It*. Harvard Business Review. https://hbr.org/2018/06/25-years-ago-i-coined-the-phrase-triple-bottom-line-heres-why-im-giving-up-on-it

Elkington, J. Hailes, Julia., & Makower, J. (1990). The green consumer. Penguin Books.

Elkington, J. (1997). *Cannibals with forks: The Triple Bottom Line of 21st Century Business*. Capstone Publishing Limited.

Eltis. (2019). *SUMP Glossary*. Eltis. https://www.eltis.org/mobility-plans/glossary#

Emmanuel, I., & Stanier, C. (2016). Defining Big Data. In *Proceedings of the International Conference on Big Data and Advanced Wireless Technologies - BDAW '16*. ACM Press. 10.1145/3010089.3010090

Enerdata. (2019). *Odyssee-Mure - Sectoral Profile – Transport*. Enerdata. https://www.odyssee-mure.eu/publications/efficiency-by-sector/transport/passenger-mobility-per-capita.html

Energy Information Administration. (2022). *Electricity explained - U.S.* EIA. https://www.eia.gov/energyexplained/electricity/#:~:text=Electricity%20is%20a%20secondary%20energy%20source&text=The%20electricity%20that%20we%20use,wind%20energy%2C%20into%20electrical%20power

ENTSO-E. (2021). *ENTSO-E Position Paper: Electric Vehicle Integration into Power Grids*. ENTSO-E. https://eepublicdownloads.entsoe.eu/clean-documents/Publications/Position%20papers%20and%20reports/210331_Electric_Vehicles_integration.pdf

EPA (United States Environmental Protection Agency). (2022). *Local Renewable Energy Benefits and Resources*. Retreived June 20, 2022 from https://www.epa.gov/statelocalenergy/local-renewable-energy-benefits-and-resources

EPA. (2011). Guide to sustainable transportation performance measures. EPA 231-K-10-004. https://www.epa.gov/sites/default/files/2014-01/documents/sustainable_transpo_performance.pdf

Erokhina, O. V., & Brega, A. V. (2020). Intelligent transport technologies in "smart" cities. In 2020 Systems of Signals Generating and Processing in the Field of on Board Communications. IEEE.

Esztergár-Kiss, D., & Lizarraga, J. C. L. (2021). Exploring user requirements and service features of e-micromobility in five European cities. *Case Studies on Transport Policy*, 9(4), 1531–1541. doi:10.1016/j.cstp.2021.08.003

Eteme, A. A., & Ngossaha, J. M. (2020). The contribution of ICTs to sustainable urbanization and health in urban areas in Cameroon. In Waste Management: Concepts, Methodologies, Tools, and Applications (pp. 624-641). IGI Global. doi:10.4018/978-1-7998-1210-4.ch030

EU Parliament. (2018). Directive 2018/2001 of the European Parliament and of the Council on the promotion of the use of energy from renewable sources. *Official Journal of the European Union.* https://eur-lex.europa.eu/legal-content/EN/TXT/?uri=uriserv:OJ.L_.2018.328.01.0082.01.ENG

EU. (2014). Directive 2014/94/EU of the European Parliament and of the Council of 22 October 2014 on the deployment of alternative fuels infrastructure. *Official Journal of the European Union L, 307*(1). https://eur-lex.europa.eu/legal-content/en/TXT/?uri=CELEX%3A32014L0094

EUGPUT. (2021). *Energy usage and green public transportation in future smart cities: An innovative teaching program for students, stakeholders and entrepreneurs.* EUGPUT. https://upb.ro/wp-content/uploads/2020/03/Comunicat-EUGPUT.pdf

Eureletric (2015). *Prosumers: an integral part of the power system and the market.* Eureletric. https://www.eurelectric.org/media/1945/prosumers_an_integral_part_of_the_power_system_and_market_june_2015-2015-2110-0004-01-e.pdf (Accessed 1 August, 2021).

European Alternative Fuels Observatory (EAFO). (2021). *Country detail vehicles and fleet.* EAFO. https://www.eafo.eu/countries/european-union-efta-turkey/23682/vehicles-and-fleet

European Bank for Reconstruction and Development (EBRD). (2017). *On the move: delivering automated fare collection.* EBRD. https://www.google.com/url?sa=t&rct=j&q=&esrc=s&source=web&cd=&ved=2ahUKEwiPgcHM6Lj2AhVxk_0HHRupAX0QFnoECAYQAQ&url=https%3A%2F%2Fwww.ebrd.com%2Fdocuments%2Fadmin%2Fon-the-move-delivering-automated-fare-collection.pdf&usg=AOvVaw0eN3cc-C-QU99j1bHITudv

European Commission (EC). (2019). *Your guide to IP commercialisation.* Executive Agency for Small and Medium-sized Enterprises. Retrieved December 6, 2022, from https://op.europa.eu/en/publication-detail/-/publication/a75b3213-ebf4-11e9-9c4e-01aa75ed71a1/language-en/format-PDF/source-search

European Commission (EC). (2019). *Your Guide to IP in Europe.* Executive Agency for Small and Medium-sized Enterprises. Retrieved December 6, 2022, from https://op.europa.eu/en/publication-detail/-/publication/ddf8fb93-ec0e-11e9-9c4e-01aa75ed71a1/language-en/format-PDF/source-164620483

European Commission (EC). (2020). *European IP Helpdesk: Your guide to IP management in International Business.* Executive Agency for Small and Medium-sized Enterprises. Retrieved December 6, 2022, from https://op.europa.eu/en/publication-detail/-/publication/bb7327c0-12a2-11eb-9a54-01aa75ed71a1/language-en/format-PDF/source-188386935

European Commission (EC). (2020). *Sustainable and Smart Mobility Strategy–putting European transport on track for the future.* EC.

European Commission. (2009). Directive 2009/28/EC of the European Parliament and of the Council of 23 April 2009 on the promotion of the use of energy from renewable sources and amending and subsequently repealing Directives 2001/77/EC and 2003/30/EC. *Official Journal of the European Union, L, 140*, 1–148.

European Commission. (2018). Directive (EU) 2018/2001 of the European Parliament and of the Council on the promotion of the use of energy from renewable sources. Official Journal of European Union, 328.

European Commission. (2021). *Transportation and the green deal.* Europa. https://ec.europa.eu/info/strategy/priorities-2019-2024/european-green-deal/transport-and-green-deal_en

European Environment Agency (EEA). (2022). *Annual European Union greenhouse gas inventory 1990–2020 and inventory report 2022. Submission to the UNFCCC Secretariat, May 2022.* EU NIR.

European Environmental Agency (EEA). (2022). *Share of energy consumption from renewable sources in Europe.* EEA. https://www.eea.europa.eu/ims/share-of-energy-consumption-from

Compilation of References

European Federation for Transport and Environment AISBL. (2020). *TE Infrastructure Report*. AISBL. https://www.transportenvironment.org/wp-content/uploads/2021/07/01%202020%20Draft%20TE%20Infrastructure%20Report%20Final.pdf

European Parliament. (2014), *Social impact bonds: private finance that generates social returns*. European Parliament. https://www.europarl.europa.eu/EPRS/538223-Social-impact-bonds-FINAL.pdf

European Parliament. (2015). *Bridging the digital divide in the EU*. European Parliamnet. https://www.europarl.europa.eu/RegData/etudes/BRIE/2015/573884/EPRS_BRI(2015)573884_EN.pdf

Eurostat - Information society. (2021). *E-government activities of individuals via websites*. Eurostat. https://appsso.eurostat.ec.europa.eu/nui/show.do?dataset=isoc_ciegi_ac&lang=en

Eurostat (2021). *Passenger mobility statistics*. Eurostat. https://ec.europa.eu/eurostat/statistics-explained/index.php?title=Passenger_mobility_statistics

Eurostat (2022). *Renewable energy statistics*. Eurostat. https://ec.europa.eu/eurostat/statistics-explained/index.php?title=Renewable_energy_statistics

Ewing, R., & Handy, S. (2009). Measuring the Unmeasurable: Urban Design Qualities Related to Walkability. *Journal of Urban Design, 14*(1), 65–84. doi:10.1080/13574800802451155

Faivre C.G. (Coord.). (2015). *Chaine de déplacement et pôles d'échanges multimodaux: diagnostics de situations [Travel chain and multimodel exchange hubs: situation diagnosis]*. Projet TIMODEV, Programme PREDIT.

Faivre d'Arcier, B. (Coord.) (2012). *Measure de la performance des lignes de transportation public urbain [Measurement of the performance o furban public transportation lines]*. APEROL.

Fazeli, S. M., Zangeneh, A., & Kalantar, M. (2014). Optimal Operation of Smart Grids Based on Power Loss Minimization Using Distribution Optimal Power Flow Model. *International Journal of Scientific Engineering and Technology, 3*(7), 978–982.

Fazio, M., Giuffrida, N., Le Pira, M., Inturri, G., & Ignaccolo, M. (2021). Planning Suitable Transportation Networks for E-Scooters to Foster Micromobility Spreading. *Sustainability, 13*(20), 11422. doi:10.3390u132011422

Federal Republic of Germany. (2021). *Green bond investor presentation*. BDF GmbH. https://www.deutsche-finanzagentur.de/fileadmin/user_upload/institutionelle-investoren/pdf/Green_Bond_Investor_Presentation_2021.pdf

Fernández-Portillo, A., Almodóvar-González, M., & Hernández-Mogollón, R. (2020). Impact of ICT development on economic growth. A study of OECD European union countries. *Technology in Society, 63*, 101420.

Ferrari, L., Cavaliere, A., de Marchi, E., & Banterle, A. (2019). Can nudging improve the environmental impact of food supply chain? A systematic review. *Trends in Food Science & Technology, 91*, 184–192.

Ferron, M., & Massa, P. (2013). Transtheoretical model for designing technologies supporting an active lifestyle. *Proceedings of the Biannual Conference of the Italian Chapter of SIGCHI on - CHItaly '13*, 1–8. doi:10.1145/2499149.2499158

Filimonau, V., & Krivcova, M. (2017). Restaurant menu design and more responsible consumer food choice: An exploratory study of managerial perceptions. *Journal of Cleaner Production, 143*, 516–527. https://doi.org/10.1016/j.jclepro.2016.12.080

Filimonau, V., Lemmer, C., Marshall, D., & Bejjani, G. (2017). 'Nudging' as an architect of more responsible consumer choice in food service provision: The role of restaurant menu design. *Journal of Cleaner Production, 144*, 161–170. https://doi.org/10.1016/j.jclepro.2017.01.010

Firoiu, D., Ionescu, G. H., Băndoi, A., Florea, N. M., & Jianu, E. (2019). Achieving sustainable development goals (SDG): Implementation of the 2030 Agenda in Romania. *Sustainability*, *11*(7), 2156. doi:10.3390u11072156

Fishman, T. D. (2012). *Digital-Age Transportation: The Future of Urban Mobility*. Deloitte University Press.

Fitzová, H., Matulová, M., & Tomeš, Z. (2018). Determinants of urban public transport efficiency: Case study of the Czech Republic. *European Transport Research Review*, *10*(2), 42. doi:10.118612544-018-0311-y

Flaherty, M., Gevorkyan, S., Radpour, S., & Semmler, W. (2017). Financing climate policies through climate bonds – A three stage model and empirics. *Research in International Business and Finance*, *42*(C), 468–479. doi:10.1016/j.ribaf.2016.06.001

Flath, C., Ilg, J., & Weinhardt, C. (2012). Decision support for electric vehicle charging. *AMCIS Proceedings*. AIS. https://aisel.aisnet.org/amcis2012/proceedings/GreenIS/14

Fogg, B. (2009). A behavior model for persuasive design. *Proceedings of the 4th International Conference on Persuasive Technology - Persuasive '09*, 1. doi:10.1145/1541948.1541999

Fonesca, F., Papageorgiou, G., Tondelli, S., Ribeiro, P., Conticelli, E., Jabbari, M., & Ramos, R. (2022). Perceived Walkability and Respective Urban Determinants: Insights from Bologna and Porto. *Sustainability*, *4*(15), 1–19. doi:10.3390u14159089

Forsyth, A. (2015). What is a walkable place? The walkability debate in urban design. *URBAN DESIGN International*, *20*(4), 274–292. doi:10.1057/udi.2015.22

Franssens, S., Botchway, E., de Swart, W., & Dewitte, S. (2021). Nudging Commuters to Increase Public Transport Use: A Field Experiment in Rotterdam. *Frontiers in Psychology, 12*. doi:10.3389/fpsyg.2021.633865

Freeman, C., & Louçã, F. (2001). As Time Goes By: From the Industrial Revolutions to the Information Revolution. Oxford University Press pp. viii, 40.

Freeman, C., & Louçâ, F. (2001). *As time goes by: from the industrial revolutions to the information revolution*. Oxford University Press.

Friebelová, J., & Klicnarová, J. (2007). *Rozhodovací modely pro economy [Decision models for economists]*. Jihočeská univerzita.

Fumagalli, L. A. W., Rezende, D. A., & Guimaraes, T. A. (2021). Challenges for public transportation: Consequences and possible alternatives for the Covid-19 pandemic through strategic digital city application. *Journal of Urban Management*, *10*(2), 97–109. doi:10.1016/j.jum.2021.04.002

Fyhri, A., Karlsen, K., & Sundfør, H. B. (2021). Paint It Red - A Multimethod Study of the Nudging Effect of Coloured Cycle Lanes. *Frontiers in Psychology, 12*. doi:10.3389/fpsyg.2021.662679

Gadepalli, G., Gumireddy, S., Bhamidipati, S., & Cats, O. (2022). Impact of introducing a metro line on urban bus services. *Case Studies on Transport Policy*, *10*(2), 940–947. doi:10.1016/j.cstp.2022.03.007

Galatoulas, N. F., Genikomsakis, K. N., & Ioakimidis, C. S. (2020). Spatio-temporal trends of e-bike sharing system deployment: A review in Europe, North America and Asia. *Sustainability*, *12*(11), 4611. doi:10.3390u12114611

Gandy, O. H., & Nemorin, S. (2019). Toward a political economy of nudge: Smart city variations. *Information Communication and Society*, *22*(14), 2112–2126. https://doi.org/10.1080/1369118X.2018.1477969

Gatautis, R., Medziausiene, A., Tarute, A., & Vaiciukynaite, E. (2015). Towards ICT Impact Framework: Private and Public Sectors Perspective. *Journal of Economics. Business and Management*, *3*(4), 465–469.

Compilation of References

Gatersleben, B., & Appleton, K. M. (2007). Contemplating cycling to work: Attitudes and perceptions in different stages of change. *Transportation Research Part A, Policy and Practice, 41*(4), 302–312. https://doi.org/10.1016/j.tra.2006.09.002

Gebhardt, L., Krajzewicz, D., & Oostendorp, R. (2017) Intermodality – key to a more efficient urban transportation system? *Proceedings of the 2017 ECEEE Summer Study Proceedings*, (pp. 759-769). ECEEE.

Gehl, J. (2010). *Cities for People*. Island Press.

Gentile, Ch., Spiller, N., & Noci, G. (2007). How to Sustain the Customer Experience: An Overview of Experience Components that Co-create Value With the Customer. *European Management Journal, 25*(5), 395–410. doi:10.1016/j.emj.2007.08.005

Gimpel, H., & Röglinger, M. (2015). *Digital transformation: changes and chances–insights based on an empirical study.* University Bayreuth. https://eref.uni-bayreuth.de/29908/

GoDigital. (2020). Smart public transport the foundation of the smart city system. *Go Digital.* https://godigital.hrvatskitelekom.hr/pametni-javni-prijevoz-temelj-sustava-pametnog-grada/

Gölcük, I., & Baykasoğlu, A. (2016). An analysis of DEMATEL approaches for criteria interaction handling within ANP. *Expert Systems with Applications, 46*, 346–366. doi:10.1016/j.eswa.2015.10.041

Goldbach, C., Sickmann, J., Pitz, T., & Zimasa, T. (2022). Towards autonomous public transportation: Attitudes and intentions of the local population. *Transportation Research Interdisciplinary Perspectives, 13*, 100504. doi:10.1016/j.trip.2021.100504

Gössling, S. (2013). Urban transport transitions: Copenhagen, city of cyclists. *Journal of Transport Geography, 33*, 196–206. doi:10.1016/j.jtrangeo.2013.10.013

Gössling, S., Choi, A., Dekker, K., & Metzler, D. (2019). The Social Cost of Automobility, Cycling and Walking in the European Union. *Ecological Economics, 158*, 65–74. doi:10.1016/j.ecolecon.2018.12.016

Gössling, S., & Cohen, S. (2014). Why sustainable transport policies will fail: EU climate policy in the light of transport taboos. *Journal of Transport Geography, 39*, 197–207. doi:10.1016/j.jtrangeo.2014.07.010

Graells-Garrido, E., Meta, I., Serra-Buriel, F., Reyes, P., & Cucchietti, F. M. (2020). Measuring Spatial Subdivisions in Urban Mobility with Mobile Phone Data. In *Companion Proceedings of the Web Conference 2020. Presented at the WWW '20: The Web Conference 2020.* ACM. 10.1145/3366424.3384370

Grand view research (2019). *Automated Fare Collection Market Size, Share & Trends Analysis Report By System (TVM, TOM), By Technology (Smart Card, NFC), By Application, By Component (Hardware, Software), And Segment Forecasts, 2019 – 2025.* Grand View Research. https://www.grandviewresearch.com/industry-analysis/automated-fare-collection-afc-system-market

Grbavec, P., Pejic Bach, M., Zoroja, J., Strugar, I., & Jaković, B. (2019). Digital economy and society index as the indicator of digital divide in European countries: preliminary cluster analysis. *Conference proceedings of the 8th International scientific conference, Kovač, Tatjana; Cingula, Marijan – Celje* (pp. 29-36). Slovenia: Fakulteta za komercialne in poslovne vede.

Greene, D. L., & Wegener, M. (1997). Sustainable transport. *Journal of Transport Geography, 5*(3), 177–190. doi:10.1016/S0966-6923(97)00013-6

Grigorieva, O., & Nikulshin, A. (2022). Electric buses on the streets of Moscow: Experience, problems, prospects. *Transportation Research Procedia, 63*, 670–675. doi:10.1016/j.trpro.2022.06.061

Guerrero-Ibanez, J. A., Zeadally, S., & Contreras-Castillo, J. (2015). Integration challenges of intelligent transportation systems with connected vehicle, cloud computing, and internet of things technologies. *IEEE Wireless Communications*, *22*(6), 122–128. doi:10.1109/MWC.2015.7368833

Guthrie, J., Mancino, L., & Lin, C.-T. J. (2015). Nudging Consumers toward Better Food Choices: Policy Approaches to Changing Food Consumption Behaviors. *Psychology and Marketing*, *32*(5), 501–511. https://doi.org/10.1002/mar.20795

Guttikunda, N., Gota, S., & Chanda, J. (2019). Air quality, emissions, and source contributions analysis for the Greater Bengaluru region of India. *Atmospheric Pollution Research*, *10*(3), 941–953. doi:10.1016/j.apr.2019.01.002

Guzman, L. A., Arellana, J., & Alvarez, V. (2020). Confronting congestion in urban areas: Developing Sustainable Mobility Plans for public and private organizations in Bogotá. *Transportation Research Part A, Policy and Practice*, *134*, 321–335. doi:10.1016/j.tra.2020.02.019

Hachenberg, B., & Schiereck, D. (2018). Are green bonds priced differently from conventional bonds? *Journal of Asset Management*, *19*(6), 371–383. doi:10.105741260-018-0088-5

Hader, M., Tchoffa, D., El Mhamedi, A., Ghodous, P., Dolgui, A., & Abouabdellah, A. (2022). Applying integrated Blockchain and Big Data technologies to improve supply chain traceability and information sharing in the textile sector. *Journal of Industrial Information Integration*, *28*, 100345. doi:10.1016/j.jii.2022.100345

Hall, C. M., & Ram, Y. (2018). *Walk score® and its potential contribution to the study of active transport and walkability: A critical and systematic review. Transportation Research Part D*, 61(B).

Halt, G. B., Donch, J. C., Stiles, A. R., & Fesnak, R. (2017). *Intellectual property and financing strategies for technology startups*. Springer.

Halt, G. B., Donch, J. C., Stiles, A. R., & Robert, F. (2014). *Intellectual property in consumer electronics, software and technology startups*. Springer. doi:10.1007/978-1-4614-7912-3

Hämäläinen, M. (2020). A framework for a Smart City design: digital transformation in the Helsinki Smart City. In *Entrepreneurship and the Community* (pp. 63–86). Springer.

Hamurcu, M., & Eren, T. (2017). *Toplu Taşıma Türünün Seçiminde Çok Kriterli Karar Verme Uygulaması. International Conference on Advanced Engineering Technologies, Bayburt, Türkiye.*

Handy. (2005). Planning for accessibility: In theory and in practice. In *Access to Destinations*. Elsevier.

Hanson, S. (2004). *The Geography of Urban Transportation*. Guilford Press.

HanY.LiP.WuS. (2020). Does Green Bond Improve Portfolio Diversification? Evidence from China. Retrieved from doi:10.2139/ssrn.3639753

Haque, M. M., Chin, H. C., & Debnath, A. K. (2013). Sustainable, safe, smart-three key elements of Singapore's evolving transport policies. *Transport Policy*, *27*, 20–31. doi:10.1016/j.tranpol.2012.11.017

Harris, N., Shealy, T., & Klotz, L. (2017). Choice architecture as a way to encourage a whole systems design perspective for more sustainable infrastructure. In *Sustainability (Switzerland)* (*Vol. 9,* Issue 1). doi:10.3390/su9010054

Helluin, J.-J., (2018). *La planification de la mobilité urbaine dans les pays en développement pour des villes plus économes en énergie : la nécessaire alliance entre objectifs globaux et besoins locaux*. Academic Press.

Herrmann-Lunecke, M. G., Mora, R., & Sagaris, L. (2020). Persistence of walking in Chile: Lessons for urban sustainability. *Transport Reviews*, *40*(2), 135–159. doi:10.1080/01441647.2020.1712494

Compilation of References

Heuberger, R. (2017). Achieving the shared sustainable development goals: How the ICT sector can drive the renewable energy revolution. *Connect World Magazine*. https://connect-world.com/achieving-shared-sustainable-development-goals-ict-sector-can-drive-renewable-energy-revolution/

He, W., Wang, X., Han, J., Xiao, X., & Sheng, X. (2022). Study on the influence of resilient wheels on vibration and acoustic radiation characteristics of suburban railway concrete box girder bridges. *Applied Acoustics, 187*(February), 108529. doi:10.1016/j.apacoust.2021.108529

Hickman, R., Mella Lira, B., Givoni, M., & Geurs, K. (Eds.). (2019). *A Companion to Transport, Space and Equity*. Edward Elgar. doi:10.4337/9781788119825

Hilbert, M. (2022). Digital technology and social change: The digital transformation of society from a historical perspective. *Dialogues in Clinical Neuroscience, 22*(2), 189–194.

Hilbert, M., López, P., & Vásquez, C. (2010). Information societies or "ICT equipment societies?" Measuring the digital information-processing capacity of a society in bits and bytes. *The Information Society, 26*(3), 157–178.

Hiramatsu. (2022). Inter-metropolitan regional migration galvanized by high-speed rail: A simulation analysis of the Linear Chuo Shinkansen line in Japan. *Socio-Economic Planning Sciences*, 101268.

Hitachi-UTokyo Laboratory. (2018). *Society 5.0: A People-centric Super-smart Society*. Springer. https://doi.org/10.1007/978-981-15-2989-4

HM Treasury and UK Debt Management Office. (2021). Green gilts investor presentation. HM Treasury and UK Debt Management Office. https://assets.publishing.service.gov.uk/government/uploads/system/uploads/attachment_data/file/1033194/Green_Gilt_Investor_Presentation.pdf

Holbrook, M. B., & Hirschman, E. C. (1982). The experiential aspects of consumption: Consumer fantasy, feelings and fun. *The Journal of Consumer Research, 9*(2), 132–140. doi:10.1086/208906

Hollenstein, D., & Bleischa, S. (2016). Walkability for Different Urban Granularities. *The International Archives of the Photogrammetry, Remote Sensing and Spatial Information Sciences, Volume XLI-B2, 2016 XXIII ISPRS Congress*.

Hong, S., & Ryu, J. (2019). Crowdfunding public projects: Collaborative governance for achieving citizen co-funding of public goods. *Government Information Quarterly, 36*(1), 145–153. doi:10.1016/j.giq.2018.11.009

Hopkins, D. (2016). Can environmental awareness explain declining preference for car-based mobility amongst generation Y? A qualitative examination of learn to drive behaviours. *Transportation Research Part A, Policy and Practice, 94*, 149–163. doi:10.1016/j.tra.2016.08.028

Hörisch, J. (2015). Crowdfunding for environmental ventures: An empirical analysis of the influence of environmental orientation on the success of crowdfunding initiatives. *Journal of Cleaner Production, 107*, 636–645. doi:10.1016/j.jclepro.2015.05.046

Hozjan, V. (2022). GEN-I razbremenjuje omrežje z zamikom vklopa toplotnih črpalk [GEN-I relieves the grid by delaying the start-up of heat pumps]. *Energetika*. https://www.energetika.net/novice/en.vizija/gen-i-razbremenjuje-omrezje-z-zamikom-vklopa-toplotnih-crpal

Hribernik, U. (2020). *Passenger Information Systems (PIS): Your top 8 questions answered*. Lit Transit. https://lit-transit.com/insights/passenger-information-systems-pis-your-top-8-questions-answered/

Hsu, C.-C., Liou, J. J. H., Lo, H.-W., & Wang, Y.-C. (2018). Using a hybrid method for evaluating and improving the service quality of public bike-sharing systems. *Journal of Cleaner Production, 202*, 1131–1144. doi:10.1016/j.jclepro.2018.08.193

Huajie (2020). *Bus Smart Card Payment Ticketing System*. Sinalbolr. https://en.wxhjic.com/b070c208-ccfa-c7d3-c271-bb71a6e5df2a/9322782a-b69d-a348-6f6f-0a98f98aa9a4.shtml

Huang, Q., & Wong, D. W. S. (2015). Modeling and Visualizing Regular Human Mobility Patterns with Uncertainty: An Example Using Twitter Data. *Annals of the Association of American Geographers, 105*(6), 1179–1197. doi:10.108 0/00045608.2015.1081120

Huber, J., & Weinhardt, C. (2018). Waiting for the sun-can temporal flexibility in BEV charging avoid carbon emissions? *Energy Informatics, 1*(1), 115-126. https://energyinformatics.springeropen.com/articles/10.1186/s42162-018-0026-2

Huber, J., Schaule, E., Jung, D., & Weinhardt, C. (2019). Quo vadis smart charging? A literature review and expert survey on technical potentials and user acceptance of smart charging systems. *World Electric Vehicle Journal, 10*(4), 85. doi:10.3390/wevj10040085

Hyde, R. A., & Karney, B. W. (2001). Environmental education research: Implications for engineering education. *Journal of Engineering Education, 90*(2), 267–275. doi:10.1002/j.2168-9830.2001.tb00602.x

Hynes. (2022). Walk a Mile in My Shoes! An Autoethnographical Perspective of Urban Walkability in Galway. *Journal of Contemporary Ethnography, 51*(5), 619-644.

Ibraeva, A., & de Sousa, J. F. (2014). Marketing of public transport and public transport information provision. *Procedia: Social and Behavioral Sciences, 162*, 121–128. doi:10.1016/j.sbspro.2014.12.192

Ikerd, J. (2012). *The essentials of economic sustainability*. Kumarian Press.

Imberg, M., & Shaban, M. (2019). *A generational shift: Family wealth transfer report 2019*. Wealth-X. https://thehome-trust.com/wp-content/uploads/2019/11/Wealth-X_Family-Wealth-Transfer-Report_2019.pdf

İnaç, H., & Tanyaş, M. (2012). *İstanbul'un kentsel lojistik analizi ve çözüm önerilerinin AHP ile değerlendirilmesi*. Ulusal Lojistik ve Tedarik Zinciri Kongresi, Konya, Türkiye.

Indiamart (2021). Iot Automation Projects. Retrieved March 9, 2022 from https://www.indiamart.com/proddetail/factory-iot-automation-project-21653851388.html

Inglesi-Lotz, R. (2016). The Impact of Renewable Energy Consumption to Economic Growth: A Panel Data Application. *Energy Economics, 53*, 58–63.

Innovate U. K. (2021). *UK TRANSPORT VISION 2050: investing in the future of mobility*. Innovate UK. https://www.ukri.org/wp-content/uploads/2022/01/IUK-110122-UK-Transport-Vision-2050.pdf

Intelligent Transport. (2021). *Moscow using green bonds to finance sustainable transport projects*. Intelligent Transport. https://www.intelligenttransport.com/transport-news/128394/moscow-green-bonds/

International Association of Public Transport. (2018, July 18). *Customer Service Excellence: A word from our members* [Video]. YouTube. https://www.youtube.com/watch?v=4EZvb-kSllE&

International Capital Market Association. (2021). *Green bond principles voluntary process guidelines for issuing green bonds june 2021*. ICMA. https://www.icmagroup.org/assets/documents/Sustainable-finance/2021-updates/Green-Bond-Principles-June-2021-100621.pdf

International Chamber of Commerce (ICC). (2019). *Handbook on Valuation of Intellectual Property Assets*. Retrieved December 6, 2022, from https://iccwbo.org/publication/icc-handbook-valuation-intellectual-property-assets/

International Electrotechnical Commission. (2022). *Medium voltage*. Electropedia. https://www.electropedia.org/iev/iev.nsf/display?openform&ievref=601-01-28

Compilation of References

International Energy Agency. (2022a). *Electricity*. IEA. https://www.iea.org/fuels-and-technologies/electricity

International Energy Agency. (2022b). *World Energy Investment 2022*. IEA. https://iea.blob.core.windows.net/assets/b0beda65-8a1d-46ae-87a2-f95947ec2714/WorldEnergyInvestment2022.pdf

International Financing Review. (2022). *Airport authority HK sells controversial green bond*. IFR. https://www.ifre.com/story/3196600/airport-authority-hk-prices-us4bn-144areg-s-four-tranche-senior-bond-tnp3jy9rns

International, I. C. F. (2010). Livability in transportation guidebook. FHWA-HEP-10-028. https://www.recpro.org/assets/Library/Livability/livability_in_transportation_guide_072910_lowres.pdf

Investment Partners, N. N. (2021). *Spain's first green bond to pay for clean transport and climate change plan*. NNIP. https://www.nnip.com/en-INT/professional/insights/articles/spains-first-green-bond-to-pay-for-clean-transport-and-climate-change-plan

ISS-oekom. (2021). *Methodology: ISS-oekom corporate rating*. ISS-oekom. https://www.deka-etf.de/documents/iss_oekom_47_latest_de.pdf

ITSO. (2018). *What is smart ticketing?* ITSO. https://www.itso.org.uk/about-us/what-is-smart-ticketing/#:~:text=ITSO%20Smart%20ticketing%20is%20a,usually%20embedded%20on%20a%20smartcard

Jagiello, A., Wojtach, A., & Łuczak, A. (2018). *Report benchmarks for the current public transport systems*. Inno Baltica. http://interconnect.one/images/PDFs/report-Interconect-4-2.pdf

Jamei, E., Ahmadi, K., Chau, H. W., Seyedmahmoudian, M., Horan, B., & Stojcevski, A. (2021). Urban Design and Walkability: Lessons Learnt from Iranian Traditional Cities. *Sustainability*, *13*(10), 1–14. doi:10.3390u13105731

Jardim, B., & de Castro Neto, M. (2022). Walkability Indicators in the Aftermath of the COVID-19 Pandemic: A Systematic Review. *Sustainability*, *14*(17), 1–24. doi:10.3390u141710933

Jašić, T. (2021). *Suvremeni informacijski sustavi u javnom prijevozu u pametnim gradovima [Modern Information Systems in Public Transport in Smart Cities]*. [Unpublished master's dissertation, University of Split, Croatia].

Jayaprakash, P., & Radhakrishna Pillai, R. (2022). The Role of ICT for Sustainable Development: A Cross-Country Analysis. *European Journal of Development Research*, *34*, 225–247.

Jiang, Y., Wang, J., Ao, Z., & Wang, Y. (2022). The relationship between green bonds and conventional financial markets: Evidence from quantile-on-quantile and quantile coherence approaches. *Economic Modelling*, *116*, 106038. doi:10.1016/j.econmod.2022.106038

Jochem, P., Frankenhauser, D., Ewald, L., Ensslen, A., & Fromm, H. (2020). Does free-floating carsharing reduce private vehicle ownership? The case of SHARE NOW in European cities. *Transportation Research Part A, Policy and Practice*, *141*, 373–395. doi:10.1016/j.tra.2020.09.016 PMID:33052178

Johnson, D. B., & Sveen, L. W. (2020). Three key values of Generation Z: Equitably serving the next generation of students. *College and University*, *95*(1), 37–40. https://www.proquest.com/scholarly-journals/three-key-values-generation-z-equitably-serving/docview/2369316081/se-2?accountid=14965

Jylhä, A., Nurmi, P., Sirén, M., Hemminki, S., & Jacucci, G. (2013). MatkaHupi: a persuasive mobile application for sustainable mobility. *Proceedings of the 2013 ACM Conference on Pervasive and Ubiquitous Computing Adjunct Publication*, (pp. 227–230). ACM. https://doi.org/10.1145/2494091.2494164

Kager, R., Bertolini, L., & Te Brömmelstroet, M. (2016). Characterization of and reflections on the synergy of bicycles and public transportation. *Transportation Research Part A, Policy and Practice*, *85*, 208–219. doi:10.1016/j.tra.2016.01.015

Kaldellis, J. K., Spyropoulos, G., & Liaros, St. (2017). Supporting electromobility in smart cities using solar electric vehicle charging stations. Mediterranean green buildings and renewable energy: Selected papers from *the world renewable energy network's med green forum* (pp. 501-513). Springer. doi:10.1007/978-3-319-30746-6_37

Kamargianni, M., Li, W., Matyas, M., & Schäfer, A. (2016). A critical review of new mobility services for urban transport. *Transportation Research Procedia, 14*, 3294–3303. doi:10.1016/j.trpro.2016.05.277

Kang, C.-D. (2018). The S + 5Ds: Spatial access to pedestrian environments and walking in Seoul, Korea. *Cities (London, England), 77*, 130–141. doi:10.1016/j.cities.2018.01.019

Kaplan, H., & Ulukavak, H. G. (2013). Kentlerimizde sürdürülebilir bütünleşik ulaşıma doğru: Sorun ve olanakların irdelenmesi. *TRANSİST 6. Ulaşım Sempozyumu ve Fuarı*, 181-195.

Kaplan, S. M. (2009, April). *Electric power transmission: background and policy issues*. Library of Congress, Congressional Research Service. https://www.nosue.org/app/download/7244200729/2009-04-14-09+CRS+18743.pdf

Kappel, K., & Grechenig, T. (2009). "Show-Me": water consumption at a glance to promote water conservation in the shower. *Proceedings of the 4th International Conference on Persuasive Technology - Persuasive '09*, 1. ACM. doi:10.1145/1541948.1541984

KarpfA.MandelA. (2017). Does it pay to be green? A comparative study of the yield term structure of green and brown bonds in the US municipal bonds market. https://ssrn.com/abstract=2923484

Kasperbauer, T. J. (2017). The permissibility of nudging for sustainable energy consumption. *Energy Policy, 111*, 52–57. https://doi.org/10.1016/j.enpol.2017.09.015

Kass, A. (2020). *Bike sharing benefits and disadvantages*. Kass and Moses. https://kassandmoses.com/bicycle/blog/bike-sharing-benefits-and-disadvantages

Kato, H. (2020). Effect of Walkability on Urban Sustainability in the Osaka Metropolitan Fringe Area. *Sustainability, 12*(21), 1–17. doi:10.3390u12219248

Kaur, I. (2021). Metering architecture of smart grid. In Design, Analysis, and Applications of Renewable Energy Systems (pp. 687-704). Academic Press. doi:10.1016/B978-0-12-824555-2.00030-7

Kazhamiakin, R., Marconi, A., Martinelli, A., Pistore, M., & Valetto, G. (2016). A gamification framework for the long-term engagement of smart citizens. *2016 IEEE International Smart Cities Conference (ISC2)*, (pp. 1–7). IEEE.

Keizer, B., Kouwenhoven, M., & Hofker, F. (2015). New Insights in Resistance to Interchange. *Transportation Research Procedia, 8*, 72–79. doi:10.1016/j.trpro.2015.06.043

Kempton, W., & Tomić, J. (2005a). Vehicle-to-grid power fundamentals: Calculating capacity and net revenue. *Journal of Power Sources, 144*(1), 268–279. doi:10.1016/j.jpowsour.2004.12.025

Kempton, W., & Tomić, J. (2005b). Vehicle-to-grid power implementation: From stabilizing the grid to supporting large-scale renewable energy. *Journal of Power Sources, 144*(1), 280–294. doi:10.1016/j.jpowsour.2004.12.022

Kerin, P. D. (1987). Why Subsidize State Transport Authorities? *The Australian Quarterly, 59*(1), 60–72. doi:10.2307/20635413

Kerstens, K. (1999). Decomposing Technical Efficiency and Effectiveness of French Urban Transport. *Annales d'Economie et de Statistique, 54*(54), 129–155. doi:10.2307/20076181

Kestrel Verifiers. (2022). *Second party opinions on green, social and sustainability bonds*. Kestrel Verifiers. https://kestrelverifiers.com/second-party-opinions/

Compilation of References

Khalifa, A. (2010). Vehicle tracking system for sugarcane. API. http://api.uofk.edu:8080/api/core/bitstreams/81315bda-39e5-4487-8a02-75867d444104/content

Khavarian-Garmsir, A. R., Sharifi, A., & Sadeghi, A. (2023). The 15-minute city: Urban planning and design efforts toward creating sustainable neighborhoods. *Cities (London, England), 132*.

Kim, J., Schmöcker, J. D., & Fujii, S. (2016). Exploring the relationship between undergraduate education and sustainable transport attitudes. *International Journal of Sustainable Transportation, 10*(4), 385–392. doi:10.1080/15568318.2014.961108

Kim, S. H., Chung, J.-H., Park, S., & Choi, K. (2017). Analysis of user satisfaction to promote public transportation: A pattern-recognition approach focusing on out-of-vehicle time. *International Journal of Sustainable Transportation, 11*(8), 582–592. doi:10.1080/15568318.2017.1280715

Kioupi, V., & Voulvoulis, N. (2019). Education for sustainable development: A systemic framework for connecting the SDGs to educational outcomes. *Sustainability, 11*(21), 6104. doi:10.3390u11216104

Kittilaksanawong, W. & Liu, H. (2021). Mobike China: competing through the giant's ecosystem. *Emerald Emerging Markets Case Studies, 11*(1).

Klaus, P., Jaakkola, E., Gustafsson, A., & McColl-Kennedy, J. R. (2015). Fresh perspectives on customer experience. *Journal of Services Marketing, 29*(6/7), 430–435. doi:10.1108/JSM-01-2015-0054

Klaus, P., & Maklan, S. (2013). Towards a better measure of customer experience. *International Journal of Market Research, 55*(2), 227–246. doi:10.2501/IJMR-2013-021

Klieber, K., Luger-Bazinger, C., Hornung-Prähauser, V., Geser, G., Wieden-Bischof, D., Paraschivoiu, I., Layer-Wagner, T., Möstegl, N., Huemer, F., & Rosan, J. (2020). Nudging sustainable behaviour: Data-based nudges for smart city innovations. *The ISPIM Innovation Conference – Innovating in Times of Crisis*, (pp. 1–18). www.simplicity-project.eu

Knapskog, M., Hagen, O. H., Tennøy, A., & Rynning, M. K. (2019). Exploring ways of measuring walkability. *Transportation Research Procedia, 41*, 264–282. doi:10.1016/j.trpro.2019.09.047

Knoch, M., & Van der Plasken, C. (2020). *The green finance market emerging in Brazil leading players, products, and main challenges*. GmbH. https://www.giz.de/en/downloads/the-green-finance-market-emerging-in-brazil-oct-2020-final.pdf

Kohout, J. (2019, 25 November). *Automatické počítání cestujících – nový kontinent příležitostí [[Automatic passenger counting- a new contineny of opportunity*. [Conference presentation]. Veřejná doprava, Prague, Czech Republic. http://www.telematika.cz/download/doc/10_Kohout_PMDP_APC.pdf

Komarčević, M., Dimić, M., & Čelik, P. (2017). Challenges and impacts of the digital transformation of society in the social sphere. *SEER: Journal for Labour and Social Affairs in Eastern Europe, 20*(1), 31–48.

Koo, T. K., & Li, M. Y. (2016). A Guideline of Selecting and Reporting Intraclass Correlation Coefficients for Reliability Research. *Journal of Chiropractic Medicine, 15*(2), 155–163. doi:10.1016/j.jcm.2016.02.012 PMID:27330520

Koschinsky, J., Emily Talen, E., & Alfonso, M. (2016). How walkable is Walker's paradise? *Environment and Planning. B, Planning & Design*, 1–21.

Kraska-Miller, M. (2014). *Nonparametric Statistics for Social and Behavioral Sciences*. CRC Press.

Kresa, Z. (2019). *Comparison of customer experience among selected transport companies* [Master's thesis, University of West Bohemia, Czech Republic.]. https://dspace5.zcu.cz/bitstream/11025/39300/1/DP-Kresa.pdf

Kristensson, P., Wästlund, E., & Söderlund, M. (2017). Influencing consumers to choose environment friendly offerings: Evidence from field experiments. *Journal of Business Research, 76*, 89–97. https://doi.org/10.1016/j.jbusres.2017.03.003

Kuo, N.-W., Sharifi, A., & Li, C.-E. (2022). Smart Cities and Urban Resilience: Insights from a delphi survey. *The Urban Book Series*, 119–138. doi:10.1007/978-3-030-95037-8_6

Kuznetsov, S., & Paulos, E. (2010). UpStream: motivating water conservation with low-cost water flow sensing and persuasive displays. *Proceedings of the 28th International Conference on Human Factors in Computing Systems - CHI '10*, 1851. ACM. doi:10.1145/1753326.1753604

Kwon, Y.-I., Kyun-Kim, Ch., Kim, T., Hagen, J., Barone, R., & Joaquin, D. (2015, June). *Improving the Customer Experience* [White paper]. Transit Leadership Summit. https://s3.us-east-1.amazonaws.com/rpa-org/pdfs/TLS-WP-Improving-the-Customer-Experience.pdf

Kylili, A., & Fokaides, P. A. (2015). European smart cities: The role of zero energy buildings. *Sustainable Cities and Society, 15*, 86–95. doi:10.1016/j.scs.2014.12.003

Lam, A., Leung, Y., & Chu, X. (2016). Autonomous-Vehicle Public Transportation System: Scheduling and Admission Control. *IEEE Transactions on Intelligent Transportation Systems, 17*(5), 1210–1226. doi:10.1109/TITS.2015.2513071

Lambert, F. (August 22, 2022). Small Vermont utility quietly builds fleet of 4,000 Tesla Powerwalls. *Electrek*. https://electrek.co/2022/08/22/small-vermont-utility-builds-fleet-4000-tesla-powerwalls/

Lane, C., Hidalgo, D., Schleeter, R., & Mackie, K. (2017). On the move: Car-sharing scales up. *Smart Cities Dive*. https://www.smartcitiesdive.com/ex/sustainablecitiescollective/move-car-sharing-scales/208451/

Larcker, D. F., & Watts, E. M. (2020). Where's the greenium? *Journal of Accounting and Economics, 69*(2-3), 101312. doi:10.1016/j.jacceco.2020.101312

Larkin, C. M., Jancourt, M., & Hendrix, W. H. (2018). The Generation Z world: Shifts in urban design, architecture and the corporate workplace. *Corporate Real Estate Journal, 7*(3), 230-242. https://www.ingentaconnect.com/content/hsp/crej/2018/00000007/00000003/art00005

Le Corbusier. (1971). La Charte d'Athènes. [The Athens Charter]. Points.

Lee, E. J., Choi, H., Han, J., Kim, D. H., Ko, E., & Kim, K. H. (2020). How to "Nudge" your consumers toward sustainable fashion consumption: An fMRI investigation. *Journal of Business Research, 117*, 642–651. https://doi.org/10.1016/j.jbusres.2019.09.050

Lefevre, B. (2010). Urban Transportation Energy Consumption: Determinants and Strategies for its Reduction, *S.A.P.I.EN.S. 2*(3). https://journals.openedition.org/sapiens/914

Lehner, M., Mont, O., & Heiskanen, E. (2016). Nudging – A promising tool for sustainable consumption behaviour? *Journal of Cleaner Production, 134*, 166–177. https://doi.org/10.1016/j.jclepro.2015.11.086

Lemon, K. N., & Verhoef, P. C. (2016). Understanding Customer Experience Throughout the Customer Journey. *Journal of Marketing, 80*(6), 69–96. doi:10.1509/jm.15.0420

Leon, I. D., & Donoso, J. F. (2018). *Innovation, startups and Intellectual Property Management Strategies and evidence from Latin America and other regions*. Springer International Publishing.

León, L. R., Bergquist, K., Wunsch-Vincent, S., Xu, N., & Fushimi, K. (2017). *Measuring innovation in energy technologies: green patents as captured by WIPO's IPC green inventory* (Vol. 44). WIPO.

Compilation of References

Lepri, B., Antonelli, F., Pianesi, F., Pentland, A., (2015). Making big data work: smart, sustainable, and safe cities. *EPJ Data Sci., 4*, 16. doi:10.1140/epjds/s13688-015-0050-4

Li, H. (2016). Study on green transportation system of international metropolises. Paper presented at *the Procedia Engineering, 137*, (pp. 762-771). Procedia Engineering. 10.1016/j.proeng.2016.01.314

Lin, L., & Hong, Y. (2022). Developing a green bonds market: Lessons from China. *European Business Organization Law Review, 23*(1), 143–185. doi:10.100740804-021-00231-1

Liou, J. J. H., Tamosaitiene, J., Zavadskas, E. K., & Tzeng, G.-H. (2015). New hybrid COPRAS-G MADM Model for improving and selecting suppliers in green supply chain management. *International Journal of Production Research, 54*(1), 114–134. doi:10.1080/00207543.2015.1010747

Li, S., Tong, L., Xing, J., & Zhou, Y. (2017). The market for electric vehicles: Indirect network effects and policy design. *Journal of the Association of Environmental and Resource Economists, 4*(1), 89–133. doi:10.1086/689702

Litman, T. (2012). *Toward More Comprehensive and Multimodal Transportation Evaluation.* Victoria Transportation Policy Institute. https://www.vtpi.org/comp_evaluation.pdf

Litman, T. (2015). *When Are Bus Lanes Warranted? Considering Economic Efficiency, Social Equity and Strategic Planning Goals.* Victoria Transportation Policy Institute. https://www.vtpi.org/blw.pdf

Litman, T. (2016). *When are bus lanes warranted? Considering economic efficiency, social equity, and strategic planning goals.* Victoria Transport Policy Institute. https://www.vtpi.org/blw.pdf

Litman, T. (2020). *Autonomous vehicle implementation predictions: Implications for transportation planning.* Victoria Transportation Policy Institute. https://www.vtpi.org/avip.pdf

Litman, T., & Burwell, D. (2006). Issues in sustainable transportation. *International Journal of Global Environmental Issues, 6*(4), 331–347.

Liu, X., Deng, Q., Gong, G., Zhao, X., & Li, K. (2021). Evaluating the interactions of multi-dimensional value for sustainable product-service system with grey DEMATEL-ANP approach. *Journal of Manufacturing Systems, 60*, 449–458. doi:10.1016/j.jmsy.2021.07.006

Liu, Y., Sun, Z., Wang, X., Chen, T., & Yang, C. (2022). Dose-response association between the daily step count and all-cause mortality: A systematic review and meta-analysis. *Journal of Sports Sciences, 40*(5), 1678–1687. doi:10.1080/02640414.2022.2099186 PMID:35819337

Liu, Z., Yang, H.-C., & Shiau, Y.-C. (2020). Investigation on evaluation framework of elementary school teaching materials for sustainable development. *Sustainability, 12*(9), 3736. doi:10.3390u12093736

Li, Y., Yabuki, N., & Fukuda, T. (2023). Integrating GIS, deep learning, and environmental sensors for multicriteria evaluation of urban street walkability. *Landscape and Urban Planning, 230*, 104603. doi:10.1016/j.landurbplan.2022.104603

Li, Z., Tang, Y., Wu, J., Zhang, J., & Lv, Q. (2019). The interest costs of green bonds: Credit ratings, corporate social responsibility, and certification. *Emerging Markets Finance & Trade, 56*(12), 2679–2692. doi:10.1080/1540496X.2018.1548350

Lo, H. R. (2009). Walkability: What is it? *Journal of Urbanism, 2*(2), 145–166. doi:10.1080/17549170903092867

Long, Z., & Axsen, J. (2022). Who will use new mobility technologies? Exploring demand for shared, electric, and automated vehicles in three Canadian metropolitan regions. *Energy Research & Social Science, 88*, 102506. doi:10.1016/j.erss.2022.102506

Longzhi, Y., Noe, E., & Neil, E. (2018). *Outlier discrimination and correction in intelligent transportation systems: Privacy and security aspects of e-government in smart cities.* Elsevier.

Loo. (2021). Walking towards a happy city. *Journal of Transport Geography, 93*, 1-11.

Lopes, J. A. P., Soares, F. J., & Almeida, P. M. R. (2010). Integration of electric vehicles in the electric power system. *Proceedings of the IEEE, 99*(1), 168–183. doi:10.1109/JPROC.2010.2066250

Lotgroup (2018). *Automated Fare Collection System.* Lot Group. https://lotgroup.eu/product/smart-city/afc/

Luk, J., & Olszewski, P. (2003). Integrated public transportation in Singapore and Hong Kong. *Road and Transport Research, 12*(4), 41–51.

Lund, H. (2009). *Renewable energy systems: the choice and modeling of 100% renewable solutions.* Academic Press.

Luo, X. G., Zhang, H. B., Zhang, Z. L., Yu, Y., & Li, K. (2019). A new framework of intelligent public transportation system based on the internet of things. *IEEE Access: Practical Innovations, Open Solutions, 7,* 55290–55304. doi:10.1109/ACCESS.2019.2913288

Luthra, S., Kumar, A., Zavadskas, E. K., Mangla, S. K., & Garza-Reyes, J. A. (2019). Industry 4.0 as an enabler of sustainability diffusion in supply chain: An analysis of influential strength of drivers in an emerging economy. *International Journal of Production Research, 58*(5), 1505–1521. doi:10.1080/00207543.2019.1660828

Mackevičiūtė, R., Martinaitis, Z., Lipparini, F., Scheck, B. C., & Styczyńska, I. (2020). *Social impact investment. Best practices and recommendations for the next generation.* EMPL. https://www.europarl.europa.eu/RegData/etudes/STUD/2020/658185/IPOL_STU(2020)658185_EN.pdf

Maduro, M., Pasi, G., & Misuraca, G. (2018). Social impact investment in the EU. Financing strategies and outcome oriented approaches for social policy innovation: narratives, experiences, and recommendations. Publications Office of the European Union. .. doi:10.2760/159402

Maeda, T. N., Shiode, N., Zhong, C., Mori, J., & Sakimoto, T. (2019). Detecting and understanding urban changes through decomposing the numbers of visitors' arrivals using human mobility data. *Journal of Big Data, 6*(1), 4. doi:10.118640537-019-0168-5

Ma, H., Balthasar, F., Tait, N., Riera-Palou, X., & Harrison, A. (2012). A new comparison between the life cycle greenhouse gas emissions of battery electric vehicles and internal combustion vehicles. *Energy Policy, 44*, 160–173. doi:10.1016/j.enpol.2012.01.034

Mair, J., & Laing, J. H. (2013). Encouraging pro-environmental behaviour: The role of sustainability-focused events. *Journal of Sustainable Tourism, 21*(8), 1113–1128. https://doi.org/10.1080/09669582.2012.756494

Malhotra, C., Anand, R., & Singh, S. (2018). Applying Big Data Analytics in Governance to Achieve Sustainable Development Goals (SDGs) in India. In U. Munshi & N. Verma (Eds.), *Data Science Landscape. Studies in Big Data* (Vol. 38). Springer. doi:10.1007/978-981-10-7515-5_19

Manfreda, A., Ljubi, K., & Groznik, A. (2021). Autonomous vehicles in the smart city era: An empirical study of adoption factors important for millennials. *International Journal of Information Management, 58*, 102050.

Mangla, S. K., Luthra, S., Rich, N., Kumar, D., Rana, N. P., & Dwivedi, Y. K. (2018). Enablers to implement sustainable initiatives in agri-food supply chains. *International Journal of Production Economics, 203*, 379–393. doi:10.1016/j.ijpe.2018.07.012

Compilation of References

Manjon, M., Aouni, Z., & Crutzen, N. (2021). Green and Digital Entrepreneurship in smart cities. *The Annals of Regional Science, 68*(2), 429–462. doi:10.100700168-021-01080-z

Marada, M. (2003). Transport typology of settlement centres of Czechia from public passenger transport point of view. *Acta Universitatis Carolinae. Geographica. Universita Karlova, 38*(1), 259–269. http://hdl.handle.net/20.500.11956/160824

Marchiori, D. R., Adriaanse, M. A., & de Ridder, D. T. D. (2017). Unresolved questions in nudging research: Putting the psychology back in nudging. *Social and Personality Psychology Compass, 11*(1), e12297. https://doi.org/10.1111/spc3.12297

Marsh, J. (2021). How IoT can make transportation more sustainable. The internet of all things web page. *The Internet of All Things.* https://www.theinternetofallthings.com/how-iot-can-make-transportation-more-sustainable/

Marsh, J. (2022). Will Renewables Make Public Transportation More Affordable? *Renewable Energy Magazine.* https://www.renewableenergymagazine.com/jane-marsh/will-renewables-make-public-transportation-more-affordable-20220518

Martí, P., Serrano-Estrada, L., & Nolasco-Cirugeda, A. (2019). Social Media data: Challenges, opportunities and limitations in urban studies. *Computers, Environment and Urban Systems, 74*, 161–174. doi:10.1016/j.compenvurbsys.2018.11.001

Masoumi, H. E. (2019). A discrete choice analysis of transport mode choice causality and perceived barriers of sustainable mobility in the MENA region. *Transport Policy, 79*, 37–53. doi:10.1016/j.tranpol.2019.04.005

Massot, M. H., & Orfeuil, J. P. (2005). La mobilite au quotidien, entre choix individuel et production sociale. *Cahiers Internationaux de Sociologie, 1*(118), 81–100. doi:10.3917/cis.118.0081

Matt, C., Hess, T., & Benlian, A. (2015). Digital transformation strategies. *Business & Information Systems Engineering, 57*(5), 339–343.

Mauro, S., Shinde, S., Arnone, M., Zamith, V. M., de Rosa, G., & Pietroni, D. (2022). *The role of awareness of mobility offer and nudges in increasing sustainable mobility habits of citizens: a case study from the Munich region.* Springer. doi:10.1109/COMPSACS54236.2022.00267

Mavragani, A., & Ochoa, G. (2018). Infoveillance of infectious diseases in USA: STDs, tuberculosis, and hepatitis. *Journal of Big Data, 5*(1), 30. doi:10.118640537-018-0140-9

Mayor of London. (2018). Mayor's Transport Strategy. London Assembly. https://www.london.gov.uk/what-we-do/transport/our-vision-transport/mayors-transport-strategy-2018?intcmp=46686

Mayor of London. (2021). *Travel in London. Report 14.* Mayor of London.

Mazhar Rathore, M., Ahmad, A., Paul, A., Hong, W.-H., & Seo, H. (2017). Advanced computing model for geosocial media using big data analytics. *Multimedia Tools and Applications, 76*(23), 24767–24787. doi:10.100711042-017-4644-7

McGlade, C. E., & Ekins, P. (2015). The geographical distribution of fossil fuels unused when limiting global warming to 2°C. *Nature, 517*(7533), 187–190. doi:10.1038/nature14016 PMID:25567285

McGlothin, D. (2002). Managing transit's workforce in the new millennium. *Transit Cooperative Research Program Report 77.* https://trb.org/publications/tcrp/tcrp_rpt_77.pdf

McGreevy. (2021). Cost, reliability, convenience, equity or image? The cases for and against the introduction of light rail and bus rapid transit in inners suburban Adelaide, South Australia. *Case Studies on Transport Policy, 9*(1), 271–279.

McKinsey. (2021, July). *Urban transportation systems of 25 global cities. Elements of success.* McKinsey. https://www.mckinsey.com/~/media/mckinsey/business%20functions/operations/our%20insights/building%20a%20transport%20system%20that%20works%20new%20charts%20five%20insights%20from%20our%2025%20city%20report%20new/elements-of-success-urban-transportation-systems-of-25-global-cities-july-2021.pdf

McQueen, M., Abou-Zeid, G., MacArthur, J., & Clifton, K. (2021). Transportation transformation: Is micromobility making a macro impact on sustainability? *Journal of Planning Literature, 36*(1), 46–61. doi:10.1177/0885412220972696

Meloni, I., & di Teulada, B. S. (2015). I-Pet Individual Persuasive Eco-travel Technology: A Tool for VTBC Program Implementation. *Transportation Research Procedia, 11*, 422–433. https://doi.org/10.1016/j.trpro.2015.12.035

Meyer, M. D., & Miller, E. J. (2000). *Urban transportation planning: A decision-oriented approach.* McGraw-Hill.

Michaud, Marro, & Denning, Shackleton, Toutant, & McNamee. (2022). Annoyance toward transportation and construction noise in rural suburban and urban regions across Canada. *Environmental Impact Assessment Review, 97*, 106881.

MicroProgram. (2021). *Smart Bike Solution.* MicroProblem. https://www.program.com.tw/en/solution/transportation/category/smart-bike-solution

Ministry of Health. (2022, April 13). *Mimořádné opatření, č. j.: 8789/2022-2/MIN/KAN.* Ministry of health. https://www.mzcr.cz/wp-content/uploads/2022/04/Mimoradne-opatreni-ochrana-dychacich-cest-ve-zdravotnickych-zarizenich-a-zarizenich-socialnich-sluzeb-s-ucinnosti-od-14-4-2022.pdf

Ministry of the Interior. (2012). *Videoconference with presentation of AVL system.* Ministarstco unutarnjih poslova. https://mup.gov.hr/vijesti-8/videokonferencija-s-prezentacijom-sustava-avl-a/130967

Mitra, S., Kumar, H., Gupta, M. P., & Bhattacharya, J. (2022). Entrepreneurship in smart cities: Elements of start-up Ecosystem. *Journal of Science and Technology Policy Management.* doi:10.1108/JSTPM-06-2021-0078

MixTelematics. (2021). *Fleet solutions for the public transport industry.* Mix Telematics. https://www.mixtelematics.com/industries/public-transport

Mobility Pilsen. (2022). *Pilsen Sustainable Mobility Plan – Overview of measures.* Mibillity Pilsen. https://www.mobilita-plzen.cz/prehled_opatreni

Molina-Markham, A., Shenoy, P., Fu, K., Cecchet, E., & Irwin, D. (2010, November). Private memoirs of a smart meter. In *Proceedings of the 2nd ACM workshop on embedded sensing systems for energy-efficiency in building* (pp. 61-66). ACM. 10.1145/1878431.1878446

Momsen, K., & Stoerk, T. (2014). From intention to action: Can nudges help consumers to choose renewable energy? *Energy Policy, 74*(C), 376–382. https://doi.org/10.1016/j.enpol.2014.07.008

Mona, I., & Raberto, M. (2018). The EIRIN flow-of-funds behavioural model of green fiscal policies and green sovereign bonds. *Ecological Economics, 144*, 228–243. doi:10.1016/j.ecolecon.2017.07.029

Montes, H., Salinas, C., Fernández, R., & Armada, M. (2017). An Experimental Platform for Autonomous Bus Development. *Applied Sciences (Basel, Switzerland), 7*(11), 1131. doi:10.3390/app7111131

Moody's Investors Service. (2018). *A greener approach to financing: green bond assessment overview.* Moody's https://www.moodys.com/sites/products/ProductAttachments/MIS_Green_Bonds_Assessment.pdf?WT.z_referringsource=TB~ESGhub~GREENBONDS

Morel, M., Balm, S., Berden, M., & Ploos van Amstel, V. (2020). Governance models for sustainable urban construction logistics: Barriers for collaboration. *Transportation Research Procedia, 46*, 173–180. doi:10.1016/j.trpro.2020.03.178

Compilation of References

Moreno, C., Allam, Z., Chabaud, D., Gall, C., & Pratlong, F. (2021). Introducing the "15-Minute City": Sustainability, Resilience and Place Identity in Future Post-Pandemic Cities. *Smart Cities*, *4*(1), 93–111. doi:10.3390martcities4010006

Morze, N. V., & Strutynska, O. V. (2021). Digital transformation in society: Key aspects for model development. *Journal of Physics: Conference Series*, *1946*(1), 012021.

Moshari, A., Yousefi, G. R., Ebrahimi, A., & Haghbin, S. (2010). *Demand-side behavior in the smart grid environment. In 2010 IEEE PES Innovative Smart Grid Technologies Conference Europe (ISGT Europe)*. IEEE. doi:10.1109/ISGTEUROPE.2010.5638956

Mott MacDonald. (2021, October 31). *Analysis - Sustainable Mobility Strategy of the Pilsen Metropolitan ITI Area*. Plzeň v pohybu. https://sump-iti.plzen.eu/wp-content/uploads/2022/05/oprava_ka01_sump-plzen-iti-analyza_2021-12-20.pdf

Mouratidis, K., & Cobeña Serrano, V. (2021). Autonomous buses: Intentions to use, passenger experiences, and suggestions for improvement. *Transportation Research Part F: Traffic Psychology and Behaviour*, *76*, 321–335. doi:10.1016/j.trf.2020.12.007

Mucunska Palevska, V., & Novkovska, B. (2021). Increasing use of digital technologies in function of economic growth in European countries. *UTMS Journal of Economics (Skopje)*, *12*(1), 84–94.

Mulley, C., Nelson, J., & Ison, S. (Eds.). (2021). *The Routledge handbook of public transport*. Routledge. doi:10.4324/9780367816698

Murdock, H. E., Collier, U., Adib, R., Hawila, D., Bianco, E., Muller, S., & Frankl, P. (2018). *Renewable energy policies in a time of transition*. IRENA.

Murshed, M. (2020). An empirical analysis of the non-linear impacts of ICT-trade openness on renewable energy transition, energy efficiency, clean cooking fuel access and environmental sustainability in South Asia. *Environmental Science and Pollution Research International*, *27*(29), 36254–36281.

Nagode, K., & Manfreda, A. (2022). IT Diffusion in the Society: The Expansion of Smart Cities and Their Impact on the Sustainable Development. *International Working Conference on Transfer and Diffusion of IT*, (pp. 177–187). Springer. https://doi.org/10.1007/978-3-031-17968-6_14

Namazu, M., Zhao, J., & Dowlatabadi, H. (2018). Nudging for responsible carsharing: Using behavioral economics to change transportation behavior. *Transportation*, *45*(1), 105–119. https://doi.org/10.1007/s11116-016-9727-1

Nanayakkara, M., & Colombage, S. (2019). Do investors in green bond market pay a premium? Global evidence. *Applied Economics*, *51*(40), 1–13. doi:10.1080/00036846.2019.1591611

Nasiri, E., Rocha-Meneses, L., Inayat, A., & Kikas, T. (2022). Impact of Policy Instruments in the Implementation of Renewable Sources of Energy in Selected European Countries. *Sustainability*, *14*(10), 6314.

National Academies Sciences Engineering Medicine. (2021). *Analysis of green bond financing in the public transportation industry*. The National Academies Press.

National Operations Center of Excellence. (2021*). Big Data and TSM & O*. National Operations Center of Excellence. https://transportationops.org/BigData/BigData-overview

NEC. (2021). *Transportation Solutions*. NEC. https://in.nec.com/en_IN/solutions_services/intelligent_transport_solutions/transportation.html

Negre L. (Coord.) (2008). *Charte des services publics locaux. Indicateurs de performance des réseaux de transportation public [Charter of local public services, Performance indicators of public transportation networks]*. Institut de la Gestion Déléguée (IDG), Association des Maires de France.

Negre, L. (Coord.) (2008). *Charte des services publics locaux. Indicateurs de performance des réseaux de transport public [Charter of local public services, Performance indicators of public transport networks]*. Institut de la Gestion Déléguée, Association des Maires de France.

Nenseth, V., Ciccone, A., & Kristensen, N. B. (2019). *Societal consequences of automated vehicles: Norwegian scenarios*. Institute of Transportation Economics. https://www.toi.no/getfile.php?mmfileid=50576

Newman, P., & Kenworthy, J. (2015). *The End of Automobile Dependence. How Cities are Moving Beyond Car-Based Planning*. Island Press. doi:10.5822/978-1-61091-613-4

Ngossaha, J. M., Ngouna, R. H., Archimède, B., Patrascu, R. G., Petrisor, A. I., & Ndjodo, M. F. (2020). Methodological Framework for Defining the Sustainability Management Process for Urban Mobility Systems Based on System Engineering. *International Journal of Digital Innovation in the Built Environment, 9*(1), 1–21. doi:10.4018/IJDIBE.2020010101

Nkoro, A. B., & Vershinin, Y. A. (2014). Current and future trends in applications of Intelligent Transport Systems on cars and infrastructure. In *17th International IEEE Conference on Intelligent Transportation Systems (ITSC)* (pp. 514-519). IEEE. 10.1109/ITSC.2014.6957741

OECD & International Transport Forum. (2017). *Managing the Transition to Driveless Road Freight Transport*. OECD. https://www.itf-oecd.org/sites/default/files/docs/managing-transition-driverless-road-freight-transport.pdf

OECD. (2018). *The shared-use city: Managing the curb, international transportation forum*. OECD. https://www.itf-oecd.org/sites/default/files/docs/shared-use-city-managing-curb_5.pdf

Oeschger, G., Carroll, P., & Caulfield, B. (2020). Micromobility and public transportation integration: The current state of knowledge. *Transportation Research Part D, Transport and Environment, 89*, 102628. doi:10.1016/j.trd.2020.102628

Office of the Government of the Czech Republic. (2017). *Strategic Framework Czech Republic 2030*. OGCR. https://www.cr2030.cz/strategie/wp-content/uploads/sites/2/2018/05/Strategic_Framework_CZ2030_graphic2.compressed.pdf

Øgaard, M. B., Riise, H. N., Haug, H., Sartori, S., & Selj, J. H. (2020). Photovoltaic system monitoring for high latitude locations. *Solar Energy, 207*, 1045–1054. doi:10.1016/j.solener.2020.07.043

Ogryzek, M., Adamska-Kmieć, D., & Klimach, A. (2020). Sustainable transport: An efficient transportation network—case study. *Sustainability, 12*(19), 8274. doi:10.3390u12198274

OICA. (2022a). Estimated worldwide motor vehicle production between 2019 and 2021, by type (in 1,000 units). *Statista*. https://www.statista.com/statistics/1097293/worldwide-motor-vehicle-production-by-type/

OICA. (2022b). Worldwide motor vehicle sales from 2005 to 2021. *Statista*. https://www.statista.com/statistics/265859/vehicle-sales-worldwide/

Oinas-Kukkonen, H., & Harjumaa, M. (2009). Persuasive systems design: Key issues, process model, and system features. *Communications of the Association for Information Systems, 24*(1), 485–500. https://doi.org/10.17705/1cais.02428

Olaverri-Monreal, C. (2016). Intelligent technologies for mobility in smart cities. *Hiradastechnika Journal, 71*, 29–34.

Olshannikova, E., Olsson, T., Huhtamäki, J., & Kärkkäinen, H. (2017). Conceptualizing Big Social Data. *Journal of Big Data, 4*(1), 3. doi:10.118640537-017-0063-x

Compilation of References

Öncü, E., & Öncü Yildiz, A. (2011). *Sürdürülebilir Ulaşım: Devlet Bunun Neresinde?* TMMOB İnşaat Mühendisleri Odası İstanbul Şubesi.

Ontario Newsroom. (2017). Green bond proceeds to fund environmentally friendly infrastructure projects. *Ontario Newsroom.* https://news.ontario.ca/en/release/43595/green-bond-proceeds-to-fund-environmentally-friendly-infrastructure-projects

Organisation for Economic Co-operation and Development. (2016). *Green bonds: country experiences, barriers and options.* OECD. https://www.oecd.org/environment/cc/Green_Bonds_Country_Experiences_Barriers_and_Options.pdf

Orji, R., & Moffatt, K. (2018). Persuasive technology for health and wellness: State-of-the-art and emerging trends. *Health Informatics Journal*, *24*(1), 66–91. https://doi.org/10.1177/1460458216650979

Orozco, L. G. N., Deritei, D., Vancso, A., & Vasarhelyi, O. (2019). Quantifying Life Quality as Walkability on Urban Networks: The Case of Budapest. *International Conference on Complex Networks and Their Applications*, 905-918.

Özgün, K., Günay, M., Doruk, B., Bulut, B., Yürüten, E., Baysan, F., & Kalemsiz, M. (2021). Analysis of PT for Efficiency. In: Hemanth, J., Yigit, T., Patrut, B. & Angelopoulou, A. (Eds) Trends in Data Engineering Methods for Intelligent Systems. ICAIAME 2020. Lecture Notes on Data Engineering and Communications Technologies, (vol 76). Springer Cham.

Öztürk, S., & Gündüz, E. (2020). Sürdürülebilir Ulaşımda Bisiklet Kullanımını Engelleyen Sebepler: Manisa Örneği. *Düzce Üniversitesi Bilim ve Teknoloji Dergisi*, *8*, 2164–2182.

Paiva, S., Ahad, M. A., Tripathi, G., Feroz, N., & Casalino, G. (2021). Enabling Technologies for Urban Smart Mobility: Recent Trends, Opportunities and Challenges. *Sensors (Basel)*, *21*(6), 2143. doi:10.339021062143 PMID:33803903

Pakere, I., Prodanuks, T., Kamenders, A., Veidenbergs, I., Holler, S., Villere, A., & Blumberga, D. (2021). Ranking EU Climate and Energy Policies. *Environmental and Climate Technologies*, *25*(1), 367–381.

Paliaga, M., & Oliva, E. (2018). Trends in the application of the concept of smart cities. *Ekonomska Misao i Praksa*, *2*, 565–583.

Papenhausen, C. (2009). A cyclical model of institutional change. *Foresight*, *11*(3), 4–13.

Pappalardo, L., Simini, F., Barlacchi, G., & Pellungrini, R. (2021). *Scikit-mobility: A Python library for the analysis, generation and risk assessment of mobility data.* Academic Press.

Parag, Y., & Sovacool, B. K. (2016). Electricity market design for the prosumer era. *Nature Energy*, *1*(4), 1–6. doi:10.1038/nenergy.2016.32

Pariser, E. (2011). *The filter bubble: What the Internet is hiding from you.* Penguin Group.

Parzonko, A. J., Balińska, A., & Sieczko, A. (2021). Pro-Environmental Behaviors of Generation Z in the Context of the Concept of Homo Socio-Oeconomicus. *Energies*, *14*(6), 1597. doi:10.3390/en14061597

Patel, M. S., Volpp, K. G., & Asch, D. A. (2018). Nudge Units to Improve the Delivery of Health Care. *The New England Journal of Medicine*, *378*(3), 214–216. https://doi.org/10.1056/NEJMp1712984

Patel, R. K., Etminani-Ghasrodashti, R., Kermanshachi, S., Rosenberger, J. M., & Foss, A. (2022). Mobility-on-demand (MOD) Projects: A study of the best practices adopted in United States. *Transportation Research Interdisciplinary Perspectives*, *14*, 100601. doi:10.1016/j.trip.2022.100601

Pawlasová, P. (2015). The Factors Influencing Satisfaction with Public City Transport: A Structural Equation Modelling Approach. *Journal of Competitiveness*, *7*(4), 18–32. doi:10.7441/joc.2015.04.02

Pedersen, T. S., Andersen, P., Nielsen, K. M., Stærmose, H. L., & Pedersen, P. D. (2011). Using heat pump energy storages in the power grid. In *2011 IEEE International Conference on Control Applications (CCA)* (pp. 1106-1111). IEEE. 10.1109/CCA.2011.6044504

Penfold, A. (2020). 5 use cases for smart cameras to improve security in public transportation. *Azena.* https://www.securityandsafetythings.com/insights/5-ways-smart-cameras-improve-public-transport

Penfold, A. (2020). Why we should not underestimate the value of smart video cameras in public. *Azena.* https://www.securityandsafetythings.com/insights/not-underestimate-smart-cameras-public

Pentland, A. (2008). *Honest Signals: How They Shape Our World*. The MIT Press. doi:10.7551/mitpress/8022.001.0001

Pérez, K., Olabarria, M., Rojas-Rueda, D., Santamariña-Rubio, E., Borrell, C., & Nieuwenhuijsen, M. (2017). The health and economic benefits of active transport policies in Barcelona. *Journal of Transport & Health*, 1–9.

Permana, Y. H., & Sanjaya, M. R. (2022). Nudging Green Preferences: Evidence from a Laboratory Experiment. *Journal of International Commerce. Economic Policy, 13*(02). https://doi.org/10.1142/S1793993322500119

Petersen, S. A., Petersen, I., & Ahcin, P. (2020). Smiling earth—raising awareness among citizens for behaviour change to reduce carbon footprint. *Energies, 13*(22), 5932.

Pharoah, T. (1992). *Less Traffic, Better Towns*. Friends of the Earth.

Pickerel, K. (May 14, 2021). Green Mountain Power will use 200 Tesla Powerwalls as virtual power plant. *Solar Power World*. https://www.solarpowerworldonline.com/2021/05/green-mountain-power-will-use-200-tesla-powerwalls-as-virtual-power-plant/

Pigeon, C., Alauzet, A., & Paire-Ficout, L. (2021). Factors of acceptability, acceptance and usage for non-rail autonomous public transport vehicles: A systematic literature review. *Transportation Research Part F: Traffic Psychology and Behaviour, 81*, 251–270. doi:10.1016/j.trf.2021.06.008

Pine, B. J. II, & Gilmore, J. H. (1999). *The Experience Economy*. Harvard Business School Press.

Pitsiava-Latinopoulou, M., & Iordanopoulos, P. (2012). Intermodal Passengers Terminals: Design standards for better level of service. *Procedia: Social and Behavioral Sciences, 48*, 3297–3306. doi:10.1016/j.sbspro.2012.06.1295

PMDP. (2013). *Annual Report of PMDP - 2012*. PMDP. https://www.pmdp.cz/WD_FileDownload.ashx?wd_systemtypeid=34&wd_pk=WzE5ODAsWzQ0XV0%3d

PMDP. (2020). *Annual Report of PMDP - 2019*. PMDP. https://www.pmdp.cz/WD_FileDownload.ashx?wd_systemtypeid=34&wd_pk=WzI3MTYsWzQ0XV0%3d

PMDP. (2022). *Annual Report of PMDP - 2021*. PMDT. https://www.pmdp.cz/WD_FileDownload.ashx?wd_systemtypeid=34&wd_pk=WzI5MDEsWzQ0XV0%3d

PNMU Cameroun - Septembre. (2019). https://www.mobiliseyourcity.net/fr/pnmu-cameroun

Poelman, H., Dijkstra, L., & Ackermans, L. (2020). *How many people can you reach by public transport, bicycle or on foot in European cities? Measuring urban accessibility for low-carbon modes*. European Commission. doi:https://doi.org/10.2776/021137

Pollard, J. A., Spencer, T., & Jude, S. (2018). Big Data Approaches for coastal flood risk assessment and emergency response. *Wiley Interdisciplinary Reviews: Climate Change, 9*(5), e543. doi:10.1002/wcc.543

Compilation of References

Portouli, E., Karaseitanidis, G., Lytrivis, P., Amditis, A., Raptis, O., & Karaberi, C. (2017). Public attitudes towards autonomous mini buses operating in real conditions in a Hellenic city. *Intelligent Vehicles Symposium* (pp. 11-14). IEEE. 10.1109/IVS.2017.7995779

Potter, S. (2003). Transport energy and emissions: urban public transport. In *Handbook of Transport and the Environment* (Vol. 4, pp. 247–262). Emerald Group Publishing Limited. doi:10.1108/9781786359513-013

Potter, S. (2007). Exploring approaches towards a sustainable transport system. *International Journal of Sustainable Transportation*, *1*(2), 115–131. doi:10.1080/15568310601091999

Pourhashem, G., Malichova, E., & Kovacikova, T. (2021). The role of participation behavior and information in nudging citizens sustainable mobility behavior: A case study of Bratislava region. *ICETA 2021 - 19th IEEE International Conference on Emerging ELearning Technologies and Applications, Proceedings*, (pp. 300–306). IEEE. doi:10.1109/ICETA54173.2021.9726681

Praha.eu. (2010, February 18). *Prague Public Transport Stands Shoulder to Shoulder with the Best in Europe*. Praha eu. https://www.praha.eu/jnp/en/transport/getting_around/prague_public_transport_stands_shoulder.html

Pratiwi, P. U. D., Landra, N., & Kusuma, G. A. T. (2018). The Construction of Public Transport Service Model to Influence the Loyalty of Customer. *Scientific Research Journal, 6*(2), 56-63. http://www.scirj.org/feb-2018-paper.php?rp=P0218502

Prochaska, J. O., & Velicer, W. F. (1997). The Transtheoretical Model of Health Behavior Change. *American Journal of Health Promotion*, *12*(1), 38–48. https://doi.org/10.4278/0890-1171-12.1.38

PSItraffic. (2020). *In 5 Steps to a Depot Management System for Transport Companies*. PSI. https://www.psi.de/en/blog/psi-blog/post/in-5-steps-to-a-depot-management-system-for-transport-companies/

PSItraffic. (2021). *Depot Management - A clear overview of all processes*. Retrieved March 10, 2022 from https://www.psitrans.de/en/solutions/depot-management/

Pucher, J., & Buehler, R. (2016). Safer cycling through improved infrastructure. *American Journal of Public Health*, *106*(12), 2089–2091.

Quigley, M. (2013). Nudging for health: On public policy and designing choice architecture. *Medical Law Review*, *21*(4), 588–621. https://doi.org/10.1093/medlaw/fwt022

Racca, D. (2004). Cost and Benefits of Advanced Public Transportation Systems at Dart First State. *Center for Applied Demography and Survey Research*, p. 20. https://udspace.udel.edu/handle/19716/1100

Raicu, R., & Raicu, S. (2005). Complex aspects of transport quality. In C. A. Brebbia & L. Wadhwa (Eds.), *Urban Transport XI. WIT Transactions on The Built Environment* (Vol. 77, pp. 281–290). WIT Press.

Raicu, S. (2007). *Transportation Systems*. AGIR Press. (*In Romanian*)

Raicu, S., & Costescu, D. (2020). *Mobility. Traffic Infrastructures*. AGIR Press. (*In Romanian*)

Raicu, S., & Costescu, D. (2021). Mobility - polysemy with interdisciplinary valences. *Journal of Engineering Sciences and Innovation, 6*(4), 459–472.

Raicu, S., Dragu, V., Popa, M., & Burciu, S. (2009). About the high capacity public transport networks territory functions. In C. A. Brebia (Ed.), *Urban Transport XV. WIT Transactions on The Built Environment* (pp. 41–50). WIT Press. doi:10.2495/UT090051

Raicu, S., Popa, M., & Costescu, D. (2022). Uncertainties Influencing Transportation System Performances. *Sustainability, 14*(13), 7660. doi:10.3390u14137660

Raj, A., Dwivedi, G., Sharma, A., Lopes De Sousa Jabbour, A. B., & Rajak, S. (2020). Barriers to the adoption of industry 4.0 technologies in the manufacturing sector: An inter-country comparative perspective. *International Journal of Production Economics*, *224*, 107546. doi:10.1016/j.ijpe.2019.107546

Rajanen, D., & Rajanen, M. (2019). Climate change gamification: A literature review. *GamiFIN*, 253–264.

Rajesh, R., & Ravi, V. (2015). Modeling enablers of supply chain risk mitigation in electronic supply chains: A Grey–DEMATEL approach. *Computers & Industrial Engineering*, *87*, 126–139. doi:10.1016/j.cie.2015.04.028

Rajwanshi, Y. (2019). Are green bonds as good as they sound? *Econ Review*. https://econreview.berkeley.edu/are-green-bonds-as-good-as-they-sound/

Ranchordás, S. (2020). Nudging citizens through technology in smart cities. *International Review of Law Computers & Technology*, *34*(3), 254–276. https://doi.org/10.1080/13600869.2019.1590928

Rassafi, A. A., & Vaziri, M. (2005). Sustainable transport indicators: Definition and integration. *International Journal of Environmental Science and Technology*, *2*(1), 83–96.

Ratten, V. (2017). *Entrepreneurship, innovation and smart cities*. Routledge.

Rauch, F. (2002). The potential of education for sustainable development for reform in schools. *Environmental Education Research*, *8*(1), 43–51. doi:10.1080/13504620120109646

Ren, J., Liang, H., Dong, L., Gao, Z., He, C., Pan, M., & Sun, L. (2017). Sustainable development of sewage sludge-to-energy in China: Barriers identification and technologies prioritization. *Renewable & Sustainable Energy Reviews*, *67*, 384–396. doi:10.1016/j.rser.2016.09.024

Replogle, M. A. (1991). Sustainable transportation strategies for third-world development. *Transportation Research Record: Journal of the Transportation Research Board*, 1294. https://onlinepubs.trb.org/Onlinepubs/trr/1991/1294/1294-001.pdf

Richardson, D. B. (2013). Electric vehicles and the electric grid: A review of modeling approaches, Impacts, and renewable energy integration. *Renewable & Sustainable Energy Reviews*, *19*, 247–254. doi:10.1016/j.rser.2012.11.042

Richer, C. (2008). L'émergence de la notion de pôle d'échanges, entre interconnexion des réseaux et structuration des territoires [The emergence of the notion of exchange hub, between interconnection of netweks and structuring of territories]. *Les Cahiers scientifiques du transportation [The scientific papers of transportation]*, AFITL, 101-123.

Richter, M. (2013). Business model innovation for sustainable energy: German utilities and renewable energy. *Energy Policy*, *62*, 1226–1237. doi:10.1016/j.enpol.2013.05.038

Rid, W. (2017). Human dimensions approach towards integrating sustainable transportation and urban planning policies: A decision support system (DSS) based on stated preferences data. *Theoretical Economics Letters*, *7*(04), 814–833. doi:10.4236/tel.2017.74059

Rietmann, N., Hügler, B., & Lieven, T. (2020). Forecasting the trajectory of electric vehicle sales and the consequences for worldwide CO2 emissions. *Journal of Cleaner Production*, *261*, 121038. doi:10.1016/j.jclepro.2020.121038

Ritchie, H., & Roser, M. (2022b). Electricity Mix. *Our World in Data*. https://ourworldindata.org/electricity-mix#:~:text=In%202019%2C%20almost%20two%2Dthirds,and%20nuclear%20energy%20for%2010.4%25

Ritchie, A. G., Lakeman, B., Burr, P., Carter, P., Barnes, P. N., & Bowles, P. (2001). Battery degradation and ageing. In *Ageing Studies and Lifetime Extension of Materials* (pp. 523–527). Springer., doi:10.1007/978-1-4615-1215-8_58

Riter, S., & McCoy, J. (1977). Automatic vehicle location - An overview. *IEEE Transactions on Vehicular Technology*, *26*(1), 7–11. doi:10.1109/T-VT.1977.23649

Compilation of References

Rodrigue, J. P. (2020). *The geography of transport systems.* Routledge. doi:10.4324/9780429346323

Rodrigues, A. L. P., & Seixas, S. R. C. (2022). Battery-electric buses and their implementation barriers: Analysis and prospects for sustainability. *Sustainable Energy Technologies and Assessments, 51*, 101896. doi:10.1016/j.seta.2021.101896

Romero, Zamorano, & Monzon. (2021). Can rail infrastructure determine perceived quality of service of suburban trains? Insights from Cercanias Madrid. *Transportation Research Procedia, 58*, 567–574.

Rončák, M., Scholz, P., & Linderová, I. (2021). Safety concerns and travel behavior of generation Z: Case study from the Czech Republic. *Sustainability, 13*(23), 13439. doi:10.3390u132313439

Rose, G., & Marfurt, H. (2007). Travel behaviour change impacts of a major ride to work day event. *Transportation Research Part A, Policy and Practice, 41*(4), 351–364. https://doi.org/10.1016/j.tra.2006.10.001

RoseIndia. (2018). Automatic Vehicle Location Advantage. *Rose India.* https://www.roseindia.net/technology/vehicle-tracking/automatic-vehicle-location-advantage.shtml

Rote, L. (2017). FutureBuilt is Changing the Way Buildings are Built in Oslo. *Gb&d.* https://gbdmagazine.com/futurebuilt/

Rozga, A. (2015). *Multiavariate anaylsis (authorised lectures).* Faculty of Economics, Business and Tourism.

Rubiano, L. Canon, & Darido G. (2019*). The ticket to a better ride: How can Automated Fare Collection improve urban transport?* World Bank blogs. https://blogs.worldbank.org/transport/ticket-better-ride-how-can-automated-fare-collection-improve-urban-transport

Ruoso, A. C., & Ribeiro, J. L. D. (2022). The influence of countries' socioeconomic characteristics on the adoption of electric vehicle. *Energy for Sustainable Development, 71*, 251–262.

Rupprecht Consult. (2019). *Guidelines for Developing and Implementing a Sustainable Urban Mobility Plan* (2nd ed.). Rupprecht Consult.

Rydén, C., & Morin, E. (2005). *Mobility Services for Urban Sustainability: Environmental Assessment. Report WP 6.* Trivector TrafficAB.

Rzędowski, H., & Sendek-Matysiak, E. (2021, September). *Evaluation of BEV and FCHEV Electric Vehicles in the Creation of a Sustainable Transport System* [Conference presentation]. Scientific And Technical Conference Transport Systems Theory And Practice. Katowice, Poland. doi:10.1007/978-3-030-93370-8_4

Saad, S., Aisha Badrul Hisham, A., Ishak, M., Mohd, F., Mohd, H., Baharudin, M., & Idris, N. (2018). Real-time on-campus public transportation monitoring system. *2018 IEEE 14th International Colloquium on Signal Processing & Its Applications (CSPA),* (pp. 215-220).

Sachs, D. D. (2015). *The age of sustainable development.* Columbia University Press. doi:10.7312ach17314

Sahu & Verma. (2022). Quantifying wider economic impacts of high-speed connectivity and accessibility: The case of the Karnataka high-speed rail. *Transportation Research Part A, Policy and Practice, 158*, 141–155.

SAIC (2007). Public transportation's contribution to US greenhouse gas reduction. *Growing Cooler.*

Salonen, A. O., & Haavisto, N. (2019). Towards autonomous transportation. Passengers' experiences, perceptions and feelings in a driverless shuttle bus in Finland. *Sustainability, 11*(3), 588. doi:10.3390u11030588

Samalna, D. A., Ngossaha, J. M., Ari, A. A., & Kolyang. (2023). Cyber-Physical Urban Mobility Systems: Opportunities and Challenges in Developing Countries. *International Journal of Software Innovation, 11*(1), 1–21. doi:10.4018/IJSI.315662

Saman control (2018). *Passenger Information System*. Saman Control. https://samancontrol.com/solutions/passenger-information-system-onboard-pis/

Samspon, E., Signor, L., Flachi, M., Hemmings, E., Somma, G., Aifadopoulou, G., Mitsakis, E., & Sourlas, V. (2019). The role of Intelligent Transport Systems (ITS) in sustainable urban mobility planning. European platform on sustainable mobility plans.

Sangameswar, M. V., Nagabhushana Rao, M., & Satyanarayana, S. (2017). An algorithm for identification of natural disaster affected area. *Journal of Big Data*, *4*(1), 39. doi:10.118640537-017-0096-1

Santi, P., Resta, G., Szell, M., Sobolevsky, S., & Strogatz, S. H. & C. Ratti C. (2014). Quantifying the benefits of vehicle pooling with shareability networks. *Proceedings of the National Academy of Sciences of the United States of America (PNAS)*, *111*(37), 13290-13294. PNAS. 10.1073/pnas.1403657111

Santos, G. (2017). Road transport and CO2 emissions: What are the challenges? *Transport Policy*, *59*, 71–74. doi:10.1016/j.tranpol.2017.06.007

Santos, G., Behrendt, H., Maconi, L., Shirvani, T., & Teytelboym, A. (2010). Part I: Externalities and economic policies in road transport. *Research in Transportation Economics*, *28*(1), 2–45. doi:10.1016/j.retrec.2009.11.002

Sarkar, S., Pratihar, D. K., & Sarkar, B. (2018). An integrated fuzzy multiple criteria supplier selection approach and its application in a welding company. *International Journal of Industrial and Manufacturing Systems Engineering*, *46*, 163–178.

Savrun, B., & Mutlu, H. M. (2019). Kent Lojistiği Üzerine Bibliyometrik Analiz. *Kent Akademisi*, *12*(2), 364–386. doi:10.35674/kent.534729

Schaeffer, K. H., & Sclar, E. (2002). The automobile era: a cultural analysis. In A. Root (Ed.), *Delivering Sustainable Transport* (pp. 116–126). Emerald Group Publishing Limited., doi:10.1108/9780585473956-007

Schmalfuss, F., Mair, C., Döbelt, S., Kaempfe, B., Wuestemann, R., Krems, J. F., & Keinath, A. (2015). User responses to a smart charging system in Germany: Battery electric vehicle driver motivation, attitudes and acceptance. *Energy Research & Social Science*, *9*, 60–71. doi:10.1016/j.erss.2015.08.019

Schmidt, R. C. (1997). Managing Delphi surveys using nonparametric statistical techniques. *Decision Sciences*, *28*(3), 763–774. doi:10.1111/j.1540-5915.1997.tb01330.x

Schuller, A., Flath, C. M., & Gottwalt, S. (2015). Quantifying load flexibility of electric vehicles for renewable energy integration. *Applied Energy*, *151*, 335–344. doi:10.1016/j.apenergy.2015.04.004

Schwertner, K. (2017). Digital transformation of business. *Trakia Journal of Sciences*, *15*(1), 388–393.

Schwertner, K. (2021). The Impact of Digital Transformation on Business: A Detailed Review. In J. Metselaar (Ed.), *Strategic Management in the Age of Digital Transformation* (pp. 1–29). Proud Pen.

Scrudato, M. (2018). Smart Mobility Reinventing insurance for the future of mobility. *Munichre*. https://www.munichre.com/content/dam/munichre/contentlounge/website-pieces/documents/SmartMobility_06-18-2019.pdf/_jcr_content/renditions/original.media_file.download_attachment.file/SmartMobility_06-18-2019.pdf

SDP ČR. (n. d.). *Annual Reports of the Association of Transport Companies of the Czech Republic 2001-2021*. SDP CR. http://www.sdp-cr.cz/o -nas/vyrocni-zpravy/

Seemiller, C., & Grace, M. (2016). *Generation Z goes to college*. John Wiley & Sons.

Segal, T. (2022). Green Bond. *Investopedia*. https://www.investopedia.com/terms/g/green-bond.asp

Compilation of References

Senin, S. N., Fahmy-Abdullah, M., & Masrom, M. A. N. (2021). The implementation of green transportation towards low carbon city. Paper presented at the *IOP Conference Series: Earth and Environmental Science, 736*(1).IOP Science. doi:10.1088/1755-1315/736/1/012063

Shabanzadeh, M., & Moghaddam, M. P. (2013, November). What is the smart grid? Definitions, perspectives, and ultimate goals. In *28th International Power System Conference*.

Shaheen, S. A., & Cohen, A. P. (2007). Growth in Worldwide Carsharing: An International Comparison. *Transportation Research Record: Journal of the Transportation Research Board, 1992*(1), 81–89. doi:10.3141/1992-10

Shaheen, S., Cohen, A., Chan, N., & Bansal, A. (2020). Sharing strategies: Carsharing, shared micromobility (bikesharing and scooter sharing), transportation network companies, microtransit, and other innovative mobility modes. In E. Deakin (Ed.), *Transportation, Land Use, and Environmental Planning* (pp. 237–262). Elsevier. doi:10.1016/B978-0-12-815167-9.00013-X

Shaheen, S., & Martin, E. (2015). Unravelling the modal impacts of bikesharing. *Access, 47*, 8–15.

Shah, K. J., Pan, S.-Y., Lee, I., Kim, H., You, Z., Zheng, J.-M., & Ciang, P.-C. (2021). Green transportation for sustainability: Review of current barriers, strategies, and innovative Technologies. *Journal of Cleaner Production, 326*, 129392. doi:10.1016/j.jclepro.2021.129392

Shankar, V., Smith, A. K., & Rangaswamy, A. (2003). Customer satisfaction and loyalty in online and offline environments. *International Journal of Research in Marketing, 20*(2), 153–175. doi:10.1016/S0167-8116(03)00016-8

Sharma & Newman. (2018). Does urban rail increase land value in emerging cities? Value uplift from Bangalore Metro. *Transportation Research Part A, Policy and Practice, 117*, 70–86.

Shaw, C., & Ivens, J. (2002). *Building great customer experiences*. Palgrave. doi:10.1057/9780230554719

Shen, Wei, & Wei. (2020). Study of trackside photovoltaic power integration into the traction power system of suburban elevated urban rail transit line. *Applied Energy, 260*, 114177.

Shibayama, T. (2011). Organizational Structures of Urban Public Transport-A Diagrammatic Comparison and a Typology. *Journal of the Eastern Asia Society for Transportation Studies, 9*, 126–141. doi:10.11175/easts.9.126

Shields, R., da Silva, E. J. G., Lima, T. L., & Osorio, N. (2021). Walkability: A review of trends. *Journal of Urbanism*, 1–24.

Shinde, Dikshit, Singh, & Campana. (2018). Life cycle analysis based comprehensive environmental performance evaluation of Mumbai Suburban Railway, India. *Journal of Cleaner Production, 188*, 989–1003.

Shishlov, I., Morel, R., & Cochran, I. (2016). *Beyond transparency: Unlocking the full potential of green bonds*. Institute for Climate Economics Report. https://www.i4ce.org/wp-content/uploads/2022/07/I4CE_Green_Bonds-1-1.pdf

Siebenhofer, M., Ajanovic, A., & Haas, R. (2022). On the Future of Passenger Mobility and its Greenhouse Gas Emissions in Cities: Scenarios for Different Types of Policies. *Journal of Sustainable Development of Energy. Water and Environment Systems, 10*(4), 1100424.

Silva, B. V. F., & Teles, M. P. R. (2020). Pathways to sustainable urban mobility planning: A case study applied in São Luís, Brazil. *Transportation Research Interdisciplinary Perspectives, 4*, 100102. doi:10.1016/j.trip.2020.100102

Singapore Ministry of Finance. (2022). *Green bonds*. MOF. https://www.mof.gov.sg/policies/fiscal/greenbonds#:~:text=Examples%20of%20eligible%20green%20SINGA,the%20greenest%20ways%20to%20move

Singh & Gupta. (2020). Urban rail system for freight distribution in a mega city: Case study of Delhi, India. *Transportation Research Procedia, 48*, 452–466.

Singh, R. (2016). Factors Affecting Walkability of Neighborhoods. *Procedia: Social and Behavioral Sciences, 216,* 643–654.

Sinha, S., Swamy, H. S., & Modi, K. (2020). User perceptions of public transport service quality. *Transportation Research Procedia, 48,* 3310–3323. doi:10.1016/j.trpro.2020.08.121

Si, S. L., You, X. Y., Liu, H. C., & Zhang, P. (2018). DEMATEL technique: A systematic review of the state-of-the-art literature on methodologies and applications. *Mathematical Problems in Engineering, 2018,* 2018. doi:10.1155/2018/3696457

Sivarajah, U., Kamal, M. M., Irani, Z., & Weerakkody, V. (2017). Critical analysis of Big Data challenges and analytical methods. *Journal of Business Research, 70,* 263–286. doi:10.1016/j.jbusres.2016.08.001

Sivasubramaniyam, R. D., Charlton, S. G., & Sargisson, R. J. (2020). Mode choice and mode commitment in commuters. *Travel Behaviour and Society, 19,* 20–32. doi:10.1016/j.tbs.2019.10.007

Slavík, J. (2014). *Marketing a strategické řízení ve veřejných službách. Jak poskytovat zákaznicky orientované veřejné služby.* Grada Publishing.

SLOCAT Foundation. (2021). *Partnership on Sustainable, Low carbon transport. Renewable Energy in Transport.* SLOCAT Foundation. https://tcc-gsr.com/responses-to-policies/renewable-energy-in-transport/

Smart Cities Connect. (2020). *Transport for London Expands Use of Traffic Sensors Using AI.* Smart Cities Connect. https://smartcitiesconnect.org/transport-for-london-expands-use-of-traffic-sensors-using-ai/#:~:text=Transport%20 for%20London%20(TfL)%20is,of%20transport%20they%20are%20using.&Text=The%20sensors%20are%20also% 20able, trucks%2C%20motorcyclists%2C%20and%20buses

Smith, G., Sochor, J., & Karlsson, I. M. (2018). Mobility as a Service: Development scenarios and implications for public transport. *Research in Transportation Economics, 69,* 592–599. doi:10.1016/j.retrec.2018.04.001

Smith, R., Meng, K., Dong, Z., & Simpson, R. (2013). Demand response: A strategy to address residential air-conditioning peak load in Australia. *Journal of Modern Power Systems and Clean Energy, 1*(3), 219–226. doi:10.100740565-013-0032-0

Sochor, J., Arby, H., Karlsson, I. M., & Sarasini, S. (2018). A topological approach to Mobility as a Service: A proposed tool for understanding requirements and effects, and for aiding the integration of societal goals. In *1*st *international conference on mobility as a service (ICoMaaS) Proceedings (vol. 27,* pp. 3-14). Chalmers university of technology.

Sociedad Ibérica de Construcciones Eléctricas. (2016). *Automatic Fare Collection (AFC).* SICE. https://www.sice.com/sites/Sice/files/2016-12/TR_TICKETING_0.pdf

Sokač Š. (2017). *Perspectives for investments and realization of development projects based on the concept of "Smart Cities" in Croatia,* 15-30. Varaždin: University North, final paper.

Sokač, Š. (2017). Perspektive za ulaganja i realizacije razvojnih projekata baziranih na konceptu "Pametnih gradova" u Hrvatskoj [Perspectives for investments and implementation of development projects based on the concept of 'smart cities' in Croatia. [Doctoral Dissertation, Sveučilište Sjever, Croatia.].

Solactive. (2021). Shining green: bonds to tackle climate change. *Solactive.* https://www.solactive.com/wp-content/uploads/2021/09/Solactive-Green-Bonds-September-2021.pdf

Sovacool, B. K., Axsen, J., & Kempton, W. (2017). The future promise of vehicle-to-grid (V2G) integration: A socio-technical review and research agenda. *Annual Review of Environment and Resources, 42*(1), 377–406. doi:10.1146/annurev-environ-030117-020220

Split Tourist Board. (2021). *Public bicycles.* Split. https://visitsplit.com/hr/4280/javni-bicikli

Compilation of References

Standard&Poor's Global. (2017). *Frequently Asked Questions: S&P Global Ratings' Analytical Approach In Evaluating Green Transactions.* S&P Global. https://www.maalot.co.il/Publications/GRB20171207111217.pdf

Standard&Poor's Global. (2020). *Swiss prime site issues chf 300m green bond.* S&P Global. https://www.spglobal.com/marketintelligence/en/news-insights/latest-news-headlines/swiss-prime-site-issues-chf-300m-green-bond-61504351

Staricco, L., & Brovarone, E. V. (2018). Promoting TOD through regional planning. A comparative analysis of two European approaches. *Journal of Transport Geography, 66,* 45–52. doi:10.1016/j.jtrangeo.2017.11.011

Statista. (2022). Users of selected segments of the mobility services market worldwide from 2017 to 2025 (in millions). *Statista.* https://www.statista.com/forecasts/1182725/users-mobility-services-worldwide

Stevic, Z., Pamucar, D., Vasiljevic, M., Stojic, G., & Korica, S. (2017). Novel Integrated Multi-Criteria Model for Supplier Selection: Case Study Construction Company. *Symmetry, 9*(11), 279. doi:10.3390ym9110279

Stickdorn, M., & Schneider, J. (2011). *This is service design thinking: basics, tools, cases.* John Wiley & Sons.

Stikvoort, B., Bartusch, C., & Juslin, P. (2020). Different strokes for different folks? Comparing pro-environmental intentions between electricity consumers and solar prosumers in Sweden. *Energy Research & Social Science, 69,* 101552. doi:10.1016/j.erss.2020.101552

Store, J. (2022, June 29). *Fit for 55 package: Council reaches general approaches relating to emissions reductions and their social impacts.* Council of the EU. https://www.consilium.europa.eu/en/press/press-releases/2022/06/29/fit-for-55-council-reaches-general-approaches-relating-to-emissions-reductions-and-removals-and-their-social-impacts/

Sun, Z., Strang, K., & Li, R. (2018). Big Data with Ten Big Characteristics. In *Proceedings of the 2nd International Conference on Big Data Research - ICBDR 2018.* ACM Press. 10.1145/3291801.3291822

Sunstein, C. R. (2015). The Ethics of Nudging. *Yale Journal on Regulation, 32,* 413–450. https://www.cdc.gov/media/releases/2011/pO5

Sustainalytics. (2020). *The ESG risk rating: frequently asked questions for companies.* Sustainalytics. https://connect.sustainalytics.com/hubfs/SFS/Sustainalytics%20ESG%20Risk%20Rating%20-%20FAQs%20for%20Corporations.pdf

Tabrizi, B., Lam, E., Girard, K., & Irvin, V. (2019). Digital transformation is not about technology. *Harvard business review.* https://hbr.org/2019/03/digital-transformation-is-not-about-technology

Tang & Xu. (2022). Optimization for operation scheme of express and local trains in suburban rail transit lines based on station classification and bi-level programming. *Journal of Rail Transport Planning & Management, 21,* 100283.

Tang, Ariano, & Xu, Li, Ding, & Sama. (2021). Scheduling local and express trains in suburban rail transit lines: Mixed–integer nonlinear programming and adaptive genetic algorithm. *Computers & Operations Research, 135,* 105436.

Taniguchi, E., & Van Der Heijden, R. E. C. M. (2000). An Evaluation Methodology for City Logistics. *Transport Reviews, 20*(1), 65–90. doi:10.1080/014416400295347

Tao, Ma, Shen, & Chai. (2022). Neighborhood effects on health: A multilevel analysis of neighborhood environment, physical activity and public health in suburban Shanghai. *Cities (London, England), 129,* 103847.

Tech Moukthika. (2016). Vehicle (fleet) management system. *Tech Moukthika.* https://techmoukthika.com/vms.html

TechTarget. (2020). Automatic vehicle locator (AVL). *Tech Target.* https://whatis.techtarget.com/definition/automatic-vehicle-locator-AVL#:~:text=An%20automatic%20vehicle%20locator%20(AVL,fleet%20by%20using%20the%20Internet

Thakuriah, P., Sila-Nowicka, K., Hong, J., Boididou, C., Osborne, M., Lido, C., & McHugh, A. (2020). Integrated Multimedia City Data (iMCD): A composite survey and sensing approach to understanding urban living and mobility. *Computers, Environment and Urban Systems*, *80*, 101427. doi:10.1016/j.compenvurbsys.2019.101427

Thaler, R. H., & Sunstein, C. R. (2008). *Nudge: improving decisions about health, wealth and happiness.* Yale University Press.

The Association of Southeast Asian Nations (ASEAN). (2019). *Handbook on IP Commercialisation Strategies for Managing IPRS and Maximising Value.* Retrieved December 4, 2022, from https://aanzfta.asean.org/uploads/2020/12/IPPEA-FINAL-HANDBOOK-ON-IP-COMMERCIALISATION.pdf

The European Automobile Manufacturers' Association. (2022a). *New Car Registrations by Fuel Type, European Union. ACEA.* https://www.acea.auto/files/20220202_PRPC-fuel_Q4-2021_FINAL.pdf (Accessed 1 August 2022).

The European Automobile Manufacturers' Association. (2022b). *Progress Report 2022. Making The Transition to Zero-Emission Mobility.* ACEA. https://www.acea.auto/files/ACEA_progress_report_2022.pdf

The World Bank. (2016). *Public Transport Automatic Fare Collection Interoperability: Assessing Options for Poland,* p. 13. World Bank. https://openknowledge.worldbank.org/handle/10986/24931?show=full

Thoughtfull Design Limited. (2013, November 21). *PT Customer Experience Project - Update. Mission to close the gap.* https://at.govt.nz/media/311248/Item-no-9i-PT-Customer-Experience-Project-Update-final.pdf

Tiseo, I. (2022). *EU-27: CO2 emissions shares by sector 2020.* Statista. https://www.statista.com/statistics/1240108/road-transportation-greenhouse-gas-emissions-eu/

Toader, E., Firtescu, B. N., & Roman, A., Anton, & S. G. (2018). Impact of Information and Communication Technology Infrastructure on Economic Growth: An Empirical Assessment for the EU Countries. *Sustainability*, *10*, 3750.

Toh, C. K., Sanguesa, J. A., Cano, J. C., & Martinez, F. J. (2020). Advances in smart roads for future smart cities. *Proceedings of the Royal Society of London. Series A*, *476*(2233), 20190439. doi:10.1098/rspa.2019.0439 PMID:32082053

Tomat, L., & Trkman, P. (2019). Digital transformation–the hype and conceptual changes. *Economic and Business Review*, *21*(3), 2.

Torrisi, V., Inturri, G., & Ignaccolo, M. (2021). Introducing a mobility on demand system beyond COVID-19: Evidences from users' perspective. *AIP Conference Proceedings*, *2343*(1), 090007. doi:10.1063/5.0047889

Toutanji, H. A., Anderson, M., & Leonard, K. M. (2013). *Developing sustainable transportation performance measures for ALDOT. UTCA theme: Management and safety of transportation systems.* UTCA Report Number 12302.

Tranfield, D., Denyer, D., & Smart, P. (2003). Towards a methodology for developing evidence-informed management knowledge by means of systematic review. *British Journal of Management*, *14*(3), 207–222.

Trubia, S., Curto, S., Severino, A., Arena, F., & Zuccalà, Y. (2021). Autonomous vehicles effects on public transport systems. *AIP Conference Proceedings*, *2343*(1), 110014. doi:10.1063/5.0048036

Tsiompras, A. B., & Photis, Y. N. (2017). What matters when it comes to "Walk and the city"? Defining a weighted GIS-based walkability index. *Transportation Research Procedia*, *24*, 523–530.

Tumlin, J. (2011). *Sustainable transportation planning: Tools for creating vibrant, healthy, and resilient communities.* John Wiley & Sons.

Compilation of References

Turner, P., Dommergues, E., Mayer, T., Murdock, H. E., & Ranalder, L. *A smooth ride to renewable energy*. Policy brief. https://www.ren21.net/wp-content/uploads/2019/05/Policy-Brief-A-Smooth-Ride-to-Renewable-Energy-REN21-UITP.pdf

Turochy, R. E. (2006). Determining the content of the first course in transportation engineering. *Journal of Professional Issues in Engineering Education and Practice, 132*(3), 200–203. doi:10.1061/(ASCE)1052-3928(2006)132:3(200)

Tyrinopoulos, Y., & Antoniou, C. (2008). Public transit user satisfaction: Variability and policy implications. *Transport Policy, 15*(4), 260–272. doi:10.1016/j.tranpol.2008.06.002

UIC. (2020). *Number of high-speed rail lines in operation worldwide as of 2020. Statista.* https://www.statista.com/statistics/1126292/high-speed-rail-lines-in-the-world/

UITP (Union Internationale des Transports Publics). (2021). *A smooth ride to renewable energy: 7 actions for public transport to address emissions and air pollution by advancing renewables.* Advancing Public Transportation. https://www.uitp.org/publications/a-smooth-ride-to-renewable-energy-7-actions-for-public-transport-to-address-emissions-and-air-pollution-by-advancing-renewables/

UITP. (2017). *Autonomous vehicles: A potential game changer for urban mobility.* UITP. https://www.uitp.org/publications/autonomous-vehicles-a-potential-game-changer-for-urban-mobility/

UK. G. (2022). Greenhouse gas reporting: conversion factors 2019. UK Government. https://www.gov.uk/government/publications/greenhouse-gas-reporting-conversion-factors-2022

Ulahannan, A., & Birrell, S. (2022). Designing better public transport: Understanding mode choice preferences following the COVID-19 pandemic. *Sustainability, 14*(10), 5952. doi:10.3390u14105952

UNCED. (1992). Agenda 21, New York. UNCED. https://sustainabledevelopment.un.org/content/documents/Agenda21.pdf

UNESCO. (2005). United nations decade of education for sustainable development: Draft international implementation scheme (2005-2014): International implementation scheme. UNESCO. https://unesdoc.unesco.org/ark:/48223/pf0000148654

UNESCO. (2015). *UNESCO science report: towards 2030.* UNESCO. https://unesdoc.unesco.org/ark:/48223/pf0000235406

UN-Habitat. (2013). *Planning and Design for Sustainable Urban Mobility, Global Report on Human Settlements 2013.* United Nations Human Settlements Programme.

United Nations (UN). (2018). *World Urbanization Prospects: The 2018 Revision-Highlights.* UN.

United Nations Department of Economic and Social Affairs (UNDESA). (2018). *E-government survey 2018: gearing e-government to support transformation towards sustainable and resilient societies.* UNDESA. https://publicadministration.un.org/egovkb/portals/egovkb/documents/un/2018-survey/e-government%20survey%202018_final%20for%20web.pdf

United Nations Department of Economic and Social Affairs (UNDESA). (2020). *E-Government Survey 2020: Digital Government in the Decade of Action for Sustainable Development.* UNDESA. https://publicadministration.un.org/egovkb/Portals/egovkb/Documents/un/2020-Survey/2020%20UN%20E-Government%20Survey%20(Full%20Report).pdf

United Nations digital Library. (n.d.). *The World's cities in 2018.* Retrieved December 4, 2022, from https://digitallibrary.un.org/record/3799524

United Nations. (2015). *Transforming our world: the 2030 Agenda for Sustainable Development (A/RES/70/1).* UN. https://sdgs.un.org/2030agenda

United Nations. (2018). *World urbanization prospects: The 2018 revision.* UN. https://www.un.org/development/desa/pd/content/world-urbanization-prospects-2018-revision

United Nations. (2018, May 16). *68% of the world population projected to live in urban areas by 2050.* UN. https://www.un.org/development/desa/en/news/population/2018-revision-of-world-urbanization-prospects.html

United Nations. (2021). Sustainable Transport, Sustainable Development. *Interagency Report for Second Global Sustainable Transport Conference*, (pp. 59-68).

United Nations. (2022). *Do you know all 17 SDGs?* UN. https://sdgs.un.org/goals

United Nations. (2022). Sustainable development goals report. UN. https://unstats.un.org/sdgs/report/2022/The-Sustainable-Development-Goals-Report-2022.pdf

US Department of Homeland Security. (2009). *Automatic Vehicle Locating Systems.* DHS. https://www.dhs.gov/sites/default/files/publications/AVLSys-TN_0609-508.pdf

USDOT. (2022). *The US Department of Transportation.* US DOT. https://www.transportation.gov/

USEPA. (2011). *Guide to Sustainable Transportation Performance Measures.* USEPA. https://www.epa.gov/sites/default/files/2014-01/documents/sustainable_transpo_performance.pdf

USEPA. (2022). *US HUD-DOT-EPA Partnership for Sustainable Communities.* USEPA. https://19january2017snapshot.epa.gov/smartgrowth/hud-dot-epa-partnership-sustainable-communities_.html

USHUD. (2022). *The US Department of Housing and Urban Development.* USHUD. https://ushud.com/

Vale, D. S., Saraiva, M., & Pereira, M. (2016). Active accessibility: A review of operational measures of walking and cycling accessibility. *Journal of Transport and Land Use*, *9*(1), 209–235.

Van Audenhove, F. J., Korniichuk, O., Dauby, L., & Pourbaix, J. (2014). *The Future of Urban Mobility 2.0. Imperatives to shape extended mobility ecosystems of tomorrow.* Arthur D. Little & The International Association of Public Transport (UITP). http://www.adlittle.com/downloads/tx_adlreports/2014_ADL_UITP_Future_of_Urban_Mobility_2_0_Full_study.pdf

Van Audenhove, F. J., Korniichuk, O., Dauby, L., & Pourbaix, J. (2014). *The Future of Urban Mobility 2.0. Imperatives to shape extended mobility ecosystems of tomorrow.* Arthur D. Little & The International Association of Public Transportation (UITP). https://www.adlittle.com/en/insights/viewpoints/future-urban-mobility-20-%E2%80%93-full-study

van den Akker, M., Blok, H., Budd, C., Eggermont, R., Gutermon, A., Lahaye, D., & Wadman, W. (2012). *A case study in the future challenges in electricity grid infrastructure.* Research Gate. https://www.researchgate.net/figure/Typical-daily-power-production-profile-from-solar-panels-1_fig7_325951690

van Dijk, J. (2009). The Digital Divide in Europe. *The Handbook of Internet Politics, Routledge, London and New York.* https://www.researchgate.net/publication/265074677_The_Digital_Divide_in_Europe

Van Egmond, P., Nijkamp, P., & Vindigni, G. (2003). A comparative analysis of the performance of urban public transport systems in Europe. *International Social Science Journal*, *55*(176), 235–247. doi:10.1111/1468-2451.5502005

Van Lierop, D., & Bahamonde-Birke, F. J. (2021). Commuting to the future: Assessing the relationship between individuals' usage of information and communications technology, personal attitudes, characteristics and mode choice. *Networks and Spatial Economics.* doi:10.1007/s11067-021-09534-9

van Marrewijk, M. (2003). Concepts and Definitions of CSR and Corporate Sustainability: Between Agency and Communion. *Journal of Business Ethics*, *44*(2), 95–105.

Compilation of References

Van Nes, R. (2002). *Design of multimodal transportation networks. A hierarchical approach.* [Doctoral Thesis, Delft University, The Netherlands].

Vandenbroele, J., Slabbinck, H., van Kerckhove, A., & Vermeir, I. (2021). Mock meat in the butchery: Nudging consumers toward meat substitutes. *Organizational Behavior and Human Decision Processes, 163,* 105–116. https://doi.org/10.1016/j.obhdp.2019.09.004

Vanek, F., Angenent, L., Banks, J., Daziano, R., & Turnquist, M. A. (2014). *Sustainable transportation systems engineering.* McGraw-Hill Education.

Verina, N., & Titko, J. (2019). Digital transformation: conceptual framework. In *Proc. of the Int. Scientific Conference "Contemporary Issues in Business, Management and Economics Engineering'2019",* (pp. 9-10). Vilnius, Lithuania.

Veryard, D., & Perkins, S. (Coord.) (2018) *Integrating Urban Public Transport Systems and Cycling. Summary and Conclusions. ITF Round Table 166.* International Transport Forum.

Vickerman, R. (2021). Will Covid-19 put the public back in public transport? A UK perspective. *Transport Policy, 103,* 95–102. doi:10.1016/j.tranpol.2021.01.005 PMID:33558796

Victoria Transport Policy Institute. (2019). Public Transit Improvements. *Transport Demand Management Encyclopedia.* VTPI. https://www.vtpi.org/tdm/tdm100.htm

Virtru. (2018). What are the Benefits of Digital Transformation? *Virtu.* https://www.virtru.com/blog/8-benefits-digital-transformation

Vuchic, V. R. (2002). Urban public transportation systems. *University of Pennsylvania, 5,* 2532-2558. https://citeseerx.ist.psu.edu/viewdoc/download?doi=10.1.1.362.6956&rep=rep1&type=pdf

Vuchic, V. (2005). *Urban transit: Operations, planning, and economics.* John Wiley & Sons Inc.

Vuchic, V. (2007). *Urban Transit Systems and Technology.* Wiley. doi:10.1002/9780470168066

Vu, K., Hanafizadeh, P., & Bohlin, E. (2020). ICT as a driver of economic growth: A survey of the literature and directions for future research. *Telecommunications Policy, 44*(2), 101922-1–101922-20.

Wang, J., Kong, X., Xia, F., & Sun, L. (2019). Urban Human Mobility: Data-Driven Modeling and Prediction. *SIGKDD Explorations, 21*(1), 1–19. doi:10.1145/3331651.3331653

Wardman, M., & Hine, J. (2000). *Costs of Interchange: A Review of Literature.* (Working Paper 546). Institute of Transportation Studies, University of Leeds, Leeds, UK.

Watkins, K., La Mondia, J., & Brakewood, C. (2015). Developing a new course for public transportation education. *Southeastern Transportation Research, Innovation, Development, and Education Center Final Report.* https://rosap.ntl.bts.gov/view/dot/29100

Watkins, K. (2018). Does the future of mobility depend on public transportation? *Journal of Public Transportation, 21*(1), 6. doi:10.5038/2375-0901.21.1.6

Wawer, M., Grzesiuk, K., & Jegorow, D. (2022). Smart Mobility in a Smart City in the Context of Generation Z Sustainability, Use of ICT, and Participation. *Energies, 15*(13), 4651. doi:10.3390/en15134651

Weijers, R. J., de Koning, B. B., & Paas, F. (2021). Nudging in education: From theory towards guidelines for successful implementation. *European Journal of Psychology of Education, 36*(3), 883–902. https://doi.org/10.1007/s10212-020-00495-0

Weiss, R. L., Maantay, J. A., & Fahs, M. (2010). Promoting Active Urban Aging: A Measurement Approach to Neighborhood Walkability for Older Adults. *Cities and the Environment*, *3*(1), 1–12.

Wheels for Wishes. (2021). *11 Car sharing benefits*. Wheels for Wishes. https://www.wheelsforwishes.org/11-car-sharing-benefits/

Will, C., & Schuller, A. (2016). Understanding user acceptance factors of electric vehicle smart charging. *Transportation Research Part C, Emerging Technologies*, *71*, 198–214. doi:10.1016/j.trc.2016.07.006

Witkowski, J., & Kiba-Janiak, M. (2014). The role of local governments in the development of city logistics. *Procedia: Social and Behavioral Sciences*, *125*, 373–385. doi:10.1016/j.sbspro.2014.01.1481

Witzel, S. (2018). *MaaS in Europe Part 1: Helsinki, Lisbon, Paris*. SkedGo. https://skedgo.com/maas-in-europe-part-1-helsinki-lisbon-paris/

Woetzel, J., Remes, J., Boland, B., Lv, K., Sinha, S., Strube, G., Means, J., Law, J., Cadena, A., & von der Tann, V. (2022, September 7). *Smart cities: Digital Solutions for a more Livable Future*. McKinsey & Company. Retrieved December 4, 2022, from https://www.mckinsey.com/capabilities/operations/our-insights/smart-cities-digital-solutions-for-a-more-livable-future

Wołek, M., Jagiełło, A., & Wolański, M. (2021). Multi-criteria analysis in the decision-making process on the electrification of public transport in cities in Poland: A case study analysis. *Energies*, *14*(19), 6391. doi:10.3390/en14196391

Wong, C.-Y., Ng, B.-K., Azizan, S. A., & Hasbullah, M. (2017). Knowledge structures of City Innovation Systems: Singapore and Hong Kong. *Journal of Urban Technology*, *25*(1), 47–73. https://doi.org/10.1080/10630732.2017.1348882

Wood, A. (2022). Problematizing the concept of walkability in Johannesburg. *Journal of Urban Affairs*.

Woodrow, C. I., & Grant, C. (2016). *Smart green cities: toward a carbon neutral world*. Routledge: Taylor and Francis.

World Bank Group. (2016). *Sustainable Urban Transport Financing from the Sidewalk to the Subway: Capital, Operations, and Maintenance Financing*. World Bank. doi:10.1596/978-1-4648-0756-5

World Bank. (2022). *Mobilité urbaine dans les villes africaines: Élaboration d'une politique nationale de mobilité urbaine et mise en œuvre au niveau de la ville - Rapport de synthèse*. World Bank.

World Intellectual Property Organization (WIPO). (n.d.). Retrieved December 4, 2022, from https://www.wipo.int/patents/en/topics/integrated_circuits.html

World Trade Organization (WTO). (n.d.). Retrieved December 4, 2022, from https://www.wto.org/english/tratop_e/trips_e/intel2_e.htm#patents

Wulandari, F., Schäfer, D., Stephan, A., & Sun, C. (2018). *Liquidity risk and yield spreads of green bonds, DIW Discussion Papers, No. 1728, Deutsches Institut für Wirtschaftsforschung*. DIW.

Wu, Y. C. J., Lu, C. C. J., Lirn, T. C., & Yuan, C. H. (2014). An overview of university-level sustainable transportation in North America and Europe. *Transportation Research Part D, Transport and Environment*, *26*, 27–31. doi:10.1016/j.trd.2013.10.006

Wu, Y. C. J., Shen, J. P., & Kuo, T. (2015). An overview of management education for sustainability in Asia. *International Journal of Sustainability in Higher Education*, *16*(3), 341–353. doi:10.1108/IJSHE-10-2013-0136

Xhafka, E., Teta, J., & Agastra, E. (2015). Mobile Environmental Sensing and Sustainable Public Transportation Using ICT Tools. *Acta Physica Polonica A*, *128*(2B), 128. doi:10.12693/APhysPolA.128.B-122

Compilation of References

Xia, X., Govindan, K., & Zhu, Q. (2015). Analyzing internal barriers for automotive parts remanufacturers in China using grey-DEMATEL approach. *Journal of Cleaner Production, 87*, 811–825. doi:10.1016/j.jclepro.2014.09.044

Xia, Z., Li, H., & Chen, Y. (2018). Assessing Neighborhood Walkability Based on Usage Characteristics of Amenities under Chinese Metropolises Context. *Sustainability, 10*, 1–18.

Yang, Y.-P. O., Shieh, H.-M., Leu, J.-D., & Tzeng, G.-H. (2008). A Novel Hybrid MCDM Model Combined with DE-MATEL and ANP with Applications. *International Journal of Operations Research, 5*(3), 160–168.

Yelloz, G., & Charon, P. (2008). Re-signaling the Paris line 1: From driver operated line to driverless line. *International Conference on Railway Engineering - Challenges for Railway Transportation in Information Age*, (pp. 1-4).

Yera, A., Arbelaitz, O., Jauregui, O., & Muguerza, J. (2020). Characterization of e-Government adoption in Europe. *PLoS One, 15*(4), e0231585.

Yıldız, B., Kütahyalı, D. B., & Çavdar, E. (2021). Şehir Lojistiği: Nicel Bir Araştırma. *Van Yüzüncü Yıl Üniversitesi Sosyal Bilimler Enstitüsü Dergisi, 53*, 303–334.

Yin, Li, & Han, Dong, & Liu. (2022). Maximizing network utility while considering proportional fairness for rail transit systems: Jointly optimizing passenger allocation and vehicle schedules. *Transportation Research Part C, Emerging Technologies, 143*, 103812.

Yu, Chen, Long, & Mansury. (2022). Urbanization, land conversion, and arable land in Chinese cities: The ripple effects of high-speed rail. *Applied Geography (Sevenoaks, England), 146*, 102756.

Zerbib, O. D. (2019). The effect of pro-environmental preferences on bond prices: Evidence from green bonds. *Journal of Banking & Finance, 98*(C), 39–60.

Zhao, J., & Melaina, M. W. (2006). Transition to hydrogen-based transportation in china: Lessons learned from alternative fuel vehicle programs in the United States and china. *Energy Policy, 34*(11), 1299–1309. doi:10.1016/j.enpol.2005.12.014

Zheng, H. (2013). On the move: Car-sharing scales up. *CityFix.* https://thecityfix.com/blog/on-the-move-car-sharing-scales-up-heshuang-zeng/

Zoroja, J. (2011). Internet, E-commerce and E-government: Measuring the Gap between European Developed and Post-Communist Countries. *Interdisciplinary Description of Complex Systems, 9*(2), 119–133.

Zoroja, J., & Pejić-Bach, M. (2016). Impact of Information and Communication Technology to the Competitiveness of European Countries - Cluster Analysis Approach. *Journal of Theoretical and Applied Electronic Commerce Research, 11*(1), 1–10.

About the Contributors

Zafer Yilmaz received his PhD degree from Turkish Military Academy Defense Sciences Institute, Department of Supply and Logistics Management. Before joining to TED University, he was a post-doctoral researcher at McGill University for 1.5 year. He taught Operations Management and Logistics Management Courses at McGill University. His interests include Operations Management, Management Science, Supply Chain Management, Inventory Management, Network Analysis, Modelling and Simulation. His current researches focuses on Green Transportation, E-Commerce, Multi Criteria Decision Making, and Green Consumption.

Silvia Golem is an associate professor at Faculty of Economics, Business and Tourism Split, University of Split and CERGE-EI Teaching Fellow. At the present time, she teaches different courses: Methodology of Economic Research, Urban Economics, Spatial Economics and Macroeconomic Planning. She actively participates in scientific projects mainly related to methodology of economic research, urban and public economics.

Dorinela Costescu is a professor, Faculty of Transports, Polytechnic University of Bucharest. She has over 25 years of academic and research experience in the Transport Engineering domain. Her teaching has covered Transport Systems, Geographic Information Systems for Transport (GIS-T), Transport Geography, Public Transport, and Management of Transport Projects. As a researcher, she has worked on studies concerning intermodal transport, city logistics, and transport terminals. In the period 2012 – 2016, she coordinated a multidisciplinary research team for studies regarding road safety in the urban environment and traffic risk estimates. Since 2017 her primary interests have focused on sustainable technologies for urban transport systems (mobility and public transport solutions for passengers and city logistics). In 2021 she achieved the habilitation in the Transport Engineering domain with the thesis "Urban Mobility: A Main Theme of the Sustainable Development."

* * *

Aysenur Budak graduated from Industrial Engineering Department of Sabanci University in 2010. She got M.Sc. degree from Istanbul Technical University (ITU) in 2013 and completed her doctoral studies at the Department of Industrial Engineering of ITU in 2017, and currently she is an associate professor at Gebze Technical University. Her current research interests include technology management, Supply chain management and logistics.

About the Contributors

Gizem Çelik graduated from Middle East Technical University in 2018, Department of Business Administration. In 2021, she received her MS degree from İstanbul Technical University, Business Administration Department. She continues to her PhD studies in Business Administration Graduate Program at Hacettepe University. She has been working as a Research Assistant at TED University since February 2019. Her main research interests are sustainable mobility, supply chain and logistic management.

Maja Ćukušić is professor at Faculty of Economics, Business and Tourism, University of Split, Department of Business Informatics. Before employment at the University of Split, she worked for three years in a Dutch company and was involved in the design and implementation of complex ICT solutions for domestic and foreign markets. She is the manager of the project financed by Croatian Science Foundation (User-oriented process (re)design and information systems modelling – a case of smart city services) and a key expert for e-learning in the SEA-EU European University Alliance. In her teaching (courses OLAP systems, ERP systems, E-business), she uses studies on different business intelligence technologies, visualization tools (open data), smart devices and similar.

Nida Durmaz completed her bachelor's degree in Industrial Engineering at Dokuz Eylül University with a third degree in 2019. In the same year, she was accepted to Graduate Programme of Industrial Engineering at Institute of Natural and Applied Sciences in Dokuz Eylül University. In 2020, she was assigned as a research assistant at Department of Industrial Engineering in Gebze Technical University and continued her Master of Science Programme there. Since 2020, she has been working at Gebze Technical University Industrial Engineering Department as a research assistant. Her research interests include Logistics and Supply Chain Management, Optimization and Operations Management.

Jure Erjavec is an assistant professor at School of Economics and Business, University of Ljubljana (SEBLU). He teaches undergraduate and graduate courses in the fields of business informatics, business logistics and supply chain management at SEBLU. Currently he is the director of Supply Chain and Logistics programme. His main research interests are digital transformation, technology adoption, supply chain management and business process management.

Jacques Etame is a professor and researcher at the University of Douala in the Department of Earth Sciences. Geochemistry of superficial formations belonging to the laboratory of geosciences natural resources and environment in which he supervised several Master II and PhD in collaboration with external researchers including the University of Sorbonne Paris. Director of the University Institute of Technology of the University of Douala. Previously Vice Dean in charge of research and cooperation at the Faculty of Science. His research activities are focused on the alteration of formations and on the dynamics of chemical elements. In collaboration with the chemistry laboratories, his research focuses on the chemistry of materials and particularly on the valorisation of local materials, notably on innovative materials (manufacture of ecological bricks and others).

Séverin Bertand Etémé Bessala is an assistant lecturer and researcher at the Computer Engineering Department of the University Institute of Technology, University of Douala. He is a PHD student at the Laboratory of Transport and Applied Logistics, University Institute of Technology, University of Douala, Cameroon. His research activities focus on sustainable urban mobility, knowledge engineering, decision support systems, big data, information systems, data analysis and transportation.

About the Contributors

Silvia Golem is an associate professor at Faculty of Economics, Business and Tourism Split, University of Split and CERGE-EI Teaching Fellow. At the present time, she teaches different courses: Methodology of Economic Research, Urban Economics, Spatial Economics and Macroeconomic Planning. She actively participates in scientific projects mainly related to methodology of economic research, urban and public economics.

Aleš Groznik is a full professor in the Department of Business Informatics at the Faculty of Economics, University of Ljubljana. His research interest is in the areas of long range planning of IT and logistics. His research area also covers studies on supply chain management, e-business and information technology management in ever changing business environments. He published over 150 papers in international journals and conferences, amongst them in Supply chain management journal, Journal of enterprise information management and Government information quarterly journal.

Adam Heyes recieved Bachelor's degree in Business Management in year 2022 at Faculty of Economics University of West Bohemia in Pilsen. As an active student, he is further studying for a master's degree Master's degree (economics). He is interested in sustainable behaviour and urban mobility (with emphasis on urban public transport). He is further interested in the impact of the aftermath of the Covid-19 epidemic on these areas. As part of his research, he has also focused on the phenomenon of carsharing - especially the knowledge of this phenomenon, the relationship of the young and older generation to carsharing and its use, etc.

Pelin Irgin, Ph.D., is an independent researcher of English Language Education in London, Ontario, Canada. She received her Ph.D. degree in English Language Teaching at Hacettepe University. She was a visiting scholar at University of Reading during her doctoral studies. Her research focuses on second language learning and teaching with particular emphasis on L2 listening, language teacher education and critical reading and writing. She has led several research projects in the field of second language education, exploring teaching and learning in a range of multicultural and multilingual contexts.

Tea Jašić is master's student of IT management at the Faculty of Economics, Business and Tourism, University of Split. She was declared as the best student of the generation for Undergraduate studies. Currently working as a student assistant at the Faculty of Economics, Business and Tourism in courses Information technologies and Basics of informatics.

Zdeněk Kresa graduated in the field of Business Economics and Management his higher education (Ing. - 2019) at the Faculty of Economics of the University of West Bohemia in Pilsen. He is now continuing his studies in the doctoral program. His main area of interest is sustainable urban transport and sustainable behaviour. He studies transport issues both from a marketing perspective and from the perspective of quantitative methods for transport management. During his studies at the Faculty of Economics he has been involved in several practice-oriented projects. In the field of sustainable transport, he also cooperates closely with practice (especially with the urban transport operator in Pilsen).

Bor Krizmanič is a teaching assistant at the School of Economics and Business, University of Ljubljana, where he is a member of the Academic Unit for Business Informatics and Logistics. Prior his employment at the University of Ljubljana, he worked in the field of information systems auditing and

394

About the Contributors

consulting. He is currently pursuing a PhD in Information Management. His main research interests are technology adoption and digital transformation with a focus on electromobility.

Anton Manfreda is an assistant professor in the Department for Business Informatics and Logistics at the School of Economics and Business, University of Ljubljana, Slovenia. His main research interests are technology adoption and digital transformation from various perspectives with special emphasis on smart cities and smart communities. He has published his research in the International Journal of Information Management, Journal of Retailing and Consumer Services, Journal of Enterprise Information Management and other international and national journals.

Justin Moskolai Ngossaha is a lecturer and researcher in the Department of Mathematics and Computer Science at the Faculty of Sciences of the University of Douala. PhD in Computer Science, he graduated from the Institut National Polytechnique de Toulouse - INPT (France). He is qualified CNU of France from the 27th session. His research activities focus on interoperability, knowledge engineering, distributed systems, decision support systems, sustainable systems, data analysis and transport. He participates actively in the field of research through conference organizing committees and reading committees of scientific journals.

Kristina Nagode is a teaching assistant and a young researcher in the Department of Business informatics and Logistics at the School of Economics and Business, University of Ljubljana, Slovenia. Currently, she is a Ph.D. student with the main research interest in smart city services adoption and sustainability-oriented behavior change of individuals. She has published her research in IFIP advances in information and communication technology and participated with chapters in the book Smart cities development and trends: cases and research opportunities.

Ivana Ninčević Pašalić is a Research and Teaching Assistant at Faculty of Economics, Business and Tourism, University of Split at Department of Business Informatics, and a PhD candidate at the University of Split. She teaches lab classes for the courses Multidimensional Information Systems, Smart city management and E-business. Her previous working positions include being Internal Auditor for a US based international organization and Operations Manager at a Croatian private company. Her research is focused on G2C and C2G interactions in smart cities, with a special focus on citizen engagement via different information and communication technologies.

Mihaela Popa has more than 30 years of academic and research experience in transportation. Professor Mihaela Popa has more than 30 years of academic and research experience in transportation. Currently, she has a teaching position in the Department of Transport, Traffic and Logistics and is Director of the Doctoral School of Transport, Polytechnic University of Bucharest. Her primary research interests and respective teaching disciplines are "Technologies in Transport Terminals", "Traffic Timetable in Networks with Controlled Access", and "Strategic Management in Transportation". Professor Popa is author or co-author of more than 70 papers, books and book-chapters in traffic and transport domain. She also acts as an independent evaluator for proposed research projects in different calls for funding of the European Commission, since 2012.

Șerban Raicu initiated and developed the Transport and Traffic Engineering Domain in research and higher education in Romania. He is a founder member of the Romanian Academy of Technical Sciences. He was intensely involved in academic management at the Polytechnic University of Bucharest (Director of Doctoral School of Transport 2012-2016; Vice-Rector for Research Activities 2004 – 2010; Dean of Faculty of Transports 1996 – 2004). He founded the Transportation Research and Consulting Centre and managed grants and research projects involving multidisciplinary teams (engineers in different fields, urban planners, geographers, economists, sociologists, and statisticians). The interrelationships between transport/traffic and the socio-economic environment, in correlation with the natural environment, are present in most of his publications and the doctoral theses he coordinated.

Alina Roman, Senior Lecturer, PhD, has more than ten years of academic and transport research experience. Currently, she has a teaching position in the Transport Faculty, Department of Transport, Traffic and Logistics, Polytechnic University of Bucharest. Her primary teaching and research areas are Transport Economics, Transport Demand Modelling, Transport Logistics and Sustainable Urban Mobility. She published more than 15 scientific papers in journals and conference volumes and participated as a team member in more than 10 research projects in the Transport Engineering domain.

Aditya Singh is a Civil Engineer, Independent Researcher, Ad Hoc Reviewer in 2 American International Journals (IJSSMET and IJRLEDM) and Alumni Mentor(LPU). He had completed his regular Bachelor of Technology degree in Civil Engineering from Lovely Professional University, India, in 2020. He had 9 publications under his name, in which 5 of them are published in national and international journals in the years 2018 and 2019, 2 as book chapters in international books for unpaid publication in USA in Nov 2021(already Scopus Indexed now) and 2022, and 2 international conference papers in (Springer Nature) LNNS Vol 371 and Vol 569 conference proceedings in 2022. Out of his 9 publications, he is a single author in 6 of them, whereas in one of them he is the main author and in other two he is the second author. He had also worked as a Peer Reviewer or Sub Reviewer or Ad Hoc Reviewer for 41 times so far in international conferences, international books and international journal.

Jean Gaston Tamba is an Associate Professor and Head of the Laboratory of Transport and Applied Logistics, University Institute of Technology of Douala. PHD in Energy and Environment at the Faculty of Sciences of the University of Yaoundé. He is the Deputy Director at the University Institute of Technology, University of Douala.

Jan Tlučhoř completed his higher education (Ing. - 2005 and Ph.D. - 2012) at the Faculty of Economics of the University of West Bohemia in Pilsen in the field of Business Economics and Management. He focuses on regional development, marketing and management in services and marketing analysis. His professional life is connected mainly with the Faculty of Economics of the University of West Bohemia and its Department of Marketing, Trade and Services. He also held and still holds some academic and managerial positions within the faculty (currently he serves as the Vice Dean for Academic Affairs). In his more than ten years of experience as an academic, he has been a researcher and co-investigator in international and national projects, applied and contract research. He often acts as a consultant or member of working groups in the field of development and implementation of strategic documents.

About the Contributors

Luka Tomat, Ph.D., is a regular member of Academic Unit for Business Informatics and Logistics at Faculty of Economics, University of Ljubljana, where he teaches several information management related courses on graduate and after-graduate level. In his research, he focuses on digital transformation, smart cities, information management, optimization, electronic business, business process management, big data analytics, IT in tourism and IT in healthcare. He also participates at several commercial projects.

Öykü Yücel graduated from Bilkent University, Faculty of Business Administration with a BS degree in Management. Upon completing her thesis on the application of the Capital Asset Pricing Model and Fama-French 3-Factor Model, she received her MSc degree from Ankara University Business Administration Department. She continues her Ph.D. studies at Ankara University Business Administration Department. Her thesis is on the merit order effect of renewable energy usage on electricity prices. She is working at TED University as a Research and Teaching Assistant mainly in accounting and finance courses. Her research interests are sustainable finance, electricity market pricing, and renewable energy sources.

Seda Damla Yücel has been working in TED University-Directorate of Research, Technology and Innovation (ATİD) since 2019 and in charge of project preparation, submission and evaluation of projects for various funding mechanisms and also management of Intellectual Property Rights (IPR). She has Bachelor's Degree in Business Administration and Master's Degree in Intellectual Property, Technology Policy and Innovation Management at Ankara University. Ms. Yücel has 15 years of general professional experience which is mostly related with preparation of project proposals for national and international institutions such as FP7, Horizon2020, MSCA, Erasmus+, TÜBİTAK, etc. and also project management and reporting. Addition; Ms. Yücel supports faculty members and students to structure their idea as a project proposal and also guide them to apply the appropriate funding program. Ms. Yücel has more than 10 years of professional experience in Technology Transfer Offices in management of patent portfolio, technology commercialization, mentoring for entrepreneurs, start-ups, SMEs and other TTOs about IPR, marketing, market research, commercialization strategy, development national and international collaborations, project preparation for various funding mechanisms and development of university-industry collaboration. She had various experience as internship at National Institutes of Health (NIH) OTT in the scope of the international mentoring program and also visiting scholar at Max Planck Institute for Innovation and Competition. She also hold a patent attorney license.

398

Index

15-Min City 342-343, 345

A

Accessibility 20, 28, 31, 33, 39-41, 43, 74, 83, 100, 103-104, 106, 110, 115-116, 119, 138, 168, 205, 235, 241, 243, 254-255, 279, 291, 294, 298-299, 305, 314, 322, 335-337, 340, 342, 344-346
ANP 293-294, 296, 300, 302, 307-308, 310, 312
Assessment 26, 32, 39, 57, 96, 100, 148, 162, 188, 198, 201, 244, 258, 265-266, 291, 334
Automated Fare Collection 81, 83, 93-94, 96-97, 269
Automated Fare Collection Service 81, 97
Automated Passenger Counting (APC) 223, 231, 235, 249
Automatic Vehicle Location System 68, 70, 97
Autonomous Vehicle 68, 73, 117

B

Behavior Change 121, 127-128, 132, 139
Behavioral Economics 125, 127, 138, 140
Bengaluru City 267-268, 270-273, 280, 282-283, 285-286, 288-290
Bibliometric Analysis 5, 11, 15, 24
Bond 141-152, 154-163
Bond Yield 163

C

Capital Market Association 141-142, 145, 156, 161
Capstone 22
Car-Oriented Urban Design 334, 346
Case Study 12, 41, 66, 138-139, 203-204, 211-212, 218-219, 221, 229, 247-248, 250, 263, 266, 292, 294-295, 312, 343
Choice Architecture 120, 128, 130-131, 137, 139-140
City Logistics 293-300, 304-305, 307-309, 312
Clean Mobility 29, 43

Climate Bonds Initiative 141, 143, 148
Cluster Analysis 182, 184, 188-189, 191-192, 195, 200, 202
CO2 Emission 169, 208, 212-216, 218-219, 222
Commercial Efficiency 25-26, 32-40, 43
Commercial Efficiency of Public Transportation 43
Commercialization of Intellectual Property Rights 313
Competencies 31, 115, 319
Co-occurrence Analysis 1, 4-5, 11, 15
Coronavirus Epidemic (CE) 224, 249
Coupon Payment 163
COVID-19 Pandemic 6, 19, 122-123, 125, 173, 177, 206, 244, 248, 344
Cultural Values 251, 296
Customer Experience (CX) 4, 7, 24, 223, 225, 227-229, 231, 233-234, 243-246, 248-249
Customer Surveys 223

D

Decision Support 63, 178, 250, 252, 261
Depot Management System 68, 79-80, 95, 97
Digital Divide 12, 183, 189, 195, 199-200, 202
Digital Transformation 1-6, 8, 16, 20-24, 137, 184, 199
Diversity 30, 114, 133, 166, 185, 188, 336, 339, 342

E

Ecological Sustainability 166, 176, 180
Economic Sustainability 10-11, 166, 168, 177, 180, 258
Effectiveness 13, 21, 25-27, 30, 32-33, 35-36, 39-41, 43, 100, 129, 149, 196-197, 241, 337
E-Government 12, 23, 183-185, 187-189, 191-195, 198-202
Electric Vehicles (EV) 19, 44, 46, 53-57, 59-62, 64-67, 133, 154, 169, 187, 195, 197, 207-208, 247, 294, 299, 326
Electromobility 44-46, 55, 57, 62, 67, 221, 241
Energy Consumption 16, 25, 27, 54, 75, 100, 104, 110,

Index

117, 130, 133, 137, 182-185, 187-188, 194-198, 200, 203-205, 207-208, 219-220, 222, 254-255, 299, 305

Entrepreneurial Ecosystem 314, 322, 324-326, 328-329

Entrepreneurship 10, 13, 137, 314, 322, 325-326, 329, 331

Epidemiological Measures 224, 236, 238-240, 249

ESG 141-142, 145, 148-150, 156-157, 159, 163

Ethics 10-11, 21, 24, 131, 139, 171

European Institute of Innovation and Technology (EIT) 326, 332

European Patent Office (EPO) 331

External Motivation 140

F

Face Value 156, 163

Feeder Service 102, 119

Fixed Income Securities 141

Fleet Management System 77-79, 97

Functions of the Public Transportation 25

G

Generation Z 223-225, 229, 241-249

Globalization 327

Graduate Programs 169-172

Green Bond Principles 141-142, 145, 154, 156-158, 161

Green Bonds 142-153, 155-163

Green Energy 144-145, 157, 182, 184, 196, 198-199, 328

Green Public Transportation 68, 73, 177, 203-204, 207-209, 211, 219, 328

Green Transportation 135, 154-155, 203-204, 208-210, 219, 221-222, 312, 328-329

Green Vehicles 203, 207, 210-211

Greenium 141, 150-151, 157-159, 161, 163

Grey-DEMATEL 293, 296, 312

H

Health 8-9, 15-16, 20-21, 31, 39, 90, 99, 129, 138-139, 165, 171, 174-175, 177, 197, 236, 238, 246, 253, 258, 264, 272, 279, 292, 294, 299, 334, 342, 345

Health and Wellness 138

Higher Education 12, 164, 167-169, 171-175, 179

Hybrid 55, 62, 67, 90, 148, 155, 169, 197, 207-208, 211, 219-220, 310, 312

I

Inclusion 8-9, 46, 54, 62

Information and Communication Technologies (ICTs) 182-183, 202, 251, 255

Integrated Public Transportation 98, 100, 117

Intellectual Property (IP) 314, 322, 332

Intellectual Property Rights (IPR) 313-315, 319, 332

Intermodal Passenger Transportation 272-273, 290

Intermodality 30, 98-100, 103, 110, 117, 119, 228, 231

Internal Motivation 140

International Patent Classification (IPC) 332

Internet of Things 16, 69, 73, 97, 129, 132, 183, 198, 210, 221, 257, 264, 324, 327

K

Kano Model 228

L

Leadership 6, 21, 168, 171, 199, 246, 343

Level of Service 33-34, 118, 333, 337

M

Maturity 141, 148-149, 151-152, 155-156, 163, 199, 332

Metrics 43, 119, 142, 146, 156, 333, 335, 341

Micro-Mobility Vehicle 222

Micro-Scale Factors of Walkability 346

Mobility 1-2, 15-21, 23-24, 26-34, 36-43, 45-46, 55, 59, 61-62, 66, 68-70, 75, 84, 87, 91, 93, 96-123, 125, 128, 131, 133-139, 166-171, 176-177, 180, 198-199, 201, 203-206, 208-211, 220-222, 224-226, 240-246, 248, 250-266, 268, 294, 296, 298-299, 311, 325-326, 328, 331, 333-336, 338-339, 341-342, 345

Mobility as a Service (MaaS) 18, 222, 225

Mobility Services 69-70, 96, 98, 100, 104, 106-110, 113, 116, 122-123, 125, 139, 208-210, 221, 240, 250, 254, 259, 261-263

Modal Share 25, 28, 34, 106

Mode of Transportation 90, 98-99, 110, 119, 124, 204

Multi Criteria Decision Making 293

Multimodality 99-100, 119, 125

N

Nudge 128-132, 134-140

399

O

On-Demand Transport 75, 249

P

Passenger Information Systems 72, 84, 94, 97
Passenger-Kilometer / Person-Kilometer 249
Patent 313, 316-320, 323-324, 328-329, 331-332
Pedestrian Planning 333, 346
Pedestrian-Oriented Urban Design 346
Performance Indicators 26, 33, 40, 42, 118, 325
Pilsen 224-227, 229, 231, 233-236, 239-242, 244, 246, 249
Power Grid 44-47, 49, 51-55, 57, 60-62, 65, 67
Production Efficiency 32-34, 36, 39, 43
Production Efficiency of Public Transportation 43
Prosumer 44, 51, 65, 67
Public Administration 175, 187, 189
Public Transportation 17-20, 25-27, 29, 31-32, 37, 43, 68-70, 73, 81, 84-86, 91, 94-100, 103-110, 112-125, 127-134, 162, 164, 166-180, 182, 184, 196-198, 200-205, 207-211, 213, 217, 219-223, 226, 244, 248, 267-268, 270, 272-273, 290, 294-296, 298-299, 328, 342
Public Transportation Line 37
Public Transportation Performance 27, 32, 43

R

Renewable energy 44-47, 49, 51-52, 54, 62-66, 138, 146, 148, 155-157, 167, 182-188, 194-202, 208, 221, 310, 326
Renewables 48, 59-60, 182, 196, 200-201
Rush Hour 234, 249

S

Shared Mobility 106, 116, 119, 209-210, 240, 255
Sharing System 75-78, 90, 93, 117
Skills 4, 8, 175, 196, 322
Small and Medium-Sized Enterprises (SMEs) 332
Smart Charging 44, 59-61, 63-64, 66-67
Smart City 1-3, 11, 14-16, 20-21, 23-24, 68-69, 91, 93-94, 121, 133, 135-137, 155-156, 171, 224, 241, 248, 299, 324-326, 330, 333, 342
Smart Grid 44, 51-54, 61-67
Smart Meter 44, 53, 65
Smart Mobility 1-2, 16-18, 20-21, 24, 40, 68-69, 91, 93, 96, 116, 133, 135, 198, 220, 241, 248, 255, 265, 325, 331

Smart Society 1-2, 13-16, 20-21
Smart Station Hubs 268-269, 273
Smart Transportation 15, 92, 328, 341
Social Big Data 250, 252, 256-258, 263
Social Impact Bond 163
Social Justice 294
Social Sustainability 10, 12-13, 165-166, 180
Socio-Economic Effectiveness 26, 43
Suburban Rail 267-276, 278, 280-286, 288-290, 292
Sustainable Behavior 120, 127, 129, 133, 240
Sustainable Development 10-15, 22, 24-26, 40, 62, 98-99, 104, 122, 138, 154, 165, 175, 177-179, 183, 196, 198-201, 203-204, 220, 222, 250-252, 255, 258-259, 265, 279, 290, 310-311
Sustainable Mobility 27, 34, 84, 96, 98-100, 102, 110, 121, 128, 134-135, 137-139, 167, 176, 199, 211, 226, 246, 258, 264, 268, 296, 311
Sustainable Transport 19, 21, 23, 41, 160, 167-168, 177-178, 207, 221-222, 224-225, 247, 272-273, 290, 293, 297-298, 300, 309
Sustainable Transport Practices 272-273, 290
Sustainable Transportation System 105, 180, 298
Sustainable Urban Mobility 36, 96, 100, 103-104, 118, 225, 250, 252, 255, 259-260, 266, 342, 345
Synchronous 46
Systems Engineering 23, 173, 179, 250, 309, 311

T

Technology Readiness Level (TRL) 321, 332
Traditional Transportation Vehicle 222
Traffic Congestion 18, 20-21, 25, 28, 77, 133, 166, 168-170, 204, 208, 211, 267, 270-271, 283, 286, 289, 294, 299, 305, 308-309, 334
Transportation 2, 15-27, 29, 31-34, 37, 39-43, 55, 59, 66, 68-70, 73, 75, 81, 83-86, 89-100, 102-110, 112-125, 127-136, 138-139, 145-146, 149, 154-156, 162, 164-180, 182, 184, 187, 196-207, 209-213, 217, 219-224, 226-228, 240, 243-249, 264, 266-268, 270, 272-274, 279, 283, 288-299, 304-305, 307-312, 314, 325-326, 328-329, 333, 338, 341-342, 344-345
Transportation Network 97, 100, 112, 115-116, 118, 221
Trunk-and-Feeder Service 119

U

Urban Environment 26, 39, 43, 70, 77, 103-104, 113, 196, 202
Urban Intermodal Hub 119
Urban Intermodality 119

Index

Urban Mobility 27-28, 30, 32-34, 36, 38-40, 42-43, 69-70, 91, 93, 96-100, 103-104, 106, 108, 110, 115-116, 118-119, 121-122, 221, 224-225, 250-266, 326, 333-335, 338, 341-342, 345

Urban Mobility System 32, 34, 43, 70, 106, 108, 115, 119, 250, 254, 262

Urban Multimodality 119

Urban Transportation 25, 39, 75, 114, 116-117, 122, 164, 166, 171-172, 174, 177-178, 180, 182, 204, 208, 210, 246, 294-296, 333, 341

V

Vehicle Sharing Systems 97

Vehicle-Kilometer 249

Vehicle-to-Grid (V2G) 59-61, 64, 66-67

W

Walkability 333-346

Walking Environment 333, 336-339

WalkScore 336, 346

Wellness 138

Recommended Reference Books

IGI Global's reference books are available in three unique pricing formats:
Print Only, E-Book Only, or Print + E-Book.
Shipping fees may apply.
www.igi-global.com

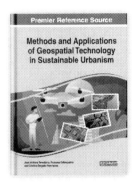

ISBN: 9781799822493
EISBN: 9781799822516
© 2021; 684 pp.
List Price: US$ **195**

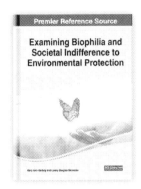

ISBN: 9781799844082
EISBN: 9781799844099
© 2021; 279 pp.
List Price: US$ **195**

ISBN: 9781799884262
EISBN: 9781799884286
© 2021; 461 pp.
List Price: US$ **295**

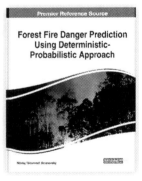

ISBN: 9781799872504
EISBN: 9781799872528
© 2021; 297 pp.
List Price: US$ **195**

ISBN: 9781799875123
EISBN: 9781799875192
© 2021; 416 pp.
List Price: US$ **295**

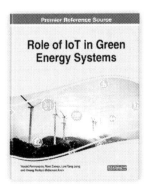

ISBN: 9781799867098
EISBN: 9781799867111
© 2021; 405 pp.
List Price: US$ **195**

Do you want to stay current on the latest research trends, product announcements, news, and special offers?
Join IGI Global's mailing list to receive customized recommendations, exclusive discounts, and more.
Sign up at: **www.igi-global.com/newsletters**.

Publisher of Timely, Peer-Reviewed Inclusive Research Since 1988

www.igi-global.com   Sign up at www.igi-global.com/newsletters   facebook.com/igiglobal   twitter.com/igiglobal   linkedin.com/igiglobal

Ensure Quality Research is Introduced to the Academic Community

Become an Evaluator for IGI Global Authored Book Projects

 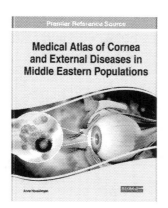  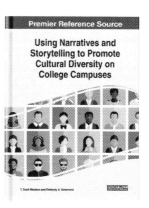

The overall success of an authored book project is dependent on quality and timely manuscript evaluations.

Applications and Inquiries may be sent to:
development@igi-global.com

Applicants must have a doctorate (or equivalent degree) as well as publishing, research, and reviewing experience. Authored Book Evaluators are appointed for one-year terms and are expected to complete at least three evaluations per term. Upon successful completion of this term, evaluators can be considered for an additional term.

If you have a colleague that may be interested in this opportunity, we encourage you to share this information with them.

Easily Identify, Acquire, and Utilize Published Peer-Reviewed Findings in Support of Your Current Research

IGI Global OnDemand

Purchase Individual IGI Global OnDemand Book Chapters and Journal Articles

For More Information:
www.igi-global.com/e-resources/ondemand/

Browse through 150,000+ Articles and Chapters!

Find specific research related to your current studies and projects that have been contributed by international researchers from prestigious institutions, including:

- Accurate and Advanced Search
- Affordably Acquire Research
- Instantly Access Your Content
- Benefit from the InfoSci Platform Features

"It really provides an excellent entry into the research literature of the field. It presents a manageable number of highly relevant sources on topics of interest to a wide range of researchers. The sources are scholarly, but also accessible to 'practitioners'."

- Ms. Lisa Stimatz, MLS, University of North Carolina at Chapel Hill, USA

Interested in Additional Savings?

Subscribe to
IGI Global OnDemand *Plus*

Learn More

Acquire content from over 128,000+ research-focused book chapters and 33,000+ scholarly journal articles for as low as US$ 5 per article/chapter (original retail price for an article/chapter: US$ 37.50).

6,600+ E-BOOKS.
ADVANCED RESEARCH.
INCLUSIVE & ACCESSIBLE.

IGI Global e-Book Collection

- **Flexible Purchasing Options** (Perpetual, Subscription, EBA, etc.)
- Multi-Year Agreements with **No Price Increases** Guaranteed
- **No Additional Charge** for Multi-User Licensing
- No Maintenance, Hosting, or Archiving Fees
- Transformative **Open Access Options** Available

Request More Information, or Recommend the IGI Global e-Book Collection to Your Institution's Librarian

Among Titles Included in the IGI Global e-Book Collection

Research Anthology on Racial Equity, Identity, and Privilege (3 Vols.)
EISBN: 9781668445082
Price: US$ 895

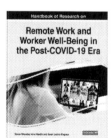

Handbook of Research on Remote Work and Worker Well-Being in the Post-COVID-19 Era
EISBN: 9781799867562
Price: US$ 265

Research Anthology on Big Data Analytics, Architectures, and Applications (4 Vols.)
EISBN: 9781668436639
Price: US$ 1,950

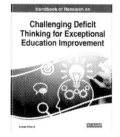

Handbook of Research on Challenging Deficit Thinking for Exceptional Education Improvement
EISBN: 9781799888628
Price: US$ 265

Acquire & Open

When your library acquires an IGI Global e-Book and/or e-Journal Collection, your faculty's published work will be considered for immediate conversion to Open Access *(CC BY License)*, at no additional cost to the library or its faculty *(cost only applies to the e-Collection content being acquired)*, through our popular **Transformative Open Access (Read & Publish) Initiative**.

For More Information or to Request a Free Trial, Contact IGI Global's e-Collections Team: eresources@igi-global.com | 1-866-342-6657 ext. 100 | 717-533-8845 ext. 100

Printed in the United States
by Baker & Taylor Publisher Services